EDUCATIONAL

and

PSYCHOLOGICAL

MEASUREMENT

and

EVALUATION

*Prentice-Hall Series
in Educational Measurement, Research,
and Statistics*

GENE V GLASS, *Editor*

John W. Best RESEARCH IN EDUCATION,
2nd Edition

Glenn H. Bracht, Kenneth D. Hopkins, and Julian C. Stanley, Editors
PERSPECTIVES IN EDUCATIONAL AND
PSYCHOLOGICAL MEASUREMENT

Gene V Glass and Julian C. Stanley
STATISTICAL METHODS IN EDUCATION
AND PSYCHOLOGY

Emil F. Heermann and Larry A. Braskamp, Editors
READINGS IN STATISTICS FOR THE
BEHAVIORAL SCIENCES

Patricia A. Kearney PROGRAMMED REVIEW
OF FUNDAMENTAL MATHEMATICS FOR
ELEMENTARY STATISTICS

Julian C. Stanley and Kenneth D. Hopkins
EDUCATIONAL AND PSYCHOLOGICAL MEASUREMENT
AND EVALUATION,
(*5th Edition of* MEASUREMENT IN TODAY'S SCHOOLS)

Julian C. Stanley

DEPARTMENT OF PSYCHOLOGY
THE JOHNS HOPKINS UNIVERSITY

Kenneth D. Hopkins

LABORATORY OF EDUCATIONAL RESEARCH
UNIVERSITY OF COLORADO

prentice-hall, inc., englewood cliffs, n. j.

EDUCATIONAL

and

PSYCHOLOGICAL MEASUREMENT

and

EVALUATION

EDUCATIONAL AND PSYCHOLOGICAL MEASUREMENT
AND EVALUATION
Julian C. Stanley and Kenneth D. Hopkins
is the fifth edition of the book formerly titled
MEASUREMENT IN TODAY'S SCHOOLS, 4th ed.

ISBN: 0–13–236281–3
Library of Congress Catalog Card Number: 70–154674
Printed in the United States of America

10   9   8   7   6   5   4   3   2   1

PRENTICE-HALL INTERNATIONAL, INC., London
PRENTICE-HALL OF AUSTRALIA PTY. LTD., Sydney
PRENTICE-HALL OF CANADA LTD., Toronto
PRENTICE-HALL OF INDIA PRIVATE LIMITED, New Delhi
PRENTICE-HALL OF JAPAN, INC., Tokyo

To Rose and Suzy
Colleen, Jonathan, and Beata

CONTENTS

part one

Basic Concepts

ix

part two

The Development of Educational Measures

10 CONSTRUCTING SPECIFIC TYPES OF OBJECTIVE TEST, 217

11 ITEM ANALYSIS FOR CLASSROOM TESTS, 267

12 THE ASSESSMENT OF THE AFFECTIVE DOMAIN, 282

13 GRADING, REPORTING, AND PROMOTING, 303

part three

Standardized Measures

14 MEASURING INTELLIGENCE, 323

15 STANDARDIZED ACHIEVEMENT TESTS, 360

16 INTEREST, PERSONALITY, AND SOCIAL MEASUREMENT, 380

17 THE TESTING PROGRAM, 417

Appendixes

PREFACE

This volume was originally planned as the Fifth Edition of *Measurement in Today's Schools*, which has been a standard textbook in educational measurement for the past three decades. It soon became clear that certain proposed modifications were so basic and extensive that it would be inaccurate to describe the volume as a fifth edition of *Measurement in Today's Schools*. Ten of the seventeen chapters are new; five others have been extensively modified and updated. Only two chapters (9 and 17) have not been altered substantially. The selection and treatment of topics were guided by two general considerations: (1) knowledge and skills that are necessary for the *development* of valid evaluation measures, and (2) knowledge and competences that are required for a proper *interpretation* of informal and standardized tests.

The chapters are divided into three major parts: Basic Concepts (One), The Development of Educational Measures (Two), and Standardized Measures (Three). The basic concepts of measurement and evaluation are treated in Part One (Chapters 1–5). Since testing and related topics have been attacked as an enemy of education, we have considered the various purposes of assessment carefully in Chapter 1.

In Chapter 2 we have incorporated an innovation designed to reduce the inordinate amount of time frequently devoted to statistics in introductory measurement courses. In addition to the usual narrative treatment of the statistical concepts, we have interspersed self-instructional material so that the reader is exposed to the same concepts via two different, but complementary, approaches. We have also eliminated obsolete material devoted to computing statistics from data grouped into intervals, since such grouping is an unnecessary procedural step which results in formulas that obscure the conceptual meaning of the concepts. Certain statistical techniques (such as Fisher's z-transformation) have been replaced with the concepts of statistical significance and confidence intervals that are more relevant for test users.

The chapters on norms, validity, and reliability (3–5) were greatly influenced by the 1966 APA–AERA–NCME *Standards for Educational and Psychological Tests and Manuals*.

The most fundamental change from earlier editions is in the greater emphasis given to standardized testing (Part Three). Although most pupils are tested repeatedly with standardized tests, few teachers for whom this information is primarily intended have the background required to interpret this information properly.

The new chapters on intelligence assessment and achievement testing (14 and 15) are not catalogs of information about specific tests. Rather, they provide a consideration of the more basic issues on which the proper evaluation and use of test results are contingent. Special sections are devoted to problems unique to elementary or secondary schools. Interest, personality, and sociometric measures are also treated (Chapter 15), but at a survey level appropriate for typical classroom teacher understanding and use.

We have also attempted to acquaint the reader with rather neglected topics pertaining to "Factors That Influence Test Performance" (Chapter 6), and with the relative magnitude of associated effects, so that allowance for these factors can be made in test interpretation.

The increased emphasis on standardized tests has not reduced the attention given to test development (Part Two). On the contrary, two new chapters have been added: "Item Analysis for Classroom Tests" (Chapter 11) and "The Assessment of the Affective Domain" (Chapter 12). The latter chapter reflects the increased importance of attitudes, interests, and values in contemporary education. Material in the present edition is extensively documented to allow the reader to pursue topics of special interest independently.

Parts Two and Three are essentially independent; Part Three might well be omitted in courses devoted exclusively to test construction. Instructors of courses oriented primarily to standardized tests might omit Part Two on test development.

An additional unique aspect of this book is the availability of a companion volume of parallel, integrated readings entitled *Perspectives in Educational and Psychological Measurement* (Prentice-Hall, 1972), which we edited with Glenn H. Bracht. Certain of the recommended readings following each chapter in this text are reproduced in the book of readings.

During the three years we spent developing this textbook, numerous individuals contributed in many ways to our efforts. We cannot name them all here, but several colleagues deserve special thanks. The administrative support provided by Stephen A. Romine facilitated the project substantially. Gene V Glass read the entire manuscript and contributed many helpful suggestions. Patricia Webster, Rose Stanley, and Lynne Rienner made numerous stylistic improvements. The author and subject indexes were prepared by B. R. Hopkins. The following persons assisted in various ways during their graduate training. Beverly Anderson, Richard Bennet, Nancy Burton, Joan Finucci, Arlen Gullickson, Stephen Jurs, Daniel Keating, Norris Harms, Gerry Hendrickson, Samuel Livingston, Larry Nelson, Todd Rogers, James Sanders, Charles Thomas, and Victor Willson. The task of deciphering and typing the various drafts of the manuscript was shared by Anita Dunlevy, Nancy Gallagher, Virginia Grim, Linda Johnson, Heidi Meyer, and Linda Venter.

JULIAN C. STANLEY
KENNETH D. HOPKINS

TABLES

FIGURES

part one

Basic Concepts

MEASUREMENT AND EVALUATION
IN THE EDUCATIONAL PROCESS

Are you aware of how widely various "measures"—such as tests of achievement, intelligence, interest, and aptitude—are used in American schools? Goslin (1963)[1] estimated that 200 million standardized ability tests are administered annually in addition to many times that number of classroom tests. Are you aware of how extensively schools depend on a related procedure called *evaluation*? Throughout this book, we use the word evaluation to designate summing-up processes in which value judgments play a large part, as in grading and promoting students. We consider the construction, administration, and scoring of tests as the *measurement* process. Interpreting such scores—saying whether they are good or bad for a specific purpose—is evaluation.

A simple illustration may clarify the distinction. Miss Roe gives her class a spelling test consisting of 25 difficult words. She finds that the number of words spelled correctly ranges from 6 to 25, and that the average number correct is 15. Will Miss Roe stop here? The mother of one of her pupils may ask, "How *well* is David doing in spelling?" Miss Roe may show her his paper and explain that he spelled 16 words correctly out of 25 on the test last Friday. David's mother may press for—in effect, demand—an evaluation of the measurement (score of 16) by replying: "Nine words wrong, 64 percent right; is that as terrible as it sounds?"

If Miss Roe answers, "More than half the pupils missed a greater number than he did," she is confining her remarks to the distribution of scores on the test—that is, staying within the area we call measurement. If, however, she agrees that 16 is indeed a "poor" score, or if she insists that in view of his verbal

---

[1] For references cited in the text, please see the listing on pages 469-507.

ability David is spelling about as well as can be expected, then Miss Roe is evaluating the score.

We consider the conversion of test scores to grades such as A, B, C, D, F; "Excellent," "Good," "Fair," "Poor"; or "High," "Average," "Low" as evaluation rather than measurement, because value judgments are made. Important value judgments are made in selecting the items and the time and method of giving the test and scoring it, but the process of attaching value judgments to *performance* on the measure is uniquely evaluation. Whether a student's score is good or bad for a given purpose cannot be determined solely from the score itself. An interpretation must be made. The score is often interpreted in terms of fixed standards, such as 80–89 percent equals B, or in terms of the student's rank on the test in his class or his rank in relationship to his estimated potential for learning. Interpreting one student's test score is evaluation at an elementary level. Evaluating a curriculum or special program is very complex. Procedures for complex program evaluations are treated in the American Educational Research Association monograph series on curriculum evaluation and *The sixty-eighth yearbook of the National Society for the Study of Education* (R. W. Tyler, 1969).

It is evident throughout this book that distinctions between measurement and evaluation, although often clarifying, are not always sharp or meaningful. Evaluation usually involves more subjectivity than measurement, but a little subjectivity occurs in even the most "objective" measurement. For example, measuring a person's height is quite objective, but it may be affected by how straight he stands, how hard the measuring instrument is pressed against the hair, and so on. An evaluation is subjective to the extent that the results depend on *who* is evaluating rather than on *what* is being evaluated. Little subjectivity is involved in determining the fastest runner in Mr. Smith's fourth-grade class, but considerable subjectivity is involved in *deciding* who should receive the best citizenship award. If a rating remains constant irrespective of the rater, the rating is said to be objective. The extent to which a measurement or evaluation is subjective is the degree to which personal bias and prejudice can influence scores. It is desirable to increase the objectivity of testing, interviewing, rating, and similar enterprises that often are pursued quite subjectively. *Increasing the objectivity of the assessment and evaluation of human behavior in the school is a chief aim of this book.*

We are interested in increasing objectivity not for its own sake but because, as later chapters will make clear, the validity of a measure or evaluation is usually enhanced as it becomes less subjective.

Educational Decisions Founded on Evaluation

If we view "tests and measurements" narrowly as the preparing, administering, scoring, and norming of objective tests, we are likely to overlook important ways in which evaluation supports the entire educational system. Why do we have schools? Obviously, society has decided that without them many people would probably not acquire essential knowledge, understanding, skills, and attitudes. Schools are organized as they are because, on the basis of much experience, current patterns appear to "work best"—at least in the eyes of those who make educational decisions. Why is a particular school built where it is, as large as it is, and with certain facilities? Why are some teachers hired to staff it, others not? What determines salaries, the choice of textbooks and other instructional aids, grades, promotions, reports to parents, grouping patterns, the community's reactions to the school and its products, recommendations for college and for jobs? All of these decisions involve evaluations. Objective measurement is usually an essential prerequisite for sound evaluation, but it is by no means sufficient.

Most educators consider that a school's main business is promoting "growth" toward desirable individual and societal objectives; fewer agree on who should judge the desirability of these objectives. However, since all schools focus on pupil progress as the ultimate criterion, it is important to evaluate the status and gains of pupils expertly. How well are Mary and Paul doing? Should they be doing better?

Measurement and evaluation encompass such subjective aspects as the judgments made by teachers and administrators. Let us not fall into the trap of asking whether we should use teacher judgments *or* test scores. Faced by complex problems of measurement and evaluation of pupil growth and influences affecting it, we cannot reject any promising resource. Various sorts of information *supplement* each other.

Are today's educators being equipped adequately for performance of their evaluation responsibilities? Mayo (1967) found that graduating seniors in 86 teacher-training institutions did not demonstrate a very high level of measurement competence. Goslin (1967b), in a study of the social consequences of testing and the development of talent, found that about 60 percent of all teachers had only minimal exposure to training in test and measurement techniques. The unsatisfactory quality of the majority of teacher-made tests no doubt reflects this inadequacy in training. Not surprisingly, Goslin also found that teachers who had little preparation in tests and measurements tended to make little use of the pupil information obtained from standardized tests. We are in complete sympathy with Goslin's concluding statement from his comprehensive study (1967b, p. 140): "The role of teachers in testing is too important to be left to chance." Unfortunately, in view of studies by Mayo (1967) and Goslin (1967b), Conant's recommendation (1963, p. 171) that instruction in tests and measurements be one of the essentials in teacher-training programs appears not to have been implemented adequately at many institutions.

Essential Knowledge and Skills

What should school personnel know about measurement and evaluation, and what abilities do they need in this area? Figure 1–1 presents the three primary aspects of the educational process—a process for changing the behavior and attitudes of students. First, educational goals[2] are established either explicitly

---

[2] *The taxonomy of educational objectives, cognitive domain* (Bloom et al., 1956) has had an important, salutary effect on both the development of appropriate curricular objectives and the designing of measures for evaluating these objectives. These subjects receive extensive treatment in Chapter 8.

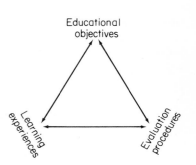

FIGURE 1–1 *A graphic representation of the three interacting aspects of the educational process. (Reproduced from E. J. Furst, Constructing evaluation instruments [New York: David McKay Company, Inc., 1958], p. 3, by permission of David McKay Company, Inc.)*

or (more often) implicitly. Learning experiences are then designed to promote the attainment of the goals. Finally, an evaluation is conducted to determine the extent to which the objectives have been attained. The results of the evaluation may affect the objectives and the instruction. The double-directed vectors of Figure 1–1 indicate the interacting nature of the entire process. If our evaluation procedures are poor, then the quality of the information on which we must make judgments cannot be adequate.

The measurement and evaluation skills needed depend partly on the position one holds. The skills needed for kindergarten and primary-school teachers differ from those needed by high-school physics and English teachers. Principals, counselors, and school psychologists need certain competencies besides those essential for teachers.

Fortunately, *certain concepts, principles, and skills are useful at all levels* and in nearly all positions. Even parents and others not professionally concerned with individual appraisal would benefit from a clear understanding of such concepts as "validity," "reliability," "IQ," and "norms." By concentrating on fundamental concepts and skills, we present in one basic textbook the *essentials* for most teachers. Ebel (1961a, p. 68) has outlined six requisites for a teacher to be competent in educational measurement:

1. Know the educational uses, as well as the limitations, of educational tests.
2. Know the criteria by which the quality of a test should be judged and how to secure evidence relating to these criteria.
3. Know how to plan a test and write the test questions to be included in it.
4. Know how to select a standardized test that will be effective in a particular situation.
5. Know how to administer a test properly, efficiently, and fairly.
6. Know how to interpret test scores correctly and fully, but with recognition of their limitations.

Throughout this book these fundamentals are carefully illustrated with examples from various age and grade levels. No single book can present all of the specialized phases of measurement and evaluation, but it should, as *Educational and Psychological Measurement and Evaluation* does, refer the reader to good supplemental sources.

As Ebel (1961c) indicated, teachers must know how to perform certain   **6** aspects of measurement and evaluation themselves, such as constructing tests, giving grades, assessing potentialities, and interpreting standardized intelligence and achievement tests. They should know how to select from the many available tests, inventories, questionnaires, rating scales, check lists, and the like those most suitable for a particular purpose. Besides being able to understand directions for administering, scoring, and interpreting tests, teachers should possess the higher ability to compare the most promising ones before the choice itself is made. This requires attaining various concepts necessary to understand test publishers' literature, reviews, and articles reporting test research. *Educational and Psychological Measurement and Evaluation* is designed to help you toward this important objective.

The Goals and Functions of Testing

Tests serve a variety of functions. The purpose for which a test is given determines not only the appropriate *type* of test but also the test's *characteristics* (such as difficulty and reliability). A measure designed for accurate assessment of individual differences in arithmetic fundamentals requires very high test reliability, whereas a much shorter (and hence, less reliable) test might suffice for a *class* or program evaluation. Findley (1963b) classified the purposes served by tests in education under three *interrelated* categories: (1) instructional, (2) administrative, and (3) guidance. Standardized measures provide the basis for most of the guidance and administrative test roles, whereas teacher-made tests are used principally for instructional functions. In the sections that follow we discuss each of these three categories.

INSTRUCTIONAL FUNCTIONS

The Process of Constructing a Test Stimulates Teachers to Clarify and Refine Meaningful Course Objectives   If teachers are continually reminded of their destination, they are more apt to stay on course. Bloom (1961, p. 60) observed that:

> Participation of the teaching staff in selecting as well as constructing evaluation instruments has resulted in improved instruments on one hand and on the other hand it has resulted in clarifying the objectives of instruction and in making them real and meaningful to teachers. . . . When teachers have actively participated in defining objectives and in selecting or constructing evaluation instruments they return to the learning problems with great vigor and remarkable creativity. . . . Teachers who have become committed to a set of educational objectives which they thoroughly understand respond by developing a variety of learning experiences which are as diverse and as complex as the situation requires.

Tests Provide a Means of Feedback to the Teacher   Feedback from tests helps the teacher provide more appropriate instructional guidance for individual students as well as for the class as a whole. Well-designed tests may also be of value for pupil self-diagnosis, since they help students identify areas of specific weaknesses.

Properly Constructed Tests Can Motivate Learning   As a general
rule, students pursue mastery of objectives more diligently if they expect to be
evaluated. In the intense competition for a student's time, courses without *Measurement
and
Evaluation
in the
Educational
Process*
examinations are often "squeezed" out of high-priority positions. When queried,
students have consistently reported greater study and learning with periodic
testing (Feldhusen, 1964). The anticipation of a forthcoming test may also
affect pupils' "intention to remember" instructional content. H. B. White (1932)
found that students expecting a final examination performed much better
than students in the same classes who thought they had been exempted from
the final. (The research on this point does not make it clear whether the mental
"set" or the induced study accounts for the superiority of students expecting
an examination. See Cook, 1951; and Ross and Stanley, 1954, pp. 312–315.)

Examinations Are a Useful Means of Overlearning   When we review,
interact with, or practice skills and concepts even after they have been mastered,
we are engaging in what psychologists call *overlearning.* Even if a student correctly answers every question on a test, he is engaging in behavior that is instructionally valuable, *apart from the evaluation function being served* by the test.
Scheduled examinations not only stimulate review (relearning and overlearning)
but also foster overlearning through the process of reacting to test questions
that assess content already completely mastered. The value of overlearning
for long-term retention is apparent in Figure 1–2, which presents the results
of the classic study by Krueger (1929). The degree of retention of the meaning
of a learned set of nouns was very slight for the no-overlearning group (bottom
line), whereas the overlearning groups had a much superior degree of retention.
Underwood (1964, p. 140) stated, "The evidence that such continued repetition
does influence retention performance is so strong that it cannot be dismissed."

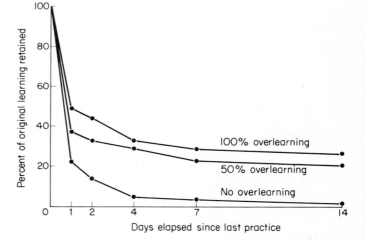

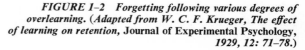

**FIGURE 1–2 *Forgetting following various degrees of
overlearning. (Adapted from W. C. F. Krueger, The effect
of learning on retention, Journal of Experimental Psychology,
1929, 12: 71–78.)***

Although most of the research on overlearning has been based on the learning of mazes and nonsense syllables, it is probable that the forgetting curves for meaningful materials follow a similar but less dramatic pattern.

ADMINISTRATIVE FUNCTIONS

Tests Provide a Mechanism for "Quality Control" for a School or School System   National or local norms can provide a basis for assessing certain curricular strengths and weaknesses. If a school district does not have a means for periodic self-evaluation, instructional inadequacies may go unnoticed.

Tests Are Useful for Program Evaluation and Research   Outcome measures are necessary to determine whether an innovative program is better or poorer than the conventional one in facilitating the attainment of specific curricular objectives. Standardized achievement tests have been the key sources of data for evaluating the success of federally funded programs (Jacobs and Felix, 1968, p. 19), although several other criteria are required for any comprehensive evaluation.

Much of teaching consists of searching for better ways to help students learn. For example, if three different methods for aiding seventh-graders to solve arithmetic reasoning problems are readily available to the teacher, which one or ones should be used? Is one of the methods superior to the other two for all seventh-graders, or is one of them better for slow learners and another better for fast learners? This question suggests an experiment in which nine groups are used, comprising all combinations of three levels of ability (low, medium, and high) with the three methods. Tests would play a prominent part in such a study, but experimentation involves much more than just testing.

More generally, how does one evaluate the effects of new curricula and various "social reforms"? (See D. T. Campbell, 1969.) An innovation such as team teaching, computer-assisted instruction, compensatory preschool education, an eleven-month school year, or a radically different physics course may seem obviously promising to those who propose it, but skeptics will demand more evidence of its effectiveness than mere enthusiasm. In recent years much has been written about how to evaluate attempted improvements in school settings and elsewhere.

In this book we cannot consider evaluation of curricula further; the interested reader will want to consult especially the articles by Glass (1971), Hastings (1966), Scriven (1967), Stake (1967), and Stufflebeam (1966).[3] Bracht and Glass (1968) and Campbell and Stanley (1966) offered many pertinent principles of educational evaluation and research.

Tests Enable Better Decisions on Classification and Placement   Grouping children by their ability levels is an example of classification for which tests can be of value. Reading readiness tests can be helpful for placing first-grade pupils in the proper classes.

---

[3] These and related articles on evaluation are reproduced by Worthen and Sanders (1972).

Tests Can Increase the Quality of Selection Decisions   Scholastic-

aptitude and achievement-test scores have repeatedly demonstrated their value in identifying students who are or are not likely to succeed in various colleges. Certain jobs require special skills that are best assessed by well-designed tests. Tests are the primary criteria for identifying gifted or retarded children.

A test designed especially for a particular selection purpose may have quite different characteristics than one to be used for classification. For example, to select the sixth-grade pupils who are proper candidates for a special remedial-reading program would not require a test that would reliably detect differences between average and superior readers. However, to *classify* all pupils into high, average, and low reading groups would require a test that reliably differentiated among students along the entire reading-ability continuum. Classification is the process of deciding which "treatment" a person should receive, whereas the selection decision is concerned with whether the person should be treated, employed, admitted, or the like. The distinguishing feature of selection decisions is that some persons are rejected. A test that identifies kindergarten pupils who will have difficulty in reading (selection) may not be helpful in deciding which instructional strategy is best for a given pupil (classification).

Tests Can Be a Useful Means of Accreditation, Mastery, or Certification Tests on which standards of performance have been established allow the demonstration of competence or knowledge that may have been acquired in an unconventional way. The examinee may thereby receive some deserved credit or authorization. For example, the Tests of General Educational Development (GED tests) were designed to allow men returning from military service to receive formal credit for demonstrated proficiency in various areas of academic achievement. This provision expedited the acquisition of a high-school diploma for thousands of World War II veterans (Dressel and Schmidt, 1951; Lindquist, 1944). Students who have taken college-level courses in secondary schools can receive advanced placement in college if they demonstrate adequate competence on the *Advanced Placement Examination* of the College Entrance Examination Board (CEEB). In 1966 the CEEB began an extensive *College Level Examination Program* based on the principle of credit by examination (Flaugher, Mahoney, and Messing, 1967); CEEB's goal was to provide a national program of general and subject examinations so that persons who have reached a college level of achievement outside the classroom can receive college credit or placement. Tests on which there is an established standard for acceptable performance are often referred to as mastery or criterion-referenced tests.

Perhaps the most common example of a test serving as a means for demonstrating mastery or proficiency is that required for obtaining a driver's license. Additional examples are the state board examinations required for licensing physicians, dentists, lawyers, and psychologists.

GUIDANCE FUNCTIONS

Tests Can Be of Value in Diagnosing an Individual's Special Aptitudes and Abilities   Obtaining measures of scholastic aptitude, achievement,

11

*Measurement
and
Evaluation
in the
Educational
Process*

interests, and personality is often an important aspect of the counseling process. The use of information from standardized tests and inventories can be helpful for guiding the selection of a college, the choosing of an appropriate course of study, discovering unrecognized abilities, and so on. Of course there are poor tests just as there are good ones—they can be misused and misinterpreted, and in the wrong circumstances a test can become a weapon rather than a tool. In recent years attacks of various types have been made on tests (for example, Black, 1963; Gross, 1962; Hoffman, 1962; La Fave, 1966). An editorial in *Science* (Wolfle, 1965) indicated that there are two general kinds of criticism. Some critics have taken to task one or more published tests and have shown them to lack validity. Failing to separate the wheat from the chaff, critics have drawn the erroneous conclusion that because certain tests have major defects, all tests are poor. Other critics have found examples of inappropriate use or interpretation of the results from good tests and have "thrown out the baby with the bathwater." One of the objectives of this book is to reduce the number of such errors that its readers will make.

> When a student, because of proper use of test results, is well adjusted and challenged in his school classes, happy with his curriculum, and aware of his abilities and interests with respect to his educational and vocational future, then not only he himself benefits, but in the long run, teachers, counselors, schools administrators, college personnel, employers, and others benefit [Frickle and Millman, 1957, p. 74].

Post-Organizer [4]

Tests play an important role in today's schools and other aspects of life. Thus teachers, especially, as well as others must know how to use and interpret tests correctly.

Tests provide objective measurements upon which school decisions are based. *Instructionally*, tests provide for feedback, motivation, and overlearning. *Administratively*, tests facilitate "quality control," program evaluation and research, classification and placement, selection, accreditation, mastery, and certification. In *guidance*, tests serve to diagnose special aptitudes or abilities.

The plan of this book is to provide the necessary tools for proper selection and use of these various types of test. However, it is up to you to make competence in educational measurement a reality.

Plan of the Book

We hope that this book will contribute to your thinking and actions. You should finish it with more *knowledge* about the special concepts and principles

---

[4] Ausubel (1961) has used the term "organizer" to denote a passage containing relevant subsuming concepts. Rothkopf (1966) has labeled material designed to facilitate learning by a focusing effect as "mathemagenic." The work of these researchers and others (Frase, 1967; Grotelueschen and Sjogren, 1968) indicates that attention-directing mechanisms can be useful aids to learning, especially if the organizer follows the reading of new material (Baumann, Glass, and Harrington, 1969).

12

*Measurement
and
Evaluation
in the
Educational
Process*

of measurement and evaluation than you may now possess. You will learn to *apply* your knowledge to new problems that confront you, to *analyze* situations efficiently, to *synthesize* (put ideas together creatively) well, and to *evaluate* soundly on the basis of internal evidence (for example, within a test itself) and outside information (such as published standards for tests).

This book is important only to the extent that you permit it to *change* you. Your altered thoughts and actions are the sole objectives of instruction. Your continuous increase in measurement competence during the years following the first use of *Educational and Psychological Measurement and Evaluation* is the ultimate criterion.

In this chapter you have glimpsed a few of the ways in which measurement and evaluation figure prominently in the educative process. The ideas and operations we have mentioned will receive detailed treatment in the chapters that follow.

Educational and Psychological Measurement and Evaluation contains three main sections: the first five chapters deal with fundamental principles and concepts of measurement and evaluation; the next eight chapters are concerned with the construction, evaluation, and use of measuring instruments, and the final five chapters pertain to the use of various types of standardized test and other measures. Appendix A offers a glossary of measurement terms along with other technical material that can be used during the course and later.

If you use *EPME* as a textbook in a course (rather than for private study), your instructor may omit certain chapters, reflecting local needs and objectives. The extensive author and subject indexes should help you bridge any discontinuity that might result.

IMPORTANT TERMS AND CONCEPTS

evaluation	classification
measurement	selection
subjectivity	mastery test
objectivity	criterion-referenced test
overlearning	

SUGGESTED READINGS

BARCLAY, J. R. 1968. *Controversial issues in testing.* Boston: Houghton Mifflin Company.

Chapter 2, "Testing and culture," is a discussion of the role of assessment in society and illustrates the social impact of testing. Barclay feels that the treating of test scores as criteria rather than as fallible predictors of criteria is the chief threat to proper, beneficial social consequences of testing.

CHAUNCEY, H., and J. E. DOBBIN. 1963. *Testing: Its place in education today.* New York: Harper & Row, Publishers.

Chapters 6, 7, and 8 present a concise, readable overview of the role of tests (1) as tools in the teaching-learning process, (2) in selection and admission, and (3) in guidance.

DYER, H. S. 1967. The discovery and development of educational goals. *Proceedings of the 1966 Invitational Conference on Testing Problems.* Princeton, N.J.: Educational Testing Service, pp. 12–24. Reprinted in G. H. Bracht, K. D. Hopkins, and J. C. Stanley. 1972. *Perspectives in educational and psychological measurement.* Englewood Cliffs, N.J.: Prentice-Hall, Inc., Selection 2.

EBEL, R. L. 1962. Measurement and the teacher. *Educational Leadership*, October, **20**: 20–24.

———. 1964. The social consequences of educational testing. *Proceedings of the 1963 Invitational Conference on Testing Problems.* Princeton, N.J.: Educational Testing Service. Reprinted in G. H. Bracht, K. D. Hopkins, and J. C. Stanley. 1972. *Perspectives in educational and psychological measurement.* Englewood Cliffs, N.J.: Prentice-Hall, Inc., Selection 1.

FINDLEY, W. G., ed. 1963. The impact and improvement of school testing programs. *The sixty-second yearbook of the National Society for the Study of Education, Part II.* Chicago: University of Chicago Press.

Each chapter in this volume is written by a recognized testing specialist. The first three chapters are especially appropriate for supplementary reading for Chapter 1: R. L. Ebel, The relation of testing programs to educational goals, pp. 28–44; W. G. Findley, Purpose of school testing programs and their efficient development, pp. 1–27; and J. W. Wrightstone, The relation of testing programs to teaching and learning, pp. 45–81.

GOSLIN, D. A. 1967. *Teachers and testing.* New York: Russell Sage Foundation.

This volume presents the findings of an elaborate sociological survey concerning (1) the use of tests in the schools, (2) the training and competence of teachers in testing, and (3) teacher practices and opinions regarding a variety of testing issues.

HAWES, G. R. 1964. *Educational testing for the millions: What tests really mean for your child.* New York: McGraw-Hill Book Company.

This book is written primarily for parents who are confused about the role of standardized testing in the schools. Hawes has done an excellent job of answering most of the questions parents may raise regarding intelligence, achievement, and personality tests, and their educational uses and misuses.

THORNDIKE, R. L. 1964. Educational decisions and human assessment. *Teachers College Record*, **66**: 103–112.

WRIGHTSTONE, J. W. 1957. Do students benefit from testing? *The High School Review*, **41**: 75–78.

2

STATISTICAL CONCEPTS IN
TEST INTERPRETATION

Measurement and evaluation, which involve the assigning of numbers to observed data and the interpretation of those numbers, are coming more and more to depend on statistical procedures.[1] Nearly all of today's test manuals refer to central tendency, variability, percentiles, standard scores, reliability, and validity. It is usually presumed that the reader is at least familiar with the most commonly used statistical terms and concepts. Some understanding of these concepts is essential for proper use and evaluation of standardized tests. In addition, at least a rudimentary grasp of basic statistical concepts is required for comprehending much of the current educational literature. The use of statistical methods is not restricted to bureaus of educational testing and research; they may, when properly understood, be put to good use by educators. People in virtually *all* fields of education and psychology can expect increased emphasis on, and use of, statistical techniques in the future.

The view emphasized some years ago by a renowned teacher of educational statistics (Walker, 1950, p. 31) is even broader: "The conclusion seems inescapable that some aspects of statistical thinking which were once assumed to belong in rather specialized technical courses must now be considered part of general cultural education." Even to be an intelligent reader of the popular press frequently requires knowledge of certain statistical concepts.

Nearly all elementary measurement texts and most general psychology textbooks include a chapter on statistics, hopefully designed to teach in a week

---

[1] Unfortunately, some persons have equated the use of numbers with dehumanization. To hold that quantification is tantamount to impersonalization imputes virtue to ignorance. Categories of performance, whether reported in terms of numbers, letters, or words, have precisely the same function—to describe and evaluate as accurately as possible.   *14*

or two material usually covered in an entire course. Though some of these chapters are very good, they inevitably fail to attain their unrealistic goal, for it is virtually impossible to teach much about statistics in such a short period of time. The situation becomes doubly frustrating when we realize that it is neither appropriate, practicable, nor justifiable to devote a *major* portion of a measurement course to statistics.

We have tried to solve this dilemma in several ways. We have interspersed sequences of programmed material on statistics throughout the chapter. This type of material lends itself especially well to self-instructional methods. The same concepts are also presented in the usual narrative manner. This dual presentation, approaching the concepts from different perspectives, should reduce the amount of instructional time required for mastery of these concepts.

We have omitted unnecessary and obsolete technical material and procedures and have attempted to emphasize concepts more than computations. An instructional mastery test of twenty-five multiple-choice items at the end of this chapter will help you assess your grasp of basic principles and assist you in identifying topics in need of further study. A summary of common statistical terms and symbols and a selected list of statistical textbooks appear at the end of the chapter. Appendix A gives a glossary of measurement terms and concepts.

Despite these aids, you will probably find that you cannot read this chapter quickly and easily. It will require the same sort of careful study you would use in preparing a mathematics or physics assignment. This effort, however, should result in a considerable improvement of your ability to understand statistical communication.

Frequency Distributions, Central Tendency, and Skewness[2]

1. Many individuals, including teachers, falsely assume that one must have a good mathematical background and high quantitative ability to learn and to use statistics. Everyone makes frequent use of statistics whether he is aware of it or not. Most teachers at some time require statistical computations from their pupils. When one discusses topics such as the average rainfall, temperature, and income, he is dealing with statistical data. When the weather man records a new high or low temperature for a given day of the year, he is conveying statistical information. If a child's reading achievement is evaluated in relation to his IQ, the statistical concept of correlation is implicit. So, although we may not be statisticians in a technical sense, we all use and are benefited by _____ in our work and recreational activities.

statistics

[2] To obtain maximum educational benefit from the programmed instruction, the student should cover the answer with a card and view it only after he has responded.

2. Statistics have many functions. They summarize and simplify otherwise unwieldy kinds and quantities of data. They help bring order out of chaos. For example, suppose John obtained a raw score of 15 on a 20-word spelling test. This score cannot be directly evaluated in terms of quality of performance relative to that of other pupils, since we know nothing about the difficulty of the test. His score may have been the best or even the poorest score in the class. When we examine the scores of the entire class of 30 pupils, John's score begins to acquire meaning. These scores, in haphazard order, were 13, 12, 15, 13, 14, 18, 13, 13, 12, 14, 16, 17, 14, 15, 11, 16, 15, 14, 19, 14, 16, 17, 11, 9, 18, 12, 17, 16, 15, and 20. It can be seen that John's score of 15 is somewhere in the middle range of the group. A more accurate interpretation is possible if the raw scores above are tallied into a *frequency distribution*. A frequency distribution shows the number of persons obtaining each score. If we listed each score with the number of times it was obtained, we would be making a _____ _____.

frequency distribution

3. The spelling scores from the frame above are partially tallied in the frequency distribution below. Complete it:

Score	Frequency	
20	/	
19	/	
18	/ /	
17	/ / /	
16	/ / / /	
15	/ / / /	
14	/ / / / /	
13	/ / / /	
12		12–///
11		11–//
10		10–
9		9–/

4. The frequency distribution facilitates a more meaningful interpretation of John's score. We can see at a glance that the lowest score was 9 and the highest was ____, a range of ____ points. (To obtain the range, simply subtract the lowest score from the highest.)

20, 11

5. The range gives us some idea about the variability of a set of scores, but one also wants information regarding the point about which the scores tend to cluster—that is, a measure of average or *central tendency*. There are three common measures of central tendency—the *mean*, *median*, and *mode*. The most frequently occurring score is called the mode. On the spelling test more pupils earned the score of ____ than any other one score; therefore, the mode of that distribution is ____.

14
14

6. One can quickly determine the mode by finding in a distribution the score that has the greatest _____.

frequency

7. The mode of the following set of scores is ____. 1, 3, 4, 4, 4, 5, 5, 6

4

8. Another measure of central tendency is the median. The median is the point that divides the scores of the examinees into two halves. The median is another name for the fiftieth percentile, because 50 percent of the frequencies lie above the median and 50 percent below it. The median of the seven scores [11, 12, 12, 13, 14, 15, 17] is ____, but the mode is ____.

13, 12

9. The simplest way to determine the median is to arrange the raw scores from low to high and then count up to the middle "score"—that is, to the point at which one-half of the scores are exceeded. The median for the following distribution of scores [52, 59, 61, 66, 68, 75, 77, 84, 88] is ____.

68

10. In the distribution above, were there an equal number of scores above and below the median? ____.

Yes

11. When there are an even number (N) of examinees, the median is halfway between the two middlemost scores. For example, the median of the four scores [21, 23, 24, 25] is ____.

23.5 (or $23\frac{1}{2}$)

12. If one additional score, 30, were added to the distribution above, the median would be ____.

24

13. If one additional score, 50, were added to the distribution in frame 9, the median would be ____.

67

14. In the frequency distribution below, the mode is ____. How many of the examinees earned the score of 6? ____ From the frequency column we can determine that there is a total of ____ scores in the distribution. The median of the distribution is ____.

7
2
9
7

Score X	Frequency f
9	1
8	2
7	3
6	2
5	1

15. We have been discussing the mode and median, but the mean is the most widely used and, generally, the best measure of central tendency. It is simply the sum of the scores divided by the number of scores. The formula for computing the mean reads:

$$\bar{X} = \frac{\Sigma\, X}{N},$$

where: $\bar{X}$ = the symbol for mean,
Σ = a symbol meaning "the sum of,"
X = any one of the scores, and
N = the number of scores.

The formula above, if expressed in words, would read: the mean equals the _____ of the raw scores divided by the _____ of scores.   sum, number

---

16. Here is an example. Find the mean of these scores: 2, 3, 5, 7, 8, 9. $\Sigma\, X =$ 2 + 3 + 5 + 7 + 8 + 9 = 34, $N = 6$, and therefore $\bar{X} = 34/6$ or 5.67. For the following set of scores: 3, 2, 5, 8, 2, $\Sigma\, X =$ ____, $N =$ ____, and   20, 5
$\bar{X} =$ ____.   4

---

17. When the term "average" is used, it usually refers to the mean. The mean is the most stable or reliable measure of central tendency; the mode, the least stable. In other words, if a group was randomly divided into halves and the measure of central tendency was computed separately for each half, the difference between the modes would tend to vary most. Since modes are highly unstable, large samples are required before modes can be meaningfully interpreted. If a choice were available, one generally would prefer the _____ over the median, and the median in turn over the _____.   mean, mode

---

18. Let us review. There are three commonly used measures of central tendency. Usually, the scores will cluster around the most frequently occurring score, called the _____. The point that separates the frequency distri-   mode
bution into two equal-sized groups (halves) is called the _____.   median
The most dependable or stable measure of central tendency is the _____,   mean
which is affected by the precise value of every score in the set.

---

19. Many of the distributions we will consider will be rather symmetrical and *"bell-shaped."* The distributions of many human traits such as height, weight, IQ score, and reaction time tend to be rather symmetrical and "bell-shaped." Distributions that are symmetric and have a certain "peakedness" are termed *normal distributions*. In a perfectly normal distribution the mode, median, and mean have the same value. Since IQ scores tend to be approximately normally distributed with a mean IQ of 100, the median and the mode of IQ scores both have the values of _____ also.   100

20. If the mean of a distribution differs considerably from the median, the shape of the distribution is not symmetrical, and therefore cannot be _____. normal

21. The shape of a distribution can provide some useful clues about the adequacy of a test. If the test has inadequate ceiling (is too easy), the scores will pile up toward the high end of the distribution as shown in the distribution below. Such asymmetrical distributions are said to be *skewed* (it appears as if a normal curve has been pushed to one side). When the "tail" points to the left, the curve is said to be skewed negatively or skewed to the left. In this distribution there were many rather _____ scores, but high
relatively few _____ scores; and the distribution would be described low
as being _____ negatively. skewed

Low   High
−   +
Scores

22. A test may be so difficult that there are many low scores and few high scores. Such a distribution would be described as being skewed
_____. Draw a distribution with positive skewing. (Low positively
scores are always placed to the left, and high scores to the right, just as

was done in the previous frame.) _____.

23. When skewing is present and the samples are large enough to make the measures of central tendency stable, those measures will differ systematically. As shown in the diagrams below, the mean is always "pulled" most toward the tail and the mode the least; the median is between the mean and the mode. Since the height of the curve represents frequency, the highest point in the curve indicates the _____ of the distribution. mode

$\bar{X}$ Md Mo   Mo Md $\bar{X}$

24. If the mean has a lower value than the median, the distribution is probably skewed _____. If the mean has the highest value of the three negatively
measures of central tendency, the distribution is probably skewed
_____; if the mean, median, and mode have the same value, positively
the shape of the distribution is probably _____. normal

25. Which one of the following four terms is most out of place with the other three?

normal   skewed   bell-shaped   symmetrical   skewed

---

26. Let us return to the common situation in which a test was too easy for a given group of examinees. The actual shape of the curve for the group of test scores will be skewed _____. The measure of central tendency that will have the largest value is the _____; the measure of central tendency with the smallest value is the _____.

negatively
mode
mean

Actual distribution of scores

Distribution of true ability

---

27. The measurement of individual differences with this easy test was adequate for examinees of low ability, but true ability differences were obscured for the more capable examinees, since an adequate test ceiling was lacking. A test with inadequate ceiling is like a high-jump apparatus that does not allow the crossbar to go beyond a certain height, a height below the jumping ability of many participants. (The psychological effect on the talented *may* be similar in both situations; that is, challenge and motivation for improvement are decreased.) Ideally, the distribution of observed scores and the distribution of the examinees' true abilities should be similar. Distributions of the true abilities are rarely significantly skewed unless some deliberate selection of the group has taken place.

    A crude indication of skewness can be obtained by comparing the measures of central tendency, especially the mean and the median. (The mode is quite unreliable unless the sample is very large; consequently, it is not very useful for indicating skewness.) If the mean and median are close in value, the distribution is probably not seriously skewed. If the mean IQ for a class is found to be 110 and the median, 100, the distribution is probably skewed _____. If a class had a mean of 89.3 and a median of 90.1, do you think serious skewing would be present? _____

positively
No.

---

28. Sketch a distribution having a mean of 70, a median of 65, and a mode of 55. The distribution is skewed _____. (As a rule, the mean and median will differ less than will the median and the mode.) _____.

positively

$Mo \mid \bar{X}$
Md

29. If the mean of a large distribution is 40 and the median 50, would the mode probably be above or below 50? _____   above

These and additional concepts will now be developed in conventional narrative style.

Classification and Tabulation

Before test scores or other quantitative data can be clearly understood and interpreted, it is usually necessary to organize and summarize them. Table 2–1 shows a class record for a reading readiness test administered to a first-grade class at the beginning of the school year. The names appear in alphabetical order, together with scores, as they are recorded in the teacher's class

TABLE 2–1
A Class Record for a Reading Readiness Test (36 Pupils)

Pupil	Score	Pupil	Score	Pupil	Score	Pupil	Score
David A.	90	Don F.	95	Jerome L.	75	Mary S.	75
Barbara B.	66	Larry F.	78	Mary M.	75	Paul S.	81
Charles B.	106	Richard G.	70	Billy N.	51	Richard S.	71
Robert B.	84	Grover H.	47	Nancy O.	109	Robert S.	68
Mildred C.	105	Robert H.	95	Carrie P.	89	William S.	112
Robbin C.	83	Sylvia H.	100	Ralph R.	58	Jean T.	62
Robert C.	104	Warren H.	69	George S.	59	Adolfo W.	91
Diney D.	82	Clarence K.	44	Gretta S.	72	Dolores W.	93
Jim D.	97	Jack K.	80	Jack S.	74	Richard W.	84

roll book. However, the scores do not mean very much in this form. For example, we can tell only with some difficulty whether David, with a score of 90 points out of a possible 128, is a very superior or just an average pupil, compared with his classmates.

RANK ORDER

Ordinarily the first step is to arrange the scores in rank order, usually from the highest to lowest. This is called a *rank-order distribution*. The first column of Table 2–2 shows the same 36 scores as Table 2–1, arranged in order of size from 112 to 44. This table also gives the *rank* of the pupils in order (1st, 2nd, ..., 36th). It is now easy to see that David A.'s score of 90 gives him a rank of 12 in the class of 36, or about one-third of the way from the top. Similarly, it is easy to interpret each of the other scores in terms of rank. But ties are likely to occur, especially in classes of 20 or more pupils. Notice, for example, that two pupils made a score of 95. Since it is not correct to say that one ranks higher than the other, we must assign them the same rank. Since there are seven pupils who rank higher (1, 2, 3, 4, 5, 6, 7), the next two ranks, 8 and 9, are

TABLE 2-2

**Reading Readiness Scores from Table 2–1 Arranged in Rank Order
and Tabulated into an Ungrouped Frequency Distribution**

Rank-Order Distribution		Ungrouped Frequency Distribution			
Score	Rank	Score	Frequency	Score	Frequency
112	1	112	1	76	0
109	2	111	0	75	3
106	3	110	0	74	1
105	4	109	1	73	0
104	5	108	0	72	1
100	6	107	0	71	1
97	7	106	1	70	1
95	8.5	105	1	69	1
95	8.5	104	1	68	1
93	10	103	0	67	0
91	11	102	0	66	1
90	12	101	0	65	0
89	13	100	1	64	0
84	14.5	99	0	63	0
84	14.5	98	0	62	1
83	16	97	1	61	0
82	17	96	0	60	0
81	18	95	2	59	1
80	19	94	0	58	1
78	20	93	1	57	0
75	22	92	0	56	0
75	22	91	1	55	0
75	22	90	1	54	0
74	24	89	1	53	0
72	25	88	0	52	0
71	26	87	0	51	1
70	27	86	0	50	0
69	28	85	0	49	0
68	29	84	2	48	0
66	30	83	1	47	1
62	31	82	1	46	0
59	32	81	1	45	0
58	33	80	1	44	1
51	34	79	0	$N = $	36
47	35	78	1		
44	36	77	0		

averaged, giving a rank of 8.5 for each score of 95. In like manner the average of ranks 14 and 15 is 14.5, and so on for the other pupils with tied scores. There are *three* pupils with scores of 75, and there are 20 pupils who rank above this score; the average of the next three ranks (21, 22, and 23) is 22, which is the rank assigned to each of the scores of 75. In addition to the time and bother required to determine these ranks, the list is long, unwieldy, and inadequate for making comparisons with other classes that are much larger or much smaller; ranking 19th in a class of 36 pupils is poorer than ranking 19th in an equally capable class of 70. This method of organizing scores into rank order tends to conceal the magnitude of ability differences between ranks at the extremes (highest or lowest ranks) and to exaggerate small ability differences in performance near the middle.

THE UNGROUPED FREQUENCY DISTRIBUTION

An *ungrouped* frequency distribution can be a useful way of presenting data for certain purposes. If we start with the lowest score and list every *possible* score with its frequency until we have included the highest score, we will construct an ungrouped *frequency distribution*,[3] also shown in Table 2–2. The various scores are arranged in order of size, here from 112 to 44, and to the right of each score is recorded the number of times it occurs. Each entry to the right of a score is called a *frequency*; the total of the frequencies is represented by N, which here is 36.

If marks or other categorizations of the scores are to be assigned, it is preferable (if there is no fixed standard of performance, such as 70–79 percent = C) to establish the cutting scores for the groupings at a point where there will be a "gap" between the lowest score in one category and the highest score in the next lower category. Recall that the data in Table 2–2 represent scores on a reading readiness test, and suppose that the pupils were to be grouped "homogeneously" into reading groups on the basis of the reading readiness test scores. It would be much better to set a score of 89 to be the minimum for the top group, rather than 90 or 91, since a break occurs between 89 and 84.

If the scores in Table 2–2 represented composite scores for students in a course, it would often be more defensible to set 104 as the minimum for a grade of A rather than 105 or 106. If one had only a rank order of scores, a failure to make this kind of reasonable distinction would be more likely.

Central Tendency and Variability

Two of the most important concepts that apply to various kinds of test data are central tendency and variability. These abstract notions are useful in summarizing the main features of a bewildering mass of figures. It is possible to understand them fairly well at a conceptual level apart from the computational details. The computations do, however, further enrich one's understanding of the statistical concepts.

A tendency for the scores to concentrate somewhere near the "center" is characteristic of most frequency distributions, as typified in the data shown in Table 2–2. An important statistic is, therefore, the point on the scale around which the scores tend to be grouped or centered. This is a measure of *central tendency*; it is the value that typifies and best represents the whole distribution.

We might want to know which of several schools or classes made the "best" record on a certain test, and which the "poorest." To determine this, we would compute an average for each school, and then note which had the

---

[3] In the past, considerable attention has been given to the mechanics of grouping into fewer and larger-sized intervals for "computational convenience." With the limited numbers of scores that confront most teachers, together with the widespread availability of calculating machines or computers, the student no longer need be burdened with rote computational mechanics, which obscure the logical meaning of various statistical measures.

highest average and which had the lowest.[4] Statisticians use several different "averages." Three of the most useful are the median, the mean, and the mode.

A widely used average in educational measurement is the *median. The median is the score point that divides the distribution into halves.* Of the 36 frequencies in Table 2–2, half (18) are for scores of 112 through 81; the other half are for scores of 80 through 44, as shown. Thus, the midpoint of the frequencies lies between 81 and 80, or at 80.5. This is the same point we would arrive at by arranging the 36 test papers in decreasing order by score (112, 109, . . . , 47, 44) and then counting halfway down in the pile. The average of the score on the 18th test paper (81) and the score on the 19th paper (80) is 80.5, the point in the test-score distribution above and below which half of the scores lie. This point is called the *median.*

In an ungrouped distribution, the *midscore* may be called the median. For example, if 31 students took a test, the 16th highest score would be the median—15 scores would be above it and 15 scores below it. Strictly speaking, when N is an even number, there is no midscore. In that case it is customary to average the middle pair of scores as we did in the example given in Table 2–2. The median of the distribution of the 36 scores shown in Table 2–2 is 80.5, the average of the middle pair of scores.

The median is often used as a reference point for describing the location of individual pupils in a distribution. A pupil in the higher half is said to be "above the median," one in the lower half "below the median." If John received a score of 29 on a test with a median of 26, he scored in the upper half of the class. Since the median is the point that divides a distribution into two equal-sized groups, 50 percent of the scores are below the median; therefore, *the median is always the fiftieth percentile* (to be discussed later).

If scores are ranked or in an ungrouped frequency distribution, the median is easier to obtain than is the arithmetic mean, which, for the data in Table 2–2, is found by adding together all 36 scores and dividing by 36. For most of the classroom teacher's purposes, the median provides a sufficient indication of the *central tendency* of the test scores.

The most familiar average is the arithmetic *mean.* This measure is in such common use that many people regard it as *the* average because it is the only average they know anything about. When the term "average" is used in ordinary conversation or in newspapers in such statements as "average temperature," "average rainfall," "average yield of corn and wheat," and "average price," it is likely that the arithmetic mean is meant.

The mean can be computed by simply obtaining the sum of the measures and dividing by their number. The measure so obtained is then the value that each individual would have if all shared equally. Unlike the median, the mean is affected by the *magnitude* of every score in the distribution. Increase any

[4] Obviously, in order to be statistically *and* educationally significant, the difference between high and low schools should be fairly large.

score by 10 points and you increase the mean by 10/N points, where N is the number of scores in the distribution. Decrease any score by 20 points and you lower the mean by 20/N points. Increase the highest score (112) in Table 2–2 and decrease the lowest score (44) all you please, and not only will the *median* remain unchanged, but so will all the ranks.

If scores are not grouped into a distribution and one has access to an adding machine, computing the mean of 25 or more scores may require less time than computing the median. *On well-constructed tests designed to measure individual differences, the mean will usually differ little from the median.* The formula for the mean is given below:

$$\bar{X} = \frac{\Sigma X}{N},$$

where: $\bar{X}$ = the mean,
X = a score,
Σ = a symbol meaning "the sum of," hence,
ΣX = the sum of all scores, and
N = the number of scores.

The symbol Σ (Sigma) means "the sum of." The symbol X is consistently used to represent scores.

Using the data given in Table 2–2, we find the sum of all 36 ($N = 36$) scores, ΣX, to be 2894. Substituting these values into the formula for the mean, we find that:

$$\bar{X} = \frac{\Sigma X}{N} = \frac{2894}{36} = 80.39 \qquad \text{or about 80.4.}$$

You will notice that here the mean (80.39) and median (80.5) are quite close in value. This will be the case in any approximately symmetrical distribution. The most common symmetrical distribution is the so-called *normal curve*, the type of distribution that describes many human characteristics and abilities. Characteristics of the normal distribution will be discussed later in this chapter.

THE MODE

The most frequent score is called the *mode*. It is determined by inspection. In Table 2–2 the mode of the scores is 75, because more pupils (3) made that score than any other. The crude mode is not a very reliable average, especially with small groups. In our example the changing of two scores could shift the mode considerably. If one of the pupils who made 75 had made 76, and if the one who made 97 had made 95, the mode would increase from 75 to 95, since more pupils (3) would then have made that score than any other. Largely because of its fickleness, the mode is not highly regarded as a measure of central tendency for small groups.

COMPARISONS OF
THE MEAN, MEDIAN, AND MODE

The sum of the deviations (differences) of all scores from the arithmetic mean is always precisely zero (provided that one does not lose sight of the plus and

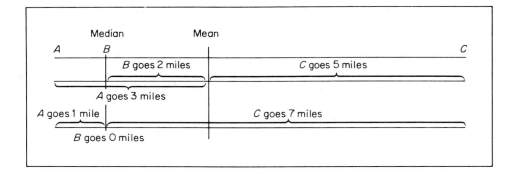

FIGURE 2–1 Travel distance (sum of deviations) is less to median than to mean. (From an example suggested by Eells, 1961.)

minus signs). When we consider only the *size* of the difference between each score and the "average," we will observe that the sum of these differences is less from the median than from any other score or point[5]—a fact that gives some logical appeal to the median as a measure of "average" or central tendency. These characteristics of the mean and median can be shown clearly with an example, illustrated in Figure 2–1. Suppose that three men (A, B, and C) live beside an 8-mile-long straight road at distance 0, 1, and 8 miles from its "origin"—that is, A at the beginning, B 1 mile from the beginning, and C at the end. The mean of 0, 1, and 8 is 9/3 = 3, whereas the median (here also the midscore) is 1. If these men desire to meet at some one point along the road, where should it be? If they meet at the mean point, 3 miles, then A will drive 3 miles, B 2 miles, and C 5 miles, a total of 3 + 2 + 5 = 10 miles. If they meet at the median, which is B's house, A will drive 1 mile, B 0 miles, and C 7 miles, 8 miles in all. Thus they drive 10 − 8 = 2 miles less to the median than to the mean, though C may point out that only A and B benefit, because *he* has to drive two miles further to reach the median than the mean. A and B each save 2 miles if the median is used, while C loses 2, resulting in the net saving of 2 + 2 − 2 = 2 miles.

If we took an 8-inch ruler and put equal weights at 0, 1, and 8 inches, it would balance if a fulcrum were placed at 3. "Weight" on one side of the mean is equal to that on the other side. If we think of frequencies as being weights, we see immediately that any score distribution balances at its mean ("center of gravity"), but not at its median unless mean and median happen to be the same.

We have already recommended use of the median for most practical work with the test scores of less than 50 or so students. If a mean is desired, we can readily compute it from scores using an electric desk calculator that multiplies, adds, and divides—or even by using an adding machine. The main office of most school systems, even small ones, usually has such equipment.

Which average is best? Overall, *the mean is regarded as the best measure*

[5] It should be clear that in this case we are considering the *absolute* values of the deviations—that is, the magnitude of the differences irrespective of sign.

of central tendency—it is the most *reliable* average. Reliable means stable. If you gave two equivalent tests to a class, as a general rule the two means would differ less than the two medians, which would differ less than the two modes. The mean, however, is greatly influenced by skewness. (See Figure 2–3, p. 49.) Whenever we wish to avoid this influence, the median is best. Since such situations often arise in educational measurement, the median is widely used. For example, if a test is too difficult, there may be several zero or chance scores; if a test is too easy, there may be several perfect scores. But in neither case are the pupils at the extremes correctly measured. In such situations, the median is usually the best or most descriptive average to use. The median is also easier to find than the mean if there are more than 50 scores (unless an electric calculator or electronic computer is available).

An illustration may help to indicate appropriate uses of these measures of central tendency. Suppose that a school district employs 100 persons, all of whom earn between $6,000 and $12,000 per year, except for five administrators who each earn more than $20,000. The *mean* salary for the district is likely to be misleadingly high, since it does not adequately characterize the 95 nonadministrators. However, the *median* will not be sensitive to the great discrepancy of the few high salaries. In fact, we can determine the median without even knowing the actual salaries of the administrators by just having a top category of "more than $12,000" whose frequency is 5. In such instances, it may be desirable to use both the median and the mean. It would probably be even more meaningful to exclude the five administrators from the distribution and to report their salaries separately. The 95 teachers represent a more homogeneous group, yet even here there would probably be skewing in the distribution, with new teachers near the bottom of the salary schedule far outnumbering old-timers who are receiving the maximum. A "manipulating" superintendent might use the mean as the "average" salary when recruiting teachers and the mode as the "average" when trying to obtain public support for an increase in teachers' salaries. In skewed distributions, the median is usually the best single measure, although each average conveys some complementary information. A church might find that over a period of a year the average member gave $0 or $300, depending on whether the mode or the mean was used.

An improbable anecdote will illustrate further the unique aspects of each average. Five men once sat together on a park bench. Two were vagrants, each with total worldly assets of 25 cents. The third was a workman whose bank account and other assets totaled $2,000. The fourth man had $15,000 in various forms. The fifth was a multimillionaire with a net worth of $5,000,000. Therefore, the modal assets of the group were 25 cents. This figure describes two of the persons perfectly, but is grossly inaccurate for the other three. The median figure of $2,000 does little justice to anyone except the workman. The mean, $1,003,400.10, is not very satisfactory even for the multimillionaire. If we *had* to choose one measure of central tendency, perhaps it would be the mode, which describes 40 percent of this group accurately. But if told that "the modal assets of five persons sitting on a park bench are 25 cents," we would be likely to conclude that the total assets of the groups are approximately $1.25, which is more than $5,000,000 lower than the correct figure. Obviously, no measure of central tendency whatsoever is adequate for these "strange benchfellows," who simply do not "tend centrally." Fortunately, in such situations we need not choose one, but can report two or three different measures of central tendency as needed to summarize the distribution accurately.

Measures of Variability

---

30. Although measures of central tendency indicate the scores of the average performers and the values about which the scores tend to cluster, they provide no information on the degree of individual differences or variability that exists among students. We have already been introduced to one measure of variability, the difference between the highest score and the lowest score, which is called the _____ .

range

---

31. The range, however, is crude and gives only a rough measure of variability or dispersion. The two distributions shown below have the same mean and median and the same _____ , yet are markedly different.

range

---

32. Curve A in the frame above is a *rectangular distribution* and might represent the ages of a large group of entering kindergarten pupils (excluding early and late entrants). Curve B appears to be a _____ distribution.

normal

---

33. To emphasize the need for measures of variability as well as measures of central tendency, consider the three normal distribution curves below, each having identical means, modes, and _____ . Although their averages are the same, they differ greatly in their degree of dispersion or _____ .

medians

variability

---

34. In the previous frame, the curve with the greatest amount of variability is
_____. The curve with the least spread in scores is _____.

A, C

35. Since the range is a crude, undependable indicator of variability, more
refined measures of dispersion have been devised. The most widely used
is the *standard deviation*, symbolized for a population by the Greek letter
σ (sigma), or for a sample by s. We know now that the mean, median,
and mode are measures of _____ _____, and the range and
standard deviation are measures of _____.

central tendency
variability

36. A simple example will illustrate the direct computation of the standard
deviation from its definitional formula. The formula for the standard deviation[6] is:

$$s = \sqrt{\frac{\sum x^2}{N}},$$

where: s = the standard deviation,
$\quad\quad N$ = the number of scores, and
$\quad\sum x^2$ = the sum of the squared deviation of the scores from the mean,
$\quad\quad\quad$ with $x = X - \bar{X}$.

The scores of five examinees on a test are 40, 35, 30, 25, 20.

X	x	x^2
40		
35		
30		
25		
20		

You recall that to compute the mean, one finds the sum of the raw scores
and divides by the number of scores.

$$\bar{X} = \frac{\sum X}{N}, \quad \text{or} \quad \bar{X} = \frac{(\quad)}{(\quad)}, \quad \text{or} \quad \bar{X} = \underline{\quad}.$$

$\frac{150}{5}$, 30

---

[6] For purposes of this course, no computational distinction will be made between the
sample standard deviation, s, and the population value, σ. When a class of students includes
all persons about whom we want to make inferences, it is then the *population* in a statistical
sense. In all computations, the maximum-likelihood variance estimate is employed; that is,
$\sum x^2$ is divided by N and not by $N - 1$. Contrary to popular opinion, even when $N - 1$ is
used in computing the standard deviation, the resulting s is not an unbiased estimate of the
standard deviation in the population (see Glass and Stanley, 1970, p. 253). Unless N is very
small (ten or less), the computed values using N and $N - 1$ will not differ meaningfully.
We shall divide by N throughout and designate all computed standard deviations with the
symbol s.

29

37. Since x is the difference between X and $\bar{X}$, we simply subtract $\bar{X}$ from every raw score; that is, $x = X - \bar{X}$, to obtain the corresponding x-values. For the score of 40, $x = ($ ___ $) - ($ ___ $)$ or ____.

40, 30, 10

38. For the score of 20, $x = 20 - ($ ___ $)$ or ____.

30, -10

39. Enter the x values for 40 and 20 in the x column. The x values for 25, 30, and 35 are ____, ____, and ____, respectively.

-5, 0, 5

40. The column x^2 represents the squared deviations from the mean for each score. [When a number is *squared*, it is multiplied by itself.] For example, three squared (3^2) means 3 times 3, which equals 9. The x value for the score of 40 was found to be 10; therefore the square of 10 will be entered into the corresponding row of the x^2 column. $(10)^2 = $ ____.

100

41. The corresponding x^2 values for scores 35, 30, 25, and 20 are 25, ____, ____, and _____.

0, 25
100

42. The formula calls for N, which in this problem is ____, and for $\sum x^2$. We remember that $\sum$ means _____ _____ ____.

5
the sum of

43. The sum of x^2 is the total of the x^2 column. $\sum x^2$ for this problem is _____.

250

44. Let's "plug in" our numerical values for N and x into the formula:

$$s = \sqrt{\frac{(\quad)}{(\quad)}} = \sqrt{(\quad\quad)}$$

$\sqrt{\dfrac{250}{5}}$, $\sqrt{50}$

45. We shall not review here the process of extracting a square root. For our purposes an approximation is satisfactory. Most statistics books contains square-root tables if you desire an accurate value. Our present problem is to estimate the square root of 50. We know that the square root of 49 is ____ (that is, $7 \times 7 = 49$); therefore we conclude that the square root of 50 is slightly more than ____.

7
7

46. To summarize: the mean of the distribution with which we have been working—that is, 40, 35, 30, 25, 20—is ____; and the standard deviation is approximately ____.

30
7

47. Let's review the steps we have taken in the computation of a standard deviation.

1. First the mean is computed.

30

2. Next, the deviation (x) of each score from the mean is found by subtracting the mean from each of the scores.

3. Finally, these deviations are squared and placed in the x^2 column. When this column is totaled, we have the value indicated by the symbols _____, which is then divided by the number of scores (N). The square root of the resulting value is the _____ _____ of the distribution.

Σx^2

standard
deviation

---

48. In frames 48–52 you will compute the standard deviation for the distribution of scores below.

X	x	x^2
7		
4		
3		
3		
2		
2		
0		

$\Sigma X =$ _____

21

---

49. The mean of the distribution is _____. The values for the x column from top to bottom are 4, 1, 0, 0, -1, _____, and _____.

3

$-1, -3$

---

50. The corresponding x^2 values from top to bottom are: 16, 1, 0, 0, 1, _____, and _____. The value for $\Sigma x^2 =$ _____.

1

9, 28

---

51. The standard deviation is then the square root of the value

$$\sqrt{\frac{(\quad)}{(\quad)}} \quad \text{or} \quad \sqrt{(\quad)}.$$

$\sqrt{\dfrac{28}{7}}, \sqrt{4}$

---

52. The square root of 4 and consequently the standard deviation for the distribution is _____ points.

2

Now that we have found the standard deviation, you might ask, "So what?" You will soon see how the standard deviation is of great value in interpreting pupil performance, especially in standardized tests. This will become clear when you are more familiar with the normal distribution and its relationship to the standard deviation.

Knowledge of central tendency and variability convey important information about the quality of a test. Central tendency depicts a test's difficulty level, and variability indicates the degree to which individual *differences* are reflected among these scores.

You are now ready to read and overlearn these and related concepts, which are presented next in narrative style.

No distribution is described completely by a measure of central tendency. The mean intelligence in two classes may be the same, and yet the classes may be very unlike. Whereas the members of one class, assigned randomly, may vary all the way from being mentally retarded to being intellectually gifted, the members of the other class (homogeneously arranged) may differ little from each other intellectually. Obviously, these two classes present contrasting instructional problems because they differ in *variability*. Variability is the extent to which the scores of a group tend to scatter (disperse, spread) above and below a central point in the distribution. Clearly, it is important to have some convenient method for determining the variability of a group. Three common measures of variability are the *range*, the *quartile deviation*, and the *standard deviation*. All these measures represent distances rather than points, and the larger they are the greater the variability (scatter, spread, heterogeneity, dispersion) of the scores.

THE RANGE

The range is simply the distance between the highest score and the lowest score.[7] From the data given in Table 2–2 (p. 22) the range can be readily determined:

Range = the highest score (112) *minus the lowest score* (44) = 68 points.

Since the range depends solely on the two most extreme scores, it is a very untrustworthy, unreliable measure of variability. The shift in a single score may greatly alter the range, thereby substantially increasing or reducing the apparent variability of the group. In addition, the range is highly dependent on the number of scores in the set of scores. As the size of the group increases, the range will tend to increase; therefore the ranges of groups of unequal size cannot be meaningfully compared. Nevertheless, the range can serve as a "quick and dirty" (that is, approximate) measure of dispersion.

THE QUARTILE DEVIATION
AND PERCENTILES

A proper understanding of the quartile deviation as a measure of variability depends on a knowledge of percentiles.[8] You will recall that the median is the 50th percentile; that is, 50 percent of all the frequencies lie below that point and 50 percent lie above it. A percentile is a score point in the score distribution below which the stated percentage of all measures lies. Thus an individual who scores at the 30th percentile of his class has done better than 30 percent of the students and poorer than 70 percent. Percentiles are computed in much the same manner as the median; the only difference is that the number of frequencies to be counted up (or down) varies with the percentile desired.

---

[7] In some books, the range is defined as the difference between the highest score and lowest score, plus one point to allow for exact upper and lower limits of the obtained scores. This, however, does not reflect the range in the scores *actually obtained*, and has no real advantage over the simpler definition.

[8] Referred to in some sources as centiles

1. Find 25 percent (or $\frac{1}{4}$) of N; $\frac{1}{4}N = \frac{1}{4}(36) = 9.0$. Therefore, there will be 9 scores below and 27 above the 25th percentile. (It is necessary to bear in mind that a test score represents an *interval* of one point in a continuous distribution. That is, a score of 62 actually extends from 61.5, its lower limit, to 62.5, its upper limit.)

2. Count frequencies beginning with the lowest score to the point below which one-fourth ($N/4$) of the scores fall. In our example we find that the ninth score is 69; hence to include "all" of it below the 25th percentile we must go to its upper limit, 69.5, which then is the 25th percentile—that is, the point below which 25 percent of the scores fall. This point is also called the first *quartile* (Q_1), the point below which the first quarter of the scores fall. Had there been 38 scores rather than 36 in the set, the 25th percentile would have exceeded $38/4 = 9.5$ scores. Therefore, we would have added one-half (.5) of the tenth score interval to the upper limit of the ninth score (69.5); thus the 25th percentile would have equaled $69.5 + .5 = 70.0$.

It is important to distinguish between percent and percentile. *Percentiles* pertain to points that exceed a certain *percent of the scores*; it is not to be confused with the *percent of the items* or questions correctly answered on the examination. *The percentile rank of a score is the percent of scores that were exceeded (or equaled) by the particular score.*[9]

The quartile deviation (Q) has been extensively used in the past. Q is defined as one-half the distance between the first and third quartiles. It is often referred to as the semi-interquartile range (that is, half the range of the extreme quartiles).

The formula used for obtaining Q is:

$$Q = \frac{Q_3 - Q_1}{2} = \frac{75\text{th percentile} - 25\text{th percentile}}{2}.$$

Since 25 percent of the scores fall below the first quartile, Q_1, and 25 percent of the scores lie above the third quartile, Q_3, the interquartile range is the range of the middle 50 percent of the scores. The whole interquartile range might be used to express the variability of the group, but it is customary to take half this distance and to set up a new middle-half range extending from Q below the median to Q above the median:

$$\text{Mdn} \pm Q = Q_2 \pm \frac{Q_3 - Q_1}{2}.$$

As already noted, the middle of the interquartile range will usually not be exactly the median, but it will be close to the median unless the distribution

---

[9] It is not appropriate to pursue the computation of percentiles and percentile ranks extensively in a measurement course. Any elementary statistics textbook will give further details not presented here. The primary use to be made of percentiles by test users is in the *interpretation* of standardized test results. The typical teacher is rarely involved in direct *computation* of percentiles, but often he must interpret percentile ranks from standardized tests. The computational process is illustrated, however, in Table 2-3 in the calculation of the 25th and 75th percentiles (Q_1 and Q_3).

TABLE 2–3

The Process of Computing the Quartile Deviation, Q
(Distribution from Table 2–2)

Scores		Steps in Process
112		1. Computing Q_1, the 25th percentile:
109		$\frac{1}{4}N = \frac{1}{4}$ of 36 = 9.
106		Nine scores fall below 69.5 = Q_1.
105		
104	9 scores	
100		
97		
95		
95		
$Q_3 = 94$		
93		2. Computing Q_3, the 75th percentile:
91		$\frac{3}{4}N = \frac{3}{4}$ of 36 = 27.
90		At or below a score of 93 are found 27 scores;
89		at or above a score of 95 are found 9 scores.
84		"Splitting" the difference yields 94, the 75th
84		percentile or Q_3.
83		
82		
81		
80	18 scores	
78		
75		
75		
75		
74		
72		
71		
70		
$Q_1 = 69.5$		
69		3. Substituting in the formula $Q = (Q_3 - Q_1)/2$:
68		$Q = \dfrac{94.0 - 69.5}{2} = \dfrac{24.5}{2} = 12.25.$
66		
62		
59	9 scores	For practical use, round this off to 12.
58		
51		
47		
44		

is severely skewed. Exactly half of all the frequencies lie within the interquartile range and exactly half outside it, but this does not hold precisely for Mdn $\pm Q$ unless the distribution is perfectly symmetrical.

Table 2–3 illustrates the computation of Q using the scores given in Table 2–2. Notice that the process of locating quartiles is like that of locating any other percentile. In the first step, the fractional part of N indicates the proportion of the distribution that falls below the desired point; that is, for Q_1 it is $\frac{1}{4}N$ and for Q_3 it is $\frac{3}{4}N$. There are three steps, as follows:

1. *Compute* Q_1, *the 25th percentile.* To begin with, one-fourth of 36 is **34**

9.0. The next three steps in locating this point are exactly the same as those locating any percentile. *Check your work* by counting downward from the top of the distribution $\frac{3}{4} \times 36 = 27.0$ frequencies.

2. *Compute Q_3*, the 75th percentile. Here the first step is to take $\frac{3}{4}N$; $\frac{3}{4}$ of 36 is 27.0. The other three steps are identical with those in locating any percentile. *Check your work* by counting downward $\frac{1}{4}$ of $36 = 9.0$ frequencies.

3. Insert Q_1 and Q_3 values into the formula, $Q = (Q_3 - Q_1)/2$, to obtain Q. Q_3 is 94.0, and Q_1 is 69.5. The difference between them is 24.5. Half of this difference is 12.25, the value of Q. You will notice that the value of $Q_1 + Q$ (that is, $69.5 + 12.25 = 81.75$) is not precisely equal to Q_2 (80.5), although the difference is slight, since the distribution of the sample scores is relatively symmetrical. In fact, the difference between Q_2 and $Q_1 + Q$ is a rough measure of the degree of skewness in a distribution.

The use of Q as a measure of variability has steadily decreased over the past several decades because it lacks some of the important features of the next measure we shall consider—the standard deviation.

THE STANDARD DEVIATION

A third measure of variability, which has many uses in educational measurement, is the *standard deviation*. Customarily represented by the letter s for samples and σ (the Greek letter "sigma") for populations, it is defined as the square root of the mean of the squares of the deviations of the scores from their mean.

Let us illustrate the computation of the standard deviation of a set of test scores directly, following the definition above. The formula below shows the standard deviation to be the square root of the average squared deviation of each score from the mean:[10]

$$s = \sqrt{\frac{\Sigma\, x^2}{N}} \quad \text{or} \quad \sqrt{\frac{\Sigma\, (X - \bar{X})^2}{N}}.$$

Using the 36 scores of Table 2–1, whose mean we already know to be 80.4, the standard deviation is:[11]

$$s = \sqrt{\frac{(90 - 80.4)^2 + (66 - 80.4)^2 + \cdots + (84 - 80.4)^2}{36}}$$

$$= \sqrt{\frac{10,688.56}{36}} = \sqrt{296.9044} = 17.2.$$

You can save much time by working directly with "raw" scores instead

---

[10] See footnote 6, page 29, for distinction between σ and s.

[11] The majority of readers of this book will have forgotten or repressed the computational details for determining square roots. The computations are so tedious and time-consuming that, in our opinion, it is an unwarranted expenditure of your time to relearn the computational mechanics. It will usually take less time to consult a square-root table than it will to perform the required arithmetic operations. By trial and error, one can usually obtain a reasonably accurate value.

of deviations from means, using an electric calculator and the following formula:

$$s = \frac{\sqrt{N \sum X^2 - (\sum X)^2}}{N},$$

or

$$s = \frac{\sqrt{36(90^2 + 66^2 + \cdots + 84^2) - (90 + 66 + \cdots + 84)^2}}{36}$$

$$= \frac{\sqrt{8,760,024 - (2894)^2}}{36} = 17.2.$$

(Will s computed by these two methods always be identical? Yes, except possibly for a slight difference due to rounding-off errors. The two formulas are algebraically equivalent.)

Persons who really need to compute standard deviations will usually be able to find an electric calculator. For most teachers, bothering with such things as "arbitrary-origin" computational procedures and those involving negative deviations is probably too time-consuming to be practicable. There are several shortcut procedures for computing s or σ, but we will consider only one of them, which has been shown to be very accurate (Jurs and Hopkins, 1971; McMorris, 1971; Mason and Odeh, 1968; Sabers, 1970).

Diederich (1964, p. 19) proposed a quick estimate of the standard deviation for classroom use by teachers.[12] It is simply the *difference* in the sums of the top and bottom one-sixth of the scores divided by $N/2$. His formula is:

$$s' = \frac{\sum (\text{upper } N/6 \text{ scores}) - \sum (\text{lower } N/6 \text{ scores})}{N/2}.$$

In our sample data given in Table 2–2, $N/6 = 36/6 = 6$, so the highest and lowest six scores will be used.[13]

$$\sum \longrightarrow (\text{upper 6 scores}) = 112 + 109 + 106 + 105 + 104 + 100 = 636,$$

$$\sum \longrightarrow (\text{lower 6 scores}) = 44 + 47 + 51 + 58 + 59 + 62 = 321.$$

Therefore:

$$s' = \frac{636 - 321}{N/2} = \frac{315}{18} = 17.5.$$

The value of s' (17.5) is a good approximation of s (17.2). The values of s' and s will usually differ by less than 2 percent on classroom tests (Sabers, 1970).

When high precision is required, one should find a calculator and use the raw-score-formula computations for s. Have someone who is familiar with the machine show you how to square scores and sum them at the same time. Be sure, however, that you actually need the standard deviation. Unless you wish to estimate test reliability or validity, you probably do not. The greatest

---

[12] Diederich's method is a slight simplification of a method originally proposed by Jenkins (1946). The rationale for these shortcut methods is given by Lathrop (1961). The derivation assumes scores are normally distributed, although it appears to work quite well on nonnormal distributions (Jurs and Hopkins, 1971).

[13] If $N/6$ is not a whole number, Ebel (1965) recommends that the number of scores in the upper and lower sixths be rounded to the nearest whole number. This procedure appears to be sufficiently accurate for classroom use (Sabers and Klausmeier, 1971).

use of the standard deviation by the classroom teacher will be in the interpretation of norms that use the standard deviation as a unit (that is, standard scores), which are considered later in this chapter.

The standard deviation is the most important measure of the variability of test scores. A small standard deviation indicates that the group has small variability —that is, it is relatively homogeneous with respect to the characteristic—whereas a large standard deviation indicates the opposite condition, heterogeneity.

The standard deviation also has certain other important uses, besides being a measure of dispersion of scores within a group. For example, the position of a pupil in a distribution is often expressed in terms of standard-deviation units. In the distribution used in Table 2–2, where the mean is approximately 80 and the standard deviation is approximately 17, a pupil whose score is 97 is said to be one standard deviation above the mean; his score may be written $+1s$. In like manner, a pupil with a score of 63 would be approximately one standard deviation below the mean, and his score is written $-1s$. Such scores are called *standard scores* or *z-scores*, which we discuss below.

Which measure of variability is best? As a rule, the standard deviation is considered the best and most reliable measure of variability; the range is undoubtedly the poorest. The range is subject to many of the limitations that the mode has as a measure of central tendency. Whenever it is desirable, therefore, to avoid the influence of skewing, the median is employed as a measure of central tendency, and with it a percentile measure of variability, such as Q. Similarly, when the mean is used, s is the appropriate measure of variability, because like the mean it is a function of all the scores in the distribution.

The standard deviation will be of interest chiefly because it is used a great deal by test publishers and educational researchers. You need to understand what it means far more than how to compute it. Part of the next chapter is devoted to a study of test manuals in order to reveal what statistics are mentioned there and how such statistics help you understand the tests better. First, however, we will discuss standard scores and several other topics.

The Normal Distribution

53. Since many traits are normally distributed, or approximately so, it is desirable to become acquainted with the properties of the normal curve. Look at the normal curve below. It is unimodal (scores cluster around a single point) and symmetric (if the portion to the left of the mean were folded over upon the right half, there would be an exact "fit"). Notice that

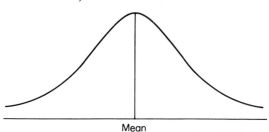

Mean

the "tails" never quite touch the baseline, although they continue to approach it more closely as one moves further from the _____.

mean

---

54. We have previously learned that in normal distributions, the mode, _____, and _____ are identical in value.

median
mean

---

55. If we begin at the mean and mark to the left and to the right in units of one standard deviation, we find that a normal distribution spans approximately ____ standard deviations (see curve below). That is, very few scores deviate by more than ____ standard deviations above or below the mean.

6
3

---

56. Since the curve is symmetric, the area to the left of the mean equals the area to the _____ of the mean. Therefore, the area between the mean and one standard deviation above the mean is the same as that between the mean and one standard deviation _____ the mean.

right

below

---

57. Remembering that the height of the curve at a given point denotes the frequency of scores at that point, we can say that in a normal distribution there are as many scores that are one standard deviation above the mean as there are that are _____ standard deviation below the mean.

one

---

58. It should be clear that the area of the curve between two points represents the number or frequency of scores falling between those two points. In a normal distribution, 34 percent of the scores fall between the mean and one standard deviation above the mean; therefore, between the mean and one standard deviation below the mean fall ____ percent of the scores.

34

---

59. In the normal curve below, the percent of the area (or the percent of the cases) falling in the shaded area between one σ below the mean *and* one σ above the mean is ____ percent + ____ percent, or ____ percent.

34, 34, 68

60. The area under the curve from mean -1σ to mean $+1\sigma$ includes approximately two-thirds of the scores. About one-_____ of the scores fall outside this range.

third

61. We have seen that approximately one-third of the scores lie more than one standard deviation from the mean. Consequently, one-_____ of the total scores fall above mean $+1\sigma$ and one-sixth fall below _____.

sixth

mean -1σ

62. The standard deviation on the Wechsler Intelligence Scale for Children (WISC) (and several other intelligence tests) is 15, and the mean is 100. By applying what we have just learned about the normal curve, we can say that about two-thirds of all IQ scores obtained on this test fall between 85 and _____; one-sixth of the population receive IQ's above _____; one-_____ have IQ's below 85.

115, 115
sixth

63. In the previous frame, we interpreted the WISC IQ's in terms of approximate fractions. To be more precise, assuming the IQ scores to be normally distributed, we would say that ____ percent of the examinees taking this test obtain IQ's between 85 and 115; ____ percent would have IQ's above 115; and 16 percent would have IQ's below ____. Eighty-four percent have IQ's above ____.

68
16
85
85

64. A common method of reporting test scores is percentiles (often called centiles—that is, hundredths). A person obtaining an IQ of 85 on the WISC exceeds 16 percent of the population—that is, his score is at the 16th percentile; the percentile *rank* of the 85 is 16. An individual obtaining an IQ of 100 exceeds ____ percent of the population and therefore is said to be at the _____ percentile. If a student obtains a WISC IQ of 115, he scores one standard deviation above the mean, and since the percent of the IQ's that fall between the mean and one standard deviation distant from it is ____, he exceeds ____ percent more scores than did the person with an IQ of 100. Therefore the percentile rank of his IQ score is ____.

50
50th

34, 34
84

65. Complete the fractions that approximate the portion of the curve in the corresponding segments shown below. Only 2 percent of the cases in a normal distribution fall below the point -2σ, two standard deviations below the mean. The corresponding percentile equivalent of -2σ to be inserted in the appropriate blank below the point on the curve is 2. Since the curve is symmetrical, can you determine the corresponding percentile value for $+2\sigma$? If 2 percent of the population fall below -2σ, then ____

2

percent fall above $+2\sigma$. Consequently $+2\sigma$ exceeds 98 percent of the scores and is at the _____ percentile.

98th

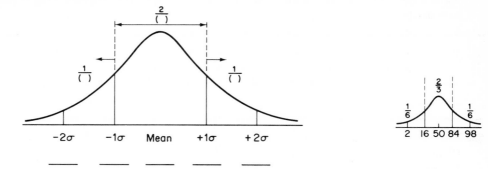

Percentile rank: _____ _____ _____ _____ _____

---

66. If the WISC IQ distribution exactly followed the normal probability curve, and if persons having IQ scores below 70 were arbitrarily classified as mentally retarded, about ____ percent of the population would meet this criterion for mental retardation.

2

---

67. Remembering that for a random sample of children the mean IQ on the WISC is _____ and the standard deviation is ____, insert the missing percentile ranks and corresponding WISC IQ's in the rows provided below the normal curve.

100, 15

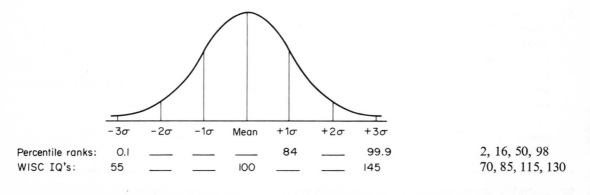

	-3σ	-2σ	-1σ	Mean	$+1\sigma$	$+2\sigma$	$+3\sigma$	
Percentile ranks:	0.1	____	____	____	84	____	99.9	2, 16, 50, 98
WISC IQ's:	55	____	____	100	____	____	145	70, 85, 115, 130

---

68. Assuming a perfect normal distribution, if 100 randomly selected children were given the WISC, we would expect approximately:

  _50_ percent to have IQ scores above 100
  ____ percent to have IQ scores above 115   16
  ____ percent to have IQ scores below 115   84
  ____ percent to have IQ scores below 85   16
  ____ percent to have IQ scores below 130   98

40

_____ percent to have IQ scores above 70   98
_____ percent to have IQ scores between 85 and 115   68
_____ percent to have IQ scores between 100 and 130   48
_____ percent to have IQ scores between 70 and 130   96
_____ percent to have IQ scores above 130   2
_____ percent to have IQ scores between 85 and 130   82
_____ percent to have IQ scores below 145   100 (99.9)

69. The mean (in grade-equivalent scores) for the California Reading Test at the beginning of the third grade is 3.0; the standard deviation is 1.0. Complete the grade-equivalent blanks below on the normal curve for the points extending two standard deviations in each direction from the mean.

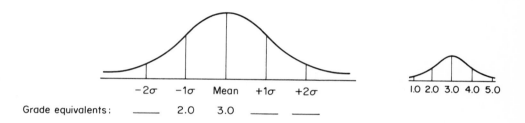

Grade equivalents: _____   2.0   3.0   _____   _____

70. The curve above shows that at the beginning of grade 3, 50 percent of the pupils obtain a grade-equivalent score of _____ or better. Bob's score on the test was 3.0, which has a percentile rank of _____. Approximately one-sixth of the children receive scores above _____. About 1 pupil in 6 obtains a score of below _____. A score of 4.0 is at the _____ percentile; a score of 2.0 is at the _____ percentile. In a class of 30 typical students, approximately 5 will have grade equivalents above _____ and 5 below _____. What score places a pupil at the 98th percentile? _____ This means that he probably reads better than about _____ out of every 100 students across the nation who are entering grade 3. The middle two-thirds of a typical class will probably receive grade-equivalent scores between _____ and _____.

3.0
50
4.0
2.0, 84th
16th
4.0, 2.0
5.0
98

2.0, 4.0

71. On the California Reading Test above, the average beginning fourth-grade student would be expected to receive a score of _____. Approximately what percent of beginning third-grade pupils achieve scores higher than the average beginning fourth-grade student? _____ This demonstrates the substantial overlap in achievement between the grades.

4.0

16

72. If the standard deviation at grade 4 were the same as that for grade 3 (it is actually slightly larger), the *average* entering third-grade student would score higher than what percent of the students in grade 4? _____

16

73. Suppose a pupil received a score of 72 on a 100-item test. Does this really give any indication of the quality of his performance relative to that of the students tested? This could be the highest or the lowest score for the group of examinees. What additional information is needed before the score of 72 begins to take on meaning? You probably are thinking that knowledge of the mean or median would help, and of course it would. Suppose the mean on the test was 62. You now know that the score of 72 is a better-than-average score; but how much better? It is probably between the 51st and 99.9th percentile, but at what point within the interval? It is evident that, in addition to having information on central tendency, you also need data regarding _____.

variability

74. You remember that the most reliable measure of central tendency is the _____, and the most reliable measure of variability is the _____ _____. If we know these two measures we can evaluate the above score of 72 more accurately. Assume that the distribution of test scores was approximately normal in form (which is common on well-constructed tests) and that the standard deviation was 5. Since the mean was 62, the score of 72 was how many standard deviations above the mean? ____. This is equivalent to a percentile rank of ____. Now the score of 72 has taken on more concrete meaning.

mean, standard deviation

2
98

75. Fortunately, statisticians and psychometricians have devised a system of reporting test scores on standardized tests so the interpreter always knows the mean and standard deviation because they are constant. Such types of score are called *standard scores*. Regardless of what the raw-score mean and standard deviation on a given test happen to be, they are converted to a *common* mean and a *common* standard deviation and are expressed in terms of standard-deviation units; hence they are called standard scores. Since the standard-score mean and standard deviation are known and fixed, any given score automatically takes on meaning. Standard scores are especially useful for standardized tests. It is impractical for a teacher to continually refer back to a test manual to remind himself what were the values for the mean and standard deviation. Scores expressed in terms of a standard, constant mean and a standard, constant standard deviation are called _____ _____.

standard scores

76. Look at Figure 2–2 (p. 47), showing the normal curve. Notice the section illustrating typical standard scores. The *z*-score type of standard score is simply a standard score in which a raw score is expressed in terms of the number of standard deviations it deviates from the mean. A raw score one standard deviation above the mean is equivalent to a *z*-score of +1. If a score is one-half of a standard deviation below the mean, in *z*-score units it would be —.5. A minus value for a z-score indicates that the score falls below the _____. A z-score of +2 is two _____ _____ above the mean.

mean, standard
deviations

---

77. A score of 72 on the test having a mean of 62 and a standard deviation of 5 is ____ standard deviations above the mean. Expressed as a z-score, the same score of 72 is ____.

2
+2

---

78. Obviously, the mean deviates not at all from itself; therefore, the mean of any z-score distribution is ____.

0

---

79. The standard deviation of the z-score distribution is ____. If the mean of a raw-score distribution is 80 and the standard deviation is 8, a score of 72 will be ____ on the z-score scale.

1

—1

---

80. The z-score system itself is not widely used in reporting test results, but it does enable us to better understand the standard scores that are. Notice the T-score row of Figure 2–2 (p. 47). The T-score type of standard score has a mean of ____. If we move to a point one standard deviation above the mean, we can see that the standard deviation of the T-score system is ____, since we move up ten units in going from the mean (50) to one standard deviation above the mean (60).

50

10

---

81. We remember that a score at the second percentile is about ____ standard deviations below the mean. Expressed in T-score units this would be ____, since it is two standard deviations (or $2 \times 10 = 20$) below the T-score mean of ____.

2
30

50

---

82. If two tests present results in the same standard-score system, an examinee's relative level of performance can be compared directly without any additional information, since the mean and the _____ _____ for both sets of scores will be the same.

standard
deviation

---

83. Consider the following example, which illustrates the advantages of standard-score norms: Miss Martin teaches sixth grade. Suppose one of her pupils, Tommy, obtained an IQ of 132 on a group intelligence test and a grade-equivalent score of 7.6 on a reading test. (Both tests were normed on the same group of examinees.) Is his reading relatively better or poorer than his performance on the intelligence test? Miss Martin no doubt knows that an IQ of 132 is a high score and that 7.6 is a good reading score, but are they equally good? Is a grade-placement score of 7.6 relatively better or poorer than an IQ of 132? Are their percentile ranks equivalent? As it stands, Miss Martin has no way of knowing without obtaining

information regarding the central tendency and variability of the respective tests. Suppose she finds from the tests' manuals:

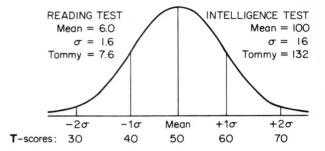

READING TEST
Mean = 6.0
σ = 1.6
Tommy = 7.6

INTELLIGENCE TEST
Mean = 100
σ = 16
Tommy = 132

	-2σ	-1σ	Mean	$+1\sigma$	$+2\sigma$
T-scores:	30	40	50	60	70

Tommy is ____ standard deviations above the mean on the intelligence test, which would be equivalent to a T-score of ____. On the reading test he is only ____ standard deviation(s) above the mean, equivalent to a T-score of ____. Now it is obvious that his reading performance is considerably below his performance on the intelligence test, although he is well above the group's means on both.

2
70
1
60

---

84. Notice that the teacher had to go to the test manuals to determine the relative status of 132 and 7.6. If both tests had used the same standard score system, such as T-scores, the relative status would have been apparent at a glance. Since the standard deviation for the T-score type of standard score is 10, the T-score of ____ on the intelligence test would exceed the reading-test T-score of ____ by 10 points or by ____ standard deviation(s).

70
60, 1

---

85. It is evident that Miss Martin's task of equating or comparing scores would be much easier and more accurate if the results were expressed in _____ scores, since the scores have the same meaning relative to their common norm or reference group. A reference group is the group from which the norms were derived.

standard

---

86. Assume that a given raw score was 45 in a distribution having a mean of 33 and a standard deviation of 12. The score of 45 would be ____ standard deviation(s) above the mean, which would place it at the _____ percentile. This would be equivalent to a z-score of ____ and a T-score of ____.

1
84th
1, 60

---

87. Most, but not all, intelligence tests report IQ's that are also a type of standard score called deviation IQ's. Referring again to the normal curve in Figure 2–2 (p. 47) we can see that the mean IQ on the Wechsler Intelligence Scales is _____, and the standard deviation is ____. Since 1960, when the L-M form of the Stanford-Binet Intelligence Scale was published, the mean of that test is 100 and the standard deviation is 16. If a person

100, 15

scores one standard deviation below the mean of his age group, his Wechsler IQ is ____, and his Stanford-Binet IQ is ____. If one is three standard deviations above the mean on the Wechsler, his IQ score is _____, whereas a score three standard deviations above the mean on the Stanford-Binet results in an IQ score of _____.

85, 84
145

148

88. Let us review some of the characteristics of standard scores. A given standard score has a fixed mean and _____ _____. Because of this, individual scores can be compared directly and easily interpreted. A disadvantage is that many users have not been introduced to them and consequently do not understand them. This situation is changing, however, and in the future we shall probably find that standard scores are being increasingly used in reporting results on standardized tests.

standard
deviation

89. Suppose Jon had the following percentile ranks (PR) from five standardized tests:

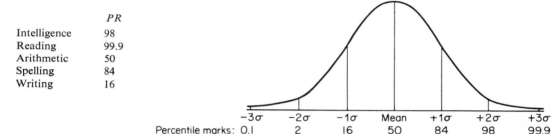

	PR
Intelligence	98
Reading	99.9
Arithmetic	50
Spelling	84
Writing	16

Look at the normal curve with the accompanying percentile ranks marked off in standard deviation units from the mean. From the percentile ranks it appears that Jon performed at about the same relative level on the intelligence and reading tests, whereas the difference is actually the same as that between the intelligence and spelling tests, assuming the scores were normally distributed. In both instances there was a difference of ____ standard deviation; yet in percentile units the difference was only 1.9 in the first comparison, but ____ in the second—again illustrating that equal differences in standard scores or raw scores do not yield equal differences in the corresponding percentile ranks, and vice versa.

1

14

90. Another example: If Jon improved his writing score by two standard deviations, his percentile rank would increase ____ percentile units; the same improvement in spelling would cause an increase of only ____ percentile units.

68
15.9

91. If, on the other hand, the scores had been expressed in standard score norms, no such problem of interpretation would have been present. Using normalized T-scores, the results would have been as follows:

	PR	T-score	
Intelligence	98	70	
Reading	99.9	____	80
Arithmetic	50	____	50
Spelling	84	____	60
Writing	16	____	40

92. We have mentioned two specific types of standard score: z-scores and T-scores. We will mention briefly one additional type, *stanines*, since several standardized tests employ it. Notice from Figure 2–2 (p. 47) that the stanine is a normalized standard score in which the mean is 5 and the standard deviation is 2. If a person scores at the 84th percentile (one standard deviation above the mean), his stanine score is ____.

7

93. Notice from Figure 2–2 (p. 47) that the stanine units are of equal width except in stanines 1 and ____. By using the normal-curve figure, indicate Jon's test performance using the stanine scale.

9

	PR	Stanine	
Intelligence	98	____	9
Reading	99.9	____	9
Arithmetic	50	____	5
Spelling	84	____	7
Writing	16	____	3

94. The different standard-score systems are special cases of the general expression[14]:

standard score = standard-score mean
+ (z-score)(standard-score standard deviation).

Figure 2–2 (p. 47) illustrates several typical standard-score systems. A score that is one standard deviation above the mean can be represented by a z-score of 1.0; a T-score of ____; a GRE score of _____; or a Wechsler IQ score of _____.

60, 600
115

The "Normal Curve"

If a test is neither too easy nor too hard for the group tested, scores will usually be distributed approximately "normally" (Lord, 1955)—that is, somewhat in the bell-shaped pattern of Figure 2–2. Notice that the curve is symmetrical (the

[14] The z-score in the expression is sometimes normalized (for example, with *true* stanines and T-scores); that is, the *obtained* percentile ranks are converted to the corresponding z-scores that exist in a normal distribution. If the transformation of the raw scores (X's) to z-scores is via the formula $z = (X - \bar{X})/s$, the z-score distribution is not normalized. (Of course, the X's themselves may be normally distributed, or nearly so, in which event the z-scores will be also.) Normalizing can be accomplished in several ways. One method is to compute the percentile for each score and convert it to a z-score via a normal-curve table, included in most elementary statistics books.

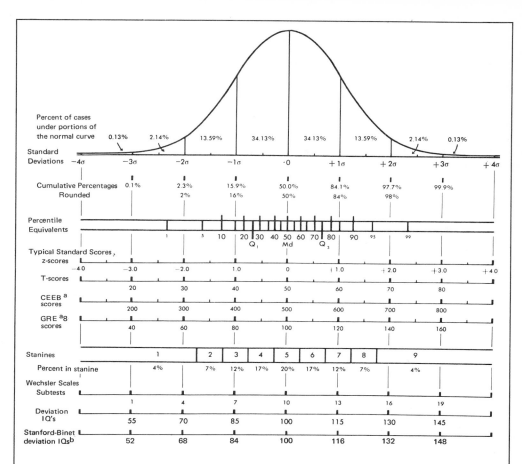

Percent of cases under portions of the normal curve	0.13%	2.14%	13.59%	34.13%	34.13%	13.59%	2.14%	0.13%

Standard Deviations: -4σ -3σ -2σ -1σ $\cdot 0$ $+1\sigma$ $+2\sigma$ $+3\sigma$ $+4\sigma$

Cumulative Percentages: 0.1% 2.3% 15.9% 50.0% 84.1% 97.7% 99.9%
Rounded: 2% 16% 50% 84% 98%

Percentile Equivalents: 1 5 10 20 30 40 50 60 70 80 90 95 99
Q_1 Md Q_3

Typical Standard Scores,
z-scores: -4.0 -3.0 -2.0 1.0 0 $+1.0$ $+2.0$ $+3.0$ $+4.0$

T-scores: 20 30 40 50 60 70 80

CEEB [a] scores: 200 300 400 500 600 700 800

GRE [a]g scores: 40 60 80 100 120 140 160

Stanines: 1 2 3 4 5 6 7 8 9

Percent in stanine: 4% 7% 12% 17% 20% 17% 12% 7% 4%

Wechsler Scales Subtests: 1 4 7 10 13 16 19

Deviation IQ's: 55 70 85 100 115 130 145

Stanford-Binet deviation IQs[b]: 52 68 84 100 116 132 148

THE NORMAL CURVE, PERCENTILES AND STANDARD SCORES

Distribution of scores of many standardized educational and psychological tests approximate the form of the NORMAL CURVE shown at the top of this chart. Below it are shown some of the systems that have been developed to facilitate the interpretation of scores by converting them into numbers which indicate the examinee's relative status in a group.

The zero (0) at the center of the baseline shows the location of the mean (average) raw score on a test, and the symbol σ (sigma) marks off the scale of raw scores in STANDARD DEVIATION units.

Cumulative percentages are the basis of the PERCENTILE EQUIVALENT scale.

Several systems are based on the standard deviation unit. Among these STANDARD SCORE scales, the z-score, the T-score and the stanine are general systems which have been applied to a

variety of tests. The others are special variants used in connection with tests of the College Entrance Examination Board, the Graduate Records Examination, and other intelligence and ability scales.

Tables of NORMS, whether in percentile or standard score form, have meaning only with reference to a specified test applied to a specified population. The chart does not permit one to conclude, for instance, that a percentile rank of 84 on one test necessarily is equivalent to a z-score of +1.0 on another; this is true only when each test yields essentially a normal distribution of scores and when both scales are based on identical or very similar groups of people.

Most of the scales on this chart are discussed in greater detail in Test Service Bulletin No. 48, copies of which are available on request from the Psychological Corporation, 304 East 45th St., New York, N.Y. 10017.

[a] Score points (norms) on the scales refer to university students and not to general populations.

[b] Standard-score "IQ's" with $\sigma = 16$ are also used on several other current intelligence tests, e.g., California Test of Mental Maturity, Kuhlmann-Anderson Intelligence Test, and Lorge Thorndike Intelligence Test.

FIGURE 2–2   Types of standard-score scales. The figure is adapted from Test Service Bulletin No. 48, The Psychological Corporation, New York, by permission of The Psychological Corporation.

left half is the mirror image of the right half) and unimodal (just one mode). In any symmetrical unimodal distribution, mean = median = mode. The "normal curve" is a special kind of symmetrical unimodal distribution whose relationship of height to width at every score is mathematically specified. (If you are curious, you can find the mathematical formula in most statistics books—for example, in Glass and Stanley, 1970, p. 97.)

In a normally distributed set of scores the 16th percentile (more precisely the 15.87th percentile) lies one standard deviation below the mean, and the 84th percentile lies one standard deviation above the mean. You can readily see this in Figure 2–2. Similarly, a score two standard deviations below the mean has a percentile rank of approximately 98 (97.72). The corresponding *PR*'s for -3σ and $+3\sigma$ are .13 and 99.87, respectively. The areas under various portions of the normal curve have been tabled in detail by Glass and Stanley (1970, pp. 513–519) and others; similar tables are found in most elementary statistics textbooks. From these tables we can readily ascertain the distance from the mean in standard deviation units that corresponds to any percentile rank, from no deviation, which corresponds to a *PR* of 50, to -3.719σ and $+3.719\sigma$, which are at the 0.01th and 99.99th percentiles, respectively.

Standard Scores

We have already wrestled with the problem of giving meaning to a student's raw test score, relative to his peers. One way is to express his score as a deviation from the mean of the group tested, such as -12 points if his score is 12 points below the mean. How low is his score? Twelve points below the mean might be the lowest score among 1,000 persons tested, if the standard deviation were small (3 or 4) and the scores distributed approximately normally. On the other hand, it would be the 16th percentile if the standard deviation were 12 and the scores normally distributed. Sixteen percent of the students would score more than 12 points below the mean. Therefore, it seems desirable to divide the deviation of a student's raw score from the mean by the standard deviation of the group to secure a "standard score" that indicates how many standard deviations above or below the mean he scored.

z - S C O R E S

The basic standard score is defined as

$$z = \frac{\text{raw score} - \text{mean}}{\text{standard deviation}} ; \qquad \text{that is, } z = \frac{X - \bar{X}}{s}$$

and is called a *z*-score.

The mean of a full set of *z*-scores is zero, because, of course, the mean does not deviate from itself. If a test had a mean of 62 and a standard deviation of 9, a raw score of 71 would be equivalent to a *z*-score of 1, since it is one standard deviation above the mean. In other words, *z*-scores are simply raw scores expressed in standard-deviation units from the mean. Therefore the standard deviation of a full set of *z*-scores is 1. If we plot the distribution of

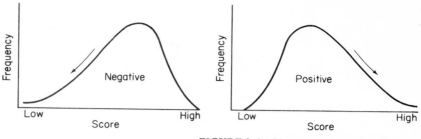

FIGURE 2–3 Negative and positive skewness.

z-scores, we find that it has exactly the same shape as the distribution of the original raw scores. Computing z-scores does *not* change the shape of the distribution. Skewed distributions—tailing off in one direction or the other, as in Figure 2–3—remain skewed; symmetrical distributions remain symmetrical.

Of course, z-scores below the mean are negative. Also, in order to get enough precision we must use at least one decimal place. This makes for such hard-to-handle z's as —2.3—negative and fractional. We can avoid minuses and decimals by simply setting up a distribution of standard scores with a mean sufficiently greater than 0 to avoid minuses, and a standard deviation sufficiently greater than 1 to make decimals unnecessary.

The general formula for any computed standard score is:

$$\text{standard score} = M + S(z)$$

$$= M + S\left(\frac{\text{raw score} - \text{mean of raw scores}}{\text{standard deviation of raw scores}}\right)$$

—that is,

$$= M + S\left(\frac{X - \bar{X}}{s}\right),$$

where: M = the standard-score mean,
S = the desired standard deviation of the standard scores, and
z = the z-score.

Wechsler's intelligence tests use the standard-score formula: IQ score = 100 + 15z. The 1960 Stanford-Binet Intelligence Scale has the standard-score formula: IQ score = 100 + 16z.

Is a score of 145 on the Wechsler Adult Intelligence Scale (WAIS) as rare as a score of 145 on the Stanford-Binet? It should be rarer, because (145 — 100)/15 = 3 is greater than (145 — 100)/16 = 2.81. If scores are normally distributed, 0.135 percent lie 3 or more standard deviations above the mean, whereas 0.248 percent lie above 2.81 standard deviations. The percentages themselves are small, but the ratio of 135 to 248 shows that only 54 percent as many IQ's of 145 or higher should occur on the WAIS as on the 1960 S-B. For each of his *subtests*, Wechsler chose an M of 10 and an S of 3 (see Figure 2–2, p. 47), terminating his scores at 0 and 20. Certain test results are reported on a $M = 500$, $S = 100$ scale, such as the Graduate Record Examinations and the College Entrance Examination Board's aptitude and achievement tests.

49

The T-scale employs a mean of 50 and a standard deviation of 10. This scale has all the properties of the *z*-scale without the awkwardness resulting from negative scores and decimal fractions. Any score can be converted to a nonnormalized T-score by using the formula

$$\text{T} = 50 + 10z \qquad \text{—that is, } 50 + 10\frac{(X - \bar{X})}{s}.$$

Normalized T-scores can be secured by converting raw scores to percentile ranks and then to the corresponding *z*-scores that these percentiles would have in a normal distribution, and then applying the formula above.[15] On well-constructed tests normalized and nonnormalized T-scores will differ little (unless the examinees are a select group, such as a class of gifted pupils). The T-scale is used for several standardized tests such as the Differential Aptitude Tests.

A dramatic advantage of using standard scores for reporting results is that the mean and the standard deviation can be the same for all tests, so that the pupil's relative performance on various tests can be directly compared. The percentile scale also has this advantage, but the marked inequality of percentile units makes the comparison of performance more imprecise (cf. Figure 2–2, p. 47). A raw-score difference corresponding to a difference of 14 percentile units (for example, 84th to 98th percentile) at one location in the distribution may be as large as a difference of 34 percentile points at another location in the distribution (for example, 50th to 84th percentile).

STANINES

Another common standard-score system is the "stanine" scale (standard scores with nine categories), which was developed and used extensively by the Army Air Force during World War II. Stanines are normalized standard scores with a mean of 5 and a standard deviation of 2.[16] Consequently, all stanines except 1 and 9 are one-half a standard deviation in width. The nine stanines 1, 2, 3, 4, 5, 6, 7, 8, and 9 are shown in Figure 2–4 in relation to the normal curve. Corresponding *z*-score and T-score limits are also given in Figure 2–4.

To convert a raw score to a stanine score one arranges the test papers in order from highest to lowest score. Pick the top 4 percent and assign them a stanine score of 9. The next 7 percent receive a stanine score of 8; the next 12 percent fall in stanine 7; the next 17 percent fall in stanine 6; the next 20 percent are in the 5th stanine, and so on. Sound simple? With a little practice, it is. Any conscientious clerk can secure stanine scores this way, and at the same time the scores are being *normalized*. Normalizing occurs when we squeeze the raw scores into an approximately bell-shaped form, as specified by the normal

[15] As originally proposed, the T-score scale was a normalized standard score. Some writers denote nonnormalized T-scores as *Z*-scores. Since on standardized tests and in several statistics and measurement textbooks the use of "T-score" is not delimited to normalized standard scores, we have not adhered to the original definition.

[16] The standard deviation of normalized stanine scores is not exactly 2.0, but 1.96, as shown by Kaiser (1958), who suggested a slight modification that would yield a standard deviation of precisely 2.0. For practical purposes the difference in the resulting scores is inconsequential.

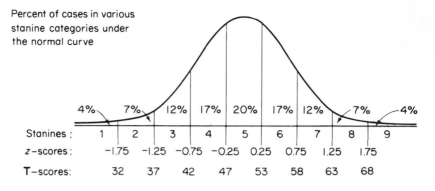

Percent of cases in various stanine categories under the normal curve

	4%	7%	12%	17%	20%	17%	12%	7%	4%
Stanines :	1	2	3	4	5	6	7	8	9
z–scores :		−1.75	−1.25	−0.75	−0.25	0.25	0.75	1.25	1.75
T–scores:		32	37	42	47	53	58	63	68

FIGURE 2–4   The stanine scale related to T-scores, z-scores, and the normal distribution.

distribution and illustrated in Figure 2–4. This makes it easier to compare scores in, say, arithmetic and English for the same group of students, where the arithmetic test was too difficult for some of the class, producing positively skewed raw scores, and the English test was too easy for some, producing negatively skewed scores; the stanine scores for arithmetic will have more nearly the same shape as the stanine scores for English than the raw scores for arithmetic and English did. This does not excuse careless or inept choosing of tests. For differentiating among a group of examinees, try to select tests with enough "floor" (easy enough so that few, if any, of the poorest students will make zero or pure-chance scores) and enough "ceiling" (hard enough so that few, if any, of the ablest students will make perfect scores).

National norms for standardized tests are often reported as stanines. Also, local norms can be reported as stanines in a school system to supplement the "national norms" offered in test manuals. In order to better understand the stanine score let us convert the raw scores in Table 2–2 into a stanine scale. Our first task is to set up a list of the frequencies desired for stanines 9, 8, and so on down. For stanines 1 and 9 we see from Figure 2–4 that we need 4 percent, or .04 of 36 scores or 1.44 scores, as shown in the top and bottom entries of the second column of Table 2–4.[17] The 1.44 is slightly closer to 1 than it is to 2, so we assign a stanine of 9 to just the highest raw score, 112. We also assign a stanine of 1 to the lowest raw score, 44. Then we work with stanines of 8 and 2 (working down from the top and up from the bottom). We need 7 percent of the 36 scores for stanines 8 and 2; .07 × 36 = 2.52. Noticing that the frequencies for raw scores of 109, 106, and 105 in Table 2–2 are 1 each, and that 2.52 is a bit closer to 3 than to 2, we assign stanine 8 to raw scores of 109, 106, and 105. Similarly, since raw scores of 47, 51, and 58 have frequencies of 1, 1, and 1, respectively, we assign stanine 2 to those three scores of 47, 51, and 58.

Stanines of 7 and 3 each require 12 percent of the 36 scores; .12 × 36 = 4.32. Since 104, 100, 97, and 95 have 1 + 1 + 1 + 2 = 5 frequencies,

[17] When the number of scores is very large or when greater accuracy is needed, the percentages of scores assigned to each stanine are 4.01, 6.55, 12.10, 17.47, 19.74, 17.47, 12.10, 6.55, and 4.01 for stanines 1 through 9, respectively.

Stanine	Theoretical Frequency for 36 Scores	Actual Frequency	Equivalent Raw Scores
9	1.44	1	112
8	2.52	3	109, 106, 105
7	4.32	5	104, 100, 97, 95, 95
6	6.12	6	93, 91, 90, 89, 84, 84
5	7.20	8	83, 82, 81, 80, 78, 75, 75, 75
4	6.12	5	74, 72, 71, 70, 69
3	4.32	4	68, 66, 62, 59
2	2.52	3	58, 51, 47
1	1.44	1	44
Total	36.00	36	

which is closer to 4.3 than the 3 that would be obtained by excluding 95 and its frequency of 2, we assign the stanine 7 to 104, 100, 97, and 95. Similarly, stanine 3 is assigned to 59, 62, 66, and 68.

Stanines 6 and 4 each need 17 percent of the 36 scores, or 6.12. The raw scores 93, 91, 90, 89, and 84 have a total frequency of 6, so stanine 6 is assigned to them. Stanine 4 is assigned to scores 69, 70, 71, 72, and 74, which have a total of 5 frequencies. Obviously, 5 is closer to 6.12 than 6.12 is to the 8 frequencies that would result if the score of 75 were included.

Which raw scores remain for the middle stanine category? Scores of 83, 82, 81, 80, 78, and 75, with 8 frequencies, contrasted with the 7.20 [.20 × 36 = 7.20] theoretically needed. Because it has the highest theoretical frequency, the middle category (5) of the stanine scale can tolerate a larger discrepancy between actual and theoretical frequency than the other categories.[18]

The final stanine distribution shown in Table 2–4 is roughly symmetrical: 9 and 1 have the same frequency (1), 8 and 2 have the same frequency (3), 7 and 3 differ in frequency by only one, as do categories 6 and 4. *Perfect* symmetry is rare and accidental, but the normalized stanine method does tend to normalize or "unskew" skewed distributions. Normalization is justified when the deviation from normality results from defects in the measure itself, but it is *not* appropriate when the true scores of the sample are nonnormal in form (cf. Anastasi, 1968, p. 56).

Some persons have advocated the stanine scale as the standard general system of reporting results from all standardized tests. Although the stanine scale has an advantage of a one-digit index, it pays a price for this convenience, namely some loss of information. If intelligence-test results were reported in stanines, we would not be able to distinguish between persons having IQ's of 128 or above or 72 and below—a significant shortcoming[19] since the use of

---

[18] Additional discussions of the uses and computation of stanines can be obtained from Test Service Notebooks Nos. 23 (by Durost) and 28 (by Englehart), which are furnished on request by Harcourt Brace Jovanovich, Inc., 757 Third Ave., New York, N.Y.

[19] If greater differentiation is desired at extremes, the sta-eleven scale breaks stanine 1 into sta-elevens 0 and 1, and stanine 9 into sta-elevens 9 and 10. The sta-eleven scale breaks

standardized intelligence tests in the identification of gifted, educable, and trainable pupils is one of their important functions.

It is true that the stanine scale helps convey the important concept that scores on a test should be viewed as *bands* rather than *points*, but the fixed bands of the stanine scale are the best band width only for those examinees who scored near the middle of the stanine. Some examinees will earn scores that differ by 2 stanines when their performance on two tests varies only slightly more than .5 standard deviations, whereas other students whose performance differs by .9 standard deviations (or even much more if stanines 1 or 9 are involved) will have stanine scores that differ by only 1. Although the stanine scale is the most widely used standard score and even appears to be increasing in popularity, we feel that its disadvantages are such that it is a second choice to the T-scale for most educational uses. Two-digit accuracy seems needed.

There are two important things to keep in mind regarding standard scores: (1) the mean and the standard deviation of the standard-score scale may have any value one chooses, without any resemblance to the mean and standard deviation of the raw scores themselves; and (2) computed standard scores are no more or less normally distributed than are the raw scores from which they were obtained, unless they were "normalized."

We are now ready to supplement the concepts of central tendency and variability with the important concept of correlation.

Correlation and Prediction

95. Most people have a general understanding of the meaning of correlation (that is, co-relationship or co-variation). Two traits are correlated if they tend to "go together." If high scores on variable X tend to be accompanied by high scores on variable Y, then the variables X and Y are correlated, since the scores co-vary. For example, there is a tendency for tall people to weigh more than short people. Since height and weight tend to co-vary, they are said to be _____.

correlated

96. We can describe the degree of correlation between variables by such terms as strong, low, or moderate, but these terms are not sufficiently explicit. A more precise method is to compute a coefficient of correlation between the sets of scores. A coefficient of correlation is a statistical summary of the degree of relationship or "going-togetherness" between two variables. Correlation coefficients range in magnitude from $+1.0$ to -1.0. A positive correlation coefficient means that high scores on one measure tend to be associated with high scores on another measure, and low scores on one tend to be associated with low scores on the other. For example, there is a tendency for individuals who score high on a scholastic aptitude test to

---

up the 4 percent in the extreme stanines into 1 percent and 3 percent. In all other respects the two scales are equivalent. (See Stanley, 1964, pp. 78–85 and 139–143, for a comprehensive treatment of the sta-eleven and sta-nineteen scales.)

receive better marks than those who score low on it. The correlation coefficient for this example would be _____ (positive or negative).

positive

---

97. On the other hand, for adults age correlates negatively with certain psychomotor abilities. The sign ($+$ or $-$) of the correlation coefficient indicates the *direction* of the relationship. When low scores on A are accompanied by low scores on B, and high scores on A by high scores on B, r_{AB} (the coefficient of correlation between A and B) is _____; if high scores on A are associated with low scores on C, and vice versa, r_{AC} would be _____.

positive

negative

---

98. Often the sign of r is an arbitrary matter. For example, if test scores correlate $-.3$ with number of days absent for a group of third-grade pupils, then the correlation between tests scores and days present would be ____.

$+.3$

---

99. The numerical value of r denotes the degree of the relationship; the higher the absolute value (the value irrespective of the sign) the stronger is the relationship. If $r_{AB} = +.55$ and $r_{AC} = -.70$, there is a stronger relation between A and ____ than there is between A and ____.

C, B

---

100. When $r = +1.0$ or -1.0, there is a perfect relationship between the two variables. In both cases a knowledge of one of the variables makes it possible to predict the second variable without error. With $r = +1.0$, the z-scores of each individual would be the same on both tests or traits. With $r = -1.0$, the highest score on one test would be associated with the lowest score on the second test, and so on. Any pair of z-scores would be identical in value, but opposite in sign, perhaps $+2.3$ and -2.3. If two tests intercorrelated $+1.0$ and John ranked third on test I, he would also rank _____ on test II. If his z-score on test I was $+1.8$, his z-score on test II would be _____.

third
$+1.8$

---

101. Although usually a correlation coefficient cannot be interpreted as the percent of agreement or the percent of possible agreement, it does reflect the expected percentage of deviation from the mean of the second variable. For example, fathers' IQ's tend to correlate about .5 with offsprings' IQ's in the general population (Jensen, 1968). The .5 correlation indicates that the best prediction we can make of a child's IQ score is that it will be only 50 percent as far from the population mean as was his father's. If one selected from a representative sample 100 fathers scoring 130 on an intelligence test, then tested one child of each father, the children's mean would be expected to be only one-half (.5) as far from the population

54

mean (100) as were the fathers'. The mean of the children would be expected to be about _____.[20]

102. On the other hand, if we selected a group of fathers from the general population with IQ scores of 80, and then examined their fathers, we would expect the mean IQ score of the fathers to be about _____.

90

103. It is important to bear in mind that a correlation coefficient expresses the ratio of the average or expected deviation from the mean on the predicted variable (y) to the known deviation from the mean on the predictor variable (x) in standard-deviation units. The following regression equation makes this clear:

$$z'_y = rz_x,$$

where: z'_y = expected or predicted z-score on variable Y,
r = the correlation between variables X and Y, and
z_x = the known z-score on variable X.

If distances that a group of children can high-jump and long-jump correlate .6, then we can say that, on the average, those who are two standard deviations from the mean in long-jumping are only ____ standard deviation(s) above the mean in high-jumping.

1.2

104. Grade-point average (GPA) in college correlates about .5 with the Verbal portion of the Scholastic Aptitude Test (SAT-V). For College A, suppose you have the following information about this year's freshman class:

	SAT-V	GPA
$\bar{X}$	500	2.5
s	100	.7
	$r = .5$	

In this class, a certain freshman has an SAT-V score of 660—that is, 1.6 standard deviations above the mean of the class. You expect his GPA to be ____ standard deviations above the mean GPA of the class. Therefore, his predicted GPA is 2.5 + ( )( ) = 3.06.

.8

.8, .7

105. In any elementary statistics course you will learn how to compute r, the Pearson product-moment coefficient of correlation. The rank-difference correlation coefficient is a very close relative. It is easy to compute, and

[20] An erroneous conclusion, often drawn when one is first introduced to the regression phenomenon (be it illustrated with IQ scores, height, or any other variable), is that successive generations become less variable. This is not the case, as illustrated in frame 102. There are enough individual exceptions to the general trend to preserve the equality of the standard deviations for the two groups. In our example you will note that $\sigma = 15$ for both fathers and children; hence the children are not more homogeneous in IQ scores than are their fathers.

its computation helps you to understand the meaning of correlation. The rank-difference correlation coefficient (r_{Ranks}), also known as Spearman's rank-difference correlation, will be approximately the same as the Pearson r for the same data.

Correlation can be viewed simply as the degree to which persons maintain their same relative positions or ranks on two variables. If there is much change, the correlation coefficient will be low; if there is little change, the coefficient will be high. A correlation coefficient can be obtained between any two variables if scores or ranks are available on both for a group of individuals.

Example: Two of the tests from the Primary Mental Abilities (PMA) battery, the Verbal Meaning (VM) and the Word Fluency (WF) tests, were given to the students in a measurement class. To simplify our illustration, only 11 of the pairs of scores are used to illustrate the computation of the rank-difference correlation coefficient, _____.

---

106. To compute a rank-difference coefficient correlation, follow the procedure outlined below:

1. Rank the individuals on the first variable (VM) from the highest score (1) to the lowest score (N). N is the number of pairs of scores (in this example $N = 11$). The VM score of 50 (see table below) is the highest score and receives a rank of 1; 49 is the next highest score and receives a rank of 2, and so on; 35 is the lowest VM score and hence ranks number 11.

2. Rank the individuals on the second variable in the same way. The highest WF score is 67, which receives a rank of 1, and so on; the lowest WF score is 25, which ranks 11.

3. Take the difference between ranks for each individual, putting this value in the column headed "rank difference" (D). The sign of the difference is unnecessary, since all values will be squared.

4. Square the rank-difference (D) column and place the value in column "D^2."

5. Total the D^2 column to get $\sum D^2$.

6. Compute the coefficient (r_{Ranks}) using the formula given below the table.

Student	Score VM	Score WF	Rank VM	Rank WF	Rank Difference (D)	D^2
A	50	51	1	5	4	16
B	49	56	2	4	2	4
C	48	59	3	2	1	1
D	47	48	4	6	2	4
E	46	37	5	9	4	16
F	45	25	6	11	5	25
G	44	58	7	3	4	16
H	43	44	8	8	0	0
I	42	34	9	10	1	1
J	41	67	10	1	9	81
K	35	46	11	7	4	16

$$\sum D^2 = 180$$

$$r_{Ranks} = 1 - \frac{6 \sum D^2}{N(N^2 - 1)}$$

$$= 1 - \frac{6(180)}{11(121 - 1)}$$

$$= 1 - \frac{1080}{1320}$$

$$= 1 - \underline{},$$ .82

$$r_{Ranks} = \underline{}.$$ .18

107. The low relationship (.18) between the VM and WF scores can also be illustrated graphically by a scatterplot—a plot showing the performance on both variables. To complete the scatterplot below, first find the person's rank on the horizontal axis (VM in this example) and then move up vertically from that point until you coincide with his rank on the vertical variable (WF in this example). Persons with ranks of 1, 2, and 7 on VM have already been entered. Complete the plot of the corresponding ranks.

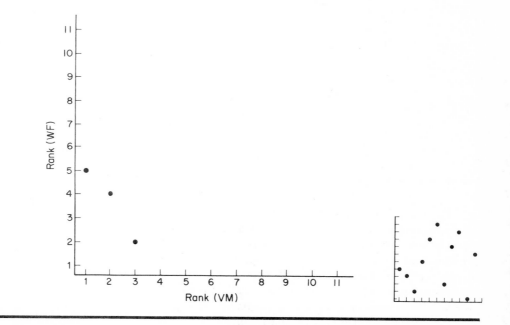

108. Compute the rank-difference correlation coefficient between the following 15 pairs of arithmetic and IQ scores:

Pupil	Score		Rank		D	D^2
	Arith.	IQ	Arith.	IQ		
A	30	105	8			
B	38	120		4		
C	16	83				
D	37	137				
E	32	114		7		
F	25	96				
G	19	107				
H	45	117	1			
I	33	108	6			
J	29	130				
K	26	88				
L	24	129		3		
M	13	76				
N	41	118				
O	36	112	5			

$$\sum D^2 = \underline{\qquad} \qquad\qquad 220$$

$$r_{\text{Ranks}} = 1 - \frac{6 \sum D^2}{N(N^2 - 1)}$$

$$= 1 - \frac{6(220)}{(\quad)[(15)^2 - 1]} \qquad\qquad 15$$

$$= 1 - \underline{\quad}, \qquad\qquad .4$$

$$r_{\text{Ranks}} = \underline{\quad}.^{21} \qquad\qquad .6$$

The core of the elementary statistical concepts needed to understand the basic principles of measurement has now been covered in the programmed-instruction portion of this chapter. The interpretation of standardized tests requires an understanding of the various measures of central tendency and variability, together with the normal curve and associated standard scores and percentile ranks. A proper understanding of test reliability and validity demands some grasp of correlation. The narrative treatment of correlation should enhance and extend your knowledge of this basic concept.

The Concept of Correlation

During the latter part of the nineteenth century, Sir Francis Galton and the pioneer English statistician Karl Pearson succeeded in developing the theory

---

[21] Actually, the two computations of r_{Ranks} above were simplified by not having any tied scores. Suppose in frame 108 two persons had earned the same top score on arithmetic, 45, and three had earned the next highest score, 41. The ranks for these five scores would have been 1.5, 1.5, 4, 4, 4. This is because when ties occur, all scores receive the average of the associated ranks, in this case, $(1 + 2)/2 = 1.5$, and $(3 + 4 + 5)/3 = 4$.

and mathematical basis for what is now known as *correlation* (Walker, 1929). They were concerned with relationships between two variables—for example, height and weight. It is easy to see that tall people usually weigh more than short ones, suggesting that above-average height tends to go with above-average weight. Height and weight vary together (that is, correlate positively), though certainly not perfectly; there are "beanpoles" and "five-by-fives," which explains why the relationship is not higher than it is. It would be possible to select a group so that the taller a person in the group is the less he weighs, but this negative correlation between height and weight would not be expected for individuals picked at *random* from the general population.

Let us examine some other factors that usually vary together. There is a substantial, but again by no means perfect, positive correlation between intelligence-test scores at the end of high school and grades earned during the freshman year of college. The higher the score obtained by an entering freshman, the higher his later grades are *likely* to be. The lower his score is, the poorer a student he will *probably* make. This relationship has been found with all sorts of intelligence tests used in a great number of different colleges ever since such tests first became available commercially shortly after the end of World War I. (One of the most complete summaries of research on predicting college success was compiled by Lavin, 1967).

Husbands and wives *tend* to be more like each other with respect to age, amount of education, and many other factors than they are like people in general. The sons of tall fathers tend to be taller than average, and the sons of short fathers tend to be shorter than average. Likewise, the fathers of tall sons tend to be above average height. Children resemble their own parents in intelligence more closely than they resemble other adults. Some degree of positive correlation between members of families is usually found for almost any characteristic—such as personality, attitude, interest, or ability (Anastasi, 1958, pp. 266–316).

To quantify Galton's concept of co-relationships among traits, Pearson devised as a measure of relationship the *product-moment coefficient of correlation*, r. Since about 1900 r has been a widely employed statistic—virtually all test manuals are sprinkled plentifully with r's, as is most educational research literature.

Pearson's original r (and several other related measures of correlation) summarizes the magnitude and direction of the relationship between two sets of measurements, such as height and weight based on the *same* persons, or between the same measurement on *pairs* of persons, like the fathers and sons mentioned above. It makes no difference whether the measures correlated are history grades and geography grades, speed of running the hundred-yard dash and skill in playing the violin, or speed of tapping and age. In such situations, r can have values that range from -1 for a perfect inverse (negative) relationship through 0 for no systematic correlation to $+1$ for perfect direct relationship; the r's between radically different kinds of variables are wholly comparable.[22] For example, it is meaningful to say that for the pupils of a

_____

[22] The r's cannot attain the value of precisely $+1.0$ unless the shapes of the two distributions of measures being correlated are identical.

certain group, reading ability and intelligence are more closely related than height and weight.

The chief purpose of a two-way scatterplot of dots or tallies, each of which represents the two scores of one student or pair (such as father-son), is not—as some discussions might imply—to simplify computation of r. With electric calculators and electronic computers, we no longer need to use the tedious hand-computational methods of the past. The scatter diagram, however, enables us to study the nature of the relationship between the two variables. It also enables us to surmise whether or not a computed r will accurately summarize the relationship between the two variables. For *linear* correlation it will. (The relationship between two variables is linear if a straight line more closely fits the dots of the scatterplot than any curved line does.) A perfect positive linear relationship ($r = 1.00$) is shown in Figure 2–5, where the dots move in a straight line from low-low to high-high, with no dots in the low-high and high-low quadrants. (When the sign of a correlation coefficient is not specified, it is always positive.) A perfect negative relationship ($r = -1.00$) occurs in Figure 2–6.

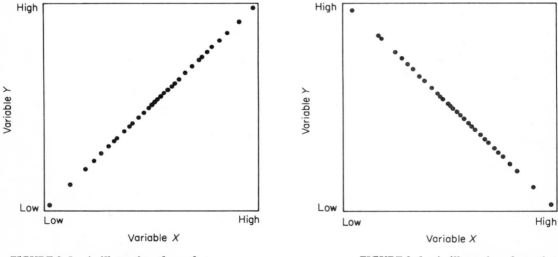

FIGURE 2–5 *An illustration of a perfect positive correlation, r = 1.00.*

FIGURE 2–6 *An illustration of a perfect negative relationship, r = -1.00.*

Figure 2–7 depicts no relationship between two variables, resulting in an r of zero. No prediction of a student's score on one test from his score on the other test can be made at better than the chance level. No matter how he scored on one test, our best prediction is that he would score at the mean of the group on the other test. Actually obtained relationships rarely yield r's of exactly $-1, 0,$ or 1.

A perfect curvilinear relationship ($r = 0$) is shown in Figure 2–8. If one score of an individual is known, it is possible to predict his other score perfectly, despite the (Pearson) r of 0. For scatterplots of this sort, r is not the appropriate summarizing statistic (see Glass and Stanley, 1970, pp. 124–125).

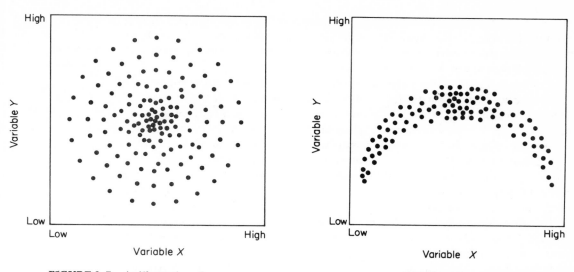

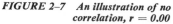

FIGURE 2–7 An illustration of no
correlation, r = 0.00

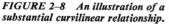

FIGURE 2–8 An illustration of a
substantial curvilinear relationship.

INTERPRETING r

Two cautions should be observed. First, *r cannot be interpreted directly as a percentage in the usual sense.* An *r* of 0 represents no linear relationship at all, but an *r* of .66 does *not* usually indicate a 66 percent relationship.[23] For large *r*'s, a small gain in the value of *r* indicates a considerable increase in the degree of association. An *r* of .66 usually indicates more than twice the relationship shown by an *r* of .33. Suppose traits A and B correlate .66, and A and C correlate .33. On the average a person will be 66 percent as far from the B mean as he is from the A mean (in standard-score units); he will be expected to be only 33 percent as far from the C mean as he is from the A mean (in standard-score units). The *accuracy* of our prediction of B from A, however, will be considerably greater than for our prediction of C from A.

It is critical to understand that correlation does not necessarily mean causation. Often variables other than the two under consideration are responsible for the association. Furthermore, problems in the social sciences, the field in which correlation is most often employed, are usually too complex to be explained in terms of a single cause. The fact that persons who have taken driver training have fewer automobile accidents than those without such training is a far cry from establishing a causal relationship between accidents and driver training.

Let us take several examples. It is probably true that in the United States there is some positive correlation between the average salaries of teachers in various high schools and the percentages of the schools' graduates who go on to college, but to say that these students attend college *because* their teachers are well paid is as inaccurate as to say that their teachers are well paid *because*

[23] In some applications of *r* in genetics and test theory the value of *r* does indicate percent of common elements.

many of the graduates attend college. The relationship is not simple, but one prominent factor is the financial condition of the community, which, to a considerable extent, determines its ability to pay *both* teachers' salaries and college tuitions and fees.

It has been found that the percentage of pupil "dropouts" occurring in high schools varies inversely with the number of books per pupil in the libraries of those schools (Ferrell, 1951). But common sense tells us that merely piling more books into the library will no more affect the dropout rate than hiring a better attendance officer will bring about a magical increase in the number of books.

Many investigators make a two-stage assumption. They assume both causation and direction of causality. Suppose, for instance, that among a large group of pupils the linear relationship between a measure of anxiety while taking an intelligence test and scores on the intelligence tests yields an r of $-.31$. What does this mean? We might surmise that underlying characteristics of pupils besides these two response variables tend to make some anxious and unintelligent, others calm and intelligent. We would then say, loosely, that some other variables "cause" the negative relationship between anxiety and intelligence. Or we might reject this and assume that there is a causative relationship between anxiety and intelligence: pupils are anxious *because* they are unintelligent, or pupils appear unintelligent *because* they are anxious (that is, low intelligence makes them anxious while taking intelligence tests, but does not actually interfere seriously with their performance, versus the interpretation that their intelligence-test scores are greatly lowered by high anxiety). There is no simple answer to this response-response situation. "Causation" is a treacherous concept, as David Hume forcefully showed long ago. Suffice it to say here that studies of association alone, without experimental substantiation, are most difficult to interpret causally (see Lerner, 1965). The measurement of anxiety should be supplemented by the study of experimentally created anxiety states. For example, when students are experimentally made anxious in a testing situation, do their intelligence-test scores suffer? This question is considered more fully in Chapter 6.

Failure to recognize that correlation may not mean causation is, in its broadest sense, a widespread logical error, for the fundamental notions of co-relationship affect our lives at many points. Going to Sunday school is generally believed to be valuable from many standpoints, but a positive relationship between the rate of attendance and a characteristic such as honesty does not *necessarily* imply that children are honest because they attend Sunday school. Underlying and causing both attendance and honesty may be home training, for example.

If honest children tend to go to Sunday school and less honest ones tend not to go, would it follow logically that children attend Sunday school *because* they are honest? (This is the reverse of the contention that they are honest because they attend.) Note several possible interpretations: H $\longrightarrow$ SS, SS $\longrightarrow$ H, and H $\longleftarrow$ T $\longrightarrow$ SS, where H stands for "honesty," SS for "Sunday school," T for "home training," and $\longrightarrow$ for "leads to." H $\longleftarrow$ T $\longrightarrow$ SS means that a third variable, home training, leads to both honesty and Sunday-school attendance.

Note carefully that while correlation does not directly establish a "causal" relationship, it may furnish *clues* to causes—and these clues can be formalized as hypotheses in planning controlled experimentation (see Campbell and Stanley, 1966). Therefore, r is useful primarily for exploratory purposes. Hence, it is used much more widely in the newer sciences such as sociology, psychology, and education than in physics and chemistry.

Just what is r? Thus far we have talked about correlation and the statistic r without defining it or exhibiting computational formulas—intentionally so, because knowing technical arithmetic details is far less important than appreciating the pitfalls you may encounter in test manuals and professional articles. Perhaps the simplest definition of r is that it is the mean z-score product, merely the arithmetic mean of the N products of the two sets of computed z-scores. One can actually obtain r by means of that definitional formula, though it requires far more tedious computation than less direct methods do. Let's go through the process, however, for in this way you may come to appreciate some of the mathematical aspects of r relatively painlessly, and at the same time you can review computation of the arithmetic mean, standard deviation, and z-scores.

Methods of Obtaining r

We begin with "real" data in Table 2–5 for pretest scores (X) and midterm examination scores (Y) of 43 graduate students. We find that the mean

TABLE 2–5

*Pretest and Midterm Scores of 43 Graduate Students
on Two Teacher-Made Objective Tests in Intermediate Statistics*

Student	Pretest Score (X)	Midterm Examination Score (Y)	Student	Pretest Score (X)	Midterm Examination Score (Y)
a	62	51	w	53	56
b	55	66	x	62	56
c	55	40	y	49	54
d	49	38	z	52	56
e	46	51	aa	44	39
f	67	57	bb	60	49
g	32	42	cc	47	55
h	42	35	dd	44	45
i	67	61	ee	49	39
j	55	46	ff	36	38
k	44	33	gg	40	15
l	46	58	hh	53	50
m	37	48	ii	44	47
n	57	44	jj	49	41
o	34	55	kk	49	35
p	57	44	ll	44	43
q	58	59	mm	53	60
r	58	45	nn	53	52
s	49	51	oo	42	35
t	40	32	pp	57	45
u	73	54	qq	49	41
v	62	65			

of the X's, denoted by the symbol $\bar{X}$, equals $(62 + 55 + \ldots + 49)/43 = 2184/43 = 50.79$, and the mean of the Y's, $\bar{Y}$, equals $(51 + 66 + \ldots + 41)/43 = 2026/43 = 47.12$. Then:

$$s_x = \sqrt{43(62^2 + 55^2 + \cdots + 49^2) - (62 + 55 + \cdots + 49)^2/43}$$
$$= \sqrt{156,654}/43 = 395.79540/43 = 9.205.$$

Also

$$s_y = \sqrt{43(51^2 + 66^2 + \cdots + 41^2) - (51 + 66 + \cdots + 41)^2/43}$$
$$= \sqrt{186,208}/43 = 431.51825/43 = 10.035.$$

Now that we have the two means and the two standard deviations, we can compute two z-scores for each student, one for his pretest score and the other for his midterm score. For the pretest scores, the z-score on the pretest (X) is

$$z_x = \frac{X - \bar{X}}{s_x},$$

meaning simply that from the student's raw pretest score we subtract the mean of the pretest scores and then divide this deviation from the mean by the standard deviation of the pretest scores. We could do just this for each of the 43 students. Consider the highest pretest score in Table 2–5, which is 73. Compute z_{73}, the z-score corresponding to this raw score of 73:

$$z_{73} = \frac{73 - \bar{X}}{s_x} = \frac{73 - 50.79}{9.205} = \frac{22.21}{9.205} = 2.41.$$

Similarly we could compute z-scores for each of the pretest scores.[24]

We repeat the above operations for Y, where the raw scores range from 66 to 15.

In Table 2–6 appear the 43 pairs of z's for students a through qq (rounded to two decimal places). We have arranged the z_x's in rank order from student u with the highest pretest z_x-score ($z_x = 2.41$) to student g with the lowest pretest z_x-score ($z_x = -2.04$). If the correlation were perfect ($r_{xy} = 1.0$), the z_x and z_y scores of any given student would be identical, meaning that he did equally well on the pretest and midterm tests. A glance at Table 2–6 reveals that this is not true. A considerable amount of change occurred—greatest for student o, whose z-score changed from -1.82 to $.79$, and least for student hh, whose z-score varied only from $.24$ to $.29$.

Let us multiply each student's z_x by his z_y, paying attention to plus and minus signs. If the signs of z_x and z_y agree, the product (z_x times z_y) will be positive; if the signs differ (one is $+$ and the other $-$), the product will be negative. If we add these 43 products and divide their sum ($\sum z_x z_y = 22.57$) by N (43), we find $r = .525$—that is:

$$r_{xy} = \frac{\sum z_x z_y}{N} = \frac{22.5662}{43} = .5248.$$

This illustration demonstrates that correlation is directly related to the

---

[24] A check on the accuracy of all your computations can be made by computing both the sum of these 43 z-scores and their standard deviation. You have already learned that the sum (or the mean) of *any* full set of z-scores is 0, and the standard deviation is 1.

Student	z-Score on Pretest (z_x)	z-Score Midterm Examination (z_y)	Student	z-Score on Pretest (z_x)	z-Score Midterm Examination (z_y)
u	2.41	.69	s	− .19	.39
i	1.76	1.38	jj, qq	− .19	− .61
f	1.76	.99	ee	− .19	− .81
v	1.22	1.78	d	− .19	− .91
x	1.22	.89	kk	− .19	−1.21
a	1.22	.39	cc	− .41	.79
bb	1.00	.19	l	− .52	1.08
q	.78	1.18	e	− .52	.39
r	.78	− .20	ii	− .74	− .01
pp	.68	− .20	dd	− .74	− .21
n, p	.68	− .31	ll	− .74	− .41
b	.46	1.88	aa	− .74	− .81
j	.46	− .11	k	− .74	−1.41
c	.46	− .71	h, oo	− .96	−1.21
mm	.24	1.28	t	−1.17	−1.50
w	.24	.89	gg	−1.17	−3.20
nn	.24	.49	m	−1.50	.09
hh	.24	.29	ff	−1.61	− .91
z	.13	.89	o	−1.82	.79
y	− .19	.69	g	−2.04	− .51

way in which students maintain their *relative* positions in the group on both variables.

There are many approaches for computing r. One of the simplest methods requires an electric calculator and utilizes the "raw" scores themselves, without any frequency distributions or scatterplots. It is seldom feasible unless a calculator is available, because the arithmetical operations involve large numbers and therefore become quite tedious. Almost all other computational procedures require a scatterplot. Many routinized "correlation charts" are available commercially, and nearly every statistics book and teacher has a pet version, usually to some extent original.

This diversity of computing aids is probably indicative of basic difficulties inherent in the process of computing r "by hand." There is no really simple way to do it. The chief difficulty is that r indicates a relationship between paired scores, so in order to obtain r by hand without undue labor we must find the sum of the products of the paired scores by some *indirect* method.

A complication in the attempt to simplify the computation of r without a calculator is that to make the numbers involved as small as possible, most chart designers set up procedures that result in many negative numbers. Unfortunately, negative numbers are likely to confuse most students, large positive ones are tedious to handle, and both invite sizable errors. We think that it is better for persons who are getting their introduction to r in this book to refrain from computing r unless they have compelling reasons for doing so and understand how to interpret and use the value computed. High-speed electronic digital computers calculate r's and other statistics quickly and inexpensively.

To compute r, we go back to the raw scores in Table 2–5 and proceed in the following manner.[25]

$$r_{xy} = \frac{43[(62)(51) + (55)(66) + \cdots + (49)(41)] - (62 + 55 + \cdots + 49)(51 + 66 + \cdots + 41)}{\sqrt{43(62^2 + 55^2 + \cdots + 49^2) - (62 + 55 + \cdots + 49)^2} \sqrt{43(51^2 + 66^2 + \cdots + 41^2) - (51 + 66 + \cdots + 41)^2}}$$

$$= \frac{43(104,987) - (2184)(2026)}{\sqrt{43(114,570) - (2184)^2} \sqrt{43(99,788) - (2026)^2}} = \frac{89,657}{\sqrt{156,654} \sqrt{186,208}}$$

$$= \frac{89,657}{\sqrt{29,170,228,032}} = \frac{89,657}{170,793} = .5249.$$

The figure obtained is the same, to three decimal places, as the r secured by averaging the products of z-scores, above. (A rounding-off "error" caused the .0001 discrepancy.) The coefficient of .52 is moderately large but not extremely high, since a considerable number of students shifted position substantially from the pretest to the midterm. We see this clearly with plotted z's in Figure 2–9. We can also tell from the z's of Table 2–6 that the student (g) who scored lowest on the pretest ranked 30th on the midterm examination, whereas the student (u) who scored highest on the pretest ranked 12.5th at the midterm.

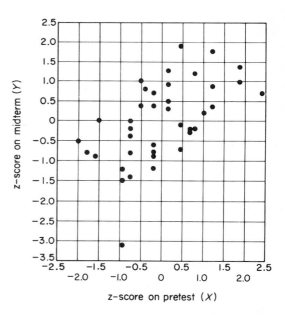

FIGURE 2–9 *z-scores for each of 43 students for pretest and midterm examination scores from Table 2–5.*

Without access to a computer or an electric calculating machine, an easier method for estimating the correlation is via the Spearman rank correlation.

[25] A useful general raw-score formula for computing r is

$$r = \frac{N(\sum XY) - (\sum X)(\sum Y)}{\sqrt{[N \sum X^2 - (\sum X)^2][N \sum Y^2 - (\sum Y)^2]}}.$$

If the measures to be correlated are placed in rank order, a relatively simple method of computing the correlation coefficient, r_{Ranks}, is possible. The steps are as follows

Statistical Concepts in Test Interpretation

1. Rank scores on X and on Y.
2. Take the difference in ranks for each individual (D).
3. Square each difference and find the sum of the squared differences ($\sum D^2$).
4. Insert $\sum D^2$ into the following formula and perform the arithmetic computation.

$$r_{\text{Ranks}} = 1 - \frac{6 \sum D^2}{N(N^2 - 1)},$$

where: $\sum D^2 =$ the sum of squared rank differences, and
$N =$ the number of *pairs* of scores.

An illustration will show how simple the computational procedure is.

A certain test question requires that six historical events be ranked without ties in chronological order, 1 representing the earliest and 6 the most recent. Table 2–7 shows the events, the ranks assigned by Richard and by John, and the correct ranks. Note that each boy has six "errors," because each one "missed" all six questions. You can see readily that John's rank order was closer to the correct ranks than was Richard's, however.

TABLE 2–7

The Computation of the r_{Ranks} for Each of Two Students Who Arranged Six Historical Events in Chronological Order

Events to Be Ranked (1 = earliest)	Correct Ranks	Richard's Ranks	D	D^2	Correct Ranks	John's Ranks	D	D^2
French Revolution	6	2	4	16	6	5	1	1
Magna Charta	3	4	1	1	3	4	1	1
Pompeii destroyed by Vesuvius	1	3	2	4	1	2	1	1
Columbus discovers America	4	1	3	9	4	3	1	1
Fall of Roman Empire	2	5	3	9	2	1	1	1
Spanish Armada destroyed	5	6	1	1	5	6	1	1

$$\sum D^2 = 40$$

$$r_{\text{Ranks}} = 1 - \frac{6(\sum D^2)}{N(N^2 - 1)}$$

$$= 1 - \frac{6 \times 40}{6 \times [(6 \times 6) - 1]}$$

$$= 1 - \frac{40}{35} = 1 - 1.14 = -.14.$$

$$\sum D^2 = 6$$

$$r_{\text{Ranks}} = 1 - \frac{6 \times 6}{6 \times 35}$$

$$= 1 - \frac{6}{35}$$

$$= 1 - .17$$

$$= .83.$$

The first correlation coefficient is secured by summing the squared differences between Richard's ranks and the correct ranks and then substituting in the formula. This r_{Ranks} equals $-.14$. Like r_{xy}, the correlation between two quantitative variates, r_{Ranks} can vary from -1 to $+1$. The negative r_{Ranks} found for Richard probably indicates a chance departure from 0, rather than actual misinformation. Notice that John, with an r_{Ranks} of .83, seems to have had a fairly good general knowledge of the correct chronology, even though he did not rank any one of the six events precisely. Many teachers would give him no credit at all, despite his superiority to Richard on this ranking item. He deserves 4 or 5 points out of the possible 6. Richard, of course, deserves none.

If the number of ranks is odd, the worst possible ranking, exactly opposite to the key (say, 5, 4, 3, 2, 1 instead of 1, 2, 3, 4, 5 for 5 events), actually yields one "correct" ranking; here the student's 3 matches the key's 3. Yet in the overall ranking sense misinformation is perfect ($r_{Ranks} = -1$). A simplified scoring procedure for "sequence" (chronology, rearrangement) items, instead of a right-wrong method (no credit at all for being close), should be used for scoring ranking items. Actually, r_{Ranks} is simply a Pearson r on which ranks of the scores are employed rather than the actual scores themselves (see Glass and Stanley, 1970, pp. 172–175). The ranking is a computational shortcut that sacrifices only a small amount of accuracy. Had dates rather than ranks been used in the above example, the r's would probably have differed little from the r_{ranks}.

When N is as great as 25 or 30, the ranking process will be time-consuming and the fractional ranks that result from ties will be tedious to square. In such a case, it is better to use an electric calculator and compute r directly from the raw scores using the formula given in the footnote on page 66.

Interpreting the Coefficient of Correlation

In interpreting a coefficient of correlation, several factors must be considered. The first is the *sign* of the coefficient; the second is the coefficient's *magnitude* or size. The sign indicates the *direction* of the relationship. Positive coefficients indicate direct relationship—that is, tendency for two series of values to vary in the same direction. High values in one column are associated with high values in the other column, low values in one column are associated with low values in the other column, and so on. Negative coefficients indicate inverse relationship, which is a tendency for the two series of values to vary in opposite directions, with high values in one column associated with low values in the other column, and high values in that column associated with low values in the first column.

The second aspect, equally important but far more difficult to interpret, is the coefficient's *size*, which indicates the *degree* or closeness of the relationship, just as the *sign* indicates the *direction* of the relationship. The minimum coefficient is .00, which indicates no consistent relationship whatsoever. From this minimum value, the coefficients increase in both directions until -1.00 is reached for one limit and 1.00 for the other. It should be noted that both -1.00 and 1.00 indicate equally close relationship, for both are perfect. Their one important difference is in direction, the former being inverse and the latter direct. Similarly, all other values of the same size, such as $-.50$ and .50, indicate equally close relationship. The size, not the sign, of the coefficient indicates the closeness or degree of relationship.

The problem, then, is to know how close a relationship is indicated by a coefficient of correlation of a given magnitude, regardless of sign. For example, how close a relationship is indicated by a coefficient of .60? Unfortunately, there is no simple way of answering such a question. Attempts to indicate this relationship by some descriptive adjective such as "high" or "marked," are vague and often misleading, to say the least. A coefficient of .60 might be regarded as high for one type of situation and low for another. For example, a coefficient of .60 between a general intelligence test administered at the beginning of the year and school marks recorded at the end of the year might be regarded as high, because the correlation between that particular predictor and criterion usually falls below .60. But a coefficient of .60 between scores on two forms of this intelligence test administered the same day to a typical school class would be unusually low. In other words, "high" and "low" have only *relative* meaning; before an interpretation can be made of a coefficient on this basis, the reader must at least know what the *central tendency* of such coefficients for similar data is. He needs to have "antecedent expectations."

Another important factor in interpreting correlation coefficients pertains to the size of the sample on which the correlation coefficient was determined. For example, consider the correlation between IQ and height with $N = 2$. The computed r must be either $+1.0$ or -1.0 (unless it is a rare case in which the two persons would be precisely the same height or have identical IQ scores). The higher-ranking person in IQ will be either the taller of the two (hence $r = 1.0$) or the shorter of the two (hence $r = -1.0$).

To keep us from being misled by high correlation coefficients resulting from small samples, statisticians have developed procedures to assist in determining whether a given correlation coefficient can be attributed to chance (sampling error) or whether a genuine relationship exists. If a correlation is *statistically significant*, it is probable that there is some degree of true relationship between the two variables. For example, if you encountered in your reading of professional literature a statement such as, "For first-grade boys the correlation between height and IQ was statistically significant at the .01 level," the statement means that there is only a 1 percent chance (or less) that the true correlation in the population of which the subjects in the study were representative is zero. Hence, we could be quite confident that some genuine relationship exists between the two variables. A common error in interpreting such *statistically significant* relationships is to assume that they are therefore *large* relationships. "Statistically significant" indicates only that it is unlikely that the true correlation in the population (that is, the parameter) is 0.00. A relationship may be statistically significant and have no practical significance. For example, the relationship between height and IQ, though statistically significant, is too low to be of value for most practical purposes.

To guard against the error of interpreting statistically significant relationships as large relationships, researchers are increasingly using *confidence intervals*. These give the upper and lower limits of the range within which the true correlation coefficient in the population can be expected to fall. For example, if an investigator observed a highly significant correlation of .60 between variables *A* and *B* with a sample of 100 subjects, he might report the .95 confidence interval (in this case, .46 to .71), as well as the obtained correlation coefficient. The confidence interval gives a reasonable estimate as to how high or how low the value of r might be if the entire population in question were included. Consequently, the confidence interval gives us some assurance (for example, "95 percent confidence") that, in spite of the N of only 100, we can expect the true correlation coefficient in the population to be somewhere in the .46 to .71 range. If we repeatedly used this strategy, we would be correct 95 percent of the time; that is, in the long run the parameter would fall outside the .95 confidence interval only on one occasion in twenty (.05).

It should be clear that statistical significance and confidence intervals have much in common. For instance, if the .95 confidence interval for an observed r-value does not encompass the value of 0.00, then r is statistically significant at the .05 level.

Table 2–8 was constructed to illustrate the relationship between sample size and statistical significance. Since very high values for r are much more likely to occur by chance with small N's, very high values of r are required for statistical significance (as illustrated in Table 2–8). Table 2–8 shows that correlation coefficients based on small samples are not very reliable and that

TABLE 2–8

Minimum Absolute Values of r [a] Required to Be Statistically Significant at the .05 Level for Various Sample Sizes (N)

N	Minimum r for Statistical Significance
5	.878
10	.632
25	.396
100	.197
1000	.062

[a] The values above are for Pearson r correlation coefficients. The corresponding values of the rank correlation r_{Ranks} required for statistical significance are very similar. (See Glass and Stanley, 1970, pp. 536–539, for critical values for both r and r_{Ranks}.)

very low relationships can be statistically significant with a very large N. Table 2–9 was constructed to illustrate the information conveyed by correlation coefficients and the influence of sample size on these values. Since height is a variable that we can observe directly, it serves as a good illustration. We know that tall parents are more likely to have children who are taller than the average. The correlation coefficient quantifies this relationship. The confidence interval makes allowances for sampling error (chance); it is the "band" of values within which we can expect the true correlation—that is, the parameter—to lie. Since the sample on which the value of .5 was based was quite large ($N = 176$), the confidence interval is quite narrow. As you recall, the .5 value indicates that, on the average, children tend to be only about one-half as far from the mean height as their parents.

TABLE 2–9

	r	N	.95 Confidence Interval
Identical twins reared together[a]	.96	83	.93–.97
Identical twins reared apart[a]	.94	30	.88–.97
Height at age 3 vs. height at maturity (males)[b]	.75	66	.62–.84
Height at age 3 vs. height at maturity (females)[b]	.70	70	.56–.77
Fraternal twins[c]	.58	235	.49–.66
Siblings[a]	.50	853	.45–.55
Parent and child[a]	.51	374	.43–.59
Husband and wife[c]	.34	320	.24–.43
Grandparent and grandchild[a]	.32	132	.18–.47
First cousins[a]	.24	215	.11–.36
Height and IQ[d]	.20	4061	.17–.23

[a] Burt, 1955, and correspondence from Burt 1970.
[b] Tuddenham and Snyder, 1954.
[c] Meade and Parkes, 1966.
[d] Husen, 1951.

It is not appropriate to pursue other technicalities in an elementary measurement text. It is important to develop through experience a general understanding of *r*-values, so that the degree of relationship denoted by a given value of *r* is commensurate with the interpretation we associate with it.

VALIDITY AND RELIABILITY COEFFICIENTS

One of the most important uses of the coefficient of correlation is in determining the validity of a test. As we shall see in Chapter 4, *predictive validity* is determined by setting up a criterion to be predicted and then computing the coefficient of correlation between the predictor scores and the scores on the criterion—for example, rank in high-school graduating class correlated with college freshman gradepoint average. The *r* so obtained is called a predictive *validity coefficient* and is interpreted in the same way as other coefficients of correlation.

A second use of the coefficient of correlation is in determining the comparable-forms or the test-retest "reliability" of a test. *Reliability is the degree of consistency with which a test measures.* Three types of reliability coefficients are obtained by computing the *r* between two forms of the same test, two comparable halves of a test, or two administrations of the same test. Such *r*'s usually vary between 0 and 1. For further discussion, see Chapter 5.

OTHER COEFFICIENTS OF CORRELATION

The *r* discussed above is by far the most common type of correlation coefficient, but there are several other types. A distribution of test scores can be expressed in various ways, such as the scores themselves, as ranks, or as a dichotomy (a division into two categories, such as dead vs. alive, female vs. male, incorrect vs. correct, or below the median vs. above the median). We could have a "natural" dichotomy such as male vs. female sex or one representing an underlying normally distributed attribute, such as height in inches dichotomized at the median. If both distributions are in score form, their correlation is represented by r_{xy}, the standard Pearsonian coefficient of correlation. If both distributions are natural dichotomies such as sex and albinism, or are treated as such, scores on the x distribution may be called 0 and 1 (say, arbitrarily, 0 = female and 1 = male), and scores on the y distribution also 0 and 1 (say, 0 = nonalbinism, 1 = albinism). Then the correlation between the two distributions is simply an r_{xy}, usually called a *phi* coefficient and designated ϕ. Fortunately, it is easier to compute *phi* from a special formula than by means of the usual correlational procedure, as Glass and Stanley (1970, p. 158) explain.

The two coefficients of correlation most used in item analysis are r_{bis} and $r_{p\ bis}$. The *biserial r* (r_{bis}) represents the correlation between total scores on the test and the dichotomous "scores" on the test item (wrong = 0, right = 1), the 0's and 1's being treated as if the item actually measured a *normally distributed variable*. The term "*bis*erial" is used because, in this illustration, there are two series of total scores—one for those who answered the item correctly and another for those who did not. If we do not assume that the ability measured by the item is distributed normally, we compute the ordinary Pearson r between the test scores and the 0, 1 item scores; this is called *point* (that is, two discrete points 0 and 1) biserial r, abbreviated $r_{p\ bis}$. Both r_{bis} and $r_{p\ bis}$ are widely used for item-analysis purposes.

Thus far we have dealt with only two variables (x and y) at a time. Suppose, for instance, that there are two predictors—rank in high-school graduating class and score on a vocabulary test—and one criterion—grade-point average (GPA) during the freshman year of college. Label these variables 1, 2, and 3, respectively. We can compute three r's: r_{12}, r_{13}, and r_{23}. The relationship between the predictors is expressed by r_{12}, whereas the other two r's show how well each of the predictors predicts the criterion, freshman-year GPA. How well do the two predictors *together* predict the criterion? A simple way to answer this question would be to convert each rank in a high-school graduating class into a z-score and each vocabulary-test score into a z-score, average the two z-scores for each student, and correlate this average z-score with the GPA's. In this way you give equal "weight" to high-school achievement and vocabulary, because your averaging formula is $(1z_1 + 1z_2)/2$. That procedure works well if the two predictors are equally useful for predicting the criterion, but of course they may not be. Usually, high-school achievement correlates better with college grades than do scores on a general vocabulary test (which, incidentally, is a pretty good verbal "intelligence" test), though both correlate appreciably with GPA.

We do not discuss the technical details of *multiple correlation*, but it may be that those equal, 1 and 1, weights for the two predictor z-scores are not optimal for predicting college grades. Perhaps 4 and 1 would be better—that is, computing for each student $(4z_1 + 1z_2)/5$ would yield new predictor scores that correlate higher with college grades than the $(1z_1 + 1z_2)/2$'s do. The best possible z-score weighting of this sort for predicting the criterion scores (college grades in this case) produces the multiple coefficient of correlation, symbolized by $R_{3.12}$, where the subscript 3 represents the criterion. How does one find the optimal weights for two or more predictors? Most statistics textbooks give procedures.[26]

Occasionally one wishes to estimate the correlation between two variables, 1 and 2, free from the influence of a third variable, 3. For example, suppose that reading speed (1) and reading comprehension (2) correlate .4 ($r_{12} = .4$) and that they correlate .4 and .7, respectively, with IQ. An obvious question is, for persons of the same IQ, do the faster readers comprehend more? By using partial correlation ($r_{12.3}$) one can estimate the correlation between reading speed and comprehension with the predictable effects from IQ *partialed* out.[27] In this hypothetical example, $r_{12.3} = .18$, considerably lower than the .4 for r_{12}. In other words, for persons having the same IQ score, the estimated correlation between reading speed and comprehension is very low (only .18).

Post-Organizer

The following is an outline summary of three important concepts and some statistics useful in connection with test scores and other quantitative data:

1. *Central tendency*
   a. The arithmetic *mean*, usually called the "average" in everyday life, is obtained by adding all the scores and dividing the sum by the number of scores. For many purposes it is the "best" measure of central tendency.
   b. The *median* is the point above which half of the scores lie and below which the other half lie. Thus, it is the 50th percentile, also called Q_2.
   c. The *mode* is the most frequent score, a rather crude measure.
2. *Variability*
   a. The *standard deviation*, involves every measure in the distribution. Approximately two-thirds of all scores in a "normal" distribution lie within plus or minus one standard deviation from the mean.
   b. *Q*, the *quartile deviation* or *semi-interquartile range*, is half of the distance between Q_3 (the 75th percentile) and Q_1 (the 25th percentile). *Q* is usually a poorer measure of variability than *s*.
   c. The *range* is the distance between the highest score and the lowest score. For most purposes it is a very inadequate measure of variability.
3. *Correlation.* There are numerous ways of expressing co-relationship. The most common statistic is Pearson's *r*. A simplification of *r*, appli-

---

[26] The formula that gives the correlation of two *optimally* weighted variables, 1 and 2, for predicting a criterion, 3 is

$$R_{3.12} = \sqrt{\frac{r_{13}^2 + r_{23}^2 - 2r_{12}r_{13}r_{23}}{1 - r_{12}^2}}.$$

[27] The formula for estimating the correlation of variables 1 and 2 that would be expected if all persons had the same score on variable 3 is

$$r_{12.3} = \frac{r_{12} - r_{13}r_{23}}{\sqrt{(1 - r_{13}^2)(1 - r_{23}^2)}}.$$

cable chiefly to data originally secured in the form of ranks, is r_{Ranks}. Both r and r_{Ranks} have values of -1 for perfect inverse relationship, 0 for sheer chance association, and $+1$ for perfect direct relationship.

The concepts of *statistical significance* and *confidence interval* are helpful aids in interpreting correlation coefficients. If a given r-value is not statistically significant, no true relationship between the variables has been established. The confidence interval gives the range of r-values within which the true correlation coefficient in the population will usually be found.

The concept of correlation is necessary for understanding reliability and validity coefficients, which are vital in evaluating the quality of a test or measurement procedure.

IMPORTANT TERMS AND CONCEPTS

frequency distribution
  normal distribution
  skewness
central tendency
  mean ($\bar{X}$)
  median
  mode
variability
  range
  standard deviation (s or σ)
  quartile deviation (Q)

percentile and percentile rank
raw score
standard score
  z-score
  T-score
  stanine
  normalized score
correlation
statistical significance
confidence interval
parameter

MASTERY TEST TO HELP YOU LEARN AND OVERLEARN STATISTICS

The following test contains 25 five-option multiple-choice items covering the material in this chapter. The questions have been designed to assist you in identifying concepts you need to review. Each has five options, only *one* of which is correct or the best answer. After you have attempted each item, turn to the answers in Appendix B and obtain immediate feedback.

  1. The *arithmetic mean* of the scores 4, 5, 7, 6, 4 is
    A. 6.0.
    B. 5.5.
    C. 5.2.
    D. 5.0.
    E. 4.8.

2. The measure of *central tendency* to use when reporting data concerning wages in order to avoid the undue influence of a few extreme salaries is the
A. standard deviation.
B. quartile deviation.
C. median.
D. range.
E. mean.

3. The *median* of the scores 4, 6, 7, 5, 4 is
A. 6.0.
B. 5.5.
C. 5.2.
D. 5.0.
E. 4.8.

4. The 60th *percentile* is the point in a distribution
A. where a student has answered 60 percent of the questions correctly.
B. which marks the distance from the median that includes 60 percent of the cases.
C. below which are 40 percent of the cases.
D. below which are 60 percent of the cases.
E. above which are 60 percent of the cases.

5. $Q = (P_{75} - P_{25})/2$. Q is a direct measure of
A. variability.
B. correlation.
C. central tendency.
D. skewness.
E. modality.

6. The percentage of scores lying between Q_3 and the median is
A. 25.
B. 34.
C. 50.
D. 68.
E. a variable quantity that depends on the score distribution.

7. What is the mean of the following distribution? 1, 1, 3, 3.
A. 0.0.
B. 1.0.
C. 2.0.
D. 3.0.
E. None of the answers above.

8. What is the standard deviation of the distribution given in question 7?
A. 0.0.
B. 1.0.
C. 2.0.
D. 3.0.
E. 4.0.

9. On a test with a standard deviation of 20 and an arithmetic mean of 80, an individual with a raw score of 70 will have a z-score of
   A. −10.0.
   B. −0.5.
   C. −0.1.
   D. 0.5.
   E. 5.0.

10. ... and a T-score ($\bar{X} = 50$, $\sigma = 10$) of
   A. 55.
   B. 50.
   C. 49.
   D. 45.
   E. 40.

11. What *rank* should be assigned to a score of 95 in the following distribution?

Score
97
97
96
95
95
95
94
94
93

   A. 5.5.
   B. 6.0.
   C. 7.0.
   D. 4.0.
   E. 5.0.

12. The Pearson product-moment *coefficient of correlation*, r_1, may vary between
   A. −2.00 and +2.00.
   B. −1.00 and +1.00.
   C. −0.92 and +0.92.
   D. 0.00 and +1.00.
   E. 0.00 and infinity.

13. A teacher computed a correlation coefficient between scores on a reading test and scores on a test of current affairs, obtaining a value of .92. He was justified in concluding that, as measured by these two tests,
   A. knowledge of current affairs and reading ability are closely related.
   B. knowledge of current affairs and reading ability are unrelated to each other.
   C. knowledge of current affairs and reading ability are perfectly related.
   D. the coefficient must have been computed incorrectly.
   E. wide knowledge of current affairs is the result of good reading ability.

14. Which one of the following r's has the *least* predictive value?
   A. .91.
   B. .50.
   C. .17.
   D. −.23.
   E. −1.00.

15. A student computed a Pearson product-moment coefficient of correlation, r_{xy}, between 30 paired scores and found it to be 1.05. We are *absolutely* certain that
   A. he has freakish data.
   B. he should have computed r_{Ranks} instead.
   C. the means of the two distributions differ.
   D. the correlation between X and Y is high.
   E. the r has been computed incorrectly.

16. Suppose five boys ran a race on two consecutive days. The order of finishing is given below. What is the correlation (r_{Ranks}) between the ranks?

	Day 1	Day 2
Bob	1	2
Dale	2	1
Jon	3	5
Jim	4	4
Ken	5	3

   A. .40.
   B. .50.
   C. .60.
   D. .80.
   E. None of these.

17. A researcher reported a statistically significant (.05 level) correlation of .31 between two variables. This means that in the population:
   A. the true value is .31.
   B. the true value is 0.0.
   C. the true value is *not* 0.0.
   D. it is unlikely that the true value is 0.0.
   E. the .95 confidence interval for r includes the 0.00 value.

18. Which one of these distributions is skewed negatively to the greatest extent?
   A.
   B.
   C.
   D.
   E. None of these.

Analogies: These terms are designed to reinforce your knowledge of various interrelationships between concepts.

DIRECTIONS: Each of the following seven items represents an analogy. In every case the first two terms of the item are related to each other in some way, and the third term is related in the same way to *one* of the other alternatives.

EXAMPLE: Shoe is to foot as hat is to

A. arm.
B. hair.
C. hand.
D. head.
E. leg.

Option D, "head," is of course correct.

19. Arithmetic mean is to central tendency as standard deviation is to
   A. average.
   B. variability.
   C. Q.
   D. percentile.
   E. relationship.

20. Q_3 is to 75th percentile as median is to
   A. 90th percentile.
   B. 75th percentile.
   C. 50th percentile.
   D. 16th percentile.
   E. 10th percentile.

21. Arithmetic mean is to standard deviation as median is to
   A. standard deviation.
   B. Q_3.
   C. Q_2.
   D. Q_1.
   E. Q.

22. $Q_3 - Q_1$ is to 50 percent as mean $\pm 1\sigma$ is to (assume normal distribution)
   A. 32 percent.
   B. 34 percent.
   C. 50 percent.
   D. 68 percent.
   E. 84 percent.

23. Arithmetic mean is to mode as standard deviation is to
   A. range.
   B. median.
   C. midscore.
   D. percentile.
   E. Q.

24. Median is to point as standard deviation is to
   A. volume.
   B. distance.
   C. square.
   D. score.
   E. area.

25. Positive correlation is to direct relationship as negative correlation is to
   _____ relationship.
   A. incomplete
   B. inconsequential
   C. incorrect
   D. inadequate
   E. inverse

22–25, excellent
20–21, very good; review the concepts in the missed items.
15–19, satisfactory initial mastery; the chapter should be reviewed carefully.
Below 15, start again.

SUGGESTED READINGS

ANASTASI, A. 1968. *Psychological testing*, 3rd ed. New York: The Macmillan Company.

Chapter 3 gives a good noncomputational presentation of the important statistical concepts covered in this chapter.

EBEL, R. L. 1965. *Measuring educational achievement*. Englewood Cliffs, N.J.: Prentice-Hall, Inc.

Chapter 8, "Describing test scores statistically," is an excellent alternative presentation of the concepts introduced in this chapter.

GLASS, G. V, and J. C. STANLEY. 1970. *Statistical methods in education and psychology*. Englewood Cliffs, N.J.: Prentice-Hall, Inc.

Chapters 4 through 7 give a more thorough treatment of the topics of this chapter.

THE MEANING AND APPLICATION
OF NORMS

Test scores are of little value unless they can be interpreted in terms of aptitudes, abilities, and accomplishments of educational significance. The value of test scores will depend not only on what the scores represent, but also on how well they are understood and interpreted. In Chapter 2 we discussed the summarization of scores by statistical methods as an aid to their interpretation. Now let us consider some closely related problems of interpreting scores with the aid of norms.

Standardized and Nonstandardized Tests

It is important for us to distinguish clearly between a *norm* and a *standard*, because these terms are frequently used interchangeably. The confusion doubtless arises because norms are used with standardized tests, and the development of norms is a part of the process of standardization. Test norms are based entirely upon actual performance of pupils and not upon predetermined levels or standards of performance.

Some standardized tests began as informal objective tests made by classroom teachers. An informal test that has undergone the usual process of standardization differs from the original class test in four essential aspects. First, the content has been refined. Each item has been carefully scrutinized, and the difficulty and discriminating value of each item have been determined by statistical processes that have eliminated weaker items. Second, the method of administration has been standardized, and explicit directions have been formalized, usually with appropriate time limits and instructions. Third, the method of scoring has been standardized. Scoring keys have been prepared, and definite rules have been formulated for marking the papers and determining the scores for each part and for the whole test. Finally, tables of norms have been provided to facilitate interpreting the various scores made on the test. These norms are merely transformations of the raw scores to a more meaningful scale derived from the performance of large numbers of pupils distributed over wide geographic areas and representing various types of school. The norms are expressed in relation to school grade or age.

Norms

The word *standard* implies a *goal* or *objective to be reached*. Thus, a norm is *not* a measure of what ought to be—that is, not a goal—but a measure of what is: the *status quo*. When a school or class scores at the national median on a test, it is just an average or typical group. Of course, this performance level may in some sense be satisfactory for the group under the circumstances, but whether it is satisfactory cannot be determined from the norms themselves. That the class median corresponds to the 50th percentile in the norm group does not of itself establish anything other than that the performance is that of a typical group. It is obvious that a group of students with superior opportunities and capacities should be expected to perform better than a representative group (the norm group), whereas a group of low ability and opportunity might find it virtually impossible to do well.

Most current standardized tests give norms based only on the total reference group, all types of pupil and school being lumped together. Regional, provincial, or state norms would often be more valuable in several achievement areas, since there are often wide curriculum differences among regions, provinces, and states, particularly in social studies and the sciences. Norms could also be developed for other special kinds of pupil or course, such as gifted students or Algebra I classes. The objective of a meaningful reference group, however, is largely accomplished by the dual standardization of intelligence and achievement tests. When the tests are normed on the same group of students, a sounder basis for evaluating pupil or school achievement is facilitated by comparing the achievement with the measured intelligence. (The evaluation of achievement in relation to aptitude is considered more extensively in Chapter 15.)

Definitive standards, or goals of attainment, are almost altogether lacking in education. An adequate technique for establishing standards has yet to be worked out. It is conceivable that such standards might be established and expressed in numerical units on existing tests, or on tests yet to be devised, but such a process is inherently difficult. The process of building norms, although time-consuming and laborious, is simple and straightforward. An understanding of the way norms are determined should make it obvious that norms make no claims to be goals of performance, unless perhaps one is willing to accept mediocrity as a goal.

The point that norms should not be viewed as standards does not preclude such use when the standards have been established on some other basis. For example, persons who did not graduate from high school can receive a certificate of equivalency, which is generally accepted as a high-school diploma, if proficiency equivalent to the average of a representative group of high-school graduates is demonstrated on the *General Educational Development Tests* (GED) (Graff, 1965). In this instance a certain predetermined *norm* value is a minimal *standard* of performance. The validity of the standard has been supported by studies showing that persons receiving high-school accreditation via GED tests perform as well as regular high-school graduates in industrial and public employment and almost as well in college work (Peters, 1956; L. E. Tyler, 1956). Without norms of some form there would have been no logical way for establishing equivalent proficiency acquired outside the school setting.

NORMS AS A MEANS OF COMPARISON WITH AN EXTERNAL GROUP

A school's instructional strengths and weaknesses become evident when its performance is viewed in terms of a larger, representative reference group. Figure 3–1 contains the test results reported by Durost (1962) of eighth-grade students in a large school who took the *Metropolitan Achievement Tests*. It appears that the students' achievement in science and social studies may be suffering because of the strong curricular emphasis on word knowledge, spelling, and language.

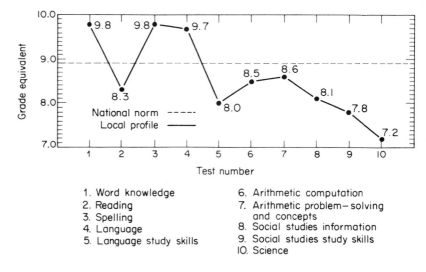

1. Word knowledge
2. Reading
3. Spelling
4. Language
5. Language study skills
6. Arithmetic computation
7. Arithmetic problem–solving and concepts
8. Social studies information
9. Social studies study skills
10. Science

FIGURE 3–1 *Average grade-equivalent score of eighth-grade students tested in June. (Reproduced from* **Manual for Interpreting Metropolitan Achievement Tests** *[New York: Harcourt Brace Jovanovich, Inc.], Fig. II, p. 12, by special permission of the publisher. Copyright © 1958–1962 by Harcourt Brace Jovanovich, Inc.)*

The identification of an individual pupil's instructional accomplishments and needs likewise can be expedited via appropriate, properly used standardized tests, as we shall see later in the chapter.

*The Meaning
and Application
of Norms*

The size of the group on which norms are established is much less important than the degree to which it is representative of the relevant population. On measures of scholastic aptitude and achievement there are marked differences across geographic region, socioeconomic status, urban–rural residence, and other factors. Data on 1,000,000 pupils from a "grab" sample are much less

TABLE 3–1
Standardization Data on the WPPSI at Age Six

A.   By Geographic Region and Color

Geographic Region	Percent in U.S.[a] Population			Percent in WPPSI Age 6 Sample		
	White	Nonwhite	Total	White	Nonwhite	Total
Northeast	20.8	1.9	22.7	22.0	2.0	24.0
North Central	26.8	2.6	29.4	26.5	2.5	29.0
South	23.7	8.2	31.9	23.0	7.5	30.5
West	14.5	1.5	16.0	14.5	2.0	16.5
Total sample	85.8	14.2	100.0	86.0	14.0	100.0

B.   By Color and Urban–Rural Residence

Residence	Percent in U.S.[a] Population			Percent in WPPSI Age 6 Sample		
	White	Nonwhite	Total	White	Nonwhite	Total
Urban	58.0	10.0	68.0	57.0	11.0	68.0
Rural	27.8	4.2	32.0	29.0	3.0	32.0
Total sample	85.8	14.2	100.0	86.0	14.0	100.0

C.   By Father's Education

Years of School Completed	Percent in U.S.[a] Population	Percent in WPPSI Age 6 Sample
8 or less	26.1	20.0
9–11	21.9	20.5
12	29.2	31.5
13–15	10.2	8.0
16 or more	12.6	17.0
Not reported	—	3.0

D.   By Father's Occupation

Occupational Category	Percent in U.S.[a] Population	Percent in WPPSI Age 6 Sample
I	13.1	11.5
II	9.6	11.5
III	12.7	12.5
IV	20.9	22.0
V	22.8	23.0
VI	4.3	5.5
VII	4.6	5.5
VIII	8.8	8.5
Not reported	3.1	—

SOURCE: Wechsler, 1967, pp. 16–18.

[a] Differential birth rates cause the overall U.S. population values to deviate from completely accurate parameters for the U.S. population of children at any given age. This difference rarely has serious consequences, however.

valuable than data on 1,000 representative pupils.[1] Samples for standardization purposes are often selected to correspond to the U.S. population in geographic region, urban–rural residence, community size, father's occupational and educational level, and/or ethnic-group membership. One of the most carefully selected norm samples was used in the standardization of the popular *Wechsler Preschool and Primary Scale of Intelligence* (WPPSI) (Oldridge and Allison, 1968). The data in Table 3–1 were abstracted from the WPPSI manual (Wechsler, 1967); they illustrate the comparabilities of the six-year sample with national population as described by the 1960 census data. Although the number of six-year-old children involved in the standardization was only 200 (100 boys and 100 girls), the sample was carefully selected to be representative—note the close correspondence between certain of their characteristics and those of the whole United States. Scores from tests that have been carefully standardized can be interpreted with much greater confidence than those based upon a group of uncertain representativeness.

Another example of a norm sample is depicted in Figure 3–2, which illustrates the selection of samples for a standardization of the *California Achievement Tests* (CAT). Figure 3–2 illustrates that geographic region, size of community, and grade level were the only factors involved in selection of the sample. Although approximately 5,000 students were tested at each grade level, we have less confidence in the representativeness of these achievement-test norms than

---

[1] Most of Gallup's surveys are based upon a representative sample of 1,500 respondents, which is about .001 percent of the adult population of the United States.

FIGURE 3–2   Standardization procedure for the California Achievement Tests. Geographical: Schools from eighteen geographical areas included at each grade. All states represented in total norming sample. Community size: Schools from community areas with populations under 2,500, 2,500–9,999, 10,000–99,999, and over 100,000 represented at each grade for each geographical area. Grades and levels: Schools at one grade entirely different from schools selected for next higher and lower grades. Sample pattern eliminates cumulative bias resulting when consecutive grades in the same school are tested. Weighting: Test results weighted in exact proportion to United States Office of Education enrollment data for total pupils at each grade, by geographical area and community size. (Reproduced from 1957 Technical Report on the California Achievement Tests, Fig. 1, p. 15, by permission of the publisher, CTB/McGraw-Hill, Monterey, California.)

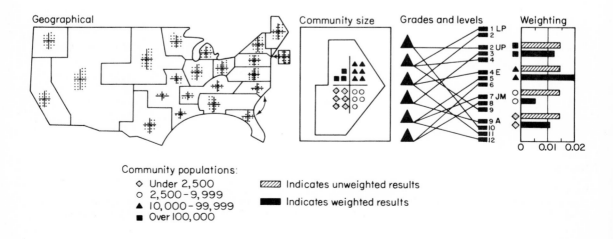

Community populations:
◇ Under 2,500
○ 2,500–9,999
▲ 10,000–99,999
■ Over 100,000

▨ Indicates unweighted results
■ Indicates weighted results

we do for the WPSSI, in which more relevant variables were considered. The mean from the WPPSI sample of 200 will almost certainly (.95 confidence) be not more than 2 points from the mean that would have been obtained if every six-year-old in the United States had been tested.[2] We are much less certain of the accuracy of the 1957 norms on the CAT[3] and most other standardized achievement tests even though they have much larger numbers of pupils involved. The *size* of the standardization sample is much less critical than its *representativeness*.[4]

KINDS OF NORM

National norms are the most common type used in education. Some states and provinces, however, have established norms on various achievement tests for their particular domains. Many school districts have established local achievement norms, which they use in addition to national norms. Figure 3–3 shows the hypothetical performance of Sam Smith in terms of national and local norms along with an interpretation.

Norms are often based on a highly select, but relevant, group of persons. Norms on the *Graduate Record Examination* (GRE) are, of course, not based on a representative sample of the nation's population, but on the performance of graduating seniors at certain colleges (Schultz and Angoff, 1956). Hence an "average" score on the GRE represents aptitudes far above an average score on a general intelligence test such as the *Stanford-Binet Intelligence Scale* or the *Wechsler Adult Intelligence Scale* (WAIS) or even the *Scholastic Aptitude Test* (SAT) of the *College Entrance Examination Board* (CEEB).

In addition to the total group norms, standardized tests often offer separate norms for each sex, as illustrated by the GRE data in Tables 3–2 and 3–3. Table 3–2 gives percentile norms for both sections on each of the three GRE general achievement "area" tests. Note the considerable difference between the performance of men and women across the three areas—females performing better on the Humanities test but less well on the Social Science and Natural Science tests. A scaled score of 500 on the Natural Science section places a female at the 71st percentile of her sex, yet the identical score is only at the 43rd

---

[2] In an elementary statistics course you would learn that the .95 confidence interval is approximately $\bar{X} \pm 2s_X$ (s_X is the standard error of the mean). For the WPPSI, $s_X = \sigma/\sqrt{n} = 15/\sqrt{200}$, or about 1 IQ point. The .95 confidence interval is based on the assumption that the sample was selected completely at random. The stratification illustrated in Table 3–1 would further reduce the value of s_X, which makes it *very improbable* that the sample mean ($\bar{X}$) is as much as 2 points from the mean that would have resulted if the entire national population of six-year-old children had been tested.

[3] In fact, studies of the 1957 CAT norms showed that they consistently yielded higher grade-equivalent scores than other competing standardized achievement-test batteries (Stake, 1961; Taylor and Crandall, 1962). This problem appears to have been corrected in the current 1963 norming (Millman and Lindlof, 1964).

[4] It appears likely that in the future test norms will be established by Lord's (1962a) item-sampling method rather than by examinee sampling; that is, each student will answer only a few items, while other students are attempting different items. Empirical studies indicate that norms developed in this way are essentially equivalent to the more time-consuming and expensive examinee-sampling approach (Cook and Stufflebeam, 1967; Owens and Stufflebeam, 1969; Plumlee, 1964).

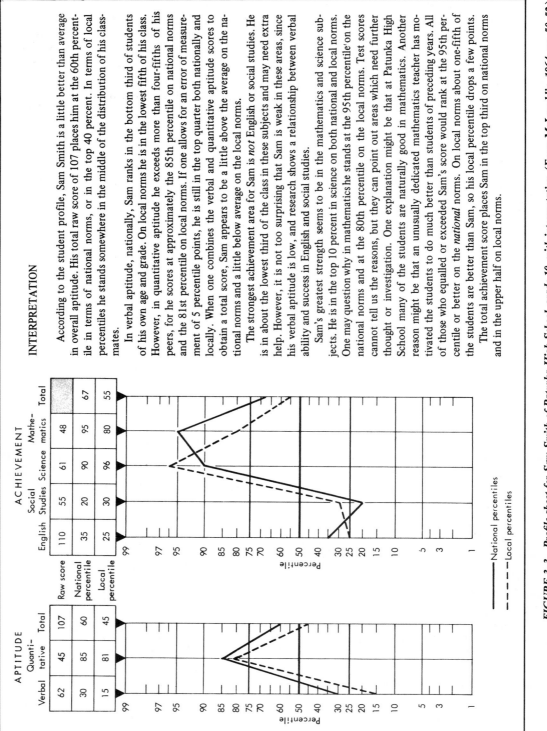

APTITUDE

	Verbal	Quantitative	Total
Raw score	62	45	107
National percentile	30	85	60
Local percentile	15	81	45

ACHIEVEMENT

	English	Social Studies	Science	Mathematics	Total
Raw score	110	55	61	48	
National percentile	35	20	90	95	67
Local percentile	25	30	96	80	55

Percentile (vertical axis): 99, 97, 95, 90, 85, 80, 75, 70, 60, 50, 40, 30, 25, 20, 15, 10, 5, 3, 1

———— National percentiles
– – – – Local percentiles

INTERPRETATION

According to the student profile, Sam Smith is a little better than average in overall aptitude. His total raw score of 107 places him at the 60th percentile in terms of national norms, or in the top 40 percent. In terms of local percentiles he stands somewhere in the middle of the distribution of his classmates.

In verbal aptitude, nationally, Sam ranks in the bottom third of students of his own age and grade. On local norms he is in the lowest fifth of his class. However, in quantitative aptitude he exceeds more than four-fifths of his peers, for he scores at approximately the 85th percentile on national norms and the 81st percentile on local norms. If one allows for an error of measurement of 5 percentile points, he is still in the top quarter both nationally and locally. When one combines the verbal and quantitative aptitude scores to obtain a total score, Sam appears to be a little above the average on the national norms and a little below average on the local norms.

The strongest achievement area for Sam is *not* English or social studies. He is in about the lowest third of the class in these subjects and may need extra help. However, it is not too surprising that Sam is weak in these areas, since his verbal aptitude is low, and research shows a relationship between verbal ability and success in English and social studies.

Sam's greatest strength seems to be in the mathematics and science subjects. He is in the top 10 percent in science on both national and local norms. One may question why in mathematics he stands at the 95th percentile on the national norms and at the 80th percentile on the local norms. Test scores cannot tell us the reasons, but they can point out areas which need further thought or investigation. One explanation might be that at Patunka High School many of the students are naturally good in mathematics. Another reason might be that an unusually dedicated mathematics teacher has motivated the students to do much better than students of preceding years. All of those who equalled or exceeded Sam's score would rank at the 95th percentile or better on the *national* norms. On local norms about one-fifth of the students are better than Sam, so his local percentile drops a few points.

The total achievement score places Sam in the top third on national norms and in the upper half on local norms.

FIGURE 3–3 Profile sheet for Sam Smith of Patunka High School, grade 10, with interpretation. (From McLaughlin, 1964, pp. 50–52.)

TABLE 3–2

Norms on the Area Tests of the Graduate Record Examinations[a]
(Percent of Seniors Scoring Lower than Selected Scaled Scores)

Scaled Score	Social Science			Humanities			Natural Science		
	Men	Women	Total	Men	Women	Total	Men	Women	Total
740					99		99		
720	99		99	99	98	99	98		99
700	98		98	98	97	98	96		98
680	96	99	97	96	94	95	94	99	96
660	94	97	95	95	92	94	90	98	94
640	91	94	93	93	89	91	86	97	91
620	86	91	88	91	85	88	83	96	89
600	82	88	85	87	79	83	75	93	84
580	75	84	79	83	74	79	71	92	80
560	69	79	74	78	68	74	64	88	75
540	60	74	66	72	58	66	57	82	69
520	53	68	60	67	53	61	50	77	62
500	46	60	52	58	43	51	43	71	55
480	39	53	46	52	36	45	36	64	49
460	32	46	38	45	29	38	30	58	42
440	25	39	31	36	22	30	24	50	36
420	19	32	25	30	18	24	19	39	28
400	13	25	19	21	11	16	14	29	21
380	9	19	13	15	7	12	8	19	13
360	7	12	9	10	4	7	4	10	7
340	4	9	6	6	2	5	2	4	3
320	3	5	4	3	1	2			
300	1	3	2	2		1			
280		1	1	1					

SOURCE: Copyright © 1968 by Educational Testing Service. All rights reserved. Reproduced by permission.

[a] The scaled scores on the Area Tests may range from 220 to 910. The data in this table are based on the performance of a reference group of seniors tested in selected colleges in 1954. Estimated data on the performance of representative groups of freshmen and sophomores are given in a separate publication, *Institutional Testing Program Score Interpretation Leaflet for Freshmen and Sophomores, 1968–1969.*

percentile for males, or at the 55th percentile in terms of the total group.[5] Even more specific normative data are illustrated in Table 3–3, which gives senior (S) and graduate (G) norms in addition to sex norms. A scaled score of 500 has a percentile rank of 43 for both the Verbal and Quantitative Aptitude Tests

[5] The GRE norms are based on the performance of 2,095 graduating seniors in the spring of 1952 at eleven colleges, which were generally representative of schools that normally administer the tests to their students. The norms on the advanced tests were adjusted to reflect differences in aptitude-test scores such that, if all students elected a given major, the mean scaled score would be expected to be 500, with a corresponding standard deviation of 100. Thus the mean score of graduating seniors majoring in physics on the Advanced Physics Test was 546, since as a group physics majors did much better on the aptitude sections of the GRE than did the entire group of graduating seniors. Thus the scale scores are not contaminated from differences in aptitude levels associated with major field of study (Schultz and Angoff, 1956).

TABLE 3–3

Norms on the Aptitude Tests of the Graduate Record Examinations[a]
(Percent of Students Scoring Lower than Selected Scaled Scores)

Scaled Score	Verbal						Quantitative					
	Men		Women		Total		Men		Women		Total	
	S	G	S	G	S	G	S	G	S	G	S	G
800								99				99
780		99		99		99	99	96				97
760		98		97		98	98	94		99		96
740	99	96	99	96	99	96	98	90		98	99	93
720	98	94	98	94	98	94	97	86		97	98	90
700	97	92	97	91	97	91	96	81		96	97	87
680	95	89	94	87	95	88	94	78		94	96	84
660	93	86	92	83	93	85	92	73		92	95	80
640	90	82	89	79	90	81	91	68	99	90	94	76
620	88	77	87	74	88	76	88	63	97	87	92	72
600	84	73	83	69	83	71	83	58	95	84	89	67
580	80	67	77	63	79	66	77	53	93	80	84	63
560	75	62	73	57	74	60	70	48	89	76	79	58
540	70	56	68	51	69	54	66	43	87	70	76	53
520	64	50	62	45	63	48	59	38	82	65	70	47
500	56	44	55	40	56	43	50	34	75	60	61	43
480	47	38	48	34	47	37	40	29	66	54	52	38
460	40	33	41	29	41	31	29	24	55	48	41	33
440	31	27	35	24	33	26	24	20	49	41	35	27
420	23	22	26	19	24	21	17	16	38	35	26	23
400	15	18	17	15	16	17	10	12	28	28	18	18
380	10	14	13	12	11	13	6	9	19	22	12	14
360	5	10	7	9	6	10	3	6	11	17	7	10
340	2	8	4	7	3	7	2	5	7	13	4	8
320	1	6	1	5	1	5	1	3	3	9	2	5
300		4		4		4		2		6		3
280		2		2		2		1		4		2
260		2		2		2				2		1
240		1		1		1				1		

[a] Scaled scores on the Aptitude Test may range from 200 to 900. The data in the shaded areas (column "S") are based on the performance of a reference group of seniors in selected colleges; the data in the unshaded areas (column "G") are based on the performance of a group consisting of graduate students and applicants for admission to graduate school tested from May 1965 through April 1968.

when the total group of graduate student norms are used. When compared with college seniors, however, this same score (500) is at the 56th and 61st percentiles on the Verbal and Quantitative sections, respectively. A score of 500 on the Quantitative section also corresponds to the 60th percentile for female graduate students but only the 34th percentile for male graduate students. It is clear that

88

for a correct interpretation of any test, the precise nature of the reference group and the kinds of norm used must always be borne in mind.

FLUCTUATIONS IN NORMS

Society in general and education in particular are continually undergoing change. For norms to be representative of current populations, they must be continually reestablished.[6] For example, on the *Stanford-Binet Intelligence scale*, the word "Mars" was far more difficult when the test was normed in 1937 than it was in 1960 when the current norms were established. The question of interest is not how intelligent the child is in relation to children of the same age in 1937, but in relation to his contemporaries. The older the norms are, the more caution must accompany their interpretation. In the late 1950's it was necessary to increase the margin of error in interpreting performance on the Stanford-Binet because the norms were outdated.

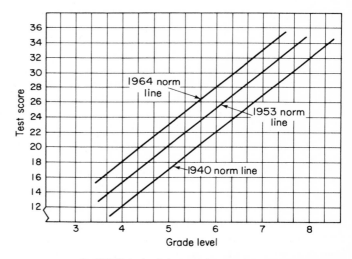

FIGURE 3–4 *Schematic illustration of upward shift in general achievement level of school population. (Reproduced from* Stanford Achievement Tests, *Technical Supplement [New York: Harcourt Brace Jovanovich, Inc.], Fig. 17, p. 29, by special permission of the publisher. Copyright © 1964–1966 by Harcourt Brace Jovanovich, Inc.)*

Bloom (1956) found that high-school seniors in 1955 were achieving better in all areas than were comparable seniors in 1943. This upward shift is further documented by the data depicted in Figure 3–4, which was taken from

[6] Some tests such as the GRE serve an important function in the assessment of trends or changes in student ability or aptitude; hence it is necessary to keep the norms based on the same reference group even though it may no longer be representative. For example, Klinger and Gee (1960), using data on the *Medical College Admissions Test* (MCAT), were able to establish that the quality of medical-school students did not change over a period of several years.

the *Stanford Achievement Test: Technical Supplement* of 1966. The figure shows the apparent increase in school achievement that the test publishers have observed during recent years on successive standardizations. Related research also tends to show generally superior academic performance by current students over their predecessors at the same grade levels, even though a greater proportion of students are remaining in school longer. The lesson is clear: norms must be kept current if they are to be interpreted properly. This shift is probably the result of changes in nonschool factors in addition to better schooling.

NORMS CAN BE EXPRESSED IN MANY DIFFERENT UNITS

Raw scores must be converted to *other* units to be meaningful. But to which other units? In Chapter 2 we discussed percentiles and various types of standard score—*z*-scores, T-scores, and stanines—which (except for *z*-scores) are all widely used in various standardized tests. In addition, there are quotient norms, which describe a ratio of two variables. The *classic* example is

$$IQ = \frac{Mental\ Age}{Chronological\ Age} \times 100.$$

Age norms and grade-equivalent units are also quite common. John's mental age of nine and one-half years means that his score on an intelligence test was the average score for persons 9.5 years of age. Likewise, a grade equivalent of 5.1 for Ann means that her score was equal to the average score of students at the end of the first month of grade five.[7]

To illustrate the advantages and disadvantages of various units used for reporting a pupil's performance on a test, suppose that Joe obtained a score of 40 on a spelling test of 50 items. What does his score of 40 mean? To say that it represents an achievement of 80 percent has little meaning. How were the 50 words for the test chosen? Were they the 50 most frequently misspelled words for the grade in which the test was administered? Or were they a random sample from a certain dictionary, so that we can predict that the pupil can spell correctly 80 percent of the words in that dictionary? Was a correction for "guessing" employed? How well did the average pupil spell?

If the spelling test is standardized, we would be interested in the "grade equivalent" of Joe's score of 40 on this test. That is, when during the school grades does the average score equal 40 for a typical group of pupils? It might, for instance, be listed in the test manual as 5.7, meaning the seventh month of the fifth grade. If Joe has an actual grade placement of, say, 4.2 (second month of the fourth grade), then he is a good speller compared with the group on which the grade equivalents are based, being 5.7 − 4.2 = one year and five months beyond the average grade equivalent of 4.2.

Suppose the national norms show that the average raw score for pupils in the second month of grade four (4.2) was 25, with a standard deviation of 10. The raw score of 40 would correspond to a *z*-score of +1.5 or a T-score of

---

[7] Since no schooling normally occurs in July and August, only ten months are considered with the grade equivalent scale; each school month is viewed as one-tenth of a school year. The error resulting from this approximation is negligible. Grade-equivalent norms receive extensive additional treatment in Chapter 15.

65 or a stanine of 8. The test manual would also provide tables for converting raw scores directly to percentile ranks. Joe's percentile rank on the spelling test will be about 93 if the raw scores are approximately normally distributed, as they usually are on well-designed standardized tests.

A few decades ago, test scores were often converted to an age scale. If the age at which 40 is the average score is ten years, ten months, Joe's "spelling age" would be ten years, ten months. This is the manner in which the mental-age scale has been developed and continues to be defined on intelligence tests.[8]

CALIBRATED NORMS

If a carefully standardized ability test were available and were used by publishers of "standardized" tests, test norms would probably be more comparable from test to test than they are now. Lennon (1964) suggests that this "anchor" test could be given with a new test to a calibration sample and norms could be obtained using the *equipercentile* method. If the norms on the anchor tests are representative, national or other norms on the new test can be calibrated vicariously on a smaller and not necessarily representative sample. If the median raw score on the new test for this calibration sample is 73, and the national percentile rank of the median score for the calibration sample on the anchor test is 65, then a national percentile rank of 65 is assigned to the score of 73 on the new test. In like manner, other percentiles, grade equivalences, and the like can be obtained. This same basic procedure was used to obtain norms on the advanced tests of the Graduate Record Examinations (see footnote 5, p. 87). Cronbach (1970a) suggests that the tests given to the excellent Project Talent sample (see Chapter 7) could serve as useful anchor tests, provided that certain difficulties are recognized (see Angoff, 1971). One current set of standardized tests, the *Evaluation and Adjustment Series* (Harcourt Brace Jovanovich, Inc.), has made extensive use of the anchor-test method of establishing norms. More tests are expected to employ this norming procedure in the future.

More about Standard Scores

Percentile ranks (PR's) are easy to understand, but their units are not equal, in the sense that for normally distributed raw scores the difference between PR's of 10 and 20 is almost twice as great, in raw score or standard-deviation units, as is the distance between PR's of 50 and 60, even though $20 - 10 = 60 - 50 = 10$ (see Figure 2–2, p. 47). A difference of one standard deviation between a student's reading and arithmetic scores could show up as a difference in percentile ranks anywhere from 38 (for $-.5\sigma$ to $+.5\sigma$) to 2 (for 2σ to 3σ). Because equal raw- or standard-score ranges produce grossly unequal differences in percentile ranks, it is usually desirable for

---

[8] Age and grade scales have some distinct disadvantages, which will be discussed in Chapter 14. Our present purpose is to become more familiar with the quantitative characteristics of various scales. The special problems of various types of scales from an educational or psychological viewpoint will be treated in the chapters dealing with the tests that employ those scales.

standardized tests to use standard scores rather than percentile ranks. A joint committee of the American Psychological Association, the American Educational Research Association, and the National Council on Measurement in Education to establish standards for educational and psychological tests has recommended that "Standard scores should in general be used in preference to other derived scores" (American Psychological Association, 1966, p. 33).

You are already familiar with several standard-score scales. The two most widely used types are the stanine and the T-score systems. The stanine system has a mean of 5 and a standard deviation of 2; each stanine unit represents half a standard deviation (except at the two extremes). The T-score system has a mean of 50 and a standard deviation of 10.

For most current intelligence tests, the ratio IQ [that is, $IQ = 100(MA/CA)$] has been replaced by a standard-score scale. The Wechsler intelligence scales (WPPSI, WISC, and WAIS) use the standard-score formula: $IQ = 100 + 15z$. For the 1960 *Stanford-Binet Intelligence Scale* the formula is only slightly different: $IQ = 100 + 16z$.

In the general standard-score formula, the mean and standard deviation can assume any values that we desire. For example, for each of his *subtests* Wechsler chose a mean of 10 and a standard deviation of 3 (that is, $Score = 10 + 3z$), terminating his scores at 0 and 20. The CEEB tests and the GRE tests are reported on a scale having a mean of 500 and a standard deviation of 100 for certain norm groups. Other tests employ other standard-score systems. For most purposes the T-score, with $\bar{X} = 50$ and $s = 10$, is satisfactory.

There are two important facts to bear in mind: (1) the mean and standard deviation of the standard-score scale may have any value you choose, without any resemblance to the mean and standard deviation of the raw scores themselves, and (2) computed standard scores are no more or less normally distributed than are the raw scores from which they were obtained, unless they have been normalized—that is, "squeezed" to fit the normal distribution.

When reporting standardized test results, be sure to record both the raw scores and the derived scores for each individual tested. Also, list the name, level, form, and edition of the tests administered, and the date of testing. Perhaps it would be desirable to keep the test booklets and answer sheets so they could be available for study.

If tests are worth administering, they are worth recording properly so results can be used effectively and not misinterpreted. Too many test records, still consist solely of entries such as "Otis 72," with no date, form, level, or norm type indicated; 72 might be the student's percentile rank (in which grade and on what norms?), his deviation IQ or his raw score. Fortunately, most commercial test-scoring services now provide self-adhesive score report labels that can be easily transferred to students' cumulative record folders.

Presenting Test Results Graphically

A graph is often an effective method of communicating otherwise cumbersome information. One small chart can often make a point clearer than a dozen tables or paragraphs. It is sometimes said that the facts speak for themselves.

In reality, statistics often stand speechless and silent, tables are tongue-tied, and only the figure or chart expresses the message to the audience. Ordinary numerical data are quite abstract. The average mind grasps their meaning only vaguely and with effort. The picture or graph is a more concrete representation.

Profiles for a Single Subject   A graph is the most striking way of representing the test record of an individual pupil. Such a graphic picture of the strong and weak points of a single person is usually called a *profile*. Many publishers of standard tests provide blank forms for showing these profiles. Sometimes the blanks appear on the first page of the test, from which they can be detached easily for filing.

Profiles are especially useful for representing a pupil's scores on achievement-test batteries. Most test publishers provide a convenient form for such a profile. Figure 3–5 depicts the profile for a third-grade pupil on the *California Achievement Tests, Upper Primary Battery.* We see that the examinee is well above the typical beginning third-grade student in reading and arithmetic, but only average in language. The asterisks in the figure indicate his "anticipated achievement," the score earned on this test by pupils in the standardization sample who have the same IQ, age, and grade level. Figure 3–5 then presents a rather rosy picture for the student in question—he is achieving better than most like him in the reading and arithmetic areas, though not as well in language. Unless a difference in two or more tests is large, no interpretation of the difference should be made. A profile emphasizes test differences that tend to be unreliable unless they are substantial (Gardner, 1970). Another illustration is provided by the Individual Profile Chart in Figure 3–6. The publisher's interpretation is adjacent to the figure.

The *Iowa Test of Basic Skills* provides an individual cumulative record form that graphically depicts a pupil's sequential progress, as illustrated in Figure 3–7. A profile of the student's performance is given for grades 4, 5, and 6. At grade 4, John's Reading Comprehension and Capitalization appear to be his weak areas. Although his performance in Capitalization was considerably better at grade 5, Reading Comprehension continued to be low in comparison to his other scores. This "storybook" example shows that by grade 6, John's slight deficiency in Reading Comprehension was eliminated. The sequential plotting of his scores for grades 7, 8, 9, and 10 hopefully would show that John continued to achieve well ever after.

The profile chart can be quite revealing when school or district averages are used in the manner illustrated in Figure 3–1. Areas of curricular weakness can be diagnosed and remediation strategies sought. Without standardized testing, a disproportionate division of instructional time and resources might never be identified. Whether this is a desirable emphasis depends to some extent on the objectives and philosophy of education subscribed to by the school.

Even when the technical meaning of test scores is clear, we must be cognizant of other important psychological factors if we are to make proper use of the results. Ohlsen (1963, p. 254) listed ten excellent principles concerning the interpretation of test scores for students and their parents.

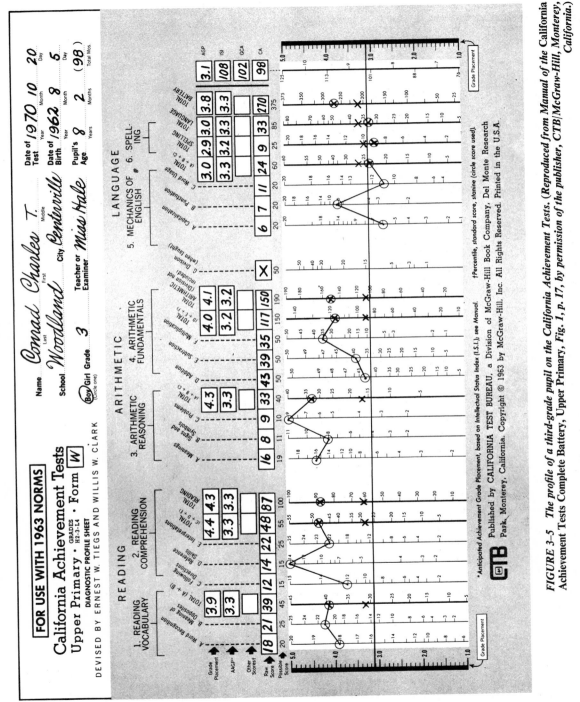

FIGURE 3–5 The profile of a third-grade pupil on the California Achievement Tests. (Reproduced from Manual of the California Achievement Tests Complete Battery, Upper Primary, Fig. 1, p. 17, by permission of the publisher, CTB/McGraw-Hill, Monterey, California.)

94

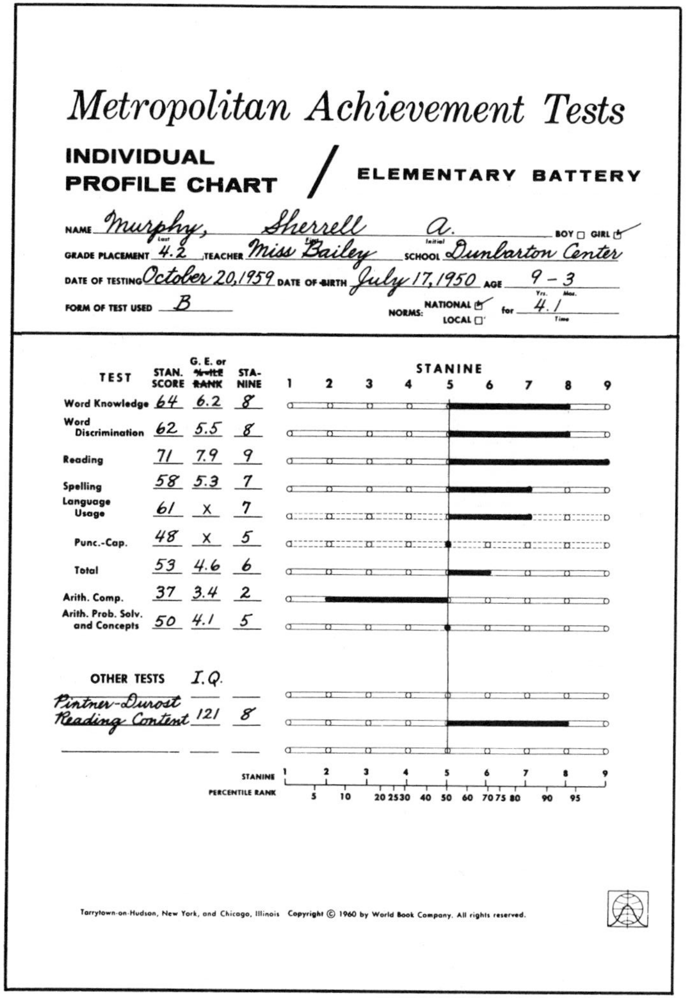
Metropolitan Achievement Tests

INDIVIDUAL PROFILE CHART / ELEMENTARY BATTERY

NAME Murphy, Sherrell A. (Last, First, Initial) BOY ☐ GIRL ☑

GRADE PLACEMENT 4.2 TEACHER Miss Bailey SCHOOL Dunbarton Center

DATE OF TESTING October 20, 1959 DATE OF BIRTH July 17, 1950 AGE 9 – 3 (Yrs. Mos.)

FORM OF TEST USED B NORMS: NATIONAL ☑ LOCAL ☐ for 4.1 (Time)

TEST	STAN. SCORE	G. E. or ~~%-ILE RANK~~	STA-NINE
Word Knowledge	64	6.2	8
Word Discrimination	62	5.5	8
Reading	71	7.9	9
Spelling	58	5.3	7
Language Usage	61	X	7
Punc.-Cap.	48	X	5
Total	53	4.6	6
Arith. Comp.	37	3.4	2
Arith. Prob. Solv. and Concepts	50	4.1	5

OTHER TESTS	I.Q.	
Pintner-Durost Reading Content	121	8

Murphy, Sherrell A., age 9 years and 3 months, is slightly below the median age for her grade. Her Pintner-Durost IQ of 121 (on Scale 2) has a corresponding IQ stanine of 8 which indicates a high level of school learning potential. Her median standard score of 153 corresponds to a stanine of 7, but this score is the topmost score in the range assigned to this stanine level. One more point earned in median standard score terms would have placed her at the 8th stanine. One would expect a close correspondence of IQ stanine and mental ability (standard score) stanine in this case since Sherrell was almost precisely at grade for her age. A substantial difference between the two can result if a child has been retarded two or more years and thus is old for his grade.

Except for Punctuation and Capitalization and the two arithmetic tests, deviation from expected performance is well within chance limits, if one assumes that Sherrell's capacity lies somewhere between a 7 and an 8. It would appear to be a good working hypothesis that Sherrell needs to do some additional work in the punctuation and capitalization area. Understanding the pupil's work may be facilitated by carefully examining her paper for clues as to possible reasons for the poor performance.

It would seem to be quite clear that Sherrell is a handicapped child in the area of arithmetic. The very low stanine of 2 in Arithmetic Computation suggests that the difficulty lies in her failure to master fundamentals. Her performance is just average in Arithmetic Problem Solving. Since this test involves more reasoning ability, it is logical for her stanine to be higher here than in Computation. One cannot tell from the profile alone the nature of her difficulty, but an alert teacher would consider this to be a danger signal calling for careful study.

FIGURE 3–6 The profile of a fourth-grade pupil on the Metropolitan Achievement Test. (*Reproduced from* Metropolitan Achievement Tests*: Individual Profile Chart (New York: Harcourt Brace Jovanovich, Inc.), Fig. 1, by special permission of the publisher. Copyright © 1958–1962 by Harcourt Brace Jovanovich, Inc.*)

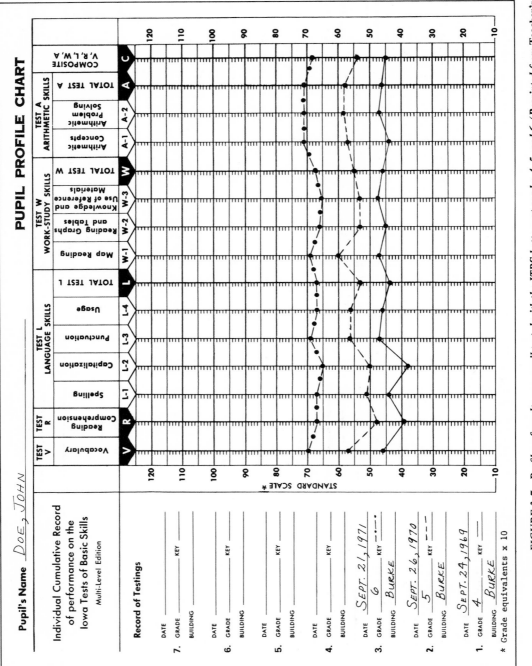

FIGURE 3-7 *Profiles of results on a pupil tested with the ITBS battery at grades 4, 5, and 6. (Reprinted from Teacher's Manual, Iowa Test of Basic Skills, p. 22, by permission of the publisher, Houghton Mifflin Company. Copyright © 1955 by the State University of Iowa.)*

1. Orientation for acceptance and use of test results should precede testing.
2. Until someone is qualified to use and interpret a test, that test should not be given.
3. Tests and test scores should be released to only those persons who are qualified to use and interpret the tests.
4. Test scores should be interpreted to only appropriate individuals, e.g., students and their parents or legal guardians. In all instances, the pupils' scores should be interpreted within a setting in which unauthorized persons cannot listen in on the interpretation or see the results.
5. Inasmuch as test scores are often misinterpreted by laymen, scores should be interpreted for pupils and parents, not merely distributed to them. Furthermore, scores should be interpreted when pupils or their parents request information. Unless there is a genuine felt need for information, the odds are against an increase in self-understanding on the part of the pupil or understanding on the part of the parent or even against the acceptance by the parent of information about his child.
6. Before interpreting a test, a teacher or counselor should familiarize himself with the nontest data available on the student. During the test interpretation he also should encourage the pupil to supplement the test results with nontest data.
7. A test-interpreter should encourage student participation in interpreting test scores. To help a student recall what a test, or a part of a battery, was like, the teacher or counselor can describe it in nontechnical language, and he will usually find that it is helpful to show the student sample items from the test, before encouraging the student to estimate how well he did on it. If the counselor is to do this successfully, it is obvious that he must know the student and be thoroughly familiar with the tests in order to communicate accurate information to the student.
8. The test-interpreter must be very sensitive to cues which suggest that the student does not comprehend the information which is being given him.
9. The student should be encouraged to react to the test results—to raise questions or to comment on how he feels about the way the test or tests describe him. When he feels that interpreted remarks are appropriate, he will often respond to data quite spontaneously—telling how pleased he is with some scores or how he does not like or cannot accept others. For the test-interpreter it is important that he detect these feelings and that he be able to respond to them. Helping a student examine these feelings increases the chances for helping him understand and accept himself as he is.
10. There is no justification for arguing with a student about his test scores. Moreover, little can be accomplished by either defending a test or criticizing it. What test-interpreters should do is explain how the results may be used by the student to understand himself and to make certain predictions, and with what certainty.

norm
standard
standardized test
normative sample
national norms
grade equivalent

calibrated norms
anchor test
equipercentile method
normalize
profile

Return to Table 3–2 (p. 87) and answer the following questions.

1. What are the percentile ranks of a scaled score of 500 on the Humanities test of the GRE
   A. for men?
   B. for women?
   C. for the total group?

2. Which sex has the higher average on the
   A. Humanities test?
   B. Social Science test?
   C. Natural Science test?

3. Suppose you received scores of 600 on all five tests. Convert your scale scores to percentile ranks, using total group norms for college seniors.

4. From Figure 3–4 (p. 89) estimate the grade equivalents of a raw score of 28 according to
   A. the 1940 norms.
   B. the 1953 norms.
   C. the 1964 norms.

5. From Figure 3–5 (p. 94), if a third-grade student answers 50 percent of the items correctly, what will his grade-equivalent score be in
   A. total reading (possible score 100)?
   B. total arithmetic (possible score 190)?
   C. total language (possible score 85)?

1. A. 58.
   B. 43.
   C. 51.

2. A. Women.
   B. Men.
   C. Men.

3. SS:85, H:83, NS:84,
   V:83, Q:89.

4. A. 7.2.
   B. 6.6.
   C. 6.0.

5. A. 2.9
   B. 3.0
   C. 3.5

ADAMS, G. S. 1964. *Measurement and evaluation in education, psychology, and guidance.* New York: Holt, Rinehart and Winston, Inc.

> Chapter 2 (pp. 17–67) is a thorough presentation of various types of units used in standardized tests.

AMERICAN PSYCHOLOGICAL ASSOCIATION, AMERICAN EDUCATIONAL RESEARCH ASSOCIATION, and the NATIONAL COUNCIL ON MEASUREMENT IN EDUCATION. 1966. *Standards for educational and psychological tests and manuals.* Washington, D.C.: American Psychological Association, Inc.

> Section F (pp. 33–36) contains the recommendations of the joint committee representing APA, AERA, and NCME pertaining to scales and norms for standardized tests.

ANGOFF, W. H. 1971. Test scores and norms. In R. L. Thorndike, ed., *Educational measurement*, 2nd ed. Washington, D. C.: American Council on Education, Chap. 15.

FINLEY, C. J. 1963. A comparison of the California Achievement Test, Metropolitan Achievement Test and Iowa Test of Basic Skills. *California Journal of Educational Research* (March), **14**(2): 79–88.

GARDNER, E. F. 1970. Interpreting achievement profiles—uses and warnings. *NCME Measurement in Education: A Series of Special Reports of the National Council on Measurement in Education,* **1**(2).

LENNON, R. T. 1964. Norms: 1963. *Proceedings, invitational conference on testing problems, 1963.* Princeton: ETS, pp. 13–22. Reprinted in G. H. Bracht, K. D. Hopkins, and J. C. Stanley. 1972. *Perspectives in educational and psychological measurement.* Englewood Cliffs, N.J.: Prentice-Hall, Inc., Selection. 4.

———. 1969. Scores and norms. In R. L. Ebel, ed., *Encyclopedia of educational research*, 4th ed. New York: The Macmillan Company.

LORD, F. M. 1959. Test norms and sampling theory. *Journal of Experimental Education,* **27**: 247–263.

LYMAN, H. B. 1971. *Test scores and what they mean.* 2nd ed. Englewood Cliffs, N. J.: Prentice-Hall, Inc.

OHLSEN, M. M. 1963. Interpretation of test scores. In W. G. Findley, ed., The impact and improvement of school testing programs, *The sixty-second yearbook of the National Society for the Study of Education, Part II.* Chicago: University of Chicago Press, pp. 254–294.

SEASHORE, H. G., and J. H. RICKS, Jr. 1950. Norms must be relevant. *Test Services Bulletin* No. 39. New York: The Psychological Corporation. Free.

SYMPOSIUM: Standard scores for aptitude and achievement tests. 1962. *Educational and Psychological Measurement,* **22**: 5–39.

> See especially E. F. Gardner, Normative standard scores, 7–14; and R. L. Ebel, Content standard test scores, 15–25.

TIEDEMAN, D. V. 1952. Has he grown? *Test Service Notebook* No. 12. New York: Harcourt Brace Jovanovich, Inc. 4 pp.

WOMER, F. B. 1965. *Test norms: Their use and interpretation.* Washington, D.C.: National Association of Secondary-School Principals.

> A very readable, practical and nontechnical treatment of appropriate uses of norms, stressing those aspects that bear most directly upon proper test interpretation.

4

TEST VALIDITY

The validity of a measure is how well it fulfills the function for which it is being used—the degree to which it is capable of achieving certain aims. Regardless of all other merits of a test, if it lacks validity for a particular task, the information it provides is useless. The validity of a test is the accuracy of specific predictions made from its scores. These inferences will pertain to: (1) future performance on some criterion (criterion-related validity), (2) the extent of knowledge of a universe of curricular content and processes (content validity), or (3) the degree to which certain psychological traits or constructs are actually represented by test performance (construct validity). During the process of test validation one examines the relationships between test scores and other empirical data and logical considerations.

It should be evident that validity is a multifaceted concept. In Chapter 1 several different uses of tests were described. The extent to which a test improves the accuracy of decisions is the extent to which it provides useful information and, hence, has practical validity.

The common question, "Is the test valid?" is not directly answerable. A test possesses many validities—it may be highly valid for one purpose but not for others. The question of test validity is always particularized; it can be answered only in relation to a given specific task for a given population of examinees.

A joint committee of the American Psychological Association, American Educational Research Association, and National Council on Measurement in Education has prepared a set of recommendations to improve the quality of validity data and other information on published tests (APA, 1966). In this chapter validity is classified into three subtypes: content, criterion-related, and construct, as outlined in the APA-AERA-NCME recommendations. The three types subsume the three principal purposes for which tests are used.

Content Validity

The relevant type of validity in the measurement of academic achievement is content validity. In assessing the content validity of an achievement test one asks, "To what extent does the test require demonstration by the student of the achievements which constitute the objectives of instruction in this area?" (Ebel, 1956, p. 269). For a test to have high content validity it should be a representative sample of both the *topics* and the *cognitive processes* of a given course or unit; that is, as Cureton (1969, p. 798) suggests, it should possess topic validity and process validity. Test publishers are increasingly providing such information on their tests. Figure 4–1, from the *Teacher's Guide* accompanying the *Sequential Tests of Educational Progress* (STEP), illustrates both the content and skill required for the STEP Science test. This kind of information is very helpful in assessing the test's content validity for a given curriculum.

An achievement test should *re-present* the content universe about which one wishes to make an assessment (Lennon, 1956). It is axiomatic that the content validity of a test must always be viewed in relation to the particular objectives to be assessed.

How does one determine the content validity of a measure? Content validation is primarily a process of logical analysis. By carefully and critically examining the test items in relation to the objectives and instruction, one must make the following professional judgments:

1. Does the test content parallel the curricular objectives in content and processes?
2. Are the test and curricular emphases in proper balance?
3. Is the test free from prerequisites that are irrelevant or incidental to the present measurement task? (For example, are the reading and vocabulary levels of the test appropriate for the examinees?)

It is crucial that a school or teacher systematically study each of the points in question before making a selection of a standardized test. School districts too often make only a cursory examination of published tests before formulating their district-wide testing programs. Small wonder, then, that teachers complain, "The test doesn't measure what we're teaching." They feel that the test does not "mirror" the curriculum. This is not to suggest that such objections be taken at face value. Some teachers think it is unfair to include any item that has not been covered in the course of study for the class—a very narrow view of an appropriate content universe for a standardized test. Nevertheless, those who select standardized tests for a district testing program are often much too casual. A systematic study of the available standardized tests will not usually identify a test that is a perfect "fit" for a district's curriculum; only tests constructed carefully by a team of curriculum and test experts (an expensive task) can approach

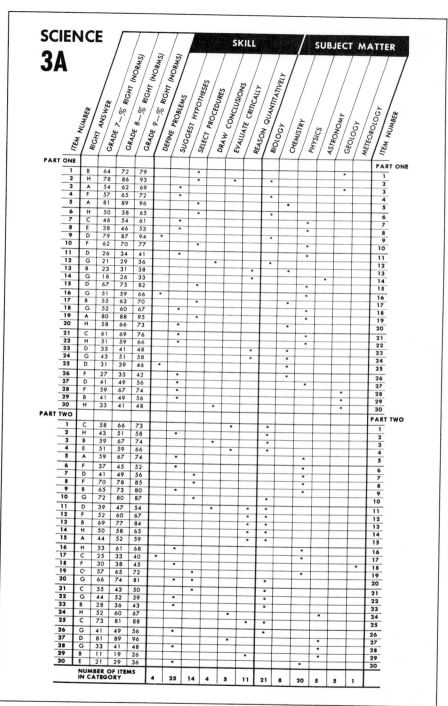

FIGURE 4–1 An illustration of topic and process information on a standardized achievement test. (Reprinted from Teacher's Guide for the Cooperative Sequential Tests of Educational Progress, STEP Science Test, Form A, Level 3, p. 77, by permission of the Educational Testing Service. Copyright © 1959 by Educational Testing Service. All rights reserved.)

this objective. However, some of the published tests will be more relevant for the district's objectives than others—even though none will measure all of the cognitive objectives, not to mention the affective objectives. This and related problems are considered more extensively in Chapters 15 and 17.

Besides providing norms, standardized achievement tests differ from locally constructed tests in at least two important respects: (1) standardized tests measure larger blocks of content because they are administered at intervals of a year or more, and (2) standardized achievement tests attempt to measure general, broad objectives and to minimize any special local, state, or regional emphases. Consequently, these tests are more process-oriented and less topic-oriented than are teacher-made tests. Standardized achievement tests are not substitutes for teacher-developed tests—they complement each other.

It is impractical to conduct an *extensive* content-validity analysis on all or even on most teacher-constructed tests, but the teacher should systematically examine each classroom test before its administration to insure a good sampling from the content universe. He should ask himself: "Are all the important instructional topics represented in about the correct proportions on the test?"; "Is there a proper balance of cognitive processes required or is there an over-emphasis on rote knowledge?"; and "Are all of the questions relevant—are there trivial items that should be eliminated?" Such elementary questions as these, if raised systematically by teachers at all educational levels, would greatly improve the quality of educational measurement.

Content validity should not be confused with "face" validity, which lacks the systematic logical analysis required by content validation. A test is said to have face validity if on first impression it appears to measure the intended content or trait. It is important that tests have face validity; otherwise students may feel they are being unfairly assessed. Typically, a content-valid test will also have face validity, but it is possible to have one without the other. Essay tests usually have high face validity, especially for persons unfamiliar with related research, but they may lack reliability, an indispensable prerequisite for valid measurement of individual differences. Conversely, a test item that is not presented in a practical context may actually measure an important concept or ability, but it may lack face validity for some examinees. For example, consider the following item:

Which of these least belongs with the other three?
(a) 84%ile, (b) $T = 60$, (c) stanine 8, (d) $z = 1.0$.

The item requires a knowledge of the normal curve in relation to percentiles and some understanding of standard scores of the T, z, and stanine types as well. Options (a), (b), and (d) describe the identical point in a normal distribution, whereas stanine 8 is above this point. Some students might respond, "If that's what you wanted to know, why didn't you ask?" If the item were recast into the form, "Which one of the following is not one standard deviation above the mean in a normal distribution?", much of the cognitive synthesis and induction of the item would be destroyed, and hence its potential for measuring higher levels of understanding would be attenuated.

When properly used, the kind of item that requires the student to find the concept being assessed as well as the answer *can* measure a high level of conceptual comprehension and application. Such items may lack face validity for examinees who are unsophisticated in measurement. Face validity is important for the test's clientele, be they students or job applicants. Otherwise they may feel they are being treated unfairly. Tests with good content validity will *usually* have face validity; the reverse, however, is much less likely to be true.

Criterion-Related Validity

In contrast to content validity, which is based almost entirely on logical considerations, criterion-related validity is an empirical matter. There are two subclasses of criterion-related validity; the more common is predictive validity, in which the test has the task of predicting some subsequent measure of performance. For example, an employer wishes to identify which applicants are most likely to be productive workmen. He is not primarily concerned with whether the test is a representative sample of some universe (content validity) nor is he necessarily concerned with whether the test is a good indicator of some psychological trait (construct validity); he wishes to select the applicants who are good risks and reject those who are poor risks. If persons who indicate that they prefer strawberry to vanilla ice cream become more successful salesmen, then that would be a relevant item for inclusion in the screening test for salesmen. It is relevant because it contributes to a more accurate decision for the selection task at hand, regardless of whether the items appear to be logically related to the job. In most instances, however, predictors are related logically as well as empirically to the criterion.

A measure's predictive validity, then, is how well its predictions agree with subsequent outcomes. The type of validity that is relevant for the *Scholastic Aptitude Test* (SAT) of the "College Board" entrance examinations is predictive validity. The extent to which scores on the tests are related to success in college is the extent to which the test fulfills its predictive function. The accuracy of the predictions is usually represented by the correlation coefficient between test scores and the criterion. This coefficient is a validity coefficient, since it defines the degree of criterion-related validity of the test. Decisions involving selection (for example, to admit an applicant or not) and classification (such as major field of study) are predictive in nature. The extent to which the use of tests can improve the accuracy of the decision is the extent to which the tests are of value.

The principal function of reading readiness tests administered in kindergarten or early in grade one is to identify (predict) those pupils who are likely to perform well, or not so well, in reading in the first grade. The role of the test is to assist the teacher in deciding which children are ready to begin reading and which should be continued on readiness activities for some time. Figure 4–2 shows the validity of scores on a reading readiness test given at the beginning of grade one for predicting subsequent reading performance on a standardized reading test (data from Hopkins and Sitkie, 1969). Notice that, as a general rule, high scores on the readiness test (the predictor) are associated with good performance on the reading test (the criterion) administered several months later.

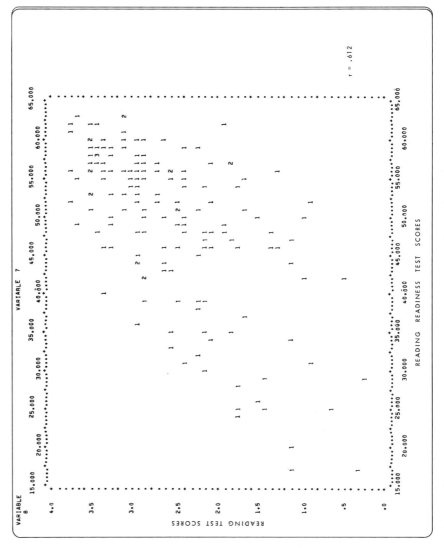

FIGURE 4–2   An illustration of criterion-related validity for a reading readiness test predicting subsequent scores on an end-of-year standardized reading test.

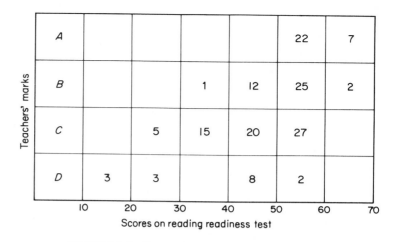

A					22	7
B			1	12	25	2
C		5	15	20	27	
D	3	3		8	2	

Teachers' marks

10   20   30   40   50   60   70

Scores on reading readiness test

FIGURE 4–3   Scatterplot showing relationship (r = .57) between reading readiness test scores at the beginning of grade 1 and teachers' marks at the end of grade 1 (N = 157). (Data from Hopkins and Sitkei, 1969.)

Figure 4–3 also shows the predictive validity of the reading readiness test, but using a different criterion for reading success, teachers' marks. Figure 4–3 shows that the pupils with low scores on the reading readiness test did not read well at the end of grade one, as judged by their teachers. Only one of the 28 pupils with scores below 40 received a grade of B. The pupils with high scores generally read well, but there were some pupils with good readiness scores who subsequently did not perform well in reading. Of the 76 pupils with readiness scores between 50 and 60, there were 22 (29 percent) who received A's, 25 (33 percent) who received B's, 27 (36 percent) who received C's, and 2 (3 percent) who received a D grade in reading. From studying Figure 4–3, it is evident that failure was more predictable than success.

The predictive validity of a test is always in relation to a *particular* criterion. Teachers' marks may be influenced by factors not associated with performance on the standardized reading test (such as deportment and effort); thus to some extent marks may represent different factors. The two criteria depicted in Figures 4–2 and 4–3 correlated substantially ($r = .75$), but are not interchangeable.[1] By looking at both criteria we get a more complete picture than we could by considering only one.

EXPECTANCY TABLES

For most consumers, predictive validity can be represented most meaningfully by an expectancy table. If, in Figure 4–3, we convert the frequencies within each score interval to proportions, we obtain probabilities for various degrees

[1] Some of the lack of correlation between the two criteria is due to errors of measurement (unreliability). If the reliabilities of both criteria were known, one could estimate the extent to which the two criteria measure different factors, apart from measurement error (see p. 340).

of performance for any score. For example, if a pupil earned a score of 45 on the reading readiness test, it is extremely unlikely that he would receive an end-of-year grade of "A"; the probabilities of receiving grades of B, C, and D, respectively would be .30 (12 of 40), .50 (20 of 40), and .20 (8 of 40).

Table 4–1 contains another example of an expectancy table (from Michael, 1969, p. 989). The table gives the probability of various grade attainments from college aptitude ratings, which were based upon various kinds of student data. The value of this information for selection and counseling purposes is obvious.

An expectancy table need not be limited to a single predictor. An illustration (from W. B. Michael, 1969, p. 989) in which three predictor variables were used is shown in Table 4–2. The table gives the probability of satisfactory performance in college (C average or higher) based upon knowledge of an applicant's high-school rank, aptitude-test performance, and sex. For example, if a girl was in the upper quarter in both high-school rank and test score, the probability she would attain at least a "C" average is .94. Fortunately, statistical knowledge of correlation is not necessary for proper use of expectancy tables.

TABLE 4–1

Expectancy Table of Freshman Scholarship according to College Aptitude (Women)

College Aptitude Ratings	Probability of Grade Attainments				
	F	D	C	B	A
91–100		.02	.42	.55	.02
81– 90		.06	.65	.29	
71– 80	.04	.23	.59	.14	
61– 70	.08	.41	.49	.01	
51– 60	.08	.55	.37		
41– 50	.10	.59	.30	.02	
31– 40	.26	.54	.20		
21– 30	.23	.74	.03		
11– 20	.31	.69			
1– 10	.60	.40			

Source: W. B. Michael (1969).

TABLE 4–2

Probability of Attaining a Grade of C or Higher for Male and Female Freshmen

High School Rank Percentile	ACE Percentile							
	0–24		25–49		50–74		75–100	
	M	F	M	F	M	F	M	F
75–100	.63	.68	.75	.80	.83	.90	.90	.94
50– 74	.46	.40	.55	.52	.66	.65	.69	.72
25– 49	.29	.44	.33	.50	.48	.29	.64	—
0– 24	.17	.31	.30	.33	.47	.50	.42	—

Source: Given in W. B. Michael (1969), based on 1789 students at the University of Wisconsin as reported by Lins (1950).

Criterion-related validity is not always predictive in nature. Occasionally our purpose is to substitute one measure for another. In this situation, little or no time interval is desired between the administration of the new test and the established test. It would be quite useful to find a short, inexpensive reading test that would correlate highly with experts' ratings or with a valid individual (and hence expensive to use) test. The new test would be said to have *concurrent* validity to the extent that it correlates with the established test or some other concurrently obtained criterion. For example, the *Wide Range Reading Test* requires only a few minutes to administer and correlates highly (about .8) with teachers' ratings of reading ability (Hopkins, Dobson, and Oldridge, 1962) and with other standard individual reading tests (Garlock, Dollarhide, and Hopkins, 1965).

Concurrent validity is often the initial step for establishing predictive validity. In the early development of the *Strong Vocational Interest Blank*, studies of concurrent validity demonstrated that the interest scores could, for example, differentiate physicians from men in general. Only after twenty years of additional research could Strong provide evidence that interest scores of college freshmen did *predict* their adult occupations (Campbell, 1968b).

In determining criterion-related validity we are usually most concerned with the test, but it is equally important to consider the qualities of the criterion. To be predictable, a criterion must be fairly reliable; even highly relevant and reliable tests cannot predict a criterion that lacks reliability. If a variable does not predict itself—that is, lacks self-correlation—it cannot be predicted by any other variable. This is probably a principal reason why the many attempts to predict teacher success have been so fruitless. The common measures of teacher success are quite unreliable, hence essentially unpredictable. For example, Walberg (1967) found only a .21 correlation between supervisor and principal ratings of the teaching success of 280 teacher trainees. This is no doubt an important reason why logically relevant factors such as GPA and intelligence have yielded such low correlations with ratings of teacher effectiveness.

The present predictability of grades in college is probably about as high as it can be without an improvement in the reliability of the criterion. Walberg (1967) found a .6 correlation between students' grade-point averages (GPA's) obtained during the first and seventh academic terms in college. It is a statistical fact that the *maximum* criterion-related validity any test can have is the square root of the reliability coefficient of the test. This maximum value will be obtained only if the test is itself perfectly relevant (it measures nothing but what is reflected in the criterion) and the criterion is perfectly reliable. It should be obvious that in practice even this maximum value is rarely approached.

One final point should be made regarding criterion-related validity. When a test is used for selective purposes, such as admission to graduate school, much of its predictive value is used at that point. To correlate scores for the selected group with a subsequent criterion will underestimate the test's predictive value— that is, its value as a selection measure. For example, suppose that no pupil with a readiness score below 40 was admitted to grade one, but instead all of them had to repeat kindergarten. When all scores below 40 in Figure 4–2 are covered, the resulting figure is much "fatter"; hence the correlation coefficient for those with scores of 40 and above would be much less than for the total group. In fact the validity coefficient of .61 for the entire group drops to only .44 for the 40+ group.

Figure 4–4 is an extreme illustration of the common phenomenon of range restriction and its consequences on validity coefficients. There is little relation between the criterion and test scores within the selected group, yet there is a substantial relationship for the entire group. For example, Roemer (1965) underrated the value of the *Medical College Admission Test* (MCAT) considerably because he failed to recognize this important point. If test scores correlate, say, only .3 with subsequent GPA's for the admitted group, they may still be of great value for admission purposes (especially when the limited reliability of the criterion is borne in mind).

The effect that restricting the range of scores has on the obtained validity coefficient is further illustrated by R. L. Thorndike (1949), who compared validity coefficients for a total group ($N = 1,031$) of aspiring pilots to those for the groups that were successful ($N = 136$). The validity coefficient for the composite score on the predictors was .64 for the total group, but a correlation of only .18 remained for those who qualified.

Research on the National Merit Scholarship Program also illustrates the strong effect the range of scores or talent has on validity coefficients. Among scholarship winners, a highly select group, there is little relationship between scores on the National Merit examinations and whether or not the recipients

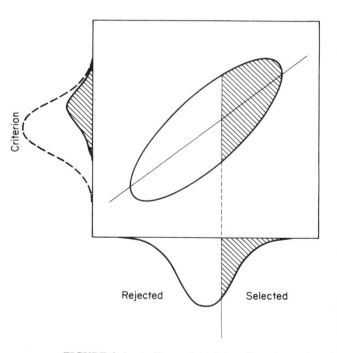

FIGURE 4–4 *An illustration of the effect of selection on the correlation between test scores and a criterion. The validity coefficient within the selected group underestimates the actual predictive value of the test.*

completed college (the criterion). Nevertheless, the strong relationship between ability and obtaining a college degree is illustrated by the fact that the mortality in the Merit group was only 8 percent compared to 50 percent in an unselected population (Stalnaker, 1961).

When a test is used to describe the degree to which an individual manifests an abstract psychological trait or ability, the construct validity of the measure is the relevant concern. Psychological constructs are unobservable, postulated variables that have evolved either informally or from psychological theory. Intelligence, anxiety, mechanical aptitude, critical thinking, ego-strength, dominance, and achievement motivation are examples of commonly used constructs. Construct validation is an analysis of the meaning of test scores in terms of psychological constructs (Cronbach and Meehl, 1955). If a test is designed to measure emotional stability, what kinds of evidence are necessary before we can have confidence that the information provided by the test reflects this factor? We make certain predictions or statements that should be correct if, indeed, the test does measure the construct in question. For example, if the scale actually measures emotional stability, one would expect: (1) some correlation between inventory scores and psychologists' ratings, (2) some difference between scores of persons in and not in mental hospitals, (3) some relationship between peer ratings and inventory scores, and so on. However, we might expect little or no relationship between inventory scores and sex, IQ, GPA, and the like. In a sense, every bit of information about a test has relevance for construct validity—that is, in establishing what it does and does not measure. In construct validation there is no single criterion, as there often is with criterion-related validity; many criteria are required to confirm what the test does and does not measure.

The measurement of intelligence provides the classic example of construct validation. Early attempts to measure "intelligence" using reaction time, auditory memory, and other psychomotor and psychophysical measures were discarded because performance on these measures did not correlate with other behavioral evidence of intelligence, such as school grades. The expected and logical relationships between relevant variables were not confirmed. Later, tasks were constructed that were logically related to intelligence; they were cognitive in nature, and many of them were found to be related to other variables in a manner expected of a measure of intelligence.

Gradually, through a continual process of research and revision, these scales yielded scores that agreed closely with logical and theoretical expectations: (1) the scores correlated with age until maturity and then leveled off, in the manner of other directly measurable human abilities; (2) the scores had a substantial relationship with academic achievement; (3) children who repeated grades scored much lower on these measures than those who were promoted; (4) the IQ scores yielded by these tests showed some stability for a period of years; (5) persons with clinical types of mental subnormality (such as mongolism) performed poorly on the tasks; and (6) the correlation of identical twins was extremely high—much higher than for fraternal twins, even when they were reared separately. Such information illustrates the unending procedure of construct validation.

Certain tests such as the *Stanford-Binet* became accepted as excellent measures of intelligence because persons who obtained high scores on the test tended to behave intelligently in situations in which such behavior was required. Although certain predictions can be made regarding future performance from tests designed to measure psychological constructs, their primary function is to assess the degree of some variable or trait within the individual.

If two pupils are achieving at the same level, but one has an IQ of 90 and the other 130, we may be relatively satisfied with the educational success of the one but quite concerned about the other, who appears to have more scholastic aptitude. However, if our sole task is to predict subsequent performance, there would be little point in administering intelligence tests, because achievement tests usually predict subsequent achievement better than intelligence tests do (Bracht and Hopkins, 1970b; Churchill and Smith, 1966). Intelligence or scholastic-aptitude tests are the only type of test taken by virtually all pupils for which validation rests in the construct-validity domain.

The process of developing a measure of a psychological construct and establishing its validity proceeds as follows:

1. Develop a set of tasks or items based on a rational analysis of the construct.
2. Derive testable predictions regarding the relationship between the construct and other variables; for example, if the test measures anxiety, we should expect to find some relationship between test scores and clinical ratings of anxiety level, and so on.
3. Conduct empirical studies of these theoretical predictions.
4. Eliminate items or tasks that operate contrary to theory (or revise the theory) and proceed again with steps 2 and 3.[2]

Post-organizer

We have discussed three rather distinct classes of validity. *Content* validation is relevant for achievement testing; it consists of a logical study of the relationship of the topics and processes included on a test to the corresponding curricular objectives and instruction. *Predictive* validation is basic to selection and classification decisions and results from an empirical study of the extent to which performances on a measure and a criterion are related. *Construct* validity pertains to the extent to which a test reflects an abstract psychological trait or ability. Both logical and empirical means are used to establish the validities of a test. All three types of validity are crucial for certain, although different, purposes.

[2] The interested reader should be informed of the more elaborate scheme for construct validation using a *multitrait-multimethod matrix* proposed by Campbell and Fiske (1959). From a matrix of correlation coefficients that describe the relationships among the same and different traits using a variety of assessment methods, certain criteria are suggested for establishing the validity of a construct and its measurement.

criterion-related validity
predictive validity
concurrent validity
content validity

construct validity
expectancy table
range restriction

SUGGESTED READINGS

ANASTASI, A. 1964. Some current developments in the measurement and interpretation of test validity. *Proceedings of the 1963 Invitational Conference on Testing Problems.* Princeton, N.J.: Educational Testing Service.

AMERICAN PSYCHOLOGICAL ASSOCIATION, AMERICAN EDUCATIONAL RESEARCH ASSOCIATION, and NATIONAL COUNCIL ON MEASUREMENT IN EDUCATION. 1966. *Standards for educational and psychological tests and manuals.* Washington, D.C.: American Psychological Association, Inc.

Section C (pp. 12–24) contains APA-AERA-NCME recommendations regarding test validity.

ASTIN, A. W. 1970. *Predicting academic performance in college.* New York: The Free Press.

CAMPBELL, D. T., and D. W. FISKE. 1959. Convergent and discriminant validation by the multitrait-multimethod matrix. *Psychological Bulletin,* **56:** 81–105.

CRONBACH, L. J. 1969. Validation of educational measures. *Proceedings of the 1969 Invitational Conference on Testing Problems.* Princeton, N.J.: Educational Testing Service, pp. 35–52. Reprinted in G. H. Bracht, K. D. Hopkins, and J. C. Stanley. 1972. *Perspectives in educational and psychological measurement.* Englewood Cliffs, N.J.: Prentice-Hall, Inc., Selection 9.

———. 1971. Test validation. In R. L. Thorndike, ed., *Educational measurement,* 2nd ed. Washington, D.C.: American Council on Education, Chap. 14.

———, and P. E. MEEHL 1955. Construct validation in psychological tests. *Psychological Bulletin,* **52:** 281–302.

CURETON, E. E. 1969. Measurement theory. In R. L. Ebel, ed. *Encyclopedia of educational research,* 4th ed. Toronto: The Macmillan Company, pp. 785–804.

EBEL, R. L. 1956. Obtaining and reporting evidence on content validity. *Educational and Psychological Measurement,* **16:** 294–304.

———. 1961. Must all tests be valid? *American Psychologist,* **16:** 640–647. Reprinted in G. H. Bracht, K. D. Hopkins, and J. C. Stanley. 1972. *Perspectives in educational and psychological measurement.* Englewood Cliffs, N.J.: Prentice-Hall, Inc., Selection 8.

———. 1962. Content standard test scores. *Educational and Psychological Measurement,* **22:** 15–25.

LENNON, R. T. 1956. Assumptions underlying the use of content validity. *Educational and Psychological Measurement,* **16:** 294–304.

SECHREST, L. 1963. Incremental validity: a recommendation. *Educational and Psychological Measurement,* **23:** 153–158.

5

TEST RELIABILITY

To do its job well, a test should yield results that are consistent and pertinent to the specific purpose the tester has in mind.

A test cannot be of much value if the score it yields for Bill today is quite different from the score it would have yielded for him under similar conditions yesterday or tomorrow. It is theoretically possible, however, for a test to yield highly consistent results from day to day without having any other known value. A highly reliable test such as reaction time may be useful in predicting the quickness with which one applies an automobile brake, but it is useless for indicating how well one reads or works arithmetic problems. *Reliability is a necessary but not sufficient condition for validity.*

The concepts of reliability and validity are, in their various forms, central to the theory and practice of educational and psychological testing. Like many basic concepts, these two are not especially simple. Reliability is for a particular purpose, just like validity. For example, a test may have substantial short-term reliability, yet little long-term stability. This chapter offers an overview of the current ways of thinking about the consistency and interpretation of test scores.

The Concept of Reliability

Suppose a simple questionnaire study was designed to estimate the mean age of female teachers in the United States. If we had a list of all women teaching in the U.S., we could take a *random* sample and send each woman in that sample a double postal card asking her month, day, and year of birth. Suppose that each woman returned the postal card stating her birthday. We could average the ages and estimate the mean reported age of all the female teachers   *114* in the U.S. We might ask, however, how reliable and valid the reported ages are. If we had written each woman's name and address on the return card, we would know to whom each reported date of birth belonged. Suppose we then sent a *second* postal card to each, asking the same question as before. If each woman responds again, we shall have for each woman two birthdates that should agree perfectly. If the two dates for each woman *do* agree exactly, then we have a perfectly reliable measure of birthdate "scores."

If we compare the two birthdates each woman reported on the postal cards with her birthdate determined from correct birth certificates, we will be able to estimate the *validity* of the reported ages. If one woman reported "June 5, 1929" both times, but her birth certificate shows "June 5, 1919," the reported dates have perfect consistency but lack validity. She has "lost" 10 years of age. The agreement of her reliably reported birthdate with her actual birthdate is poor. Another teacher reported "January 30, 1942" both times, and her birth certificate showed the same date. Her report was both reliable and valid. A third woman put "December 12, 1922" on the first card and "December 12, 1927" on the second; her birth certificate showed "December 12, 1920." Her reported birthdate is unreliable as well as invalid—that is, the reported dates do not agree with each other or with the correct date.

A coefficient of reliability of the birthdates would be the correlation between the two sets of birthdates reported—first card vs. second card over the entire sample. It would no doubt be somewhere between 0 and 1, depending on how and by whom the inquiry was conducted. One might expect the figure to be very close to 1.0 in a well-conducted study, especially if results were to be strictly confidential. A crucial point to remember is that even if each woman had reported the same birthdate both times, we would still not be sure this was her *true* birthdate. The coefficient of reliability would be 1.0, but the coefficient of validity would be less than 1 to the extent that the reported ages differed from those reflected on the birth certificates. The coefficient of validity for the first set of birthdates reported would be their r with the birth-certificate dates (the criterion), and the coefficient of validity for the second set of birth dates reported would also be their r with the birth-certificate dates. Each of these two r's could theoretically range from -1 to $+1$. If the reported birthdates and the birth-certificate dates were identical, the validity coefficient would be 1.0. Validity coefficients can be small, zero, or negative, even though the reliability coefficients are very high or perfect (1.0).

In a study of this sort the older women might "forget" their birthdates more than the younger ones, or perhaps the middle-aged ones would have the largest discrepancies between reports and certificates. Anonymous replies might be more correct than signed or well-identified ones. The point we again make is that *reliability is necessary for validity but not sufficient*; it is impossible to know a woman's true age solely from her assertions if she never uses the same figure twice, but it is possible to be deceived systematically even if she always reports the same birthdate. We work for reliability of measurement as an essential prerequisite, but we check further to ascertain validity. We want to know how old each female teacher really is as shown on a correct birth certificate. This is the *criterion*. The reported birthdates are the two predictors; probably neither is perfectly reliable nor totally valid.

Assume that your instructor lends each of you a new quarter, coined at the same mint in the same year, and says: "Today we shall have a coin-flipping test. Please go to an uncrowded room and bounce your quarter against the ceiling. Do this 100 times, and each time observe whether the coin lands 'heads' up. You receive one point for each 'head' you obtain. Your score is the number of 'heads' obtained; this may be anywhere from 0 to 100, of course, but will almost always be between 35 and 65."[1]

After the "test" is over, the instructor computes the class mean "score," which happens to be 50. He then asks you to estimate the number of heads you will obtain the next time you flip your coin against the ceiling 100 times. Suppose that your score the first time was 60, very high in the group of coin-flippers. Would you consider yourself expert at flipping heads and so estimate that your score the next time will again be about 60? Not if you know much about the laws of chance and the reliability of coin-tossing. All deviations from 50 (for an unbiased coin) are random events. The best estimate of your "true score" and the true score of each of your classmates is 50, regardless of your "obtained score" (number of heads). Your luck score of 10 points (60 − 50) the first time is technically called a 10-point "error of measurement." An individual's error of measurement is generally the discrepancy between his *obtained* (that is, actual) score and his *true* score. Such errors of measurement are normally distributed around the true scores with a mean of 0, so your best bet is that your error of measurement the second time you make 100 tosses will be 0, and that your obtained score the second time will be 50.

For a fairly large class, the correlation between the number of heads obtained by you and your classmates the first and second time will be very nearly 0 (and not statistically significant), indicating that a coin-flipping test yields scores whose reliability coefficient is 0. Are the coin-tossing scores useful for predicting students' ages? IQ's? Knowledge of English grammar? Anything at all? Most assuredly not. If scores one time will not predict scores another time, how can they possibly predict anything external to the coin-tossing itself? If a test will not predict a strictly comparable form of itself, how can it predict anything else? Test scores whose reliability is nil cannot predict better than random guessing will.

Thus we have defined the ends of the reliability continuum: 0 for the coin-tossing "test" and 1.0 for the same birth certificates examined twice without clerical or computational errors. Between these two points lie the reliability coefficients for most test scores, usually closer to 1.0 than to 0.0. A psychomotor (say, handwriting) test, for example, can be made quite reliable (perhaps .95) if the recording apparatus is accurate and if the test is of sufficient length. The scores may not correlate significantly, however, with things we desire to predict, such as college grades, job success, or high-jumping ability. A psychomotor test

---

[1] The standard deviation of the "scores" would equal $\sqrt{Npq}$, where N is the number of tosses, p the probability of one event (heads), and q the probability of the other event (tails). Since *for an unbiased coin* both p and q are .5, the standard deviation is $\sqrt{100(.5)(.5)}$, or 5. Therefore, applying our knowledge of the normal curve, we expect about 68 percent of the coin-flippers to obtain between 45 and 55 heads. Only about 3 persons in 1,000 (.27 percent) would be expected to obtain "scores" below 35 or above 65.

may be fine for predicting one's psychomotor ability at some other time under
similar circumstances (that is, self-prediction or reliability), but it may not be
useful for predicting most other criteria. Thus, a certain psychomotor test can
have high reliability (perhaps .95), but low predictive validity for the criteria
of interest. Reliability is necessary, but validity of some sort is the real aim of
testing. Reliability does not guarantee validity, although validity does guarantee
some degree of reliability.

Reliability and True Scores

"An investigator asks about the precision or reliability of a measure
because he wishes to generalize from the observation in hand to some class of
observation to which it belongs" (Cronbach, Rajaratnam, and Gleser, 1963,
p. 144). Rarely is our interest in the scores *per se* on a given test. A test should
ordinarily be viewed as a *sample* from a *population* of items. Many other items
similar to those that appear on a test could have been employed. Suppose we
randomly selected 100 words from *Webster's Third New International Dictionary*
for a vocabulary test. We may be interested in the percent of the 100 words
that a person knows, but our principal interest is in estimating the number or
percent of the words he knows in the population (the dictionary). If we randomly selected another 100 words from the dictionary for a second form of the test,
few (if any) examinees would receive scores identical to the scores they obtained
on the initial form.

Most examinees will know by chance a few more or less on the first form,
A, than on the second, B. Our real interest is in what an examinee's average
score would be on many (theoretically an infinite number) forms of 100 randomly selected words each; this average is known technically as his "true" score.
True scores are free from good or bad "luck" associated with chance factors
in the selection of the items appearing on a given form as well as from other

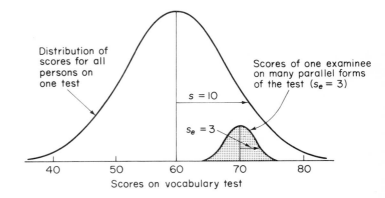

FIGURE 5-1   *A hypothetical distribution of scores of one*
examinee on many parallel forms of a test in relation to the
distribution of scores for all examinees on one form of the test,
assuming a test reliability of .91. (Adapted from Cronbach,
1970, p. 157.)

random sources of variation such as "luck" in guessing. In classical test theory

a person's obtained score is said to be composed of two independent parts: his true score and a random error of measurement.

On parallel forms of the 100-item vocabulary test, Jim might obtain scores of 72 on form A, 67 on form B, 71 on C, and so on. If we constructed a frequency distribution of these obtained scores over a large number of the parallel forms, we might end up with the data illustrated in Figure 5–1.

Occasionally Jim was "lucky"; the form included more words that he knew, and he scored 75 or more; sometimes he knew only 65 words or less. Obviously, our interest is not in the idiosyncrasies of a particular form of the test, but in his general word knowledge (his true score). In this illustration his true score is 70, the mean of his obtained scores, and all deviations from this score are called *errors of measurement*. Sometimes the error of measurement was large, but usually it was small. *Other things being equal*, the smaller the errors of measurement, the greater the reliability of the measure.

THE STANDARD ERROR OF MEASUREMENT

The standard deviation of these errors of measurement is called the standard error of measurement (s_e). Because it is a measure of the discrepancies between obtained and true scores, it is a very useful statistic in test interpretation. Approximately two-thirds of the examinees on any test will have obtained scores that differ one s_e or less from their true scores.

The concepts of reliability and the standard error of measurement are closely associated, as Figure 5–2 illustrates. Figure 5–2 shows that, when the standard deviation of a test is held constant (by the use of a standard-score

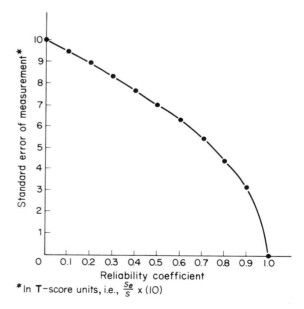

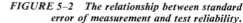

*In T-score units, i.e., $\frac{S_e}{S}$ x (10)

FIGURE 5–2 The relationship between standard error of measurement and test reliability.

T-scale), the value of the standard error of measurement is completely determined by the test's reliability coefficient and vice versa. The figure also illustrates that this relationship is not linear. A change of .1 in a test's reliability coefficient has a much greater effect on the standard error of measurement when the coefficient is large than when it is small. An increase in reliability from .8 to .9 decreases s_e by about 1.3 points (.13s), but an increase from .1 to .2 decreases s_e only about .6 (.06s) points.

The Standard Deviation and the Standard Error of Measurement   Figure 5–2 also indirectly depicts the relationship among a test's standard deviation (s), standard error of measurement (s_e), and reliability coefficient. If a measure has no reliability, its s and s_e are equal; that is, individual differences on the test are totally the result of errors of measurement. When reliability is perfect, all differences in scores are totally due to differences in true scores. Between these extremes are found all measures employed in education and psychology.

The reliability of a test indicates how nearly the distribution of obtained scores coincides with the distribution of true scores. If the measure has a reliability of 1.0, the obtained scores it yields are the true scores. If the reliability is 0, there is only a chance relationship between the examinees' true scores and the obtained scores. More explicitly, the reliability coefficient (r_{xx}) of a test is that portion of the total variance (s^2) that does *not* result from errors of measurement; that is,

$$r_{xx} = \frac{s^2 - s_e^2}{s^2} = 1 - \frac{s_e^2}{s^2}.$$

The last expression is quite revealing: the extent to which intraperson (within persons) variability in scores is less than interperson (between persons) variability in scores (see Figure 5–1) is the extent to which the test is reliable (see Stanley, 1971a). That portion of the total variance not the result of errors of measurement is called true-score variance (s_t^2)—that is, the variance of examinees' true scores. An equivalent definition of the reliability of a measure is that proportion of the total variance that is true variance:

$$r_{xx} = \frac{s_t^2}{s^2}.$$

TRUE SCORES

Figure 5–3, using IQ scores as an example, depicts the interrelationship among true scores, obtained scores, and errors of measurement. True scores are given along the horizontal axis (X axis) and obtained scores along the vertical axis (Y axis). The correlation between true and obtained scores is termed the *index of reliability* and should not be confused with its square, the reliability coefficient.

Figure 5–3 shows that on this hypothetical intelligence test the obtained IQ scores for examinees with true IQ scores of 100 have a mean of 100 but some variation above and below 100. What is the standard error of measurement—that is, the standard deviation of obtained scores for a given true score? In this example, it is 5 points. This s_e of 5 indicates that about two out of three

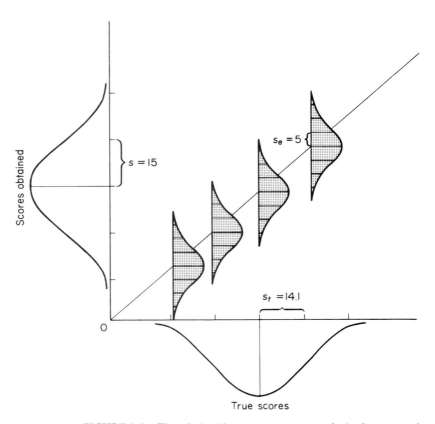

FIGURE 5–3 The relationship among true scores, obtained scores, and standard error of measurement in IQ units, illustrated using a test having a reliability coefficient of .89 (that is, $r_{xx} = 1 - (s_e^2/s^2) = .89$).

examinees (68 percent) will obtain IQ scores that fall within 5 points of their true IQ score. Half of the examinees will have an obtained score above their true score and vice versa (ignoring the cases in which the two are equal). About 95 percent received IQ scores that were within 10 points ($\pm 2s_e$) of their true scores. The s_e helps us to know how much elasticity should accompany our interpretations of test scores.

It is important to remember that a true score in measurement does *not* usually mean a perfectly valid score. True scores represent the average score a person would obtain on an infinite number of parallel forms of the test, assuming that he is unchanged by taking the tests (that is, no practice effect). Any source of invalidity that is systematic, one that remains constant over the tests, is defined as being a part of an examinee's true score.

MORE ABOUT s_e

In measurement theory, *the variance of the obtained scores (s^2) of a large group of students equals the variance of the true scores of those students plus the variance of their errors of measurement; that is,*

$$s^2 = s_t^2 + s_e^2.$$

120

We can estimate directly the variance of the obtained scores (the square of the standard deviation). Also, we can estimate the *variance error of measurement* (s_e^2). If only an unspeeded test has been administered, the test can be split into two comparable halves, and a score for each student can be found on half *a* and half *b*. If we obtain the difference in scores on half *a* and half *b* for each student, the variance of these differences is the variance error of measurement (s_e^2) for the entire test. An alternative method is the use of the formula

$$s_e^2 = s^2(1 - r_{xx}),$$

where r_{xx} is the reliability coefficient of the test.

If two comparable whole-forms A and B of the same test have been given to a group of students, we find for each student his score on form A minus his score on form B. The (variance of these differences)/2 is the variance error of measurement for either form A or form B, where variance errors of measurement for the two forms are assumed to be equal. The square root of this variance is the standard error of measurement of either form A or form B.

A standard error of measurement is used to infer the range within which the student's true score probably lies; thus 68 percent of the obtained scores are within one standard error of measurement (s_e) of corresponding true scores, and 95 percent are within $2s_e$ of their respective true scores.

For most purposes little is gained by predicting true scores. Most standardized test results are interpreted in terms of obtained scores and s_e's. Thus if the student has an obtained IQ score of 106, and the standard error of measurement for that test is 5 points, we infer that his true IQ score probably lies somewhere from 101 to 111. There is one chance in six that it is lower than 101, and one chance in six that it is higher than 111.

Since an individual's test score is considered to be composed of two independent parts, his "true" score and a random error component, the obtained test score is used in some way (usually directly) to estimate his true score. A difficulty arises, however, because obtained scores correlate positively with the errors of measurement that they contain; therefore an obtained score that is high or low in the obtained-score distribution tends to have a larger error than do test scores near the center of the distribution. This leads to a phenomenon called "regression toward the mean," which occurs when the group is retested with a comparable form of the same test. The very high scorers on the first form will tend, on the average, not to be quite as high (though still high) on the retest because their measurement errors will tend to be smaller the second time. The initially low scorers will tend to "improve" their scores by sheer chance on the retest because their errors the first time were too large negatively and will tend to be smaller the second time, which makes their obtained scores larger. (These changes occur because errors of measurement on the first test are uncorrelated with errors of measurement on the second test.) Therefore, although over the entire range the obtained scores are unbiased estimators of true scores (that is, they have no systematic tendency to be too high or too low), they tend to be underestimates at the bottom of the distribution and overestimates at the top of the distribution. By how much? That depends on the reliability coefficient of the test. Perfectly reliable scores do not regress toward the mean at all on retest; perfectly unreliable ones would be expected to regress all the way to the mean on retest. Moderately reliable scores regress that fraction of the way toward the mean that one minus the reliability coefficient represents $(1 - r_{XX})$, such as 25% for a reliability coefficient of .75 or 40% for a reliability coefficient of .60.

Two illustrations may be clarifying. Ascertain the correct ("true") chronological age "score" of each of your classmates to the nearest month. Repeat this 3 months later. Each person is exactly 3 months older, so his two z-scores are

$$z = \frac{\text{age} - \text{mean age}}{s_{\text{age}}}$$

and

$$z = \frac{(\text{age} + 3) - (\text{mean age} + 3)}{s_{(\text{age}+3)}} = \frac{\text{age} - \text{mean age}}{s_{\text{age}}},^2$$

precisely the same; hence, the correlation between age initially and age 3 months later is 1.00. No regression occurred; there were no measurement errors.

Now consider the illustration of the class flipping the same type of coin 100 times in random fashion. Each student obtains a number-of-heads score somewhere between 0 and 100, the score probably averaging about 50 for the class as a whole. Let each of them flip his coin 100 times again, thereby obtaining a second score for each person. How highly will the two sets of scores correlate? Zero, on the average, because the number-of-heads scores vary from person to person, or from one time to the next for a given person, in purely chance fashion. No matter how many "heads" one individual flips the first time, we predict 50 for him the second time. Reliability of "measurement" is nil, and regression toward the mean is expected to be total.

Regression toward the mean caused by errors of measurement has implications for measurement and experimentation. For discussion of these consequences, see articles by Rulon (1941), R.L. Thorndike (1963a), Campbell and Stanley (1966), and Hopkins (1969).

Types of Reliability Coefficient

Different methods of estimating the reliability of an instrument take into account different sources of error. The test-retest *reliability* coefficients for the birth-certificate and coin-flipping illustrations are sometimes called *coefficients of stability*. By stability we mean that an individual's score may change from one time to the next, not because of a change in the "test," which remains constant (the same question regarding the same coin both times, the same apparatus, and so on), but because of fluctuations in some aspect of the measurement of a characteristic such as coin-flipping "ability" or birthdate reporting. Since coin-flipping ability does not vary from one person to another,

---

[2] The denominator simplifies because

$$s_{(\text{age}+3)} = \sqrt{s_{\text{age}}^2 + s_3^2 + 2r_{\text{age},3}\, s_{\text{age}} s_3}$$
$$= \sqrt{s_{\text{age}}^2 + 0 + 2(0)} = \sqrt{s_{\text{age}}^2} = s_{\text{age}}.$$

variation within a given tosser from one set of tosses to another is as great as variation among tossers (that is, $s_e = s$); hence reliability equals 0.0. Conversely, variation *within* individuals with respect to true birthdate is nil, while variation *among* individuals can be great. Once we introduce the possibility of errors of measurement in ascertaining birthdates by asking each person his birthdate at two different times, we may discover that some within-individual variability exists. The same correct birth certificate has no error of measurement from one time to the next unless it is misread, because it is the same "test" both times, but each time we ask a woman her age we are to some extent giving her another test because the situation may change from the first questioning to the next.

Recall the illustration in which a student took many parallel forms of a 100-item vocabulary test. If the test-retest method of estimating reliability were used, the chance factors (sampling errors) involved in the particular set of 100 items would be constant on both occasions. Perhaps in the dictionary 10 percent of the words are technical in nature. On given forms of a test, the number of scientific words appearing might vary from 1 to 18.[3] If form A, which has 15 percent, were repeated, the person whose technical knowledge is extensive would be overrated; "lady luck" was good to him as she as-

[3] The standard deviation of the number of technical words that would be found on the 100-item test, assuming that the words were selected randomly from a large unabridged dictionary in which technical words represented 10 precent of the entries would be $\sqrt{Npq}$ (see footnote on p. 116) or $\sqrt{100(.1)(.9)} = 3$.

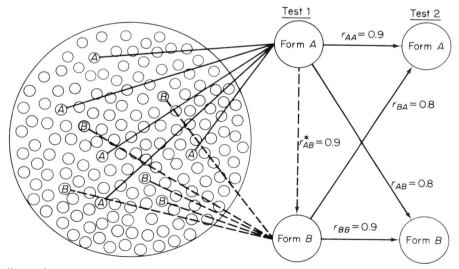

Item universe
(e.g., all words in Webster's dictionary)

*This coefficient illustrates the split-half reliability estimate. The hypothetical test is composed of items, half from form A and half from form B, administered as a single test.

FIGURE 5–4 Graphic illustration of test-retest reliability and parallel-form reliability estimates.

sembled form A. If form A is given a second time, the test content is fixed; hence the consistency between scores is higher than it would be if different forms were administered. Therefore the reliability coefficient tells only the test-retest stability of performance on this particular test, which may be much less interesting and relevant than the stability of performance on tests "like these." Test-retest reliability coefficients are usually higher than parallel-form coefficients because the latter permit item content to vary.

Figure 5-4 shows two equally representative parallel forms of a test from the same universe of content. The test-retest method of estimating reliability does not permit a new sample of items to be used in the second testing. Therefore, the reliability coefficients, r_{AA} and r_{BB}, will be higher, but usually less meaningful, than the parallel-form reliability estimate (r_{AB} or r_{BA}) in which randomly different sets of items have been selected from the same item universe. Forms A and B are both random samples from the universe of content, yet r_{AA} will be greater than r_{AB} because the sample of test content is not allowed to vary in the test-retest method.

An important point in evaluating reliability coefficients is illustrated in Figure 5-4: if the procedure used to estimate reliability does not allow certain factors to vary (for example, sampling error in item selection), then of course they are constant and cannot be categorized as errors of measurement, even though they may logically belong in that category. The figure also demonstrates that the term "reliability coefficient" is ambiguous when the method used to estimate it is unknown. For further discussion, see Stanley (1971a, 1971b).

PARALLEL-FORM RELIABILITY

Since 1910, the parallel-form approach has been the preferred method of estimating the reliability coefficient of a test. With the parallel-form reliability coefficient, r_{AB}, the reliabilities of the two forms are considered to be equivalent because they were constructed carefully to be parallel. Forms are parallel if a person's true score is the same on both and if the standard error of measurement (in the population) for one form is the same as for the other. To determine the parallel-form reliability coefficient of a test requires two or more forms of that test. For many tests this has been impracticable—for example, when the user needs just one form or does not have the financial resources to develop alternate forms. Since both test-retest and parallel-form methods require two administrations, pupil motivation, fatigue, boredom, and the like can present additional practical obstacles. Methods of estimating a test's reliability that require only one administration are more commonly employed, especially for teacher-made tests.

SPLIT-HALF METHOD

To avoid two test administrations, an unspeeded test can (as noted earlier) be split into two parts. For example, one might put the odd-numbered items (1, 3, 5, . . .) into half *a* and the even-numbered items (2, 4, 6, . . .) into half *b*. From one test administration a total score for each half for each examinee can be obtained and the half-scores can be correlated to secure a coefficient that could be labeled r_{hh}—that is, the "parallel-form reliability" of a test half as long as form A. Fortunately, from r_{hh} one can estimate r_{XX} via the formula $r_{XX} = 2r_{hh}/(1 + r_{hh})$, which is one version of the Spearman-Brown step-up or prophecy formula.[4] The halving procedure is called the split-half method, and the stepped-up r_{hh} is usually referred to as a "corrected" split-half reliability coefficient. (The splitting procedure should throw comparable types of item into both halves. The odd-even method will not always accomplish that [see R.L. Thorndike, 1951].) Thorndike and Hagen (1969, p. 193) note that split-half estimates tend to exceed parallel-form estimates .03–.11 on selected standardized tests.

RELIABILITY VIA INTERNAL CONSISTENCY

Many years ago two measurement specialists (Kuder and Richardson, 1937) devised a procedure for estimating the *internal consistency* of a test (that is, the extent to which all items in the test measure the same abilities) without splitting it into halves. Kuder and Richardson's most commonly used procedure, KR formula 20, is roughly equivalent to (1) securing the mean intercorrelation of the k items in the test, (2) considering this as the reliability coefficient of the typical *item* in the test, and (3) stepping up this average r with the general Spearman-Brown formula to estimate the coefficient of equivalence of a test consisting of k items (see Stanley, 1957).[5] Since there are 45 item intercorrelations for a 10-item test and 1,225 for a 50-item test, it is fortunate that we do not actually have to compute all 45 or 1,225 r's, but can instead estimate the reliability coefficient fairly easily. It can theoretically vary from 0 to 1.

In a test that has perfect internal consistency each item measures without error exactly the same thing as every other item; thus every item correlates $+1$ with every other item. Item intercorrelations near 1 are rarely obtained, however, for three reasons:

1. One item does not measure precisely the same "thing" as another.

---

[4] Although this has been the most commonly used split-half procedure and has been empirically shown to yield accurate results when its assumptions are satisfied, methods proposed by Flanagan (1937) and Rulon (1939) are simpler because they do not require the computation of a correlation coefficient or the use of the Spearman-Brown formula. In addition they do not assume $\sigma_a^2 = \sigma_b^2$, which is required by the Spearman-Brown formula, but yield identical results when this condition is met. Rulon's formula is

$$r_{XX} = 1 - \frac{s_d^2}{s^2},$$

where s_d^2 is the variance of the *differences* in scores on the two halves. Flanagan's formula is

$$r_{XX} = 2\left(\frac{s_a^2 + s_b^2}{s^2}\right),$$

where: s_a^2 and s_b^2 are the variances of halves a and b, and s^2 is the variance of total scores on the test.

[5] Stanley (1957) showed that if $\bar{r}$ is the average intercorrelation of the k items, then the reliability coefficient estimated via the Kuder-Richardson formula is very nearly $k\bar{r}/[1 + (k-1)\bar{r}]$, the general Spearman-Brown formula, a formula that estimates the reliability of a test whose length is changed by adding or removing homogeneous items. If r_{XX} denotes the reliability coefficient of a test of known length, and r'_{XX} denotes the reliability coefficient of a test n times as long, then

$$r'_{XX} = \frac{nr_{XX}}{1 + (n-1)r_{XX}}.$$

2. Errors of measurement in items are usually appreciable.
3. When the responses to two dichotomously scored items are correlated, r will not be able to reach 1 if the items are of different difficulty. For example, if 50 percent of the examinees correctly answer item 1, and 80 percent answer item 2 correctly, at least three-fifths of those who missed item 1 must answer item 2 correctly.

Kuder-Richardson Formula 20   Even when the average intercorrelation of items is rather small, the internal consistency of the test in the Kuder-Richardson sense will be *much* higher than this $\bar{r}$ if the test is composed of a fairly large number of items. When the average intercorrelation of the 20 items in a test is .10, the KR 20 coefficient for the test will be approximately $20(.10)/[1 + 19(.10)] = .69$, as estimated by the Spearman-Brown formula. For 50 items that intercorrelate .10, on the average, it would be .85. The more items of a given quality, the higher will be the KR 20 coefficient. Therefore, other things being equal, *long tests are more reliable than short tests.*

A desirable feature of the KR 20 reliability estimate is that it is essentially the mean of all possible split-half reliability estimates (see Cronbach, 1951, and Novick and Lewis, 1967). It also tends to provide a good estimate of parallel-form reliability (Cronbach and Azuma, 1962). Its computation is straightforward, but too time-consuming to be recommended for classroom purposes.[6]

Kuder-Richardson Formula 21   Because computing $r_{KR_{20}}$ by hand is tedious, Kuder and Richardson (1937) proposed a second formula. KR 21 is less accurate but simple to compute. It requires only the test mean ($\bar{X}$), the variance (s^2), and the number of items on the test:

$$r_{KR_{21}} = \frac{ks^2 - \bar{X}(k - \bar{X})}{(k - 1)s^2}.$$

For example, on a 50-item test with a mean of 30 and a standard deviation of 10, this reliability estimate is:

$$r_{KR_{21}} = \frac{50(100) - 30(50 - 30)}{49(100)} = \frac{5000 - 600}{4900} = \frac{4400}{4900} = .898.$$

The values of $r_{KR_{21}}$ are always below the more accurate $r_{KR_{20}}$ value, but the differences are usually not great on *well-constructed* tests (Lord, 1959; Cronbach and Azuma, 1962; Payne, 1963). Figure 5–5 depicts the high relationship between $r_{KR_{20}}$ and $r_{KR_{21}}$ on 58 carefully developed tests; $r_{KR_{20}}$ consistently exceeds $r_{KR_{21}}$, but usually by .05 units or less. The Kuder-Richardson formula 21 assumes

---

[6] The formula is

$$r_{KR_{20}} = \frac{k}{k - 1}\left(1 - \frac{\Sigma pq}{s^2}\right),$$

where: $p =$ is the proportion passing a given item, and $q =$ the proportion not passing that item ($q = 1 - p$), and these pq values are summed over all k items. to obtain Σpq. Cronbach (1951) developed a more general coefficient, α, of which $r_{KR_{20}}$ is a special case:

$$\alpha = \frac{I}{I - 1}\left(1 - \frac{\Sigma s_i^2}{s^2}\right)$$

where s_i^2 is the variance of scores on the ith part of the test, composed of I parts. When the parts are individual items, $\alpha = r_{KR_{20}}$. When parts of halves, α is the split-half reliability coefficient yielded by the Flanagan formula (see p. 125, footnote 4).

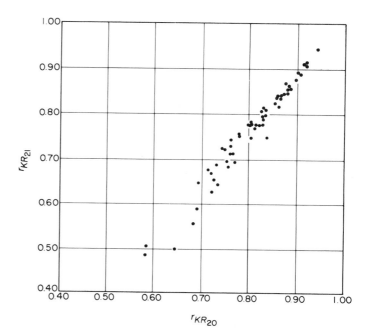

FIGURE 5-5 Relation between Kuder-Richardson formulas 20 and 21 reliability coefficients for 58 tests. (Reprinted from F. M. Lord, Tests of the same length do have the same standard error of measurement, Educational and Psychological Measurement, 1959, 19(2): Fig. 2, p. 237, by permission of the author and publisher.)

that the items on the test are equally difficult; it is lower than $r_{KR_{20}}$ to the extent that item difficulties vary greatly within a test (see Stanley, 1968). On mastery or teacher-made tests that have many very easy items, $r_{KR_{21}}$ becomes quite conservative and may underestimate $r_{KR_{20}}$ by as much as .15 (Cronbach and Azuma, 1962). On unspeeded tests $r_{KR_{21}}$ is often given as a lower-bound (minimal) estimate of reliability, but where computational ease is not a major consideration, $r_{KR_{20}}$ is preferable.

SPEEDED TESTS

Split-half and Kuder-Richardson procedures are appropriate only for *power tests*, tests, in which each student has enough time to show what he knows (though he may not mark all items). These procedures are not proper for *speed* tests, tests in which he does not have time to respond to some questions for which he knows the correct answer. If a test begins with items so easy that nearly everyone marks them correctly and ends with items so difficult that nearly everyone misses them, it may not be a speed test even though few students actually have time to try all the items. When questions are ordered by degree of difficulty, a student may run out of ability long before he completes the test, and thereafter he may merely guess.

The "split-half reliability coefficient" of a *pure* speed test is virtually 1.0. For example, on a highly speeded clerical speed and accuracy test, the split-half reliability estimate was .99, whereas the parallel-form value was about .85 (Bennett, Seashore, and Wesman, 1966, p. 6-6). The following hypothetical illustration shows the influence of speed on split-half reliability.

George marks the first 40 of 90 items, all correctly, during the short time limit. His split-half score is 20 on one half and 20 on the other half. Jill marks 72, so her half-scores are 36 and 36. For all even-number total scores, the half scores on odd-numbered items are identical with those on even-numbered items because by definition we are considering a test in which no items are marked incorrectly. If within-individual variation is 0, the correlation between halves will be perfect. Most ability tests lie much nearer the power than the speed end of the continuum if the time limit is not severe. Rarely is an educational test strictly a "power" test or only a "speed" test. Educational tests usually contain elements of both. Many students fail to answer or even to read some items; but at the same time, few respond correctly to all items they attempt.

The moral is clear: speeded tests usually yield spuriously high reliability coefficients when split-half or internal consistency methods are employed. To assess the reliability of speeded tests, one should administer separately timed comparable halves *a* and *b*, correlate the half-scores, and step-up the correlation coefficient with the Spearman-Brown formula $2r_{ab}/(1 + r_{ab})$ (or use the Rulon or Flanagan method; see footnote 4, p. 125).

Of course the test-retest and parallel-form methods of estimating reliability are also legitimate for speeded tests. Internal-consistency reliability methods have no useful meaning in situations, such as the measurement of height, in which the items (say, the inches) comprising the score are not subject to errors. Inches on a ruler are internally consistent. A 71.9-inch-tall man today may be measured as 71.8 or 72.0 tomorrow, but if he got Inch No. 71 "right," he also got Inches No. 1, 2, . . . , 70 right. The ruler is a near-perfect scale. We merely need read off the last fraction of an inch of height to know that all items below it were "correct." To find the error of measurement at the top of his head we need a second, *independent* measurement of his height. Physical measurement is usually more reliable than psychological measurement, because the units and scales of psychological measurement—the items themselves—are subject to substantial errors of measurement.

Usability

Among the tests that will do what we want done reliably and validly we choose those that offer the most *convenience, economy,* and *interpretability.* A test may yield more than one reliable score during a single testing period. It may be available in more than one form at more than one grade level. It may be easy to administer properly and to score or have scored quickly. Its cost per student tested may be lower than most other similar tests. Results may be expressible conveniently and clearly on forms provided by the publisher. Such considerations of usability are important, but only after questions of reliability and validity have been answered satisfactorily.

The advent of high-speed electronic test-scoring devices has made it usually undesirable for teachers themselves to score the standardized tests administered in their classes, except in the primary grades where separate answer sheets may be confusing to pupils. Otherwise, handscoring is a waste of teachers' energies, and is expensive when the value of their time (and morale) is considered. Most major test publishers now offer to score standardized tests at reasonable rates and to provide extensive interpretative information about scores for students, grades, and schools. Some publishers offer "package" deals in which school systems do not even have to buy and store the test booklets.

Rarely does the teacher gain enough diagnostic information about a pupil or class by handscoring a standardized test to make the effort worthwhile. He would usually be better advised to spend that time studying machine-scored answer sheets, perhaps with a scoring stencil (key) in hand to spot-check answers.

Whether the results of a test are easy to interpret and apply depends primarily on the adequacy of the manual accompanying the test. The manual should contain complete norms to facilitate interpretation. Whenever possible, all derived scores should be obtainable from tables of norms without the necessity of computation or interpolation.

Illustration from a Test Manual

In order to make the concepts of reliability and validity more understandable, let's look at a test manual to see what is said there about these characteristics. We consider the 75-page 1965 Manual for the *Academic Promise Tests* (APT), designed for grades 6–9 and published by The Psychological Corporation. These tests measure abstract reasoning (AR), numerical ability (N), verbal ability (V), and language usage (LU). In the section entitled "Reliability of the APT" on pages 59–62, we read that "The coefficients of reliability . . . are based on scores from alternate forms administered with an intervening time interval. Such reliability coefficients may be described as coefficients of equivalence and stability . . . the range of reliability coefficients for the single tests, within each of the four grades, is .81 to .90. For the subtotals, AR + N and V + LU, the reliability coefficients range from .88 to .92, with only one of the eight coefficients below .90. The APT Total has extremely high reliability, .93 or .94 for each single grade . . . a rule-of-thumb estimate of the standard errors of measurement would be: 4 points of raw score for each of the four tests, 6 points for either subtotal, and 8 points for the APT Total, regardless of grade."

For example, in grade 6 (444 students tested) the reliability coefficient of the abstract-reasoning test scores—the coefficient of correlation between scores on the two comparable forms—was .87. The mean of the sixth-grade group on the form given first was 28.0, with standard deviation 11.6. The standard error of measurement for this grade would be $11.6\sqrt{1 - .87} = 4.2$; thus, if a student's obtained score is 28, there are two chances in three (odds of 2:1) that his true score lies within the 8.4-point range 28 ± 4.2, or 23.8–32.2, for which the percentile ranks are approximately 59–71. There is one chance in six that his true score is less than 23.8 and one chance in six that it is more than 32.2. The authors of the APT battery point out the desirability of the parallel-form reliability estimates that they provide, versus test-retest and split-half or other internal-consistency coefficients:

> Procedures which analyze the student's performance on a single administration of one form of a test take advantage of some kinds of irrelevant influences. For example, if odd and even scores on a test are correlated, scores on each half will be similarly affected by whether or not the student is specially alert on the day of the testing. This procedure provides no evidence concerning the stability of the student's performance from day to day. Administering the same form on two different occasions would permit variations in the student's day-to-day performance to be reflected in the reliability coefficient. However, this procedure provides evidence only on the specific items which happen to be included in that one form. Whether or not the student would have scored similarly had a different but equally appropriate sample of items been included, can not be ascertained by retesting with the same form [p. 59].

The Kuder-Richardson formula 20 may yield a good approximation of the comparable-forms reliability that would be obtained with a small time interval between administration of the two forms (Stanley, 1957), but the comparable-forms coefficient is often preferable for the reasons given by the authors of the Academic Promise Tests.

The authors state on page 33 that "The characteristic of a test which is of primary interest to the test user is validity; i.e., to what extent will the test predict future performance?" This is predictive validity, of course. They then write:

> For academic aptitude tests, the criteria to be predicted usually are grades awarded by teachers or scores on an appropriate achievement test, which may in turn be a final school examination or a standardized test. . . . The predictor tests are designed solely to appraise intellectual abilities; grades often are assigned not only for what the student has learned, but also for effort, diligence, active participation in discussion, and less relevant (to actual achievement) personal characteristics. Grades are sometimes unreliable; it is not reasonable to expect any test to predict beyond the reliability of the criterion. Despite these deficiencies, however, grades are the basic currency in which school success is evaluated, and tests should therefore be appraised in terms of their effectiveness in forecasting grades.

After discussing the limitations and advantages of grades as the criterion, the authors present 15 pages of tables showing how well the tests, singly and in combinations, predict grades in various courses for grades 6–9 in a number of communities. These are admirably detailed and complete. For example, on page 36 the predictive validity coefficients for 194 students in an English course in community 13, grade 7, North Central region of the U.S., community of 5,000 to 99,000 residents, are as follows: AR, .49; N, .58; V, .53; LU, .67; AR + N, .61; V + LU, .68; and APT Total, .70. For this particular subject and situation, the language-usage test alone predicts about as well (.67) as the APT total (.70).

On page 58 the APT authors present expectancy tables for predicting grades in English, social studies, mathematics, and science from scores on the tests of language usage, verbal ability, numerical ability, and abstract reasoning, respectively. They also provide tables of coefficients of correlation of APT scores with intelligence, scholastic aptitude, and other aptitude tests (pp. 64–66), and with achievement tests (pp. 67–68). In addition, they enable one to estimate the Wechsler Intelligence Scale for Children (WISC) full-scale IQ from the APT total raw score, taking into consideration chronological age.

This clear, complete manual contains much valuable information, such as the "probability that a difference of one inch between APT scores plotted on student report form is due to chance" (p. 32), which of course is based on the standard error of measurement of the difference between APT scores. The probability that a difference of one inch or more is due to chance ranges from .016 for (V + LU) versus (AR + N) in grade 8 to .096 for V versus N in grade 6. As we have seen, the APT Manual covers predictive validity extensively for the grade criterion and gives attention to construct validity. A diligent user of the APT Manual can learn much from it about the test's quality and relevance for various purposes.

What are the earmarks of a good measuring instrument? In brief, it possesses three outstanding qualities: validity, reliability, and usability. *A good test helps the user attain a specific goal, consistently, and with a reasonable expenditure of time, energy, and money.* The first consideration in educational and psychological testing is always validity. Reliability is a crucial prerequisite for validity, but it is only a means toward that end.

When a test is administered to an examinee, he obtains a score. If he had been tested on some other occasion, he probably would not have earned exactly the same score. The score that he would have earned, on the average, if he had been tested at various times under exactly the same testing conditions is called his *true score*. Although we can never actually know his true score, we can be aware of the discrepancy between his obtained score (which we know) and his true score (which we do not know). This difference, the obtained score minus the true score, is called error of measurement.

The standard deviation of an examinee's obtained scores about his true score is the standard error of measurement (s_e). About two-thirds of the examinees will have obtained scores that are within one s_e of their true scores. Only about one person in twenty will obtain a score that varies from his true score by as much as $2s_e$.

The reliability coefficient of a test represents the relationship between true scores and obtained scores. The square root of the reliability coefficient (known as the index of reliability) is the correlation between obtained and true scores.

There are several methods for estimating the reliability of a test. The test-retest and parallel-form methods have the practical disadvantage of requiring two administrations, and the latter requires the construction of two forms. Although the parallel-form method is theoretically best, split-half and internal-consistency methods are more common because only one test and one admin- istration are required. These one-form methods are inappropriate for speeded tests, however, because they give inflated results to the extent that speed rather than power influences test scores. The split-half (usually odd-even item split) reliability estimates tend to be higher than those yielded by the Kuder- Richardson formulas. Kuder-Richardson formula 20 yields the average of all possible split-half coefficients and is usually a good estimate of parallel-form reliability when the time interval between forms is short. Kuder-Richardson formula 21 yields conservative values, but requires only the number of items on a test, the mean, and the variance.

elevenEven though a test produces valid and reliable scores, it may still not be functional because of some practical problem. If the test is too expensive, requires too much time to administer or score, or is difficult to interpret, its real value is reduced accordingly.

IMPORTANT TERMS AND CONCEPTS

sample
population or universe
errors of measurement
standard error of measurement
reliability coefficient
index of reliability
true score
variance

parallel-form reliability
test-retest reliability
split-half method
Spearman-Brown formula
internal consistency
Kuder-Richardson formulas 20 and 21
usability

SUGGESTED READINGS

AMERICAN PSYCHOLOGICAL ASSOCIATION, AMERICAN EDUCATIONAL RESEARCH ASSO- CIATION, and NATIONAL COUNCIL ON MEASUREMENT IN EDUCATION. 1966. *Standards for educational and psychological tests and manuals.* Washington, D.C.: American Psychological Association, Inc., Section D (Reliability), pp. 25–32.

CRONBACH, L. J., and H. AZUMA. 1962. Internal-consistency reliability formulas applied to randomly sampled single-factor tests: An empirical comparison. *Educational and Psychological Measurement*, **22**: 645–665.

CURETON, E. E. 1969. Measurement theory. In R. L. Ebel, ed., *Encyclopedia of educational research*, 4th ed. Toronto: The Macmillan Company, pp. 785–804.

HOPKINS, K. D. 1964. Extrinsic reliability: Estimating and attenuating variance from response styles, chance, and other irrelevant sources. *Educational and Psychological Measurement*, **24**(2): 271–281. Reprinted in G. H. Bracht, K. D. Hopkins, and J. C. Stanley. 1972. *Perspectives in educational and psychological measurement.* Englewood Cliffs, N.J.: Prentice-Hall, Inc., Selection 10.

LIVINGSTON, S. A. 1972. Criterion-referenced applications of classical test theory. *Journal of Educational Measurement*, **9** (in press).

STANLEY, J. C. 1971a. Reliability. In R. L. Thorndike, ed., *Educational Measurement,* 2d ed. Washington, D.C.: American Council on Education, Chap. 13.

——. 1971b. Reliability of test scores and other measurements. In L. C. Deighton, ed., *The Encyclopedia of education.* New York: The Macmillan Company. Reprinted in G. H. Bracht, K. D. Hopkins, and J. C. Stanley. 1972. *Perspectives in educational and psychological measurement.* Englewood Cliffs, N.J.: Prentice-Hall, Inc., Selection 6.

THORNDIKE, R. L. 1964. Reliability. *Proceedings of 1963 Invitational Conference on Testing.* Princeton, N.J.: Educational Testing Service. Reprinted in G. H. Bracht, K. D. Hopkins, and J. C. Stanley. 1972. *Perspectives in educational and psychological measurement.* Englewood Cliffs, N.J.: Prentice-Hall, Inc., Selection 7.

WESMAN, A. G. 1952. Reliability and confidence. *Test Service Bulletin* No. 44, The Psychological Corporation.

part two

The Development of Educational Measures

6

6

PSYCHOLOGICAL AND CULTURAL FACTORS THAT INFLUENCE PERFORMANCE ON COGNITIVE TESTS

Cronbach (1970) distinguished between measures of *maximum performance* (achievement, intelligence, and aptitude tests) and measures of *typical performance* (attitude, interest, and personality inventories). The object of cognitive measures is to obtain an evaluation of an examinee at his best (maximum); the desired result of affective measures is a sample of usual or representative behavior. The measurement problems are very similar within each of the two categories, but quite different between the classes. In this chapter, we discuss influences of certain irrelevant factors on the measurement of maximum performance.

In addition to the trait that is to be measured, many other factors may be related to or affect an examinee's performance on a test. To evaluate test results properly, one should not only be aware of the existence of extraneous variables, but also be able to make appropriate allowances for such factors in the interpretation of the results.

Test Sophistication, Practice, and Coaching

TEST SOPHISTICATION

A general "know-how" of taking tests can affect test performance. Persons who are familiar with taking objective or essay tests usually perform better than persons who lack experience with such tests. Slakter, Koehler, and Hampton

137

(1970) have demonstrated that test-wiseness increases progressively in grades 5 through 11. It has been demonstrated (Moore, Schutz, and Baker, 1966; Wahlstrom and Boersma, 1968) that junior-high-school pupils can be taught principles of "test-wiseness" from a programmed instruction sequence based on the general formulation of test sophistication proposed by Millman, Bishop, and Ebel (1965). Such test-taking skills improved the scores of unsophisticated examinees on poorly constructed test items, although no effect was found on well-constructed items.

Since poor items are found on almost all teacher-made tests and on many standardized tests, test sophistication is probably a factor on most tests. It apparently is a major factor only with naive examinees on poor tests or on tests given under conditions in which certain response styles play a significant role.

PRACTICE

Several studies provide data on the effects that taking a test has on the examinee's subsequent performance on that test or on its parallel form. Almost all studies consistently show a general "improvement" in score on the retest. Most studies have used intelligence tests; the gains are usually reported in IQ units. Rodger (1936) gave six different intelligence tests to the same group of children and found an average gain of 8 points (about $.5\sigma$) from the first to the last test. A mean gain of 2.5 IQ points (about $.2\sigma$) was observed on the Stanford-Binet when the forms were counterbalanced (Terman and Merrill, 1937). Kreit (1968) observed a practice factor of 7 IQ points (about $.4\sigma$) when third-grade pupils were administered four intelligence tests during a five-month interval.

The practice factor on tests used for admission to college or graduate school is important to note. Levine and Angoff (1958) investigated the effect of repetition on the College Entrance Examination Board (CEEB) *Scholastic Aptitude Test* for high-school juniors and seniors. The authors found an average gain of only 10 points ($.1\sigma$) for the first retest after a two-month interval and an additional gain of 10 points for the second retest, but no further gain for a third retest. (Angoff, 1971, provides detailed information about changes in *Scholastic Aptitude Test* scores over longer periods of time.) Campbell, Hilton, and Pitcher (1967) compared the performance of a large group who had repeated the aptitude sections of the *Graduate Record Examination* after a three-month interval. Unlike the sample in Levine and Angoff's (1958) study, these examinees had elected to repeat the test on their own initiative; they apparently felt that the first test score did not accurately reflect their abilities. An average gain of only approximately 20 points ($.2\sigma$) was observed on each of the verbal and quantitative aptitude sections. Thus it appears that the practice effect is a very minor factor on these important tests. A similar gain of 25 points ($.25\sigma$) was observed for medical-school applicants on the *Medical College Admission Test* (MCAT) (Schumacher and Gee, 1961).

A study by Knapp (1960) illuminates several factors pertaining to the practice effect and its ally, test-wiseness. Knapp found a greater practice effect for Mexicans than for Americans on the *Cattell Culture Free Intelligence Test*. The practice effects were much larger when speed was a factor, especially for the Mexicans, who were less experienced in taking tests.

The review of the above and related studies of the practice effect on cognitive tests supports the following generalizations:

1. Practice effects are more pronounced with persons of limited educational background or experience.
2. The effects are greater on speeded tests.
3. The effects are greater on a repeated test than on a parallel form of the test. There is little or no practice effect after the second retest.
4. The greater the time interval between tests, the smaller the effect. There appears to be little practice effect for an interval greater than three months.
5. Other things being equal, the effects appear to be slightly greater for examinees of high mental ability (Weiss, 1961).
6. For a group of typical examinees, the average practice effect is usually $.2\sigma$ or less in magnitude.

COACHING

The topic of coaching is difficult to treat because it may mean anything from drill on the same items that were missed on a test to a general remedial course. In addition to the kind of coaching given, the amount of time spent varies considerably in the published studies. Consequently, the results from "coaching" studies are quite varied. Greene (1928) reported the following results on the Stanford-Binet for three groups of school children. The control group, which received no coaching (practice effect only), on the average gained 2–3 IQ points (about $.2\sigma$) on retesting. A second group received two hours of training on similar but not identical material to that appearing on the test; this group had an average gain of 7–8 IQ points (about $.4\sigma$–$.5\sigma$). A third group, which was coached on identical material, reflected a mean gain of about 30 points (about 2σ)! These differences declined with time for three years, at which time no coaching advantage remained. When the term "coaching" as used by Yates et al. (1953, 1964) is properly interpreted, the results are remarkably consistent with those of Greene. Vernon (1954) observed an average gain of 2–3 IQ points (about $.2\sigma$) for a control group on the second testing, a mean gain of about 6 points ($.4\sigma$) on the third retest, and no additional gain thereafter. When coached examinees had numerous representative items explained by the teacher, they gained 5–6 IQ points (about $.4\sigma$) on the first retesting. This increased to 8–10 points (about $.6\sigma$) for the third retesting, and there was no additional gain thereafter.

Several studies have been conducted on the effect that coaching has on the *Scholastic Aptitude Test* (CEEB, 1968). The studies reveal a small 5–20 point ($.05\sigma$–$.2\sigma$) gain from special coaching. Frankel (1960) compared students who took a commercial coaching course with a group matched on initial SAT score who merely repeated the test. The coached students gained less than 10 points ($.1\sigma$) more than the matched group.

From the results of these and related studies, we can draw the following generalizations pertinent to the effects of coaching on test performance:

1. Coaching usually results in small (often negligible) gains in test performance, over and above the practice effect.

2. The magnitude of the gain rarely exceeds $.2\sigma$ unless the examinees have been coached on the actual test items. Somewhat larger gains (often $.3\sigma$) may result on achievement tests for those examinees who have not had recent association with the content area.

Anxiety and Motivation

Obviously, a poorly motivated pupil will not give his maximum effort on a test. Most examinees are intrinsically motivated to succeed in test situations, although the degree of motivation varies widely in different ethnic and socio-economic groups (Anastasi, 1958, p. 551). Incentives such as cash, grades, and special urging have little or no effect on normal students who are already motivated to do well (Klugman, 1944; Sinick, 1956). When the test content is not intrinsically interesting or examinees are not ego-involved with their performance, effects can be sizable (Duncan, 1947; Yamamota and Dizney, 1965).

If an examinee is too ego-involved with his performance on a test, he may become anxious. There have been dozens of research studies relating anxiety and test performance (see Ruebush, 1963). Almost all of this research is consistent in showing a small negative ($-.1$ to $-.3$) correlation between paper-and-pencil self-report test anxiety measures and performance on intelligence and achievement tests. Too often these findings have been incorrectly interpreted—that is, they have been assumed to show that "test anxiety depresses ability test performance." Correlation may reflect causation, but does not *necessarily* do so. One would be equally unjustified in concluding from the negative correlation that "poor performance on ability tests generates high test anxiety." A brief look at some of the items used on the self-report scales designed to measure test anxiety (Sarason et al., 1960) will show that both explanations are logically plausible:

> When the teacher says she is going to find out how much you have learned, does your heart begin to beat faster?
> While you are taking a test, do you usually think you are not doing well?

As French (1962, p. 555) stated, "Evidence that anxiety is usually found to accompany low test scores proves nothing about the part that anxiety plays in bringing about the low scores."

In a few studies, researchers have attempted to ascertain experimentally whether high anxiety impairs test performance. In these studies, subjects were randomly assigned to various anxiety-inducing or anxiety-reducing treatments. The evidence obtained thus far has failed to support the common contention that such experimentally induced "anxiety" depresses test performance (Allison, 1970; Chambers, Hopkins, and Hopkins, 1972; French, 1962; Silverstein, 1964). However, in tests requiring psychomotor performance in addition to cognitive performance (such as mazes), anxiety-inducing instructions did cause more errors to be made by high-anxiety examinees (Sarason, Mandler, and Craighill, 1952).

It can be concluded that *although measured test anxiety is inversely associated with cognitive test performance, the available research fails to establish a causative relationship with the usual kind of cognitive test of maximum performance*. This generalization does not necessarily apply to psychomotor measures, nor even to individual tests in which the examiner plays a more active role in the testing process.

Response Styles

Cronbach (1946, 1950, 1970) defined *response sets* or *styles* as test-taking habits that cause persons of equal ability to earn different scores on a test or inventory. An examinee may bring to a test some patterns of test-taking behavior that influence his performance but are unrelated to his ability.

THE SPEED-VS.-ACCURACY SET

Some examinees have a test-taking set that causes them to work slowly and carefully; others have a tendency to work quickly and with less caution (Guilford and Lacey, 1947). The correlation between ability and working rate on tests has been shown to be very low (Tate, 1948; Ebel, 1954; Hopkins, 1964). Some examinees respond slower than others irrespective of item difficulty or test content (Bennett and Doppelt, 1956; Davidson and Carroll, 1945; Tate, 1948). Barch (1957) and Michael and Michael (1969) have found little or no relationship between the examinee's order of finishing and his score on a test. When tests are pure power tests, the effects from this response style are negligible. (Power tests are tests given with ample time for all examinees to demonstrate how well they can perform.)

Teacher-made and standardized tests (Boag and Neild, 1962; Kahn, 1968; Knapp, 1960) frequently have inadequate time limits, which allows the irrelevant effects from the speed-vs.-accuracy response set to contaminate the validity of test scores. Lord (1956) and Mollenkopf (1960) found that tests may measure different mental functions when administered under power and speed conditions. Older persons tend to work more slowly, a factor which led to a gross overestimation of the degree of intellectual decline with age in some early studies (Lorge, 1952).

Except for those educational objectives for which speed of response is an important objective (such as typing, reading), tests should be constructed and administered so that virtually all examinees (perhaps 90 percent) complete the examination. Special directions or periodic announcements during the test may help pace the examinees and reduce the contamination resulting from the speed-vs.-accuracy set.

THE ACQUIESCENCE SET

If one is uncertain about a true-false item, there is a significant tendency to choose the "true" option (Cronbach, 1942, 1950). Gustav (1963) found that 62 percent of a group of college students had marked more items "true" than there were true items on the test. This is particularly interesting since some instructors have a tendency to include more true than false items on their tests (Metfessel and Sax, 1957). The acquiescence set allows more persons to get undeserved credit for true items than for false items; thus, true items tend to be easier and less discriminating (Ebel, 1960; Storey, 1968).

THE POSITIONAL-PREFERENCE SET

Guilford (1965, p. 490) stated that

> when examinees are ignorant of the answer to an item, their habits of taking tests are such that they do not choose among the alternatives entirely at random. Certain positions in a list of five responses may be favored by habits of reading or attention.

Recent evidence has consistently failed to find any significant position factor (Hopkins and Hopkins, 1964; Marcus, 1963; Wevrick, 1962; and Wilbur, 1969). The scoring pattern on certain standardized tests has reflected a keying bias toward certain option positions. The bias most often results in fewer correct answers for the initial and, to a lesser extent, the final response options (Metfessel and Sax, 1957). This condition appears to be corrected on more recently published tests (Jacobs, 1968).

THE OPTION-LENGTH SET

Chase (1964) found a set favoring the longest option on difficult multiple-choice tests. The set was easily removed by inserting some long incorrect options on easy items early in the test.

THE SET TO GAMBLE

The topic of examinee guessing has received extensive attention during the past several decades. There would be no serious problem if all pupils of equal ability guessed with equal frequency, but it has been well established that there are great individual differences in the tendency to guess on test items, that these differences are reliable within a test, and that they are generally consistent from one test to another (Granich, 1931; Jackson, 1955; Slakter, 1967, 1969; Swineford, 1938, 1941). The tendency to gamble varies from the person who will not guess even when told he must answer every question to the "gambler" who attempts almost every item regardless of penalties or directions (Waters, 1967). This response style is particularly evident when students are told there is a "penalty for guessing." There are those, however, who omit some items even when assured of no penalty.

Because most standardized tests do not employ correction for chance (Womer and Wahi, 1969), the "gambler" is given an advantage over the more deliberate student. In one study (Davis, 1951, p. 277) that illustrates the potential magnitude of this factor, a standardized reading test was administered to approximately 400 high-school students. Those examinees who obtained scores below the twelfth percentile ($N = 47$) were told they might have done better if they had marked an answer for every item, whether they knew the answer or not. When they were then given an alternate form of the same test, their mean score increased from 25.53 on the first test to 46.32 on the second test, with an average grade-placement gain of 2.7 grades according to the published norms![1]

The gambling set has been found to have little or no relationship to ability (Swineford and Miller, 1953) and to be related to certain personality traits that are irrelevant on ability tests (Hamilton, 1950; Sherriffs and Boomer, 1954; Votaw, 1936; Ziller, 1957).

Examinees with personality scores indicating introversion and low self-esteem tend to omit more items, and to omit more items for which they know the answers. On most tests examinees can "guess" better than chance because (1) they may have partial information on several items, and (2) on many items not all of the distracters are plausible. Little and Creaser (1966) asked examinees to indicate whether they guessed, were uncertain of their answers, or were certain on each item of a test containing three-option questions; the percentages of correct answers were 55, 67, and 93, respectively, for the three categories. If the examinees possessed no partial information and guessed randomly, they would have been expected to have answered correctly only 33 percent rather than 55 percent for items in the "guessed" category. Jackson (1955) similarly found that students correctly answered one-third of the five-option items on which they reported guessing rather than the one-fifth expected solely from chance.

Corrective Measures for the Gambling Set   The most widely used method to reduce the effects of guessing is the "correction for chance," often erroneously referred to as the "penalty for guessing."

The correction-for-chance formula actually corrects for omissions rather than for guessing as such. If the students omit no items or if they all omit the same number of items, their relative scores (that is, the z-scores or percentile ranks) will be the same, whether or not the formula is applied (Stanley, 1954). The most commonly used formula is

$$S = R - \frac{W}{k-1},$$

where: S = the examinee's score corrected for chance,
R = the number of right responses marked by the examinee,
W = the number of wrong responses, *not* including omitted items, and
k = the number of options presented for each item.

For two-option items, including true-false, this becomes

$$S = R - \frac{W}{2-1} = R - W.$$

For three-option items the formula is

$$S = R - \frac{W}{3-1} = R - \frac{W}{2}.$$

[1] Although some portion of this difference can be attributed to the regression effect (see Campbell and Stanley, 1966; Hopkins, 1969), the increase is substantially greater than the regression effect alone.

For four-option items the formula is

$$S = R - \frac{W}{4 - 1} = R - \frac{W}{3}.$$

For five-option items it is

$$S = R - \frac{W}{5 - 1} = R - \frac{W}{4}.$$

It should be evident that the greater the number of options per item, the less likely it is that one will select the correct option by chance, and, hence, the less the magnitude of the weighting of an incorrect response.[2]

These formulas theoretically reduce to zero the scores of students who, totally ignorant of the material presented in the test, guess with a chance degree of success that depends only on the number of options each item has. If a test contains 100 true-false items and a student guesses an answer to each of these, he should, by chance, answer about 50 items "correctly." Thus, we expect the typical totally uninformed person to score 50 wrong. However, since he richly deserves a final score of zero, which by our definition represents his true knowledge of the material, 50 wrongs are subtracted from 50 rights: $R - W = 50 - 50 = 0$.

If he answers 50 items correctly and *omits* the other 50, his score will be $50 - 0 = 50$. Had he tried the 50 omitted items he would, on the average, by chance have answered half of them (25) correctly and missed the other 25; his "rights score" would be 50 known + 25 guessed = 75, and his "wrongs score" would be 25. He would therefore receive $75 - 25 = 50$, the same score he would have obtained without any guessing. The possible fallacy in this procedure has already been discussed. Because of poor distracters in some items and the partial information possessed by examinees, they can usually do better than chance when forced to guess at items that they have omitted (Ebel, 1968; Jackson, 1955; Little and Creaser, 1966; Wiley, Collins, and Glass, 1970). Consequently, even when the correction formula is used, the gambler usually obtains a higher score than does an equally knowledgeable but more cautious person.

Traub, Hambleton, and Singh (1968) reported slightly better results obtained from using a positive rather than a negative correction approach. Even though the formulas yield scores that correlate 1.0, they appear to have different psychological effects on examinees. The following formula was used:

$$S = R + \frac{O}{k},$$

where S, R, and k are defined as before and O is the number of omitted items. This procedure yields scores that lack the logical meaning of the usual procedure; for example, a person who omitted all 100 T-F items on a test would nevertheless receive a score of 50.

---

[2] If not all items on a test have the same number of options, each subset of items with the same number of options should be treated separately with the appropriate formula. For example, a test composed of 25 true-false items and 30 four-option multiple-choice questions would use $S = R - W$ for the true-false items, and $S = R - W/3$ for the multiple-choice questions. The corrected scores for the two subtests would sum to the corrected-for-chance score for the entire test.

The consequences of correction formulas are not consistent across tests, although perhaps a majority of the studies show a negligible decrease in reliability (Glass and Wiley, 1964). The evidence on validity is also inconclusive, although the evidence slightly favors the corrected scores (Cureton, 1969; Lord, 1963; Sax and Collet, 1968).

It should be reemphasized that the correction formula is needed *only* when some students omit a fairly large number of items and others omit few. When this does not occur, the student ranking will be virtually unchanged whether or not the scores are corrected for "chance." For psychological reasons, the teacher may wish to return corrected scores to the students even though few items have been omitted. This is especially advisable with two-option tests, since the poorest students may not realize the extent of their ignorance and may protest if they are given low grades on the basis of uncorrected test scores that to them seem to indicate considerable knowledge (Stanley, 1954). For example, 60 correct of 100 two-option items marked may represent only 20 percent knowledge of content, but the student may think that he knew 60 percent.

If every student tested answers every item, the standard deviation of scores corrected for chance is $k/(k-1)$ times the standard deviation of the rights scores. From this relationship, it is apparent that correcting scores for a test with no omissions composed of two-option items will double their standard deviation:

$$\frac{k}{k-1} = \frac{2}{2-1} = 2.$$

If there are no omissions, the standard deviation of corrected-for-chance five-option-item test scores is $\frac{5}{4} = 1\frac{1}{4}$ times the standard deviation of the uncorrected scores. The correction formula with true-false and two- and three-option multiple-choice test scores more accurately emphasizes the range of knowledge within the group tested even when omissions are negligible.

The Educational Testing Service uses the $R - W/4$ formula to obtain raw scores on the *Preliminary Scholastic Aptitude Test* (PSAT), *Scholastic Aptitude Test* (SAT), and *Graduate Record Examination* (GRE), which are all composed of five-option multiple-choice items. Negative SAT scores can result if an examinee's "true" ability on the SAT is near 0; the score he will obtain may (if he marks many items) depart by chance from 0 in either direction.

Most students grossly overestimate the role of chance on multiple-choice tests. Unless a test contains very few items, it is virtually impossible to receive a satisfactory score by chance alone. Suppose many students have absolutely no knowledge of the material on a 100-item test on which each item contains only two options (perhaps T-F). They choose one option for each item entirely by chance. The righthand distribution, curve 2 of Figure 6-1, shows various scores that would result. The average score is 50 out of 100 (that is, 50 percent) correct by chance alone, because one-half of 100 is 50 (the mean chance score). The standard deviation of the scores is approximately 5 (see footnote, p. 116). About two-thirds of scores group themselves in a rather narrow (50 ± 5) range on both sides of this most likely score of 50. A score above 60 correct could be expected to occur by chance about as frequently as would a score below 40 correct—for about 2 percent of the examinees' trials. For 98 students in 100

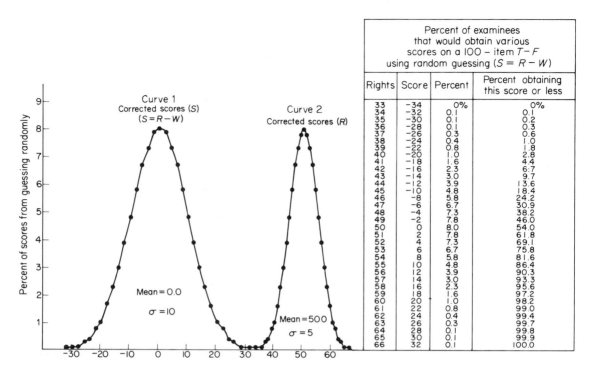

	Percent of examinees that would obtain various scores on a 100 – item $T-F$ using random guessing ($S = R - W$)		
Rights	Score	Percent	Percent obtaining this score or less
33	−34	0%	0%
34	−32	0.1	0.1
35	−30	0.1	0.2
36	−28	0.1	0.3
37	−26	0.3	0.6
38	−24	0.4	1.0
39	−22	0.8	1.8
40	−20	1.0	2.8
41	−18	1.6	4.4
42	−16	2.3	6.7
43	−14	3.0	9.7
44	−12	3.9	13.6
45	−10	4.8	18.4
46	−8	5.8	24.2
47	−6	6.7	30.9
48	−4	7.3	38.2
49	−2	7.8	46.0
50	0	8.0	54.0
51	2	7.8	61.8
52	4	7.3	69.1
53	6	6.7	75.8
54	8	5.8	81.6
55	10	4.8	86.4
56	12	3.9	90.3
57	14	3.0	93.3
58	16	2.3	95.6
59	18	1.6	97.2
60	20	1.0	98.2
61	22	0.8	99.0
62	24	0.4	99.4
63	26	0.3	99.7
64	28	0.1	99.8
65	30	0.1	99.9
66	32	0.1	100.0

FIGURE 6–1 *Frequency distributions of corrected-for-chance scores ($S = R - W$) (curve 1) and of number-right scores (curve 2) resulting from guessing answers to test of 100 two-choice items.*

the scores will occur in the range of 40 to 60 correct answers as shown. The most probable individual score is 50, which would be obtained by 8 percent of a large group of guessers. There is less than one chance in three million that an examinee would select the correct answer on 75 or more of the 100 items by chance alone! Only about one examinee in a thousand would score 65 or higher by chance alone.

Notice what happens to the range of chance scores when the correction-for-guessing formula (in this case $R - W$) is applied (curve 1). The most probable no-information score appropriately becomes 0. Also possible, though less probable, are scores lower than −20 or higher than +20; each of these has a probability of approximately .01 (one in a hundred). Ninety-eight times in 100 the student's score will occur within the range of −23 to +23, with a most probable individual score of 0. The figure shows graphically two important results of applying the correction for guessing to chance scores even when no omissions occur: (1) the average chance score is reduced to 0, and (2) the variability of possible scores is doubled. The standard deviation of the "number-right" distribution when there are no omissions is 5. The standard deviation of a corrected-for-chance distribution is $[k/(k − 1)]\sigma$ or, in this illustration, 2σ or 10.

Although guessing may produce variations among the scores, one should not pay serious attention to the beaming student who insists that he "guessed his

way" to a high score on a long test (even on one composed of two-option items).
The probability is great that he approached the items with considerable knowledge or test-wiseness, although he may not have been aware of it (unless
the test was poorly constructed, in which case test-wiseness could be an important factor).

In summary, the correction for chance may have some slight advantage over
"rights only" scoring. The correction is especially useful when tests are difficult
or speeded, situations in which the speed-vs.-accuracy and gambling response
styles are operative. However, as Mollenkopf (1960) suggested, it is only fair
to inform the examinees that such *a correction is not a penalty* because, as we
documented earlier, it usually undercorrects. Of course, if an examinee is more
*mis*informed than partially knowledgeable, his score may be unduly lowered
by the correction. For example, a person who believes that "separate" is spelled
"seperate" will choose that distracter deliberately but be penalized $-1/(k-1)$
points for "guessing."

Confidence Scoring　　　　Another approach designed to remove the
consequences of guessing (first proposed by Soderquist, 1936) asks students to
indicate how certain they were of the correctness of their answers. Students
received more credit for answers given with confidence than for those of which
they were uncertain. The penalty for an incorrect response rated as highly
confident was greater than for one rated uncertain. Soderquist found that confidence scoring yielded slightly higher test reliability than did conventional
scoring. Interest in Soderquist's approach has been revived by several investigators who have also found higher test reliability with confidence scoring
(Armstrong and Mooney, 1969; Ebel, 1965a; J. J. Michael, 1968a). The effects
of confidence scoring on test validity are much less certain, although the
available evidence is disappointing (Hopkins, Hakstian, and Hopkins, 1973).

It seems likely that the increase in reliability that results from confidence
scoring may be due to its encouraging a reliable response style of gambling or
"bravado" (i.e., examinee rates his choices with high confidence). Consequently,
the procedure offers no clear advantages at the present time.[3]

SOME CONCLUSIONS REGARDING
RESPONSE SETS

1. Response styles are reliable. They tend to show consistency from test
to test and from item to item, which may allow their effects to contribute
to increased test reliability even though validity may or may not be
affected.
2. Knowledge of response sets can be used to improve teacher-constructed
tests. For example, the tendency to use too many "true" items can be
eliminated in order to increase test validity. Liberal or generous time
limits can be established to minimize effects from the speed-vs.-accuracy
set. Special directions can reduce the role of the gambling set.
3. Response sets, if unchecked, can reduce the validity of test scores. An
ability assessment should be as free as possible from personality factors.

[3] See Stanley and Wang (1970) and Wang and Stanley (1970) for a review of research
on other scoring strategies.

147

*Psychological
and Cultural
Factors that
Influence
Performance on
Cognitive Tests*

4. The need for control of response sets is greatest with difficult and speeded tests. When an examinee does not know the answer to an item, he can make a guess, skip the item, or spend more time trying to find a solution. Appropriate directions, time limits, and scoring procedures can reduce possible contaminating effects from response styles.

Administrative Factors

A number of miscellaneous variables associated with the administration of a test have been explored.

MODE OF ADMINISTRATION

Several studies have shown that tests administered via television (Burr, 1963; Curtis and Kropp, 1961; Fargo et al., 1967) or overhead projector (Schwarz, 1967) yield results comparable to those obtained on conventionally administered tests, provided that speed is not a factor, and when other conditions are held constant.

EXAMINER

Masling (1959) found only slight effects of a hostile and a congenial tester on the results obtained from an individual adult intelligence test. Under certain conditions the sex or race of the examiner has resulted in some small differences (Abramson, 1969; Stevenson, 1961). The teacher can be a significant variable in the administration of standardized tests (Hopkins, Lefever, and Hopkins, 1967); when teachers administered standardized achievement tests, the grade equivalents of pupils averaged .2 years higher than when the test administration was controlled via TV. Goodwin (1966) also found that classes in which the teacher administered the test averaged .2 grade placements higher than when an outsider administered the tests.

To reduce possible contamination from administration error, some current tests offer recorded directions that control time and other relevant factors; these should reduce the effects of errors in test administration. In many instances the validity of scores on standardized tests has been reduced by errors in administration such as extending the time limits, giving nonstandardized directions about guessing, or even more flagrant deviations from the standard procedure.

PREANNOUNCEMENT

Little is known about the potential effects of informing students of a forthcoming *standardized* test. A study conducted in Japan showed that the announcement resulted in slightly higher scores (Hashimoto, 1959). Goodwin (1966), however, found no significant difference between groups that received a preannouncement and groups that did not. If the scores are to be unambiguously interpreted, the procedures that are used in obtaining test norms should also be followed when the tests are administered in the schools.

Although many test publishers give the user the option of marking in the test booklet or on a separate answer sheet, the separate answer sheets cause more difficulty on timed tests (Whitcomb, 1958), especially for low-ability students (Clark, 1968). In several studies it has been found that college students perform equally well on the new 1230, 85, and mark-sense cards and answer sheets (Dizney, Merrifield, and Davis, 1966; Hayward, 1967; Slater, 1964). Differences among three answer-sheet formats (805, 1230, and Digitek) were found, however, for fourth-grade children, especially boys (Hayward, 1967).

SCORING

Unless examinees are given explicit directions and follow them carefully, substantial errors in machine-scored tests can result (Burack, 1961; Durost, 1954). Teacher scoring is likely to result in even more errors. Phillips and Weathers (1958) found that 28 percent of approximately 5,000 *Stanford Achievement Tests* scored by fifty-one teachers contained errors. The most frequent errors were an incorrect counting of marks (45 percent) and a failure to follow directions (26 percent). Goodwin (1966) did not find that clerks were significantly more accurate in test scoring than were teachers. Whenever it is practical, tests should be machine-scored, and they should be administered only after special directions about marking and erasures have been given to pupils.

DISTURBANCE

An interesting study by Super, Braasch, and Shay (1947) explored the effects that a combination of various disruptions had on test performance. One random group of graduate students took a standardized intelligence test under normal conditions. While another random group took the same test, the following sequence of prearranged events occurred:

1. While marking the answer to the third question, one student deliberately broke her pencil point with a loud snap. She made a mild exclamation as she dropped the pencil, slid her chair back with a scraping noise, got up and walked ostentatiously to the examiner to get another pencil.
2. At the end of the fourth minute two persons walked down the stairs from the fourth floor; they were arguing loudly about a suggested ban of the Communist Party. The discussion near the door lasted for about one minute. The examiner had placed himself on the far side of the room so he would arrive at the door at about the time the two persons were ready to walk away.
3. At the end of ten minutes, a trumpeter played six bars of "Home Sweet Home," faltered, recovered, and then finished the melody. The trumpeter gave the impression that the melody was being played by a novice. The inclusion of musical distractions was not incongruent because music students used nearby rooms for practice.

4. At the beginning of the test, the examiner set the timer to ring at fifteen instead of twenty minutes. When the bell rang, the examiner picked up the timer, looked at it, looked at his stopwatch, and announced "Go on with the test."

Despite these irregularities, the disrupted group's mean score was not significantly lower than that of the control group. Similar findings with college students were reported by Ingle and de Amino (1969). It is unlikely, however, that younger examinees would possess the powers of concentration necessary to maintain their composure under such circumstances.

Several factors such as time of day, physical conditions (lighting, temperature, and so on), and number of tests per day have been essentially unexplored. The safest procedure for administering standardized tests is to approximate norming conditions as closely as possible (although often, unfortunately, many details concerning the norming procedure are not reported in test manuals). These administrative factors are much less important on teacher-made tests because norms are not involved.

Cultural Influences on Test Scores

An examinee's test score reflects all the experiences the individual has had from conception to time of testing, including the effects of the particular genes he inherited. Genetic potential interacts with environmental stimulation or lack of it to produce a person who scores high, average, or low on a particular test at a particular time.

There are no "culture-*free*" tests that measure only genetic potential. A child at age five or even much younger has been exposed to so many strong environmental influences that most "innate" abilities have probably been overlaid and modified considerably. Even his speed of tapping or his eye-blink frequency is likely to be different from what it would have developed into in a quite different environment (including nutrition and medical care).

Even if culture-free tests could not be devised, early measurement specialists hoped that culture-*fair* ones might be. Is it fair to expect a child living among uneducated people to understand the meaning of words such as "sonata" and "flaunt" as well as will a child of the same age whose parents are college graduates? Will not the former child be able to compete better if concepts more common to both cultures are used?

Despite its desirability, attempts to produce an intelligence test in which "culturally disadvantaged" persons perform as well as those from enriched backgrounds have been largely unsuccessful. A long, major study at the University of Chicago at midcentury (Eells et al., 1951) resulted in a specially designed test, the *Davis-Eells Test of General Intelligence or Problem-Solving Ability*, which did not reduce the difference among the means of the separate socioeconomic groups from that reflected in the usual intelligence tests (Ludlow, 1956). Later results with other tests have been similar. (See Cleary and Hilton, 1968, for an example.) Youngsters from educationally unstimulating environments tend, on the average, to have more poorly developed intellectual abilities than do youngsters from stimulating environments. The difference is noticeable during preschool years and tends to increase thereafter. Of course, there are some high-scoring examinees in the less-privileged groups and some low-scoring ones among the children of well-educated parents, even though their *means* differ considerably.

For many years there has been much discussion about the extent to which culturally disadvantaged persons, especially blacks, tend to score low on intelligence tests because of genetic factors. The "nature versus nurture" argument continues to rage in the United States and elsewhere. If you have plenty of time and much energy, study the pros and cons in Jensen (1969) and subsequent commentaries in the *Harvard Educational Review* and the *Review of Educational Research*. Also see Stein and Susser (1970).

It seems clear that *within* Caucasian groups intelligence-test ability is rather strongly, but by no means completely, a function of heredity. No study of the heritability of intelligence within a black population had been published at the time this volume went to press.[4]

Culturally disadvantaged groups tend to score low on measures of academic aptitude; they also tend to make poor grades. This is not surprising, because most of the abilities needed to score well on such tests are also required to achieve well in class. Cleary (1968), Hills and Stanley (1970), Kendrick and Thomas (1970), Stanley and Porter (1967), Thomas and Stanley (1969), Stanley (1971a), and others have shown that academic-aptitude test scores predict the college grades of blacks at least as well as they predict the grades of whites. Analogous results have been secured in at least one employment situation (ETS, 1969) and one military application (Gordon, 1953).

Someone *might* construct tests that do not discriminate among socioeconomic classes but that do predict academic achievement well; however, the many rather fruitless efforts thus far make this seem unlikely unless a fundamentally different method of measuring academic aptitude is discovered.[5]

The United States Employment Service has taken steps to improve the assessment of culturally disadvantaged applicants—experimenting with novel tests, improved test-orientation and practice, development of nonreading forms of existing tests, and so on (Jurgensen, 1966).

Tests are not the enemies of the culturally disadvantaged. As Anastasi (1968, p. 563) stated, "When social stereotypes and prejudice may distort interpersonal evaluation, tests provide a safeguard against favoritism and arbitrary and capricious decisions." J. A. Fishman et al. (1964, p. 139) in "Guidelines for testing minority group children" also commented: "Without the intervention of standardized tests, many such [bright, nonconforming, and culturally handi-

[4] The heredity-environmental correlates of IQ scores are considered more extensively in Chapter 14.
[5] The reader may have read reports of a widely disseminated study by Rosenthal and Jacobson (1968), in which experimenter-induced teacher expectancies are purported to have resulted in significant gains in IQ scores in certain students. The interested reader should consult critical reviews of the study (Snow, 1969; R. L. Thorndike, 1968) which raise some serious questions regarding its validity. At least four subsequent attempts to generate a related effect have not been successful (Fleming and Anttonen, 1970; Gozali and Meyer, 1970; Haberman, 1970; José and Cody, 1971).

capped] children would be stigmatized by the adverse subjective ratings of teachers who tend to reward conformist behavior of middle-class character."

Tests should be used as an aid in understanding pupils. No responsible person should fail to take into consideration a student's background in making an interpretation of a test score. The fact that undernourished children weigh less than those who are well fed hardly builds a case to eliminate scales.[6]

Post-organizer

Many irrelevant factors can influence test performance. Test-wiseness can be a factor; it is especially influential on poorly constructed tests and for examinees unfamiliar with objective tests. The practice effect is greatest on speeded tests; however, it seldom accounts for more than $.2\sigma$ improvement. Coaching produces small gains in performance (usually less than $.2\sigma$); larger gains may result if the examinee has not had recent contact with the test content. Most effects of practice and coaching are temporary; they dissipate after a few months.

The response styles of gambling and speed-vs.-accuracy can have a major effect on test scores, especially on speeded tests or on very difficult tests. Response sets tend to be stable personality characteristics. The correction for chance can be valuable when the nature of the correction is carefully explained. Administrative factors usually have only minor influence on test performance. Standardized instructions and procedures must be followed explicitly if results are to be interpreted in terms of the published norms.

IMPORTANT TERMS AND CONCEPTS

maximum performance
typical performance
test sophistication
response styles
    speed-vs.-accuracy
    acquiescence
    positional preference

correction for guessing
confidence scoring
culture-fair test

SUGGESTED READINGS

ANASTASI, A. 1964. Culture-fair testing. *Educational Horizons*, **43**: 26–30. Reprinted in G. H. Bracht, K. D. Hopkins, and J. C. Stanley. 1972. *Perspectives in educational and psychological measurement.* Englewood Cliffs, N.J.: Prentice-Hall, Inc., Chap. 20.

[6] For further discussions of related issues, see Fishman et al. (1964) and Millman and Pauk (1970).

————. 1968. Social implications of psychological testing. Chapter 21 in *Psychological testing*, 3d ed. New York: The Macmillan Company.

CLEARY, T. A. 1968. Test bias: Prediction of grades of Negro and white students in integrated colleges. *Journal of Educational Measurement*, **5**: 115–124.

———— and T. L. HILTON. 1968. An investigation of item bias. *Educational and Psychological Measurement*, **28**: 61–75.

CLEMANS, W. V. 1971. Test administration. In R. L. Thorndike, ed., *Educational measurement*, 2d ed. Washington, D.C.: American Council on Education, Chap. 6.

COLLEGE ENTRANCE EXAMINATION BOARD. 1968. *Effects of coaching on Scholastic Aptitude Test scores*. New York: CEEB.

CRONBACH, L. J. 1946. Response sets and test validity. *Educational and Psychological Measurement*, **6**: 475–494.

————. 1950. Further evidence on response sets and test design. *Educational and Psychological Measurement*, **10**: 3–31.

EDUCATIONAL TESTING SERVICE. 1966. Are aptitude tests unfair to Negroes? ETS investigates two kinds of "Bias." *Educational Testing Service Developments* **14** (1): 1–4.

EDUCATIONAL TESTING SERVICE. 1969. Bias in selection tests and criteria studies by ETS and U.S. Civil Service. *ETS Developments*, **17**: 2.

    This is a brief summary of ongoing research by J. T. Campbell, F. R. Evans, R. L. Flaugher, M. H. Mahoney, L. Norris, L. W. Pike, and D. A. Rock of the Educational Testing Service, Princeton, N.J.

FRENCH, J. W. 1963. Effect of anxiety on verbal and mathematical examination scores. *Educational and Psychological Measurement*, **22**: 553–564.

FRENCH, J. W., and R. E. DEAR. 1959. Effect of coaching on an aptitude test. *Educational and Psychological Measurement*, **19** (3): 319–330.

HILLS, J. R., and J. C. STANLEY. 1970. Easier test improves, prediction of Black students' college grades. *Journal of Negro Education*, **39**, 320–324. Reprinted in G. H. Bracht, K. D. Hopkins, and J. C. Stanley. 1972. *Perspectives in educational and psychological measurement*. Englewood Cliffs, N.J.: Prentice-Hall, Inc., Selection 11.

HOPKINS, K. D. 1964. Extrinsic reliability: Estimating and attenuating variance from response styles, chance, and other irrelevant sources. *Educational and Psychological Measurement*, **24**: 271–281. Reprinted in G. H. Bracht, K. D. Hopkins, and J. C. Stanley. 1972. *Perspectives in educational and psychological measurement*. Englewood Cliffs, N.J.: Prentice-Hall, Inc., Selection 10.

JENSEN, A. R. 1968. Another look at culture-fair testing. In Thomas A. Shellhammer (chairman), Measures for educational planning. *Seventeenth annual western regional conference on testing problems*. Princeton, N.J.: ETS, pp. 50–104.

————. 1969. How much can we boost IQ and scholastic achievement? *Harvard Educational Review*, **39**: 1–123. Reprinted in G. H. Bracht, K. D. Hopkins, and J. C. Stanley. 1972. *Perspectives in educational and psychological measurement*. Englewood Cliffs, N.J.: Prentice-Hall, Inc., Selection 19.

KENDRICK, S. A., and C. L. THOMAS. 1970. Education for socially disadvantaged children: Transition from school to college. *Review of Educational Research*, **40**: 151–179.

KREIT, L. H. 1968. The effects of test-taking practice on pupil test performance. *American Educational Research Journal*, **5**: 616–625.

LUDLOW, H. G. 1956. Some recent research on the Davis-Eells Games. *School and Society*, **84**: 146–148.

LYMAN, H. B. 1968. *How to take a test.* New York: McGraw-Hill Book Company. tape recording (♯75488, 21 minutes).

MILLMAN, J., C. H. BISHOP, and R. EBEL. 1965. An analysis of test-wiseness. *Educational and Psychological Measurement*, **25**: 707–726.

MILLMAN, J., and W. PAUK. 1969. *How to take tests.* New York: McGraw-Hill Book Company, 176 pp.

NUNNALLY, J. C. 1967. Contingent variables. Chapter 15 in *Psychometric theory.* New York: McGraw-Hill Book Company.

STANLEY, J. C., 1971. Predicting college success of the educationally disadvantaged. *Science*, **171**: 640–647.

STEIN, Z., and M. SUSSER. 1970. Mutability of intelligence and epidemiology of mild mental retardation. *Review of Educational Research*, **40**: 29–67.

SUPER, D. E., W. F. BRAASCH, and J. B. SHAY. 1947. The effects of distractions on test results. *Journal of Educational Psychology*, **38**: 373–377.

THOMAS, C. L., and J. C. STANLEY. 1969. Effectiveness of high school grades for predicting college grades of black students: A review and discussion. *Journal of Educational Measurement*, **6**: 203–215.

7

A BRIEF HISTORY OF
EDUCATIONAL MEASUREMENT

Measurement and evaluation have played a far more prominent role in human history than is generally recognized. The historical origins of testing and measurement are lost in antiquity. There was an elaborate system of civil service examinations in China several centuries before Christ (DuBois, 1966). Testing was a part of the normal educational process of the ancient Greeks (Chauncey and Dobbin, 1963). The Socratic method involves the skillful interspersing of instruction with oral testing. Some of the earliest records of the use of various testing devices are found in the Bible, although they generally have no reference to education. One illustration will suffice:

> And the Gileadites took the passages of Jordan before the Ephraimites: and it was so, that when those Ephraimites which were escaped said, Let me go over; that the men of Gilead said unto him, Art thou an Ephraimite? If he said, Nay; Then said they unto him, Say now Shibboleth: and he said Sibboleth: for he could not frame to pronounce it right. Then they took him, and slew him at the passages of Jordan: and there fell at that time of the Ephraimites forty and two thousand.[1]

Here indeed is an old "final examination," though in a field other than education. Today's measurement experts no doubt would point out that, in spite of its high degree of objectivity, it had certain questionable features: it was oral, it was very short, and the "mortality rate" was excessively high!

The sole test of a man's being a Gileadite was his using the *h* sound in the word *Shibboleth*. It was a one-question test that yielded for each examinee

---

[1] Judges, 12: 5–6, King James Version.

a score of "right" or "wrong," and the consequences of failing the exam were rather extreme. It is possible, however, that other paths might have been taken if the Gileadites had held different attitudes toward the Ephraimites, which illustrates that measurement is always a means to an end but never an end in itself. The uses made of measurement always depend on the broader contexts of the of values, goals, and purposes of the measurers. The Gileadites seem to have been satisfied with their examination, although a modern-day tester would have his doubts. Isn't it possible that some true Gileadites failed and some true Ephraimites passed? Isn't it possible that an examiner might have made a wrong judgment on the basis of only one question? These are questions touching the principles of test validity and reliability.

In education, some form of measurement is inevitable; it is inherent in the teaching-learning process. Consider the constant evaluative role of the classroom teacher as he attempts to determine the degree of scholastic and social status and the growth of pupils that will help him make hundreds of major and minor educational decisions each year. Measuring devices are indispensable to the teacher, the guidance counselor, the school administrator, the curriculum planner, and the professional researcher.

Early Scientific Measurement in American Education

Oral questioning dates back to the beginnings of human language. Socrates (469?–399 B.C.) used it effectively to "draw out" his students, as many good teachers do today, but it is important to distinguish between the instructional value of an activity and its evaluation merits. A spelling "bee" may be useful as a motivation technique, but its measurement merits are few. Until the availability of inexpensive pencils and paper after the middle of the nineteenth century, oral examinations were standard in American schools. Some countries by law still require oral final examinations (Stanley, 1960a). American universities harbor vestiges of this in the form of "thesis orals."

A job interview often is nothing more than an oral test that assesses an applicant's cognitive and affective characteristics. From time to time, oral-quiz "giveaway" programs appear on radio and television, though the contestants are often chosen in advance for their proficiency on written tests. Not until the latter half of the past century did writing instruments largely replace glib or faltering tongues as a basis for educational decisions.

The first important steps toward the scientific use of measurement in education were taken by Horace Mann (1845) more than a century ago. This prominent New England educator, famous for his doctrine of free, compulsory, and universal education, had a remarkable understanding of the importance of examinations and of the limitations of the ones then being used. His penetrating analysis of the weakness of the oral examinations then in vogue and of the superiority of written examinations can hardly be improved by today's specialist in educational measurement. Mann showed clearly where oral examinations were lacking; he used the concepts that have become the cornerstones of today's theories, and which are now known as validity, reliability, and usability. (These concepts were discussed in Chapters 4 and 5.)

Another American educator who understood both the value and the limitations of examinations was Emerson E. White, educational writer and school administrator. He wrote, "It may be stated as a general fact that school instruction and study are never much wider or better than the tests by which they are measured" (E. E. White, 1886). In the same volume he enumerated several "special advantages" of the written test:

> It is more impartial than the oral test, since it gives all the pupils the same tests and an equal opportunity to meet them; its results are more tangible and reliable; it discloses more accurately the comparative progress of the different pupils, information of value to the teacher; it reveals more clearly defects in teaching and study, and thus assists in their correction; it emphasizes more distinctly the importance of accuracy and fullness in the expression of knowledge . . . ; it is at least an equal test of the thought-power or intelligence of pupils . . . [pp. 197–198].

These views of Mann and White seem surprisingly modern; they show how far general practice is apt to lag behind the theory of the pioneer thinker. Even though measurement specialists now tend to shy away from the early enthusiasm for the ordinary written test, pointing out that many of the cited limitations of oral tests also hold in some degree for certain written tests, the best thinkers of yesteryear were often far ahead of many educators today.

The actual improvement of existing tests and other measuring instruments has always lagged far behind theory, and school practice has been the farthest behind of all. Despite the marked superiority of written examinations over oral ones, which Mann pointed out in 1845, in some cases teachers have not moved either to adopt the former or to improve the latter. It is interesting to note, however, that by 1864 an enterprising English schoolmaster, the Reverend George Fisher, had proposed the widespread use of objective and standardized measures of academic attainment. Reverend Fisher outlined the practice of the new system in his school as follows:

> A book, called the "Scale-Book," has been established, which contains the numbers assigned to each degree of proficiency in the various subjects of examination: for instance, if it be required to determine the numerical equivalent corresponding to any specimen of "writing," a comparison is made with various standard specimens, which are arranged in this book in order of merit; the highest being represented by the number 1, and the lowest by 5, and the intermediate values by affixing to these numbers the fractions $\frac{1}{4}$, $\frac{1}{2}$, or $\frac{3}{4}$. So long as these standard specimens are preserved in the institution, so long will constant numerical values for proficiency in "writing" be maintained. And since facsimiles can be multipled without limit, the same principle might be generally adopted.
>
> The numeral values for "spelling" follow the same order, and are made to depend upon the percentage of mistakes in writing from dictation sentences from works selected for the purpose, examples of which are contained in the "Scale-Book," in order to preserve the same standard of difficulty.
>
> By a similar process, values are assigned for proficiency in mathematics, navigation, Scripture knowledge, grammar, and composition, French, general history, drawing, and practical science, respectively. Questions in each of these

subjects are contained in the "Scale-Book," to serve as types, not only of the difficulty, but of the nature of the question, for the sake of future reference . . . [Chadwick, 1864].

Apparently, Fisher was too far advanced for his times, since his incisive work seems not to have attracted a widespread audience. As Leonard P. Ayres (1918) expressed it, "progress in the scientific study of education was not possible until people could be brought to realize that human behavior was susceptible of quantitative study, and until they had statistical methods with which to carry on their investigations."

Although Ayres felt that the statistical contributions of Sir Francis Galton had largely met these two needs, he credited Joseph M. Rice with being the "real inventor of the comparative test." A young American physician turned zealous researcher, Rice had studied pedagogy in Germany and had been influenced by experimental psychologists at the Universities of Leipzig and Jena. His great concern for the quality of contemporary education prompted him to conduct two large studies of spelling achievement in various U.S. cities. In each study, he administered his own specially constructed tests to all students under uniform conditions. The volume of his purely personal delving is awesome even in this day of mass research; he secured test results on 13,000 children under his own direction and on 16,000 more by mail, his researches spanning 16 months and 21 cities (Rice, 1897). Though of course this first approach to test standardization is inferior to modern practice, it promoted Rice's aim of making education more scientific.

The conclusion to the first article by Rice (1897, p. 172) on the results of his investigations sets forth the value of what we now call "norms": "Whether or not the spelling in a particular locality is actually below the average can be learned only by comparing the results of an examination conducted *on the same basis* in many localities. By examining children in any one city on a set of arbitrarily selected words, the question cannot be solved, because the results in other places on the same list of words would remain an unknown quantity. A common standard is offered, however, by a . . . test such as I have undertaken" (italics added). How obvious that statement is to us now, but how radical it was then!

Rice was much more than just a tester; he was a pioneer in what later came to be known as progressive education. He was, during the years 1891–1899, a relentless investigator of American education. He published a series of 20 articles in the *Forum*, a leading literary magazine. The educational leaders of the time were anything but cordial to him, and for many years little progress was made beyond Rice's own work.[2]

STUDIES OF THE UNRELIABILITY OF SCHOOL MARKS AND TESTS

Only in the last half-century or so have techniques been developed to increase the objectivity in the assessment of school achievement. We have already sketched some of the scientific and practical concerns that established the

---

[2] See Cremin (1961), Chaps. 1 and 5, and Stanley (1966) for a more extensive treatment of Rice's effect on educational change.

intellectual climate for a tremendous blossoming of educational measurement. But good arguments in favor of new methods do not always assure the adoption of those methods—the inadequacy of existing methods must first be shown. The development and use of standard tests was greatly spurred on by a series of studies begun after the turn of the nineteenth century. These studies clearly documented the questionable status of the forms of educational measurement then in use.

Course marks proceed directly from some forms of measurement by the teacher. Sometimes the measurement procedures are explicit, but a mark often may be the result of a tacit and subjective value scale peculiar to the particular teacher or department. The need for reform in college marking was forcefully brought to the attention of the public by Professor Max Meyer (1908), an experimental psychologist educated at the University of Berlin. Meyer reported on the marks assigned by 40 teachers during a five-year period at the University of Missouri. He found such astonishing variations as 55 percent of A's in philosophy and only 1 percent in Chemistry III, while there were 28 percent of failures in English II and none in Latin I. Franklin Johnson (1911) found a similar situation at the University of Chicago High School, where he was the principal; in a two-year period the marks in German showed 17.1 percent A's and 8.4 percent F's, whereas the marks in English showed 6.5 percent A's and 15.5 percent F's. Even when the ability differences of the various groups were allowed for, more of this inconsistency in marking was cause by varying marking severity than by varying subject difficulty. In short, school marks appeared to be highly subjective and arbitrary; the mark assigned often seemed to be more a function of the *personality of the instructor* than of the *performance of the student*. Without exception, further studies conducted elsewhere showed similar results. The findings were certainly disturbing, if not, as E. L. Thorndike (1922) suggested, actually "scandalous."

The evidence presented by later studies was even more damaging. Although the departmental variations in grading could be partially accounted for by variations in the background, intelligence, and application of the students in those departments, such factors clearly could not be responsible for differences when several persons were marking the same student's paper and, least of all, when the same person marked the same paper on two different occasions. Many convincing studies revealed great variability of marks under both conditions.

Perhaps the most striking of the early investigations were those of Daniel Starch, a pioneering applied psychologist. In one of these studies Starch and Edward Elliott (1913) analyzed facsimiles of the same geometry paper marked independently by 116 high-school teachers of mathematics. The grades given ranged from a low of 28 per cent to a high of 92. If high-school teachers could not agree any more closely in mathematics, supposedly one of the most objective subjects, the situation was indeed poor.

Later studies confirmed the early findings. In one of the most spectacular studies (Falls, 1928), 100 English teachers were asked to mark a composition and to indicate the grade level in which they would expect to find that quality of work. The percentage values (see Table 7–1) varied from 60 to 98, averaging about 87 percent, and the estimated grade location varied from the fifth grade

TABLE 7–1

The Estimated Grade-Value and Percentage Marks
Assigned to an English Composition by 100 Teachers

Estimated Grade-Level	Percentage Mark								
	60–64	65–69	70–74	75–79	80–84	85–89	90–94	95–99	Total
Coll. Jr.								2	2
Coll. So.									0
Coll. Fr.							1	2	3
12th					1		2	3	6
11th			2			6	5	2	15
10th			1	3	8	4	7	1	24
9th	1		1	1	8	4	4	3	22
8th			2	2	2	3	4	3	16
7th				2	2	2	1		7
6th	1				1	1		1	4
5th	1								1
Total	3		6	8	22	20	24	17	100

SOURCE: After Falls (1928).

to the junior year of college, averaging about the beginning of the tenth grade. The composition used was the best one found by a survey committee at Gary, Indiana, and was written by a high-school senior whose special interest was journalism and who was already a correspondent for some of the Chicago newspapers. It seems reasonable to suppose that many of these English teachers would seldom, if ever, have as good a composition submitted by one of their own pupils. Yet the typical one of these teachers considered it "B" quality for the tenth grade!

Starch (1913) also presented the problem in a different and even more un-favorable light. He found that college instructors assigned different marks when they *regraded their own papers* without knowing what marks they had formerly assigned to those papers. Later, Ashbaugh (1924) had 49 college seniors and graduate students, the latter with teaching experience, rate a seventh-grade arithmetic paper on a percentage basis three times, at intervals of four weeks between ratings. The lack of consistency in scoring can be appreciated when it is mentioned that only one of the 49 students gave the same total score on all three trials and only seven gave the same total score on any two successive trials. The average variation between pairs of scores on successive trials was 8.1 points between the first and second trials, and 7.3 points between the second and third trials. These are *averages*. Many of the markers had considerably larger discrepancies.

In a similar study, Hulten (1925) found that 28 experienced high-school English teachers differed widely, after an interval of two months, in their grading of an English composition which they believed was written by an eighth-grade pupil, but which actually was part of a new and still unfamiliar standard composition scale. He found that 15 teachers who gave passing marks the first time failed the paper the second time, and that 11 teachers who gave failing marks the first time passed the paper the second time. Studies involving English composition are especially significant because an essay examination is a series of

160

compositions; and when English teachers who presumably have more than ordinary skill in this field can find only limited agreement both with others, and with themselves in a second trial, a more refined technique is needed.

The History of Modern Achievement Tests

Ayers credited Rice with the invention of educational measurement, but he awarded the title "father of the educational testing movement" to Edward L. Thorndike. During his distinguished and prolific career at Columbia University's Teachers College, Thorndike was concerned with many phases of the measurement movement. In addition to his very influential publications on statistical methods in education and his pioneer work on intelligence tests, Thorndike and his students were responsible for nearly all of the early standard achievement tests and scales. The modern achievement-testing movement was initiated in 1904 when Thorndike published the first textbook on educational measurement. In 1910 the Thorndike Handwriting Scale (E. L. Thorndike, 1910) was published—the first of its kind. It consisted of formal writing samples of children in grades five through eight; the samples were arranged in an equal-unit, 15-category scale of increasing quality (see Figure 7–1), in much the manner suggested 46 years earlier by the Reverend Fisher (Chadwick, 1864).

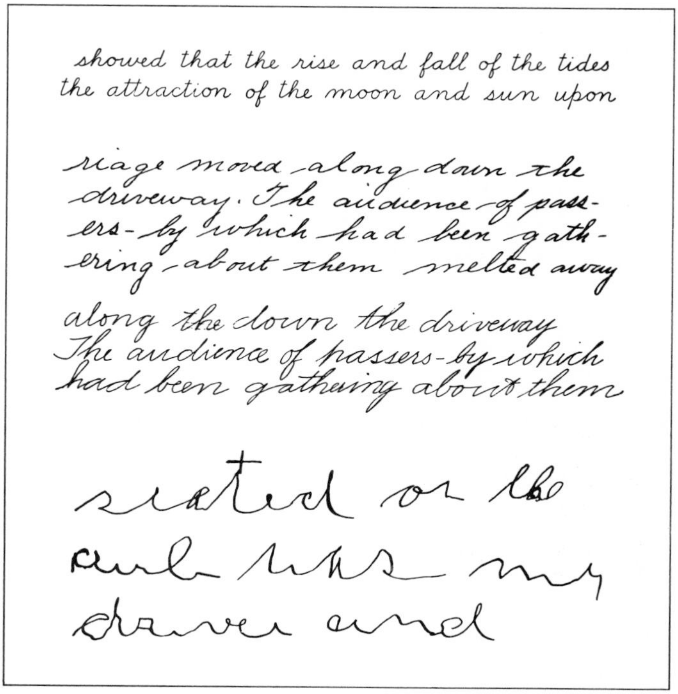

FIGURE 7–1 *Excellent, average, and poor handwriting. (Reproduced from E. L. Thorndike, Handwriting [New York: Bureau of Publications, Teachers College, Columbia University, 1910], by permission of Teachers College Press.)*

C. W. Stone (1908) conducted his dissertation research on elementary-school arithmetic with instruments that evolved into a portion of "Stone's Standard Tests" (J. C. Stone, 1922). A section from an early derivative of the Stone test is reproduced in Figure 7–2.

COURTIS STANDARD RESEARCH TESTS

Arithmetic   Test No. 1   Addition

Series B   Form 1

SCORE

No. Attempted_____

No. Right_____

You will be given eight minutes to find the answers to as many of these addition examples as possible. Write the answers on this paper directly underneath the examples. You are not expected to be able to do them all. You will be marked for both speed and accuracy, but it is more important to have your answers right than to try a great many examples.

927	297	136	486	384	176	277	837
379	925	340	765	477	783	445	882
756	473	988	524	881	697	682	959
837	983	386	140	266	200	594	603
924	315	353	812	679	366	481	118
110	661	904	466	241	851	778	781
854	794	547	355	796	535	849	756
965	177	192	834	850	323	157	222
344	124	439	567	733	229	953	525
537	664	634	572	226	351	428	862
695	278	168	253	880	788	975	159
471	345	717	948	663	705	450	383
913	921	142	529	819	174	194	451
564	787	449	936	779	426	666	938
932	646	453	223	123	649	742	433
559	433	924	358	333	755	295	599
106	464	659	676	996	140	187	172
228	449	432	122	303	246	281	152
677	223	186	275	432	634	547	588
464	878	478	521	876	327	197	256
234	682	927	854	571	327	685	719
718	399	516	939	917	394	678	524
838	904	923	582	749	807	456	969
293	353	553	566	495	169	393	761
423	419	216	936	250	491	525	113
955	756	669	472	833	885	240	449
519	314	409	264	318	403	152	122

FIGURE 7–2 *A speed test of arithmetic, composed of exceedingly homogeneous items and published in 1913. (Reproduced from the Courtis Standard Research Tests [1913] by permission of Stuart A. Courtis.)*

The decade before 1920 represented a period of slow but substantial development of printed, objectively scored, and standardized instruments for achievement testing in a number of subject areas. The major problems facing the early test-makers were not so much those of theory and technique as of gaining a more favorable opinion among educators as to the value of standardized measuring instruments. The outlook of those early educational psychologists who championed the use of precise measurement in education was expressed by Thorndike (1918, p. 16) in a now classic paper:

Whatever exists at all exists in some amount. To know it thoroughly involves knowing its quantity as well as its quality. Education is concerned with changes in human beings; a change is a difference between two conditions; each of these conditions is known to us only by the products produced by it—things made, words spoken, acts performed, and the like. To measure any of these products means to define its amount in some way so that competent persons will know how large it is, better than they would without measurement. To measure a product well means so to define its amount that competent persons will know how large it is, with some precision, and that this knowledge will be conveniently recorded and used.

Large-scale testing was first done in the City of New York Survey, 1911–1913, and soon afterward in other large cities (Scates, 1947). In 1915 the National Educational Research Association was founded. Among its constitutional goals was the "promotion of the practical use of educational measurement in all educational research" and, by 1918, a substantial bibliography of tests and test-oriented research had appeared (Bryner, 1918). Monroe (1945), an effective promoter of educational research, saw 1920 as marking the "beginning of the widespread use of objective tests in American schools." By the end of that decade more than 1300 tests were available to teachers and researchers (W.W. Cook, 1952, p. 1461). Investigators became less concerned with stressing scoring objectivity; they concentrated more on developing the wider range of item forms needed for tests of higher mental abilities. The true-false item form may have been objective, but usually it required little more than rote memorization by the pupil. For educators interested in measuring such abilities as understanding, comprehension, and critical analysis, new types of item had to be developed. For the first time, questions were raised as to the reliability and validity of the standard tests: Is this test a consistent measure of a student's knowledge of arithmetic, or will his score fluctuate greatly? Does this test adequately cover the subject matter presented by the teacher? Are the scores obtained in accord with the teacher's own judgments? New statistical methods and research techniques had to be designed to help answer such questions.

In the 1920's a number of textbooks were published that supplemented or replaced E. L. Thorndike's (1904) original *Introduction to the Theory of Mental and Social Measurements*. Teachers were urged to construct their own achievement examinations for subject areas not covered by published and standardized tests. W.A. McCall (1920) was among the first to suggest that classroom teachers should use the so-called "new-type" examination, and, in effect, that they should adopt the objective measurement principles of the professional. Those were days of consolidation, extension, and innovation in achievement testing. The first comprehensive battery of standardized tests, the *Stanford Achievement Tests*, was published in 1923.

In the 1930's, educational measurement passed from adolescence into maturity (Monroe, 1945, p. 340). The number of tests developed, standardized, and published increased tremendously. Organizations such as the Cooperative Test Service were established to supply, administer, and score achievement tests. By 1940, over 2,600 achievement tests were available (Cook, 1952, p. 1461) for all the traditional subject areas—reading, mathematics, science, and language—and for such areas as health, commerce, aeronautics, and engineering

(Woodruff and Pritchard, 1949). J.P. Guilford's *Psychometric Methods* (1936) had a widespread impact on the attention given to technical and theoretical aspects of testing. Evidence that educational measurement was coming of age is found in the extensive bibliographies of tests and scales that appeared in this decade; the outstanding volumes are listed in Buros' *Mental Measurements Yearbook* series (1936–1972), which offers timely catalogs of published tests with expert critiques and extensive research bibliographies. The *MMY*'s (the most recent of which is the Seventh, published in 1972) are invaluable reference books.

The first machine for the scoring of answer sheets, the IBM 805, was developed in 1935. This machine facilitated greater use of item analysis in test development. It was superseded by the optical test-scoring equipment developed by E. F. Lindquist at the University of Iowa that became operational in 1955. [3]

Educational measurement specialists began to think differently in the thirties. Lindquist, later to become one of the country's outstanding leaders in measurement, warned (1935, p. 519) that "it is . . . important that the *limitations* of present measuring instruments be more adequately recognized. Even the best of the tests now being provided fall far short of measuring all of the desirable outcomes of instruction in any field of subject matter." Reports of the famed Eight Year Study, under the auspices of the Progressive Education Association (Smith and Tyler, 1942), similarly declared that educational measurement had overemphasized the testing of limited areas of knowledge and skills and had excluded other important educational objectives. Tyler pointed out that educational objectives must ultimately be conceived of as changes in pupil behavior patterns and that adequate "evaluation" of pupil progress requires devices capable of measuring broad areas of learning. Accordingly, these investigators showed how assessment procedures could be developed to measure the attainment of such objectives as critical thinking, social sensitivity, aesthetic appreciation, and personal and social adjustment.

The so-called "pupil evaluation movement" is exemplified in the work of Lindquist and Tyler, who became quite prominent; it had a profound influence on educational measurement. It not only indicated that existing testing devices neglected significant realms of student behavior, but it led to more adequate assessment of higher mental processes, such as application and analysis, and broad areas of intellectual skills and learnings, such as interests and attitudes.

World War II, like World War I, stimulated the further development of rigorous measurement practices, not only through the demands of military classification, but also because the war unified many research efforts under the auspices of the government. Construction of all the College Entrance Examination Board examinations, some of which were inaugurated at the beginning of the twentieth century, was taken over by the Educational Testing Service in 1947. ETS is responsible for many important examinations used in selection, such as the *Scholastic Aptitude Test* (SAT), CEEB achievement tests, the

---

[3] For a more extensive treatment of scoring machines, materials, and procedure, see Baker (1971).

Graduate Record Examination (GRE), *Medical College Admission Tests* (MCAT), *Law School Admission Test* (LSAT), the Advanced Placement Testing Program, and the College-Level Examination Program. ETS was responsible for the development of the *Sequential Test of Educational Progress* (STEP), a "battery" of tests designed to measure achievement in several broad areas at various levels from grade 4 through the sophomore year of college. This followed the tradition of the well-known *Stanford Achievement Tests, Metropolitan Achievement Tests, Iowa Every Pupil Tests*, and *California Achievement Tests*, which have been revised periodically.

From 1932 until 1969, a summary of research on educational measurement was published in a three-year cycle in the *Review of Educational Research*. Since World War II, measurement specialists have worked to increase the precision and usefulness of their instruments and to improve educational and psychological measurement theory. The momentum toward rigorously scientific methods was increased by the founding of two quarterly professional journals in the late thirties and early forties: *Psychometrika*, "devoted to the development of psychology as a quantitative rational science," and *Educational and Psychological Measurement*, "devoted to the development and application of measures of individual differences." In 1956 Bloom's *Taxonomy* was published, having an important impact on the quality of items on objective tests. This taxonomy receives extensive treatment in Chapter 8. A related taxonomy of the affective domain published in 1964 (Krathwohl et al., 1964) stimulated efforts toward measuring pupil attitudes and interests, as well as cognitive skills.

In 1940 the National Council on Measurement in Education (NCME) was founded "to promote a greater understanding and improved use of measurement techniques in education." In 1955 the *Technical Recommendations for Achievement Tests* was produced by NCME and AERA (American Educational Research Association). This document had an important impact on the standards to be employed on published tests. A revision of this document was produced by NCME, AERA, and APA (American Psychological Association). It gives the newer criteria by which published tests should be evaluated (APA, 1966).

In 1964 NCME began publishing the *Journal of Educational Measurement*, which soon became a leading quarterly. In 1969 the American Personnel and Guidance Association (APGA) began to publish a journal devoted exclusively to measurement techniques and problems in guidance, *Measurement and Evaluation in Guidance*.

THE NATIONAL MERIT SCHOLARSHIP PROGRAM

In 1955, under the auspices of the National Merit Scholarship Corporation, a program was initiated to provide scholarship aid for talented college-age youth. Each year all secondary schools in the United States and its territories are invited to identify able pupils to take the Preliminary Scholastic Aptitude Test, which measures both verbal and quantitative abilities. On the basis of these results semifinalists are named, who then take the SAT. These results, along with other relevant data—recommendations, past school performance, non-academic activities, and so on—are employed to award scholarships in each state roughly proportional to the number of high-school graduates in that state.

PROJECT TALENT

In 1959 a large-scale, long-range educational measurement project was initiated to determine the best methods for "the identification, development, and utilization of human talents" (Flanagan et al., 1962); this has become known as Project TALENT. In 1960 some 440,000 students in more than 1,300 secondary schools in all parts of the country took 23 aptitude and achievement tests plus five other inventories. These students are being followed longitudinally to ascertain the types of ability that are associated with success and failure in various careers. See Flanagan et al. (1962), Flanagan and Cooley (1966), and publications by the American Institutes for Research

NATIONAL ASSESSMENT OF
EDUCATIONAL PROGRESS (NAEP)

The U.S. Office of Education was formed "for the purpose of collecting such statistics and facts as shall show the condition and progress of education in the several States . . . and of diffusing such information"—Act of Congress, March 2, 1867. Despite that century-old charge, the Federal Government has collected few meaningful facts on the quality of education in U.S. schools.

In 1964 the Carnegie Corporation and the Ford Foundation were instrumental in the establishment of a committee under the chairmanship of Ralph W. Tyler to explore the feasibility of procedures for securing dependable information that could become a barometer of the progress of education. The committee developed a careful plan to assess achievement at four age levels: 9, following the primary grades; 13, following elementary school; 17, the last age before heavy dropout from school occurs; and young adults. Public, private, and parochial schools are sampled, as well as youth not in school at all. Not only are the achievements of the total U.S. population considered, but certain subpopulations in the country can be viewed separately. The sample of 20,000 to 30,000 persons at each age level is broken down by sex, region of the country (northeast, southeast, central, and west), type of community (large city, urban fringe, smaller city, and rural small town), and socioeconomic level. The sampling plan is such that no single student is likely to encounter more than a single hour of testing.

Ten areas (reading, writing, science, mathematics, social studies, citizenship, literature, art, music, and vocational education) are to be covered by means of a cycling approach calling for exercises from three or four subjects each year and then return to each subject-matter field every three to five years.

Results of the tests are not pinpointed by class, school district, or states to prevent any invidious comparisons and pressures to "teach for the tests." Misunderstandings about the use of the findings resulted in considerable controversy during the developmental stages of the National Assessment Program, but now the program has received widespread acceptance by professional educators and laymen alike.

In 1970 the first exercises in three subject areas—science, writing, and citizenship—were administered with more than 95 percent cooperation rate from the schools. Two illustrative items with corresponding findings are given below (from NAEP, 1970, pp. 1–2):

A. Does the President have the right to do anything affecting the United States that he wants to do?
☐   Yes (Go to B)
☐   No (Go to C)

B. (If "Yes") Why?

C. (If "No") Why not?

Nationally, the correct answer ("No" to A) was given by 49 percent of the 9-year-olds in the National Assessment sample, 73 percent of the 13s, 78 percent of the 17s, and 89 percent of the adults. The correct response and at least one acceptable reason why were given by 18 percent of the 9s in the sample, 53 percent of the 13s, 68 percent of the 17s, and 80 percent of the adults.

Examples of responses scored acceptable were: people could stop him; elected officials could stop him; checks and balances system of government; laws stop him; country would be a dictatorship; not the democratic way.

A science exercise asked:

Whenever scientists carefully measure any quantity many times, they expect that
☐   **A.** all of the measurements will be exactly the same.
☐   **B.** only two of the measurements will be exactly the same.
☐   **C.** all but one of the measurements will be exactly the same.
☐   **D.** most of the measurements will be close but not exactly the same.
☐   **X.** I don't know.

Nationally, the correct response (D) was selected by 69 percent of the 13s, 72 percent of the 17s, and 57 percent of the adults. Nineteen percent or more of all the respondents chose the incorrect response, "all of the measurements will be exactly the same."

The assessment reporting plan calls for the withholding of part of the exercises in each subject area so that they may be reused in the next assessment cycle for purposes of comparison. The National Assessment Program promises "to provide useful indicators of educational progress."

The concerns of today's specialist in educational measurement are many. Continued efforts are being made to develop and standardize new and more efficient achievement tests, to carry on research concerned with their reliability and validity, and to develop new statistical procedures for use in test construction and data analysis. The measurement of abilities and achievements is a vast topic. We hope that this volume will add to your understanding of it.

The appraisal of educational achievement in the United States relied primarily upon oral examinations until about 1850. Written tests, which allowed all students to answer the same questions, largely replaced the oral examinations during the latter half of the nineteenth century. The development of quantitative and statistical methods stimulated research designed to improve educational appraisal. Standardized and objective tests began to be developed shortly after the turn of the nineteenth century. Objective tests have largely replaced essay tests as selective measures for college admission, since they tend to have greater reliability and predictive validity. They are widely used in the National Merit Program, Project TALENT, and the National Assessment of Educational Progress. Figure 7–3 presents a historical timeline of major events in the recent history of educational measurement.

IMPORTANT PROJECTS AND ORGANIZATIONS

Mental Measurements Yearbooks (MMY's)
National Council on Measurement in Education (NCME)

National Merit Program
Project TALENT
National Assessment of Educational Progress

SUGGESTED READINGS

AYRES, L. P. 1918. History and present status of educational measurements. *Seventeenth yearbook of the National Society for the Study of Education, Part II.* Bloomington, Ill.: Public School Publishing Company, p. 10.

CHAUNCEY, H., and J. E. DOBBIN. 1963. Testing has a history. Chapter 1 in *Testing: Its place in education today.* New York: Harper & Row, Publishers.

COLEMAN, W. E. 1969. History of achievement tests. In R. L. Ebel, ed., *Encyclopedia of educational research*, 4th ed., pp. 8–9.

COOK, W. W. 1952. Achievement tests. *Encyclopedia of educational research*, rev. ed. New York: The Macmillan Company, p. 1461.

CREMIN, L. A. 1961. *The transformation of the school.* New York: Alfred A. Knopf.
    A lucid treatment of educational change, including measurement, during the period 1876–1957.

CURETON, L. W. 1971. The history of grading practices. NCME *Measurement in Education*, **2**, No. 4 (May), pp 1–8.

DuBois, P. H. 1970. *A history of psychological testing.* Boston: Allyn and Bacon Inc.

———. 1966. A test-dominated society: China, 1115 B.C.–A.D. 1905. In A. Anastasi, ed., *Testing problems in perspective.* Washington, D.C.: American Council on Education, pp. 29–38.

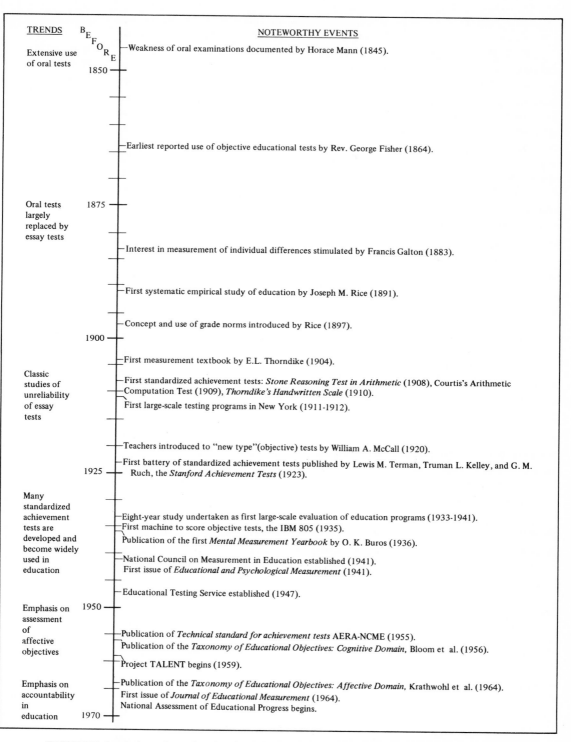

TRENDS   B
    E
     F
      O
       R
        E   NOTEWORTHY EVENTS

Extensive use   ──Weakness of oral examinations documented by Horace Mann (1845).
of oral tests

1850 ──

──Earliest reported use of objective educational tests by Rev. George Fisher (1864).

Oral tests   1875 ──
largely
replaced by
essay tests

──Interest in measurement of individual differences stimulated by Francis Galton (1883).

──First systematic empirical study of education by Joseph M. Rice (1891).

──Concept and use of grade norms introduced by Rice (1897).

1900 ──

──First measurement textbook by E.L. Thorndike (1904).

Classic   ──First standardized achievement tests: *Stone Reasoning Test in Arithmetic* (1908), Courtis's Arithmetic
studies of   ──Computation Test (1909), *Thorndike's Handwritten Scale* (1910).
unreliability   First large-scale testing programs in New York (1911-1912).
of essay
tests

──Teachers introduced to "new type"(objective) tests by William A. McCall (1920).
──First battery of standardized achievement tests published by Lewis M. Terman, Truman L. Kelley, and G. M.
1925 ── Ruch, the *Stanford Achievement Tests* (1923).

Many
standardized
achievement   ──Eight-year study undertaken as first large-scale evaluation of education programs (1933-1941).
tests are   ──First machine to score objective tests, the IBM 805 (1935).
developed and   Publication of the first *Mental Measurement Yearbook* by O. K. Buros (1936).
become widely
used in   ──National Council on Measurement in Education established (1941).
education   First issue of *Educational and Psychological Measurement* (1941).

──Educational Testing Service established (1947).

Emphasis on   1950 ──
assessment
of
affective   ──Publication of *Technical standard for achievement tests* AERA-NCME (1955).
objectives   Publication of the *Taxonomy of Educational Objectives: Cognitive Domain*, Bloom et al. (1956).

               Project TALENT begins (1959).

Emphasis on   ──Publication of the *Taxonomy of Educational Objectives: Affective Domain*, Krathwohl et al. (1964).
accountability   First issue of *Journal of Educational Measurement* (1964).
in   National Assessment of Educational Progress begins.
education   1970 ──

**FIGURE 7–3 A chronology of major events in the history of educational measurement. (*Information drawn
primarily from Kelley [1927], Chauncey and Dobbin [1963], and DuBois [1970].*)**

169

EBEL, R. L., and D. E. DAMRIN. 1960. Tests and examinations. In C. W. Harris, ed., *Encyclopedia of educational research*, 3d ed. New York: The Macmillan Company, pp. 1502–1517.

KATZMAN, M. T., and R. S. ROSEN. 1970. The science and politics of national assessment. *The Record*, May, **70**: 571–586.

LESSINGER L. M. 1970. Accountability in public education. *Proceedings of the 1969 invitational conference on testing problems*. Princeton, N.J.: Educational Testing Service, pp. 109–111. Reprinted in G. H. Bracht, K. D. Hopkins, and J. C. Stanley. 1972. *Perspectives in educational and psychological measurement*. Englewood Cliffs, N.J.: Prentice-Hall, Inc., Selections 26 and 27.

LINDEN, K. W., and J. D. LINDEN. 1968. *Modern mental measurement: A Historical perspective*. Boston: Houghton Mifflin.

LINDQUIST, E. F. 1968. *The impact of machines on educational measurement*. Bloomington, Ind.: Phi Delta Kappa, Inc.

McCALL, W. A. 1920. A new kind of school examination. *Journal of Educational Research*, **1**: 33–46.

MONROE, W. S. 1945. Educational measurement in 1920 and 1945. *Journal of Educational Research*, **38**: 334–340.

ROBERTSON, G. J. n.d. Innovation in the assessment of individual differences: Development of the first group mental ability test. *Normline*, **1**(2). New York: Harcourt Brace Jovanovich, Inc. Reprinted in G. H. Bracht, K. D. Hopkins, and J. C. Stanley. 1972. *Perspectives in educational and psychological measurement*. Englewood Cliffs, N.J.: Prentice-Hall, Inc., Selection 18.

ROBINSON, D. 1970. National assessment assessed: General optimism, but doubts linger on. *Phi Delta Kappan*, **52**(1): 67–68.

SAYLOR, G. 1970. National Assessment: Pro and con. *The Record*, May, **70**: 588–597.

SCATES, D. E. 1947. Fifty years of objective measurement and research in education. *Journal of Educational Research*, **41**: 241–264.

THORNDIKE, E. L. 1918. The nature of purposes, and general methods of measurements of educational products. *Seventeenth yearbook of the National Society for the Study of Education, Part II*. Bloomington, Ill.: Public School, Publishing Company, p. 16.

TESTING: toward national assessment. 1967. *Time Magazine*. January 27, p. 61.

WOMER, F. B. 1970. *What is National Assessment?* Ann Arbor, Mich.: National Assessment of Educational Progress. Reprinted in G. H. Bracht, K. D. Hopkins, and J. C. Stanley. 1972. *Perspectives in educational and psychological measurement*. Englewood Cliffs, N.J.: Prentice-Hall, Inc., Selection 3.

WOODRUFF, A. D., and M. W. PRITCHARD. 1949. Some trends in the development of psychological tests. *Educational and Psychological Measurement*, **9**: 105–108.

GENERAL PRINCIPLES OF TEST CONSTRUCTION: COGNITIVE DOMAIN

There are important reasons teachers must become proficient in constructing classroom tests. They develop most of the tests they use. In the hands of an untrained teacher, essay and objective tests will usually produce unsatisfactory results. The volume of writing on essay examinations has repeatedly demonstrated this fact. Novices often do worse with an objective test than with an essay examination; it is possible to make objective tests of even lower reliability than essay examinations (Stalnaker, 1951). Finally, logical considerations and research have shown that skillfully prepared informal tests can be as reliable as some standardized tests, and often more valid for a particular class or student. Standardized tests rarely assess the objectives for a particular unit of instruction. Standardized tests tend to be focused upon broad, general objectives that cover a wide range of content because they are usually designed primarily to assess a full year of instruction. A teacher needs to evaluate frequently so he can identify the specific learning difficulties of individual children and of the class as a whole. Periodic testing is also needed to permit more valid reporting of pupil progress, a topic receiving attention in Chapter 13.

In this chapter we consider the general principles of constructing informal tests; the following are four essential steps: (1) planning the test; (2) preparing the test; (3) trying out the test; and (4) evaluating the test.

Planning the Test

Constructing a satisfactory test is one of the hardest jobs a teacher has to perform; good tests do not just happen. Test construction remains largely an art rather than a science, but there are well-established, valid principles of test development that are all too frequently unknown or ignored. The process of constructing a *good* test item is deliberate and time-consuming; it demands an understanding of the objectives being assessed and of the examinees and their test-taking behavior.

If a test is to be successful, careful planning must precede its construction. One must consider the objectives to be measured, the purpose the scores are to serve, and the conditions under which testing will occur. The following four rules should be followed:

1. Adequate provision should be made for evaluating all the important outcomes of instruction.
2. The test should reflect the approximate typical emphasis in the course.
3. The nature of the test should reflect its purpose.
4. The nature of the test should reflect the conditions under which it will be administered.

EDUCATIONAL OBJECTIVES

In Figure 1–1 (p. 6) we illustrated the interrelationships among roles of objectives, instruction, and evaluation in the total educational process. The objectives should give direction to the curricular methods and content. The evaluator seeks to ascertain the degree to which the objectives have been attained, both collectively and individually. The results of the evaluation thus provide feedback that may suggest modification of either the objectives or the instruction or both. For example, for a group taking a communications skills course, Bird (1953) found no significant improvement in listening comprehension, which was one of the important objectives of the course. With careful assessment, a course's unfulfilled "promises" can be discovered.

Historically, objectives have been stated as broad, ultimate goals. One of the earliest statements of educational objectives is the Yale report of 1830, which emphasized the importance of exercising the mental functions of "reasoning," "imagination," "taste," and "memory" (Ammons, 1969). The "Seven Cardinal Principles of Secondary Education" from 1918 are generally accepted today: good health, command of fundamental processes, worthy home membership, vocational efficiency, good citizenship, worthy use of leisure time, and ethical character. The same can be said for the four objectives of education formulated in 1938 by the Educational Policies Commission (EPC) of the National Education Association: self-realization, human relationship, economic efficiency, and civic responsibility.

The Educational Policies Commission (1961, pp. 4, 5) stresses "the central role of the rational powers" and devises its own categories:

The cultivated powers of the free mind have always been basic in achieving freedom. The powers of the free mind are many. In addition to the rational powers, there are those which relate to the aesthetic, the moral, and the religious. There is a unique, central role for the rational powers of an individual, however, for upon them depends his ability to achieve his personal goals and to fulfill his obligations to society.

These powers involve the processes of recalling and imagining, classifying and generalizing, comparing and evaluating, analyzing and synthesizing, and deducing and inferring. These processes enable one to apply logic and the available evidence to his ideas, attitudes, and actions, and to pursue better whatever goals he may have.

These ultimate aims are too vague to give focused direction to curriculum development. In addition, they cannot possibly be realized or assessed until long after formal education has been concluded. It is therefore necessary to establish intermediate objectives that are logically derived from and related to these accepted ultimate objectives (Lindquist, 1951, Krathwohl and Payne, 1971). Whenever possible, these intermediate objectives should be stated in terms of student behavior that can be observed or measured.

Adequate Provision Should Be Made for Evaluating All the Important Outcomes of Instruction From the start, a precise statement of the objectives of the school and of the particular course should be available. Most courses of study contain some statement of objectives, but, to be helpful in teaching and testing, they should be stated as specifically as possible. The expected *pupil behaviors* that exemplify the sought-after objectives must be stated. Such commonly offered objectives as "good citizenship" and "an integrated personality" are of little *practical* value. Educational goals must be stated in more precise and observable form to give direction to the important tasks of curriculum development and evaluation.

Teachers at all levels of education too often instruct and evaluate without giving careful thought to the educational objectives. The objectives are frequently undefined and vague (Ammons, 1969). Without critical, periodic reexamination, a course is likely to drift "off target." Boersma (1967) found that teachers who were systematically involved in applying evaluative criteria had a clearer perception of the curriculum. Bloom (1961) noted that when teachers participated in the construction of tests in a systematic way, not only were the objectives clarified, but more relevant instruction also occurred.

Armed with a clear and specific list of teaching objectives, a teacher may consider the most appropriate procedures for evaluating progress made towards each objective. He attempts to test what he has tried to teach by using techniques best suited to determine how well each objective is attained.

TAXONOMY OF OBJECTIVES

An important forward step in providing a framework within which educational objectives could be organized and measured was the publication of *The Taxonomy of Educational Objectives* by Bloom, Engelhart, Furst, Hill, and Krathwohl (1956). They classified instructional objectives into what they call three major "domains"—*cognitive*, *affective*, and *psychomotor*. Handbooks for the classification of the first two domains have been produced (Bloom et al., 1956; Krathwohl et al., 1964).

The cognitive domain includes those objectives that deal with the recall or recognition of learned material and the development of intellectual abilities and skills. This domain is the core of much current curriculum and test development. The clearest definitions of objectives for the cognitive domain are phrased as descriptions of desired student behavior—that is, in terms of knowledge, understanding, and abilities to be acquired. The largest proportion of educational objectives fall into the cognitive domain (Krathwohl et al., 1964, p. 6). The affective domain includes objectives that emphasize interests, attitudes, and values, and the development of appreciations and adequate adjustment. "Objectives in this domain are not stated very precisely; and, in fact, teachers do not appear to be very clear about the learning experiences which are appropriate to these objectives" (Bloom et al., 1956, p. 7). Chapter 12 deals with the evaluation of objectives in this domain. The psychomotor domain is concerned with physical, motor, or manipulative skills. Handwriting is an example of a common skill in the psychomotor domain.

The taxonomy of objectives in the cognitive domain has had a major impact on the development of educational curricula and on the methods by which they are assessed. The taxonomy categorizes behavior into six hierarchical categories from simple to complex as illustrated in Figure 8–1. These six ascending levels are *knowledge, comprehension, application, analysis, synthesis,* and *evaluation.*

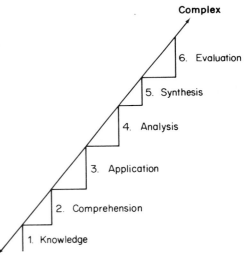

FIGURE 8–1 *An illustration of the six hierarchical levels of Bloom's taxonomy. (Adapted from B. S. Bloom et al.* **Taxonomy of Educational Objectives: Handbook I, The Cognitive Domain** [*New York: David McKay Company, Inc., 1956*], *by permission of David McKay Company, Inc. and Longman Group Ltd.*)

The rationale for the hierarchy is based upon the assumption that each level is an extension of all previous levels. For example, to attain an objective in the *application* category requires (in theory, at least) that certain comprehension goals were achieved, which in turn can be achieved only if certain information in the *knowledge* category is acquired. A rather sharp line is suggested in the taxonomy between "knowledge" and the five higher levels, which involve "intellectual abilities and skills" in addition to simple knowing. We shall discuss and illustrate each of the six levels briefly:

175

*General
Principles of
Test
Construction:
Cognitive
Domain*

Knowledge involves "the recall of specifics and universals, the recall of methods and procedures, or the recall of a pattern, structure, or setting. For measurement purposes, *the recall situation involves little more than bringing to mind the appropriate material....* The knowledge objectives emphasize most the psychological processes of *remembering....* To use an analogy, if one thinks of the mind as a file, the problem in a knowledge test situation is that of finding in the problem or task the appropriate signals, cues, and clues which will most effectively bring out whatever knowledge is filed or stored." Persons may have various kinds and levels of knowledge, from "knowledge of terminology," such as "familiarity with a large number of words in their common range of meanings," to "knowledge of theories and structures," such as "knowledge of a relatively complete formulation of the theory of evolution" (Bloom et al., 1956, pp. 201–204).

Examples of objectives within the knowledge category are the knowledge of specific facts, terminology, dates, persons. Below are two of many examples given by Bloom et al.[1] (1956, p. 79) of test items designed to measure an objective in the knowledge category.

1. The Monroe Doctrine was announced about ten years after the
   a) Revolutionary War.
   b) War of 1812.
   c) Civil War.
   d) Spanish-American War.

To answer the question requires no reasoning, only a simple knowledge of the date 1823 or knowledge that the event occurred after (b) but before (c).

2. If the volume of a given mass of gas is kept constant, the pressure may be diminished by
   a) reducing the temperature.
   b) raising the temperature.
   c) adding heat.
   d) decreasing the density.
   e) increasing the density.

The item requires only a knowledge of the relationship among pressure, volume, and temperature of gases as described by Boyle's and Charles' laws.

Although basic and essential, knowledge is not sufficient for *comprehension*, which represents the lowest level of understanding; translation, interpretation, and extrapolation are common behaviors at this taxonomy level. Comprehension is evidenced by "the care and accuracy with which the communication is paraphrased or rendered from one language or form of communication to another." Some instructional objectives at the comprehension level

---

[1] All items illustrating the various taxonomy levels are from *The taxonomy of educational objectives: Handbook I, Cognitive domain*, by B. S. Bloom et al., (New York: David McKay Company, Inc., 1956). Reprinted by permission of David McKay Company, Inc.

are "the ability to understand non-literal statements (metaphors, symbolism, irony, exaggeration)"; "skill in translating mathematical verbal material into symbolic statements and vice versa"; "the ability to grasp the thought of the work as a whole at any desired level of generality"; and "skill in predicting continuation of trends" (Bloom et al., 1956, pp. 204–205).

Here are two examples of items from the comprehension level (pp. 100, 104):

1. Which of the following represents the *best* definition of the term "protoplasm"?
   a) A complex colloidal system made up of water, proteins, and fats.
   b) Anything capable of growth by a regular progressive series of changes into a more complex unit.
   c) A complex mixture of proteins, fats, and carbohydrates, capable of responding to changes in its environment.
   d) A complex colloidal system of proteins, fats, carbohydrates, inorganic salts, and enzymes which manifests life.

The exercise requires the examinee to judge the "best" of the four definitions, which vary in correctness and completeness. Had three of the choices been totally incorrect, the item would be functioning only at the knowledge level of Bloom's taxonomy.

2. "Milton! thou shouldst be living at this hour: England hath need of thee; she is a fen of stagnant waters"—Wordsworth.
   The metaphor, "She is a fen of stagnant waters," indicates that Wordsworth felt that England was
   a) largely swampy land.
   b) in a state of turmoil and unrest.
   c) making no progress.
   d) in a generally corrupt condition.

The correct answer (c) requires the *translation* of one verbal form to another. If this question had been used directly in instruction, it would of course require only knowledge rather than comprehension skills.

The third taxonomy level is *application*, which requires not only comprehension (to know an abstraction well enough to use it correctly when required) but a step beyond this. Given an unfamiliar problem, the student must select and apply the appropriate abstraction. "The fact that most of what we learn is intended for application to problem situations in real life is an indication of the importance of application objectives in the curriculum. The effectiveness of a large part of the school program is therefore dependent upon how well the students carry over into situations applications which the students never faced in the learning process" (Bloom et al., 1956, p. 122).

Three illustrative objectives at the application level are: "the ability to relate principles of civil liberties and civil rights to current events"; "the ability to apply the laws of trigonometry to practical situations"; and "the ability to apply Mendel's laws of inheritance to experimental findings on plant genetic problems." Two illustrative test items at this level (p. 136) follow:

1. Suppose an elevator is descending with a constant acceleration of gravity "g." If a passenger attempts to throw a rubber ball upward, what will be the motion of the ball with respect to the elevator? The ball will
   a) remain fixed at the point the passenger releases it.
   b) rise to the top of the elevator and remain there.
   c) not rise at all, but will fall to the floor.
   d) rise, bounce off the ceiling, then move toward the floor at a constant speed.
   e) rise, bounce off the ceiling, then move toward the floor at an increasing speed.

2. If a person is planning to sunbathe, at what time of day is he most likely to receive a severe sunburn? *He is most likely to receive a severe sunburn in the middle of the day* (11 A.M. to 1 P.M.) because:
   a) We are slightly closer to the sun at noon than in the morning or afternoon.
   b) The noon sun will produce more "burn" than the morning or afternoon sun.
   c) When the sun's rays fall directly (straight down) on a surface, more energy is received by that surface than when the sun's rays fall obliquely on that surface.
   d) When the sun is directly overhead, the sun's rays pass through less absorbing atmosphere than when the sun is lower in the sky.
   e) The air is usually warmer at noon than at other times of the day.
   f) The ultraviolet of the sunlight is mainly responsible for sunburn.

The examples illustrate that a "parroting" of textbook definitions, and the like, would not be sufficient to enable the student to arrive at the correct answer in a fresh, applied setting.

Analysis is defined as "the breakdown of a communication into its constituent elements or parts such that the relative hierarchy of ideas is made clear and/or the relations between the ideas expressed are made explicit." Typical objectives at this level are: "skill in distinguishing facts from hypotheses"; "ability to recognize unstated assumptions"; and "ability to recognize the point of view or bias of a writer in a historical account" (Bloom et al., 1956, pp. 146–148). Illustrative analysis items are (pp. 158–159, 161):

A group of college students were discussing the relative merits of two grading systems. It had been suggested that only two grades be used: S (satisfactory) and U (unsatisfactory), instead of the A-B-C-D-F system then in use at the college. One student made the following statement:

"People go to college to learn, not just to get grades. Grades are no indication of absolute degree of learning, they are purely relative and then mostly determined by chance or probability (guessing, multiple-choice tests, etc.). The student is a better judge of how he is doing than the professor. Therefore, an S-U system would be better since it would cut down the amount of differentiation between grades and give a better picture of how the student is doing."

1. The conclusion depends fundamentally on the proposition that
   A. people do not go to college just to get grades.
   B. the student is the best judge of how he is doing.
   C. grades are very inaccurate indications of what students have learned.

D. one grading system is better than the other.

E. multiple-choice tests are used in determining grades.

178

*General
Principles of
Test
Construction:
Cognitive
Domain*

2. Which of the following statements is *least* essential as a part of the argument?

A. Grades are no indication of absolute degree of learning.

B. An S-U system would cut down the amount of differentiation between grades.

C. An S-U system would give a better picture of how the student is doing.

D. Grades are determined by chance or probability.

E. The student is a better judge of how he is doing than the professor.

The next two items are based on a composition that is played during the test.

3. The general structure of the composition is

A. theme and variations.

B. theme, development, restatement.

C. theme 1, development; theme 2, development.

D. introduction, theme, development.

4. The theme is carried essentially by

A. the strings.

B. the woodwinds.

C. the horns.

D. all in turn.

Synthesis involves "the putting together of elements and parts to form a whole . . . not clearly there before." Sample instructional objectives at this level are: "skill in writing, using an excellent organization of ideas and statements"; "ability to plan a unit of instruction for a particular teaching situation"; and "ability to formulate a theory of learning applicable to classroom teaching" (pp. 169–172). Examples of synthesis exercises are (p. 179):

1. Add three lines to complete this verse:
   "I saw old autumn in the misty morn."

2. Set a poem to music.

3. Here are some general findings comparing babies who have colic and those who do not. Formulate a theoretical explanation and at least one testable hypothesis derived from the theory.

Evaluation includes "the making of judgments about the value, for some purpose, of ideas, works, solutions, methods, materials, etc." Examples of this, the highest level of cognitive ability in the taxonomy, are: "the ability to indicate logical fallacies in arguments"; "the ability to evaluate health beliefs critically"; and "skills in recognizing and weighing values involved in alternative courses of action" (pp. 189–192). An example is (p. 200):

1. Jane is faced with the problem of selecting material for a school dress. The dress will receive lots of wear and will be laundered frequently. Which of the fabrics would be her best choice? (The test should include examples of fabrics. . . . This would allow more reasons to be given below.)
   Check the qualities the fabric you choose possesses which make it superior for Jane's purpose.

179

*General
Principles of
Test
Construction:
Cognitive
Domain*

_____ (a) Material is colorfast to washing
_____ (b) Material is crease resistant
_____ (c) There is little or no sizing in the material
_____ (d) Material is easily cared for
_____ (e) Weave is firm, close and smooth
_____ (f) Material is soft and will drape easily
_____ (g) Material is colorfast to sunlight
_____ (h) Material will not show soil easily
_____ (i) Design is *printed* with the grain

Many excellent examples can be found in two current paperbacks: *Classroom questions: What kinds?* (Sanders, 1966) and *Testing and evaluation for the sciences* (Hedges, 1966). Sanders provides an illustration of how a concept such as gerrymandering can be measured at each level of the taxonomy.

The taxonomy levels of analysis, synthesis, and evaluation have been of much less value for curriculum development and educational evaluation than those of the knowledge, comprehension, and application categories. There is nothing in the taxonomy per se to suggest that all good tests or evaluation measures will have items from every taxonomy level. The logic of the unitary underlying hierarchical continuum of complexity also is less compelling (J. J. Michael, 1968b) beyond the application level.

Research on the Taxonomy Rationale　　Krathwohl and Payne (1971) summarized the available research on the taxonomy of the cognitive domain and concluded that the rationale has been generally supported for the first three categories. Support for the order of the more complex categories has largely failed to develop. Experience with the taxonomy has demonstrated that it is very difficult to reliably distinguish many application items from those in the higher levels. Several investigators (McGuire, 1963; Kropp, Stoker, and Bashaw, 1966; Poole, 1969; Stanley and Bolton, 1957) have reported that persons frequently disagree on the taxonomy level represented by many items, except those at the knowledge level.

The principal contribution of the taxonomy has been its impact on the quality of educational measures. A teacher who has been exposed to the taxonomy, with illustrations of how higher mental processes can be objectively measured, can no longer be satisfied with a test that measures only rote learning of isolated facts. Much of the criticism of objective tests has arisen because many objective tests are of a very low quality and too often emphasize only the knowledge level of the taxonomy.

The *instructional value* that can result from examinations composed of items from the higher taxonomy levels was shown by Hunkins (1969). Sixth-grade students exposed to tests containing many items from the higher taxonomy levels performed equally well on the knowledge-type items on the final examination, but those students were significantly superior on items measuring higher-level instructional objectives.

For any course the particular objectives under each classification must be expressed in terms of the specific changes that the teacher is trying to bring about in the mental and physical behavior of pupils. A detailed statement of the particular facts, principles, concepts, and skills of the course is also required, as well as of the levels of cognition the pupils will be expected to employ. In questioning the pupils to see whether *comprehension* actually occurred, teachers must try to avoid using both the wording of the text and that of earlier class discussion. Otherwise, they will test only rote memory. Opportunities should be provided to apply the material learned to new problems and situations. The center of gravity is the mental activity of the pupils themselves. The teacher must not confuse ends and means. Many years ago a leading psychometrician, E. F. Lindquist (1944, p. 366), stated this point well: "The real ends of instruction are the *lasting* concepts, attitudes, skills, abilities and habits of thought, and the improved judgment or sense of values acquired; the detailed materials of instruction—the specific factual content—are to a large extent only a means toward these ends."

OTHER CLASSIFICATIONS

Bloom's six-level classification of the cognitive domain is not the only useful scheme available to us, though it is the most extensive attempt thus far. Ebel (1956) offered six ascending levels and attached to them "ideal" percentages he recommended for a good achievement test: content details, 0 percent; vocabulary, less than 20 percent; facts, less than 20 percent; generalizations, more than 10 percent; understanding, more than 10 percent; and applications, more than 10 percent.

In addition to the various schemes discussed above, J. J. Michael (1968b) suggested the structure of intellect proposed by Guilford as a comprehensive basis for achievement examinations. Scriven (1967) suggested a comprehensive system of educational objectives that encompasses cognitive, attitudinal, psychomotor, and social dimensions.

Why bother to use these classifications in constructing an achievement test? The chief reason is to insure the measurement of objectives higher than simple knowledge. The Educational Testing Service prepared a booklet, "ETS Builds a Test" (Katz, 1959), in which the grid method shown in Table 8–1 for constructing the National Teacher Examination in biology and general science was proposed. The rows consist of twelve subject-matter areas, the top five for general science and the other seven for biology. The nine columns define the different levels of cognitive abilities to be tested in each subject-matter area. Thus there are 108 (12 × 9) "cells" in the grid. The committee of science specialists preparing the test decides in advance how many questions of each kind should be included.

Specifications ("dimensions") for the Mathematics section of the College Entrance Examination Board's *Scholastic Aptitude Test* illustrate this systematic approach to test construction. They consist of seven classifications, with from two to six levels or types within each:

1. Content: (a) arithmetic or algebra, (b) geometry, (c) other;
2. Context of presentation: (a) unusual, (b), familiar;
3. Process for solution: (a) novel, (b) straightforward;
4. Type of thinking: (a) computation, (b) numerical judgment, (c) relational thinking, (d) other;

TABLE 8–1

Specifications for a Science Test

NTE — Biology and General Science — Item Distribution — SUBJECT MATTER	ABILITIES										TOTAL
	Understanding of basic scientific concepts and principles	Ability to distinguish basic concepts from those which are irrelevant or inappropriate	Ability to anticipate and diagnose concepts likely to prove easy or difficult for students	Ability to select and devise appropriate demonstrations for effective teaching	Ability to recognize and utilize appropriate sources of information	Ability to give a lucid explanation of scientific concepts and principles	Ability to apply scientific concepts and principles to everyday experience	Ability to evaluate student learning	Ability to stimulate and guide the individual student		
Chemistry											
Physics											
Astronomy											
Geology											
Meteorology											
Histology											
Botany											
Zoology											
Human anatomy and physiology											
Biology and human welfare											
Ecology											
Heredity and evol.											
TOTAL											

SOURCE: M. R. Katz, ed., *ETS builds a test* (Princeton, N.J.: Educational Testing Service, 1959). Reprinted by permission of the Educational testing Seruice.

5. Characteristics of data: (a) adequate, (b) excess, (c) question of sufficiency;
6. Form of presentation: (a) verbal, (b) tabular or graphic;
7. Difficulty: (six classifications from easy to hard).

If just one question of each kind were used, there would be $3 \times 2 \times 2 \times 4 \times 3 \times 2 \times 6 = 1,728$ items on the test. Actually, the SAT quantitative test usually has less than 4 percent of that number, so only some kinds can be represented. The committee might decide to include two questions dealing with **181** geometry, in an unusual context, requiring a straightforward process for solution, evoking a relational type of thinking, involving excess data, presented in graphic form, classified as "easy."

How, according to the above seven-point scheme, would you classify the following item (Educational Testing Service, 1960, p. 47, problem No. 60)?

> In which one of the following ways could 168 pencils be packaged for shipping?
> (A) 11 boxes with 18 pencils in each
> (B) 14 boxes with 12 pencils in each
> (C) 17 boxes with 14 pencils in each
> (D) 24 boxes with 12 pencils in each
> (E) 28 boxes with 11 pencils in each

One can readily see that there are many ways to classify educational objectives and test items; each way has its advantages and disadvantages. The simpler plans tend to be too general, but the more extensive plans are usually too complex to be used extensively by classroom teachers. No plan thus far proposed—not even the 207-page Bloom *Taxonomy* for the cognitive domain—fully covers all situations. Perhaps a reasonable compromise between completeness and usability is to blend the three-domain viewpoint (cognitive, affective, psychomotor) with the hierarchy for the cognitive domain: knowledge, comprehension, application, analysis, synthesis, and evaluation. Adding Guilford's distinction between convergent and divergent thinking[2] guards against the strong tendency to teach and test primarily at the rote-knowledge, undigested-fact level.

PLANNING A TEST FOR A TEACHING UNIT

Stanley (1960b) urged that a test on a teaching unit be cooperatively prepared by two or more teachers in the following way:

1. A team of teachers planning a teaching unit lists a complete set of *specific objectives*—that is, changes in the mental, physical, and affective behavior of the students that constitute the goals of instruction. Two or more teachers independently *classify the objectives* into Bloom's three domains: cognitive, affective, and psychomotor. Still working independently, they further classify the cognitive objectives according to some scheme such as Bloom's, Guilford's, Ebel's, or ETS's. Then they compare their classifications and try to reconcile differences.

Anyone who has tried knows how hard it is to write readily classifiable objectives. Many of these become so complex, grandiose, or vague that they can barely be classified in one of the three major domains, much less in one of the levels within a domain. Complex, general objectives should be used as major headings under which more specific, classifiable objectives may be

---

[2] Thinking is convergent when "the conclusion or other outcome is a unique one that is essentially determined by the information given . . . [Thinking is divergent when] the generated information can be varied or must be varied, alternative outcomes being not only possible but also sometimes demanded. . . . [C]onvergent thinking . . . converges upon the unique consequence. . . . [D]ivergent thinking . . . goes searching, changes route, and yields multiple answers. It is in the divergent-thinking category that we find the abilities most clearly associated with creative performance—fluency of thinking, flexibility of thinking, and originality" (Guilford, Fruchter, and Kelley, 1959, p. 28).

183

*General
Principles of
Test
Construction:
Cognitive
Domain*

grouped. Compound or multiple objectives should be rewritten as two or more objectives. Vague and grandiose objectives should either be brought down to earth or modified if they prove to be unassessable.

Relatively successful attempts to deal with educational objectives for observable and testable behavior have been made at the elementary-school level (Kearney, 1953), the secondary-school level (French, 1957), and the college level (H. Smith, 1955).

The key to good objectives is the verb that describes what the child will be able to do (R. D. Anderson, 1967). Words that have a discrete, definite meaning should be used rather than those open to many interpretations. The words "to identify," "to solve", or "to construct" are preferable to "to understand" and "to appreciate" (Mager, 1962). The phrase "to understand magnets" is vague, but the phrase "to know the kinds of materials that are attracted by magnets" gives clear direction to instruction and to evaluation (R. D. Anderson et al., 1970, Chap. 2).

Even though one has specifically defined educational objectives in terms of student behavior, classification will not necessarily be easy. Systems such as Bloom's *Taxonomy* fall far short of perfection; furthermore, the mental activity of classifying is itself rather high in the levels of the cognitive domain. It is certainly well beyond the rote-knowledge level. Close observation of what happens in classrooms, even at the graduate level, reveals that teaching and testing often occur to a considerable extent at the lowest level, rote knowledge, so students probably are not encouraged to use their minds enough at the higher levels. This seems least true in mathematics and the physical sciences, in which application and analysis must play a large part. This may partially explain the great attraction these fields have for bright youngsters.

A task even more difficult than obtaining classifiable objectives is that of listing all the objectives for a teaching unit. Even though presenting a unit may take only a few weeks' time, that unit will suggest an almost infinite number of immediate, intermediate, and "ultimate" goals. A teacher, however, will usually most concern himself only with those immediate objectives that will, in his experience, lead to important intermediate and ultimate objectives; attainment of these immediate objectives supposedly will show growth toward the more distant objectives. It is quite important that the teachers try to specify the changes in behavior—cognitive, affective, and psychomotor—that should result from the unit.

2. After stating and classifying objectives, the teachers *weight each objective according to its relative importance* by determining how much time and effort each one requires. Total unit time, including both class activities and homework, is set at 100 percent; each objective receives a percentage equivalent to its determined importance. (It may be helpful to reserve a percentage for such "lost motion" as the routine of washing laboratory equipment; making this stolen time explicit may increase teacher and student efficiency.)

3. Teachers work toward attainment of the objectives in ways deemed most likely to produce the desired changes in the students' behavior (whether mental, physical, or both). This is *the* crucial step, based firmly upon the prior stating, classifying, and weighting of objectives.

4. Teachers *devise evaluative procedures suitable for determining how well each objective has been attained by each pupil.* Ideally, these procedures will evaluate progress toward every stated objective, but will not confine attention to the cognitive domain. For simplicity and clarity, first consider only paper-and-pencil tests calling for cognitive responses. The items that comprise these tests should cover the cognitive objectives at the same levels as were originally specified for those objectives, if the teachers are to determine how well the objectives were attained.

In the plan of the unit, one must include time for enough evaluation to yield data adequate for assessing the achievement mastery of individual students. Reliable total scores may not be sufficient. Reliable subscores may also be needed to determine whether particular objectives have been attained adequately by each student. This is the diagnostic function of the test.

A teacher will often require complete mastery of certain objectives before permitting a student to attempt later material. Thus, the immediate outcome of evaluation may be remedial assignments—for example, to study lists of spelling words, basic vocabulary, chemical symbols, fundamental arithmetic operations—which usually fall into the *Taxonomy's* lowest level, *knowledge.* However, the balancing of unfamiliar chemical equations, which would be classified as application, could be treated similarly, since students might be required to be proficient in balancing easier equations before being allowed to proceed with more difficult ones.

Even when the teacher *does* succeed in writing test questions at what he considers to be the same cognitive level as the particular objective, there still remains the question of whether the items are actually tests of that objective and not of some other. Another teacher, working independently, can help by classifying the test items as to level and objective tested. This second teacher should also write test questions and have them classified by the first teacher. Such cross-classification serves three purposes: (a) to verify the objective of each item; (b) to determine that the items and the objectives are on the same level; and (c) to provide a wider variety of items testing the objective than one teacher would probably prepare, because each item writer tends to write certain types of item more frequently than others. Preparation of tests by teams of two or more teachers appears to be a desirable safeguard. Of course, often it is not possible to have a team develop a test. With a little carefully evaluated experience, a single teacher can produce a satisfactory test by following the same procedures.

The suggested steps for constructing achievement tests are:
1. List or consult teaching goals—that is, the instructional objectives.
2. Classify them according to domain and level by means of a systematic scheme.
3. Determine the relative importance of each objective.
4. Devise and prepare learning experiences that will accomplish the objectives.
5. Select evaluative procedures that are appropriate to the domains and levels of the objectives.

Appendix C shows how two mathematics teachers applied this procedure in a two-week introductory algebra unit. Because of the unit's introductory nature, none of their objectives were at the two highest levels, synthesis and evaluation. Of the 10 listed, 8 objectives are in the cognitive domain. Objectives 9 and 10 are affective: to develop a realization of the importance of algebra in the modern world and to create a friendly attitude toward mathematics. Notice that all 10 could have been subdivided and made to specify more fully the behaviors desired. For such a two-week unit, however, their 10 objectives would be adequate to guide teaching and testing.

It must be remembered that the *objectives of a course represent directions of progress rather than destinations to be arrived at by individual pupils at a particular time.* As far as possible, the progress of each pupil should be measured in terms of his own abilities, interests, and needs. How well this aim of the modern school is accomplished depends not only on the material resources available, but also on the educational philosophy and skill of the teaching staff.

The Test Should Reflect the Approximate Proportion of Emphasis in the Course Proper balance of question emphasis requires the outlining of a "job analysis" or "table of specifications"[3] that will guide the test-maker, just as blueprints and specifications guide the building contractor. It is valuable to indicate not only the various objectives in mind, but also, at least roughly, the relative amount of emphasis each objective has received in the actual teaching of the course. For example, the same test might not be equally valid for two teachers of a course in general science using the same textbook if the teachers are not pursuing common objectives. This would occur if one teacher emphasized the memorization of isolated facts, while the other stressed understanding of facts in relation to each other and in their application to practical problems. The test should be a faithful mirror of the instructional objectives reflected in the teaching emphasis. The amount of time devoted to the different phases of the course is usually a fair indication of their relative importance. The content of the test should show similar proportion. The time devoted to a topic can indicate only the *proportion* of test items to be included and not the *type* of item (such as essay, multiple-choice, matching, ranking, performance). The type of item will depend on the nature of the objective to be measured. The table of specifications should also indicate the approximate teaching emphasis from the standpoint of the cognitive, affective, and psychomotor skills that have been sought.

The Nature of the Test Should Reflect Its Purpose If the purpose of the test is to provide a basis for school marks or classification, it will rank the pupils in order of their total achievement. But if its purpose is diagnostic, it will be valuable for its capacity to reveal specific weaknesses in individual pupil achievement. Diagnostic tests cover a limited field but in much greater detail than general achievement tests; they are designed to yield scores on the separate

[3] For a systematic approach to specifying the content of individual items see Flanagan (1951b).

parts. The range of item difficulty and the individual discriminating power[4] of the items are relatively less important in diagnostic tests. This is also true of mastery or criterion-referenced tests administered at the end of a teaching unit to determine whether the minimum essentials have been achieved.

MASTERY AND CRITERION-REFERENCED TESTING

In recent years there has been renewed interest in the concept of mastery or criterion-referenced tests—that is, measuring instruments constructed to yield measures directly interpretable in terms of specified performance standards (Glaser, 1963; Glaser and Nitko, 1971; Lindvall and Nitko, 1969; Mayo, 1970; Mayo, Hunt, and Tremmel, 1969; Popham and Husek, 1969). The mastery test is given to identify those who have or have not acquired the basal competencies. Differential consequences for instruction may result. The rationale underlying much computer-assisted instruction, programmed instruction, and systems approaches to education is based largely on this concept.

There are a few competencies for which complete mastery is possible; for example, everyone should *know* the multiplication table through 10×10 perfectly. Perhaps everyone should be able to identify the major parts of speech of a sentence and write legibly, know all the laws pertaining to motor vehicles, and so on. It is possible on logical grounds to set absolute standards for performance in these areas. The examinee has or has not reached the particular performance criterion required. In some contexts these absolute standards can be established on definitive empirical grounds. We discussed earlier the *General Educational Development* (GED) tests, which use the actual achievement of high-school graduates to establish the minimum *standard* that must be reached for one to obtain the GED high-school equivalency certificate. The same principle is used on the advanced placement tests administered by the Educational Testing Service to many high-school seniors, and accepted at many colleges and universities.

Individual differences are of no concern in criterion-referenced testing— if everyone scores 100 percent on the test, so much the better.

Certain serious problems greatly restrict the value and utility of mastery tests in most curricular areas. Rarely is there a definitive logical basis for establishing the standard. The obsolete standard of 70 percent for a passing grade has been discarded as completely arbitrary by thoughtful teachers. It is no difficult task to write two sets of items on identical concepts, one set being composed of very easy items and another set of very difficult items. A score of 70 percent on the easy test may reflect extremely poor achievement, whereas on the difficult items a 70 percent score may represent superior mastery. Consider the following two items, both designed to measure a sixth-grade science objective.

1. Dark colors absorb heat faster than lighter colors. (True or False)

---

[4] If an item is marked correctly more often by pupils with high total scores on a test than by pupils with low total scores, we say that the item discriminates between high scorers and low scorers, or simply that it has discriminating value or power. See Chapter 11 for treatment of item analysis.

2. Suppose we have two identical balloons except that one is white and one is black. Both are filled with the same amount of air and are tied so that no air can get in or out. What will happen if both balloons are put in the direct sunlight?

    (a) The black balloon will become larger.
    (b) The white balloon will become larger.
    (c) Both balloons will get smaller.
    (d) Both balloons will stay the same size.

Both items are designed to measure the same concepts, yet item 2 requires a much greater understanding than item 1. Item 2 would fall in the application taxonomy level, whereas item 1 is only a knowledge-level question. Obviously, criteria for mastery such as 90 percent of the items on the criterion test are arbitrary, since item complexity has no definitive external reference point.

As another illustration consider the following two questions, designed to measure the concept of reliability.

1. If scores on two forms of a test correlate highly, the test will have high reliability. (True or False)

2. Other things being equal, which one of the following will *not* tend to increase the obtained reliability coefficient of a test?

    (a) Increase the test's standard deviation.
    (b) Increase the correlation among items.
    (c) Decrease the uniqueness in the items.
    (d) Increase the objectivity of the scoring.
    (e) Increase the number of examinees.
    (f) Use the split-half rather than the parallel-form method of estimation.
    (g) Give the test to a more heterogeneous group.

This is a deliberately extreme example to make the following point: probably all readers would correctly answer the first question measuring the concept of reliability, but many would not be able to select the correct answer (e) to the second question designed to measure the same concept.

What is mastery? How does one logically establish an absolute standard or criterion of mastery? How does one justify a criterion of, say, 80 percent as the cutting score for mastery of some concept or domain? When does one have a proper understanding? How does one establish a level of minimal competence in reading, spelling, speaking, writing, listening, or even test construction or interpretation? Many concepts are virtually inexhaustible, so how does one draw an arbitrary line at some minimum point? R. Anderson (1967) showed that even the phrasing and format of items employed in the measurement of a given concept can influence the examinee's performance. Thus, although the concept of mastery testing or criterion-referenced testing has strong logical appeal, at least initially, its practicability for most educational purposes is greatly restricted because of the unavailability of definitive means of establishing performance standards.

Mastery testing has considerably more relevance where psychomotor objectives are involved, in areas such as developmental tasks, driver training, and industrial arts, in which a minimal level of satisfactory performance can often be established on logical or empirical grounds. As Ebel (1970b) and Davis

(1970) pointed out, the rationale for criterion-referenced testing is not new; it is not fundamentally different from the discarded percentage grading system of the past that required a score of 70 percent for passing, and so on. More than a century ago Chadwick (1864) described a "scale book" prepared by the Reverend George Fisher "which contains the numbers assigned to each degree of proficiency in various subjects of examinations." That system was abandoned because examinees' scores were a function of two rather arbitrary factors—whether the test was easy or difficult, and the generosity (or lack of it) of the scorer. Obviously a criterion for mastery lacks credibility if it cannot be based on strong logical or empirical grounds. Criterion-referenced tests should be used when a definitive criterion is available, as with the GED and CEEB advanced placement illustrations, or perhaps in a carefully developed instructional program in which a performance criterion (for example, 90 percent) has been empirically shown to be sufficient to progress sequentially through the program in a satisfactory manner. Most classroom testing, however, should not be geared only to determining whether students meet the minimum, basal levels of achievement, but should assess the individual differences that inevitably are present among the students. (See Glaser and Nitko, 1971, for a more extensive treatment of criterion-referenced testing.)

Preparing the Test

The following suggestions are helpful in the actual preparation of the test:

1. *Begin the preliminary draft of the test as soon as possible.* Many teachers find it helpful to jot down possible test questions as they teach. In this way, they make sure that no important points are omitted, and avoid overlooking supplementary material not found in the textbook (but which can be of unusual value). This practice also permits the material to "cool off" and to be appraised more correctly before it is included in the final draft of the test. Experienced teachers often develop large item pools that can be of great value when used properly.

2. *The test may include more than one type of item.* A test with a variety of item-types is less likely to be monotonous than one with a single form. This is especially true of long tests. The requirement that the question types be suited to the material covered may automatically require that a number of objective item-forms be used. These varied objective items are frequently teamed with one or more discussion questions to make up the test.

3. *Most of the items in the final test should be in the 50–80 percent difficulty range.* Maximum test reliability requires questions so difficult that only about half of the group responds correctly. Lord (1952) demonstrated that reliability will be maximum when item difficulties are approximately midway between chance success and 100 percent. Optimal difficulty for true-false items is about 75 percent, for five-option multiple-choice questions about 60 percent, and approximately 50 percent for completion items. This condition is hard to satisfy in the typical school situation. A rule-of-thumb method for constructing the test is this: (1) For motivational purposes, let items 1 and 2 be easy so that almost nobody will miss them; (2) discard all previously used items answer-

ed correctly by less than 20 percent or more than 90 percent of the tryout group unless they are mastery type items—that is, items that measure minimum skills that everyone should have; (3) let item 3 be the easiest of the remaining items, perhaps correctly answered by about 90 percent of those tested, and (4) arrange the remaining items in an ascending order of difficulty with the hardest ones at the end of the test.

For maximum reliability in measuring the individual differences among the students tested, the difficulty of the entire test should be such that, when allowance is made for chance, the mean score for the group is about 50 or 60 percent of the possible score. Thus, a test that is of ideal difficulty for one class may be too easy or too difficult for other classes of abler or less able students.

One of the worst and most common defects of teacher-constructed tests is the lack of relevant yet difficult items. This is probably due to the influence of the "70 percent is passing" tradition. To pass all but a few students, the teacher who grades on a 100-base, percentage-right system must build tests for which the average score is 80 percent or more. The result is a test that is too easy for efficient measurement.

Teachers too often fail to realize that on very easy tests only the very few difficult items do all the "work" in assessing individual differences; hence, the scores lack reliability. Sax and Reade (1964) found that college students who were given difficult tests had greater general achievement than students in the same class who took easier tests.

A difficult item is not necessarily a good item. It is simple to ask trivial questions that are difficult. A degree of difficulty is a necessary but not sufficient condition for a discriminating item. A few exceptions to this principle should be noted. When the objective is *rate* rather than extent of knowledge, as in speed tests in simple arithmetic and routine clerical work, all items should be quite easy. For mastery and for diagnostic tests, the content should be determined by the *importance* of the subject matter, not with respect to test *difficulty*. An adequate diagnostic test in fundamental arithmetic might yield many nearly perfect scores in a strong class and scores well below 50 percent in a weak class.

4. *It is usually desirable to include more items in the first draft of the test than will be needed in the final form.* This permits a later culling of the items that appear weak or are not needed to provide proper balance. For each section of the test, from 25 to 50 percent more items should be prepared than are likely to be required.

5. *After some time has elapsed, the test should be subjected to a critical revision.* The items should be checked with the original outline to see that the test contains the desired emphasis on the various topics. A careful reading of the test at this time will usually reveal some objectionable items. It is wise to have the test criticized or edited by other teachers of the same subject, who may discover some items that test points of doubtful importance and others that are unclearly stated or about which there is disagreement on the answers. The wording of the items should be checked critically for ambiguity. A very common and serious error is wording items so one answer is correct with one interpretation but, with another interpretation, a different answer is also reasonably correct.

190

General
Principles of
Test
Construction:
Cognitive
Domain

6. *The items should be phrased so that the content rather than the form of the statement will determine the answer.* A common flaw is the telltale word or phrase that provides an unwarranted clue to the answer. These so-called *specific determiners* are especially common in true-false items. It has been found that statements containing emphatic words such as "always," "never," "entirely," "absolutely," and "exclusively" are much more likely to be false than true. On the other hand, words or expressions that weaken a statement, such as "may," "sometimes," "as a rule," and "in general," are much more likely to make it true than false. These expressions should be minimized. There should be a nearly equal number of false and true items. Avoiding the exact wording of the text will prevent pupils with good rote memories from answering items they do not understand. Sometimes even spelling or grammatical form can provide clues. Such defects, however, are not inherent in objective testing and may be avoided by the alert test maker. Administering the test to persons unfamiliar with the specific content of the course will often reveal items that can be answered from general intelligence or from knowledge of language forms and usage.

The opposite mistake is also made. Figurative language, needlessly heavy vocabulary, or involved sentence structure may so obscure the meaning of an item that it is answered incorrectly by pupils who really understand the point questioned. Double negatives should be avoided. Care should be taken to see that one item does not give away the answer to another item. Unless a test is definitely supposed to measure reading ability or general intelligence, the form and wording of its items should neither block the pupil's way nor provide unwarranted clues, since these defeat the intended purpose of the test.

7. *An item should be so worded that its whole content, rather than only a part of it, functions in determining the answer.* There is often a wide discrepancy between what actually determines the pupil's response to an item and what the teacher intended. One of the main reasons for this is often that only a part of a question's content functions; the rest is wholly inert for the pupil concerned. Some excellent examples of this difficulty are given by Hawkes, Lindquist, and Mann (1936, pp. 73–81), two of which should clarify the problem. In the first:

> The leader in the making of the compromise tariff of 1833 was (1) Clay, (2) Webster, (3) Jackson, (4) Taylor, (5) Harrison.

There is evidence that the majority of the pupils who responded to this item correctly did so on the superficial basis of the strong verbal association between the words "compromise" and "Clay," because fewer than half of them answered correctly when the item appeared in the following form:

> The leader in the tariff revision of 1833 was (1) Clay, (2) Webster, (3) Jackson, (4) Taylor, (5) Harrison.

That the matching type of test is also subject to this error is shown by the next illustration:

DIRECTIONS: Below are two columns of items. Match the items in the two columns by placing on the line before each group of words in the "Items" column the correct *letter* from the "Options" column.

Items	*Options*
____1. a Phoenician contribution to civilization	A. Mason-Dixon Line
____2. most famous building of the ancient Greek world	B. Spanish Armada
____3. the fleet whose defeat in 1588 gave England the control of the Atlantic Ocean	C. Saratoga
	D. Dred Scott Decision
	E. Parthenon
____4. a boundary between two colonies that later became famous as the division between free and slave territory	F. Missouri Compromise
	G. alphabet
	H. printing press
	I. Ordinance of 1787
____5. the victory which caused France to come to our aid during the Revolutionary War	
____6. the law that forbade slavery north of the Ohio River	
____7. a ruling by the Supreme Court which opened all territory to slavery	

In most of these items, a single word gives the clue. "Boundary" in item 4 suggests "Line" in option A. Similarly, either "ruling" or "court" in item 7 suggests "Decision" in option D. If a pupil knows that "armada" means "fleet," he will be able to match item 3 with option B without knowing the date, the country, or the event involved. Note that even with corrected wording, this matching question will still be poor because the items included are so diverse in character.

The test maker should try to anticipate how the pupils will arrive at their answers to each item. The teacher should ask himself whether a pupil can ignore *any* part of the item and still answer correctly. What is the least amount of knowledge he will need to answer correctly?

8. *All the items of a particular kind should be placed together in the test.* Completion, true-false, and multiple-choice items (of varying numbers of choices) are sometimes thrown together in random order. This arrangement can be distracting, especially for younger pupils. Similar kinds of items should be placed together. Such an arrangement not only speeds up scoring and evaluation, but also enables the pupil to take full advantage of the "mind-set" imposed by a particular item form.

9. *The items of any particular kind in the test should be arranged in ascending order of difficulty.* It is especially important to have the easiest items at the beginning of the test and the hardest ones at the end. The psychological justification for this is the wholesome effect it has on the morale of the pupils. Placing very difficult items at the beginning may produce needless discouragement in the pupils, particularly those of average ability and below. This is certainly valid, because the only function of these items is to measure differences among the higher-ability pupils.

192

*General
Principles of
Test
Construction:
Cognitive
Domain*

Before a teacher conducts an actual tryout of the test, it is impossible for him to do more than estimate the difficulty order of the items, unless he has the time to obtain the judgment of several persons (Lorge and Kruglov, 1952). The opinion of even one experienced teacher is likely to have some validity. It is usually possible to select those items that will be at the extremes of the scale and fortunately, this is what is needed most. After the test has been administered, the items can be placed in a more exact order of difficulty for later use.

Although most researchers (Brenner, 1964; Marso, 1970b; Sax and Cromack, 1966) have failed to demonstrate that any significant difference is obtained from various item arrangements under unspeeded testing conditions, the use of the difficulty gradient in item ordering is desirable because many teacher-made tests are not pure power tests. If speed is a factor, order becomes significant (Hambleton, 1968; Sax and Carr, 1962). Even when the order in which the items are arranged is of no psychometric consequence, the easy-to-difficult order should be used since no other item order has been shown to be superior to it.

10. *Classroom tests should be power rather than speed tests.* A test is speeded to the extent that it contains items known by the examinee, yet which are unanswered because of inadequate time. For most curricular areas the instructional objective of speed of response is not relevant. It happens too often that a test is too long for the time allowed; hence, the speed-vs.-accuracy response style becomes a factor. If more than 10 or 15 percent of the examinees fail to complete the test in the allotted time, speed is probably a factor for some examinees, and the test should be shortened before it is used again. In addition, the scores should be corrected for chance to help prevent the slow workers from receiving an undue penalty. For fairly short factual items, two items per minute may be reasonable for pupils above the third grade. For items above the knowledge level, the time allotments should be increased. Younger pupils and longer or harder items may demand even more time. To prevent disturbance and discipline problems, assigned readings or other work should be required for those students who complete the test early.

11. *Keep the reading level of the question low.* Unless the measurement of reading ability is your objective, do not use complex vocabulary or sentence structure. This is especially important at the elementary and junior high-school levels. For example, if an assessment in science or arithmetic reasoning is the object, the test should not require high reading ability.

12. *A regular sequence in the pattern of correct responses should be avoided.* The order of correct responses should be random rather than of a regular pattern (S. B. Anderson, 1952). If, for example, items are arranged alternately true and false, or two true and two false, the pupil is apt to discover the arrangement. In a desire to make scoring easier, some educators suggest that the correct responses to multiple-choice items be arranged in an easily remembered "date-like" pattern such as 1342. But there is still the risk that the pupil will recognize the pattern and be able to answer without even considering the content of the item. Metfessel and Sax (1958) found several standardized tests that had systematic keying biases; frequently the correct answer did not appear in the extreme positions as often as would be theoretically expected.

13. *Provision should be made for a convenient written record of the pupil's responses.* Such a record may be a check list or some form of rating scale

that will serve as a systematic and permanent record of a pupil's behavior under specified conditions. It is particularly difficult, though not impossible, to keep a satisfactory written record of responses to oral quizzes (Kostick and Nixon, 1953). For the written test, however, the pupil makes his own record either on a test paper or a printed answer sheet. The teacher's problem is merely arranging the test to minimize the labor of scoring it. Numbering or lettering multiple-choice responses and completion-item blanks so that the responses will be recorded in a column rather than scattered irregularly over the page will save time and reduce the possibility of scoring error. Special answer sheets and punched-out scoring stencils may be helpful. Simply grouping the items by fives, instead of spacing them uniformly, reduces eyestrain in scoring the test and the likelihood of a recording error.

14. *The directions to the pupil should be as clear, complete, and concise as possible.* The teacher's aim should be to make the instructions so clear that the least able pupil in the group knows what he is expected to do, although he may not be able to do it. The pupil should know how and where to mark the items, how much time he has to do so, and the extent to which he should "guess." The amount of detail necessary will depend on the age of the pupils and their experience with that kind of test. It is better, for example, to tell very young children to "draw a line under" rather than "underline," and to "draw a ring around the right answer" rather than "encircle the correct response." In the lower grades, the teacher should read the directions aloud while the pupils silently follow the written directions on their test papers. Where the form of the test is unfamiliar or complicated, the generous use of correctly marked samples and practice exercises (or even practice tests) is recommended. Sometimes, a blackboard demonstration is the only way to make sure a procedure is clear. When the pupils become familiar with the various kinds of item, the directions may be abridged greatly.

The following directions may be considered reasonably satisfactory for a class unfamiliar with objective tests:

DIRECTIONS TO THE PUPIL: Here are thirty statements. Read each one carefully and decide whether it is true or false. In the ( ) before each statement you think is true, put +; in the ( ) before each statement you think is false, put 0. You will have ten minutes for the test. Your score will equal the number right minus the number wrong. You should mark an answer even when you have only a slight hunch, but *do not waste time.* Study the following samples. They are answered correctly.
SAMPLES:

(0) A. Beef is especially high in carbohydrates.
(+) B. Vitamins themselves have few calories.

After the pupils have become familiar with true-false tests and the method used to score them, the directions may be shortened to a form somewhat as follows:

DIRECTIONS: In the ( ) before each item put + if it is true, and 0 if false. You will have ten minutes for the test.

15. *Every reasonable precaution should be taken to insure excellent testing conditions.* This is important because the responses to any test are determined not only by the test itself, but also by surrounding conditions. It is usually best

194

*General
Principles of
Test
Construction:
Cognitive
Domain*

to administer the test to the pupils in the familiar environment of their own classroom. Any tendency to cheat should be forestalled by careful supervision. When cheating is likely to be a special problem, pupils may be seated so that every other seat is vacant, or the test items may be arranged in different orders for pupils seated close together.

16. *The scoring procedure should be fairly simple.* In most instances, the best procedure for scoring objective tests is to give the same credit for each correct response. In multiple-choice tests, this means giving the same credit for one properly marked item as for another, and in recall tests, the same credit for each correctly filled blank. It is usually unnecessary to weight the items according to estimated difficulty or importance; even in essay examinations, weighting is less important than is ordinarily assumed. Almost all pupils will be in nearly the same rank order regardless of whether the individual items are weighted alike or quite differently (Stanley and Wang, 1970; Wang and Stanley, 1970).

17. *Before the actual scoring begins, prepare answer keys and scoring rules.* Satisfactory scoring keys for teacher-made objective tests can be prepared simply by filling in the correct responses on an unused copy of the test. Scoring then consists of comparing the pupil's responses with those on the key placed beside his paper. Scoring rules for objective tests usually say merely that one point will be allowed for each correct response and that no fractional credits will be allowed, also indicating whether a correction formula will be used. In essay examinations, the key would be a paper containing a set of model answers, together with the maximum point value to be allowed for each. The scoring rules for essay examinations, besides giving the weight for each question, tell whether deductions are to be made for errors in spelling, grammar, and usage. In mathematics tests, the rules should cover such points as whether the answers to problems must be reduced to lowest terms, and whether credit will be allowed for solutions that are correct in principle but have the wrong answer.

The availability of optical test-scoring equipment such as the IBM 1230 series and the DIGITEK 100 greatly facilitates not only the scoring of tests but also item analyses, which are critical for evaluating the quality of tests and test items. Such equipment is presently being used at most universities and in many large school districts. Its availability for classroom teachers below the college level remains quite limited, but it should increase considerably, at least for large high schools, within the next few years.

Post-organizer

Tests should represent both educational objectives and classroom instruction. Tests should reflect much more than rote memory of facts. Bloom's taxonomy has been a useful scheme for increasing the cognitive complexity and content validity of achievement tests. The taxonomy postulates a continuum of complexity along which *knowledge, comprehension, application, analysis, synthesis*, and *evaluation* are ordered.

In constructing classroom tests, several procedures are recommended:

1. Items should span several cognitive levels.
2. Most items should be in the 50–80 percent difficulty range.

3. Items should be arranged on a difficulty gradient—easiest to most difficult.
4. Items should be carefully checked for clarity.
5. Most tests should be power rather than speed tests and written at an easy reading level.

Criterion-referenced tests have an established standard for satisfactory performance and are useful in situations where complete mastery is reasonable or where the criterion can be established on an a priori basis.

IMPORTANT TERMS AND CONCEPTS

cognitive
affective
psychomotor
behavioral objective
Bloom's taxonomy:
    knowledge, comprehension,
    application, synthesis,
    analysis, evaluation

mastery or criterion-referenced tests
item difficulty gradient
power test
speed test

SUGGESTED READINGS

ADAMS, G. S. 1964. The taxonomy of educational objectives and test items illustrative of its major categories. In *Measurement and evaluation in education, psychology, and guidance.* New York: Holt, Rinehart and Winston, Inc., Chap. 11.

ANDERSON, R. D. 1970. Performance objectives: A blueprint for action. In *Developing children's thinking through science.* Englewood Cliffs, N.J.: Prentice-Hall, Inc., Chap. 2.

BLOOM, B. S., ed. 1956. *Taxonomy of educational objectives: Handbook I, Cognitive domain.* New York: David McKay Company, Inc. Reprinted in G. H. Bracht, K. D. Hopkins, and J. C. Stanley. 1972. *Perspectives in educational and psychological measurement.* Englewood Cliffs, N.J.: Prentice-Hall, Inc., Selection 12.

———, J. T. Hastings, and G. F. Madaus. 1971. *Handbook on formative and summative evaluation of student learning.* New York: McGraw-Hill Book Company. See especially: Chapter 2, Defining educational objectives; Chapter 7, Evaluation techniques for *knowledge* and *comprehension* objectives; Chapter 8, Evaluation techniques for *application* and *analysis* objectives; Chapter 9, Evaluation techniques for *synthesis* and *evaluation* objectives.

EBEL, R. L. 1970. Some limitations of criterion-referenced measurement. Symposium presented at the American Educational Research Association, Minneapolis, Minn. Reprinted in G. H. Bracht, K. D. Hopkins, and J. C. Stanley. 1972. *Perspectives in educational and psychological measurement.* Englewood Cliffs, N.J.: Prentice-Hall, Inc., Selection 14.

EDUCATIONAL TESTING SERVICE. 1963. *Multiple choice questions: A close look*. Princeton, N.J.: ETS. Reprinted in G. H. Bracht, K. D. Hopkins, and J. C. Stanley. 1972. *Perspectives in educational and psychological measurement*. Englewood Cliffs, N.J.: Prentice-Hall, Inc., Selection 15.

GLASER, R., and A. J. NITKO. 1971. Measurement in learning and instruction. In R. L. Thorndike, ed., *Educational measurement*, 2d ed. Washington, D.C.: American Council on Education, Chap. 17.

HEDGES, William D. 1966. *Testing and evaluation for the sciences in the secondary school*. Belmont, Calif.: Wadsworth Publishing Co., Inc.

HILL, W. H., and P. L. DRESSEL. 1961. The objectives of instruction. In P. L. Dressel, ed., *Evaluation in higher education*. Boston: Houghton Mifflin Company, Chap. 2.

KRATHWOHL, D., and D. A. PAYNE. 1971. Defining and assessing educational objectives. In R. L. Thorndike, ed., *Educational measurement*, 2d ed. Washington, D.C.: American Council on Education, Chap. 2.

LINDQUIST, E. F. 1951. Preliminary considerations in objective test construction. In E. F. Lindquist, ed., *Educational measurement*. Washington, D.C.: American Council on Education, Chap. 5.

MCASHAN, H. H. 1970. *Writing behavioral objectives*. New York: Harper & Row, Publishers.

MAGER, R. F. 1962. *Preparing instructional objectives*. San Francisco: Fearon Publishers.

PAYNE, D. A. 1968. *The specification and measurement of learning outcomes*. Waltham, Mass.: Blaisdell Publishing Company.

POPHAM, W. J., and T. R. HUSEK. 1969. Implications of criterion-referenced measurement. *Journal of Educational Measurement*, **6**: 1–10. Reprinted in G. H. Bracht, K. D. Hopkins, and J. C. Stanley. 1972. *Perspectives in educational and psychological measurement*. Englewood Cliffs, N.J.: Prentice-Hall, Inc., Selection 13.

SANDERS, N. M. 1966. *Classroom questions: What kinds?* New York: Harper & Row, Publishers.

SCHOER, L. A. 1970. *Test construction: A programmed guide*. Boston: Allyn and Bacon, Inc.

TINKELMAN, S. N. 1971. Planning the objective test. In R. L. Thorndike, ed., *Educational measurement*, 2d ed. New York: American Council on Education, Chap. 3.

WOOD, D. A. 1960. *Test construction: Development and interpretation of achievement tests*. Columbus, Ohio: Charles E. Merrill Books, Inc.

9

CONSTRUCTING AND USING
ESSAY TESTS

Thus far we have mostly considered tests that can be scored objectively, tests with little need for teacher judgment. Essay tests are less widely used than formerly, especially by teachers trained in recent years, but they continue to be used frequently by more than half of the teachers in the public schools (Goslin, 1967). Essay questions produce answers that require subjective scoring, because each pupil's answer to a particular question will differ from those of his classmates. "What were the principal political considerations that led to the War Between the States?" "Write an essay of approximately 1,000 words about the cinema as an art form." "Distinguish between 'connotation' and 'denotation.'" "Is logic a branch of mathematics, or is mathematics a branch of logic? Why?" "Discuss the relative influence of heredity and environment on the development of verbal 'intelligence.' Support your points by citing relevant studies." Teachers usually refer to such questions or statements as "essay questions."

One or more essay questions will constitute an "essay test," if the answers are graded. (Note that teachers do not "score" essay tests in the same sense that they score objective tests, for which a key can be prepared in advance of the scoring.) An essay test differs from a short-answer-item test, in which the teacher knows the responses he expects. "Name the inert gases" permits an answer of only one set of names; it allows no display of individuality, although the student may vary the order in which he writes the names. Essay questions limit student responses less than do other item forms. The teacher does not say merely, "Write something," but neither does he completely specify the form of the answer.

Because the grading of essay questions calls for expert judgment, they   *197* cannot be graded by clerks as objective items can, nor can they be graded quickly or without thought. Even when skilled teachers expend their best efforts in grading them, the reliability of most essay tests is low. For many years, major efforts have been made to obtain adequate reliability in grading essay tests, particularly for English compositions written by high-school juniors and seniors applying for entrance to select colleges. Since its beginning early in this century, the College Entrance Examination Board (CEEB) has had the grading of essay questions as a major item on its agenda. Two "camps" have developed in recent years, one decrying objective testing and the other insisting that most important mental processes, including the composing of essays, can be measured well by objective items.

Hoffman (1962) contended that objective tests are not concerned with the examinee's quality of reasoning or his ability to conceive, design, and actually carry out a complex undertaking in an individual way, and that these tests thereby discriminate against the bright, discerning student. The empirical research on this issue contradicts Hoffman's claim (Chauncey and Hilton, 1965). The comparative evaluation of the two types of test was summarized by Chauncey and Dobbin (1963, pp. 79–80):

> Given two examiners fully trained in the arts of achievement testing, one building essay examinations and the other objective tests, the examiner with the essay tests probably can do a better job of estimating a student's present skill in creative writing, but the examiner who builds objective tests can provide more valid and reliable estimates of just about every other kind of school achievement.

Some critics (Hoffman, 1962; La Fave, 1964, 1966) have argued that the objective test can measure only a knowledge of facts but the essay test can measure more complex, higher levels of understanding. Bracht and Hopkins (1970a), after correcting for the unreliability of the tests, found that performance on objective and essay tests over the same content (educational psychology) measured essentially the same factors. Similar results have been observed in other content areas (Cook, 1955; Godshalk, Swineford, and Coffman, 1966; Horn, 1966; Stake and Sjogren, 1964; Vernon, 1962). Of course, the fact that in ordinary use the two kinds of test may not measure different factors should not be construed to mean that they cannot have unique measurement values when *used appropriately*. Whether they are objective or essay, the tests used to assess learning are too often of extremely poor quality.

Some teachers in most curricular areas use essay tests regularly or even exclusively. To limit the use of informal teacher-made tests to those classified as objective would be an unwarranted restriction. The essay test may have instructional merits apart from any evaluative weakness it possesses. The traditional essay still has a legitimate place in the modern school. In this chapter we consider some of the limitations and advantages of the essay test and offer suggestions for its improvement and use. The wise admonition offered many years ago by Hawkes, Lindquist, and Mann (1936, p. 20) is just as timely today:

> The intelligent point of view is that which recognizes that whatever advantages either type may have are *specific* advantages in *specific* situations; that while certain purposes may be best served by one type, other purposes are best served

by another; and, above all, that the adequacy of either type in any specific situation is much more dependent upon the ingenuity and intelligence with which the test is *used* than upon any *inherent* characteristic or limitation of the *type* employed.

Limitations of the Essay Test

As it is ordinarily employed, the essay test has certain serious limitations. It suffers in comparison with most forms of objective tests on the three important criteria for a satisfactory measuring instrument—reliability, validity, and usability.

READER UNRELIABILITY

The major problem with essay examinations is the lack of consistency in judgments among competent raters. The Educational Testing Service (1961) reported a study on 300 essays written by college freshmen and rated by 53 "outstanding representatives" from several fields. Each judge used a nine-point rating scale to indicate quality. *More than one-third* (34 *percent*) *of the essays received all possible ratings*! Another 37 percent received eight ratings, and 23 percent received seven. No essay received fewer than five of the possible nine merit categories. Obviously, a highly valid rating requires that the rating be a function of what is written, not of which expert happens to evaluate the response.

In a study (Coffman and Kurfman, 1968) involving the Advanced Placement Test in American History, it was found that some readers were much more lenient in their grading than others and that this trend was consistent irrespective of method of scoring (global vs. analytic).

Raters differ not only in their standards but also in how they distribute grades throughout the scale (Coffman, 1971). Some raters tend to spread scores more widely than others, even though the average scores may be equal. Good papers will receive lower scores and poor papers will get higher scores than they would from those raters who cluster scores closely around an average value— that is, whose scores have little variance.

In a study conducted at the University of West Virginia, Ashburn (1938) found that "the passing or failing of about 40 percent [of students] depends, not on what they know or do not know, but on *who* reads the papers" and that "the passing or failing of about 10 percent depends . . . on *when* the papers are read." It has been observed that the grades assigned tend to be greatly influenced by the grades given to the papers immediately preceding. One writer (Stalnaker, 1936) asserted that, "A *C* paper may be graded *B* if it is read after an illiterate theme, but if it follows an *A* paper, if such can be found, it seems to be of *D* caliber."

Scorer unreliability tends to increase when one attempts to capitalize on the essay test's unique characteristics—flexibility and freedom of choice (Coffman, 1971). This factor no doubt accounts for the great disparity in the reader reliability values reported in the literature; the disparity ranges from as low as .32 to as high as .98 (Coffman, 1969a, p. 10). It is not difficult to obtain high scorer reliability if essay questions are narrow and carefully structured.

For example, "List the four principal causes of the Civil War identified by your textbook," and "Name the countries of South America and the chief export of each," are questions that could present only minor difficulty in scoring reliability. These questions, however, could be cast more efficiently in objective form. Broader, open-ended questions designed to assess more complex concepts in the higher taxonomy levels delineated by Bloom et al. (1956) are precisely the kind of questions that tend to possess the least scorer reliability. The following essay question would probably have low reader reliability: "Defend or refute the following proposition: 'Liberty can be achieved only by an extension of governmental regulation of competitive business enterprise.'" This structural factor is probably a principal reason that essay tests in mathematics tend to be more reliable than those in history, which in turn tend to have greater reliability than those in literature (Coffman, 1971).

THE HALO EFFECT

The halo effect is the tendecy, in evaluating one characteristic of a person, to be influenced by another characteristic or by one's general impression of that person. For example, psychologists rating intelligence on the basis of observation overrated men with less outgoing personalities. This effect can seriously impair the validity of marks assigned by teachers to essay tests. If Mary Dogood is a well-behaved student who loves her teacher and tries very hard to please her, these characteristics can influence the teacher's judgment of the quality of Mary's essay test. When essay tests are not read anonymously, the halo effect can seriously contaminate the results.

CARRYOVER EFFECTS

A common contaminant in scoring essay tests results from the item-to-item carryover effect. The rater receives an impression of the student's knowledge on the initial item that "colors" his judgment of the second item. Bracht (1967) found that the carryover factor had a strong influence on the marks given to questions on an essay test. When the responses to each essay question were scored for all students before the next question was marked, the correlation between the marks on the questions was much lower than when the student's response to the first question was allowed to influence the rater's judgment of the second question. Obviously, the response to an essay question should be evaluated on its own merits and should not be influenced by preceding questions on the test.

Essay Testing in College Admission

CEEB publications, the *College Board Review* and the *Annual Report of the Director*, contain valuable reports of work with essay tests. For College Board achievement tests in English, see the current "A description of the College Board achievement tests." As of 1963, only the objectively scored English Composition Test and the essay Writing Sample were offered; recently, however, even the

Writing Sample was discontinued. The description of the Writing Sample below shows the kind of essay test of compositional ability that colleges required their applicants to take:

> The Writing Sample, as its name suggests, is an essay-writing exercise which provides colleges with direct evidence of your competence in written expression. You are given one hour to write an essay on a single assigned topic, and copies of your essay, exactly as written, are sent to your school and to the colleges you specify at the time you write the essay.
>
> The essay will not be graded by the College Board. It will be used by the college to supplement the information provided by your school grades in English, your score on the English Composition Test (if you are asked to take it), and any other evidence that may be submitted relating to your writing ability (such as teachers' recommendations or ratings).
>
> Here is an example of the kind of topic you will be asked to write on if you are requested by a college to take the Writing Sample:
>
> "Loyalty is a quality which, in the abstract, we delight to honor. In practice, however, it is something that may vary with circumstances and conditions. There is 'loyalty among thieves,' 'loyalty to self-interest,' 'loyalty to a pal at the expense of truth,' as well as 'loyalty to an ideal, to country, or to cause.'"
>
> Define your concept of loyalty and arrive at a principle regarding its use or abuse.
>
> DIRECTIONS: Express your ideas in a well-planned essay of 300 to 500 words, using several paragraphs to organize your discussion. Your point of view should be supported by and illustrated from your own experience, or by appropriate references to your reading, study, or observation. Be specific. You are expected to express your best thought in your best natural manner. After you have written your essay, *underline the sentence* which you think comes closest to *summarizing your central idea.*

The fact that the CEEB did not mark or grade the Writing Sample in any way, but allowed each college that required the Writing Sample to decide how it should be handled, emphasizes the difficulties of grading such an essay test reliably and validly. Many colleges (by no means all of them) wanted a Writing Sample from each applicant, but they differed in how these were used. Some colleges gave the papers to the English department to be graded; others made them available for scrutiny by members of the admissions committee when the applicant could not be accepted or rejected on the basis of other information.

English composition is only one subject in which subjectively graded tests are used, but even for it, Godshalk, Swineford, and Coffman (1966) were able to develop a one-hour objective measure of English composition skill that produced scores that correlated about .75 with a $2\frac{1}{3}$ hour criterion essay test that had a reliability of .84. A one-hour "parallel" essay test could not be expected to do appreciably better.[1]

---

[1] Using the Spearman-Brown formula to estimate the reliability of the $2\frac{1}{3}$-hour essay test, the reliability of a one-hour essay test would be expected to be about .70. The observed score would then be expected to correlate with true scores about .85 ($\sqrt{.70}$). The correlation between the observed scores from the one-hour objective examination with true scores on the essay test is estimated to be .82, by employing a "correction for attenuation" in the criterion (Guilford, 1954, p. 401): $75/\sqrt{.84} = .82$.

In recent years there has been considerable interest in the work of Ellis B. Page and his associates at the University of Connecticut (Garber, 1967; Page, 1966) on the incongruous task of grading essays by computer. After studying Table 9–1, you will see that such a feat is not as preposterous as it initially appears to be. The computer ("Judge C") is indistinguishable from the other four judges.

TABLE 9–1

Which One Is the Computer?

Below is the intercorrelation matrix generated by the cross-validation of PEG I in the following fashion:

All "judges" graded the overall quality of a set of 138 essays written by high school students in grades 8–12. One "judge" was a computer, the other four were independent human experts. The correlations in this table show the extent to which each "judge" tended to agree with each other in grading essays. The computer-assigned grades were based upon beta weightings generated from the multiple prediction of human judgments on 138 essays by other students randomly drawn from the same population. Which one, A, B, C, D, or E, is the computer vector?

	Judges				
	A	B	C	D	E
A		51	51	44	57
B	51		53	56	61
C	51	53		48	49
D	44	56	48		59
E	57	61	49	59	

SOURCE: Reprinted from E. B. Page, 1966, The imminence of grading essays by computer, *Phi Delta Kappan*, *47:* 238–243, by permission of the publisher.

Page has shown that computer scoring can yield scores that are *superior* to a single judge's rating for each of the following factors: (1) ideas or content, (2) organization, (3) style, (4) mechanics, and (5) creativity (see Coffman, 1971). Although the information used by the computer often lacks face validity and even logical validity (number of words in the essay, average word length, number of commas, and so on), there is strong evidence that the resulting scores are as valid as when the criterion is the average rating given by several experts. For the present, Page's research is more of a graphic illustration of the deficiencies in subjectively scored examinations than a practical "teachers' aid" for high-school English.

Reader reliability is improved when essay questions are carefully delimited and explicitly framed. Agreements are further increased when the raters are provided with a model answer that gives major points or concepts and their corresponding credit allocations. When such carefully developed analytic scoring methods are followed with clearly focused questions, it is possible to achieve high reader reliability. As Coffman (1971) cautioned, however, these methods are expensive—they require large amounts of professional time to obtain the required number of independent ratings. In an extensive study by the Educational Testing Service, Godshalk, Swineford, and Coffman (1966, pp. 39–40) found:

> If one can include as many as five different topics [of 20–40 minutes each] and have each topic read by five different readers, the reading reliability of the total score may be approximately .92 and the score [test] reliability approximately .84 . . . . In contrast, for one topic read by one reader, the corresponding figures are .40 and .25, respectively.

The order in which a paper appears also affects its score. In several studies (Bracht, 1967; Coffman and Kurfman, 1968; Godshalk, Swineford, and Coffman, 1966) a "slide effect" was observed in the scores awarded by raters. Papers read earlier tended to receive higher ratings than those nearer the end of the sequence. Perhaps readers become weary and, in this physical and mental condition, nothing looks quite as good as it otherwise might.

Even when essays are reread by the same rater, there is considerable variation in the score a given paper receives. Bracht (1967) found that the first and second scores of a single brief essay question correlated .50 when reread by the same instructor, and .47 when read by a different instructor. It is clear that there is considerable intrarater (within rater) as well as interrater (between rater) inconsistency.

Essay-Test Reliability

It is significant that most studies on the "reliability" of essay tests deal with between- or within-rater agreement in *marking the examination*—not with the reliability of the *examination* itself. Reader unreliability limits test reliability, but it is theoretically possible to have perfect reader reliability without any test reliability. A few studies have been reported on the correlation between two forms of an essay test designed for a particular purpose that were given to the same pupils and carefully marked by experienced examiners. One study (Ruch, 1929) used this procedure to study eighth-grade tests in 16 subjects taken by 952 pupils in 11 states. Each paper in the two sets of examinations was marked independently by two experienced teachers. This study made it possible to compare the reliability of the *test* with agreement in *marking the test*. The agreement of the two independent markings of the *same* papers is represented by an average correlation of .62, but the agreement of the two different sets of examinations marked by the same teacher is represented by an average correlation of only .43. One of Ruch's students, W. E. Gordon (Ruch, 1929, pp. 97–98), did a similar study of the New York Regents' Examinations; he obtained comparable results. He found the average agreement of the two independent markings of the same papers was .72, but the average agreement of the two sets of tests marked by the same teacher was only .42. Of course if the two sets were marked by different teachers, the agreement would be expected to be even lower.

Traxler and Anderson (1935) conducted a study at the University of Chicago High School in which they showed that two independent sets of marks assigned by two "experienced readers of essay examinations" agreed to the extent of .94 on form A and .84 on form B, but that the correlation between form A and form B was only .60. Coffman (1970) found that correlations between two different 45-minute essay questions with two different readers on an Advanced Placement Test in American History were .28–.48, depending on the two questions involved, whereas correlations between readers on the same questions were .54–.67. These studies illustrate an important point: *agreement in marking the essay test is higher than the reliability of the test itself.*

The reliability coefficient of an essay test is the correlation across both graders and comparable forms of the essay test. In simplest form, it is the correlation between teacher 1's grades for form A papers with teacher 2's grades for the form B papers of those same students. To improve reliability, more than one teacher would grade the form A papers and more than one other teacher would grade the form B papers. Then for each pupil his total score would be found on form A for the, say, *a* teachers who graded the form A papers, and his total score on form B for the *b* teachers (different from the form A graders) who graded form B. The total scores of the pupils on form A would then be correlated with their total scores on form B. In other words, test reliability is improved when reader reliability is increased.

Notice, however, that a student's total score on the two forms, *A* and *B* combined, would be more reliable than his total score on form *A* or form *B* alone. If r_{AB} is the reliability coefficient for either form *A* or *B*, then the reliability coefficient of $(A + B)$ is estimated by the Spearman-Brown formula in the following way: $2r_{AB}/(1 + r_{AB})$. For example, if $r_{AB} = .50$, then

$$\frac{2r_{AB}}{1 + r_{AB}} = \frac{2(.50)}{1 + .50} = .67.$$

If there were three comparable forms, A, B, and C, each with reliability coefficient .50, the reliability of total scores on all three forms combined, A + B + C, would be even higher:

$$\frac{3(.50)}{1 + (3 - 1)(.50)} = .75.$$

Therefore, *to increase the reliability of essay-test scores, increase the number of questions on the test* administered to all pupils. If the number of competent readers were increased, an additional increase in reliability would result. It is crucial that the essay questions be prepared carefully so the r_{AB} for teacher 1 grading form A with teacher 2 grading form B will be as high as possible.

Essay-Test Validity

Since test reliability is a necessary condition for a valid test and since reader reliability is a prerequisite for test reliability, all of the factors that we have been considering are also relevant to the validity of essay tests. There are additional concerns as well. Since the usual classroom essay examination has only a few questions, it tends to have low content validity. The limited subject-matter sampling of the essay test means that a large chance factor (sampling error) is operative in the selection of the questions that appear on the test. Suppose there are a large number of possible questions that might appear on a test of three questions. The test might be an essay test in social studies or three problems on a math or physics test. Suppose that you know the answers to only one-half of those that could conceivably appear on the test. Assuming a random selection of the questions, there is one chance in eight that you will know the answers to all three questions that appear on the test; there is also the same probability that the test will contain none of the problems that you can solve. This is a simplistic example because one probably knows something about most of the questions; nevertheless, it illustrates the large role that chance plays when tests consist of only a few questions. If objective tests were this short, they would be subject to the same problem. Since short tests are usually less reliable than long tests, the limited sampling—that is, the small number of questions—tends to restrict the reliability of an essay test. Accurate inferences about a population cannot be made by polling only a very small sample; in like manner an examinee's general level of mastery or understanding of a universe of content cannot be accurately predicted from a very few questions.

An early measurement specialist, Giles Ruch (1929, p. 54), produced evidence that the essay called forth less than half the knowledge the average pupil actually possessed on the subject, as determined by objective tests, and required twice the time to do it. Coffman (1971) reported that a well-constructed 45-minute objective test provided as much information as three 45-minute essay questions, each read by a different reader. The essay scorer is also confronted with many irrelevant factors such as the quality of the spelling, handwriting, and English used, as well as bluffing, for which no correction formula exists.

In recent studies, investigators have found that teachers were unable to rate essay responses to social-studies questions on content alone, independent of errors in spelling, punctuation, and grammar (Scannell and Marshall, 1966; Marshall, 1967; Marshall and Powers, 1969). Several investigators (Chase, 1968; Shepherd, 1929) also found that handwriting quality was related to scores awarded to essays. Shepherd's (1929) early study showed dramatic differences in the scores received by identical essay responses presented in good and poor penmanship. More recent studies show real but small effects on essay rating for penmanship and general appearance.

Bracht and Hopkins (1968), Klein and Hart (1968), Garber (1967), and several others found that the length of an essay response has substantial relationship (r's: .32–.56) to the rating awarded. Bracht and Hopkins (1968) noted that there was no relationship between the length of the essay response and the score received on an objective test over the same instructional unit, which suggests that those who wrote more did not know more. Even when grade-point average and scholastic aptitude were held constant, the partial correlation between the length of the response and the assigned mark was almost .5. This pattern was consistent across several raters. If this finding is typical, it seems that there is considerable support for the common student notion that instructors assign marks on the basis of the "weight" of student products. It has been suggested that the essay overrates the importance of knowing how to say a thing and underrates the importance of having something to say.

In an extensive study in England, Pidgeon and Yates (1957, p. 47) concluded:

The results of the experiments that we have outlined, however, show that even in ideal conditions, which cannot in practice be contrived—that is, with a faultless system of marking—papers of this kind [essay] do not achieve the level of reliability that is maintained by objective tests, nor do they achieve the same degree of validity.

The essay test also ranks low in usability unless the number of examinees is small. It seems inevitable that the essay test be time-consuming, both for the pupil and for the teacher. The additional expenditure of time and energy beyond that needed for objective tests is so serious a limitation that the use of essay tests as an evaluation tool can be justified only if it can be shown that the values realized are commensurate with the investment.

Advantages of the Essay Test

Even the most enthusiastic advocate of essay tests would scarcely claim they are superior to objective tests in reliability or usability. The best that can be hoped is that by constructing a long test of several carefully focused questions and by using at least two readers who have model answers as a guide, we can make the reliability of essay tests satisfactory, although it will still be below that of well-developed objective tests. That the questions of an essay test can be written on the blackboard is no longer an advantage, since few of today's schools lack duplicating facilities. The saving in time required to prepare essay tests is more than offset by the extra time required for scoring them, which is extensive if the scores are to have much validity.

It is apparent that if the use of essay tests is to be justified, it must be for their superior value for certain purposes. What are the unique functions of these tests? Guilford's distinction between divergent and convergent thinking may be relevant to the issue of essay versus objective tests. If you want novel responses to divergent question such as "List in two minutes time all the possible uses you can devise for a book," it seems necessary to seek free responses rather than to provide a large number of uses to be checked in some manner. Conversely, if you want to determine whether pupils can reason ingeniously to arrive at the "best" or "correct" solution, the multiple-choice format is usually excellent. As noted earlier, research studies have generally failed to reveal much support for the popular contention that essay and objective tests measure different abilities. Coffman (1969a, p. 10) summarized the research on this point: "It seems safe to conclude that the decision to use a particular type of question ought to be made on the basis of efficiency of the type for the particular situation and the skills of the test writer rather than in terms of supposed uniqueness of the data to be obtained."

Students have reported in several studies (see Hakstian, 1968) that the kind of test they anticipated influences the study procedures they use. An opponent (La Fave, 1964, p. 171) of objective tests contended that "when preparing for multiple choice tests the students probably spend most of their time memorizing facts; when preparing for essay exams, they will spend a considerably higher proportion of their time thinking about relations between facts, and with a problem-solving attitude." Hakstian (1971), in two separate experiments, failed to find that the kind of examination anticipated (essay, objective, or a combination) had a bearing on performance on either carefully developed and scored essay or objective tests, although the students reported some differences in study emphases. Similar findings were reported by Vallance (1947). Nevertheless, there is no reason that a teacher should not use a combination of essay and objective questions; this seems to be preferred by a majority of teachers (Hensley and Davis, 1952).

There has been little empirical research on the kind of examination preferred by students. Bracht (1967) found only 13 percent of college students preferred essay examinations exclusively, twice that number (26 percent) preferred entirely objective tests, and most (61 percent) preferred that the test format be part objective and part essay. Not surprisingly, there was a very high relationship between test preference and the kind of examination on which the student perceived his performance to be better. However, Bracht (1967) found that those who preferred essay examinations and those who preferred objective examinations performed equally well on both kinds of test.

Stanley and Beeman (1956) found that college students from most curricular areas did equally well on the objective and essay portions of a final examination in educational psychology. However, mathematics and science majors performed better on the objective part than English majors did, and vice versa.

Improving the Construction and Use of Essay Tests

Although the essay test has existed for hundreds of years, the amount of research devoted to it has been far less than that devoted to the comparatively new objective test. Furthermore, much of the research relating to essay tests has been conducted with poor, unimproved versions. However, a study of the meager experimental literature available does yield several positive suggestions, which if employed would substantially increase the validity and reliability of essay examinations.

It is just as important to know *when* to use the essay test as it is to know *how* to use it. It is wise to restrict the use of the essay test to the measurement of those organizing and expressive abilities for which it is best adapted. There seems to be no good reason for employing subjective measurement when objective tests measure the same abilities as validly. What does one attempt to have the essay test measure? Several writers have tried to answer that question.

Weidemann (1933, 1941) distinguished 11 definable types of test. Arranged in a series from simple to complex, these types are as follows: (1) *what, who, when, which,* and *where;* (2) *list;* (3) *outline;* (4) *describe;* (5) *contrast;* (6) *compare;* (7) *explain;* (8) *discuss;* (9) *develop;* (10) *summarize;* and (11) *evaluate.* The first two types are items in the *knowledge* level of Bloom's taxonomy. The others require either an essay question or very skillfully developed objective questions.

Years ago, Monroe and Carter (1923) divided essay questions into

21 types. These types, together with sample questions from the field of measurement and some discussion, appear below:

SOME TYPES OF QUESTION

1. *Selective recall—basis given*
   Name three important developments in measurement that occurred during the first decade of the twentieth century.
2. *Evaluation recall—basis given*
   Name the three persons who have had the greatest influence on the development of intelligence testing.
3. *Comparison of two things—on a single designated basis*
   Compare essay tests and objective tests from the standpoint of their effect on the study procedures used by the learner.
4. *Comparison of two things—in general*
   Compare standardized and nonstandardized tests.
5. *Decision—for or against*
   In which, in your opinion, can you do better, oral or written examinations? Why?

Score for its truth and logical relevance the evidence offered in support of the decision. There is no justification for scoring the *opinion*, since it was asked for and given.

Sometimes this kind of question appears as "What is your favorite X and why?" In this case nothing is scorable but the mechanics of composition. Notice that "why" is ambiguous because it may call either for an account of the student's psychological development or for a list of qualities of X that have special appeal for him.

6. *Cause or effects*
   How do you account for the popularity of objective tests during the last 50 years?
7. *Explanation of the use or exact meaning of some word, phrase, or statement in a passage*
   What is the meaning of "objective" in the above question?
8. *Summary of some unit of the text or of some article read*
   Summarize in not more than one page the advantages and limitations of essay tests.

A comment on the meaning of *summary* may be helpful. If a pupil responds with a mass of detail, but omits the main ideas that the details support, he has not responded adequately; the ability to summarize is a manifestation of a high order of thinking, and a properly scored summary item should have considerable discriminating power as to the degree of understanding of the matters involved.

Our example above is faulty because it specifies a quantity of verbiage ("one page"). When this is so, the scorer tends to evaluate in terms of the quantitative requirement and the pupil tends to respond in terms of it. The same comment is applicable to attempts to "limit" the discussion question (14, below). A glib student, who is acquainted with the possibilities of the English language, can use five words where two would do, thereby meeting the requirement of "in not less than 300 words."

"In my opinion, for whatever it may be worth, which probably is not very much in view of the fact that I was not present at the time and have no direct knowledge of the central issue involved in the controversy between the contending parties . . ."

This means no more than "I have no justification for thinking that . . . ," but it achieves 45 of the desired 300 words instead of just seven.

9. *Analysis (the word itself seldom appears in the question)*
Why are many so-called "intellectuals" suspicious of standardized tests?

10. *Statement of relationships*
Why is it that nearly all essay tests, regardless of the school subject, tend to a considerable extent to be measures of the learner's mastery of English?

11. *Illustrations or examples (the pupils's own) of principles in science, construction in language, etc.*

12. *Classification*
What type of error appears in the following test item? "With what country did the United States fight during World War II?"

13. *Application of rules, laws, or principles to new situations*
In the light of experience in the United States with examinations for selecting college students, what public-relations problems would you expect to arise in England because of the Age 11+ examinations there?

14. *Discussion*
Discuss the role of Sir Francis Galton in the development of the Pearson product-moment coefficient of correlation, r.

15. *Statement of an author's purpose in his selection or organization of material*
Why are individual mental tests not treated in greater detail in this book?

16. *Criticism—as to the adequacy, correctness, or relevancy of a printed statement, or a classmate's answer to a question on the lesson*
Criticize or defend the statement, "The essay test overrates the importance of knowing *how* to say a thing and underrates the importance of having something to say." "To criticize" assumes a set of standards given or known. Many persons are under the impression that it means "Tell something good about and tell something bad about, but mostly good, so that it will be constructive." Teachers should not foster this misconception. For further clarification, see Bloom et al. (1956, pp. 185–200).

17. *Outline*
Outline the principal steps in the construction of an informal teacher-made test.

18. *Reorganization of facts (a good type of review question to give training in organization)*
Name ten practical suggestions from this book that are particularly appli-. cable to the subject you teach or plan to teach.

19. *Formulation of new questions—problems and questions raised*
What are some problems relating to the use of essay tests that require further study?

20. *New methods of procedure*
Suggest a plan for proving the truth or falsity of the contention that exemption from semester examinations for the ablest students is a good policy in high school.

21. *Inferential thinking*
Are the authors of this book likely to use essay tests frequently in their measurement classes?

Notice that the classifications by Weidemann and by Monroe and Carter distinguish several rather distinct abilities that *can* be measured by essay tests that are carefully prepared and scored. To measure these abilities by objective items requires skill and careful effort in item construction. Each type of question should be studied carefully until its distinguishing characteristics are familiar; this will help determine whether the essay or objective item-type is more appropriate.

There is some evidence that a more valid sampling of the pupil's knowledge can be obtained by increasing the number of questions and reducing the length of discussion expected on each. In many cases, a well-constructed paragraph is a sufficient answer. Very few discussions need exceed one or two pages. In any case, the question should be so worded as to restrict the responses toward the objective that is to be measured. For example, the question, "Explain the reasons for the strike at Consolidated Electronics in 1972," is too general and would be improved if it were restricted by the addition of the phrases "to show (a) the labor grievances of the employees; (b) the practices of the employer; (c) related national, social, and economic factors; (d) the rival labor unions; and (e) the method of striking." It must be recognized, however, that such suggestions take away some of the "freedom" of the traditional essay examination in that, to improve its validity and reliability, they make it more like the objective test—that is, less flexible and more structured.

Many teachers, especially beginning teachers, believe that the essay test is the easiest kind to construct. As a matter of fact, *it is probably more difficult to construct essay tests of high quality than it is to construct objective tests of high quality.* Much care and thought must be given to their construction, if they are to measure anything but mere memory for factual knowledge. Many of the general principles of testing outlined in earlier chapters are as applicable to essay tests as to objective tests, and the special suggestions of this chapter should help you devise questions above the rote-knowledge level. Finally, there is always the risk that in attempting to phrase essay questions so that they can be answered more specifically and scored more objectively, the results may not even be as good as a straight objective test. In any case, it is especially important that the test be critically reviewed, with the help of a colleague's judgment if possible.

PREPARING STUDENTS TO TAKE ESSAY TESTS

Several writers have emphasized the importance of training students to take examinations of all kinds. This training can be done well by teachers in classrooms. Wider experience and training in preparing for and in taking tests of all kinds is likely to increase the accuracy of measurement and therefore the fairness of scores for the students tested. For essay tests, pupils should be taught the meanings of the words used in the various types of thought question. They should be taught that "compare" requires a statement of similarities *and* differences and that their answer to such an item is not complete if it omits either. "Contrast" requires only a statement of differences.

Pupils should be taught to apportion their time wisely to avoid spending most of it on one or two questions. A thorough and excellent response to one question will almost never receive equal credit as would good, but less elaborate, responses to two questions. Students should be cautioned about their penmanship and the general appearance of their "product." They should be aware that teachers apparently cannot ignore spelling and grammatical errors in their grading (Marshall, 1967; Marshall and Powers, 1969). They should be told to do their best to respond to every question because if they do not, the "bluffer" will be rewarded even more than he would otherwise. As we previously indicated, the length per se of a response to a question has an important relationship to its rated merit. There probably is at least as much "test-wiseness" in taking an essay test as in taking an objective test. If students are told the "tricks of the trade," the magnitude of their irrelevant effects will be minimized, particularly if the scorers also are acquainted with these factors.

CONSTRUCTING GOOD ESSAY TESTS

Suggestions for the construction and use of essay examinations are summarized as follows:

1. Make definite provisions for teaching pupils how to take examinations. Specific training in preparing for and in taking tests and examinations of the various kinds commonly encountered is a legitimate objective of instruction. Perhaps the best way is to find or devise good practice tests, administer them, and discuss the results with the students.

2. Make sure that questions are carefully focused. The following questions present freedom not only to students but also to graders: "What are the advantages of individualized instruction?" or "Discuss collective bargaining." "There must be structure or the student may readily miss the intent of the question—or be free to bluff if he understands . . . but is not prepared to deal with it" (Coffman, 1971). A common ploy of the test-wise student is to appear to have "misunderstood" the intent of the question and proceed to emphasize those aspects with which he is thoroughly familiar.

3. When questions are structured on content and length, the number of questions asked can be increased and the amount of discussion required on each reduced. Such a plan permits a better sampling of the content and, at the same time, allows the responses to be read with greater reliability; both of these increase the validity of the examination.

4. Have a colleague critique the test. The composer of a question is in a particular frame of reference that often prevents him from seeing the intrinsic ambiguity and misinterpretations that are readily apparent to another person. In addition, an opinion should be sought about (a) the emphases and breadth of coverage, (b) the appropriateness of difficulty of the questions, and (c) the the adequacy of the model answers. The small amount of effort required by this suggestion will reap disproportionately large dividends.

5. The use of optional questions should be discouraged (Stalnaker, 1951, pp. 505–506), because each student should take the same test as any other

student if their scores are to be compared. Questions are intrinsically different in difficulty. One's score should not depend on which questions he happened to elect to answer. However, if the intent is to measure writing ability per se, then a choice of topics should be allowed, since content mastery is incidental to the purpose at hand.

6. Restrict the use of the essay *test* (in contrast to its use as an instructional exercise), a measuring instrument whose results are graded, to those functions to which it is best adapted. The time required for students to write answers to a representative sample of questions and the time required to obtain satisfactory reader reliability are impractical. Nevertheless, the essay examination remains the preferred method of obtaining evidence of the candidate's ability in many contexts. When it is not clear that an essay test is required for measuring the desired instructional objective, use an objective test. This does not abrogate the use of ungraded essay *exercises* for instructional puposes. In fact, Pidgeon and Yates (1957, p. 38) reported that students in some primary schools in England that had eliminated essay examinations *because of their weaknesses as evaluation measures* frequently needed remedial instruction in written expression in the secondary schools. It almost goes without saying that one cannot learn to write well without writing.

Improving the Grading or Rating of Essay Tests

Strictly speaking, it is more correct to speak of grading or rating essay examinations than it is to speak of scoring them, because scoring is an objective process of counting right or wrong responses; grading is interpreting quality subjectively in terms of a criterion.

All claims made for the value of the essay test as a measuring instrument are, of course, based on the assumption that the papers can be read accurately. For example, not only must the essay test elicit from superior pupils responses that are consistently superior, but the teachers marking the papers must be able to *recognize* consistently that they are superior responses.

Cochran and Weidemann (1934, 1937) outlined a procedure for evaluating essay examinations; the essentials of their procedure can be taught in ten minutes. It is most impressive that the majority of the consistency coefficients of two series of scorings made five weeks apart on highly structured essay tests were between .80 and .90 for teachers with ten minutes of training. Independent scores by experienced readers showed an average agreement of .98 when the procedure given below in a slightly modified and abridged form was used. (Much depends on the particular questions used and on situational factors, such as heterogeneity of the group of students; r's *far* lower than these sometimes result despite the teacher's best efforts.)

SUGGESTIONS FOR MARKING
ESSAY EXAMINATIONS

1. Read over a sampling of the papers to obtain a general idea of the quality of answer that may be expected.
2. Score one question through all of the papers before considering another

question. There are two outstanding advantages in scoring one question through an entire set of papers. The first is that the comparison of answers appears to make the grades more exact and just. The second is that having to keep only one list of points in mind saves time and promotes accuracy.

3. Before scoring any papers, read the material in the text that covers the questions, and also the lecture notes on the subject.

4. Make a list of the main points that should be discussed in every answer. Each of these points must be weighed and assigned a certain value if the scoring is to approach accuracy. This value assigned to the main points needed for a reasonably adequate answer is designated as the minimum score. If a pupil elaborates and discusses points not required yet pertinent to the question, his answer is given an additional value, called the extra score. This extra score may vary for different pupils, but may not exceed a certain set maximum.

5. After the points have been weighed, the actual scoring begins. Read the answer through once and then check back over it for fact details. Attempt to mark every historical mistake on the paper and write in briefly the correction. As the answer is read, make a mental note of the points omitted and the value of each point, so that when the end of the question is reached, you have the minimum grade figured. If there is any additional or extra percentage to be given, it is added to the minimum score, and then the value of the question is written in terms of the percent deducted rather than the positive percent. Then when every question on a paper is scored, it is a simple matter to add the negative quantities and obtain the final grade.

One cannot overemphasize the importance of three essential steps: (1) the preparing in advance of a list of answers that are considered adequate for the objectives of the test; (2) the assigning of a specific value to each essential part of the answers; and (3) the grading of one question through all the papers before going on to another question. Most students of the problem recommend attempting to distinguish a relatively small number of degrees of merit in an answer. Perhaps as good a plan as any is to allow credit for each part of the answer considered essential to a question as follows: 4 for excellent, 3 for good, 2 for fair, 1 for inferior, and 0 for an omission or a wrong response.

GRADING BY SORTING

In addition to the points made by Cochran and Weidemann, several specialists have found that sorting is helpful. They suggest sorting the papers into three to five piles, according to the merit of the discussion of each question on the basis of a brief preliminary examination of the answers. Sims (1931) describes one such procedure as follows:

1. Quickly read through the papers and on the basis of your opinion of their worth, sort them into five groups as follows: (a) very superior papers, (b) superior papers, (c) average papers, (d) inferior papers, (e) very inferior papers.

2. Reread the papers in each group and shift any that you feel have been misplaced.

Flanagan (1952) showed that when the ability being measured is normally distributed, the optimum percentages for five groups are 9, 20, 42, 20, and 9.

Therefore, about 10 percent of the papers might be called "very superior" and 10 percent "very inferior." Twenty percent would be "superior" and a like percentage would be "inferior." The remaining 40 percent are "average." These are rough approximations, of course, dependent upon the ability level of the particular student group being graded.

The preliminary sorting of the papers into piles of approximately equal merit before assigning numerical values to them will help to avoid the difficulty pointed out by Stalnaker: namely, that the values allowed a paper are often greatly influenced by the merit of the paper that happens immediately to precede it in the order of scoring. It is also easier to locate papers distinctly unlike those in a particular group supposedly of similar quality. It is important to regroup the papers in a single stack after each question has been evaluated and before they are re-sorted into piles according to the merits of the discussions of the next question. This procedure will help prevent the score on one question from influencing the grades on subsequent questions.

ANONYMITY

The simple precaution of having the pupil write his name inconspicuously either on the back or at the end of the paper, rather than at the top of each page, will also decrease the bias with which the paper is graded.

STYLE

Each teacher should adopt a policy regarding what factors shall be considered, and what factors shall not be considered, in evaluating a written examination. *Only those factors should be taken into account that afford evidence of the degree to which the pupil has attained the objectives set for that particular course.* Except in English classes, this may rule out making arbitrary reductions for such things as faulty sentence structure, paragraphing, handwriting, and the spelling of nontechnical words. These factors will be considered only when they affect the clarity of the pupil's discussion. It is always legitimate to hold the pupil responsible for the spelling, as well as the meaning, of the vocabulary that is peculiar to the course.

This does not mean that the quality of the written English used in examinations is unimportant and should therefore be disregarded. On the contrary, it is always very important. But it should be considered only in relation to that for which it may be accepted as valid evidence: namely, in determination of the pupil's mark in English.

Proper Use of Essay Exercises

Despite the critics who have a number of valid objections to essay tests as they are often used, it seems likely that the written responses to questions are here to stay. As teachers, you can use them wisely as an essential *part* of your instructional activities and, to some extent, your measuring and evaluating equipment. You will not be misled into abandoning objective tests because of the attacks by well-intentioned persons in professional and popular magazines and in books. Some persons who wish to abolish objective testing may be confusing testing with teaching. The two are related, of course, but not completely. Compositions, essays, and discussion questions that prove to be poor *tests* may nevertheless be worthwhile *exercises*. If the teacher goes through the material carefully and makes constructive remarks, perhaps followed by oral discussion of the paper, the student may benefit greatly even though no grade is assigned— perhaps partly *because* none is. If, however, the teacher merely marks the paper "A," "B," or the like without commenting, his grading may be highly unreliable and, to boot, the student probably will not have learned how to improve his next paper. It is possible to do both, grading and commenting, in which event the comments may be helpful even if the grading is unreliable (Page, 1958).

Post-organizer

Even though essay tests, as typically used in education, have face validity, they tend to be characterized by low scorer reliability and low test reliability, both of which are essential for test validity. Scoring is often unduly contaminated by penmanship, length of response, lack of anonymity, and item-to-item and test-to-test carryover effects in grading.

The quality of essay tests can be improved if questions are carefully structured in content and length and if all students write on identical sets of questions. If possible, scoring should be done with the examinee being anonymous, with one question being evaluated on all papers before the next question is graded, and by more than one rater. Essays may be important instructional experiences apart from their use as evaluation devices.

SUGGESTED READINGS

BRACHT, G. H., and K. D. HOPKINS. 1970. The communality of essay and objective tests of academic achievement. *Educational and Psychological Measurement*, **30**: 359–364.

COFFMAN, W. E. 1966. On the validity of essay tests of achievement. *Journal of Educational Measurement*, 3(2): 151–156. Reprinted in G. H. Bracht, K. D. Hopkins, and J. C. Stanley. 1972. *Perspectives in educational and psychological measurement*. Englewood Cliffs, N.J.: Prentice-Hall, Inc., Selection 16.

———. 1969. Achievement tests. In R. L. Ebel, ed., *Encyclopedia of Educational Research*, 4th ed. New York: The Macmillan Company.

———. 1971. Essay examinations. In R. L. Thorndike, ed., *Educational measurement*, 2d ed. Washington, D.C.: American Council on Education, Chap. 10.

——— and D. KURFMAN. 1968. A comparison of two methods of reading essay examinations. *American Educational Research Journal*, 5(1): 99–107.

GODSHALK, R., F. SWINEFORD, and W. E. COFFMAN. 1966. *The measurement of writing ability*. Princeton, N.J.: College Entrance Examination Board.

HAKSTIAN, A. R. 1971. The effect on study methods and test performance of objective and essay examinations. *Journal of Educational Research*, **64**(7): 319–324.

MARSHALL, J. C. 1967. Composition errors and essay examination grades re-examined. *American Educational Research Journal*, **4**(4): 375–385.

PAGE, E. B. 1966. The imminence of grading essays by computer. *Phi Delta Kappan*, **47**: 238–243.

PIDGEON, D. A., and A. YATES. 1957. Experimental inquiries into the use of essay-type English papers. *British Journal of Educational Psychology*, **27**: 37–47.

SOLOMON, R. J. 1965. Improving the essay test in the social studies. In H. D. Berg, ed., *Evaluation in social studies*. Washington, D.C.: National Council for Social Studies, pp. 137–153.

VALLANCE, T. R. 1947. A comparison of essay and objective examination as learning experience. *Journal of Educational Research*, **41**: 279–288.

VERNON, P. E., and G. D. MILLICAN. 1954. A further study of the reliability of English essays. *British Journal of Statistical Psychology*, **7** (Part II): 65–74.

10

CONSTRUCTING SPECIFIC TYPES
OF OBJECTIVE TESTS

In the previous chapter we considered basic principles for constructing objective test items. Now we develop specific guidelines and procedures for writing good items of several types. In certain respects this chapter is the most important one in the book; if the unit of an objective test—the item itself—is prepared insightfully and skillfully, the test will yield a high-quality assessment.

No amount of statistical computation will make badly written items acceptable, but such techniques as item analysis facilitate identifying the items that should be eliminated or revised.

The main kinds of objective test item are (1) free-response items and (2) fixed-response items. Fixed-response items include multiple-choice, true-false, matching, and rearrangement exercises. Fixed-response items provide all the options among which the student must decide. The most common is the four- or five-option multiple-choice item used in most published tests. Here is an example from a social studies test (Berg, 1958, p. 9):

> The House of Representatives has the authority, within limits, to determine who shall become President in case:
>
> A. No candidate receives a majority of the popular votes.
> B. No candidate receives a majority of the electoral votes.
> C. No candidate receives a majority of both the popular and electoral votes.
> D. The elected candidate dies before he can be inaugurated.

Only one of the four options correctly completes the stem to form a "true" statement. Which one is it? The other three options are designed to detect the uninformed and are known as *distracters*. Such options must be plausible, more tempting to the less knowledgeable students and less correct in relationship to the stem than is the keyed option. There are two kinds of keyed option: correct answer and best answer. Above, *B* is the correct answer. Sometimes a student will produce what he considers to be a more "correct" option than the item provides him. If this happens, something is wrong either with him or with the item, and one of the two should be set right.

Multiple-choice items were formerly referred to simply as "recognition" items, as if they were capable of testing only rote knowledge. Obviously, they can be as high-level as the effort and ingenuity of an able item writer can make them. Even a simple arithmetical reasoning item such as "How many apples can I buy for 42¢ when each apple costs 7¢?" involves application. A teacher can leave a blank at the end of such a question, or he can provide several options and let the student choose the correct option. In neither case is "recall" alone involved, as it might be if we asked what year England entered World War I.

Free-Response Items

The *free-response* test is one in which each item is in the form of a direct question, a stimulus word or phrase, a specific direction, or an incomplete statement or question. The response must be *supplied* by the pupil rather than merely *identified* from a list of suggested answers supplied by the teacher. This kind of test differs from the essay examination primarily in the length of response required; the typical response to the free-response item is short, preferably a single word or phrase. Thus it is sometimes called a short-answer objective item. Example: Who devised the 1916 Stanford-Binet Intelligence Scale? _____

ADVANTAGES AND LIMITATIONS

The free-response test has the obvious advantage of familiarity and "naturalness." It may almost completely eliminate guessing, because the student chooses among the (usually large) number of options he can recall. The free-response test is particularly valuable for mathematics and the physical sciences when the stimulus appears in the form of a problem requiring computation. It also has wide application to test situations when it is presented in the form of maps, charts, and diagrams for which the pupil is required to supply, in spaces provided, the names of parts keyed by numbers or letters.

A limitation of the free-response test is that it tends to measure highly factual knowledge, consisting of isolated bits of information, because questions with unrelated short answers are used. The isolated-knowledge level is avoidable if the item writer is ingenious. The scoring is somewhat time-consuming and not always entirely objective. For example, which of the following answers to the above completion item ("Who devised the 1916 Stanford-Binet Intelligence Scale?") is correct? Lewis M. Terman, Professor of Psychology at Stanford University in Stanford, California; Lewis M. Terman; Lewis Terman; L. M. Terman; Terman; Louis Terman; Termen; or Tarmen. Probably most teachers will consider any of the first five responses (through "Terman") fully correct, because they indicate that the student has differentiated between Terman and, say, Wechsler. Some would want to penalize the last three for inaccurate spelling, even though the student's intent is clear. More difficult decisions about grading completion and other short-answer items must be made when several different answers to an item seem plausible. These limitations need not be serious when tests are carefully prepared.

ILLUSTRATIONS OF FREE-RESPONSE ITEMS

Below are a few sample free-response test items taken from standard tests.[1] Excellent examples of this and other test forms used in a variety of school subjects on all educational levels are given by Rinsland (1938, pp. 23–222).

stone reasoning tests in arithmetic[2]

1. James has 5 cents. He earned 13 cents more and then bought a top for 10 cents. How much money did he have left?

   Answer: _____

2. How many oranges can I buy for 35 cents when oranges cost 7 cents each?

   Answer: _____

sones-harry high school achievement test, part II[3]

1. What instrument was designed to draw a circle? _____ 1
2. Write "25% of" as "a decimal times." _____ 2
3. Write in figures: one thousand seven and four hundredths. _____ 3

cooperative general mathematics tests for college students, form 1934[4]

28. How many axes of symmetry does an equilateral triangle have? .... (   )
29. Eight is what percent of 64? .... (   )
30. Write an expression that exceeds M by X .... (   )
31. Solve the formula $V = \dfrac{Bh}{3}$ for h .... (   )

iowa placement examinations, chemistry-training[5]

1. The atomic weight of K is 39; of Cl, 35.5; of O, 16. What is the molecular weight of $KClO_3$? _____

2. If 7 gm. of iron unite with 4 gm. of sulphur, how many gm. of iron sulphide will be produced? _____

[1] In the examples of the various types of objective test that follow, an effort has been made to illustrate a wide variety of mechanical arrangements of items as well as of subject matter. It is recognized that they are not all of equal merit. Some of the tests referred to are out of print but are needed as illustrations, because recent published tests are largely of the multiple-choice variety.

[2] Devised by C. W. Stone and published by Teachers College Press.

[3] Devised by W. W. D. Sones and D. P. Harry, Jr., and published by Harcourt Brace Jovanovich.

[4] Devised by H. T. Ludholm and L. P. Siceloff, and published by Cooperative Test Division of ETS.

[5] Devised by G. D. Stoddard and J. Cornog, and published by Extension Division, State University of Iowa.

What device is used in a vacuum cleaner to pump air into the
dust bag? . . . .(15) _____

What is the pressure in pounds of ordinary air per square
inch? . . . .(16) _____

an exercise from a biology workbook[7]

DIRECTIONS: As you locate each part using a hand lens on an actual specimen, find
the corresponding part in the accompanying illustration and label it. Consider how
each part functions in the life of the grasshopper.

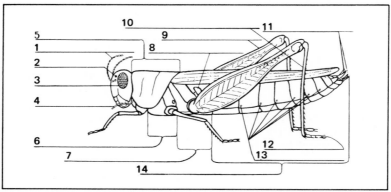

Parts of the Grasshopper.

The following items from an informal class test illustrate the possibilities
of free-response tests with more than one response to each item:

Event	*Country*	*Year*	*Person*
First psychological laboratory	_____	_____	_____
First general intelligence test	_____	_____	_____
First standardized achievement test	_____	_____	_____

RULES FOR CONSTRUCTING
FREE-RESPONSE ITEMS

The free-response is one of the most familiar test forms and one of the easiest
to prepare. The main problem is phrasing the items so they call forth responses
of a higher intellectual level than mere rote memory, and so they can be scored
with a minimum expenditure of time and effort.

1. *The direct-question form is often preferable to the statement form.* It is
more natural for the pupil and is often easier to phrase.

[6] Devised by C. J. Pieper and W. L. Beauchamp, and published by Scott, Foresman
and Company.
[7] Prepared by A. O. Baker and L. H. Mills to accompany their *Dynamic biology today*
(Chicago: Rand McNally & Company, 1943).

EXAMPLE: While it circles the sun once, the earth rotates on its axis _____ times.
BETTER: How many times does the earth rotate on its axis while it circles the sun once? _____

2. *The questions should be so worded that the response required is as brief as possible, preferably a single word, number, symbol, or at most a short phrase.* This will facilitate scoring and increase objectivity.

3. *The blanks provided for the responses should be in a column, preferably at the right of the questions.* This arrangement simplifies scoring and is more convenient for the pupil. The illustrations above show various ways of arranging the answer column.

4. *Avoid using textbook wording in phrasing items.* Unfamiliar phrasing will reduce the possibility of correct responses that represent mere meaningless verbal associations; it also will eliminate tempting pupils to memorize the exact wording of the book.

5. *The questions should be so worded that there is only one correct response.* This standard is difficult to achieve because pupils are ingenious in reading into questions interpretations that the teacher never intended.

When challenged on a history test to "name two ancient sports," one resourceful student answered "Anthony and Cleopatra." This possibility would not have arisen if the question had taken the form, "What were two popular athletic contests in ancient Greece?" When there is clearly more than one legitimate interpretation of a question, all acceptable replies must be listed on the scoring key. Extra care in wording the original questions will prevent much of this ambiguity.

If they are carefully developed, free-response questions can measure levels of understanding beyond the "knowledge" category of the *Taxonomy of Educational Objectives.* For example: what is the taxonomy level represented by the "grasshopper" item on the previous page?

Completion Tests

The *completion* item, a special form of the free-response item, may be defined as a sentence in which certain important words or phrases have been omitted, with blanks inserted for the pupil to fill in. The sentence may contain one or more blanks. The sentences in the test may be disconnected, or they may be organized into a paragraph. Each blank is usually worth one point.

Completion tests have wide applicability to subject matter. But, unless they are prepared with extreme care, they are likely to measure rote memory rather than real understanding; or they may be better measures of general intelligence or linguistic aptitude than of school achievement. This occurs when a test requires more brightness and reading ability than knowledge of the subject matter.

Scoring completion tests is likely to be even more laborious than it is with simple-recall tests, especially if the missing words are written in blanks scattered all over the page rather than in a column. Although these limitations cannot be eliminated entirely, they can be greatly reduced, as in the illustrations on the next page.

ILLUSTRATIONS OF COMPLETION TESTS

*stanford achievement test, paragraph meaning,
1940 edition*[8]

DIRECTIONS: [Abridged] Write JUST ONE WORD on each line. *Be sure to write each answer on the line that has the same number as the missing word in the paragraph.*

1–2–3   Answer

In olden days men made their own pens from the quills of feathers. It required considerable skill to cut a pen properly so as to suit one's individual taste in writing. Students were always   1 _____
on the lookout for good goose, swan, turkey, or other bird feathers. Goose quills made the most satisfactory—1—for gen-   2 _____
eral —2—, but school-masters liked pens made from the —3—
of swan feathers because they fitted best behind the ear.   3 _____

*public school attainment tests for
high school entrance*[9]

3. *Question:* Did this team have a coach?
Answer: No, they taught ____(3)____ how to play without
any coach.   (3) _____

tests of everyday problems in science, unit XI[10]

A pry-pole is an example of a machine called the.......... (11) _____
A capstan is an example of a machine called the .... (12) _____
A screw is an example of a machine called the .... (13) _____
Your teeth are examples of machines called .... (14) _____

gregory tests in american history[11]

	Write your words and dates here.
2. The man who headed the first expedition to circumnavigate the globe was	2 _____
7. The Articles of Confederation were in force from 1781 to.......................................	7 _____
9. The "Old Liberty Bell" rang out the decision of Congress to be free from England in the year....	9 _____

[8] Devised by T. L. Kelley, G. M. Ruch, and L. M. Terman, and published by Harcourt Brace Jovanovich. (Superseded by the later editions.)
[9] Prepared by H. D. Rinsland and R. L. Beck, and published by Public School Publishing Company. (This form of completion, with all responses in a column instead of staggered within sentences, was devised by Rinsland.)
[10] Devised by C. J. Pieper and W. L. Beauchamp, and published by Scott, Foresman and Company.
[11] Devised by C. A. Gregory and published by C. A. Gregory Company.

20. Write on the lines to the right the contractions—shortened forms to represent how the words are naturally spoken—for the seven groups of words underlined in the following sentences. For instance, for *do not*, you would write *don't*. You need not copy the sentence, but only the seven contractions.
I have read his story, but I *cannot* believe   _____
that *he will* get a passing grade on it,   _____
for *it is* not well written and *has not*   _____
a clear-cut plot. The characters *are*   _____
not at all interesting; *they are* not even human.   _____

RULES FOR CONSTRUCTING
COMPLETION ITEMS

Most of the suggestions on pages 220–221 for constructing free-response items apply equally to completion items. The dangers to be avoided are largely the same for both forms. A few suggestions will help you construct good completion items. The three main problems in constructing completion tests are (1) how to phrase the statements to indicate the kind of response desired, (2) how to avoid giving the pupil unwarranted clues to the correct, or keyed responses, and (3) how to arrange the items to facilitate scoring. The first two suggestions below apply to the first problem, the next five apply to the second problem, and the last six suggestions are for the third problem.

1. *Avoid indefinite statements.* A pupil has a right to know the kind of response desired; when this is explicitly stated, the scoring is far more rapid. First phrase a simple direct question; then write a complete statement in answer to the question. Use all the applicable wording of the question, but omit the crucial word or words of the answer.

EXAMPLE: When was Abraham Lincoln born? (Vague question, probably leading to the poor completion item "Abraham Lincoln was born in _____.")
BETTER: In what year was Abraham Lincoln born? (This leads to the completion item, "Abraham Lincoln was born in the year _____.")

The first example leads to a completion item that fails to indicate specifically whether the desired response is the date, the place, or the circumstances of his birth. In that form, legitimate answers might be "February" or "1809," "Kentucky," or possibly "The South," and even "poverty," or "a log cabin." By a slight change in wording the statement is made quite definite.

2. *Avoid overmutilated statements.* If too many key words are left out, it is impossible to know what meaning was intended.

EXAMPLE: The __(1)__ is obtained by dividing the __(2)__ by the __(3)__ .   1. _____
                                                                             2. _____
                                                                             3. _____

In its present form, it is impossible to tell to what the statement refers.

BETTER:

1. The IQ is obtained by dividing the __(1)__ by the __(2)__   1. _____
                                                                    2. _____

[12] Devised by S. A. Leonard and others, and published by Cooperative Test Division of Educational Testing Service, Princeton, N.J.

2. The __(1)__ is obtained by dividing the __(2)__ by the CA.   1. _____

                                                                             2. _____

    3. *Omit key words and phrases, rather than trivial details.* If this is not done the response may be as obvious as the first example below, or as unnecessarily difficult as the second example.

EXAMPLES:
1. Abraham Lincoln was born February ____, 1809.   _____
2. Abraham Lincoln was born in ____ County, Kentucky.   _____

    4. *Avoid lifting statements directly from the text.* This places too great a premium on rote memory.
    5. *Avoid grammatical clues to the correct answer.*

EXAMPLE: The authors of the first performance test of intelligence were.. _____

BETTER: The first performance test of intelligence was prepared by .... _____

    6. *Whenever the indefinite article is required before a blank, write it in the form a(n), so that the pupil must decide for himself whether the correct answer begins with a consonant sound or with a vowel sound.*

EXAMPLE: An elementary particle consisting of a charge of negative electricity is called an _____.

BETTER: An elementary particle consisting of a charge of negative electricity is called a(n) _____.

    Clearly, such words as proton, coulomb, molecule, and meson could not be used in the first statement. The second statement contains no specific determiner.
    7. *Try to choose statements in which there is only one correct response for the blanks.* The scoring is far more objective if only one specific word or phrase can be used to complete the statement.
    8. *The required response should be a single word or a brief phrase.* The more words the scorer has to read, the longer scoring will take, because the more words there are in the intended answer, the more different patterns the scorer will have to evaluate subjectively.
    9. *Make the blanks of uniform length.* If the blanks vary in length, the pupil has a clue to the length of the correct answer. Even more of a clue is afforded by using a dot or a dash for each letter in the correct word. Perhaps it is best to use an ellipsis (. . .) for each omitted word in a completion item and put standard-length answer blanks at the right of the item, each blank being long enough for the longest correct response.

EXAMPLE:
1. The second president of the United States was _ _ _ _ _ _ _ _ _ _ from the state of _ _ _ _ _ _ _ _ _ _ _ _.
2. The president in office during the Mexican War was _ _ _ _ _ _ _ _ _ _ _ from the state of _ _ _ _ _ _ _ _ _ _.

BETTER:

1. The second president of the United States was
   ...(1)... from the state of ...(2)...

   1. _____
   2. _____

2. The president in office during the Mexican War was
   ...(1)... from the state of ...(2)...

   1. _____
   2. _____

10. *Arrange the test so that the answers are in a column at the right of the sentences.* The illustrations above show how this may be done. If the sentences contain more than one blank, scoring will be faster if the blanks are numbered and the pupil is directed to write his response in the correspondingly numbered blank in the answer column at the right. The wording of the following directions should be clear to pupils above the fourth grade:

DIRECTIONS: In each of the sentences below, one or more words, numbers, or dates are needed in the numbered dotted spaces to make the sentence complete and true. Place the word or words in the same-numbered blank to the right.

11. *Prepare a scoring key that contains all acceptable answers.* Although it is desirable to have only one "correct" response for each blank, it is not always possible. A satisfactory scoring key generally can be made by writing in red all the correct answers in each blank on an extra copy of the test.

12. *Allow one point for each correctly filled blank.* Assigning fractional credits or unequal weighting of items based on difficulty or importance only complicates scoring and almost always fails to improve reliability or validity (Stanley and Wang, 1970).

At best, the completion item usually is less than fully satisfactory. Disillusioned writers of completion items may wish to try casting them into multiple-choice form. Two examples are given below from the practice booklet entitled "A Description of the College Board Scholastic Aptitude Test":[13]

Each of the sentences below has one or more blank spaces, each blank indicating that a word has been omitted. Beneath the sentence are five lettered words or sets of words. You are to choose the one word or set of words which, when inserted in the sentence, *best* fits in with the meaning of the sentence as a whole.

14. Science is always _____, expecting that modifications of its present theories will sooner or later be found necessary.
    (A) final
    (B) original
    (C) tentative
    (D) practical
    (E) improving

15. Since growth is not a _____ process for all people, the importance of studying the _____ growth pattern has been emphasized.
    (A) uniform .. individual
    (B) healthy .. normal
    (C) unique .. varying
    (D) simple .. fundamental
    (E) normal .. typical

[13] Published annually by the College Entrance Examination Board, c/o Educational Testing Service, Princeton, N.J., and obtainable without cost. These two examples are from p. 30 of the 1963 edition.

No more than two omissions appear in any of these SAT multiple-choice completion items, nor is more than one word required for any blank. Which option did you choose as being correct for item 14? The keyed option is (C). For item 15 the keyed option is (A). Any conscientious clerk can score this kind of completion item, but scoring free-response completion items usually requires expert judgment, because decisions about the correctness of various answers must be made by the scorer.

Fixed-Response Items

A fixed-response item permits only a limited number of possible responses. A common form is the familiar true-false item. Other similar forms are multiple-choice and matching.

ADVANTAGES AND LIMITATIONS

Obvious advantages of the fixed-response test are its apparent ease of construction, applicability to a wide range of subject matter, objectivity of scoring, and wide sampling of knowledge tested per unit of working time. The true-false test, a form very popular with classroom teachers, has been the object of more research and criticism than any other form of objective test. The negative-suggestion effect (that is, the presumably undesirable effect of incorrect statements on students) and the guessing factor are often pointed out as its greatest limitations. The use of the correction formula may provide a fairly satisfactory adjustment for guessing in the total score, but the true-false form is not sufficiently adapted to educational diagnosis because alternatives other than the statement itself are not specified. For instance, if a student answers "False" to the statement, "Columbus discovered America in 1492," what other date—if any—does he have in mind?

The danger of negative suggestion when pupils read statements that are false has apparently been overestimated, but perhaps it is wise not to use true-false tests as pretests when untaught points might be learned incorrectly or with young children who may be susceptible to misinformation. In such cases it is better to avoid the true-false format; instead of a declarative statement, use a question that can be answered *YES* or *NO*.

Several modifications of the true-false test have been proposed. Barton (1931), for example, suggested having students cross out the part of the statement that is in error. Curtis, Datling, and Sherman (1943) and Wright (1944) have shown that having students correct the wrong statements increases the reliability of the test. These suggestions add to the labor of scoring and have not been widely accepted. And in a strict sense, when these modifications are incorporated, the test is no longer of the alternative-response type. The most obvious way to "improve" the true-false test is also the best: *make the test longer and prepare it more carefully*. An advantage of the true-false test is that it can include more items in the same time than most other kinds can. The same-opposite vocabulary item ("Does *hot* mean the same as *cold*, or the opposite?") may be answered even faster. To achieve a satisfactory reliability, however, more true-false items are required than would be necessary with multiple-choice items.

The low regard that many test experts have for the true-false form is indicated by the absence of that form in most recent standardized achievement tests. Although this test has been overused by classroom teachers, it does have a legitimate but restricted use in informal tests. For example, the true-false test seems well adapted to testing the persistence of popular misconceptions and superstitions. In some situations, it is difficult or impossible to construct more than two plausible responses for a multiple-choice item in which one alternative is correct (or true) and the other incorrect. Common examples include the case forms of pronouns (such as *who* vs. *whom*), correct use of singular and plural verbs, confusions of past tense and past participles, the use of *sit* and *set*, *lay* and *lie*, and many others. A safe rule would be to *restrict the use of the true-false test to situations in which other test forms are inapplicable and to give particular care to the wording of the items.*

ILLUSTRATIONS OF TWO-CHOICE
FIXED-RESPONSE ITEMS

*california achievement tests—
advanced battery, form AA*[14]

DIRECTIONS: In the following sentences, mark as you have been told the number of each correct word.

Test 5—Section C

36. ([1]Isn't[2]Aren't) the baskets filled with flowers? _____ 36
47. I approve of ([1]his[2]him) going. _____ 47

For each statement given below that is a complete sentence, mark YES; for each that is not, mark NO.

51. When we approached the deserted farmhouse at night. YES NO 51
56. The mountains resounded with peals of thunder which
    indicated the storm's fury. YES NO 56

*iowa silent reading tests, new edition,
sentence meaning, elementary, form AM*[15]

DIRECTIONS: Read each question. If the answer is "Yes," fill in the space under YES in the margin. If the answer is "No," fill in the space under NO. Study the sample. Do not guess.

1. Is a dime less in value than a nickel? ....1 YES NO

2. Can we see things clearly in a thick fog? ....2 YES NO

3. Is geography studied in public schools? ....3 YES NO

[14] Devised by E. W. Tiegs and W. W. Clark, and published by California Test Bureau.
[15] Devised by H. A. Greene and V. H. Kelley, and published by Harcourt Brace Jovanovich.

DIRECTIONS: A number of controversial statements or questions with two alternative answers are given below. Indicate your personal preferences by writing appropriate figures in the boxes to the right of each question . . . . For each question you have three points that you may distribute in any of the following combinations.

1. If you agree with alternative (a) and disagree with (b), write 3 in the first box and 0 in the second box. . . .
2. If you agree with (b); disagree with (a), write [0 in the first box and 3 in the second box].
3. If you have a slight preference for (a) over (b), write [2 in the first box and 1 in the second box].
4. If you have a slight preference for (b) over (a), write [1 in the first box and 2 in the second box]. . . .

1. The main object of scientific research should be the discovery of truth rather than its practical applications.

   (a) Yes   (b) No
     a   b
    □   □

10. If you were a university professor and had the necessary ability, would you prefer to teach: (a) poetry; (b) chemistry and physics?
     a   b
    □   □

tests in english fundamentals: grammar[17]

DIRECTIONS: Classify the italicized words in the sentence below as adjectives or adverbs by placing check marks in the proper columns:

		Adjective	*Adverb*
3. That was a *silly* remark.	3		
6. Those flowers smell *sweet*.	6		
11. You can *hardly* expect him to wait.	11		

the iowa every-pupil tests in basic skills[18]

DIRECTIONS: In each of the following sentences there are two or more numbered words or phrases enclosed in brackets. If you think the *first* word or phrase is correct, place an X in the *first* box of the corresponding row on the answer sheet. If you think the *second* answer is correct, place an X in the *second* box of the proper row, etc.

7. Ted is $\begin{Bmatrix} 1.\ a \\ 2.\ an \end{Bmatrix}$ industrious man.

[16] Devised by G. W. Allport, P. E. Vernon, and G. Lindzey, and published by Houghton Mifflin Company, 1960.
[17] Devised by R. Davis and published by Ginn and Company.
[18] Devised by H. A. Greene and published by Extension Division, State University of Iowa, 1939.

54. My father 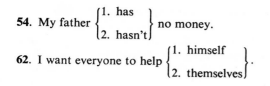 no money.

62. I want everyone to help $\begin{Bmatrix} 1.\ \text{himself} \\ 2.\ \text{themselves} \end{Bmatrix}$.

cooperative plane geometry test, revised series Q[19]

DIRECTIONS: Read these statements and mark each one in the parentheses at the right with a plus sign (+) if you think it is always true, or with a zero (0) if you think it is always or sometimes false.

1. The opposite angles of a parallelogram are equal . . 1   (   )

17. If two triangles are similar, their areas are in the same ratio as the medians drawn to corresponding sides   . . 17   (   )

2. A diameter of a circle divides the circle into two equal parts 2   (   )

18. All similar polygons are equilateral 18   (   )

tests on everyday problems in science: unit III[20]

DIRECTIONS: There are 25 incomplete statements in this test, each followed by parts (a), (b), (c), and (d). One or more of these parts, or perhaps none of them, correctly complete the incomplete statement. You are to place a plus sign (+) in the parentheses (near the right margin) opposite each part which correctly completes the statement, and a minus sign (−) opposite each part which does not correctly complete the statement.

13. Minerals in our food supply
(a) furnish heat and energy to the body . . . .(   )
(b) are the only materials of which cells can be built . . . .(   )
(c) are good regulators of certain of the body activities. . . . .(   )
(d) help particularly to build bone and blood . . . .(   )

cooperative solid geometry tests[21]

DIRECTIONS: Read these statements and mark each one in the parentheses at the right with a plus sign (+) if you think it is true, or with a zero (0) if you think it is false, wholly or in part.

4. Any number of planes may be passed through a given straight line.   (   )

27. Two planes parallel to the same straight line are parallel to each other.   (   )

41. The square of a diagonal of a cube is three times the square of its edge.   (   )

---

[19] Devised by Emma Spanney and L. P. Siceloff, and published by the Cooperative Test Division, Educational Testing Service, Princeton, N.J.

[20] Devised by C. J. Pieper and W. L. Beauchamp, and published by Scott, Foresman and Company.

[21] Devised by H. T. Lundholm and others, and published by Cooperative Test Division, Educational Testing Service, Princeton, N.J.

T   F   **1.** "Il Penseroso" describes the charms of a merry social life.
T   F   **2.** "Pilgrim's Progress" is one of the greatest prose allegories in literature.

RULES FOR CONSTRUCTING TRUE-FALSE RESPONSE ITEMS

Experienced test-makers are convinced that preparing excellent alternative-response items requires great skill. The true-false test is generally thought to be one of the easiest to prepare. This superiority is more apparent than real. Unusual care must be exercised in wording true-false statements and questions so that the *content* rather than the *form* of the statement determines the response. The test-maker's aim should be to phrase the statement so no unwarranted clues are provided, but so the meaning is not needlessly obscure. With practice and care, one can attain this balance. The following suggestions may be helpful in constructing true-false tests. Many of the suggestions for constructing multiple-choice tests (found in the next section) are also applicable here.

1. *Avoid specific determiners.* It has been found that teachers' strongly worded statements are more likely to be false than true, but moderately worded statements are more likely to be true than false. (As a wit once said, "Every generalization, including this one, is false.") Examples of the first are those statements containing "all," "always," "never," "no," "none," and "nothing"; examples of the second are those containing "may," "some," "sometimes," "often," "frequently," "generally," and "as a rule." For example, "The gas xenon never combines chemically with any other element" is a false statement, whereas "The gas xenon is generally inert" would probably be considered true, because only with certain rather active elements does it form compounds. If one carefully balances the number of true and false statements containing any one expression, that expression ceases to be a specific determiner that affords a clue to the answer.

"All" and "always" creep in because the teacher is aware of a relatively minor exception. Once the pupil has been tricked in this way, he only needs to recognize "always" as meaning there is an exception in this teacher's items; he does not need to know what that exception is. If an exception is significant, the true-false statement should be made about the exception itself and not in terms of the generalization. For example, instead of the statement "All but the smallest sea creatures lay eggs," say "Whales are mammals" or "A mammal living in the sea is the _____."

2. *Avoid a disproportionate number of either true or false statements.* In several studies it has been shown that false statements are more valid than true ones because pupils who do not know the correct answer tend to acquiesce with "true" (Cronbach, 1942). Therefore, it is sometimes suggested that a test should have more false statements than true ones. Ebel (1965b) suggested that perhaps 60 percent of the items be false. If this were overdone, however, the validity of the false statements would probably be reduced, because the pupil

---

[22] Devised by K. T. Omwake and others, and published by Center for Psychological Service.

might learn to mark all doubtful statements false. Make *approximately* half of the statements true, the other half false.

3. *Avoid the exact wording of the textbook.* Lifting true statements directly from the textbook or making true statements false by changing a single word or expression places too great a premium on rote memory.

4. *Avoid trick statements.* These are usually statements that appear to be true but that are really false because of the petty insertion of some inconspicuous word, phrase, or letter.

EXAMPLES:
1. "The Raven" was written by Edgar Allen Poe. [Notice spelling of All<u>a</u>n.]
2. The Battle of Hastings was fought in 1066 B.C. [Notice B.C.]

BETTER:
1. "The Raven" was written by Edgar Allan Poe. [True]
2. The Battle of Hastings was fought in 55 B.C. [Correct answer: A.D. 1066.]

5. *Limit each statement to the exact point to be tested.* Do not use two or more stimuli to elicit one response, as in the following partly true, partly false statement: "Poe wrote 'The Gold Bug' and *The Scarlet Letter.*"

6. *Avoid double negatives.* Such statements are especially bad because pupils well versed in English grammar might conclude that two negatives equal an affirmative, whereas other pupils would interpret such statements as emphatic negatives. Logically, "I do not have no money" means that I do have some money. A subtler version is "He was not unmindful of my poverty."

7. *Avoid ambiguous statements.* With one interpretation the statement may be true, and with another equally plausible interpretation it may be false. It is impossible to tell what is being measured when a statement has more than one legitimate interpretation. "The Aztecs were a backward people" is true if they are compared with Europeans of the same period, but false if they are compared with U. S. Indians of that time.

8. *Avoid unfamiliar, figurative, or literary language.* The experience of the learner must be considered. A statement is badly worded if a pupil who understands the point involved misses it because of the language employed. "A gorilla is hirsute" tests knowledge of the meaning of that unfamiliar adjective more than it tests knowledge of the hairiness of the gorilla.

9. *Avoid long statements, especially those involving complex sentence structure,* for the same reason as for the preceding suggestion.

10. *Avoid qualitative language wherever possible.* Quantitative language conveys more precisely the meaning intended. Expressions such as "few," "many," "large," "small," "old," "young," "important," and "unimportant" are vague and indefinite. Notice that "more than" and "most" are specific enough to make the truth or falsity of a statement containing them determinable (by measurement or counting), whereas "many" cannot be agreed upon in any way. "Many people voted for Jones in the recent election" can be replaced by "Jones received a majority of the votes cast in the recent election."

11. *Commands cannot be "true" or "false."* They do not state or assert anything; they simply *direct.* Teachers of young children are especially likely to produce such gems as, "Eat the seven basic foods," "Brush your teeth three times a day," and "Start each sentence with a capital letter."

12. *If a statement is to test for the truth or falsity of reason, the main clause should be true and the reason either true or false.* Say either "As it ages, pure copper turns green [true] because it oxidizes [true]" or "As it ages, pure copper turns green [true] because it attracts green algae [false]," and *not* "As it ages, pure copper turns brown [false] because it oxidizes [true]."

13. *Require the simplest possible method of indicating the response.* When separate answer sheets are not used, let the pupil write *T* and *F*, *Y* and *N*, or underline the correct response instead of requiring the pupil to write *True* and *False* or *Yes* and *No*. The symbols "+" for true and "0" for false are so distinct they make scoring even easier. When the pupil must choose between two words or expressions, the responses should be numbered so they simply require him to write the correct number. Indicate by a short line or by ( ) where the pupil should record the response. The responses may be arranged in a column either to the left or right of the statements. Most scorers prefer the answers to the right.

14. *Arrange the statements in groups.* There is less eyestrain for the scorer if the items are arranged in groups of five with double spacing between each group.

15. *Use true-false items only for points that lend themselves unambiguously to this kind of item.* Rarely should a major test be composed exclusively of true-false items.

Multiple-Choice Items

Definition: A multiple-choice item presents two or more responses, only one of which is *correct* or *definitely better* than the others. (It is also possible, especially in English-usage and spelling tests, to have several correct options and only one incorrect or least desirable option, which is to be chosen in each item.) Each item may be in the form of a direct question, an incomplete statement, or a word or phrase. This multiple-choice test is to be distinguished from the multiple-response test, which requires two or more responses to a single item. A simple multiple-choice item is:

The first president of the United States was
A. Lincoln
B. Kennedy
C. Grant
D. Washington
E. Jefferson

In multiple-response form, a similar question would be:

Which one(s) of the following men served as president of the United States?
A. Davis
B. Grant
C. Hamilton
D. Polk
E. Jefferson

The keyed response for the first item is D, Washington. For the second item, the keyed answer is B, D, E, because Grant, Polk, and Jefferson were presidents of the United States.

It is unfortunate that many persons assume the multiple-choice test to be popular because it is easy to score. Its major virtue is that it requires the examinee to *discriminate* among alternatives. The "best-answer" type of multiple-choice item can measure the degree of understanding of abstract concepts. Consider the item below:

2. Which one of these changes would be expected to have the greatest effect on the test-retest reliability of a typical teacher-made test of 50 items?
A) Eliminate the ten items that were answered correctly by all examinees.
B) Eliminate the ten items that had the lowest positive correlations with the total score.
C) Eliminate all ten items that correlated negatively with the total score.
D) Use the correction-for-chance scoring procedure (assume the mean number of items attempted was 48).

The item above is graphically illustrated in Figure 10–1. The "semantic space" concept being measured is reliability. If one understands the concept thoroughly, he should be able to determine that option C is clearly the *best* answer:

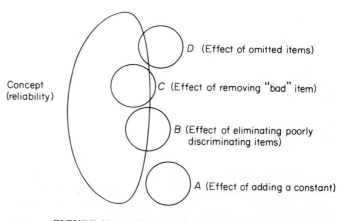

Concept (reliability)

D (Effect of omitted items)

C (Effect of removing "bad" item)

B (Effect of eliminating poorly discriminating items)

A (Effect of adding a constant)

FIGURE 10–1   Graphic illustration of semantic space for a multiple-choice item in educational measurement.

Option A has virtually no effect. These ten items serve only to add a constant to all scores.
Option B would be expected to lower reliability, but only slightly.
Option C would tend to improve reliability.
Option D would have little effect, since almost everyone attempted almost all items.

Such an item can determine whether a concept is fully understood or whether the examinee's thinking is "fuzzy." Consider the illustration in Figure 10–2 of an examinee whose thinking is fuzzy regarding the concept of reliability. The

dashes indicate the student's understanding of the concept. The item seems
ambiguous to that student, not because it is intrinsically ambiguous but because
of inadequacies in the student's knowledge—that is, extrinsic or apparent
ambiguity (Ebel, 1965b, p. 135–136). The item functioned well, since the student
may select an incorrect option and hence not receive credit. Extrinsic ambiguity
is a desirable characteristic of a test designed to measure individual differences;
items should seem ambiguous to those who have a faulty grasp of the concept
being tested.

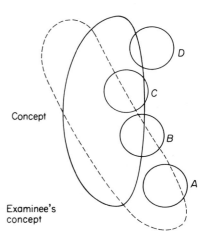

Concept

Examinee's
concept

FIGURE 10–2 *An illustration of the
semantic-space for an item that possesses
extrinsic ambiguity.*

If the students were asked whether option B or D would have the greater
effect, the test-maker may be drawing too fine a line and making a valid discrimination impossible. Such a situation illustrates intrinsic ambiguity, a highly
undesirable item characteristic. Fortunately, this intrinsic ambiguity can be
identified when an item analysis is conducted (see Chapter 11).

There are two possible explanations for item ambiguity. Extrinsic ambiguity may result when the examinee's understanding is faulty. Intrinsic ambiguity results either from imprecise wording or from requesting distinctions that
cannot be validly made with the information available. Intrinsically ambiguous items should be revised or eliminated because they reduce the reliability
and validity of tests.

In his attempt to insure against intrinsic ambiguity, the test-maker often
constructs multiple-choice items so easy that they no longer assess understanding. Consider the following item pertaining to the concept of reliability.

Which one of these changes would be expected to have the greatest effect on
the test-retest reliability of a typical teacher made test of 50 items?

A) Eliminate one item at random.
B) Give the test on Tuesday rather than Wednesday.
C) Shorten the test to 10 items.
D) Add two more easy items.

Such an item is depicted graphically in Figure 10–3.

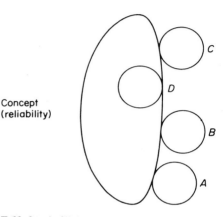

Concept
(reliability)

*FIGURE 10–3   An illustration of the semantic space
of a multiple-choice item that requires little
discrimination.*

The item will not distinguish those who have a clear understanding of the concept from those who do not. The distracters are ineffectual. They should appear plausible to examinees with an adequate grasp of the concept being tested.

Of course, items of the "correct-answer" rather than "best-answer" kind will look like the one in Figure 10–3, but the skillful test constructor will be able to develop attractive distracters; many mathematic or problem-type items require answers that cannot be arrived at by comparing the options.

One can also use the multiple-choice item to require the student to select the poorest or least accurate option. Suppose, for example, on a vocabulary test, persons were asked:

Which of the following terms is most different in meaning from *ruminate*?
a) Contemplate
b) Cogitate
c) Comprehend
d) Ponder
e) Cerebrate
f) Meditate

Option C, "comprehend," has the least overlapping "semantic space" with the term, "ruminate," and hence could be identified by examinees who correctly understand the meaning of the terms, among which they must discriminate.

Of course, if the option "comprehend" were replaced by the term "disseminate," the item would function at a more primitive level, since "disseminate" has little "semantic overlap" with the other options.

POSSIBILITIES AND LIMITATIONS

The multiple-choice item is usually regarded as the most valuable and most generally applicable test form. Prominent measurement specialist Lindquist (see Hawkes, Lindquist, and Mann, 1936, p. 138) asserted that it is "definitely superior to all other types" for measuring such educational objectives as "inferential reasoning, reasoned understanding, or sound judgment and discrimination on the part of the pupil." Another leading psychometrician (Cronbach, 1950) regarded it as less vulnerable to response sets than other item types. Mosier, Meyers, and Price (1945) suggested 14 question types that may be used in multiple-choice test items. The list is not all-inclusive and is not supposed to prescribe exact wording, but it serves as a guide in formulating questions:

1. Definition
   a. What means the same as . . . ?
   b. What conclusion can be drawn from . . . ?
   c. Which of the following statements expresses this concept in different form?
2. Purpose
   a. What purpose is served by . . . ?
   b. What principle is exemplified by . . . ?
   c. Why is this done?
   d. What is the most important reason for . . . ?
3. Cause
   a. What is the cause of . . . ?
   b. Under which of the following conditions is this true?
4. Effect
   a. What is the effect of . . . ?
   b. If this is done, what will happen?
   c. Which of the following should be done (to achieve a given purpose)?
5. Association
   What tends to occur in connection (temporal [same time], causal [one causes the other], or concomitant association [varying together]) with . . . ?
6. Recognition of Error
   Which of the following constitutes an error (with respect to a given situation)?
7. Identification of Error
   a. What kind of error is this?
   b. What is the name of this error?
   c. What recognized principle is violated?
8. Evaluation
   What is the best evaluation of . . . (for a given purpose) and for what reason?
9. Difference
   What is the important difference between . . . ?
10. Similarity
    What is the important similarity between . . . ?

11. Arrangement

   In the proper order (to achieve a given purpose or to follow a given rule), which of the following comes first (or last, or follows a given item)?

12. Incomplete Arrangement

   In the proper order, which of the following should be inserted here to complete the series?

13. Common Principle

   All of the following items except one are related by a common principle.
   a. What is the principle?
   b. Which item does not belong?
   c. Which of the following items should be substituted?

14. Controversial Subjects

   Although not everyone agrees on the desirability of _____, those who support its desirability do so primarily for the reason that _____.

In constructing multiple-choice items, one must be especially careful to avoid the inclusion of irrelevant or superficial clues and to insure that the tests measure more than the memorization of factual knowledge. The measurement value of multiple-choice tests depends more on the skillful selection of the incorrect choices presented in the items than on any other factor (Weitzman and McNamara, 1946).

ILLUSTRATIONS OF MULTIPLE-CHOICE TESTS

The items below, most taken from standardized tests, illustrate several different arrangements of multiple-choice tests in a variety of subjects.[23] The multiple-choice test is widely used in all school subjects and on all educational levels for measuring a variety of teaching objectives.

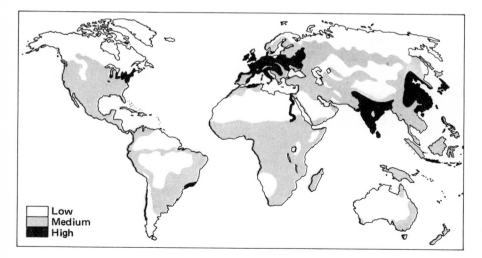

Low
Medium
High

[23] These tests are not all equally good. Also, the observant reader will note that some of them are not wholly consistent with the principles set forth in this chapter.

The shading on the above map is used to indicate
(A) population density
(B) percentage of total labor force in agriculture
(C) per capita income
(D) death rate per thousand of population

In many of the multiple-choice questions included in tests in the social sciences, an attempt is made to require the student to make use of his general background of knowledge in the interpretation of materials. Thus, this question does not simply ask: What areas of the world have the highest population densities? Rather, it presents a novel situation in which the student must infer that, of the choices offered, only population density provides a plausible explanation of the shadings on the map.

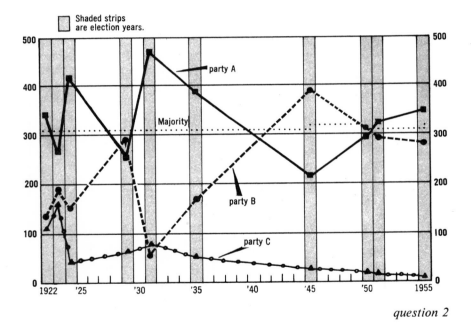

question 2

The graph above represents the political composition from 1922 to 1955 of which of the following?
(A) German Bundestag
(B) French National Assembly
(C) Italian Chamber of Deputies
(D) British House of Commons

To answer this question correctly, the student must be able to do several things. First, he must be able to read the graph. Then, using the information he can infer from it, he must interpret it in the light of his knowledge of European history and government from 1922 to 1955 and draw a conclusion concerning which legislative body may properly be so depicted. In such a process, it is possible for different students to make use of different information to arrive at the correct answer.

question 17

One method of obtaining "artificial gravity" in a space station is to have the station rotating about axis AA′ as it revolves around Earth.

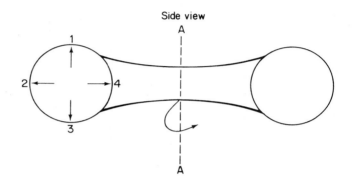

Side view

The inhabitants of the space station would call which direction "down"?
(A) Direction 1
(B) Direction 2
(C) Direction 3
(D) Direction 4
(E) Any one of the four, depending on speed of rotation

This was part of a set of questions administered to high school students who were completing a year of high school physics. The question illustrates the kind of response that can be expected of well-trained students of high school age when they are presented with a relatively novel situation which is based on fundamental concepts from the field of mechanics.

This question requires that the student consider the nature of a possible mechanism for providing a "down" direction in a space station to simulate the gravitational "down" so important in our normal activities on Earth. Choice (C) is the direction normally considered down in diagrams. Although this direction is not significant in the space station, a sizable number of the poorer physics students chose it. Other students assumed that the "down" direction would be that one toward the center of rotation of the station, choice (D). However, objects free to move in the space station behave as do particles in a centrifuge and "fall" to the outer edge. This direction, (B), then is the "down" direction in the rotating station. The other choices, (A), "up" as it is usually represented in diagrams, and (E), a direction which depends on the speed of rotation, were not selected by many students.

kuhlmann-finch intelligence tests, test IV [25]

13. **Early** is to **begin** as **late** is to
1	2	3	4	5
start	end	awake	enter	prompt

22. **Flour** is to **bread** as **sugar** is to
1	2	3	4	5
sweet	candy	fruit	cook	eat

the modern school achievement tests, language usage [26]

DIRECTIONS: In each sentence, choose the word or group of words that makes the best sentence. Then on the dotted line at the right, copy the number that is before the correct form.

              1. **off**
4. I borrowed a pen 2. **off of**   my brother.   . . . . . .
              3. **from**
              1. **your**
7. Every student must do 2. **his**   best.   . . . . . .
              3. **their**
      1. **has got**
17. He 2. **has**   his violin with him.   . . . . . .
      3. **has gotten**

the barrett-ryan literature test: silas marner [27]

A. ( ) An episode that advances the plot is the—1. murdering of a man. 2. kidnapping of a child. 3. stealing of money. 4. fighting of a duel.
B. ( ) Dolly Winthrop is—1. an ambitious society woman. 2. a frivolous girl. 3. a haughty lady. 4. a kind, helpful neighbor.
C. ( ) A chief characteristic of the novel is—1. humorous passages. 2. portrayal of character. 3. historical facts. 4. fairy element.

wesley test in political terms [28]

1. An embargo is
   1. a law or regulation
   2. a kind of boat
   3. an explorer
   4. a foolish adventure
   5. an embankment   ( )

[25] Devised by F. H. Finch, F. Kuhlmann, and G. L. Betts, and published by American Guidance Service, Inc.
[26] Devised by A. I. Gates and others, and published by Teachers College Press.
[27] Devised by E. R. Barrett, T. M. Ryan, and H. E. Schrammel, and published by Kansas State Teachers College, Emporia.
[28] Devised by E. B. Wesley and published by Charles Scribner's Sons.

2. An injunction is a
   1. part of speech
   2. wreck
   3. union of two things
   4. court order
   5. form of advice ( )

*unit scales of attainment in foods and
household management*[29]

2. The spoon should be placed
   1. at the top of the plate
   2. at the left of the fork
   3. in the spoon holder on the table
   4. at the right of the knife ( )
40. We get the most calories per pound from
   1. proteins
   2. carbohydrates
   3. fats
   4. mineral matter
   5. vitamins ( )

traxler silent reading test, word meaning [30]

8. The *commendation* is deserved.
   (1) success
   (2) blow
   (3) popularity
   (4) good fortune
   (5) praise ( )
9. His actions received *condemnation.*
   (1) approval
   (2) applause
   (3) censure
   (4) sympathy
   (5) contempt ( )

*college entrance examination board
foreign-language items*[31]

1. C'est la fin de l'entracte, et la pièce est très amusante.
   Vous dites à votre camarade:
   (A) La pièce va commencer tout de suite.
   (B) Qu'allons-nous faire maintenant?
   (C) Allons reprendre nos places.
   (D) Voulez-vous aller fumer une cigarette?

[29] Devised by E. B. Reeve and C. M. Brown, and published by Educational Test Bureau.
[30] Devised by A. E. Traxler and published by Public School Publishing Company.
[31] From *A description of the College Board achievement tests* (Princeton, N.J.: College Entrance Examination Board, 1963). The items are from pp. 33, 38, 17, and 22–23.

4. I am glad to see you.

Es freut mich, . . . zu sehen.

(A) Ihnen

(B) Sie

(C) ihn

(D) sie

college entrance examination board english items

DIRECTIONS: The following sentences contain problems in grammar, usage, word choice, and idiom.

Some sentences are correct.

No sentence contains more than one error.

You will find that the error, if any, will be underlined and lettered, and that all other elements of the sentence are correct and cannot be changed.

If there is an error, select the *one underlined part* that must be changed in order to make the sentence correct, and blacken the corresponding space on your answer sheet.

If there is no error, mark answer space E.

EXAMPLE: He spoke <u>bluntly</u> and <u>angrily</u> to <u>we</u> <u>spectators</u>. <u>No error</u>
            A   B   C   D   E

SAMPLE ANSWER: A   B   C   D   E
                    ☐   ☐   ■   ☐   ☐

---

1. <u>Had we known of</u> your desire to go with us, we <u>most</u> certainly <u>would of</u>
        A   B   C
invited you <u>to join</u> our party. <u>No error</u>
            D   E

2. Neither Harriet nor Claire <u>was</u> <u>completely</u> convinced by <u>Joan's</u> insisting
                                  A   B   C
that it was <u>them</u> who were to blame. <u>No error</u>
            D   E

3. Big Konrad's new helper, though somewhat <u>slighter</u> of build than <u>him</u>, set
                                               A   B
out <u>to prove that</u> skill <u>may</u> compensate for lack of brute strength. <u>No error</u>
    C   D   E

DIRECTIONS: Each group of sentences in this section is actually a paragraph presented in scrambled order. Each sentence in the group has a place in that paragraph; no sentence is to be left out. You are to read each group of sentences and decide the best order in which to put the sentences so as to form a well-organized paragraph.

Before trying to answer the questions which follow each group of sentences, jot down the correct order of the sentences in the margin of the test book. Then answer each of the questions by blackening the appropriate space on the answer sheet. Remember that you will receive credit only for answers marked on the answer sheet. . . .

P. The Empire State Express, loaded with passengers, left New York.

Q. Unlike the businessmen, however, a few reporters on board had been told that this run would be newsworthy and were eagerly waiting for something unusual to occur.

R. At last the big day, May 10, arrived.

S. If some of the important businessmen on board had known what was going to happen, they might have found an excuse to leave the train at Albany.

T. Her secret had been carefully kept.

U. Only a few officials knew that a record was to be tried for.

CORRECT
ORDER
OF
SENTENCES

R
P
T
U
S
Q

*Constructing
Specific
Types of
Objective Tests*

sample questions

i. Which sentence did you put first?
  (A) Sentence P
  (B) Sentence R
  (C) Sentence S
  (D) Sentence T
  (E) Sentence U

ii. Which sentence did you put after Sentence P?
  (A) Sentence Q
  (B) Sentence R
  (C) Sentence S
  (D) Sentence T
  (E) Sentence U

iii. Which sentence did you put after Sentence Q?
  (A) Sentence P
  (B) Sentence R
  (C) Sentence T
  (D) Sentence U
  (E) None of the above. Sentence Q is last.

sample answer sheet

	A	B	C	D	E
i	☐	■	☐	☐	☐
ii	☐	☐	☐	■	☐
iii	☐	☐	☐	☐	■

*cooperative test of social studies abilities,
experimental form Q*[32]

Interpreting Facts

DIRECTIONS: The exercises in this part consist of a series of paragraphs each followed by several statements about the paragraph. In the parentheses after each statement, put the number

  1. if the statement is a reasonable interpretation, fully supported by the facts given in the paragraph.

[32] Devised by J. W. Wrightstone and published originally by Cooperative Test Service.

2. if the statement goes beyond and cannot be proved by the facts given in the paragraph.

3. if the statement contradicts the facts given in the paragraph.

[*The sample exercise and its explanation are omitted.*]

I. The nineteenth century witnessed a rapid growth in Germany's industrial power. Like England, Germany came to have a fairly satisfactory balance between the amount of its export and import trade. Heavy exports of coke supplied full cargoes for ships to foreign ports and helped to balance heavy importations of raw materials. The imports especially provided a means for distributing freight rates to the advantage of the German trader competing overseas. By these means Germany was constantly obtaining larger portions of world trade. German wares were carried into every trading realm, and trade meant political as well as commercial power in foreign lands.

    1. Through growth in foreign trade, Germany's industrial power increased in the nineteenth century . . . . 1 ( )

    2. Germany had an export trade equal in volume to that of England . . 2 ( )

    3. Germany exported very little coke to foreign countries . . . . 3 ( )

    4. England was unable to balance the tonnage of her import and export shipments . . . . 4 ( )

    5. By reducing freight rates Germany was constantly gaining a greater percentage of world trade. . . . . 5 ( )

    6. The sale of German wares in every part of the world resulted in added political influence and commercial growth . . . . 6 ( )

sequential tests of educational progress (STEP), science[33]

Level 4 (Grades 4-6)

SITUATION: Tom wanted to learn which of three types of soil—clay, sand, or loam— would be best for growing lima beans. He found three flowerpots, put a different type of soil in each pot, and planted lima beans in each. He placed them side by side on the window sill and gave each pot the same amount of water.

                  LOAM   CLAY   SAND

    The lima beans grew best in the loam. Why did Mr. Jackson say Tom's experiment was **NOT** a good experiment and did **NOT** prove that loam was the best soil for plant growth?

    A The plants in one pot got more sunlight than the plants in the other pots.

    B The amount of soil in each pot was not the same.

    C One pot should have been placed in the dark.

    D Tom should have used three kinds of seeds.

Level 3 (Grades 7-9)

[33] *A prospectus for the Cooperative Sequential Tests of Educational Progress* (Princeton, N.J.: Cooperative Test Division, Educational Testing Service, 1957). We illustrate only one test item for each situation, but STEP Science itself has several.

SITUATION: Tom planned to become a farmer and his father encouraged this interest by giving Tom a part of the garden to use for studying plant life.

Tom wanted to find out what effect fertilizer has on garden plants. He put some good soil in two different boxes. To box A he added fertilizer containing a large amount of nitrogen. To box B he added fertilizer containing a large amount of phosphorus. In each box he planted 12 bean seeds. He watered each box with the same amount of water. One thing missing from Tom's experiment was a box of soil with

A both fertilizers added
B neither nitrogen nor phosphorus fertilizers added
C several kinds of seed planted
D no seeds planted

Several test publishers provide excellent practice materials. The College Entrance Examination Board's extensive booklets are splendid.[34] Although they are much shorter, the California Test Bureau's "Practice exercises for marking answers to tests on machine-scoring answer sheets, scoreze, or Cal-cards"[35] can be very helpful for introducing pupils, particularly in the lower grades, to new items and to new ways of marking them. Below is an item from the practice exercises and one from the sample test:

Thirty-four sample items from social science, natural science, and the humanities are contained in an announcement of the Area Tests of the Graduate Record Examinations of the Educational Testing Service.[36] One sample is:

[34] See the current *A description of the College Board Scholastic Aptitude Test* and *A description of the College Board achievement tests*, both obtainable without cost from the College Entrance Examination Board, Princeton, N.J. 08540.

[35] California Test Bureau, Del Monte Research Park, Monterey, Calif. Four pages, including seven practice items and a 15-item sample test to be marked on two different answer sheets.

[36] *Assessing the broad outcomes of education in the liberal arts* (Princeton, N.J.: Educational Testing Service, n.d.), 15 pp.

3. "I am tired of being lectured to about these schedules . . . Let us recognize the fact that with a tariff bill it is just as it is with the river and harbor bills. There is no use denying it. You tickle me and I tickle you."

In this statement, Senator Knute Nelson was

(A) holding that the tariff is a form of pork-barrel legislation
(B) defending protection because it unifies the country
(C) favoring internal improvements
(D) arguing for less government intervention in business
(E) questioning the usefulness of tariffs

Several multiple-choice items, including analogies, are also illustrated at the end of Chapter 2.

RULES FOR CONSTRUCTING
MULTIPLE-CHOICE ITEMS

Testing specialist Harry D. Berg (1958, 1961) gave suggestions for increasing the thought content of objective test items in the social studies, which he illustrated with four- or five-option multiple-choice items. Jason Millman (1961) listed 22 "Multiple-choice test item construction rules" under the headings "Communicate well" and "Don't give away the answer." Fourteen of Berg's rules are similar to Millman's, but the other 14 represent an ingenious attempt to pitch the level of items above rote knowledge or general intelligence. Here are 21 of Millman's rules, in expanded and somewhat altered form:

1. *The stem should contain the central problem and all qualifications*, including words that would otherwise be repeated in each alternative. For example, if the incomplete statement form is used, it must clearly imply a specific question. The pupil should not be required to construct his own question by consulting the options. In two of his examples, Berg illustrates such flaws.

I. "The study of the price system narrows down to an analysis of these two sets of prices and the interrelationships between them" (Knight, *Social Economic Organization*). The two sets of prices referred to are
(A) those for consumption goods and those for capital goods.
(B) those for consumption goods and those for productive services.
(C) those for labor and those for the other productive factors.
(D) those for economic and those for non-economic goods.

Obviously, the second sentence of the stem should have read "The two sets of prices referred to are those for," because "those for" occurs as the first two words of every option. If the incomplete form of stem is used, it must include all the language that is exactly applicable in every option, in order to avoid wasting the pupil's time by repetition in each option.

II. Consumer cooperatives
(A) are to consumers what labor unions are to laborers.
(B) have recently been declared illegal.
(C) originated in the United States and later spread to Europe.
(D) have been criticized as not paying their equitable share of taxes.

Here there are actually four true-false questions; each concerns consumer cooperatives, but only one is keyed as true. The stem, "Consumer cooperatives," does not constitute a statement of a central problem. Questions that lend themselves naturally to a true-false item form should not be forced into a multiple-choice style, and vice versa.

2. *Each item should be as short as possible*, consistent with clarity. Otherwise, it may be more a test of reading ability than is desirable, or, at least, require too much valuable testing time.

3. *Try to avoid negatively stated stems*, but if the negative form is used, emphasize the fact by underlining or using italics. As Berg (1958, p. 8) wrote, "Negative items increase testing opportunities, but it is well to group them together and to underscore such words as 'not,' 'never,' and 'least.' Another technique to use with such items is to end the stem with the words 'with one exception. Select the exception.'" For example, "Each of the following men *except one* was president of the United States. Which one was *not*?"

4. *The stem should, without aid from other items, state the problem of the question fully.* Items should be largely independent of each other whenever possible, though several of them may refer to a common passage; for instance, four or five questions can be based on the same paragraph to be read.

5. *Ask for the best answer or use terms such as "most" and "primary" if more than one answer is at least partially correct.* One alternative should clearly be best. For example, "The one factor generally considered most important in causing the United States to enter World War II at the time that it did was . . . ."

6. *The omissions in incomplete statements should usually not occur early in the stem.* This might lead to confusion and necessitate excessive rereading of the stem. There are instances in which exceptions to this and other rules should be made. Note the following item (number 20 from page 31 of the 1963 SAT sample booklet), to which the "rule" does not seem applicable:

_____ no physical basis for the disorder can be found with the tests now available, doctors refuse to say that the cause must be _____.
(A) Although . . . mental
(B) Insofar as . . . hereditary
(C) Since . . . unknown
(D) When . . . mysterious
(E) Because . . . serious

7. *The linguistic difficulty of items should be low.* Berg (1958, p. 8) explicitly stated the rule and provided an example: "The incidental vocabulary and phrasings used in items should not be above the general level, nor should technical terms which have not been studied be used.

"Of the following, the chief difference between man and the lower animals is that the lower animals
(A) are incapable of any communication.
(B) cannot develop true conditioned responses.
(C) lack adaptive instincts.
(D) do not become objects to themselves.
(E) are independent of the homeostatic principle."

"Homeostatic" and "conditioned responses" are perhaps too technical for the context.

8. *Try to test a different point with each item.* A long test may actually cover only a few points if it repeatedly tests the same point with slightly different items. Many aspects can usually be tested if some care is taken; consequently there is better sampling of instructional objectives.

9. *When there is a logical sequence in which alternatives can occur (as in order of magnitude, temporal sequence, and so on), use it,* but be sure that in the test as a whole each option occurs as the keyed response approximately as frequently as any other option. Avoid regularly recurring patterns of correct responses, for pupils are likely to detect them.

10. *Distracters must be plausible and attractive if the item is to measure real understanding.* Distracters (foils, decoys) are the incorrect options. They must be prepared at least as carefully as is the keyed option, or they will not elicit responses from the unknowledgeable. As we noted earlier, for ideal discrimination among pupils a five-option item should be of 50 percent difficulty when *corrected for chance*. Therefore, it should be answered correctly by about 60 percent of the students who mark it (because 60 percent — 40 percent/4 = 50 percent), and some of the students should mark each incorrect option. The item writer will usually try to position the various incorrect options at several levels of knowledge, from nearly enough to answer the item correctly to very little. After the item has been administered, an item analysis may be made to determine how well the distracters functioned. Then unattractive distracters can be replaced with seemingly better options, unless the item already discriminates so well between high and low scorers on the test as a whole that the test-maker considers it unwise to disturb the options.

For example, a teacher of general mathematics in a junior high school might devise the following test item because he hoped that its various options would attract students from five levels of ability in his class:

The positive fourth root of 16 is:

A 2
B 4
C 12
D 64
E 16^4

The correct answer is A (because $2 \times 2 \times 2 \times 2 = 16$), which can be expressed as $16^{1/4}$. A student who confused "root" with "power" might choose E. Perhaps such students would be abler, on the average, than students who chose option B, 4, which is the second root of 16. Students who chose D, 64, which is 4×16, might be abler than students who marked C, 12, which is $16 - 4$.

Of course, the options may not function as the teacher planned, but the item would still distinguish the able students from the less able ones if the better students on the test marked A and the poorer ones distributed their choices among options B through E.

Devising excellent multiple-choice items is a highly creative process, particularly in the preparation of distracters.

Inconsistent articles, changes in tense, and the like may nullify otherwise excellent distracters. We mentioned earlier how an item such as the following gives a strong grammatical clue to the keyed option:

Which of the following men were famous explorers?
A Lewis and Clark
B Van Gogh
C Rogers and Hart
D Aaron Burr
E Benjamin Franklin

The plural wording, me*n* and explorer*s*, points to options A and C only. One might solve this problem by substituting the following options for B, D, and E:

B Gauguin and Van Gogh
D Burr and Hamilton
E Franklin and Jefferson

12. *The length, explicitness, or degree of technicality of alternatives should not vary with correctness.* This rule is related to number 7 above, but differs in that the characteristics above give clues to the keyed answer, whereas in number 7 the technicality tended more to confuse students. A highly qualified, cautiously worded option is likely to be both long and correct. A strange technical word in an option often signifies a distracter, for if a reasonably competent student cannot recall having ever seen it before, the chances are good that it is not the keyed answer. Inexperienced item writers and item writers who are not completely familiar with the topic being tested are prone to use such options.

A general-science item may help clarify this rule:

An atom is
A an amalgam.
B a compound.
C a mixture.
D a molecule.
E the basic "building block" of matter, consisting of a nucleus surrounded by electrons in orbits.

If the class has not yet studied amalgams, the test-wise student will probably ignore option A. He will notice immediately that option E is much longer than the other answers. Even without a clear idea of the relationship of atoms to compounds, mixtures, and molecules (much less to amalgams), he will have little doubt that the keyed answer is E, because it "stands out" from the others (Chase, 1964). Some experienced item writers will occasionally choose to lure this test-wise type of student astray by making one or more of the incorrect options long and elaborate but leaving the correct option short and simple.

13. *Alternatives should be rather homogeneous in subject content, form, and grammatical structure.* The following illustration (Hawkes, Lindquist, and Mann, 1936, pp. 146–147) shows how the degree of required discrimination increases with homogeneity of the options presented:

I. Engel's law deals with
   (A) the coinage of money.
   (B) the inevitableness of socialism.
   (C) diminishing returns.
   (D) marginal utility.
   (E) family expenditures.
II. Engel's law deals with family expenditures for
   (A) luxuries.
   (B) food.
   (C) clothing.
   (D) rest.
   (E) necessaries.
III. According to Engel's law, family expenditures for food
   (A) increase in accordance with the size of the family.
   (B) decrease as income increases.
   (C) require a smaller percentage of an increasing income.
   (D) rise in proportion to income.
   (E) vary with the tastes of families.

To respond correctly to item I, the student must know only that Engel's law deals with family expenditures. For II, he must know that the specific item of expenditure is food. The maximum degree of discrimination, however, is required for answering III, in which more information is given in the stem. These three items also illustrate the last portion of rule 13: *Make all optional responses for a given item parallel in grammatical structure.* Note that grammatical consistency is least true in I, but that even there the basis of each option is a modified noun. All five responses in II are single-word nouns. All responses in III begin with a verb in the present tense, third person plural.

14. *Avoid unintentionally allowing the correct response to occur appreciably more often in one option position than in another.* This is the reverse of the logical-sequence suggestion in rule 9, above, and was covered there. Four options for a given item may occur in any one of $4 \times 3 \times 2 \times 1 = 24$ orders, five options may occur in 120 different orders, and six options can be arranged in 720 ways! (Try this with books on a library shelf. Three books can be arranged in $3 \times 2 \times 1 = 6$ ways.) See that you use the various option positions (A, B, C, . . .) approximately equally frequently for the keyed response, even when logical considerations suggest certain orders for some items. You will want to vary slightly from *exactly k/o* occurrences in each option position, where k is the number of items and o is the number of alternatives (that is, options) for each item, because having precisely the right number of options correct in each position might help the best students, who know most of the answers, to infer answers to items about which they are uncertain.

15. *Have at least four options per item* unless doing so requires using implausible options. Five alternatives per item are optimal for many situations, but sometimes six or more excellent options may be available. For certain materials, as few as two options per item may be best. The number of options from item to item may even be varied.

16. *Avoid poetic repetition of sounds or repetition of words or phrases between the stem and the correct answer.* Berg qualified the rule as follows: "It is legitimate, even desirable, to incorporate in the incorrect responses phrasing,

etc., which would be weaknesses in the correct response. Such things as lengthiness, repetition of words appearing in the stem, and 'pat' phrases are examples." Like all rules, this can be overdone. If all distracters are loaded with irrelevant lengthiness, false technicality, and words from the stem, but the correct response stands out because of clarity and simplicity, test-wise students will be able to "spot" it without much knowledge about the point being tested. The test constructer must be clever and versatile; he should be able to read the students' minds in advance (and in retrospect, too, from the item analysis) without permitting his intentions to be discernible.

For example, in the following question the word "battle" appears in the stem and in the keyed option only; thus it provides a clue for the observant pupil:

A decisive battle between United States soldiers and American Indians was the
A. battle called "Custer's last stand."
B. fighting at Yorktown.
C. War of 1812.
D. storming of the Alamo.

Notice that option C, "War of 1812," is poor because the stem specifies a single battle, whereas a war usually involves more than one battle. The test-wise student will ignore option C.

The question might be reworded as follows:

A decisive battle between United States soldiers and American Indians was the
A. last stand of Custer.
B. fighting at Yorktown.
C. Battle of Gettysburg.
D. Battle of the Alamo.

Now the word "Battle" appears in two incorrect options but not in the keyed option, so it may distract test-wise students who do not know the correct keyed answer.

17. *Avoid textbook wording or stereotyped phraseology*, except perhaps in distracters as discussed above.

18. *Avoid stems that reveal the answer to another item.* One item should not help the student answer another item that is meant to be independent of it. Therefore, the assembled items that form the test must be reviewed carefully in relation to each other. It may help, when time permits, to have a competent person check the entire test for overlapping items.

19. *Alternatives should not overlap, include, or be synonymous with one another*, especially within a given item. Consider the following item.

A substance that in its pure form is a good conductor of electricity is
A. water.
B. silver.
C. H_2S.
D. H_2O.

Since there is one correct or best answer, the alert student can eliminate options A and D immediately. His chances of getting credit for the item are greatly increased even if credit is undeserved.

Inexperienced, unimaginative, or lazy item writers sometimes reuse the same or similar alternatives in different items to such a great extent that they in effect prepare wordy matching tests (discussed in the next section) and not proper multiple-choice tests. The matching-test format is appropriately used only when the mere matching of stimuli with responses is the mental operation tested.

20. *Avoid specific determiners* such as "always" and "never," except occasionally to foil test-wise examinees who know about specific determiners; students know that few things are always true or never true. This requires that the usually determining word be employed in the nondetermined way part of the time, as for example "The product of 4 and 3 is (a) always 12; (B) not always the same as 3×4; (C) 7." Options containing "always" would have to be true statements as often as they are false, so that the student could not reject them automatically. Even then, some test-wise pupils may outsmart the teacher. The skillful use of words that are usually specific determiners is a task only for expert writers of options and stems.

21. *In testing the understanding of a term or concept, one should usually present the term first, followed by a series of definitions or descriptions from which the choice is to be made.* If the order is reversed, so the one that best fits the definition or descriptive statement is chosen from a series of terms, the selection frequently can be made on the basis of superficial verbal associations without genuine understanding.

To these 21 rules we add the following seven:

22. *Avoid arranging items in the same order as they were presented in the textbook.* This is especially important on spelling tests, multiplication tables, and other learning tasks in which serial learning is possible. Although test scores are sometimes higher (but not usually—Marso, 1970b) when items are arranged in the order they were learned (Norman, 1954), the logical validity of the test is reduced.

23. *Do not include so many items in the test that it becomes a speed rather than a power test.* Thought-provoking and problem-solving items can be time-consuming; items measuring rote knowledge can be answered quickly. If a teacher realizes that too many items have been included in the test for the time allowed, probably he should inform the class that a specified number of the last items will not be scored.

24. *"None of these" may be a useful last option* for correct-answer items, especially in mathematics (Williamson and Hopkins, 1967). Avoid using it when the keyed response is merely the *best* answer among the responses given rather than the wholly correct or best possible answer. The option saves the test-maker's time, since it can be used repeatedly. Which answer would you mark for the following item?

49 divided by 6 equals
A. 294
B.   55
C.   43
D.   .12245
E. None of the above answers.

The "none of these" option can introduce intrinsic ambiguity if it is not used carefully. In the illustrative item, if option D were changed to 8.2, which answer would you select? The exact answer is $8\frac{1}{6}$, or 8.1666.... The item would probably be keyed D, because 8.2 is the correct answer to one decimal place. How can the student who knows how to divide 49 by 6 decide whether to mark D or E? E here may serve only to introduce "frozen subjectivity" into the test.

The four distracters involve the use of an incorrect operation (multiplication, addition, subtraction, or inverted division): 49×6, $49 + 6$, $49 - 6$, and $6/49$, respectively.

Also, be careful that "None of these" is the correct response approximately $1/o$th of the time that it occurs, where o is the number of options the item has—2, 3, 4, 5 or more. If it is used as the fifth option in each of 50 five-option items, then, on the average, it should be the keyed response about 10 times. "None of these" should not be a desperation response, resorted to when inspiration fails. Apparently, it is used rather infrequently by professional item writers. The 1963 practice booklets for the College Entrance Examination Board *Scholastic Aptitude Test* and the Achievement Tests do not contain it, although the final option (E) for some geometry problems, "It cannot be determined from the information given," is an equivalent.

25. *"All of the above" or "More than one of the above" may sometimes be suitable*, but usually the alternatives are made more specific, as in the two following examples from p. 86 of the 1963 CEEB "A description of the College Board achievement tests":

Given $\triangle PQR$ with median RS. Which of the following *must* be true?
 I. RS is perpendicular to PQ.
 II. RS bisects $\angle QRP$.
 III. $\triangle PQR$ is a right triangle.
 (A) None   (B) I only   (C) II only
 (D) III only   (E) I, II and III

The keyed answer to the above question is (A) None. Does the *must* in the stem function as a specific determiner?

If h, k, m, and n are positive numbers, k is greater than m, and n is greater than h, which of the following is (are) true?
 I. $n + h$ may equal $k + m$.
 II. $k + h$ may equal $n + m$.
 III. $k + n$ may equal $m + h$.
 (A) I, II, and III   (B) I and II only   (C) I and III only   (D) I only
 (E) None

Notice that the I, II, and III above may be combined in eight ways, producing eight possible options: *none* (1), *any one* (3), *any two* (3), *and all* (1). In the first question *none*, the three *ones*, and *all* are used. In the second question *none*, *one* (once), *two* (twice), and *all* occur. Would it be desirable to offer all eight alternatives for each such item, instead of just five? If feasible from the scoring standpoint, the eight options would be useful because they include all possible alternatives and also reduce the number of chance successes. Another possibility would be to recast the item into three separate true-false questions.

FORM

26. *Paragraph each option,* unless all options are so brief that they easily fit on a single line. This reduces the time and effort needed to locate the correct answer.

27. *Number items and letter options,* as illustrated above.

28. *Punctuation for options.* If the stem of the item is an incomplete statement, each option (*not the series of options*) is by itself a possible completion of the statement. Therefore, each should begin with a lower-case letter and be followed by a terminal mark of punctuation (period, question mark, exclamation point) and not by a semicolon, as is often found. If the stem is a direct question, and each option a sentence that might possibly answer it, begin each option with a capital letter and follow it by a terminal mark of punctuation. If the stem is a question, but the options are words or phrases and not complete sentences, begin each option with a capital letter but do not put any mark of punctuation at its end. Other possibilities occur, as shown in the illustrations below from various unrevised teacher-made tests:

The defeat of the Danes by King Alfred prevented them from
(A) destroying Christianity in England.
(B) driving the older tribes from England.
(C) conquering all the Anglo-Saxons.

A rose is a
(A) box.
(B) flower.
(C) home.
(D) month.

Ingor is a new child in school. He has been in this country only a year. He can speak English but still has difficulty with some words. He also has an accent. What would be best for you to say to the boys and girls who are teasing him?
(A) He is better than you, anyway. He knows two languages.
(B) Why don't you go tease somebody else?
(C) He is trying. Why not give him a chance?
(D) You are too ignorant to listen and understand him.

The woods listed below are used in furniture construction. Which one is classified as a hardwood?
(A) White pine
(B) Walnut
(C) Red cedar

In the following group of words, one word does not belong in the group because of its part of speech. Mark the letter of that word on the answer sheet. (A) toward (B) beyond (C) before (D) running (E) on

Tommy reached greedily for his dessert, but, noticing his mother's disapproving look, he . . . pulled toward himself a half-finished dish of vegetables.
(A) slowly
(B) cautiously
(C) eagerly
(D) reluctantly
HUGE, TINY
(S) same
(O) opposite

Other kinds of multiple-choice item occur, of course. Test specialist Raymond Gerberich (1956) classified and illustrated a variety of them. You will want to try many; do not succumb to the common tendency to use only one kind of item.

Though even the best rules have exceptions and must be tempered with good judgment, careful consideration of the 28 suggestions above should help one to write better multiple-choice items. This is no substitute for practice. Practice is invaluable, especially when it is accompanied by the critical reactions of someone with expertise in measurement and item analysis.

Matching Exercises

A matching exercise typically consists of two columns; each item in the first column is to be paired with an alternative in the second column. In the simplest matching exercise, the number of responses is exactly the same as the number of items. But matching exercises that provide more responses than items are frequently used because they reduce the examinee's success by guessing. Sometimes the items in the first column are incomplete sentences, each requiring a word or phrase from the second column for its completion. Occasionally, two or more columns of responses are given, and a choice must be made from each of these response columns for each item in the first column. The matching exercise is useful for identifying numbered places or parts on maps, charts, and diagrams.

ADVANTAGES AND LIMITATIONS OF MATCHING ITEMS

Many types of learning involve the association of two things in the learner's mind. Common examples are events and dates, events and persons, events and places, terms and definitions, foreign words and English equivalents, laws and illustrations, rules and examples, and tools and their use. The matching exercise is very convenient for measuring such learning.

As Hawkes, Lindquist, and Mann (1936, p. 150) observed, "the matching exercise is particularly well adapted to testing in *who, what, when,* and *where* situations, or for naming and identifying abilities."

Its principal limitations are as follows: (1) it is not well adapted to the measurement of understanding as distinguished from mere memory—it is difficult to design a matching exercise that will measure genuine understanding of a high level or the ability to interpret complex relationships; (2) with the exception of the true-false test, the matching exercise is the form most likely to include irrelevant clues to the correct response; (3) unless skillfully made, it is time-consuming for the pupil. The suggestions that follow are designed to overcome the last two limitations.

ILLUSTRATIONS OF MATCHING TESTS

Because matching exercises usually have too many options (more than 5 or 6) for typical multiple-choice answer sheets, they appear less frequently in recently published tests than they did before 1940. Some teachers still use them, however. Following is a "square," 10-by-10, unrevised matching exercise from a social studies quiz:

_____ 1. The country that aided Columbus with money and ships	A. Philadelphia
_____ 2. The oldest town in the United States	B. St. Augustine
_____ 3. A famous Quaker	C. William Penn
_____ 4. The first English settlement in America	D. Pilgrims
_____ 5. A city in Massachusetts	E. Cartier
_____ 6. "City of Brotherly Love"	F. Spain
_____ 7. First French explorer in America	G. Jamestown
_____ 8. He founded Connecticut.	H. Magellan
_____ 9. They landed at Plymouth Rock.	I. Thomas Hooker
_____10. His ship sailed around the world.	J. Boston

Is the above material too heterogeneous to be put into a single matching exercise? Four of the options are names of cities, four are names of persons, one is the name of a country, and one is a plural noun. How much does a student have to know about early United States history to be able to puzzle out the correct answers? For item 1, he has only to recognize that Spain is the only country in the list of alternatives. His choice for item 2 lies among A, B, G, and J. For item 3, he is likely to reject Cartier and Magellan as not sounding "Quakerish," leaving just C, William Penn, and I, Thomas Hooker. Item 4 uses the same four options as item 2, and perhaps St. Augustine does not sound like an English name. Item 5 has an oddly contemporary, nonhistorical ring that is out of context with the other nine items. Item 6 is the fourth and last of the "city" items; it is automatically answerable if he surmised the correct answers to items 2, 4, and 5. In effect the city questions constitute a 4 × 4 matching exercise that might better have been presented as such, instead of being buried in the 10 × 10 format, which favors test-wiseness and clerical ability.

"Persons" also constitutes an imbedded 4 × 4 matching exercise. Item 7 contains the giveaway "French," which points to Cartier, the only French-sounding name among the four. Ignorant but shrewd pupils will probably choose the answer to item 8 from just C and I, because it seems unlikely that Connecticut was founded by a person with a name such as Cartier or Magellan. (True, that is hazardous procedure and requires a little knowledge, but with this sort of teacher-made exercise it usually pays.) Item 9 is ridiculous, for the "They" who landed at Plymouth Rock *must* be the only plural word among the 10 alternatives. By the time the average pupil comes to item 10, the fourth person in the list of 10 items (he may not save it for last), he probably feels that cunning is more important than knowledge in getting through this maze. The teacher could have prepared far better exercises to cover the material.

This 10-item matching exercise appeared in a 40-item social studies test, along with 10 three-option multiple-choice items, 10 true-false items, and 10 completion items. It was administered to 33 students who had just completed a unit of instruction on U.S. colonial history. The four teachers who constructed the test claimed that the objectives for the social studies course were: (1) to help pupils understand how America developed into a great nation, (2) to teach the children the pertinent facts about the discovery and colonization of our country, and (3) to intensify pupil interest in the workings of democracy. The matching exercise obviously emphasized the second objective.

Results of the item analysis based on the 33 pupils tested are interesting. First the papers were graded for all 40 items. They were then arranged according to total score from the highest to the lowest (33rd). Then the highest 27 percent (9 papers) and the lowest 27 percent (also 9 papers) were compared for responses to each item. The most discriminating item was number 9, "They landed at Plymouth Rock," which we have already decided could be answered solely from the correspondence of the "They" to the plural "Pilgrims" because these were the only plurals among either the items or the alternatives. The 9 top-scoring pupils on the entire test all marked this item correctly, while the 9 lowest-scoring pupils all marked it incorrectly! It *may* be that this is the central theme of the unit and that the ablest students would have got it right even without the specific determiner, but it is uncomfortable to suspect that the primary determinant of score on the test *might* be verbal ability, reading ability, and test sophistication (in various proportions, perhaps) and not specific knowledge of the topic studied.

The least discriminating of the 10 matching items and fourth from the bottom of the 40 items in discrimination was number 2, "The oldest town in the United States." Eight persons of the 9 in the low group and six of the 9 in the high group missed it. The most difficult item on the entire test was number 6, "City of Brotherly Love," missed by 9 in the low group and 6 in the high group. By looking at the actual options marked, a teacher can to some extent "read the pupils' minds" and determine what remedial teaching is needed. For example, are a number of pupils misinformed so they think St. Augustine is the City of Brotherly Love, or are they ignorantly marking number 6 at random among the four cities offered?

Despite all its limitations, suggested by our analysis of the 10 matching items, this test was of middle difficulty for the group tested (mean rights score, not corrected for guessing, 19.5), had a large standard deviation (9.1), and yielded a high estimated internal-consistency (reliability) coefficient of .92. Whatever it measured, scores on this test ranked the students reliably, and the various items measured the same kind of knowledge or ability rather accurately. With practice, the four teachers could devise items much freer of the faults we noticed. Even at its worst, the test is probably superior to a teacher's casual judgments about a pupil's knowledge.

Below is another type of matching exercise; it was devised as part of a test for a grade 9 English class:

She and Margaret have probably gone to the little grocery store around the

14   15   16   17   16   18   19   20

corner.

____14. She	A. noun	
____15. Margaret	B. pronoun	
____16. have gone	C. verb	
____17. probably	D. adjective	
____18. little	E. adverb	
____19. grocery	F. preposition	
____20. around		

This is a 7 × 6 matching item. Any number of items could be used with the 6 alternatives (that is, responses). On the test itself, 40 items were used with 15 sentences and a six-column arrangement for checking the part of speech. Items 16 and 19 were the most discriminating of the 7 above, and item 15 was the least discriminating. All 7 discriminated well between high and low scorers on the test. The most difficult of the 7 items was number 19, which was missed by 11 of the 12 lowest scorers but by only one of the 12 highest scorers. Incidentally, the only perfectly discriminating (12:0) one of the 93 items was the adjective "hearty" in the sentence "The hearty breakfast was soon finished." Most of the lowest scorers thought it was an adverb because of the "y" ending.

A little knowledge can be a dangerous thing, and student misapplication of knowledge sometimes is detectable from the item analysis. As an aside from our discussion of matching exercises, consider the following item: "No one but (A. he) (B. him) came to the meeting." Five of the 12 lowest-scoring students chose "he," but nine of the highest scorers did also. Apparently, the more able students knew that "but" is usually a conjunction and concluded that this is a compound sentence in which "he" is the subject of the verb "came." The lowest-scoring students, not knowing much about parts of speech, may have based their answer on the sound of the sentence. They were probably used to saying, "This is him," and "him" sounded right in the test sentence. To check this hypothesis, high and low scorers could be questioned about their reasons for marking A and B.

Another negatively discriminating item was the part of speech of the pronominal adjective "their" in "The strong yellow soap stung their chapped hands." It was keyed as an adjective. Whereas 7 of the 12 lowest scorers mistakenly thought otherwise, 11 of the 12 highest scorers were also in error. Most of the highest scorers noted that it precedes the adjective "chapped" and concluded incorrectly that therefore it modified "chapped" and must be an adverb! The remedy for such imperfect knowledge is not a new item, but remedial teaching.

Consider three other examples of matching exercises (Stecklein, 1955). The first goes readily with six-option printed answer sheets when options are lettered.

DIRECTIONS: Famous inventions are listed in the left-hand column below. In the right-hand column are names of famous inventors. Place the letter corresponding to the inventor in the space before the invention for which he is famous.

Inventions	*Inventors*
____1. steam boat	A. Alexander Bell
____2. cotton gin	B. George Washington Carver

_____3. sewing machine
_____4. reaper

C. Robert Fulton
D. Elias Howe
E. Cyrus McCormick
F. Eli Whitney

DIRECTIONS: Quotations from poetry written during the Romantic Period are listed in the column at the left below. In the column at the right, names of famous poets are listed. You are to indicate the author of each of the quotations by writing in the space before the number of the quotation the letter corresponding to the name of the author in the right-hand column.

Quotation (Romantic Period)

_____1. Hail to thee, blithe Spirit!
    Bird thou never wert,
    That from Heaven, or near it,
    Pourest thy full heart in profuse
    Strains of unpremeditated art.

_____2. She walks in beauty, like the night
    of cloudless climes and starry skies;
    And all that's best of dark and bright
    meet in her aspect and her eyes.

_____3. My heart leaps up when I behold
    a rainbow in the sky;
    So was it when my life began;
    So is it now I am a man;
    So be it when I shall grow old, or let me die!

_____4. A thing of beauty is a joy forever:
    Its loveliness increases; it will never
    Pass into nothingness; but still will keep
    A bower quiet for us, and a sleep
    Full of sweet dreams, and health,
    and quiet breathing.

Poet

A. Robert Burns
B. Lord Byron
C. Samuel Taylor Coleridge
D. John Keats
E. Percy Bysshe Shelley
F. Alfred Lord Tennyson
G. William Wordsworth

DIRECTIONS: Three lists are presented below. Famous English authors of plays are listed in the column farthest to the right, names of well-known plays are listed in the center column, and in the column farthest to the left are names of characters in some of these plays. You are to look at the name of the character listed, decide in which play this character appears, and identify the author of this play. Indicate your answers as follows: Place the small alphabet letter corresponding to the play in which the character appears in the first space before the name of the character; place the capital alphabet letter corresponding to the author of this play in the second space before the name of the character. Note that there are more names of plays and authors than there are names of characters, so not all answers will be used.

____ ____1. Mildred Tresham
____ ____2. Ralph Rackstraw
____ ____3. Algernon Moncrieff
____ ____4. Elizabeth Saunders
____ ____5. Marion Whittaker
____ ____6. Bartley
____ ____7. Montague
    Lushington

a. The Silver Box
b. Riders to the Sea
c. Easy Virtue
d. H. M. S. Pinafore
e. A Bill of Divorcement
f. A Blot on the
    Scutcheon
g. Our Betters
h. The Masqueraders
i. The Importance of
    Being Earnest

A. John Millington
    Synge
B. Clemence Dane
C. Robert Browning
D. W. Somerset
    Maugham
E. Henry Arthur Jones
F. Noel Coward
G. Oscar Wilde
H. W. S. Gilbert
  I. John Galsworthy

1. *Be careful in deciding what material is placed in the question column and what is placed in the option column.* It is wrong, for example, to use authors in the question column and novels in the option column; for this, in effect, asks the question, "What did Sinclair Lewis write? Guess which one of his many novels I have put over there in the option column for you to seek." Some teachers try to justify this frustrating arrangement by saying, "But I just taught them one!" Unfortunately, the absurdity of this reply is not at all apparent to some of them. For a one-to-one correspondence such as chemical element—chemical symbol, it makes no difference; for a many-to-one correspondence, it is an item of the many that belongs in the question column, with the unique correspondent in the option column. For example, *Main Street* is the item and Sinclair Lewis the option to be chosen.

2. *Include only homogeneous material in each matching exercise.* Do not mix such dissimilar items as persons and places in a single exercise. We demonstrated in the Colonial-America exercise why this heterogeneity is undesirable.

3. *Check each exercise carefully for unwarranted clues to matching pairs.* For each item ask yourself this question: What is the least amount of information that must be known to select the right response?

4. *Be sure that the students fully understand the bases on which matching is to be done.* May an option be used for more than one item? May the desired response to a given item consist of more than one option? Communicate your exact intent to the pupil.

5. *Place items on the left and number them; place options on the right and designate them by letters.* Item numbers should run consecutively throughout the test, but option letters should begin anew with each matching exercise.

6. *Arrange items and options in a systematic order.* If the list consists of dates, arrange them in chronological order. Option words may be alphabetized to make it easier for the student to locate the desired response.

7. *Place all the items and options for a matching exercise on a single page,* if possible. Turning the page back and forth in search of desired responses is confusing and time-consuming.

8. *Limit a matching exercise to not more than 10–15 items.* Longer lists tend to be too heterogeneous and afford clues for the test-wise; they waste time; and if testing time is brief, they put too much premium on the students' clerical speed and accuracy.

Rearrangement Exercises

Probably the chief difficulty in preparing rearrangement exercises is keeping the material homogeneous. Each thing to be ranked in a given set should, for the group tested, be about as difficult as every other thing. For historical chronologies, unfamiliar events should not be included with more familiar events. If one event is wholly unknown to most of the students, as compared to the rest of the events, then the location of that event in the ranked series will have to be made by sheer chance, thereby decreasing the reliability of the ranking exercise. If two events are much closer together in time than are the other events, they may be confused with each other, even though the chronological location of either with reference to the other events is known. This seems to be a lesser difficulty than the unknown event, for half the time by chance the two close-together events would be ranked correctly, and the other half of the time they would be interchanged.[37]

The rearrangement exercise is promising only for certain limited contexts in which there is an important logical sequence of steps. Home economics teachers might use it for such chronologies as steps in baking a cake. Chemistry teachers may wish to have equations for a certain process put in order. English teachers may ask (as the College Entrance Examination Board's *English Composition Test* sometimes does) that a set of randomly ordered sentences be regrouped to make the best possible paragraph, or that the sequence of events in a story be ordered. Mathematics teachers may be able to test for sequence of operations in solving a problem. Science teachers may present colors to be ranked according to wave length.

There are $N(N-1)(N-2) \cdots (1)$ possible orders for N things. For example, there are $4(4-1)(4-2)(4-3) = 24$ different orders of the letters ABCD. Ideally, each rearrangement exercise should have its components presented in a purely random order. Up through six, you can randomize by rolling a die (singular of dice) and arranging each item according to the number on the die. Suppose, for example, that a rearrangement exercise consists of five events in a story to be put into the correct order. Start with the five events listed in any order. How shall the first one be relisted? You roll the die and get a two, so the first event in your list will be placed second in the exercise. You next roll a five, so your second event will be fifth in the exercise. Continue until all five events are put in some order. If you throw a six, disregard it and roll the die again. (Should you prefer not to use a die, write the numbers 1, 2, 3, 4, and 5 on each of five slips of paper respectively, shuffle them thoroughly, and draw randomly.) Numbers from 7 through 12 can be handled by using 7–12 slips of paper.

A novel use of 15 four-item rearrangement exercises occurs in Part II of the *Study of Values*.[38] The authors pit each one of six "evaluative attitudes" against all possible combinations of three of the other five attitudes. There are 15 possible combinations of six things taken four at a time, and each possible combination is used once. Each of the four items in an exercise typifies one of the six values. The student is told, "Each of the following situations or questions is followed by four possible attitudes or answers. Arrange these answers in the order of your personal preference by writing, in the appropriate box at the right, a score of 4, 3, 2, or 1. To the statement you prefer most give 4, to the statement that is second most attractive 3, and so on."

[37] Unfortunately, although measurement specialists know how to score rearrangement exercises to take into account amount of discrepancy and degree of misinformation, little is known about how to construct them well. For that reason, our suggestions in this paragraph are few and tentative. Systematic research in the construction of rearrangement items is needed.

[38] Devised by G. W. Allport, P. E. Vernon, and G. Lindzey, and published by Houghton Mifflin Company, 1960.

Two of the 15 ranking items from the *Study of Values* follow.

2. In your opinion, can a man who works in business all the week best spend Sunday in—

a

a. trying to educate himself by reading serious books ☐

b

b. trying to win at golf, or racing ☐

c

c. going to an orchestral concert ☐

d

d. hearing a really good sermon ☐

13. To what extent do the following famous persons interest you—

a

a. Florence Nightingale ☐

b

b. Napoleon ☐

c

c. Henry Ford ☐

d

d. Galileo ☐

The four options in item 2 represent Evaluative Attitudes A, B, C, and D, while the options of item 13 represent E, B, F, and A. What do "trying to educate himself by reading serious books" and "Galileo" have in common, being representatives of Evaluative Attitude A? What do "trying to win at golf, or racing" and "Napoleon" have in common, both being items for Attitude B? If you rank "trying to educate himself by reading serious books" 4—the highest possible—you award 4 points to Attitude A. Because there is no "correct" (that is, keyed) order against which to score the *Study of Values* ranking exercises, by an r_{Ranks} formula (see Chapter 2) or otherwise, you award to the attitude (one of the six attitudes ABCDEF) represented by each item the number of points (4, 3, 2, or 1) you allotted that item.

There are 4 items per ranking exercise and 15 exercises, making a total of $4 \times 15 = 60$ items covering the 6 attitudes equally, so there are $60/6 = 10$ items per attitude. Because the maximum number of points for any item is 4, the largest possible score on the 15 ranking exercises is $10 \times 4 = 40$ for any *one* of the 6 attitudes. The smallest possible score is $10 \times 1 = 10$. There are $15 (4 + 3 + 2 + 1) = 150$ points for all 6 attitudes, so the average attitude score for any person on the ranking exercises must be $150/6 = 25$. In other words, each student has the same average (or total) attitude score as any other student. The *Study of Values* is an *ipsative* scale because of the forced-choice (that is, ranking) nature of its items; thus, it is not appropriate to compare one student's *scores* on the various attitudes with another student's scores in absolute terms. Only the *relative* positions of the subtest scores are directly interpretable. What is the student's highest attitude? His lowest attitude? Does he have the same rank-order of attitudes as some other student? Are his scores on the

6 attitude scales considerably more variable than another student's? If so, he
has more sharply differentiated evaluative attitudes.

263

*Constructing
Specific
Types of
Objective Tests*

The *Study of Values* is an interesting rearrangement and alternative-response test. There are no "right" or "wrong" answers for it, and each person who completes the SV has the same "total" score as any other person. To understand it better, you may wish to obtain a copy of the SV booklet and the Manual of Directions, fill out the booklet, score it, and study the results. In Chapter 16 we consider why inventories such as the *Study of Values* are not "tests" in the same sense that a vocabulary or an arithmetic test is.

Concluding Remarks

Item writing is an art; it is assisted but not superseded by the statistical procedures of item analysis and by evaluative reactions of subject-matter and measurement specialists. As automation takes over the scoring of tests, obtains frequency distributions and reliability coefficients, and item-analyzes (see Chapter 11), we hope that the heart of the test—its items and exercises—will not be neglected by test publishers or teachers. Great emphasis on mechanical procedures can lead to undesirable consequences. Too great a preoccupation with indices of item discrimination, for example, may result in neglect of the item's logical, motivational, and literary properties. A paragraph in a reading test should be acceptable to an expert in the subject to which it pertains, well written in an aesthetic sense, and interesting to the student. An item may discriminate well between high and low scorers on a test as a whole and still measure trivia. This situation usually arises when items are not constructed with care and consummate artistry by well trained subject-matter specialists who genuinely know the basic principles of measurement. Brightness and mastery of measurement concepts are necessary but not sufficient; knowledge of subject matter, sufficient time, and hard work are essential, too. The items should be thoroughly reviewed by other well-qualified persons *who are not aware how the items are keyed by the writer*, and the items must be edited on the basis of their comments. This must be done to compensate for the inevitable limitations of any one person. Further editing of all but the most discriminating items on the basis of a detailed item analysis (performed on the answer sheets of a substantial number of students) is an important step that is frequently omitted. This may be because items are often in short supply, and because of the usually unwelcome prospect of constructing new items.

In the future, test booklets, answer sheets, and scoring keys will give way to fully computerized testing, which will probably be tailored optimally to each individual pupil. Teachers may even be able to ask a machine, "In which section of algebra should Eric be placed?" and get an answer of stated precision on the basis of information already known about Eric as supplemented by further personalized testing via the machine. Already there are experimental efforts in which a teacher chooses, from a large pool of items, those that are relevant for the forthcoming test. The computer assembles and numbers the items and even produces a "ditto" or mimeograph master.

Probably for a long time, test items and exercises will be devised mainly by humans in the current painstaking manner, so the prospective or present teacher must decide either to learn the art or to employ inferior evaluation measures. We have presented the ABC's of test construction. With practice and further study you will be able to prepare better tests for *your* classes than anyone else can and certainly much better than anyone else will.

Post-organizer

Each kind of item has unique advantages and disadvantages. True-false items can be constructed quickly and require less examinee time than most other item types, but they usually fail to measure more complex concepts. If not prepared carefully, they often are intrinsically ambiguous.

Multiple-choice items have the greatest potential for measuring understanding. The chief feature in their effective use is the preparation of attractive distracters. This also is a great practical drawback, because constructing plausible alternatives requires a high level of skill that is developed only with time and effort.

A matching item can measure associations in an economical manner. As with multiple-choice questions, the options should be homogeneous.

IMPORTANT TERMS AND CONCEPTS

distracter

free-response items

completion items

alternative-response items

matching items

multiple-choice items

stem

intrinsic ambiguity

extrinsic ambiguity

specific determiner

SUGGESTED READINGS

ANDERSON, H. R. and E. F. LINDQUIST, revised by David K. Heenan. 1960. *Selected test items in world history*, 3d ed.: Bulletin No. 9. Washington, D.C.: National Council for the Social Studies.

———, revised by Harriet Stull. 1964. *Selected test items in American history:* Bulletin No. 6. Washington, D.C.: National Council for the Social Studies.

BERG, H. D., ed. 1967. Evaluation in social studies. *Thirty-fifth yearbook of the National Council for the Social Studies.* Washington, D.C.: NCSS.

BLOOM, B. S., J. T. HASTINGS, and G. F. MADAUS. 1971. *Handbook on formative and summative evaluation of student learning.* New York: McGraw-Hill Book Company. See special chapters devoted to certain content areas: chapters 13, 15, 16, 17, 18, 19, 20, 21, 22, and 23.

DOWNIE, N. M. 1967. Multiple-choice items; Other types of objective test items. Chapters 7 and 8 in *Fundamentals of measurement: Techniques and practices*, 2d ed. New York: Oxford University Press.

DRESSEL, P. L., ed. 1961. *Evaluation in higher education.* Boston: Houghton Mifflin Company.

EBEL, R. L. 1970. The case for true-false test items. *School Review,* **78**: 373–389.

EDUCATIONAL TESTING SERVICE. n.d. *Making your own tests.* Princeton, N.J.: ETS.
A leaflet describing an instructional kit containing three filmstrips, LP records, and related materials.

——. 1963. *Multiple-choice questions: A close look.* Princeton, N.J.: ETS. Reprinted in G. H. Bracht, K. D. Hopkins, and J. C. Stanley. 1972. *Perspectives in educational and psychological measurement.* Englewood Cliffs, N. J.: Prentice-Hall, Inc., Selection 15.

ENGELHART, M. D. 1964. *Improving classroom testing. What research says to the teacher,* No. 31. Washington, D.C.: National Educational Association.

GERBERICH, J. R., H. A. GREENE, and A. N. JORGENSEN. 1962. *Measurement and evaluation in the modern school.* New York: David McKay Company, Inc.
Has separate chapters on evaluating particular school subjects, such as foreign languages, home economics, physical education, and music.

GRONLUND, N. E. 1968. *Constructing achievement tests.* Englewood Cliffs, N.J.: Prentice-Hall, Inc.
Especially Chap. 4, "Constructing objective tests of complex achievement."

HEDGES, W. D. 1966. *Testing and evaluation for the sciences in the secondary school.* Belmont, Calif.: Wadsworth Publishing Co., Inc.

HENRY, N. B., ed. 1946. The measurement of understanding. *Forty-fifth yearbook of the National Society for the Study of Education, Part I.* Chicago: University of Chicago Press.
Separate chapters are devoted to measuring understanding in social studies, science, fine arts, health education, and so on.

KURFMAN, D. 1968. *Teacher-made test items in American history:* Bulletin No. 40. Washington, D.C.: National Council for the Social Studies.

LINDQUIST, E. F., ed. 1951. *Educational measurement.* Washington, D.C.: American Council on Education. Especially chap. 7, "Writing the test item," by R. L. Ebel.

MERWIN, J. C., and E. F. Gardner. 1962. Development and application of tests of educational achievement. *Review of Educational Research,* **32**: 40–50.

MYERS, S. S. 1961. The kinds of thinking required in current mathematics tests. *New Jersey Mathematics Teacher,* **18**: 11–15.

PALMER, O. 1961. Sense or nonsense? The objective testing of English composition. *English Journal,* **50**: 314–320.

PAYNE, D. A. 1968. *The specification and measurement of learning outcomes.* Waltham, Mass.: Blaisdell Publishing Company.

SANDERS, N. M. 1966. *Classroom questions: What kinds?* New York: Harper & Row, Publishers.
Presents item development in terms of Bloom's taxonomy, with many illustrations.

STANLEY, J. C. 1958. The ABCs of test construction. *NEA Journal,* **47**: 224–226. Reprinted in J. T. Flynn and H. Garber, eds. 1967. *Assessing behavior: Readings in educational and psychological measurement.* Reading, Mass.: Addison-Wesley Publishing Company, Inc.

STECKLEIN, J. E. *Bulletins on classroom testing* of the Bureau of Institutional Research, University of Minnesota, Minneapolis, Nos. 4, 5, and 6 (1955) and 7 (1956): "How to write multiple-choice test items," "How to write true-false test items," "How to write matching test items," and "How to measure more than facts with multiple-choice items."

WEITMAN, M. 1965. Item characteristics and long-term retention. *Journal of Educational Measurement*, **2**: 37–47.

WESMAN, A. G. 1971. Writing the test item. In R. L. Thorndike, ed., *Educational measurement*, 2d ed. Washington, D.C.: American Council on Education, Chap. 4.

WOOD, D. A. 1960. *Test construction: Development and interpretation of achievement tests*. Columbus, Ohio: Charles E. Merrill Books, Inc. Especially Chap. 7, "Constructing objective test items."

11

ITEM ANALYSIS FOR
CLASSROOM TESTS

If the procedures for test development outlined in Chapters 8, 9, and 10 are followed, the most important quality of an item will be achieved—its *relevance*. This is the *sine qua non* of any good item or test. However, logical relevance is only the first hurdle in the sequence of test-item evaluation. An item analysis is needed to indicate which items are very easy or very difficult and which are not functioning properly. It is not uncommon for an item to appear satisfactory even to an expert while being intrinsically ambiguous—that is, to elicit undesired response patterns from students (Coffman, 1969a, p. 14). The immediate purposes of an item analysis are to determine the *difficulty* and *discrimination* of each item. When an item analysis is performed on a test, one is almost certain to gain additional important insight into the examinees' thinking, understanding, and test-taking behavior. The process of item analysis should improve an instructor's skills in test construction beyond that possible otherwise (Ebel, 1965b, p. 346). Blessum (1969, p. 5) reported that item-analysis feedback to a university faculty "resulted in an improvement not only in the quality and fairness of each individual examination, but also in the technical and educational quality of successive tests."

A Simplified Test-Analysis Procedure

PREPARING THE ITEMS

In addition to relevance, the two characteristics usually desired for a test item are discrimination and difficulty: how hard is the item for the group tested, and how well does it distinguish between the more knowledgeable and the less knowl-   *267* edgeable students? These characteristics can be nearly independent of each other, except that a very easy or very hard item cannot discriminate well. If all students mark the item correctly, it has not distinguished between those who know more and those who know less about the concept. If all students mark an item incorrectly, then the item is not discriminating for the group. This information may be important to the teacher for quality-control or diagnostic purposes, but it does not help identify individual differences.

Several different item-analysis procedures have been proposed. Some of the more elaborate are appropriate for standardized tests or research projects. The procedure proposed below is simple, but adequate for most classroom purposes.[1] It works best with examinations given to large groups but it is valuable even with daily or weekly tests for a single class. To minimize response-style effects on teacher-made tests, each student should be strongly encouraged to answer every item for which he has *any* information, even a vague hunch about one of the options. The test length should be such that adequate time is available for nearly everyone to attempt every item.

The items generally should be arranged in ascending order of difficulty, although this is critical only on speeded tests (Brenner, 1964). For an untried set of items, this arrangement can be achieved fairly well on a subjective basis; if each item has been administered previously to a similar group, the original difficulty values can be used.

Note that *an item analysis is no substitute for meticulous care in planning, constructing, criticizing, and editing items*. It does supplement that intuitive process, however, by revealing unsuspected defects or virtues of specific items. The feedback on individual items can also be of instructional value to the teacher by, for example, identifying topics in need of review.

THE STEPS OF AN ITEM ANALYSIS

After the test has been given, the papers or answer sheets should be scored by marking all items incorrectly answered or omitted. Because of the instructions concerning omissions, they should be few. Each pupil's score (not corrected for "chance") will be the number of items on the test less the number of errors (wrong or omitted items) on his paper or answer sheet.

1. Order the N papers by score, placing the paper having the highest score on top and continuing sequentially until the paper having the lowest score is placed on the bottom.
2. Multiply N, the total number of students, by 0.27 and round off the result to the nearest whole number;[2] this number is called n. If N is 30, n would be 8 (8.1 rounded).

[1] A standard index of item discrimination is the coefficient of correlation of the examinees' scores on an item with their total scores on the rest of the test or subtest, but there are other possibilities (see Henrysson, 1971, and Baker, 1965). The short-cut item-analysis method explained here is the D-index for item analysis, suggested by Johnson (1951) and popularized by Findley (1956). Its values have been shown to be almost perfectly linearly correlated with biserial coefficients (Bridgman, 1964). Engelhart (1965) found D "remarkably effective" in identifying poor items. Mayo (1968, p. 93) concluded, "From a time-and-motion point of view, D is probably the most economical index to calculate."

[2] Henrysson (1971) suggests taking the upper and lower $N/3$ examinees, rather than .27N. Obviously, the smaller the percent used for the upper and lower groups, the greater will be the differentiation (D-values). However, the smaller the extreme groups, the less reliable are the resulting D-values or item-test correlation coefficients. Kelley (1939) showed that the optimum point at which these two conditions balance is reached when the upper

3. Count off the n best papers from the top of the stack. This is the "high" group.

4. Count off the n poorest papers from the bottom of the stack. This is the "low" group.

5. Determine the proportion in the high group (p_H) who answered each item correctly by dividing the number of correct answers for the high group by n; that is,

$$p_H = \frac{\text{number of correct answers}}{n}.$$

Repeat the procedure for the low group to obtain p_L for each item.

6. To obtain an item difficulty index p—that is, the proportion of the total group who answered each item correctly[3]—add p_H and p_L and divide by 2:

$$p = \frac{p_H + p_L}{2}.$$

This must be interpreted with the chance level of the item in mind. For example, $p = .5$ for a two-option item that all examinees mark probably indicates little or no knowledge of the point tested.[4]

7. To obtain a measure of item discrimination, D (that is, how well this item distinguished between the students who understand the content universe of the test well and those who do not), subtract p_L from p_H:

$$D = p_H - p_L.$$

Items that yield a discrimination index of .4 or more are high in discrimination. Those with D-values below .2 are low in discrimination (Ebel, 1954); they deserve careful scrutiny, particularly if they are revised for future use. Items that were miskeyed or that are intrinsically ambiguous will tend to have negative D-values, or other options of that item will have higher D-values than the keyed-correct option. These options usually should be double-keyed, since the distinction between the best and next-best options was too fine for the knowledgeable students to make. Of course, no item should be double-keyed if there is not logical justification in terms of the concept being measured. This logic may not be readily apparent to the test constructor, but can usually be supplied by high-scoring examinees who did not select the keyed-correct option.

---

and lower 27 percent values are used. For classroom use it makes little difference whether 25, 27, or 33 percent is selected. When the item analysis is computerized, all cases should be used in obtaining item-test correlation coefficients, or other statistics, since economy of time is not an important consideration.

[3] Michael, Haertzka, and Perry (1953) have shown that p-values computed directly, using all examinees, agree closely with the average of p_H and p_L values.

[4] The p-values used in this chapter have not been "corrected for chance" which is the common practice. Assuming all distracters are equally attractive, the proportion of examinees who know the answer (p') can be estimated by

$$p = p - \frac{1-p}{k-1}$$

where: $k =$ the number of options contained by this item. For a procedure that does not assume that the distracters are equally attractive, see Horst's method (Guilford, 1954, pp. 421–422). It is usually not practical in classroom testing to correct item difficulty indexes for chance; nevertheless the chance values for p should be borne in mind when interpreting p-values. If all examinees atempt all items, the p-values expected from chance are $1/k$, that is, .50, .33, .25, and .20 for 2–, 3–, 4–, and 5–choice items, respectively.

The relationship between item difficulty and *potential* item discrimination is illustrated in Figure 11–1. The potential measurement value of an item is at a maximum when its difficulty level is .5—that is, when only one-half of the examinees are able to answer the item correctly. The figure also shows that there is little opportunity for an item to assess individual differences if it is very easy or very difficult. Note in Figure 11–1 that in the middle range of difficulty (25 to 75 percent), all items have the potential for very high discrimination ($D \geq .5$). Of course, an item's being at an appropriate difficulty level does not insure that it is a good item. The crucial test for an item is whether those who best understand the domain of content (the high scorers on the total test) agree with the key-correct answer on the item to a greater extent than those who know least about the subject (the low scorers on the total test). This is the information conveyed by the D-value for the item. The relationship between item difficulty and observed D-values for 120 items is shown in Figure 11–2. The median D-values for the 18 difficult items ($p \leq .25$) and the 23 easy items ($p \geq .75$) are only .10 and .20, respectively, whereas the median D-values for moderately difficult items (p's of .45 to .70) was .36. Notice also that four items on this carefully prepared test (Engelhart, 1965) took away from its measurement value (that is, had negative D-values). On subsequent versions of the test, these items, as well as others, should be revised or eliminated.

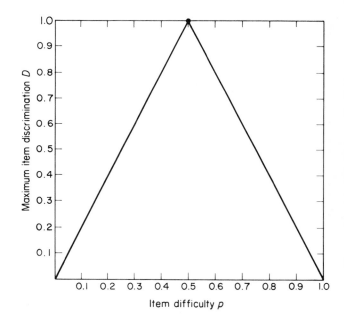

*FIGURE 11–1   The relationship between item
difficulty (p) and corresponding maximum item
discrimination (q).*

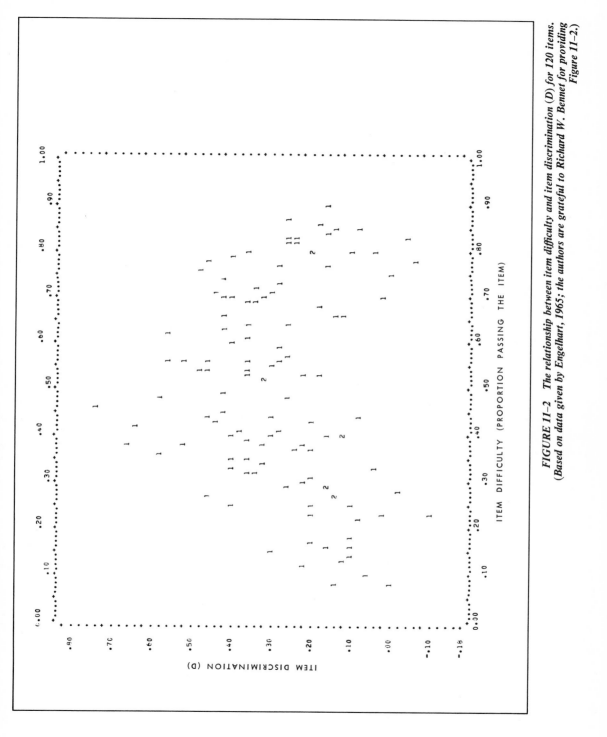

FIGURE 11–2 *The relationship between item difficulty and item discrimination (D) for 120 items. (Based on data given by Engelhart, 1965; the authors are grateful to Richard W. Bennet for providing Figure 11–2.)*

If the mean D ($\bar{D}$) on a test is .3, then the mean total score of the high group is greater than the mean for the low group by $.3k$ items, where k is the number of items on a test. For example, on a 100-item test, if $\bar{D}$ is .3, the high group's mean ($\bar{X}_H$) will exceed the low group's mean ($\bar{X}_L$) by 30 points.

The average D-value, $\bar{D}$, can be used as a quick estimate of a test's standard deviation. The differences in means of high and low groups will be about 2.45 standard deviations[5] (Kelley, 1939)—that is,

$$k\bar{D} = \bar{X}_H - \bar{X}_L \doteq 2.45s,$$

where k = the number of items and $\doteq$ means "approximately equal to");

$$s \doteq \frac{\bar{X}_H - \bar{X}_L}{2.45} = \frac{k\bar{D}}{2.45}.$$

Using the example above, in which the difference between means ($\bar{X}_H - \bar{X}_L$) was estimated to be 30, the standard deviation is approximately 30/2.45 or 12.3. If $\bar{D}$ had been .20 instead of .30, the standard deviation of the 100-item test would be approximately 20/2.45 or 8.2, which usually would bring with it a corresponding decrease in reliability[6] (see Figure 11–3). *Other things being equal, the greater $\bar{D}$ is, the greater the test's standard deviation and reliability are.*

The direct relationship between item discrimination values and a test's internal-consistency reliability ($r_{KR_{21}}$) is illustrated in Figure 11–3, which depicts the relationship between the mean D-value ($\bar{D}$) and the corresponding $r_{KR_{21}}$ coefficients for tests of 100 items (data from Ebel, 1965b, p. 366).

The reason that a 100-item test with no reliability would still have a positive mean item discrimination index of .12 is that any item whose discrimination is being assessed also contributes a fraction of the total test score, which is the basis for determining the "high" and "low" groups. This degree of internal contamination because of the overlap of item with total test is a direct function of test length—the fewer items there are, the greater is the proportion each item contributes to the total score.[7] This factor becomes serious only on very short

[5] Kelley (1939) proved that the mean of scores in the tail of a normal distribution is equal to $(y/q)\sigma$, where σ is the standard deviation, q is the proportion of the cases included in the tail, and y is the height of the ordinate of a unit normal distribution at the point of truncation. When the upper 27 percent is chosen for the high group, $q = .27$. From a normal-curve table it can readily be determined that the point of truncation must be .61 standard deviation (σ) from the mean, at which point $y = .33$. The mean score of the high group ($\bar{X}_H$) must then equal $(.33/.27)\sigma$ above the mean, or in z-score units, $(.33/.27)(1)$ or 1.225. Corresponding, the mean of the low group ($\bar{X}_L$) would be -1.225 in z-score units, or a difference in means of 2.45 σ's. The accuracy of this procedure for nonnormal distribution has not been investigated.

[6] The mean D-value, $\bar{D}$, can also be employed in estimating a test's reliability, avoiding the necessity of computing its standard deviation. Kuder-Richardson formulas 20 and 21 become, respectively:

$$r_{KR_{20}} = \frac{k}{k-1}\left[1 - \frac{6\sum pq}{(k\bar{D})^2}\right],$$

$$r_{KR_{21}} = \frac{k}{k-1}\left[1 - \frac{6\bar{p}\bar{q}}{(k\bar{D})^2}\right],$$

where: $\bar{p} = \bar{x}/k$, and $\bar{q} = 1 - \bar{p}$.

[7] Henrysson (1963) presents a procedure that gives an exact correction for this contamination. The refinement should be employed on items in standardized tests, but it is impractical for classroom testing, except at colleges and universities where computerized item analysis procedures may be available.

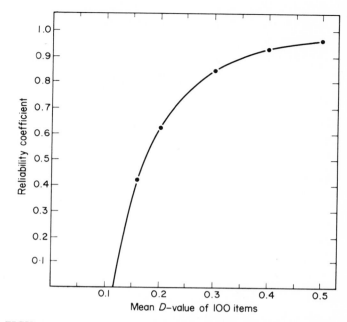

FIGURE 11–3 *The relationship between the average D-value and test reliability for a 100-item test. (Data from Ebel, 1965b, p. 366.)*

tests. Ebel (1965b, p. 364) gave the following "rules of thumb" for interpreting item-discrimination index values for classroom tests.

Index of Discrimination	Item Evaluation
.40 and up	Very good item
.30–.39	Reasonably good item but possibly subject to improvement
.20–.29	Marginal item, usually needing and being subject to improvement
below .19	Poor item, to be rejected or improved by revision

It should be noted that items with .0 or negative *D*-value probably were inadvertently miskeyed or else are intrinsically ambiguous. These interpretations are relevant only for the ability of the item to measure individual differences. Criterion-referenced or mastery items often are included in classroom tests for diagnostic or certification purposes and should be retained even if they are answered correctly by almost all students and contribute little or nothing to the measurement of individual differences among the examinees.

The four illustrative test items were selected from a test given to an introductory measurement class of thirty students. The results of the item analysis are given below for items 1, 2, 3, and 4. (Only item 1 is stated.)

Item 1. "Educational objectives are best determined from the results of objective educational measurements." (T or F)

Item Analysis Data for 4 Items

Item Number		Number of Correct Responses for Groups	Proportion of Correct Responses	Item Discrimination $D = P_H - P_L$	Item Difficulty $p = \dfrac{P_H + P_L}{2}$
1	H	7	7/8 = .88	(.88 − .38) = .5	$\dfrac{.88 + .38}{2} = .63$
	L	3	3/8 = .38		
2	H	8	1.00	.25	.88
	L	6	.75		
3	H	4	.5	.0	.5
	L	4	.5		
4	H	2	.25	−.50	.50
	L	6	.75		

$a_n = .27N = .27(30) = 8.1$ (rounded off to 8) students in the "High" group and 8 in the "Low" group.

Item 1 functioned well from a measurement perspective; it also provided diagnostic feedback for the instructor by indicating a misconception that needs to be clarified for the 38 percent of students who answered the item incorrectly (that is, True). Item 2 was too easy ($p = .88$) to permit much discrimination. Item 3 was in the appropriate difficulty range, but it failed to discriminate; it may be intrinsically ambiguous and need to be eliminated or revised. Item 4 is probably miskeyed, or at least seriously intrinsically ambiguous since the examinees appear to be in a different mental set than the instructor. The item appears to have good measurement potential (note large D-value) but should be revised, double-keyed, or excluded from the present examination. In its present form it lowers test reliability, and no doubt validity as well. Items like number 4 are often found on classroom tests—such items are miskeyed, or at least intrinsically ambiguous. They usually remain unidentified unless an item analysis is performed.

If items 3 and 4 are multiple-choice questions a further analysis is needed to identify the options that are creating the difficulty. For instructors at many colleges and universities, generalized item-analysis programs have been developed for the local computer, and provide this kind of information to the instructor. This service will probably be available to most classroom teachers eventually, *274* but even as a hand operation it can be completed fairly quickly by a teacher or even by a student.

Suppose there were four options to item 3:

**Distribution of Responses to Item 3
for High (H) and Low (L) Scoring Examinees**

Item	Group	A	B*	C	D	Omit
3	H	0	4	3	0	1
	L	0	4	0	4	0

*Keyed answer

Option "C" deserves scrutiny. It is likely that the distinction between the options B and C is too fine; perhaps the distinction has not received adequate instructional emphasis. A study of the item may reveal that both B and C are reasonable and hence each should be credited as correct. Distracter A probably should be revised for future use, since it was nonfunctional. Option D seems to be an excellent distracter.

On occasion it may not be feasible to retain an item. Not all poorly discriminating questions can be revised successfully. Sometimes the point tested is not clear or defensible enough to serve as the basis for an item. Some items, such as those for mathematics and science, are much easier to prepare well than are others, such as those for social studies and English.

Item four below appears to have been miskeyed. Only a study of the content of the item can diagnose the reason for its grave failure.

**Distribution of Responses to Item 4
for High (H) and Low (L) Scoring Examinees**

Item	Group	A	B	C	D*	Omit
4	H	0	5	1	2	0
	L	1	1	0	6	0

*Keyed answer.

Of course one would not give credit for an incorrect answer, such as might be found on an arithmetic test. When the item analysis "faults" the item, the source of the ambiguity can usually be identified, particularly if it is discussed with the class. When n is small, one will sometimes obtain peculiar results due to sampling fluctuations.

OTHER EXAMPLES

The following item was developed by Educational Testing Service (1963, pp. 12–13) and administered to 370 students:

In the following questions you are asked to make inferences from the data which are given you on the map of the imaginary country, Serendip. The answers in most instances must be probabilities rather than certainties. The relative size of towns and cities is not shown. To assist you in the location of the places mentioned in the questions, the map is divided into squares lettered vertically from A to E and numbered horizontally from 1 to 5.

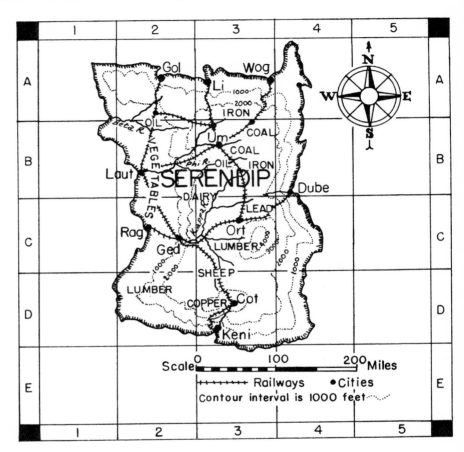

Which of the following cities would be the best location for a steel mill?
(A) Li (3A), (B) Um (3B), (C) Cot (3D), (D) Dube (4B).

The question reproduced beneath the map requires knowledge of the natural resources used in producing steel and an awareness of the importance of transportation facilities in bringing these resources together. It was part of a general achievement test given to high school seniors.

The student who knows that iron is the basic raw material of steel and that coal commonly provides the necessary source of heat would proceed to locate deposits of these resources in relation to the cities listed in the question. He would be able to eliminate Cot immediately, since there is no iron or coal in its vicinity, although Cot might be an attractive choice to students who mistakenly think that copper is a basic ingredient of steel. Both Li and Dube are located reasonably near supplies of iron, and therefore might be attractive choices. Um, however, is the more clearly "correct" response, because not only are deposits of iron and coal nearby, but they are more readily transportable by direct railroad routes.

Examinee Response to the Item

		Option				p	D
	Li A	Um B*	Cot C	Dube D	Omit		
H	2	84 $p_H = .84^a$	1	6	7		
						.62	.44
L	10	40 $p_L = .40^a$	4	9	37		

*Keyed option

$^a N = 370, n = 100.$

Although the item was rather difficult for the group (answered correctly by only 62 percent of the examinees), it did discriminate well ($D = .44$). However, some of the discrimination resulted from the fact that many (37 percent) of the low group did not attempt the item. Distracters A, C, and D functioned mildly, but in the right direction. Additional study of the test on which this item appeared revealed that the 7 omits in the high group and 29 of the 37 omits in the low group ran out of time before they had a chance to attempt the item (which appeared near the end of the test). The analysis of this item suggests that there may be a substantial speed element in the test, hence many examinees with low total scores may not be low in map-reading ability, but only slow workers who were unable to respond to many items they would have been able to answer correctly.

Another example from a writing test administered to 250 college-bound high school students is given below:[8]

In the following question you are given a complete sentence to be rephrased according to the directions which follow it. You should rephrase the sentence mentally to save time, although you may make notes in your test book if you wish.

Below the sentence and its directions are listed words or phrases that may occur in your revised sentence. When you have thought out a good sentence, find in the choices A to E the word or entire phrase that is included in your revised sentence. The word or phrase you choose should be the most accurate and most nearly complete of all the choices given.

Although the directions may require you to change the relationship between parts of the sentence or to make slight changes in meaning in other ways, make only those changes that the directions require; that is, keep the meaning the same, or as nearly the same as the directions permit. If you think that more than one good sentence can be made according to the directions, select the sentence that is most exact, effective, and natural in phrasing and construction.

[8] From *Multiple-choice questions: A close look*. Copyright © 1963 by Educational Testing Service. All rights reserved. Reproduced by permission.

Sentence: John, shy as he was of girls, still managed to marry one of the most desirable of them.

Directions: Substitute John's shyness for John, shy.

Your rewritten sentence will contain which of the following?

(A) him being married to
(B) himself married to
(C) him from marrying
(D) was himself married to
(E) him to have married

In order to select choice (A), a sentence like John's shyness with girls did not stop him being married to the most desirable of them would have to be used. To make this sentence correct, formal written English demands that the word being be preceded by the possessive pronoun his. Choice (B) presents a sentence similar to Despite John's shyness with girls, he managed to get himself married to one of the most desirable of them. This sentence is wordy and inappropriate in its tone (for formal English). Choice (C), however, yields a sentence on the order of John's shyness with girls did not prevent him from marrying one of the most desirable of them. This retains the meaning of the original sentence and contains no errors in grammar; it is the correct answer. The fourth choice might lead to John's shyness with girls did not keep him single; he was himself married to one of the most desirable of them. This sentence changes the meaning of the original sentence, and it is, at the same time, ambiguous in its own meaning. John's shyness with girls was not a reason for him to have married the most desirable of them—this sentence, an attempt to use the fifth choice, results in a complete change of meaning. It is therefore unacceptable, even though it is grammatically correct.

Examinees' Response to the Item

	Option						p	D
	A	B	C*	D	E	Omit		
H	3	0	61 $p_H = .90^a$	1	3	0	.58	.75
L	5	11	17 $p_L = .25^a$	14	15	6		

*Keyed option
[a] $N = 250$, $n = 68$.

The analysis reveals that few of the able students had difficulty with this item, whereas the low group had extreme difficulty. Distracters B, D, and E appear excellent, whereas option A contributed a bit negatively to the item.

More elaborate item analyses, such as the one shown in Table 11–1, are facilitated when a computer is available. The r-values in Table 11–1 are estimates of the item-test (biserial) coefficients of correlation. They convey the same information provided by the D-values and correlate almost perfectly with them (Bridgman, 1964), although they are in different units.

TABLE 11–1

Item Analysis of a Final Examination[a]

Item	A		B		C		D		Total		
Number	High	Low	High	Low	High	Low	High	Low	Key	p	r
1	01	03	13	17	85	79	02	02	C	82	.09
2	34	36	03	09	55	40	08	15	A	35	−.02
3	00	07	01	07	01	05	98	81	D	89	.45
4	03	04	83	59	13	30	01	07	B	71	.29
5	03	01	17	34	10	04	69	61	C	07	.19
6	79	61	19	31	01	05	01	04	A	70	.21
7	13	20	73	49	01	04	14	27	B	61	.25
8	05	08	01	11	04	43	89	35	D	62	.57
9	73	81	07	05	17	05	03	09	B	06	.07
10	01	15	76	44	21	31	02	10	B	60	.34
.											
.											
.											
81	03	11	66	39	05	13	24	37	C	09	−.21
82	81	39	01	16	11	27	07	15	A	60	.44
83	04	26	01	13	03	13	92	44	D	68	.56
84	00	07	71	33	13	31	15	25	B	52	.38

SOURCE: Reprinted from H. Grobman, *AERA Monograph series in Curriculum Evaluation*, No. 2, *Evaluation activities of curriculum projects* (Chicago: Rand McNally and Company, 1968). By permission of the publisher.

[a] High group consists of the top 27 percent of the pupils in the sample on total test score. Low group consists of the bottom 27 per cent of the pupils in the sample on total test score.

The first column, *Item Number*, refers to the number of each question on an 84-question, multiple-choice test.

Each question includes four possible alternatives; the double columns labeled *A*, *B*, *C*, and *D* across the top of the table refer to the answer options for each question. Thus, the columns labeled *A* refer to those students selecting answer alternative *A* for a given question.

Under each answer option (*A*, *B*, *C*, *D*) there are two subcolumns, *High* and *Low*. *High* refers to those students whose total scores on the test were the highest of all students taking the test. And *Low* refers to those students whose total scores on the test were the lowest of all students taking the test. Thus, for item #1, the overwhelming majority of both good and poor students (categorized on the basis of over-all success on the test) selected answer *C*; 85 percent of the high students and 79 percent of the low students selected answer *C*.

Under the *Total* heading to the far right of the table, the column labeled *Key* indicates the answer considered best by the test writers. Thus, for question #1, answer *C* is correct.

The column labeled *p* indicates the percent of all students taking the test who selected the correct answer. For question #1, 82 percent of those taking the test answered correctly. Thus, question #1 was extremely easy for all students.

The last column, *r*, is the biserial correlation (often written as r_{bis}). This is a way of stating mathematically the extent to which a question discriminates between the high-scoring students and the low-scoring students on the total test. Thus, for question #1, an r_{bis} of .09 indicates that this question did not effectively discriminate between these two groups of students. Question #83, with an r_{bis} of .56, was effective in discriminating between good and poor students. Item 81 has a negative r_{bis}. This means that the correct answer was selected more often by the poorer students than by the better students. A majority of the good students selected answer *B*, rather than keyed answer *C*. This is an indication of some kind of trouble either with the item or with the curriculum. The problem may be that the question was incorrectly keyed, that is, that the correct answer is answer *B* rather than answer *C*. Or the question may be stated ambiguously. It may have two correct or equally defensible answers. Or it may be that course materials are misleading.

Post-organizer

In this chapter we have presented the relationship between item difficulty and item discrimination. Items of moderate difficulty have the *potential* for good item discrimination. The theoretical maximum item discrimination *D*-value (1.0) is possible only when item difficulty is .5.

An item analysis—comparing the performance on each item of the most and least successful examinees on the total test—will identify items that are nonfunctional, intrinsically ambiguous, or miskeyed, so they can be revised or thrown out. Usually, not only will this procedure improve the reliability and hence the validity of a particular test, but the experience of studying the students' responses in depth will help the instructor in his teaching and in subsequent test construction.

A chain of relationships exists between certain item and test characteristics. Item difficulty affects possible item discrimination, which in turn directly determines the variance and internal-consistency reliability of the test scores. Reliability is necessary, but not sufficient, for validity.

IMPORTANT TERMS AND CONCEPTS

relevance   item analysis
item difficulty (*p*)   intrinsic ambiguity
item discrimination (*D*)   extrinsic ambiguity

SUGGESTED READINGS

EBEL, R. L. 1954. Procedures for the analysis of classroom tests. *Educational and Psychological Measurement*, **14**: 352–364.

———. 1965. How to improve test quality through item analysis. In *Measuring educational achievement*. Englewood Cliffs, N.J.: Prentice-Hall, Inc., Chap. 11.

————. 1967. The relation of item discrimination to test reliability. *Journal of Educational Measurement,* **4**: 125–128.

ENGELHART, M. D. 1965. A comparison of several item discrimination indices. *Journal of Educational Measurement,* **2**: 69–76.

FELDT, L. S., and A. E. HALL. 1964. Stability of four item discrimination indices over groups of different average ability. *American Educational Research Journal.* **1**: 35–46.

FINDLEY, W. G. 1956. Rationale for evaluation of item discrimination statistics. *Educational and Psychological Measurement,* **16**: 175–180.

HENRYSSON, S. 1971. Gathering, analyzing, and using data on test items. In R. L. Thorndike, ed., *Educational measurement,* 2d ed. Washington, D.C.: American Council on Education, Chap. 5.

JOHNSON, A. P. 1951. Notes on a suggested index of item validity. *Journal of Educational Psychology,* **42**: 499–504.

LANGE, A., I. J. LEHMANN, and W. A. MEHRENS. 1967. Using item analysis to improve tests. *Journal of Educational Measurement,* **2** (4): 65–68.

MYERS, C. T. 1962. The relationship between item difficulty and test validity and reliability. *Educational and Psychological Measurement,* **22** (3): 565–571.

12

THE ASSESSMENT OF
THE AFFECTIVE DOMAIN

Cognitive measures attempt to assess *maximum* performance (what a person *can do*); affective measures attempt to reflect *typical* performance (what a person *does do or feel*). The objectives for almost any course will include statements pertaining to attitudes, appreciations, and interests as well as knowledge and proficiencies. As Krathwohl (1965, p. 90) stated: "In spite of the lack of explicit formulation . . . nearly all cognitive objectives have an affective component if we search for it."[1] If a child is taught to read, but he reads only when forced to, an important affective educational objective was not achieved. Although much attention is given to the assessment of the cognitive objectives, rarely is any systematic effort directed toward the evaluation of affective objectives. Tuckman and Lorge (1954) found that a course on the psychology of the adult had little affect on the attitudes of graduate students toward other people, even though such an outcome had frequently been taken for granted. Jackson and Lahaderne (1967) and Bauman (1970) found that teachers were poor predictors of the affective responses of their students.

Krathwohl et al. (1964) produced a handbook and taxonomy designed to stimulate and systematize the assessment of objectives in the affective domain, as Bloom's taxonomy had done in the cognitive area.

> The taxonomy, like the periodic table of elements or a check-off shopping list, provides the panorama of objectives. Comparing the range of the present curriculum with the range of possible outcomes may suggest additional goals that might be explored [Krathwohl, 1965, p. 89].

[1] Probably the converse also holds: nearly all affective objectives have a cognitive component.

The degree of *internalization* is proposed as the unifying hierarchical factor underlying the affective taxonomy. Various affective concepts are defined in relation to the internalization hierarchy as shown in Figure 12–1. The shallowest degree of internalization of feeling is represented by *awareness*; the deepest is represented by *characterization*. Recall that we found assessment at the higher levels of the cognitive taxonomy difficult; measuring character and value often pose even greater problems. The affective taxonomy has not had the impact on education that the cognitive taxonomy had. Perhaps this is partially due to the unique assessment problems associated with affective measurement, but the basic impediment is probably ever-present inertia—things at rest remain at rest unless acted on by some external force. We hope that this book may stimulate attempts to assess affective educational objectives, in addition to the conventional cognitive outcomes. Krathwohl's taxonomy can be a useful general framework to help organize such assessment.

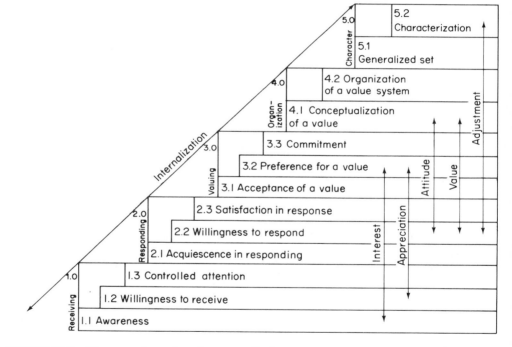

FIGURE 12–1 *The range of meaning of common affective terms as defined by the taxonomy of affective educational objectives. (Adapted from Krathwohl et al., 1964.)*

Cognitive vs. Affective Appraisal

"Who was the third President of the United States?" Historians agree that Thomas Jefferson was; thus, if you respond "Thomas Jefferson" you are correct. "Do you like spinach?" One cannot in advance designate an answer to this question that will always be correct, because there are no generally correct or incorrect responses for matters of personal preference. An in-between question that is keyed in advance would be: "How well do you like spinach? Loathe it. Dislike it. Indifferent. Like it. Love it." Scores for the five responses could be 1, 2, 3, 4, or 5.

A fourth kind of question partakes of both the knowledge aspect of the president question and the affective nature of the spinach query. If you ask a student, "Have you read any nonrequired book this semester?", his "Yes" response may be correct or incorrect. Either he did or he did not, but you may find it difficult to verify his statement. This may make you speculate about his memory and motives. *The correct answer to an affective question depends on the person queried; the correct answer to a cognitive question is the same for all respondents.* Although attitude scales are the most widely employed means of assessing affective objectives, many other means are used that involve self-reports or reports by others—interest inventories, personality inventories, questionnaires, projective techniques, systematic observation, sociometric techniques, interviews, and so on.[2] Although the names sound dissimilar, certain common difficulties occur in all such measures. Situational factors of the examiner and the assessment context have a more significant influence on the results for affective measures than they do for ability measures. (In part this instability arises from the instability of what is measured—attitudes, interests, and so on.)

Assessment Techniques

THURSTONE ATTITUDE SCALES

Ever since the groundbreaking studies by Professors Thurstone and Chave at the University of Chicago in 1929, psychologists and others have been devising scales to determine people's attitudes toward a multitude of objects and situations—everything from war to God. Psychologist Leonard Ferguson (1952) stated:

> Attitude scales developed in accord with the Thurstone equal-appearing-interval procedure have been put to many uses. There are more than 500 references to them in the literature in which they have played an important part. In these studies, Thurstone-type attitude scales have been used to determine the effects of movies on attitudes toward crime and toward nationality groups . . . the effects of social science courses upon student attitudes . . . the relative effectiveness of written and oral propaganda . . . the effect of college attendance upon attitudes . . . the degree of employee morale.

Most attitude scales were developed to answer specific research questions and therefore are not available in fully standardized commercial form. Thurstone, however, had a broader purpose. His great contributions were in showing how scales of attitude expression could be constructed for any specified topic and in developing items that revealed various strengths of feeling toward a given object or situation. The attitude-toward-movies scale is presented in Figure 12–2. Before you read further, respond to the items according to the directions at the top.

[2] These and related topics are treated in Chapter 16.

ATTITUDE TOWARDS MOVIES

This is a study of attitudes toward the movies. On the following pages you will find a number of statements expressing different attitudes toward the movies.

    ✓ Put a check mark if you agree with the statement.

    × Put a cross if you disagree with the statement.

If you simply cannot decide about a statement you may mark it with a question mark.

This is not an examination. There are no right or wrong answers to these statements. This is simply a study of people's attitudes toward the movies. Please indicate your own attitude by a check mark when you agree and by a cross when you disagree.

LIST OF OPINIONS IN THE SCALE

1. (1.5) The movies occupy time that should be spent in more wholesome recreation.
2. (1.3) I am tired of the movies; I have seen too many poor ones.
3. (4.5) The movies are the best civilizing device ever developed.
4. (0.2) Movies are the most important cause of crime.
5. (2.7) Movies are all right but a few of them give the rest a bad name.
6. (2.6) I like to see movies once in a while but they do disappoint you sometimes.
7. (2.9) I think movies are fairly interesting.
8. (2.7) Movies are just a harmless pastime.
9. (1.7) The movies to me are just a way to kill time.
10. (4.0) The influence of the movies is decidedly for good.
11. (3.9) The movies are good, clean entertainment.
12. (3.9) Movies increase one's appreciation of beauty.
13. (1.7) I'd never miss the movies if we didn't have them.
14. (2.4) Sometimes I feel that the movies are desirable and sometimes I doubt it.
15. (0.0) It is a sin to go to the movies.
16. (4.3) There would be very little progress without the movies.
17. (4.3) The movies are the most vital form of art today.
18. (3.6) A movie is the best entertainment that can be obtained cheaply.
19. (3.4) A movie once in a while is a good thing for everybody.
20. (3.4) The movies are one of the few things I can enjoy by myself.
21. (1.3) Going to the movies is a foolish way to spend your money.
22. (1.1) Moving pictures bore me.
23. (0.6) As they now exist movies are wholly bad for children.
24. (0.6) Such a pernicious influence as the movies is bound to weaken the moral fiber of those who attend.
25. (0.3) As a protest against movies we should pledge ourselves never to attend them.
26. (0.1) The movies are the most important single influence for evil.
27. (4.7) The movies are the most powerful influence for good in American life.
28. (2.3) I would go to the movies more often if I were sure of finding something good.
29. (4.1) If I had my choice of anything I wanted to do, I would go to the movies.
30. (2.2) The pleasure people get from the movies just about balances the harm they do.
31. (2.0) I don't find much that is educational in the current films.
32. (1.9) The information that you obtain from the movies is of little value.
33. (1.0) Movies are a bad habit.
34. (3.3) I like the movies as they are because I go to be entertained, not educated.
35. (3.1) On the whole the movies are pretty decent.
36. (0.8) The movies are undermining respect for authority.
37. (2.7) I like to see other people enjoy the movies whether I enjoy them myself or not.
38. (0.3) The movies are to blame for the prevalence of sex offenses.
39. (4.4) The movie is one of the great educational institutions for common people.
40. (0.8) Young people are learning to smoke, drink, and pet from the movies.

In scoring the attitude scale, we cannot say that one score is better or worse than another; we can only say that one person's attitude toward the movies is more or less favorable than another person's. It is purely arbitrary that attitudes unfavorable to the movies have lower scale values than favorable attitudes.

Any individual's attitude is measured by the average or mean scale value of all the statements he checks. The person who has the larger score is more favorably inclined toward the movies than the person with a lower score.

For the purpose of comparing groups, the distributions of attitude in each group can be plotted, and it can then be said whether and how much one group is more favorable to the movies than another group.

FIGURE 12–2 *An attitude-toward-movies scale. (Reproduced from L. L. Thurstone,* **The measurement of values** *[Chicago: University of Chicago Press, 1959], pp. 285–286, by permission of The University of Chicago Press.)*

After you have completed the scale, determine your score in finding the median scale value (given in parentheses) of all of the statements with which you agreed. Notice the difference between the very strong pro-movie statements (numbers 27 and 29) and the extreme anti-movie statements (4 and 15).

What does your score mean, and how were the item intensities secured? It would be interesting to tabulate the scores of your class, perhaps separately by sex; keep the identity of individuals anonymous so you can make a normative comparison with the absolute meaning of the mean-intensity scores. The higher your score is, the more favorable your attitude is toward movies; the lower the score, the less favorable. The scale of intensities is considered to run from 0 through 6. Do the scores in your class average approximately $(0 + 6)/2 = 3.0$? (Remember that this scale was constructed many years ago, and attitudes may have changed; or, your class may be atypical.) How far above or below the median of your class are you? In your opinion, is your attitude actually more favorable or less favorable toward movies than the average intensity for the items you checked indicates, as compared with your classmates? If so, how do you explain your score?

Thurstone-type attitude scales are developed by giving several hundred persons ("judges") a large number of statements about a topic. Each judge sorts each statement into one of several categories (usually 11, but 6 on the movie-attitude scale) that range from "extremely favorable" through "neutral" to extremely unfavorable." Each statement is written on a separate slip of paper. The judges are asked to rate the intensity of each statement, not the extent to which they agree with it. (This sorting procedure has been described as the method of "equal-appearing intervals," although the judges are not told that the intervals between categories are equal.) Those statements on which the judges agree reasonably well as to intensity are candidates for the final scale. The reliability of the scale can then be estimated on a sample of subjects. The attitude scale usually consists of from 20 to 45 statements that spread evenly over the intensity scale, in order to discriminate well the levels of "favorableness." The intensity scale value is determined by the median category to which the judges assigned a given statement. The order of these statements is random on the final printed form. As you did above, the examinee is asked to mark those statements with which he agrees; his score is the median intensity of those statements. It should be evident that considerable time and effort are required to use Thurstone's method to construct an attitude scale. This requirement limits the use of this kind of scale largely to those areas for which scales are already available. An extensive and extremely useful collection of attitude scales and discussion of many topics has been assembled by Shaw and Wright (1967).

LIKERT SCALES

There are many methods of obtaining information pertinent to affective variables. Perhaps the most widely used technique for attitude measurement is the Likert scale, on which a statement is followed by a five-response continuum such as strongly agree, agree, undecided, disagree, and strongly disagree (fewer

```
THE EDUCATION SCALE

READ EACH ITEM CAREFULLY AND UNDERLINE QUICKLY THE
PHRASE WHICH BEST EXPRESSES YOUR FEELING ABOUT THE STATE-
MENT. Wherever possible, let your own personal experience determine your
answer. Do not spend much time on any item. If in doubt, underline the phrase
which seems most nearly to express your present feeling about the statement.
WORK RAPIDLY. Be sure to answer every item.

  *1  A man can learn more by working four years than by going to high
      school. **Strongly Agree   Agree   Undecided   Disagree   Strongly Disagree**
   2  The more education a person has the better he is able to enjoy life.
   3  Education helps a person to use his leisure time to better advantage.
   4  A good education is a great comfort to a man out of work.
  *5  Only subjects like reading, writing, and arithmetic should be taught at
      public expense.
  *6  Education is no help in getting a job today.
  *7  Most young people are getting too much education.
   8  A high school education is worth all the time and effort it requires.
   9  Our schools encourage an individual to think for himself.
 *10  There are too many fads and frills in modern education.
 *11  Education only makes a person discontented.
 *12  School training is of little help in meeting the problems of real life.
  13  Education tends to make an individual less conceited.
  14  Solution of the world's problems will come through education.
 *15  High school courses are too impractical.
 *16  A man is foolish to keep going to school if he can get a job.
  17  Savings spent on education are wisely invested.
  18  An educated man can advance more rapidly in business and industry.
 *19  Parents should not be compelled to send their children to school.
  20  Education is more valuable than most people think.
  21  A high school education makes a man a better citizen.
 *22  Public money spent on education during the past few years could have
      been used more wisely for other purposes.

*These are negative items, agreement with which is considered to reflect an unfavorable
attitude. Their weights must be reversed for purposes of scoring. The same response al-
ternatives are used with all items.
```

*FIGURE 12–3   An example of a Likert scale. (Reproduced from E. A. Rundquist and
R. F. Sletto,* **Personality in the Depression** *[Minneapolis: University of Minnesota Press, 1936],
by permission of the publisher. Copyright 1936 by the University of Minnesota Press.)*

or more categories are not uncommon). The subject selects the category that
best describes his reaction to the statement.

An example of a Likert scale is *The Education Scale* developed by
Rundquist and Sletto (1936) and shown in Figure 12–3. Test-retest and split-half
reliability estimates reported for it were above 80. Another example is provided   **287**

REVISED MATH ATTITUDE SCALE

Directions: Please write your name in the upper right hand corner. Each of the statements on this opinionnaire expresses a feeling which a particular person has toward mathematics. You are to express, on a five-point scale, the extent of agreement between the feeling expressed in each statement and your own personal feeling. The five points are: Strongly Disagree (SD), Disagree (D), Undecided (U), Agree (A), Strongly Agree (SA). You are to encircle the letter(s) which best indicates how closely you agree or disagree with the feeling expressed in each statement AS IT CONCERNS YOU.

*1   I am always under a terrible strain in a math class.

SD   D   U   A   SA

*2   I do not like mathematics, and it scares me to have to take it.

3   Mathematics is very interesting to me, and I enjoy math courses.

4   Mathematics is fascinating and fun.

5   Mathematics makes me feel secure, and at the same time it is stimulating.

*6   My mind goes blank, and I am unable to think clearly when working math.

*7   I feel a sense of insecurity when attempting mathematics.

*8   Mathematics makes me feel uncomfortable, restless, irritable and impatient.

9   The feeling that I have toward mathematics is a good feeling.

*10   Mathematics makes me feel as though I'm lost in a jungle of numbers and can't find my way out.

11   Mathematics is something which I enjoy a great deal.

*12   When I hear the word math, I have a feeling of dislike.

*13   I approach math with a feeling of hesitation, resulting from a fear of not being able to do math.

14   I really like mathematics.

15   Mathematics is a course in school which I have always enjoyed studying.

*16   It makes me nervous to even think about having to do a math problem.

*17   I have never liked math, and it is my most dreaded subject.

18   I am happier in a math class than in any other class.

19   I feel at ease in mathematics, and I like it very much.

20   I feel a definite positive reaction to mathematics; it's enjoyable

*These are negative items, and must be reversed for purposes of scoring. The same response alternatives are used with all items.

FIGURE 12–4   *Another Likert scale. (Reprinted from L. R. Aiken, Jr., Personality correlates of attitude toward mathematics, Journal of Educational Research, 1963, 56: 576–580, by permission of the author and publisher, Dembar Educational Research Services, Inc.)*

by the *Revised Math Attitude Scale* (Aiken, 1963)(Figure 12—4). A test-retest reliability coefficient of .94 was reported for the scale. Many other examples can be found in Shaw and Wright's (1967) *Scales for the Measurement of Attitudes.* The sample scale illustrates that Likert scales are very flexible and can be

FIGURE 12-5 The Personality Record. Prepared by a joint committee representing high schools and colleges. (Copyright © 1958, National Association of Secondary School Principals of the NEA, and reproduced by permission.)

Personality Record (Confidential)
(REVISED)

PERSONAL CHARACTERISTICS OF ....

School................ Town or City................ State................

Last Name First Name Middle Name

Room................
Grade................

The following characterizations are descriptions of behavior. It is recommended that where possible the judgments of a number of the pupil's present teachers be indicated by the use of the following method or by checks:

Example: MOTIVATION

M (5) indicates the most common or modal behavior of the pupil as shown by the agreement of five of the eight teachers reporting. The location of the numerals to the left and right indicates that one teacher considers the pupil *vacillating* and that two teachers consider him *highly motivated*. If preferred, the subject fields or other areas of relationship with the pupil may be used to replace the numerals.

	1			2
Example: MOTIVATION	Purposeless	Vacillating √	Usually purposeful M (5) √√√√√	Effectively motivated	Highly motivated 2 √√
1. MOTIVATION	Purposeless	Vacillating	Usually purposeful	Effectively motivated	Highly motivated
2. INDUSTRY	Seldom works even under pressure	Needs constant pressure	Needs occasional prodding	Prepares assigned work regularly	Seeks additional work
3. INITIATIVE	Merely conforms	Seldom initiates	Frequently initiates	Consistently self-reliant	Actively creative
4. INFLUENCE AND LEADERSHIP	Negative	Co-operative but retiring	Sometimes in minor affairs	Contributing in important affairs	Judgment respected— makes things go
5. CONCERN FOR OTHERS	Indifferent	Self-centered	Somewhat socially concerned	Generally concerned	Deeply and actively concerned
6. RESPONSIBILITY	Unreliable	Somewhat dependable	Usually dependable	Conscientious	Assumes much responsibility
7. INTEGRITY	Not dependable	Questionable at times	Generally honest	Reliable, dependable	Consistently trustworthy
8. EMOTIONAL STABILITY	Hyperemotional / Apathetic	Excitable / Unresponsive	Usually well-balanced	Well-balanced	Exceptionally stable

constructed quickly. In the primary grades the categories should be reduced to three (Disagree, Undecided, Agree) or even to two (Disagree, Agree); the statements should be read aloud if the reading would be a problem for some students. Items generally should be a mixture of positive (pro) and negative (con) statements to add variety to the scale and reduce the student's tendency to respond perfunctorily. Likert scales can be refined through the item-analysis procedures presented in Chapter 11.

RATING SCALES

Rating scales do not differ fundamentally from Likert scales. Instead of using the standard set of response options pertaining to the degree of agreement, rating scales use descriptive terms pertaining to the factor in question.

An example of a rating scale is the *Personality Record* (Figure 12–5) used by high schools to send reports to colleges. A teacher records his judgment of a student on several factors. Such ratings can be made quickly. If they are consistent across teachers, one becomes more confident that the ratings reflect a generalized trait or traits and are not merely a function of the idiosyncracies of an individual teacher. The other side of the coin is reflected in Figure 12–6, depicting Burton's (1968) *Course Evaluation Inventory*. In a very brief period, students can provide much valuable feedback information for the teacher. The inventory is sufficiently focused so that if there is a consistently reported weakness, the results have diagnostic and remedial value for the teacher. If teachers would provide opportunity for such simple, straightforward, and systematic pupil feedback, the quality of instruction would improve substantially (Gage, Runkel, and Chatterjee, 1960). Remmers (1963, pp. 367–368) observed: "Research has shown that, taken as a group, student ratings of teachers are reliable, have little relationship to student grades or to a course's difficulty, and are higher for more experienced teachers." Empirical studies also tend to corroborate the validity of student ratings of teaching effectiveness (McKeachie *et al.*, 1971).

An example of a carefully developed numerical rating scale developed by Ryans (1960) in an extensive study of teacher characteristics is shown in Figure 12–7. (Its bipolar traits are illustrative of the semantic-differential technique, which is described in the next section.) With trained raters, inter-observer agreement is quite high (r's of .8 and above). Such a scale would also seem to have value for teacher evaluation and improvement.

SEMANTIC DIFFERENTIAL

A widely used technique was developed by Osgood and his associates (1957) during research on the psychology of meaning. Concepts are measured and portrayed in three dimensions of meaning—that is, *semantic space*. The dimensions are *evaluation* (good-bad), *potency* (strong-weak), and *activity* (fast-slow). Sample directions for the semantic differential are given in Figure 12–8. Osgood recommends that each dimension be measured by at least three separate *scales* that have been empirically shown to be relatively pure measures of that dimension. The three scales for each of the three dimensions are averaged for each

COURSE EVALUATION INVENTORY

Course: _____ Instructor: _____ Date: _____

Please be frank and objective in your responses. Omit irrelevant items. Thank you for your co-operation.

I. Student self-evaluation

1. The amount of work I did for this course was	very great	1 2 3 4 5	quite small.
2. The quality of my work for this course was	excellent	1 2 3 4 5	poor.
3. My contribution to the class as a whole was	excellent	1 2 3 4 5	poor.
4. I learned from this course	very much	1 2 3 4 5	very little.
5. The subject matter, methods, or skills learned will be	very useful	1 2 3 4 5	useless.

6. On the back of this sheet, write your evaluation of your own participation and involvement in the work of this course.

II. Instructor

7. The instructor's knowledge of the subject was	excellent	1 2 3 4 5	poor.
8. The instructor expressed his ideas clearly	always	1 2 3 4 5	never.
9. He avoided confusing or useless jargon	always	1 2 3 4 5	never.
10. His speaking ability (enunciation, volume, etc.) was	excellent	1 2 3 4 5	poor.
11. His treatment of students was	courteous	1 2 3 4 5	discourteous.
12. The instructor was	over confident	1 2 3 4 5	too unsure.
13. He was aware of students' needs and difficulties	always	1 2 3 4 5	never.
14. He was able to alleviate students' difficulties	always	1 2 3 4 5	never.
15. He encouraged students to work independently	always	1 2 3 4 5	never.
16. His reaction to differences of opinion was	encouragement	1 2 3 4 5	intolerance.

17. On the back of this sheet, indicate your opinions about the instructor of the course.

III. Organization of classroom proceedings

18. The instructor was well-prepared	always	1 2 3 4 5	never.
19. The basic concepts were clear and logically developed	always	1 2 3 4 5	never.
20. The class was	too teacher-dominated	1 2 3 4 5	too student-dominated.
21. The lectures were	stimulating	1 2 3 4 5	boring.
22. The lectures were	informative	1 2 3 4 5	wasteful.
23. The discussions were a waste of time	always	1 2 3 4 5	never.
24. The committee/lab work was a waste of time	always	1 2 3 4 5	never.
25. The instructor covered the material	too quickly	1 2 3 4 5	too slowly.
26. His coverage of material was	too superficial	1 2 3 4 5	too technical.
27. The class was most interesting at the	beginning	1 2 3 4 5	end.

IV. Requirements

28. The text, with respect to course objectives, was	relevant	1 2 3 4 5	irrelevant.
29. The text was	too difficult	1 2 3 4 5	too elementary.
30. Reference materials were useful	always	1 2 3 4 5	never.
31. The text was	up-to-date	1 2 3 4 5	outdated.
32. The assignments were clear	always	1 2 3 4 5	never.
33. The number of assignments was	too great	1 2 3 4 5	too small.
34. The assignments were	too difficult	1 2 3 4 5	too simple.
35. The assignments were necessary (not busywork)	always	1 2 3 4 5	never.

V. Evaluation

36. There was sufficient time for preparation for exams/papers	always	1 2 3 4 5	never.
37. The criteria for grading were clear in advance	always	1 2 3 4 5	never.
38. The concepts emphasized on exams/papers were relevant	always	1 2 3 4 5	never.
39. The number of exams/papers was	too great	1 2 3 4 5	too small.
40. The exams/papers were	too long	1 2 3 4 5	too short.
41. The exams/papers were	too difficult	1 2 3 4 5	too simple.
42. The instructor graded fairly	always	1 2 3 4 5	never.
43. The instructor returned papers promptly	always	1 2 3 4 5	never.

IV. Content

44. The subject matter was intellectually stimulating	always	1 2 3 4 5	never.
45. The subject matter was	up-to-date	1 2 3 4 5	outdated.
46. The course should be given to students who are	more advanced	1 2 3 4 5	less advanced.
47. Considering the credit-hours, the work required should be	more	1 2 3 4 5	less.
48. This course should be	required	1 2 3 4 5	dropped.
49. I would like to take another course in this subject area.	definitely	1 2 3 4 5	definitely not

50. Please write specific suggestions for improving the course, student participation and involvement, or instructor on the back of this sheet.

FIGURE 12–6 *Rating scale used for student evaluation of instruction. (Copyright © 1968 by Nancy W. Burton, Laboratory of Educational Research, University of Colorado. Reproduced by permission of the author.)*

CLASSROOM OBSERVATION RECORD

TEACHER CHARACTERISTICS STUDY

Teacher_____ No. _____ Sex _____ Class or Subject_____ Date_____

City _____ School_____ Time _____ Observer_____

Pupil Behavior   Remarks:

1.	Apathetic	1	2	3	4	5	6	7 N	Alert
2.	Obstructive	1	2	3	4	5	6	7 N	Responsible
3.	Uncertain	1	2	3	4	5	6	7 N	Confident
4.	Dependent	1	2	3	4	5	6	7 N	Initiating

Teacher Behavior

5.	Partial	1	2	3	4	5	6	7 N	Fair
6.	Autocratic	1	2	3	4	5	6	7 N	Democratic
7.	Aloof	1	2	3	4	5	6	7 N	Responsive
8.	Restricted	1	2	3	4	5	6	7 N	Understanding
9.	Harsh	1	2	3	4	5	6	7 N	Kindly
10.	Dull	1	2	3	4	5	6	7 N	Stimulating
11.	Stereotyped	1	2	3	4	5	6	7 N	Original
12.	Apathetic	1	2	3	4	5	6	7 N	Alert
13.	Unimpressive	1	2	3	4	5	6	7 N	Attractive
14.	Evading	1	2	3	4	5	6	7 N	Responsible
15.	Erratic	1	2	3	4	5	6	7 N	Steady
16.	Excitable	1	2	3	4	5	6	7 N	Poised
17.	Uncertain	1	2	3	4	5	6	7 N	Confident
18.	Disorganized	1	2	3	4	5	6	7 N	Systematic
19.	Inflexible	1	2	3	4	5	6	7 N	Adaptable
20.	Pessimistic	1	2	3	4	5	6	7 N	Optimistic
21.	Immature	1	2	3	4	5	6	7 N	Integrated
22.	Narrow	1	2	3	4	5	6	7 N	Broad

FIGURE 12–7 *Assessment blank employed by observers.* (*Reproduced from D. G. Ryans,* Characteristics of teachers [*Washington, D.C.: American Council on Education, 1960*], *p. 86, by permission of the author and publisher.*)

concept. The concepts can then be plotted in the semantic space of meaning. The semantic-differential format is illustrated in Figure 12–9 along with John Brown's perception of teachers. John has indicated his reaction to teachers on each of the nine seven-point scales. His responses are usually converted to   *292*

SEMANTIC DIFFERENTIAL INSTRUCTIONS

On the following pages there is either a word or an expression in capitalized letters followed by pairs of opposite words underneath the capitalized word or sentence. Between each of the pairs of opposites there are 7 dashes. You are to place a check mark on one of the 7 positions that are between the two opposite words. The check mark should indicate how you feel about the word or concept. Look at the examples below:

EXAMPLE 1:   EDUCATION

```
Good  _✓_:___:___:___:___:___:___  Bad
Slow  ___:_✓_:___:___:___:___:___  Fast
Cruel ___:___:___:_✓_:___:___:___  Kind
```

In this example EDUCATION is the concept being assessed and the pairs of opposites are Bood-Bad, Slow-Fast, and Cruel-Kind. If EDUCATION seemed to you to mean something very Good, you would make a check in position 1 of the Good-Bad scale. If EDUCATION seemed to you to mean somthing Slow, then you would place your check mark in position 2 of the Slow-Fast scale. And if you feel that EDUCATION means something which is neither Cruel nor Kind, then you would put your check mark in position 4.

In the following example a check has been placed to illustrate how someone would place his check marks if he thought that TEACHERS were very Bad, very Fast, and very Cruel:

EXAMPLE 2:   TEACHERS

```
Good  ___:___:___:___:___:___:_✓_  Bad
Slow  ___:___:___:___:___:___:_✓_  Fast
Cruel _✓_:___:___:___:___:___:___  Kind
```

On the following pages, place your check marks rapidly. What is wanted is your first impression. There are no "right" or "wrong" answers. Be sure to make only one check mark for each pair of words. Do not skip any pairs of words or pages.

FIGURE 12–8 *Directions for administering a semantic differential measure.*

1 to 7 ratings (using a consistent low-to-high direction; for example, the first position of scale 2 would receive a "7" rating, but the last position in scale 5 would receive a "7" rating) and averaged for each of the three dimensions. For John the evaluation dimension scales (scales 2, 5, and 8) average 7.0; the

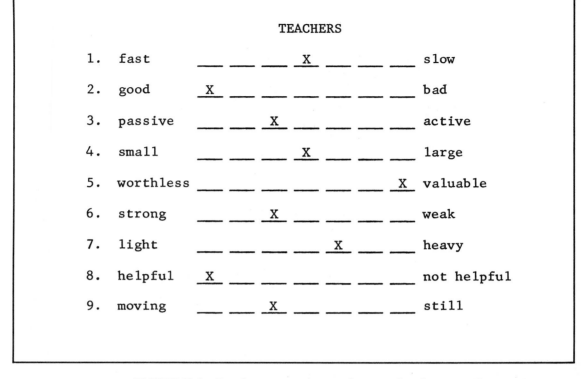

FIGURE 12-9 *Sample responses of one student regarding the concept "teachers" using the semantic-differential technique.*

potency dimension scales (scales 4, 6, and 7), 4.3; and the activity dimension scales (scales 1, 3, and 9), 4.0.

In actual practice, the major educational concern is with the *value* a concept has for a pupil—whether he likes it or not, is interested or not, and so on. Consequently, most current educational applications of the semantic differential have deviated from Osgood's orthodox approach. Scales that have intrinsic relevance for the concept in question are used whether or not they are pure measures of a given dimension. The semantic notion is thus ignored, and each scale is interpreted directly. A recent application at the elementary-school level is shown in Figure 12-10. Any relevant concept can be studied with the semantic-differential technique: "geometry," "reading," "Richard Nixon," "recess," "classmates," "school," "time," "the ideal teacher," and so on. When the integrity of the information is protected, the semantic-differential approach can yield much valuable information. Since little reading is required, it takes little time to administer. The semantic differential has been found to yield reasonably reliable information on students as low as in grade 2, but the reliability is greater with older students (Di Vesta and Dick, 1966). The semantic-differential measurement technique has been useful in a wide spectrum of applications in many fields. Despite its rather brief history, it has become a standard assessment technique.

READING A STORY

easy	___	___		___	___	hard
dull	___	___		___	___	interesting
useful	___	___		___	___	useless
worthless	___	___		___	___	valuable
unpleasant	___	___		___	___	pleasant

SPELLING

dull	___	___	___	___	___	interesting
pleasant	___	___	___	___	___	unpleasant
useless	___	___	___	___	___	useful
hard	___	___	___	___	___	easy
worthless	___	___	___	___	___	valuable

GIVING ORAL REPORTS

worthless	___	___	___	___	___	valuable
interesting	___	___	___	___	___	dull
unpleasant	___	___	___	___	___	pleasant
useless	___	___	___	___	___	useful
easy	___	___	___	___	___	hard

SCIENCE CLASS

interesting	___	___	___	___	___	dull
useless	___	___	___	___	___	useful
easy	___	___	___	___	___	hard
pleasant	___	___	___	___	___	unpleasant
worthless	___	___	___	___	___	valuable

FIGURE 12–10   Example of concepts from a semantic-differential measure administered to elementary-school pupils.

A procedure by which one can assess attitudes, interests, and other affective variables is the Q-sort technique, which was originally developed by Stephenson (1953). An individual is given a set of cards containing statements, traits, pictures, or whatever; he then sorts then into piles according to their relative standing along a single dimension. The continuum can take many forms: "most like me" to "least like me," "most important" to "least important," "best" to "worst." The number of cards allowed in each pile usually is predetermined to approximate a normal frequency distribution.

The student may describe himself, a course, his interests, his school principal, and so on. The Q-sort technique has been widely used in counseling studies in which an individual describes himself with one Q-sort and re-sorts the cards to describe his ideal self. The sorted piles can then be correlated to ascertain the degree of agreement between perceived and ideal self. As with the other methods of assessing attitude that have been discussed, the content of the Q-sort can be tailor-made to the immediate particular purpose. There are a few standard Q-sorts, the most common of which is the California Q-set. One hundred descriptive statements are sorted into nine categories ranging from "extremely characteristic" to "extremely uncharacteristic" of the person. A special feature of this Q-sort set is a description of optimal adjustment, which is consensually based on the judgments of nine clinical psychologists. This and other examples can be found in Black (1961).

The major use of the Q-sort technique has been in counseling and psychotherapy. For example, Oldridge (1963) used Q-sorts by teachers to ascertain whether pupils undergoing counseling were improving in behavior more than those who were not receiving any treatment. The potential applicability of the Q-sort is much broader. Armitage (1967) used the Q-sort technique to assess differences in the value attached to certain social studies objectives by "experts" and classroom teachers. Sheldon and Sorenson (1960) used the technique to study changes in the educational philosophy of prospective teachers during their student teaching. The time required for administering and scoring the Q-sort and its focus on a single dimension reduces its widespread usability in comparison to the Likert and semantic-differential approaches (see Bauman, 1970).

The methods of assessing affect that we have illustrated should not be considered exhaustive. When properly used, simple questionnaires (structured or open-ended) can also reveal important educational values and attitudes. A comprehensive program of affective measurement should include assessment of teachers' and students' attitudes toward various aspects of the school's program. If examinees do not respond anonymously, however, the ensuing data will usually lack credibility—probably rightly so, since the expression of negative attitudes toward school, teachers, principals, and so on can hardly be expected when one thereby places himself in jeopardy.

GUTTMAN SCALES

A rather different scaling procedure, devised by Guttman (1947), is of considerable theoretical but limited practical importance because it requires items that are more reliable than can almost ever be found. If you are especially interested in scaling, read his basic article for its nice analogy of attitude assessment to the measurement of physical characteristics such as height and weight.

ATTITUDES VS. BEHAVIOR

Attitude assessment is complex, especially because the relationship of stated attitudes to actions is uncertain—even under the most deception-free circumstances. A man who would greatly prefer that members of a certain national group not marry his daughter, belong to his club, live on his street, or even visit his country, might sit next to such a person on the bus and talk with him cordially because there was no other unobtrusively reached seat, or because he is aware of his prejudice and ashamed of it, or because he is running for political office and needs the vote, or for any of a number of other reasons. L. L. Thurstone was once heard to say that one should not expect much correspondence between scores on a paper-and-pencil attitude scale and behavior that might appear to reflect that attitude. This would seem especially likely with the largely unvalidated social-distance scale (Bogardus, 1925, 1933), where one's score may reflect at least as much geographical difference and unfamiliarity as dislike. For example, how socially distant do you feel from the inhabitants of the Republic of San Marino? (Nevertheless, *some* attitude is being measured when a person says in effect that he cannot tolerate X, of which he has no knowledge or experience.)

QUESTIONNAIRES

Sets of self-report questions are frequently used in educational surveys, and probably are considerably overused in comparison to experimentation and personal observation. The sets are usually mimeographed or printed and sent through the mail or administered to captive audiences such as groups of teachers. The questions comprising questionnaires may be any kind that we have discussed in this book. The questions may begin with background data, such as sex (Male or Female—check one), date of birth (month, day, and year), and number of years of school completed. The subsequent questions may remain factual (How many students are enrolled in your classes? Which subject do you teach?) or the instrument may become an opinionnaire, typically of the rating-scale or ranking kinds. One might, for instance, send the Thurstone-Chave "Attitude toward Movies" scale to be filled out and returned, but more likely he would use materials of his own devising instead.

Questionnaires have all the usual limitations of self-report devices, plus some special problems of their own. If they are mailed to individuals to be filled out at whatever time(s) and under whatever circumstances happen to prevail in the home or office of the recipient, the results may vary greatly from individual to individual, depending on the time and care he chooses or is able to give. Some questionnaires will probably be returned with responses made carelessly and perhaps incompletely, unless respondents are in some way wooed into giving the time and care required. Other questionnaires will not be returned unless their receivers are reminded several times. Despite the best efforts of the investigator, there will probably be some persons who do not return questionnaires in a usable condition. These nonreturners and unsatisfactory answerers are the nonrespondents who bias the generalization one can make legitimately from his survey.

Suppose, for example, that you sent out a double postal card to every female fourth-grade teacher in your state and asked her how many years she has taught in that grade. If in two weeks half of the cards have been returned, you would not be in a good position to tabulate your results and announce them because you would not know which half of the teachers had responded, the ones who have taught the shortest time in the fourth grade or those who have taught the longest. Of course, you could *assume* that you have secured a *random* 50 percent of the teachers, so far as years of teaching are concerned, but readers of your report might not be willing to permit you that assumption without further justification. That is why it is essential to build initially into your study careful plans for several *follow-ups* in order to reduce nonrespondents to as small a percentage as possible.

Even with 100 percent returns, however, you would still need to qualify your conclusions from the self-report returns. Your figures represent how long the teachers *say* they have taught in the fourth grade, not necessarily how long they have actually taught. Careless errors, fallible memories, and willful deceptions color your findings in ways largely unknown to you. The problems are much greater when the questionnaire includes sensitive attitudinal questions.

Even a simple mail survey demands great care in the construction of the questionnaire; equal care is necessary with the use of such devices with large "captive" audiences. Unless the questionnaire is carefully structured, the information yielded is very difficult to summarize into a general picture. Further intricacies are discussed in books that treat questionnaire methodology, such as Helmstadter (1970) or Mouly (1970).

Problems of Affective Measurement

There are four problems general to most affective measures: (1) fakability, (2) self-deception, (3) semantics, and (4) criterion inadequacy.

FAKABILITY

During an interview for a summer position in a music store a person's reported liking for classical music may differ greatly from what he would tell a close friend, but it is very unlikely that his score on an "ability" test of music vocabulary would be affected much by his desire for employment. To reveal his knowledge, it is only necessary that he have enough motivation to take the vocabulary test conscientiously. Even large inducements will not compensate for lack of information about fugues and Bach. Ability tests are keyed a priori; it is not possible to fake a high (that is, favorable) score, although of course one can fake a low score (that is, deliberately score poorly on the test). On affective measures one can usually fake in either direction: he can tell the music-store owner that he prefers classical music and tell his friends that he prefers jazz, when he actually dislikes both forms and prefers country music.

A few disguised self-report and other-report devices are fairly resistant to extreme faking; the individual being tested cannot readily ascertain what is being assessed. Properly constructed and administered ability tests yield measures of well-motivated performance; self-report affective devices may more nearly reflect the desire to conform to the special situation, as perceived by the examinee, because self-report devices do not lend themselves to intrinsic right-wrong scoring. Liking spinach may be "right" for one purpose and "wrong" for another, but the correct spelling of "grandiose" is independent of the context in which the word appears.

Most affective measures require self-reports that are fakable; thus if the assessment is to be valid, it must be obtained in such a way that there is no incentive to be untruthful. Anonymity is the key to valid attitude assessment of feeling in any situation in which the subject may be rewarded or punished for his responses. Anonymity precludes the use of the information for individual purposes, but it can still yield feedback invaluable for the teacher in evaluating the degree to which various affective educational objectives were achieved. When the identity of the subject is necessary, an honest sharing of one's values, attitudes, interests, and feelings can be expected only when a deep level of rapport and trust has been established between the individual and the users of the information. This was graphically illustrated in a study reported by Cronbach (1970a, p. 495) in which a group of industrial workers filled out identical health questionnaires under two conditions. One questionnaire was returned to the company medical department as a preliminary to a medical examination. The other was mailed directly to a research group at a university. Far more symptoms were indicated on the research questionnaire than on the company's, even though an honest report on the latter might facilitate medical help.

Most subjects strive to make a socially desirable impression on self-report inventories; this is sometimes referred to as the "facade" effect. However, when it is to one's advantage to "fake bad," a facade effect can also be expected (Pollaczek, 1952). A draftee who wants a medical discharge may report a staggering array of psychotic symptoms. Affective measures can be falsified, no matter how constructed; moreover, faked scores lack predictive validity (Cronbach, 1970a, pp. 495–497).

The giving of socially desirable responses on a self-report inventory does not necessarily indicate deliberate deception by the respondent, but may be an unconscious tendency "to put up a good front."

Edwards (1957) developed a special social desirability (SD) scale in order to study the effects of this factor on affective measures. This scale is of value in investigating the extent to which the social desirability facade effect contaminates scores on some other measure. If scores on the SD scale correlate highly with scores on another measure, the validity of the measure is suspect.

The forced-choice type of item can reduce the influence of the social desirability set. Items of this type require the respondent to discriminate between two or more alternatives that, ideally, are equally acceptable. The forced-choice procedure is widely used on published affective measures, and receives additional treatment in Chapter 16.

A common adjustment phenomenon in human behavior is the tendency to want to like what we see when we look at ourselves. Human defense mechanisms cushion failures, minimize faults, and maximize virtues so we maintain a sense of personal worth (which, as a consequence, is often overpriced!). When one is asked questions about himself, the validity of the responses is vulnerable to the distortions of self-deception. This "blurring" can become a major threat to the validity of self-report inventories—persons who have the greatest personality problems are those who are the least able to give an accurate self-description. If a man believes himself to be Napoleon, his nonfaked, "honest" responses to personal questions will probably reflect his delusion. The validity of the responses is, of course, another matter. Other than for school counseling and guidance, and psychological case-studies, there is rarely a need in education for assessment of such a personal nature that self-deception becomes a serious problem. There is apt to be little need for self-deceit on issues of attitudes and interests toward educational experiences. Teachers "with a little learning" should resist any temptation to play junior psychiatrist by probing into emotional matters of a very personal nature.

The Assessment of the Affective Domain

SEMANTICS

On cognitive measures, the alternatives to items are usually categorically different; one of them is the correct or best answer. On affective measures, however, the responses frequently demand differences in degree. Consequently words such as "often," "seldom," "frequently," "usually," and "sometimes" are required. Unfortunately there is considerable variation in the explicit meanings that people attach to such words (Simpson, 1944). When students were asked what percentage frequency of a particular response would correspond to what they "frequently" did, one-fourth of them applied "frequently" only to events occurring at least 80 percent of the time, while another one-fourth indicated that "frequently" could mean a frequency below 40 percent of the time. Similar semantic difficulties occur with other types of terms and expressions. A question such as "Do you find reading interesting?" seems straightforward, but how interesting is interesting? Consider "Do you make friends easily?" How easy is easily? Also, is a friend a casual acquaintance or a very intimate associate? The validity of self-report information is reduced to the extent that the descriptive terms employed do not have uniform meaning across individuals.

CRITERION INADEQUACY

Definitive criteria against which the validity of the self-report information can be checked are usually either impossible or very difficult to obtain. How is a test of emotional stability or adjustment validated? There is no definitive criterion that will demonstrate the test's validity. Only after many varied and extensive studies would it be possible to establish the construct validity of tests of this kind scientifically. Consequently, one must interpret cautiously the results of published and unpublished affective measures, since only fragmentary data with

Post-organizer

relevance for validity are available. One is on safer ground when he tries to measure attitudes and interests instead of personality traits. If there seems to be no incentive to fake, and if the nature of the question is not emotionally jeopardizing, its face value has more logical validity and an interpretation can be made with more confidence.

The appraisal of feelings, interests, and attitudes has been grossly neglected in education, even though affective objectives are implicit, if not explicit, in every educational endeavor.

Several measurement techniques have been devised for registering affect. Common examples are: Thurstone, Likert, rating, and semantic-differential scales, and the Q-sort technique. Thurstone scales for measuring "attitude toward———" (e.g., war) are expensive to construct; a number of them, generally rather outdated, are available. Likert scales are very flexible and easily constructed; they have a common scale (strongly agree to strongly disagree) for the responses, which allows a common comparison across items. Rating scales are easily constructed and have wide applicability. The semantic differential is a special type of rating scale that requires very little time and reading for administration. The Q-sort technique, although difficult to administer, facilitates an assessment of the degree of relationship (r) between persons or within the same person. Its greatest application has been in personality research, although there are many rich, untapped areas in which it might be used.

Unique assessment problems are encountered in the affective domain; the measures are fakable, vulnerable to self-deception, and usually lacking in definitive external criteria. Semantic problems exert great influence on the responses to items that reflect differences in degree rather than having a correct answer. Anonymity is usually required for valid evaluative feedback in affective assessment.

SUGGESTED READINGS

ANASTASI, A. 1968. Other techniques for personality assessment. In *Psychological testing*, 3d ed. New York: The Macmillan Company, Chap. 20.

BLACK, J. 1961. *The Q-sort method in personality assessment and psychiatric research.* Springfield, Ill.: Thomas C Thomas, Publisher.

CRONBACH, L. J. 1970. Personality measurement through self-report. Chapter 16 in *Essentials of psychological testing*, 3d ed. New York: Harper & Row, Publishers.

EISS, A. F., and M. B. HARBECK. 1969. *Behavioral objectives in the affective domain.* Washington, D.C.: National Education Association.

JOHNSON, O. G., and J. W. BOMMARITO. 1971. *Tests and measurement in child development: A handbook.* San Francisco: Jossey-Bass, Inc.

KRATHWOHL, D. R. 1965. Stating objectives appropriately for program, for curriculum, and for instructional materials development. *Journal of Teacher Education*, **16**: 83–92.

————, B. S. BLOOM, and B. B. MASIA. 1964. *Taxonomy of educational objectives: Handbook II, Affective domain*. New York: David McKay Company, Inc.

MILLER, D. C. 1967. *Handbook of research design and social measurement*. New York: David McKay Company, Inc.

Many scales are evaluated and reproduced that have been used for measuring morale, job satisfaction, community attitudes, leadership, and other factors.

REMMERS, H. H. 1963. Rating methods in research on teaching. In N. L. Gage, ed., *Handbook of research on teaching*. Skokie, Ill.: Rand McNally & Company, Chap. 7.

SHAW, M. E., and J. M. WRIGHT. 1967. *Scales for the measurement of attitudes*. New York: McGraw-Hill Book Company.

Numerous attitude scales are reproduced and evaluated. Scales include attitudes toward various social practices, issues, and institutions, political and religious issues, ethnic groups, and so on.

STERN, G. G. 1963. Measuring noncognitive variables in research on teaching. In N. L. Gage, ed., *Handbook of research on teaching*. Skokie, Ill.: Rand McNally & Company.

illustrative studies using affective measurement

JACKSON, P. W., and H. M. LAHADERNE. 1967. Scholastic success and attitude toward school in a population of sixth graders. *Journal of Educational Psychology*, **58**(1): 15–18.

SHELDON, M. S., and A. G. SORENSON. 1960. On the use of Q-techniques in educational evaluation and research. *Journal of Experimental Education*, **29**: 143–151.

SPRINTHALL, N. A. 1964. A comparison of values among teachers, academic underachievers, and achievers. *Journal of Experimental Education*, **33**(2): 193–196.

WILLIAMS, J. E., and J. K. ROBERSON. 1967. A method for assessing racial attitudes in preschool children. *Educational and Psychological Measurement*, **27**: 671–689.

ZIRKEL, P. A., and E. G. MOSES. 1971. Self-concept and ethnic group membership among public school students. *American Educational Research Journal*, **8**: 253–266.

13

GRADING, REPORTING, AND PROMOTING

Like so many other everyday practices, grading has often seemed too humble to merit the attention of high-powered test and measurement people. My feeling is that it is far more important and in more need of help than anything else they work on [Scriven, 1970, p. 114].

The process of measurement is only one aspect of evaluation. At some point the quality of students' performance should be conveyed to them, their parents, and their teachers. Converting scores and performance into grades is at best a rather arbitrary process, which is further complicated by public-relations problems in reporting to parents. Frequently these difficulties produce double-talking teachers and confused students and parents.

The converting of performance data into meaningful ratings of quality has been a hotly debated topic for many decades. Prior to objective tests, marking and grading were usually synonymous, and the infallibility of the teacher's judgment was rarely questioned. The classic studies of Johnson (1911) and Starch and Elliot (1912, 1913) revealed the gross subjectivity of teacher-assigned marks even in such clear-cut areas as geometry, initiating a series of controversial innovations in marking that continue to this day. Anderson (1966), Glasser (1969) in *Schools without failure*, and Holt (1968) in *How children fail* made emotional pleas for the abolition of grades. Such proposals are at least forty-five years old (Dadourian, 1925). The problems with grades are many, but to assert that imperfect information and feedback is worse than none at all is, as Moynihan (1971, p. 4) has emphasized, to mount an argument for ignorance:

One of the achievements of democracy, although it seems not much regarded as such today, is the system of grading and sorting individuals so that young persons of talent born to modest or lowly circumstances can be recognized for their worth. (Similarly it provides a means for young persons of social status to demonstrate that they have inherited brains as well as money, as it were.) I have not the least doubt that this system is crude, that it is often cruel, and that it measures only a limited number of things. Yet it measures valid things, by and large. To do away with such systems of accreditation may seem like an egalitarian act, but in fact it would be just the opposite. We would be back to a world in which social connections and privilege count for much more than any of us, I believe, would like. If what you know doesn't count, in the competitions of life, who you know will determine the outcomes.

Teachers and counselors should be not only reporting on pupil progress to parents but also helping parents interpret scores from teacher-made and standardized tests. Reporting of this type requires special skills of the kind that we hope you have acquired by now—especially, familiarity with percentile ranks, standard scores, errors of measurement, reliability, and validity.

Marking tests

Consider the process of assigning grades to tests. Sometimes the grade is given directly, as when an English teacher says that this is an "A" theme and that is a "C" theme. In his mind, some sort of evaluative process has occurred, moderated by his usual standards of grading. He is accustomed to giving approximately a certain percentage of A's, of B's, and so on. He is typically a "hard," an average, or an "easy" marker, as compared with other teachers of the same course in the same school. His percentages fluctuate from time to time, of course, particularly if he uses grades as a motivating or disciplining device, but year after year his grades tend to average higher or lower than the grades of certain other teachers of the same course.

Often teachers give a paper a total point score that is the percentage grade directly, as when each of 25 questions counts four points. Either percentages are used directly or the letter equivalent of a percentage is set by school regulations (for example, 70–79 = C, 80–89 = B, 90–100 = A). This can result in "adjustments" of successive tests in order not to fail most of the pupils or give most of them A's. Since the difficulty of a test depends on the particular questions that happen to be used, and since teachers are not expert judges of such difficulty (nobody is), direct percentage marking usually forces the teacher to grade some tests leniently and others severely to make the grades come out "right." If percentages are running low, he can give points for partially correct answers, unless the questions are wholly objective. If percentages are running too high for his tastes, he can choose to credit only the most unimpeachable answers and count all the others wrong. If all this adjusting of scoring methods results in a distribution of grades different from that desired by the teacher, he can make the next test easier or harder in order to bring the average grade up or down.

Changing standards from test to test in the above ways must be confusing to students, and it is unnecessary. If the teacher simply scores the test for number of points earned, expressed neither as a grade nor as a percentage (for example, with 25 items the maximum number of points might be 25, each item counting 1 point), then he can make the arbitrary conversion of points into grades according to his best judgment, rather than having it hidden by sleight-of-hand grading procedures.

No one has ever been able to devise a sure-fire way to make the savage grader more lenient and the easy one more stringent, but there may be help in faculty discussion of grading practices, together with consideration of anonymous distributions of grades assigned by various teachers. If a certain teacher insists year after year that he gets the worst students in his classes, it may be desirable to set up an explicit partitioning of available students at the beginning of the year so his contention may be shown invalid. However, it is difficult, if not impossible, to tighten the grading of the teacher who argues that his lenient grading is indicative of good teaching. (Grading differences among instructors are at least as great at the college level as they are in high schools and elementary schools.)

Grading on the Curve

In desperation, some schools have set percentages for the various grades, especially for failing grades, that all teachers are urged or even required to use: not more than 10 percent of F's in general mathematics at the end of the year, for example. Such prescription is of limited value, since the ability of students even in various sections of the same course can vary considerably because of scheduling difficulties and year-to-year variation, as when none of the pupils taking advanced mathematics can enroll for one section of physics but must all be in the other. Probably it would be unfair to require the same distribution of grades in these two sections.

Some of you may have heard of "grading on the normal curve," which became popular during the 1920's and 1930's. The most common method uses 1.5 standard deviations (s) and above for A's (about 7 percent), $.5s$ to $1.5s$ for B's (about 24 percent), $-.5s$ to $+.5s$ for C's (about 38 percent), $-1.5s$ to $-.5s$ for D's (about 24 percent), and below $-1.5s$ for F's (about 7 percent).

Stripped of its unnecessary complexities, this "grading on the curve" amounted simply to determining in advance what percentage of the class would get A's, what percentage B's, and so on. Some amusing and revealing tales are told about how this prejudgment might backfire. On the first day of class a graduate professor of Latin informed the seven students taking his advanced course that he had learned of grading on the curve the previous summer and would use it in this class, resulting in the certainty that one of the seven students would fail the course. As the students left at the close of class, one of them muttered to the other six, "I'm sure to be the one who fails, so I'm dropping the course right now."

"But you can't do that," the others exclaimed, "because we don't know which one of us would fail then."

So the six pooled their money and paid the predestined failure to stay in the course and absorb the failing grade.

Another story is similar. At a certain large state university during the first few years after World War II, the wives of veterans who were studying there enrolled for the more difficult courses in sufficient numbers to absorb all the failing grades themselves. They simply did little or no work and received F's and D's, while their husbands got grades of C or better with only moderate effort.

We deplore this rigidity, of course, but the fact remains that the number of A's or F's given is arbitrarily dependent on the philosophy or even the whim of the instructor or of some policy-making group such as a committee. Setting the percentage of each grade in advance may be justifiable for, say, the 2,000 persons enrolled for a required college course in physical science that has a common final examination for all sections. Even then, however, some discretion is usually left to the instructor of each section to count daily assignments and his own quizzes in determining the final grades. A compromise of uniformity with individuality of grading seems desirable.

Objections to Grades

Four principal allegations are offered as support for the abolition of marking. These allegations have been carefully evaluated by R.L. Thorndike (1969b); the following summary is based largely on his cogent observations.

1. Marks are inaccurate and not comparable across instructors, departments, or schools. Personality factors do influence grades (Russell and Wellington, 1955; Hadley, 1954); girls usually do get higher grades than boys of equal ability and achievement (Caldwell and Hartnett, 1967); and "at most colleges, the majority of students are given C's—whether the mean ability of the students is nationally at the 95th percentile or the 5th" (Baird, Munday, and Feister, 1969, p. 6). Unfortunately it is unlikely that a teacher's evaluation in any form can be free of considerable subjectivity. The teacher who gives more F's is the same teacher who would more frequently describe pupils' performance as "unsatisfactory," "inferior," "below acceptable standards," and so on if verbal evaluations were substituted for letter grades. It is naive to assume that a change in symbols from letters to words, percentages, or any other simple substitute would remedy the defects of the conventional system. It is easy to identify the faults in the system; it is difficult to devise a superior alternative.

2. Marks focus upon false and inappropriate objectives and have little relationship to important educational objectives. This criticism is really directed toward the assessment procedures employed by teachers rather than toward pupil evaluation itself. The evaluation procedures employed by many instructors are atrocious, but there is little reason to believe that some other method of *describing* student performance would improve the quality of the evidence upon which student evaluations are based. This book has failed in its purpose if the assessment procedures you employ will not be more valid as a consequence of your having studied it. The remedy implied in the criticism is not to eliminate formal reporting procedures, but to improve the assessment procedures.

3. Marks have limited value as a medium of communication between school and home. This allegation is certainly true. To imply that this point

justifies abolition of marks, however, is a *non sequitur*. It should be made clear to students and parents that marks reflect only certain educational factors, primarily, cognitive achievement measured by written tests. Reporting on academic performance of this kind should be only a part of the communication system between school, pupil, and the home. The school should have another systematic method, such as parent-teacher conferences, for discussing pupil performance.

4. Marks are responsible for a variety of detrimental side effects such as anxiety, dishonesty, hostility, and poor mental health; they produce negative attitudes resulting from chronic failure, encourage undesirable value patterns (striving for grades rather than learning), are incompatible with democracy, and so on. Glasser stated, "The school practice that most produces failure in students is grading" (1969, p. 59); and "Grades are also bad because they encourage cheating" (p. 64). The first contention is like claiming that "thermometers produce bad weather"; the second like, "money is bad because it encourages cheating." As Ebel (1965b, p. 440) pointed out, "There is nothing wrong with encouraging students to work for high marks if the marks are valid measures of achievement."

It is most unfortunate that some students do not read well or have trouble learning arithmetic concepts, but it is erroneous to assume that the cognitive or affective consequences are the results of employing letter grades to summarize pupil performance as evaluated by a teacher. Although pupils are not graded on attractiveness, certain unfortunate side-effects often accompany unattractive students (probably as frequently as they do the poor achiever who receives poor marks). A child's poor athletic ability may affect his self-concept adversely, but no teacher-given mark is responsible. Any first-grade child is aware of which reading group he is in (high, average, low, and so on) and even which students in his group read better than he does; he knows these facts whether marks are assigned or not. The problem is not marks; the problem is perceived inferior performance or failure. The best creative educational efforts should be directed toward finding methods by which every student can learn effectively. In any group and on any trait there are always internal comparisons within the group. For example, the lowest-achieving pupil in a class of gifted pupils is vulnerable to the same detrimental side-effects that have been attributed to marks—even though the student receives good marks and would be excellent in a representative class. To avoid this attitudinal concomitant will require a complete individualization, and probably isolation, of instruction. We should be misled if we assume that marks are the culprit. In the final analysis, a mark is a judgment of one person by another; it can provide both information and incentive (R.L. Thorndike and Hagen, 1969). It is interesting to note that Jackson and Lahaderne (1967) found that the educational values that teachers hold distort their perceptions of pupils' satisfaction with school. A teacher's estimate of a student's satisfaction was more closely related to the student's academic record than to the student's own rating of satisfaction. There was little relationship between scholastic performance and pupil's rating of satisfaction. Most individuals sooner or later accept their weaknesses and adjust to them, although exceptions to this generalization are not uncommon.

Several substitutes for marking have been proposed; most of them have created additional problems (R.L. Thorndike, 1969b, p. 761). Parent–teacher or teacher–student conferences have been suggested as a replacement for marks. Conferences have been widely and, in general, effectively used to *supplement* conventional report cards on the elementary-school level. The major disadvantages are the scheduling problem and the time required for conferences. In addition, counseling skills beyond those of many teachers are often demanded; such skills are particularly vital for students who are performing below parental expectations. The time and scheduling problems preclude individual conferences with each student's parents in the departmentalized programs that are typical in junior and senior high schools. (Departmentalization is also an increasing trend in the elementary school.) When released time has been provided and some general guidelines and orientation for parent-teacher conferences have been made available to teachers, the parent-teacher conference has usually been an effective addition to the school-home communication system, at least in the elementary school. Letters from teachers to parents have been proposed in lieu of report cards, but this would require even more teacher time and it fails to provide two-way communication. Pupil self-evaluation has been proposed, but results have not been satisfactory (Spaights, 1965). Page (1960) suggested that marks be given by someone other than the teacher; he contends that marking "kills the enjoyment of the class." It is not surprising to find substitutes proposed that relieve the teacher of the often unpleasant task of marking. But if the teacher is competent, who is in a better position to evaluate performance than he? An abdication of responsibility is the easy answer but is probably not the educationally appropriate solution.

Many current pupil report forms give the teacher an opportunity to make special comments in addition to the formal marks. Burba and Corlis (1963) found that children and parents want report cards with grades. The usefulness of the various substitutes must be evaluated from a local perspective. Teachers can hardly be expected to be enthusiastic about any alternative that adds to their already demanding duties.

Roelfs (1955), studying the marking trend during the 1925–1953 period, found a decided shift toward letter grades during the interval. The National Education Association's (1967) survey of over 600 school systems found letter or numerical grades used in almost 80 percent of public schools, except in kindergarten (17 percent) and first grade (73 percent). It is apparent that despite the continuing controversy over marking, the measurement and reporting of pupil achievement are necessary, and no substantially better or more scientific means than marks seems likely to appear (Ebel, 1965b; Engelhart, 1964). However, the validity of the information on which marks are based and hence of marks themselves can be increased substantially by improved assessment methods.

The Meaning of Marks

In assigning quarter, semester, and yearly grades for a course, many teachers consider not only achievement as measured by tests but also more   *308* subjectively evaluated characteristics such as "effort," punctuality, behavior, and neatness of written work. Usually these nontest aspects get much more weight in elementary school than in high school; in some schools children who are "working up to capacity" get the highest obtainable grade, even though they are not learning much, while those who seem not to be expending "enough" effort are graded lower despite better achievement. This extreme system is confusing to pupils and parents, especially when a child moves from elementary to junior high school and his grades change sharply because the bases for them change.

One does not average oranges and bicycles; it is wise to *keep marks for achievement separate from ratings of essentially noncognitive aspects.* Achievement can be judged from teacher-made tests, homework assignments, oral and written work in class, and standardized tests. The meaning of marks is confounded when several aspects of pupil behavior are summarized together. Most parents want to know how well the student is achieving, how much industry and effort he is giving to the subject, how regular his attendance has been, what his citizenship is, and so on. Every factor that is important should be evaluated and reported separately. If students and their parents have an accurate picture of the child's total performance and behavior, they are in a better position to understand, develop appropriate aspirations, and take appropriate action.

The Criterion of Quality

There are several questions pertaining to the criterion against which achievement is referenced: should it be performance in relation to (a) an absolute standard, (b) aptitude, (c) one's peer group, or (d) one's growth?

AN ABSOLUTE STANDARD

In the past an erroneous absolute standard was employed, and marks were considered to represent a percentage of complete or perfect mastery. Close scrutiny reveals the "absolute standard" to be the teacher and test artifact that it is. A poor teacher can give an easy test in which all pupils will score 90 percent or even higher. An excellent teacher can administer a more reliable test and have a class average of 60 percent. Test difficulty is a matter of item construction; it is far from being an absolute standard. The notion of complete mastery of a subject such as English, literature, chemistry, or social studies is illusory and should be so identified to prevent fallacious interpretations of performance.

ACHIEVEMENT IN RELATION
TO APTITUDE

Teachers have no valid basis for estimating aptitude (potential) apart from achievement, except via standardized aptitude and intelligence tests. Different school subjects require a somewhat different set of aptitudes. The technical difficulties in interpreting differences (achievement vs. aptitude) are virtually insurmountable, except when standardized achievement and aptitude tests are employed, and even then they are hazards (R.L. Thorndike, 1963a). Since the more specific educational objectives are not assessed by them, standardized achievement tests should rarely be an exclusive or even the principal basis for assigning marks. Achievement in relation to aptitude is an untenable basis for marking, despite the obvious appeal the idea has for many educators.

GROWTH

The problems of assessing improvement or progress are more difficult than those associated with contrasting achievement with aptitude (Cronbach and Furby, 1970; Harris, 1963). Even with highly refined instruments, gain scores are usually rather unreliable. When the procedure is attempted on the informal, unsystematic basis available to the teacher, such scores are almost certain to have little or no validity.

ACHIEVEMENT IN RELATION TO PEER ACHIEVEMENT

Virtually all marking is a derivative of this model. A child who reads well in the first grade is inferior if compared with tenth-graders. The teacher evaluates his performance on what she feels can reasonably be expected from a representative group of pupils his age. This "phantom" representative group usually turns out to be a crude internal standard developed through the teacher's experience. In most cases the major determiner of the assigned marks is the teacher's perception of the pupil's performance in relation to the other students in the present class and perhaps recent classes. This "internal standardization" was demonstrated by Aiken (1963) and Baird, Munday, and Feister (1969), who found that despite substantial changes in the abilities of entering college freshmen, there was no real change in the distribution of assigned marks.

In spite of the lack of a clearly and objectively defined reference group, marks have considerable meaning. This is evidenced by the predictive validity they have for subsequent academic performance. Hicklin (1962) found a correlation of .73 between marks at grade 9 and grade 12. Nell (1963) found that teacher grades in a subject correlated .64 to .81 with performance on the respective subtest of a standardized achievement-test battery. High-school grades are even better predictors of college grades than are standardized intelligence and achievement tests (for example, see Hills, 1971, and Richards and Lutz, 1968). In a study by the American College Testing Program (Hoyt and Munday, 1966) of over 100,000 students, the correlation with freshman grades was .58 and .55 for high-school marks and composite standardized test scores, respectively.

Irrespective of the facts that (1) grading standards differ among teachers, (2) grades tend to be scaled internally for a class regardless of differences in the students' aptitude levels, and (3) grades are often contaminated by deportment and crude efforts to mark in relation to aptitude or progress or an absolute standard—nonetheless, grades continue to have considerable meaning and predictive validity.

WEIGHTING COMPONENTS

To arrive at an overall summary of student performance, some means must be used to combine the various kinds of information on which the mark is based. The results from reports, homework, tests, recitations, and other sources must be pooled to form a composite succinct summary. If each of the weighting factors had the same standard deviation, they would probably contribute approximately equally to the composite score. Or, equivalently, if each ingredient were converted to a standard score (say, a T-score) and the scores then were totaled for each pupil, each factor would be weighted more nearly equally.

Intuitively, it seems as if the maximum possible score on a factor would reflect its influence, but it does not. Consider a science project with 100 possible points. Suppose that each child worked diligently and received 100 points. When these points are added to all other information on which the grade is to be based, what effect does the project have on the distribution? Every score is increased by 100 points, so the relative standing of each pupil is unchanged. The mean would be increased by 100 points, but the standard score for any pupil on the composite would be unaffected. When scores from various tests, projects, and so on are combined into a total score, each measure contributes to the composite distribution in direct proportion to its standard deviation and to its correlation with the other measures. (See Stanley and Wang, 1970.) Consider the fictitious data below:

	Project	Essay Tests	Objective Tests	Homework
Mean	80	80	80	80
Standard deviation	10	30	10	5

If the teacher simply sums the points for each student to arrive at a total score on which a final grade will be based, the essay test would tend to have more influence than the other three factors combined, even though each of the four factors might carry the identical number of maximum credits.

When scores are to be totaled, the teacher should insure that the standard deviations are at least approximately in proportion to the desired weights. Fortunately, this can be easily controlled. Recall from Chapter 2 that if every score in a distribution is multiplied by 2, the standard deviation likewise is doubled. If the teacher in the previous example wants each factor to be weighted equally, he will multiply the project scores by 3, the objective test by 3, and the homework by 6. Then, the standard deviation of the scores on each component will be 30.

Even if in practice you never bother to do this, being aware of the principle should help you score various projects and assignments that are subjectively evaluated. If the standard deviation on the objective portion of a test is 10, and you desire to weight the essay portion equally, you should scale your scoring of the essays so the middle two-thirds will fall within roughly a 20-point range, with a total range of about 40 to 60 points ($4s$ to $6s$).

If each component is converted to a mark before the information is combined, the task of arriving at a final mark is much simpler. Unfortunately, the reliability is decreased because not all information is used. For instance, students who receive the highest and lowest "B's" on a test are treated equally in this plan. If there are several components to be combined, this loss is not apt to be serious.

HOW MANY DIFFERENT MARKS?

The antiquated percentage marking system had 101 possible categories (0–100); this system continues to prevail in many countries. The most common marking system in American schools has five categories (A, B, C, D, F), although three is not uncommon (for example, O—outstanding; S—satisfactory; N—needs improvement). Some educators have favored a two-category pass-fail (P, F) or credit-no credit system. Philosophical and technical measurement issues must be considered in deciding the best number of classifications. There is a trend in higher education to allow a student the option of taking a limited number of courses outside his major and minor fields and using the pass-fail system. This proposal is designed to encourage the student to broaden his education by exposing himself to other fields without jeopardizing his academic record. Such a program has appeal for its intended purpose, but as a general reporting strategy it has major defects. Princeton students reported that they tended to study less and learn less in P-F courses than they did in conventionally evaluated courses (Karlins, Kaplan, and Stuart, 1969).

Ebel (1965b, p. 423) showed that even when the composite scores on which the marking was based had a reliability of .95, the reliability of the resulting *marks* using a two-category system would be only .63. If five categories were used, the reliability of the corresponding *marks* would be .85; if 15 categories (say, A, B, C, D, F with plus and minus signs) were used, the reliability would be .94. With fewer categories one loses all the information pertinent to individual differences within that category. There are fewer persons with errors, but when there are errors, their severity is much greater as the number of categories is reduced. It is not serious when a student who deserves a B receives a B–, but it is critical when a student who deserves a Pass receives a Fail. Reducing the number of categories to two or three clearly compounds the problem of the unreliability of marks.

It is unlikely that a widespread move to eliminate the five-category system will occur in the near future, even though the reliability of the marks could be slightly increased with more categories. The modified stanine system proposed by Ebel (1965b) for marking has some desirable features, but will probably languish along with many other attempts to reform the marking system.

Report Cards

Most report cards contain both grades and checklist items; some also contain achievement-test scores. The trend is toward informing parents more by interpreting and supplementing the grades themselves. It seems important to keep achievement separate from aptitude, judged effort, neatness, citizenship, and the like. Parents usually want to know both aspects: how is my child progressing in knowledge of each subject being studied (that is, cognitive attainments), as well as in observed affective and social characteristics? Is he doing as well as he can be expected to do on the basis of measures of general ability? How does he rank on national norms in the subject as shown by an achievement test?

No one report card can be offered as a model. Each school or school system must work out its own reporting system to suit the local situation. Figures 13–1 and 13–2 are examples of reasonably typical cards. They have the first part in common. Grades of A, B, C, D, F, Inc., or NM are given for "Scholastic Achievement" for each of the four quarters. Citizenship ratings of S, N, and U are also given each quarter. Checklists on the lower part of each card differ from subject to subject; the categories for fine arts are the most numerous and detailed.

In many schools, computer facilities have allowed the process of reporting on pupil progress to be automated. Figure 13–3 illustrates the parents' copy of a typical report card. Some explanatory information is given to the parent on the reverse side of the card. Another example is the report card shown in Figure 13–4. This card gives marks in (1) the subjects and (2) citizenship and attitudes for each quarter and semester. The pupil's GPA is given for the current grading period along with his cumulative GPA for the year.

Cumulative Records

Most secondary schools maintain a cumulative record of test scores for each student; this record can be used in parent-teacher or student-counselor conferences. A parent-teacher conference report form is shown in Figure 13–5. It is a checklist in triplicate with one copy each for the cumulative folder, the teacher, and the parent.

The illustrated report forms were devised for local use, so they should not be considered models for other situations. We emphasize again that it is important for report cards and parent-teacher conferences to be supplemented by careful reporting of standardized-test results. Much information of great value and interest to parents and pupils lies buried in test files. It should be used evaluatively and diagnostically in systematic ways, along with the results of teacher-made tests, to round out the parent's picture of the pupil's progress. This must be done skillfully and carefully, of course, but we are convinced that it should be done.

Suggestions for Improving Marking and Reporting

After ten years of experimenting with a number of ways to improve marking and reporting practices, William Wrinkle (1956), a former principal, listed the following twenty-two generalizations that seemed to him to summarize what he and his staff had learned. You will be amply repaid by improved

Report of _____

Ratings are for first quarter, first semester, second quarter, second semester	Semester I		Semester II	
Scholastic Achievement				
Citizenship				

Scholastic Achievement Ratings: A-Excellent; B-Good; C-Fair; D-Poor (D-not recommended for college entrance); F-Failure; Inc.-Incomplete; NM-Non-Mastery. Marks of Inc. and NM can be converted into passing marks through supplementary work.

Citizenship Ratings - S-Superior; N-Normal; U-Unsatisfactory.

Items checked here offer partial explanation of ratings given above	Superior	Average	Unsatisfactory

INITIATIVE
    Ability to initiate ideas with minimum stimulation from instructor
        Comment _____			

WORK HABITS
    Expresses ideas in an original, inventive and imaginative way
        Comment _____			

Demonstrates an understanding of some basic art principles Comment _____			
Uses time in an effective way Comment _____			
Cares for tools and equipment _____			
Demonstrates craftsmanship and an understanding of materials Comment _____			

EVALUATION OF WORK
    Ability to judge and improve own work
        Comment _____			

Ability to work congenially with others and accept criticism Comment _____			
Shows growth in expression Comment _____			
General quality of completed work Comment _____			

Red-1st 9 weeks; Black-1st Semester; Green-3rd 9 weeks; Purple-2nd Semester

Signature of Teacher _____

FIGURE 13-1 *A sample report card for fine arts.*

Report of _____

Ratings are for first quarter, first semester, second quarter, second semester	Semester I		Semester II	
Scholastic Achievement				
Citizenship				

Scholastic Achievement Ratings: A-Excellent; B-Good; C-Fair; D-Poor (D-not recommended for college entrance); F-Failure; Inc.-Incomplete; NM-Non-Mastery. Marks of Inc. and NM can be converted into passing marks through supplementary work.

Citizenship Ratings - S-Superior; N-Normal; U-Unsatisfactory.

Items checked here offer partial explanation of ratings given above	Semester I		Semester II	
1. Organizes material well				
2. Thinks independently and critically				
3. Has growing understanding of current problems				
4. Takes active part in class discussion				
5. Works up to capacity				

_____

_____

_____

_____

_____

_____

_____

_____

Signature of Teacher _____

FIGURE 13–2 A sample report card for social studies.

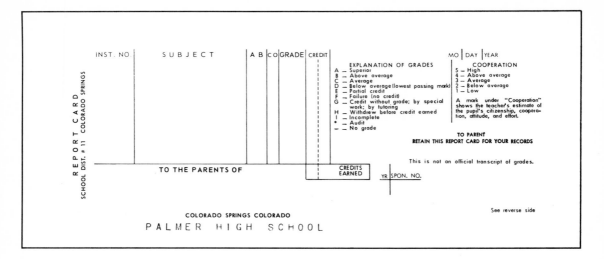

FIGURE 13-3 A sample report card (automated processing). (Reproduced by permission of Colorado Springs School District #11.)

BOULDER VALLEY SCHOOL DISTRICT RE-2

SCHOOL	GRADUATION CREDITS	SCHOOL YEAR	HOME ROOM	STUDENT NUMBER	1ST PERIOD		2ND PERIOD		3RD PERIOD		4TH PERIOD		
					DAYS A	TT	DAYS A	TT	DAYS A	TT	DAYS A	TT	
CENTENNIAL JR. HIGH		69-70	203	258000	2.0		1.0						

TO THE PARENTS OF	CLASS	SUBJECT	1ST QTR.		2ND QTR.		SEMESTER 1		3RD QTR.		4TH QTR.		SEMESTER 2		TEACHER
			SUBJ.	C	SUBJ.	C	EXAM.	GRADE	SUBJ.	C	SUBJ.	C	EXAM.	GRADE	
HIRTER NANCY L	7	ENGLISH 7	A	1	A	1		A							TONSO
2530 GLENWOOD		GEOGRAPHY	B&	2	A-	2		A							CLEMENTS
BOULDER, COLORADO 80302		LIFE SCIENCE	C&	2	C&	2		C							MACY
		BASIC MATH 7	A-	2	A	2	C&	B							GODDEN
		SPANISH 1AB	A	2	A-	2		A							TERRELL
(S) SUBJECT		ART 7	B	2	A	1		A							RICHARDSN
		ORCHESTRA	B	2	B&	2		B							FORD
A -SUPERIOR		GIRLS P E 7	A	2	A	1		A							HOBSON

(S) SUBJECT (C) SCHOOL CITIZENSHIP AND CLASS ATTITUDE

A -SUPERIOR
B -VERY GOOD — 1.-OUTSTANDING
C -AVERAGE — 2.-SATISFACTORY
D -BELOW AVERAGE — 3.-UNSATISFACTORY
F -FAILING — 4.-CONFERENCE REQUESTED
I -INCOMPLETE
S -SATISFACTORY

GRADE POINT AVERAGE	
ACCUM	CURRENT
.000	3.500

PAGE 1   LAST PAGE

SCHOLARSHIP GRADE is an evaluation of the student's achievement and progress in the subject.
CLASS ATTITUDE is an evaluation of the student's RESPECT for authority, property, fellow student and self, and his DEMONSTRATION of self-motivation, responsibility of self and others, cooperation, sportsmanship, punctuality, dependability, honesty, leadership and service.

FIGURE 13-4 A sample report card of a seventh-grade student. (Reproduced by permission of Mrs. R. M. Hirter.)

understanding of marking and reporting for the time you spend considering these statements:

1. The statement of any outcome or objective to be evaluated should be analyzed into its specific meanings so that its meaning is clearly stated.
2. The number of different forms should be kept at a minimum. If two or more short forms are to be used at the same time, they should be incorporated into a single form.
3. During a period of experimentation, unless there is plenty of money to spend on printing, forms should be produced by some inexpensive process such as mimeographing. An expensive printed form is less likely to be discarded even if it is known to be inadequate.

BIRNAMWOOD PUBLIC SCHOOLS
Birnamwood, Wisconsin

Parent-Teacher Conference Report

Teachers Name ....

Name of Student..Name of Parent.. ....

Date......................	Date......................
First Conference	**Second Conference**

PHYSICAL	PHYSICAL
General Health — — — —	General Health — — — —
Specific difficulties — —	Specific difficulties — —
Attendance record............days pres.	Attendance record............days pres.
Regular sleeping hours — —	Regular sleeping hours — —
Personal appearance — — —	Personal appearance — — —
EMOTIONAL	EMOTIONAL
Getting along at home — —	Getting along at home — —
Is he having trouble in school? ?	Is he having trouble in school? ?
Courtesy — — —	Courtesy — — —
Special friends — —	Special friends — —
WORK HABITS	WORK HABITS
Follows directions —	Follows directions —
Neatness — —	Neatness — —
Does he give up easily — —	Does he give up easily — —
Work independently?	Work independently?
Others — — —	Others — — —
ACADEMIC GROWTH	ACADEMIC GROWTH
Language ave. above below	Language ave. above below
Arithmetic ave. above below	Arithmetic ave. above below
Reading ave. above below	Reading ave. above below
Writing ave. above below	Writing ave. above below
Music ave. above below	Music ave. above below
Others ave. above below	Others ave. above below
TEACHERS COMMENTS	TEACHERS COMMENTS
Suggestions:	Suggestions:

FIGURE 13–5   *A parent-teacher conference report form. (Devised by F. O. Pappenfuss and reproduced by permission.)*

4. The basis for an evaluation of the student's achievement should be decided upon. Should the evaluation be in terms of established norms, the class average, or the ability of the student?

5. In the interpretation of a report the likelihood of misunderstanding by parents tends to increase in proportion to the number of details included in the report.

6. Students should have a real part in the development of new forms and practices.

7. The development by students of an understanding of and a favorable attitude toward new practices is a most effective approach to parent education.

8. The student's experiences, his successes, difficulties, abilities, and inabilities, should be the subject of frequent conversations between teacher and student. Students should be encouraged to take the initiative in asking for such conferences.

9. The summarization of reports on a student in a departmentalized program by a guidance counselor, a home-room teacher, a core teacher, or the principal involves too big a task and is not a workable plan.

10. Reporting on all students at one time during the school year is chiefly for the purpose of stimulating competitive comparisons; if such stimulation is not a purpose of the reporting, then reports should be made at different times to discourage such invidious comparisons.

11. The scale type evaluation form is unsatisfactory unless each scale item involves only a single outcome, the achievement of which can be expressed in degrees by clearly distinguishable descriptions.

12. The check form is simpler than the scale for use in reporting evaluations and is more economical of space on a printed form.

13. The development of highly detailed, elaborate cumulative record forms is uneconomical; if too detailed and lengthy, they will not be used by most teachers.

14. To ensure an adequate understanding by parents of the status of the student, a conference should be arranged between the parents and the counselor or teacher for the discussion of individual cases.

15. Although it has many real advantages, the conference plan is not a practical solution to the reporting problem, especially at the secondary-school level.

16. Checklists utilizing the best features of the scale-type evaluation, the anecdotal record, and the conference plan should be developed for the evaluation of (a) general outcomes with which the total school program is concerned and (b) more specific outcomes relating to each of the various areas of the curriculum.

17. Parents should be sent a summary form of evaluation focusing attention on desired outcomes of the school program which have been analyzed in detail by the check lists. The evaluation made should involve cooperative activity on the part of students and teachers.

18. Whatever forms for use in reporting are developed, a separate report involving the use of a five-point scale should be maintained for administrative record purposes. Administrative records should not be confused by shifting from A B C D F to H S U to H M L or other sets of symbols.

19. Check forms, unless they are carefully controlled, tend to become increasingly detailed and, therefore, increasingly impractical.

20. The best way to state objectives is in terms of desired behavior outcomes—what the learner should do.

21. Many teachers have difficulty in writing effective comments. A deliberate program for the improvement of the writing of informal comments is essential.

22. The most intelligible way to write supplementary comments in explaining evaluations is to tell what the student did.[1]

Post-organizer

Reports of achievement are desirable and necessary in education; marks in some form will continue to be needed.

Marks are means of feedback to students and to their parents; they should be as valid and accurate as possible. Critics of grading have failed to supply superior alternatives.

Although marks have several major defects, they have considerable meaning and predictive validity for subsequent academic performance.

The meaning of marks can be greatly improved if the basis on which they are to be assigned is clearly defined. Great difficulties arise when one attempts to evaluate achievement in relation to aptitude, to evaluate on the basis of improvement, or to mark when using an illusionary absolute standard.

Marks should reflect demonstrated achievement. Other important factors such as student attitude, effort, and citizenship should be evaluated independently.

When components are summed into total scores, one must try to make the actual weighting of factors correspond with the desired weighting; adjusting the standard deviations of the components helps to do this.

Even when the composite ratings have very high reliability, the reliability of assigned *marks* decreases, and the severity of errors increases, as the number of categories in the marking system is reduced.

Marks should be supplemented by written comments and other means of communication between teacher, student, and parents.

SUGGESTED READINGS

AHMANN, J. S., and M. D. GLOCK. 1969. Determining and reporting growth. In *Evaluating pupil growth: Principles of tests and measurement*, 3d ed., Boston: Allyn and Bacon, Inc. Chap. 16.

CURTON, L. E. 1971. The history of grading practices. *NCME Measurement in Education*, **2**, No. 4 (May), pp. 1–8.

EBEL, R. L. 1965. Marks and marking systems. *In Measuring educational achievement*. Englewood Cliffs, N.J.: Prentice-Hall, Inc., Chap. 13.

KARLINS, J. K., M. KAPLIN, and W. STUART. 1969. Academic attitudes and performance as a function of a differential grading system: An evaluation of Princeton's pass-fail system. *Journal of Experimental Education*, **37**: 38–50.

KATZ, M., D. W. SEIBEL, and J. A. CONNOLLY. 1961. Testing . . . testing . . . . *Junior Libraries*, **7**: 14–20. Reprinted, with additions, by Educational Testing Service as "Take a reading in measurement."

[1] Reprinted from W. L. Wrinkle, *Improving marking and reporting practices in elementary and secondary schools* (New York: Holt, Rinehart and Winston, Inc., 1956), by permission of the publisher. Copyright © 1956 by Holt, Rinehart and Winston, Inc.

Kurtz, A. K., and M. A. Bertin. 1958. Reappraisal of marking practices. *Educational Research Bulletin*, **37**: 67–74.

Palmer, O. 1962. Seven classic ways of grading dishonestly. *English Journal*, **51**: 464–467.

National Education Association. 1963.—Policies and exceptions. *NEA Research Bulletin*, **41**: 77–78.

Smith, A. Z., and J. E. Dobbin. 1960. Marks and marking systems. In C. W. Harris, ed., *Encyclopedia of educational research*, 3d ed. New York: The Macmillan Company.

Thorndike, R. L. 1969. Marks and marking systems. In R. L. Ebel, ed., *Encyclopedia of educational research*, 4th ed. New York: The Macmillan Company. Reprinted in G. H. Bracht, K. D. Hopkins, and J. C. Stanley. 1972. *Perspectives in educational and psychological measurement*. Englewood Cliffs, N. J.: Prentice-Hall, Inc., Selection 17.

Wrinkle, W. L. 1956. *Improving marking and reporting practices in elementary and secondary schools*. New York: Holt, Rinehart and Winston, Inc.

part three

Standardized Measures

14

MEASURING INTELLIGENCE

Probably the first systematic experimentation concerning individual differences in behavior occurred fortuitously in 1796, when astronomers at Greenwich Observatory were found to differ in the speed with which they could respond to visual stimuli (Cronbach, 1970, p. 197). Four decades later, in 1838, a French physician named Esquirol used various physical and psychological measures in an attempt to assess different degrees of feeblemindedness. (See Goodenough, 1949, pp. 3–5.) He found that language usage was the best indicator of mental level. Unfortunately Esquirol's work was not widely disseminated nor systematically continued; not until a half-century later was the importance of verbal ability as a measure of intelligence rediscovered.

The Rise of Scientific Psychology

PSYCHOPHYSICS:
"PHYSICS OF THE MIND"

A turning point in the history of psychology occurred in 1879 when Wilhelm Wundt established the first laboratory for experimental psychology at the University of Leipzig, Germany. The rise of *scientific* psychology, as opposed to the traditional *philosophic* psychology, was intimately related to the use of empirical measuring devices. Wundt was interested in questions concerning the physiology of sensory processes, reaction times, and word association, but he also inherited and extended the psychological legacy known as "psychophysics" (Murphy, 1949, pp. 155–156). This field had been opened 20 years earlier by another German, Gustav Fechner, who saw psychophysics as "an exact science of the functional relations of the dependency between mind and body" (Guilford, 1954, p. 3). Before the middle of the nineteenth century, physics had made great progress in measuring such objective attributes as length, weight, time, temperature, and volume. Fechner came to believe that certain purely "mental" or psychological processes, such as sensation, perception, and feeling, could be accurately measured. According to Fechner, scales measuring them would be definitely and mathematically related to the strength of the sensation-producing stimulus under investigation.

For example, a psychophysicist might be interested in developing a scale of brightness as perceived by a person, using units of "just-noticeable-differences" (j.n.d.'s) in the intensity of the source of light the individual sees. Fechner's law states that the degree of sensation is related to the actual magnitude of the physical stimulus in a certain specific mathematical way (Boring, 1961, pp. 238–257). In this example, the magnitude of perceived brightness, as measured in j.n.d.'s, should be that mathematical function of the actual intensity of the light, as measured in a physical unit such as candlepower.

Fechner developed several procedures now known as "psychophysical methods" for determining units of just-noticeable-differences. His basic law has not gone unscathed over the years, and its revision and extension in the light of experimental findings continue to be a lively source of debate among researchers.

In 1927 L. L. Thurstone extended the classical psychophysical measuring operations in his "law of comparative judgment," which allowed the investigator to "measure" a psychological characteristic such as "attitude toward war" for which no known corresponding physical measure could be obtained. Obviously, one could not weigh a person's attitude toward war in ounces or measure its length in inches, whereas one could determine how bright the light actually was versus how bright it seemed to the observer.

The new psychophysics asked such questions as "How strong is this man's attitude towards the Negro?" "How good are these essays relative to one another?" "What judgment factors underlie preference for movie stars: beauty? gender? kind of role? color of hair?" To answer these questions, Thurstone and others abandoned the original physical reference point.

Since the physical intensity of the psychological response was made unnecessary for certain purposes, a new field of *response-response* investigation developed. If responses made on an attitude scale indicated that an individual hated war, what did this suggest about his responses in other areas? Would he have more intensely negative attitudes than a person with neutral feelings toward war? What about his intelligence, his open-mindedness, his needs for love or dominance, his political views? Psychology thus directed some of its efforts away from the development of directional *stimulus-response* laws, in which the stimulus produces the response (S $\longrightarrow$ R), in favor of the development of *response-response* relationships (R $\longleftrightarrow$ R) that have no obvious directionality.

THE SEARCH FOR A VALID MEASURE
OF INTELLIGENCE

Individual differences in mental abilities such as comprehension, problem-solving, and analytic ability—qualities which are usually grouped under the heading of "intelligence"—were not discovered by modern psychologists; terms such as idiot, genius, bright, and dull have a long history in our language. Scientific psychology's genuine contribution to the study of intelligence has been that of heightening human understanding of that "arch-faculty," to use Sir Charles Spearman's (1923) term, particularly in devising accurate measures of the *degree* of intelligence of an individual. Cronbach (1970, p. 197) observed, "Despite occasional overenthusiasm and misconceptions, . . . the general mental test stands today as the most important technical contribution psychology has made to the practical guidance of human affairs."

Galton and the Study of Human Differences   Coincident with the blossoming of Wundt's experimental psychology laboratory in Leipzig, a slightly different tradition was developing in England under Sir Francis Galton (1822–1911). Although the psychophysicists were interested in determining universal psychological processes and treated the response differences between subjects as so much "experimental error," Galton worked in the intellectual tradition of Darwinian biology with its emphasis on *variation* between and within species. In Galton's work there is the beginning of a concern for *individual differences* that has been a keystone in the history of psychological and educational testing. From his laboratory of anthropometry (the study of human body measurements), established in London in 1882, came studies of topics such as word association, mental imagery, and the genetic basis of genius. To facilitate his research, Galton invented several statistical devices; the most important was a graphical method for depicting the degree of relationship between two variables such as height and weight. (See Murphy, 1949, pp. 117–122.) As later refined by Galton's colleague, the statistician Karl Pearson, this device led to the now-classic *product-moment coefficient of correlation* (see Chapter 2 for a discussion of this technique).

Galton also devised the earliest mental tests. He studied individual performance differences on tests of reaction time, memory, and sensory acuity. This tradition of using rather simple "sensory" and "motor" tasks as indicators of intellectual ability was continued by James McKeen Cattell, one of the earliest and best known of American psychologists. Cattell was a product of Wundt's experimental psychology laboratory at the University of Leipzig. In 1890 he suggested the term "mental test"; he described in detail a series of tests with which he attempted to measure the intelligence of his students at the University of Pennsylvania. Cattell and many of his contemporaries regarded simpler mental and motor processes such as speed of tapping, reaction time, judgment of time intervals, and keenness of vision and hearing as indications of what are now called the "higher" mental processes.[1] But, because he directed his efforts away from tests of more complex mental processes, his efforts were doomed to failure. At the turn of the century, Iowa psychologist Carl Seashore (1899) found virtually no relationship between teachers' estimates of general mental ability and children's ability to judge time intervals, to judge length of lines, and to discriminate loudness and pitch. Shortly thereafter, Bagley (1900) reported that simple motor abilities such as hand strength, trilling a telegraph

---

[1] For a review of early work with mental tests, see Spearman (1904).

key, and reaction time bore no relation to a child's actual class standing or to a teacher's judgment of that child. Clark Wissler (1901), using Cattell's tests with college students, found no significant relationship between the tests and college marks (*r*'s of —.09 to .16) and little relationship among the tests *themselves*. Consequently the attempt to measure intelligence with such tests was all but abandoned. Wissler's study was the first to apply Pearson's correlation techniques to test scores.

Binet's Breakthrough   In France incisive work was being done by a French physician named Alfred Binet (1857–1911), the father of modern intelligence testing. As early as 1896, Binet had published a proposal for a series of tests designed to measure children's intellectual capacity. Binet found that a measure, or test, of intelligence must demand a range of performances normally regarded as intelligent behavior. The test should comprise a series of tasks requiring the ability to reason, make sound judgments, recognize familiar objects, and understand commands; that is, it should call for a variety of mental skills. A child's intelligence would be represented by a summation of his scores on each separate task. For Binet, intelligence was a phenomenon requiring many different abilities. Two children might obtain the same total score on his test by scoring quite differently from each other on the subtests.

In 1904 Binet was commissioned by the French Minister of Public Instruction to extend his investigations to determining workable methods of identifying mentally retarded school children so they might be given special instruction. He tried and rejected sensory discrimination tasks, size of cranium, handwriting analysis, responses to inkblots, and several other measures. The results appeared in three classic papers published in 1905 (see Binet and Simon, 1916), in which Binet discussed a number of tasks he had found useful in approaching the problem. These had been arranged in order of difficulty and then "standardized" on a group of normal children at each age level from three to eleven years. By comparing an individual child's performance with the age of children who typically performed likewise, Binet was able to get an indication of the subject's intellectual development; that is, a child's mental age was determined by referring his performance to the chronological age at which the average child successfully completed the same tasks. Reports of further investigations and revisions of the original scale appeared in 1908 and 1911. The last version of the scale included such tasks as the following: to earn mental-age credits at the nine-year level a child must give change for 20 cents, define five words at an abstract level, recognize the value of a piece of money, name the months of the year, and understand simple questions such as "When one has missed the train, what must one do?" Similarly, five task groups were established as norms for each age level from three to sixteen years. Figure 14–1 is a reproduction of the seven-year-level "unfinished picture" task from Binet's 1908 scale. Compare this with the analogous task of the 1960 revision of the *Stanford-Binet Intelligence Scale*, known as "picture completion" and now presented at the five-year level.

Later Developments   Binet's method of assessing intelligence was met with some criticism but much acclaim. By 1916, his scales had been translated

FIGURE 14–1 *Unfinished pictures from Year VII of the 1908 Binet Scale. (From Binet and Simon, 1908.)*

into seven languages and were used in at least twelve countries (Binet and Simon, 1916). Henry Goddard (1910a,b, 1911) was probably the first American psychologist to recognize the practical value of Binet's 1908 and 1911 scales; he translated them and with minor adaptation tested them at the Vineland Training School for the mentally retarded in New Jersey. In 1911 and 1912

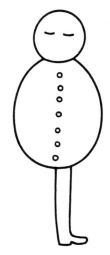

FIGURE 14–2   Picture-completion man reproduced from Year V, Test 1, of the 1960 Stanford-Binet Intelligence Scale Record Booklet ([Boston: Houghton Mifflin Company, 1960], by permission of the publisher).

Kuhlmann published his revision of the 1911 Binet scale, extending it downward to the age of three months, which is considerably below Binet's three-year limit.[2]

It remained for psychologist Lewis M. Terman of Stanford University to provide the first thorough revision of the Binet scale. Terman carefully adapted and standardized the scale for use with average, as well as deficient, American children. His scale, known as the Stanford Revision or Stanford-Binet, appeared in 1916 with a comprehensive manual, *The Measurement of Intelligence*. In 1937 and in 1960 two further revisions of the *Stanford-Binet* appeared (Terman and Merrill, 1937, 1960). This highly regarded instrument has remained a standard among individual intelligence scales for preschool and school-age children.

Performance and Group Tests   Two other distinctly American developments helped make intelligence tests more practical. The early tests had two disadvantages that limited their usefulness. (1) They were highly *verbal*; that is, their successful administration required that the subject taking the test understand spoken language. (2) The tests were *individual*; that is, only one person could be examined at a time. Reasonably satisfactory solutions were found in 1917 when the pioneering applied psychologists Rudolph Pintner and Donald Paterson found the Stanford-Binet was unsatisfactory for deaf children; Pintner and Paterson overcame this difficulty by developing a series

[2] For an excellent historical discussion, see Goodenough, chaps. 4 and 5.

of 15 manipulation or performance tests (which are used only at the preschool levels of the Stanford-Binet). The form board (an intellectual jigsaw puzzle), block design (assembling blocks to copy designs), and other nonlanguage tasks appeared in 1917 as the *Pintner-Paterson Performance Scale*. That same year the United States entered World War I and faced the necessity of training a large citizen army with too few commissioned and noncommissioned officers. In this emergency, the American Psychological Association offered its services to the War Department. The Binet-type individual intelligence tests not only were unsuitable for recruits who did not speak English but also were far too slowly administered and scored to be used with the huge number of English-speaking soldiers. To deal with this problem, a committee of psychologists headed by Robert M. Yerkes based their efforts on the unpublished work of Arthur S. Otis and prepared the *Army Alpha*, which was the first of a long series of group intelligence tests designed to receive wide use. Thus, the second problem of the early tests, their "one-at-a-time" quality, had been solved; the new group tests could be administered to almost any number of men at a time and then be objectively scored by routine clerks.

Nonverbal tests   It should be noted that the *Pintner-Paterson Performance Scale* and the *Army Alpha* group tests each solved but one difficulty at a time. Group tests of the *Army Alpha* type were generally even more verbal than the individual tests had been. Figure 14–3 shows a sample page from the *Army Alpha*. Notice that the items require reasoning and that the vocabulary is relatively simple. The early performance scales were nonverbal, but they could be administered to only one person at a time. The *Army Beta*, designed for illiterate and foreign-speaking soldiers, was the first test to combine the group and performance ideas; it also appeared in 1917. Figure 14-4 shows the picture-completion test of the *Army Beta*; the examinee must identify "what's missing" from each picture.

The *Army Alpha* and *Army Beta* proved to be a great boon to Army administrators and to researchers interested in the patterns of mental ability in our culture; as was inevitable, a large number of group intelligence tests based on the principle of the *Army Alpha* were soon made available to educators. Unfortunately, the determination of children's IQ's tended to become little more than a fashionable fetish without concern for the practical value of such a score or even for the meaning of what was being measured. Half a century of experience with such instruments has resulted in a more realistic perspective on the value of group intelligence tests; it is generally agreed, for example, that verbal, numerical, and reasoning abilities are the major determinants of scores. These abilities are certainly dependent upon past learning experiences, though of a more general nature than specific classroom learnings. The value of the tests has been demonstrated by their use in comparing general scholastic ability with specific subject-matter achievement and in predicting scholastic and occupational level. General-intelligence group tests have become important working tools for educators; some of the most familiar of these are the *California Test of Mental Maturity*, the *Henmon-Nelson Test of Mental Ability*, the *Kuhlmann-Anderson Intelligence Tests*, the *Lorge-Thorndike Intelligence Tests*, and the *Otis-Lennon Tests*.

SAMPLES {
sky—blue::grass—**table green warm big**
fish—swims::man—**paper time walks girl**
day—night::white—**red black clear pure**
}

In each of the lines below, the first two words are related to each other in some way. What you are to do in each line is to see what the relation is between the first two words, and underline the word in heavy type that is related in the same way to the third word. Begin with No. 1 and mark as many sets as you can before time is called.

1	finger—hand::toe—**box foot doll coat**	1
2	sit—chair::sleep—**book tree bed see**	2
3	skirts—girl::trousers—**boy hat vest coat**	3
4	December—Christmas::November—**month Thanksgiving December early**	4
5	above—top::below—**above bottom sea hang**	5
6	spoon—soup::fork—**knife plate cup meat**	6
7	bird—song::man—**speech woman boy work**	7
8	corn—horse::bread—**daily flour man butter**	8
9	sweet—sugar::sour—**sweet bread man vinegar**	9
10	devil—bad::angel—**Gabriel good face heaven**	10
11	Edison—phonograph::Columbus—**America Washington Spain Ohio**	11
12	cannon—rifle::big—**bullet gun army little**	12
13	engineer—engine::driver—**harness horse passenger man**	13
14	wolf—sheep::cat—**fur kitten dog mouse**	14
15	officer—private::command—**army general obey regiment**	15
16	hunter—gun::fisherman—**fish net bold wet**	16
17	cold—heat::ice—**steam cream frost refrigerator**	17
18	uncle—nephew::aunt—**brother sister niece cousin**	18
19	framework—house::skeleton—**bones skull grace body**	19
20	breeze—cyclone::shower—**bath cloudburst winter spring**	20
21	pitcher—milk::vase—**flowers pitcher table pottery**	21
22	blonde—brunette::light—**house electricity dark girl**	22
23	abundant—cheap::scarce—**costly plentiful common gold**	23
24	polite—impolite::pleasant—**agreeable disagreeable man face**	24
25	mayor—city::general—**private navy army soldier**	25
26	succeed—fail::praise—**lose friend God blame**	26
27	people—house::bees—**thrive sting hive thick**	27
28	peace—happiness::war—**grief fight battle Europe**	28
29	a—b::c—**e b d letter**	29
30	darkness—stillness::light—**moonlight sound sun window**	30
31	complex—simple::hard—**brittle money easy work**	31
32	music—noise::harmonious—**hear accord violin discordant**	32
33	truth—gentleman::lie—**rascal live give falsehood**	33
34	blow—anger::caress—**woman kiss child love**	34
35	square—cube::circle—**line round square sphere**	35
36	mountain—valley::genius—**idiot write think brain**	36
37	clock—time::thermometer—**cold weather temperature mercury** . . .	37
38	fear—anticipation::regret—**vain memory express resist**	38
39	hope—cheer::despair—**grave repair death depression**	39
40	dismal—dark::cheerful—**laugh bright house gloomy**	40

FIGURE 14–3 *Test 7 from the Army Alpha. (Reproduced by permission of the National Academy of Sciences.)*

Several tests that yield separate scores for verbal and quantitative abilities are related to the group intelligence tests but are more specifically designed **330**

FIGURE 14–4 *Test 6 from the Army Beta. (Reproduced by permission of the National Academy of Sciences.)*

to assess school-learned abilities and to predict academic success. Although they are not achievement tests in the strictest sense, they measure students' abilities to recognize, understand, and manipulate verbal and mathematical symbols. The *Cooperative School and College Ability Test* (SCAT), for example, is composed of four parts. The first contains incomplete sentences (each sentence lacks a word which the student must supply); the second consists of arithmetic computation items; the third is a vocabulary test; and the fourth consists of arithmetic reasoning items. A student's scores on the first and third parts are added together to obtain his verbal score, and his scores on the second and fourth parts are summed to obtain his quantitative score. Because these SCAT abilities, and those measured by other intelligence or scholastic aptitude tests, are considerably dependent on educational experiences, they are useful in the prediction of scholastic success in most subjects. The two score categories can be considered together or separately, depending on the area of study to be predicted. We would expect the verbal score to be the better indicator of success in the humanities and social studies and the quantitative score to be superior in mathematics and science. The *Scholastic Aptitude Test* (SAT), a major segment of the College Entrance Examination Board's widely administered test program, is an examination of the verbal-quantitative abilities type, as are the aptitude tests of the more advanced *Graduate Record Examinations*.

The Nature of Intelligence

The Binet scales and their descendants are perhaps the most publicized accomplishments of modern psychology. The term "IQ," though often misunderstood, is a household word. The practical success of the "IQ test," in its ability to place individuals along a spectrum of intelligence from dull to bright and in its relationship to school and occupational success, has overshadowed doubt about what the tests were measuring in an exact, psychological sense. Binet continually revised his estimations of the nature of intelligence as determined by his test; he finally characterized intelligence as *inventiveness* dependent upon *comprehension* and marked by *purposefulness* and corrective *judgment* (Binet, 1911). His efforts to define these abilities more exactly or to indicate the specific test behavior that demonstrated them were cut short by his untimely death in 1911.

In 1921 the *Journal of Educational Psychology* published a series of articles by fourteen prominent psychologists, each of whom presented his conception of the nature of "intelligence." Although there was some agreement, it was startling and undeniable that fourteen clearly different conceptions of intelligence emerged. Some of the participants stressed the adaptive nature of intelligence; others saw it as the ability to learn, the ability to think abstractly, or the degree of past learning. This muddle prompted later researchers to propose that since the only intelligence one can discuss objectively is the intelligence that can be measured and hence studied, one should define intelligence as "that which an intelligence test measures" (Peak and Boring, 1926). This so-called "operational definition" has been a favorite among psychometricians who are wary of theoretical disputes but very impressed with the widespread utility of intelligence tests. Instead of using the term "intelligence test," most psychologists prefer to describe such measures as tests of "general mental ability," "scholastic aptitude," or "academic aptitude."

E. L. Thorndike (1926) also recognized that "intelligence" is given meaning only by its observable consequences or, as he expressed it, by its "products." The "products" of intelligence are the tasks an individual is able to complete; the difficulty level of the tasks completed indicates the person's intellectual level. Thorndike therefore envisioned as many different types of intelligence as there are different types of tasks. For his own purposes, however, he felt that the best indicators of what is normally meant by intelligence would be the abilities to supply words to make a statement true and sensible (completion test), solve arithmetic problems, understand single words (vocabulary test), and understand connected discourse as in oral directions for paragraph reading (directions test). From this formulation, there developed his CAVD tests of mental ability, which correlated well with traditional intelligence examinations.

Some years later a clinical psychologist, David Wechsler, developed an individual intelligence examination especially for adults; Wechsler's test included a verbal and a performance measure of intelligence. First published in 1939 and revised in 1955 as the *Wechsler Adult Intelligence Scale* (WAIS), this test consists of 11 different subtests (Wechsler, 1958). The verbal subtests are Information, Comprehension, Digit Span, Similarities, Arithmetic, and Vocabulary. The nonverbal part is dependent mainly on "performance" or manipulative skills: Picture Arrangement, Picture Completion, Block Design, Object Assembly, and Digit Symbol. Each subtest yields a separate score; Wechsler feels it is important to determine an individual's *profile* of abilities. The tester is also able to compute a Verbal IQ, a Performance IQ, and a Full-Scale IQ. In 1949 the test was "scaled down" for use with children, and the *Wechsler Intelligence Scale for Children* (WISC) has become a serious competitor with the Stanford-Binet for testing at ages 5 to 15. The WISC was not very satisfactory below age 7 for below-average children, so in 1967 the scale was further extended downward (the *Wechsler Preschool and Primary Scale of Intelligence*, WPPSI) to allow testing of children in the 4 to $6\frac{1}{2}$ year age range (see Oldridge and Allison, 1968).

The leading psychometrician Louis Thurstone characterized intelligence as a series of distinct abilities. His approach was somewhat different from that of Thorndike or Wechsler, who *assumed* that their individual subtests were pure measures of the designated ability. According to Thurstone, an ability is isolated by giving mental tests to a great number of persons and then determining, through a mathematical process known as "factor analysis," the least number of abilities necessary to explain the correlations among the tests. In his pioneering study, Thurstone (1938) isolated six "factors" that accounted for most of the score similarity of 56 different tests given to a group of college students. These were verbal (V), number (N), spatial (S), word fluency (W), memory (M), and reasoning (R). The verbal factor was identified by its heavy "loadings" on tests of reading, synonyms, analogies, grammar, and vocabulary. Similarly, Thurstone's number factor was identified by its loadings on such tests as addition, multiplication, and arithmetical reasoning. Out of this research came the first of the "multi-aptitude" test batteries, the *Primary Mental Abilities Tests*. Later investigations showed, however, that the number of factors isolated depended considerably on the educational and environmental backgrounds of the subjects tested and on the number and types of tests used in the factor analysis. It was even shown that Thurstone's so-called "primary" mental abilities correlated positively with each other, which suggests the presence of a still more basic and general mental factor, as had long been argued by the British psychologist Charles Spearman (1927).

Recent thinking among factor analysts about the nature of human intelligence has led to two slightly different ideas. One is represented by Spearman's

British tradition of investigation, exemplified by Philip Vernon's (1950) structure of human abilities in which human mental abilities are arranged in a hierarchy with a broad general factor (*g*) and split into two major "group" factors, one distinguished by verbal and educational abilities (*v: ed*) and the other by practical or performance abilities (*k: m*). Each of these major group factors is then differentiated into more specific factors like Thurstone's verbal, number, and space. These finally break into factors found in specific types of test. (See Figure 14–5.) Thus any mental performance can be described as involving percentages of *g*, *v: ed*, verbal, and others until all the factors needed to account for the performance have been determined. The scheme of Raymond B. Cattell and John L. Horn has some similarity to Vernon's structure (Cattell, 1963; Horn, 1967; Horn and Cattell, 1966). Cattell distinguishes between *fluid* and *crystallized* intelligence. Crystallized intelligence is largely a function of one's environment and is much like the *v: ed* abilities. Fluid intelligence reflects more of the genetic aspect of intelligence and is more clearly reflected in nonlanguage tasks that are less related to one's background or previous experience.

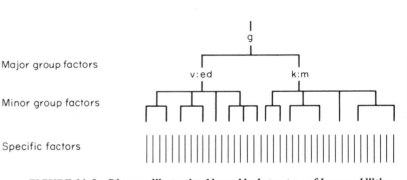

FIGURE 14–5 *Diagram illustrating hierarchical structure of human abilities.* (*Adapted from P. E. Vernon,* **The structure of human abilities** [*New York: John Wiley & Sons, Inc., 1950*], *p. 22, by permission of the publisher.*)

Another view of mental organization grows from the Thurstonian American tradition of investigation. Its chief advocate is J. P. Guilford (Guilford, 1967, 1968), who devised a theoretical structure-of-intellect model (SI) in which he classifies human mental abilities in three dimensions. The first is defined by the kind of test content confronting the individual—"figural," "symbolic," "semantic," or "behavioral." The second is defined by the types of mental "operations" necessary to deal with the various content forms—"cognition," "memorization," "convergent thinking," "divergent thinking," and "evaluation." The last deals with the outcome or "products" yielded by the various mental operations applied to the various content forms. There are six products: units of information, classes of units, relations between units, systems of information, transformations, and implications. With 4 kinds of content, 5 kinds of operation, and 6 kinds of product involved in mental performances, Guilford postulates 120 (4 × 5 × 6) distinct mental abilities in the SI model. (See Figure 14–6.) He reports that about 60 of these have been isolated through factor-analytic investigations. This analysis of the "structure of intellect" is rather complex; the reader is referred to other sources for further explication (Carroll, 1968; Guilford, 1967, 1968).

Perhaps the most important application of factor-analytic studies of mental abilities has been the increasing use of "multi-aptitude" test batteries in educational and vocational guidance. These batteries are composed of a series of individual tests built around the findings of factor analysis; to a certain degree each of the general battery's subtests assesses a specific ability. One such battery is the *Differential Aptitude Test* (DAT) for use with high-school students; the DAT contains seven subtests that measure verbal reasoning, numerical ability, abstract reasoning, space relations, mechanical reasoning, clerical speed and accuracy, and language usage. Although the DAT subtests are not intended to be "pure" measures of single "factors," they provide a profile of an individual's mental strengths and weaknesses which are designed to be more specific, descriptive, and meaningful than an omnibus test of "general mental ability." In addition to the great *descriptive* value of such a test, *prediction* of success or failure in a variety of academic or occupational endeavors can be achieved by isolating the important abilities specifically required. It was found, for example, that a combination of three of the DAT subtests correlated highly with the College Board *Scholastic Aptitude Test,* and that college graduates are high scorers on the Verbal Reasoning and Numerical Ability subtests, compared with high-school graduates. Engineers were found to be superior on all subtests—most markedly in numerical ability, abstract reasoning, and mechanical reasoning.[3]

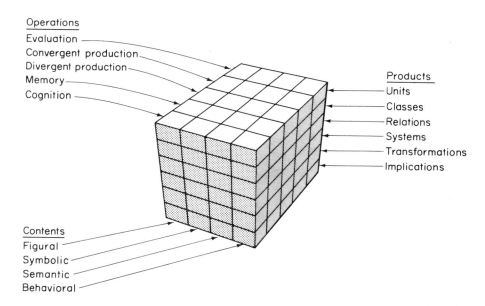

FIGURE 14–6   The theoretical model for Guilford's structure of intellect. (Reproduced from J. P. Guilford, The structure of intelligence, in Dean K. Whitla, ed., Handbook of measurement and assessment in behavioral sciences [Reading, Mass.: Addison-Wesley Publishing Company, Inc., 1968], Fig. 1, p. 220, by permission of the publisher.)

[3] For excellent coverage of the DAT and other multi-aptitude tests, see Super (1958).

INFANT INTELLIGENCE SCALES

Research findings have revealed that during the first two years of life, results from infant "intelligence" tests have little predictive validity. A child's IQ at age six can be predicted much better from his parents' education (*r* of .5–.6) than from an intelligence test or any other measure taken at two years of age or younger (Bayley, 1955). In fact, infant tests have been shown to have virtually no predictive value below 20 months of age (Escalona and Moriarty, 1961).

The lack of relationship between IQ's or DQ's (development quotients) from infant tests and later scores probably occurs because the tests are measuring in different domains. The infant scales must rely primarily on psychomotor responses because of the limited language facility of very young children. Yet abstract thinking is best reflected in language. One of the primary uses of infant scales is in the placement of children for adoption. Intelligence tests should be recognized for what they are—measures that have little or no value below age two. Knowledge of parents' education, occupational level, or IQ scores is much more useful in predicting a young child's academic success than are IQ's from tests that require little abstract thinking.

At about age two, the cognitive development of the child is such that a very crude assessment of intelligence can be made. IQ scores at 24 months correlate about .4 with IQ scores two years later, .3 with IQ scores at age six, and only .2 or less with adult IQ's (Cavanaugh et al., 1957; Honzik, Macfarlane, and Allen, 1948).

INTELLIGENCE GROWTH CURVES

Many studies have been conducted to ascertain the sequence and termination of intellectual growth. Figure 14–7 is based on cross-sectional data from Wechsler's first intelligence test in 1939 and is widely reproduced in psychological textbooks. The basic flaw in the data results from their cross-sectional nature, that is, a different sample of persons was used at each age level; consequently variables (besides age) on which they differ, such as formal educational attainment, confound the findings. In the 1958 revision and restandardization of the Wechsler Bellevue scale from which the *Wechsler Adult Intelligence Test* (WAIS) evolved, the intellectual decline with age was much less marked than that shown for the 1939 Wechsler-Bellevue data given in Figure 14–7. This supports the hypothesis that a substantial portion of the "decline" in Figure 14–7 is not a decline; it simply reflects in large measure the educational differential and, to some extent, test-taking speed among the age groups (Lorge, 1952). In several studies (Bayley and Oden, 1955; Droege, Crambert, and Henkin, 1963; Owens, 1953, 1966; Schaie and Strother, 1968; R. L. Thorndike and Gallup, 1944) no loss occurred on verbal measures, when education was controlled, until around 60 years of age. Measures that require psychomotor responses, visual perception, or an element of speed show considerable decline over the 18–70 age span even with education controlled (Droege, Crambert, and Henkin, 1963), but the difference is less than when the education factor is ignored.

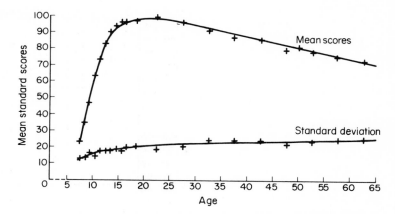

Various intellectual functions seem to have different developmental patterns. Thurstone (1955), using cross-sectional data from the *Primary Mental Abilities Tests*, reported that 80 percent of the adult-level perceptual-speed abilities was reached by age 12; for spatial abilities the 80 percent point occurred at age 14; for verbal meaning at age 18, but not until age 20 for verbal fluency.

Most studies show a marked tendency for performance on intelligence tests to begin to level off at about age 13 and 14. Performance increases little after age 16, although some slight increase in performance occurs until about age 20. The maximum performance on the *Wechsler Adult Intelligence Scale* is not reached until age 25 (Wechsler, 1958, p. 140). This increase probably reflects the effects of continued education and learning rather than an increase in capacity to learn (see Horn, 1967, Wechsler, 1958, pp. 202–205, and Birren, 1960).

The Reliability of Intelligence Tests

The reliability of *most* tests of scholastic aptitude or intelligence is satisfactory for individual use, but there are several exceptions. Reliability estimates determined by internal-consistency methods often exceed .90, and those determined by retesting with an alternate form for a brief time interval usually exceed .80. Standard errors of measurement of 5-7 *IQ* points exist, however, even with reliability coefficients in the .80–.90 range. The relationships between IQ scores on parallel forms L and M on the Stanford-Binet are shown in Figure 14–8.

IQ CONSTANCY

The constancy of the IQ has been a controversial topic since the "mental quotient" was suggested by Stern and Kuhlmann as early as 1912 (see Goodenough, 1949, p. 63) as the *ratio* of the mental age (MA) to the chronological

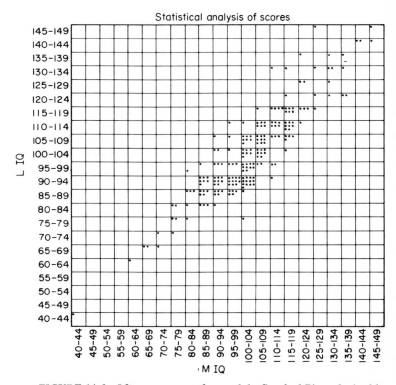

FIGURE 14–8 *IQ scores on two forms of the Stanford-Binet obtained by seven-year-old children. (Reproduced from L. M. Terman and M. A. Merrill,* Measuring intelligence *[Boston: Houghton Mifflin Company, 1960], p. 11, by permission of the publisher, Houghton Mifflin Company.)*

age (CA), multiplied by 100 to remove the decimal point. An examinee's mental age (MA) on a test is the age at which his score is the average score. If a ten-year-old correctly answers 38 items on a test, and 38 is the average score at 12.5 years of age, his MA is 12.5 and his IQ would be:

$$IQ = 100\left(\frac{MA}{CA}\right) = 100\frac{(12.5)}{10} = 125.$$

The *ratio* IQ illustrated above (the ratio of MA to CA) was popular until about 1960. Since then it has been largely replaced by the *deviation* IQ, a type of standard score.

With the ratio IQ one has no "control" over the standard deviation (σ) of the IQ value. Although a σ of 16 was a "typical" value on intelligence tests, the values varied substantially from test to test—even within well-developed tests. Figure 14–9 shows the wide variation in σ's across ages for the two forms of the 1937 Stanford-Binet. This factor would cause considerable fluctuation in IQ scores even if IQ's correlated perfectly ($r = 1.0$) from year to year! For example, as shown in Figure 14–9, a child who consistently remained at the 98th percentile in intelligence would receive ratio IQ scores of 141, 125, and 140 at ages $2\frac{1}{2}$, 6, and 12 respectively—*again, assuming that his performance is completely constant relative to that of his age peers and that the*   **338** *tests correlated perfectly*. Users of ratio IQ scores were rarely aware of this "technicality"; hence, many interpretive errors resulted, particularly in the area of "change" in intellectual status.

Another problem with the ratio IQ resulted from the use of CA in the IQ denominator. To continue to use actual CA when intellectual growth had ceased would mean a forty-year-old with a mental age of 20 would obtain an IQ of 50! To prevent such erroneous results, it was necessary to fix an age at which intellectual development is completed. For most test in which the ratio IQ is or was used, the maximum CA value was set at age 16. If the terminal CA value used is too low, the average IQ's of older subjects will be too high. If the CA value is too high, older subjects would score too low on the test. A maximum CA value of 15 was used on the 1937 Stanford-Binet, which appears to have been too low since the mean IQ's for persons 17 and 18 years old were not 100, but 105 and 107, respectively. Obviously the CA factor in the ratio IQ determination has caused unnecessary vacillation in IQ scores.

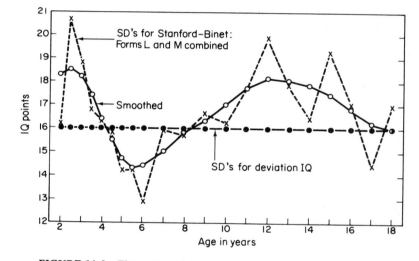

FIGURE 14-9   *Fluctuations in the size of standard deviations of conventional
(ratio) IQ's at different age levels. (Reproduced from S. R. Pinneau,
Conventional and deviation IQ's for the Stanford-Binet, Testing Today, No. 4
[Boston: Houghton Mifflin Company, n.d.].)*

THE DEVIATION IQ

The deviation IQ concept was introduced so that the σ's would have a constant value at each age (which would eliminate the aberrant variability of the ratio IQ). The deviation IQ is simply a kind of standard score with a mean of 100 and a constant value for the standard deviation (usually 15 or 16) irrespective of age. A constant σ-value of 16 deviation IQ's is illustrated in Figure 14-9. A given deviation IQ value represents the same degree of relative intellectual performance for all age levels; there is no vacillation in obtained IQ's resulting from scaling artifacts that accompany the use of the ratio IQ's.

For a proper interpretation of results from an intelligence test, the user must know whether the test employs a ratio or deviation IQ, and, if a ratio IQ is used, what the σ is for each age level in question. The ratio IQ continues to be employed for several widely used tests although this practice should soon become a rarity.

COMMON VARIANCE VS. SCORE STABILITY

We demonstrated that a test must have stable means and standard deviations for each age level if IQ scores are to be stable. The use of deviation IQ's is thus necessary but not sufficient for obtaining a high degree of stability in IQ scores. Correlation coefficients do not necessarily depict score stability. For example, Hopkins and McGuire (1966) found that two intelligence tests correlated very highly ($r = .86$), although the means differed by 8.5 points and the standard deviations differed substantially (16.0 vs. 22.7). That the tests were measuring essentially the same cognitive factors was shown by the high correlation (r, corrected for attenuation,[4] equaled .94); however, quite different numbers (IQ's) were assigned to the same relative level of performance.

In the vast majority of all studies of IQ constancy, only the Stanford-Binet test has been involved. The constancy is typically represented by a correlation coefficient. The correlation (stability) coefficient is useful because it depicts predictable variance (r^2 equals predictable variance); nevertheless, it does not explicitly depict IQ constancy. Recall that one form of the formula for a correlation coefficient is

$$r_{12} = \frac{\sum z_1 z_2}{N}.$$

This formula shows that a correlation coefficient is a function of z-scores ($\bar{X} = 0$, $s = 1.0$ for each variable) for the two measures. Thus the correlation coefficient between IQ scores at times 1 and 2 is blind to score differences in means or standard deviations. Two intelligence tests *could* correlate 1.0, and yet one could have a mean of 100 and the other 130! When deviation IQ's are used, the parallel-form or test-retest stability coefficients are more meaningful, since means and variances are the same at every age level—provided, of course, that examinees in the standardization group are comparable from one age level to another.

Figure 14–10 graphically illustrates the meaning of such coefficients. It depicts the relationship ($r = .8$, Bloom, 1964, p. 56) of Stanford-Binet

---

[4] The correction for attenuation is a statistical procedure for estimating the correlation between "true" scores on two variables—that is, what the correlation between them would be if both tests were perfectly reliable. It is useful for estimating the extent to which two tests measure the same or different factors, after allowance (compensation) has been made for errors of measurement. The formula is:

$$r_{t_1 t_2} = \frac{r_{12}}{\sqrt{r_{11} r_{22}}},$$

where: $r_{t_1 t_2}$ = the estimated correlation between true scores on variables 1 and 2,
  r_{12} = the obtained correlation between variables 1 and 2, and
  r_{11}, r_{22} = the reliability coefficients of variables 1 and 2, respectively.

In the example noted above, $r_{12} = .861$, $r_{11} = .895$, $r_{22} = .847$; hence, $r_{t_1 t_2} = .988$. For further information, see Glass and Stanley (1970), pp. 182–186.

deviation IQ's at grade 3 with corresponding IQ scores at grade 12. The coefficient of .8 indicates that the IQ predicted for an examinee at grade 12 will be only eight-tenths (.8) as far from the mean as his grade 3 IQ was. As shown in Figure 14–10, pupils who scored 125 in grade 3 tended on the average to score 120 (.8 × 25 = 20) in grade 12.[5] Those examinees who received IQ scores of 80 in grade three tended to be only 80 percent as far from the mean (.8 × 20 = 16) at grade 12 and hence to average 84 then.

The accuracy of these predictions is reflected by the standard error of estimate ($\sigma_{y.x}$), which is the standard deviation of actual scores on the criterion (y) around the predicted scores:

$$\sigma_{2.1} = \sigma_2 \sqrt{1 - r^2}.$$

In the Stanford-Binet (Figure 14–10) example where $\sigma = 16$,

$$\sigma_{2.1} = 16\sqrt{1 - (.8)^2} = 16\sqrt{.36} = 16(.6) = 9.6, \text{ or about 10 points.}$$

The standard-error-of-estimate value of 10 shows that even with a substantial degree of stability ($r = .8$), there is still considerable fluctuation in individual scores. The $\sigma_{2.1}$ value of 10 indicates that about one-third of the examinees depicted in Figure 14–10 will have IQ's that differ from their *predicted* grade 12 IQ value by 10 or more points. A .95 confidence interval for a pupil's grade 12 IQ, predicted from his grade 3 score, would be his predicted IQ at grade 12 $\pm 2\sigma_{2.1}$; in other words, it would span a range of more than 40 IQ points! Clearly, a high stability coefficient still allows considerable variation in individual performance. This fact is further illustrated in Figure 14–11, which shows the plot of the actual IQ scores obtained by 354 pupils at grades 5 and 7 on the *California Test of Mental Maturity* (CTMM). Even though the scores over the two-year period are rather stable ($r = .829$), notice that of the nine pupils who received IQ scores of 99 at grade 5, one scored 114 at grade 7, another scored 86, but the grade 7 mean (99.7) differed little from the grade 5 mean (99.0).

As we previously pointed out, almost all studies of IQ constancy have been done with individual intelligence tests (usually the Stanford-Binet); only a few studies have employed group tests. Yet it is group tests that are given to all but a very small percentage of students. Figure 14–12 illustrates the typical findings on IQ stabilities with an individual verbal test (the Stanford-Binet, see Bloom, 1964, p. 56), along with corresponding information on *group* verbal and nonverbal intelligence tests. It is evident that IQ scores from individually administered verbal tests are much more stable at younger ages than those from group tests. Whereas IQ scores on individual-verbal tests at age six correlate about .7 with corresponding IQ's at maturity, scores on *group* intelligence tests do not reflect the same degree of stability until 2–3 and 5–6 years later for verbal and nonverbal tests, respectively.

---

[5] If the means or standard deviations were not constant for each age, the prediction would have to allow for this by converting the grade 3 score to a z-score (z_1) and multiplying z_1 by r to obtain the predicted z-score (z_2') at grade 12:

$$z_2' = rz_1.$$

We convert z_2' back into the relevant units by multiplying z_2' by s_2 and adding this value to the mean of the predicted variable ($\bar{X}_2$).

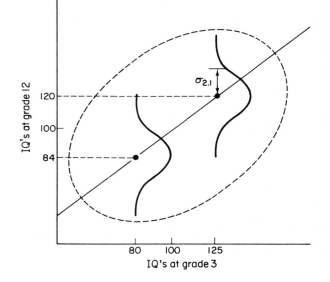

*FIGURE 14–10   The relationship (r = .8) between deviation
IQ scores obtained on the Stanford-Binet (at grades 3 and 12).
The distributions of grade 12 IQ scores obtained by examinees who
received scores of 80 and 130 at grade 3 are specifically illustrated.
(Data from Bloom, 1964, p. 56.)*

Hopkins and Bracht (1971b) studied IQ constancy and change with group intelligence tests by following a large sample of pupils in grade 1 through elementary, junior high, and high school. Figure 14–13 shows the stability coefficients for verbal and nonverbal IQ's. Each line in the figure depicts the correlation of the IQ scores from an initial grade level with scores obtained at subsequent grade levels. For example, the grade 1 verbal IQ (see bottom solid line in Figure 14–13) correlated .51 with grade 2 verbal IQ's, and .52, .50, .44, and .50 with IQ's obtained in grades 4, 7, 9, and 11, respectively. Notice that IQ's obtained for students in the primary grades have rather low correlations with their IQ scores in subsequent grades (grade 1 IQ's are not even highly related to IQ's obtained one year later). Verbal IQ's at grade 4 have considerable stability, correlating .81, .79, and .77 with IQ's in grades 7, 9, and 11, respectively. Figure 14–13 illustrates that nonverbal IQ's fluctuated significantly more than verbal IQ's and did not show much stability until grade 7. The pattern of results reported in Figure 14–13 is consistent with results of other groups using different tests (Hopkins and Bibelheimer, 1971; L. E. Tyler, 1958). When verbal and nonverbal IQ's are combined in a total IQ score, its stability closely parallels that shown for verbal IQ (stability coefficients average only about .03 higher than the verbal IQ's).

The stability of IQ scores expressed directly in IQ units is more informative for most people than stability coefficients. Hopkins and Bracht (1971b) found that the *mean* absolute change in total IQ scores from grade 1 to any grade thereafter, even for grade 2, was 10–12 points. The average absolute difference in grade 2 IQ's and IQ's from subsequent grades was 9–10 points; grade 4 IQ's   *342*

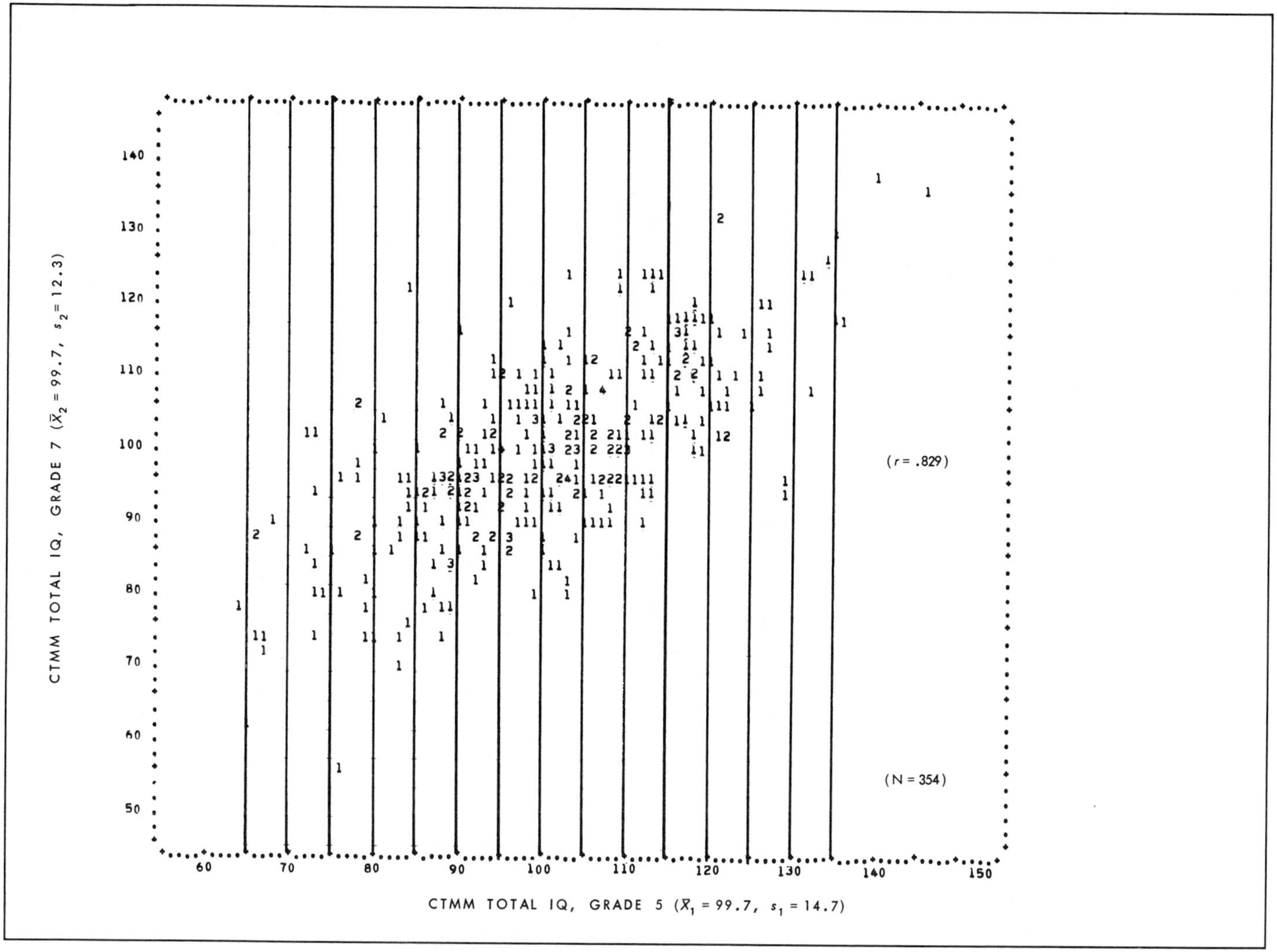

FIGURE 14-11 Scatterplot of IQ scores at grades 5 and 7 for 354 pupils. (Data from Hopkins and
Bibelheimer, 1971.)

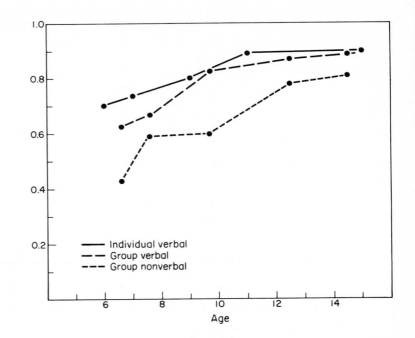

FIGURE 14–12 *Correlation coefficients between IQ scores at various ages and IQ scores at maturity (age 17, corrected to a common terminal variability) for individual verbal, group verbal, and group nonverbal intelligence tests.*

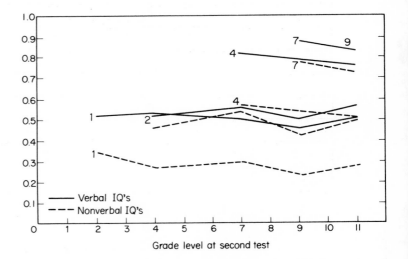

FIGURE 14–13 *Graphic representation of stability coefficients for verbal and nonverbal IQ's (CIMM used at grades 1, 2, and 4; Lorge-Thorndike at grades 7, 9, and 11). Grade level of initial testing precedes each line.*

differ 7–9 points from subsequent IQ's, on the average. The mean difference in grade 7 IQ's and IQ's in grades 9 and 11 was 5–6 points; and grade 9 IQ's averaged 5 points different from grade 11 scores. It is important to note that these are *mean* absolute differences; such differences include changes up and down. Recall that the changes are least at the mean and are expected to be progressively greater as scores deviate from the mean. The changes are usually greater when the IQ's are obtained on different tests (for example, Lorge-Thorndike vs. CTMM) than when a different level of the same series is repeated. Mouly and Edgar (1958) compared the IQ scores yielded by four widely used intelligence tests. They found that some tests consistently yielded IQ's 5–7 points higher than others. This finding shows that degree of IQ change will be even greater across different tests than within the same test.

The standard errors of estimate (standard deviation of obtained IQ scores around the most probable IQ predicted from a prior test, see Figure 14–10) were

1. 12–17 points using grade 1 or grade 2 scores as predictors,
2. 9–12 points using grade 4 scores as predictors,
3. 7–8 points using grade 7 scores for predicting scores in grades 9 and 11, and
4. about 7 points in predicting grade 11 IQ's from grade 9 IQ's.

Several conclusions can be drawn about IQ consistency:

1. The stability of IQ's from individual verbal tests is fairly high as early as age five. Infant tests have virtually no validity as predictors of later IQ scores.
2. The stability of IQ's from group tests is much less than that of IQ's from individual verbal tests until at least 10–12 years of age but becomes comparable thereafter. Accurate long-term predictions cannot be made from group intelligence tests given during the primary grades. IQ's from nonverbal group tests tend to be much less stable than those from verbal group tests.
3. Even when there is a high degree of overall stability, the scores of a few individuals will change greatly.
4. Each test varies slightly in the cognitive abilities that are tapped. An IQ score should always be interpreted in terms of the test on which it was obtained.
5. Various intelligence tests differ considerably in IQ stability. For the *Primary Mental Abilities Tests*, which yield Verbal, Numerical, Spatial, Reasoning, and Word Fluency scores, much less long-term stability is reflected in the Spatial and Word Fluency abilities than in other areas (Meyer and Bending, 1961; L. E. Tyler, 1958).
6. IQ changes are greater when the type of intelligence test used is varied. IQ differences are especially great when the type of test given (verbal vs. nonverbal) is varied. Verbal and nonverbal IQ's correlate only .4–.6 at most grade levels (Hopkins and Bibelheimer, 1971; Hopkins and Bracht, 1971b).

These conclusions indicate that great care must be taken in interpreting IQ's, especially from group tests, which are the only ones available for 95 percent of the students. Scores from group tests given during the primary grades should be viewed only as general indicators of *present* intellectual status. The findings suggest that there are great dangers in disseminating the results to parents, who may interpret results with much less tolerance for error and change than is required for a proper evaluation. Certainly no one has more right to knowledge of a child's abilities than his parents, but the information should be given in terms meaningful to parents. Perhaps percentile ranks would be more meaningful than IQ scores in this context. Fortunately many test publishers now provide report forms that interpret a student's performance in terms that he and his parents can understand (see Figures 14–15, 16–3, 16–4, 17–3, and 17–4).

Many parents are unaware that intelligence tests tend to measure primarily scholastic aptitudes and that many other cognitive abilities that can be legitimately considered to reflect intelligence and special abilities are untapped. For example, Hoepfner and O'Sullivan (1968) found that measures of social intelligence correlated only .3–.4 with scores from conventional intelligence tests.

RELATIONSHIP OF IQ AND
SCHOLASTIC ACHIEVEMENT

The data given in Table 14–1 show the relationship between IQ's from the Lorge-Thorndike Intelligence Test (LT) and various kinds of academic achieve-

TABLE 14–1

Intercorrelations of Lorge-Thorndike Multilevel and Iowa Tests of Basic Skills (Sample from National Standardization)

Iowa Tests of Basic Skills	L-T Verbal Battery: Grade						L-T Nonverbal Battery: Grade					
	3	4	5	6	7	8	3	4	5	6	7	8
Vocabulary	.71	.75	.77	.78	.80	.82	.56	.62	.62	.62	.64	.65
Reading	.68	.74	.76	.79	.81	.82	.53	.63	.65	.65	.67	.69
Language												
Spelling	.66	.67	.68	.69	.70	.69	.52	.55	.56	.55	.54	.53
Capitalization	.65	.67	.67	.67	.67	.69	.55	.61	.61	.61	.62	.64
Punctuation	.56	.63	.66	.66	.67	.69	.48	.61	.61	.61	.61	.62
Usage	.67	.70	.71	.71	.71	.69	.55	.59	.61	.60	.60	.57
Total	.73	.76	.78	.78	.79	.78	.61	.66	.67	.67	.68	.67
Study Skills												
Maps	.59	.62	.65	.66	.66	.71	.51	.58	.64	.64	.66	.70
Graphs	.63	.65	.66	.66	.69	.70	.56	.62	.62	.63	.68	.68
References	.62	.67	.71	.74	.76	.78	.53	.61	.65	.67	.72	.72
Total	.72	.75	.76	.77	.79	.81	.62	.69	.71	.71	.77	.78
Arithmetic												
Concepts	.65	.70	.71	.71	.72	.75	.61	.67	.69	.69	.71	.72
Problems	.57	.61	.61	.62	.65	.64	.51	.56	.56	.56	.61	.61
Total	.66	.71	.72	.72	.74	.75	.61	.68	.68	.69	.71	.71
Composite	.79	.82	.84	.85	.88	.88	.65	.73	.74	.75	.77	.77
N	2677	2757	2706	2584	2605	2462	2677	2757	2706	2584	2605	2462

SOURCE: Reprinted from *Technical Manual, Lorge-Thorndike Intelligence Tests,* Multilevel Edition (1966), Table 15, by permission of the publisher, Houghton Mifflin Company, Boston.

ment as measured by the *Iowa Tests of Basic Skills* (ITBS). At each grade level, each correlation is based on approximately 2,500 pupils from a nationally representative collection of schools. The results illustrate that there is a pronounced relationship between achievement in various subject-matter areas and measured intelligence. Notice that the degree of relationship tends to increase with successive grade level in every achievement area. The nonverbal IQ's have a consistently lower relationship in every achievement area, but, as would be expected, the difference is less in areas that are less verbal (such as map or graph reading and arithmetic).

Table 14–2 gives similar information at the high-school level for the LT tests and the *Tests of Academic Progress* (TAP). These findings agree with the typical results from other well-constructed intelligence and achievement tests; they confirm the substantial relationship between measured intelligence and all academic areas of scholastic achievement.

TABLE 14–2

Intercorrelations of Lorge-Thorndike Multilevel and Tests of Academic Progress (Sample from National Standardization)

Tests of Academic Progress	L-T Verbal Battery: Grade				L-T Nonverbal Battery: Grade			
	9	10	11	12	9	10	11	12
Social Studies	.807	.806	.811	.833	.658	.644	.615	.608
Composition	.750	.736	.727	.752	.648	.615	.593	.592
Science	.744	.741	.726	.742	.629	.640	.628	.639
Reading	.807	.791	.811	.833	.652	.606	.598	.590
Mathematics	.732	.748	.727	.710	.696	.715	.674	.673
Literature	.790	.785	.812	.835	.630	.596	.586	.602
Composite	.879	.869	.882	.895	.742	.718	.706	.707
N	2503	2250	2174	1684	2503	2250	2174	1684

SOURCE: Reprinted from *Technical Manual, Lorge Thorndike Intelligence Tests,* Multilevel Edition (1966), Table 16, by permission of the publisher, Houghton Mifflin Company, Boston.

Most authorities feel that current intelligence tests are more aptly described as "scholastic aptitude" tests because they are so highly related to academic performance, although present use suggests that the term "intelligence test" is going to be with us for some time. The reservation is *not* based on the opinion that intelligence tests do not reflect intelligence, but that there are other kinds of intelligence that are not reflected in current tests; the term intelligence is too inclusive. It should be clear that intelligence tests reflect abilities that are very important and relevant to educational performance. Wallen (1962, p. 17) surveyed the research pertaining to IQ scores and ability to learn and concluded: "In spite of the not uncommon statement that intelligence tests do not predict ability to learn, the evidence that they do continues to accumulate." Only when the learning tasks are of a primitive, rote type, such as with paired-associates tasks, do IQ scores have little relationship with learning behavior. When learning complex tasks, intelligence tests are substantially related to learning speed and ease (Noble, Noble, and Alcock, 1958).

The appropriate evidence for the validity of intelligence tests is of the construct-validity variety. In Chapter 4 (pp. 111–112) we used intelligence tests to illustrate the concept of construct validity. In a very real sense every bit of information one has on a test may have implications for construct validity; that is, the data respond to the question "Is the information congruent with theoretical expectations?" IQ constancy has important implications for the construct validity of a given intelligence test. The validity of IQ's from infant intelligence tests is rejected because they possess so little consistency with later cognitive performance.

The nature-nurture studies on measured intelligence have an important bearing on the construct validity of IQ scores. If there were no relationship between the IQ's of siblings reared apart and a very high relationship between their IQ's when reared together, we would either revise the theory of intelligence (the proposition that genetic factors play a significant role would have to be eliminated) or else we would reject the validity of the measurements. Either an ingredient in the theory is invalid or else the measurement of the construct must lack validity.

Contrary to indications in much of the popular literature, genetic factors definitely seem to have a strong relationship to IQ. Table 14–3 presents the median correlation between IQ scores for varying degrees of genetic similarity. The correlations are generally consistent with theoretical expectations. The correlation between IQ scores of unrelated persons reared together is only about .2, but the IQ scores of identical (monozygotic) twins reared apart

TABLE 14–3

Correlations for Measured Intellectual Ability

Correlations Between	Number of Studies	Obtained Median r
Unrelated Persons		
Foster parent and child	3	+.20
Children reared apart	4	−.01
Children reared together	5	+.24
Collaterals		
Second cousins	1	+.16
First cousins	3	+.26
Uncle (or aunt) and nephew (or niece)	1	+.34
Siblings, reared apart	33	+.47
Siblings, reared together	36	+.55
Dizygotic twins, different sex	9	+.49
Dizygotic twins, same sex	11	+.56
Monozygotic twins, reared apart	4	+.75
Monozygotic twins, reared together	14	+.87
Direct Line		
Grandparent and grandchild	3	+.27
Parent (as adult) and child	13	+.50
Parent (as child) and child	1	+.56

SOURCES: Jensen (1969, p. 49) and Burt (1966, p. 150).

correlate highly ($r = .75$). In typical environments of the U.S. and England, genetic factors bear a much stronger general relationship to IQ than do environmental factors. Of course for certain subgroups the environment may have dramatic effects on IQ—as, for example, with brain damage at birth, metabolic types of mental retardation, or extreme environmental deprivation.

Table 14–4 gives similar correlations between variables in addition to intelligence. One very critical observation is that although genetic factors are strongly related to academic achievement, that relationship is much less than with intelligence tests. The achievement scores of unrelated persons reared together are substantially related, and *it is achievement, not intelligence per se, that is socially significant.* The environment tends to have more influence on a student's academic performance than on his IQ score.

One can conclude that genetic factors have a strong relationship to measured intelligence. The relationship with scholastic achievement is considerably less. Conversely the environment has a much stronger relationship with childrens' academic achievement than with their observed scores on intelligence tests. There is little relationship among measured intelligence or physical variables among unrelated persons reared together, but there is a substantial relationship (about .5) between their educational achievement levels—about as great as for siblings reared apart.

TABLE 14–4

Correlations for Intelligence, Scholastic Assessments, and Physical Traits

	Identical Twins Reared Together, $N = 83$	Identical Twins Reared Apart, $N = 30$	Fraternal Twins Reared Together, $N = 172$	Siblings Reared Together, $N = 853$	Siblings Reared Apart, $N = 131$	Unrelated Children Reared Together, $N = 287$
Intelligence						
Group Test	.944	.771	.542	.515	.441	.281
Individual Test	.921	.843	.526	.491	.463	.252
Final Assessment	.925	.876	.551	.538	.517	.269
Mean	.929	.829	.539	.514	.473	.267
Scholastic						
General	.898	.681	.831	.814	.526	.535
Reading & Spelling	.944	.647	.915	.853	.490	.548
Arithmetic	.862	.723	.748	.769	.563	.476
Mean	.900	.683	.831	.811	.526	.519
Physical						
Height	.956	.942	.472	.503	.536	−.069
Weight	.929	.884	.586	.568	.427	.243
Head Length	.961	.958	.495	.481	.536	.116
Head Breadth	.977	.960	.541	.507	.472	.082
Eye Color	1.000	1.000	.516	.553	.504	.104
Mean	.965	.949	.522	.522	.495	.095

SOURCE: Reprinted from A. R. Jensen. 1968. Social class, race, and genetics: Implications for education. *American Educational Research Journal,* **5:** Table 1, p. 8, by permission of the author and the American Educational Research Association, Washington, D.C.

The relationship of measured intelligence to occupational level is illustrated in Figure 14–14. There data are based on the testing of approximately 90,000 white recruits during World War II; the *Army General Classification Test* (AGCT) was given to these recruits. The AGCT uses a standard score system (mean = 100, σ = 20) to describe performance. The scores are similar to IQ's except that the standard deviation is set at 20 rather than 15 or 16. As an aid in interpretation, the median AGCT scores for several different occupations were converted to corresponding IQ equivalents (mean = 100, σ = 16) in Figure 14–14. The variability within each occupation is shown by the bars that extend from the 25th and 75th percentiles in IQ units, and the lines that extend from the 10th to the 90th percentiles.

Two important generalizations are apparent from the data given in Figure 14–14. First, there is a substantial relationship between measured mental ability and various occupations. The median IQ for the highest occupational group was 35 IQ points higher than for the lowest occupational group. Second, there is a wide range of mental ability within each occupation. Although the accountant's median was 123, 25 percent of the group scored below an IQ equivalent of 117 or above one of 129. Notice that the variability within each occupational group tends to decrease as its median increases.

There are many bright persons in occupations that do not require high mental ability. One-fourth of the lumberjacks scored above the general average on the test, even though as a group they had the lowest performance. Note that we are talking about *measured intelligence*; the variation in amount of education probably makes the observed differences greater than the true differences in intellectual potential. In addition, these data were obtained about three decades ago; today, students of all interests are getting much more education, which would influence their test performance.

If school counseling programs are helping students select vocational plans commensurate with their abilities, some of the very able students who in 1940 would have become laborers will continue their education today and enter a skilled trade or profession. This would make the differences in measured intelligences among the occupations even greater. If there were no change in the occupations entered but simply an increase in the workers' education, the differences among occupational groups shown in Figure 14–14 would be decreased slightly.

It is interesting to note, as shown in Figure 14–15 (from Jensen, 1968b), that the IQ differences among the means of parents of various occupational levels in England are much greater than among the means of their children. On the average, the children tend to be only half as far from the mean as their parents (r = .5, see Table 14–3), illustrating the ubiquitous regression-to-the-mean phenomenon, originally observed by Sir Francis Galton about a century ago. The differences among the various occupational levels in the United States are probably less than those in England, where different educational philosophies and practices prevail.

350

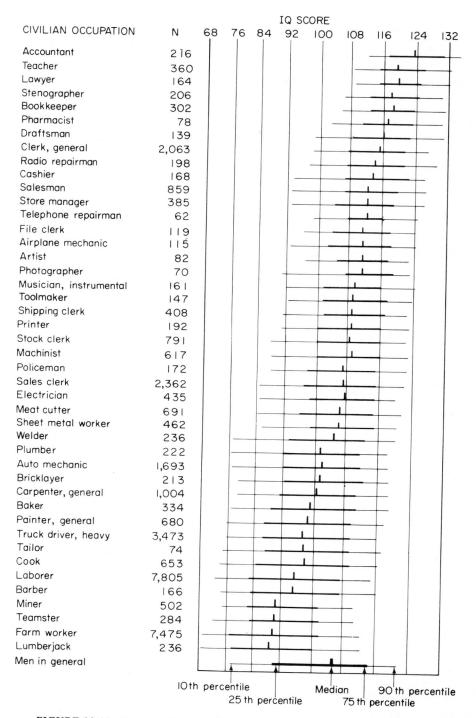

FIGURE 14-14 *Scores on the Army General Classification Test for occupational groups converted to deviation IQ equivalents. (Data from Stewart, 1947.)*

Although intelligence tests that yield a total IQ score and/or separate verbal and nonverbal IQ scores constitute the bulk of cognitive aptitude assessment in school testing programs, an increasing use is being made of tests that yield a profile of different aptitudes, especially in guidance contexts. The most popular battery of this type is the *Differential Aptitude Tests* (DAT), which yield separate scores on eight somewhat independent aptitudes or abilities: Verbal Reasoning, Numerical Ability, Abstract Reasoning, Clerical Speed and Accuracy, Mechanical Reasoning, Space Relations, and Language Usage (Spelling and Grammar). A sample DAT profile is shown in Figure 14–16.

The basic rationale underlying these tests is that various academic and occupational pursuits require different patterns of aptitude, hence a decision in which a profile of aptitudes is available should be more appropriate than a decision based upon a single "omnibus" IQ score. This assumption was strongly contested by McNemar (1964). Nevertheless Figures 14–17 and 14–18 from the DAT manual show that the various aptitude tests do have differing degrees of relationship with certain academic and occupational criteria. Notice that some of the differences are counterintuitive; for example, the girls who entered clerical work (Figure 14–18, B) tended to have substantially less clerical ability than girls who became teachers.

That the separate subtest scores can have substantial validity for certain occupational pursuits is illustrated in the following expectancy table. Table 14–5, shows the relation between the DAT Space Relations test scores obtained at the beginning of the term and final grades in a watch-repair training program.

TABLE 14–5

Space Relations (Form A) Scores at Time of Admission and End-of-Course Grades for 111 Students in the American Institute of Specialized Watch Repair (r = .69)

N	Number Receiving Each Grade					Raw Score	Percent Receiving Each Grade				
	E	D	C	B	A		E	D	C	B	A
9				3	6	80–99				33	67
33			7	19	7	60–79			21	58	21
43	1	8	17	17		40–59	2	18	40	40	
14	3	5	4	2		20–39	21	36	29	14	
12	4	3	4	1		0–19	33	25	33	9	

SOURCE: Reprinted from G. K. Bennett, H. G. Seashore, and A. G. Wesman, *Differential Aptitude Tests*, Forms L and M, Fourth Edition Manual (New York: The Psychological Corporation), Table 53, p. 5–58, by permission of the publisher. Copyright © 1947, 1952, 1959, 1963, 1966 by the Psychological Corporation, New York. All rights reserved.

Multiple-aptitude tests can provide important information for career planning; as McNemar (1964) illustrated, however, their superiority over general intelligence tests for predicting differential *academic* success remains uncertain. The great communality among the abilities required to succeed in most academic fields is no doubt a major factor that prevents multiple-aptitude tests from excelling over the omnibus intelligence test in predictive validity.

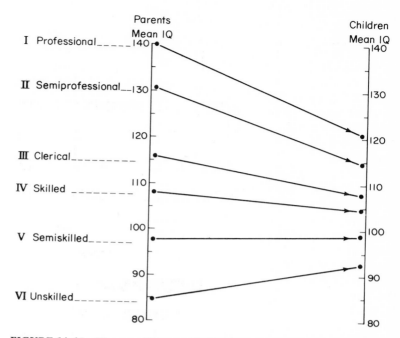

FIGURE 14–15 *The mean IQ scores for English adults at various occupational levels and the corresponding mean IQ scores of their children. (Reproduced from A. R. Jensen, Social class, race, and genetics: Implications for education, American Educational Research Journal, January 1968, p. 17, by permission of the author and the American Educational Research Association. Copyright © 1968 by the American Educational Research Association, Washington, D.C. Data from Burt, 1961.)*

Various General Ability Tests

Many different published tests purport to measure intelligence and cognitive aptitudes. The validity data on many of these are fragmentary and unconvincing. Before selecting or using the results from a test, one should read the critical reviews of that test in the *Mental Measurements Yearbooks* edited by Oscar K. Buros.[6]

The representative standardized tests given below are noteworthy and widely used. The abilities measured, their separate scores, and the ages for which norms are available are given.

Individual Tests

Stanford-Binet Intelligence Scale (Verbal), ages 2–adult.
Wechsler Preschool and Primary Scale of Intelligence (WPPSI) (Verbal and Performance), ages 4–6½.

---

[6] For a quick general evaluation of standardized tests, presented in numerical ratings, see Hoepfner and Klein (1970).

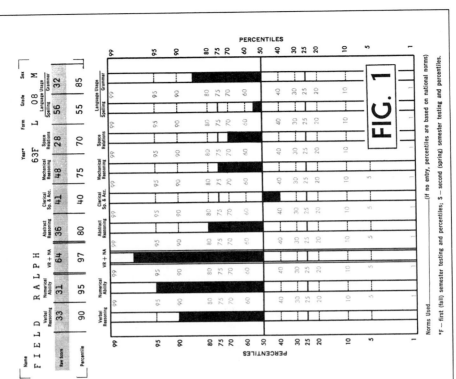

Forms L and M

INDIVIDUAL REPORT FORM

DIFFERENTIAL APTITUDE TESTS [1963 EDITION]

G. K. Bennett, H. G. Seashore, and A. G. Wesman

FIG. 1

Profiling Your DAT Scores

The numbers that tell how you did on each test are in the row marked "Percentiles." Your percentile tells where you rank on a test in comparison with boys or girls in your grade. These percentiles are based on test scores earned by thousands of students in numerous schools across the country. If your percentile rank is 50, you are just in the middle — that is, one-half of the students in the national group did better than you and one-half did less well. (If your school uses local norms, your counselor will explain the difference.)

In the columns below each percentile you can draw your aptitude profile. For each test make a *heavy short line* across the column at the level which corresponds to your percentile rank on that test.

Your aptitude profile will be more visible if you black in each column *up to* or *down to* the 50-line from the short lines

you have just made. The vertical bars on your profile show the strength of your tested aptitudes, *up* or *down* from the rank of the *middle student* of your grade and sex.

Think of "percentile" as meaning "per cent of people." In your case, the people are boys or girls in your grade in many schools across the country. The percentile shows what per cent of this group scored no higher than you did. If your percentile rank on one test is 80, you are at the top of 80 per cent of the group — only 20 per cent of the group made higher scores than yours. If you scored in the 25th percentile, this would mean about 75 per cent of the group did better than you on the test. Thus, a percentile rank always indicates your relative standing among a theoretical 100 persons representing a large "norm" group — in this case, students of your sex and grade. It does not tell how many questions (or what per cent of them) you answered correctly.

How Big a Difference Is Important?

Of course we do not want to over-estimate small differences in ability on tests because a test cannot be perfectly accurate, and your score might not be exactly the same if you could take the same test twice.

To estimate the importance of a difference between your scores on any two tests on this profile, use a ruler to measure how much higher on the chart one mark is *than* the other. It is the *vertical* distance — ⌐ that counts, of course, *not* how far *across* the chart ╱ or ╲ .

If the distance is *one inch or greater*, it is probable that you have a real difference in your abilities on the two tests.

If a difference between the two percentile ranks is *between a half inch and one inch*, consider whether other things you know about yourself agree with it; the difference may or may not be important.

If the vertical distance between two tests is *less than a half inch*, the difference between the two scores may be disregarded; so small a difference is probably not meaningful.

FIGURE 14-16 Sample student profile on the Differential Aptitude Test. (Reproduced from G. K. Bennett, H. G. Seashore, and A. G. Wesman, Differential Aptitude Tests, Forms L and M Fourth Edition Manual [New York: The Psychological Corporation], Fig. 2, p. 3-6, by permission of the publisher. Copyright © 1961, 1963 by The Psychological Corporation, New York. All rights reserved.)

Wechsler Intelligence Scale for Children (WISC) (Verbal and Performance), ages 5–15.

Wechsler Adult Intelligence Scale (WAIS) (Verbal and Performance), ages 16–adult.

Illinois Test of Psycholinguistic Abilities (ITPA), ages 3–10.

Group Tests

California Tests of Mental Maturity (CTMM) (Language and Nonlanguage), K–adult

Cooperative School and College Ability Tests (SCAT) (Verbal, Quantitative), grades 4–14

Henmon-Nelson Tests of Mental Ability (Verbal), grades 3–14

Kuhlmann-Anderson Intelligence Tests (KA) (Verbal), grades K–12

Lorge-Thorndike Intelligence Tests (LT) (Verbal, Nonverbal), grades 3–adult

Otis-Lennon Mental Ability Tests (Verbal) grades K–adult

Differential Aptitude Tests (DAT) (8 subtests), grades 8–12

Assessing Creativity

In his 1950 presidential address to the American Psychological Association, Guilford (1950) documented the dearth of attention that psychologists were giving to the study of creativity. His address stimulated interest in the topic, and since that time considerable research efforts have been directed toward the definition and assessment of creativity.

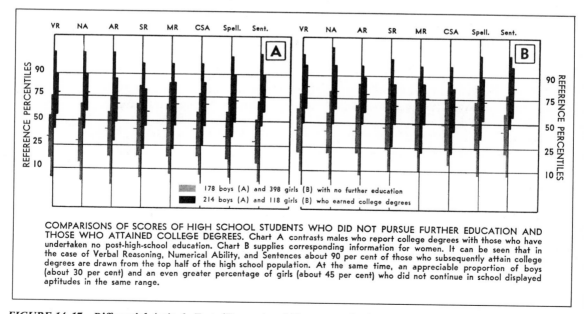

COMPARISONS OF SCORES OF HIGH SCHOOL STUDENTS WHO DID NOT PURSUE FURTHER EDUCATION AND THOSE WHO ATTAINED COLLEGE DEGREES. Chart A contrasts males who report college degrees with those who have undertaken no post-high-school education. Chart B supplies corresponding information for women. It can be seen that in the case of Verbal Reasoning, Numerical Ability, and Sentences about 90 per cent of those who subsequently attain college degrees are drawn from the top half of the high school population. At the same time, an appreciable proportion of boys (about 30 per cent) and an even greater percentage of girls (about 45 per cent) who did not continue in school displayed aptitudes in the same range.

FIGURE 14–17   Differential Aptitude Tests (Forms A and B) scores and subsequent education. (Reproduced from G. K. Bennett, H. G. Seashore, and A. G. Wesman, Differential Aptitude Tests, Forms L and M Fourth Edition Manual [New York: The Psychological Corporation], by permission of the publisher. Copyright © 1947, 1952, 1959, 1963, 1966 by The Psychological Corporation, New York. All rights reserved.)

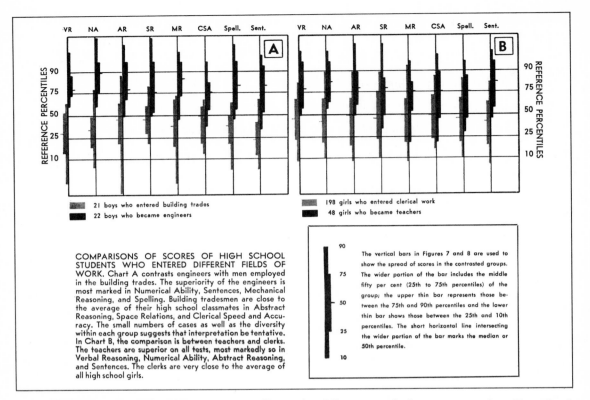

FIGURE 14–18 Differential Aptitude Tests (Forms A and B), scores and subsequent occupations. (Reproduced from G. K. Bennett, H. G. Seashore, and A. G. Wesman, Differential Aptitude Tests, Forms L and M Fourth Edition Manual [New York: The Psychological Corporation], by permission of the publisher. Copyright © 1947, 1952, 1959, 1963, 1966 by The Psychological Corporation, New York. All rights reserved.)

Creative thinking is in the *divergent* operation of Guilford's SI model, and he and others have attempted to develop tests of creativity. In these tests the examinee is asked such things as how many different uses he can think of for a brick or a tin can; "What would happen if birds could speak the language of man?"; "What might be about to happen in the picture above?"; "Make up a story to fit the title, 'The Lion That Won't Roar'"; "Just suppose that no one ever has to go to school anymore; what would happen?"; and so on. Illustrative items are given in Figure 14–19. Responses are scored by trained raters according to three criteria: originality, fluency (number of responses), and flexibility (variation in categories of responses).

The creativity tests developed to date have yet to demonstrate their practical value; their predictive validity tends to be low (Hoepfner, 1967). The tests tend to be too unreliable for individual use (Wodtke, 1964; Yamamoto, 1962); test-retest reliabilities tend to be in the .45–.75 range with a median value of perhaps .65. In addition, many creativity tests do not correlate highly with each other. R. L. Thorndike (1963) showed that tests of creativity correlate as highly with conventional "convergent" intelligence measures as they do with other "divergent" tests.

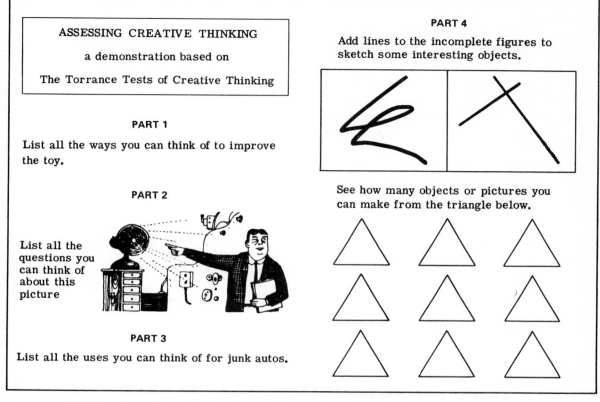

FIGURE 14–19 *Illustrative items for creativity test.* (*Reproduced by permission of the Personnel Press, Inc., Princeton, N.J., a division of Ginn and Company.*)

Continued research efforts may refine or develop creativity measures so that they have practical utility, but at present they must be viewed as bold attempts rather than successes in creativity assessment. Tryk (1968, p. 54), in concluding his survey of creativity assessment, stated: "In spite of the recent upsurge in research, the current status of instruments for assessing creativity is less than satisfactory. Evidence for the validity and reliability of creativity measures fails so far to promote much confidence in their use in assessing specific components of creativity." Even Guilford, who stimulated great interest in creativity testing, is leery of some of its developments (Guilford, 1968, p. 251).

Post-organizer

Intelligence measurement became successful shortly after 1900, when Binet employed verbal reasoning items. There continue to be several theories of intelligence, although its measurement is done principally by the use of rather heterogeneous collections of verbal or nonverbal items.

The construct-validity data for intelligence tests include: (1) age differentiation; (2) the considerable stability of IQ scores, especially from individual tests

such as the Stanford-Binet; (3) the substantial relationship of IQ scores with
academic achievement and occupational level; and (4) the apparently high
relationship of genetic factors with measured intelligence. Several conclusions
regarding the assessment of intelligence can be drawn:

358

*Measuring
Intelligence*

1. Infant intelligence tests have almost no predictive validity.
2. Intelligence continues to develop until age 18 or so.
3. Deviation IQ scores are superior to ratio IQ scores because, unlike ratio IQ's, their meaning is not obscured by fluctuations in standard deviation across various age levels.
4. A high correlation between intelligence tests indicates that they are measuring common abilities, but does not necessarily mean that the tests yield similar IQ scores.
5. High stability coefficients on intelligence tests represent the general consistency in scores, although scores for some individuals may change dramatically.
6. Individual verbal intelligence tests tend to have greater IQ stability than group verbal tests. IQ scores from verbal tests tend to have more stability than scores from nonverbal tests.
7. Intelligence-test scores have a substantial relationship to academic achievement. The relationship tends to increase with grade and is greater for verbal than for nonverbal tests.

SUGGESTED READINGS

ANASTASI, A. 1958. Heredity, environment, and the question "How?" *Psychological Review*, **65**(4): 197–208.

———. 1964. Culture fair testing. *Educational Horizons*, **43**: 26–30. Reprinted in G. H. BRACHT, K. D. HOPKINS, and J. C. STANLEY. 1972. *Perspectives in educational and psychological measurement*. Englewood Cliffs, N. J.: Prentice-Hall, Inc., Selection 20.

———. 1968. Tests and the culturally disadvantaged. *Psychological testing*, 3d ed. New York: The Macmillan Company, pp. 558–564.

BARRON, F. 1968. The measurement of creativity. In D. K. Whitla, ed., *Handbook of measurement and assessment in behavioral sciences*. Reading, Mass.: Addison-Wesley Publishing Co., pp. 348–366.

BLOOM, B. S. 1964. Intelligence. *Stability and change in human characteristics*. New York: John Wiley & Sons, Inc., pp. 52–94.

BRADWAY, K. P., C. W. THOMPSON, and R. B. CREVENS. 1958. Preschool IQ's after twenty-five years. *Journal of Educational Psychology*, **49**(5): 278–281.

BURT, C. 1966. The genetic determination of differences in intelligence: A study of monozygotic twins reared together and apart. *British Journal of Psychology*, **57**: 137–153.

CATTELL, R. B. 1963. Theory of fluid and crystallized intelligence: A critical experiment. *Journal of Educational Psychology*, **54**: 1–22.

CRONBACH, L. J. 1969. Heredity, environment, and educational policy. *Harvard Education Review*, **39**: 338–347.

DuBois, P. H. 1970. *A history of psychological testing.* Boston: Allyn and Bacon, Inc.

EYSENCK, H. J. 1971. *Race, intelligence and education.* London: Maurice Temple Smith Ltd.

GUILFORD, J. P. 1967. *The nature of human intelligence.* New York: McGraw-Hill Book Company.

HIERONYMOUS, A. N., and J. B. STROUD. 1969. Comparability of IQ scores on five widely used intelligence tests. *Measurement and Evaluation in Guidance*, **2**: 135–140.

HOPKINS, K. D., and M. BIBELHEIMER. 1971. Five-year stability IQ's from language and nonlanguage group tests. *Child Development*, **42**: 645–649.

HOPKINS, K. D., and G. H. BRACHT. 1971. *IQ constancy and change—grades 1 through 11.* Research Paper No. 51. Boulder, Colo.: Laboratory of Educational Research.

HORN, J. L. 1967. Intelligence—why it grows, why it declines. *Trans-action*, **5** (1), pp. 23–31.

JENSEN, A. R. 1968. Social class, race, and genetics: Implications for education. *American Educational Research Journal*, **5**(1): 1–42.

————. 1969. How much can we boost IQ and scholastic achievement? *Harvard Educational Review*, **39**: 1–123. Reprinted in part in G. H. BRACHT, K. D. HOPKINS, and J. C. STANLEY. 1972. *Perspectives in educational and psychological measurement.* Englewood Cliffs, N. J.: Prentice-Hall, Inc., Selection 19.

McNEMAR, Q. 1964. Lost: Our intelligence. Why? *American Psychologist*, **19**: 871–882.

NELSON, M. J. 1969. Intelligence and special aptitude tests. In R. L. Ebel, ed., *Encyclopedia of educational research,*, 4th ed. New York: The Macmillan Company.

ROBERTSON, G. J. n.d. Innovations in the assessment of individual differences: Development of the first group mental ability test. *Normline*, **1**(2). New York: Harcourt Brace Jovanovich, Inc. Reprinted in part in G. H. BRACHT, K. D. HOPKINS, and J. C. STANLEY. 1972. *Perspectives in educational and psychological measurement.* Englewood Cliffs, N. J.: Prentice-Hall, Inc., Selection 18.

SEARS, R. R. 1957. L. M. Terman, pioneer in mental measurement. *Science*, **125**: 978–979.

TERMAN, L.M. 1954. The discovery and encouragement of exceptional talent. *American Psychologist*, **9**: 221–230.

THORNDIKE, R. L. 1963. Some methodological issues in the study of creativity. *Proceedings of the 1962 Invitational Conference on Testing Problems.* Princeton, N.J.: Educational Testing Service. Reprinted in part in G. H. BRACHT, K. D. HOPKINS, and J. C. STANLEY. 1972. *Perspectives in educational and psychological measurement.* Englewood Cliffs, N. J.: Prentice-Hall, Inc., Selection 21.

THURSTONE, L. L. 1927. A law of comparative judgment. *Psychological Review*, **24**: 273–286.

TUDDENHAM, R. D. 1969. Intelligence. In R. L. Ebel, ed., *Encyclopedia of educational research*, 4th ed. New York: The Macmillan Company, pp. 654–664.

WOODRING, P. 1966. Are intelligence tests unfair? *Saturday Review* (April 16), 79–80.

15

STANDARDIZED ACHIEVEMENT
TESTS

In Chapter 8 several distinctions were made between standardized and non-standardized tests. Standardized tests tend to be focused on broader, more general skills and kinds of information than would be included among the educational objectives of most school districts. Since they are ordinarily administered annually or even less frequently, standardized achievement tests must span a much wider range of content than almost any teacher-constructed tests. Teacher-made examinations should be given often to monitor pupil and class progress, to identify the need for remediation, to motivate students, and so on. Teacher-made tests are more specific; they usually reflect only the content of a particular unit or course.

Advantages of Standardized Tests

The norms provided by standardized tests offer a comparison with an external group; such comparison is critical for such purposes as quality control, curricular evaluation, counseling, and identifying exceptional students. External comparisons cannot be made readily with nonstandardized tests. Laymen often feel that the average percent correct on a test directly reflects the quality of teaching or learning; they fail to realize that a very poor teacher can construct a test so easy and nondiscriminating that almost all students will have perfect performance, even though they have learned little. An excellent teacher can develop a difficult and discriminating test on which the average score may be only 60 percent or less.

Standardized tests impose more restrictions than teacher-made tests. The prescribed directions, time limits, and other controls of standardized tests make the conditions under which the tests are taken *standard*; thus, they afford more meaningful bases for evaluating and comparing performance.

Reliability is another point of difference between standardized and locally constructed tests. Standardized tests are usually carefully developed and refined by item analysis so that every item is functioning appropriately, most intrinsic ambiguity is removed, and implausible distracters have been deleted; consequently, the reliability of most standardized tests is (and should be) greater than that of teacher-made tests. Some standardized ability tests are not highly reliable, but they are the exception rather than the rule. The number and frequency of teacher-made tests can compensate for the lack of high reliability for a single test. Although each of ten weekly quizzes may have a reliability of only .5, the reliability of scores summed over the ten measures may exceed .90 (see Spearman-Brown formula, p. 125).

It should be clear that teacher-made and standardized tests are partners rather than competitors. They serve somewhat different purposes and provide complementary information. Both kinds of test are necessary for adequate evaluation of educational achievement by individual pupils and schools.

Aptitude vs. Achievement Tests

Intelligence and aptitude tests are future-oriented—their focus is on subsequent performance. Achievement tests are past and present oriented—they register the degree of learning or achievement after instruction. Aptitude tests are designed to reflect potential; achievement tests depict present proficiency. A valid musical-aptitude test administered prior to music instruction should predict with some degree of accuracy performance on a music proficiency measure obtained *after* some period of instruction. Aptitude tests purport to indicate what a person *could learn*; achievement tests represent what a person *has learned*.

In practice this distinction is less clear-cut than we indicated above. Educational achievement tests predict subsequent achievement better than intelligence tests do (Bracht and Hopkins, 1970b). Intelligence tests reflect a great deal of educational achievement, such as vocabulary; and some achievement tests examine factors that are usually associated with intelligence, such as abstract reasoning and deductive and inductive logic.

Both aptitude and achievement tests reflect developed ability; the primary difference between them is largely in the nature of the test content and its level of generality. An implicit assumption in selecting an achievement test is that the examinees have been directly exposed to the concepts needed—the universe of content is defined specifically. An achievement test does not indicate how or why the student performs or does not perform, but it does represent his level of developed ability.

Anastasi (1968, p. 392) and Cronbach (1970, p. 282) present figures illustrating the concept of an achievement-aptitude continuum (see Figure 15–1). Existing tests of developed abilities can be ordered along this continuum. At one extreme are teacher-made tests covering highly specific and even idiosyn-

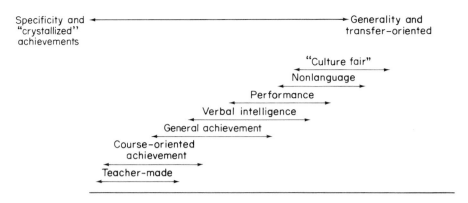

FIGURE 15–1 *Spectrum of tests of cognitive abilities.*

cratic content. Course-oriented general achievement tests are broader in objectives and content, but are more specific and more school-oriented than most verbal intelligence tests (such as the Stanford-Binet). Even more general are performance, nonlanguage, and "culture-fair" tests that may be administered to persons who are illiterate or who have language restrictions owing to physical or cultural factors.

In support of the continuum in Figure 15–1 are data showing that tests generally correlate most highly with their closest neighbors and progressively less as the separation increases. Some authorities maintain that standardized intelligence and achievement tests correlate so highly they are essentially parallel forms of measures of the same abilities. Kelley (1927) found (as have others, such as Coleman and Cureton, 1954) that correlation coefficients between certain achievement and intelligence measures were very high after allowance was made for errors of measurement (correcting for attenuation, p. 340). Kelley consequently warned of the "jangle fallacy," which is committed when one assumes that tests of different labels measure different abilities. He also coined the phrase "jingle fallacy"—the fallacy of assuming that tests with the same labels measure the same functions. For example, Hopkins, Dobson, and Oldridge (1962) found that a reading vocabulary test correlated as highly with a reading comprehension test as it did with another reading vocabulary test. It is essential that each test establish its own validity.

Figure 15–2 was constructed to illustrate the overlapping variance on well-constructed intelligence and achievement tests. Data are depicted here for two grade levels for verbal and nonverbal intelligence measures. The reliability coefficient of a test indicates what proportion of total variance is true variance —that is, is not error variance. The area depicting true variance is indicated by slanting lines. The crosshatched pattern shows the overlapping variance (r_{12}^2) for each set of tests. For example, the proportion of nonerror variance for the grade 3 tests was found to be .95, .91, and .85 for the verbal intelligence, reading, and arithmetic-concepts tests, respectively. The verbal intelligence test correlated .68 with the ITBS reading; thus, the overlapping (predictable) variance between the two tests was $(68)^2 = 46$ percent. Forty-six percent of the

362

variance of the verbal intelligence test is true (nonerror) and is not unique from the reading test.

Figures 15–1 and 15–2 illustrate that although there is a substantial relationship between the achievement and scholastic aptitude measures, they have considerable uniqueness. This could also be deferred from our discussion, in the preceding chapter, of the heritability of intelligence vs. achievement.

Content Validity

The principal validity for achievement tests is content validity, sometimes called content relevance. Does the test reflect the reading or arithmetic objectives at a given grade level? Does the math test reflect the related curriculum? Ideally, the items on an achievement test should be a representative but "miniature" sample of the content and process objectives of a curriculum. If a teacher assumes that the ABC and DEF arithmetic reasoning tests equally reflect his arithmetic reasoning objectives and are thus equally valid measures in his school district, he is guilty of the "jingle fallacy." Often tests with the same label differ greatly in content, the taxonomy levels represented by their items, the degree of speededness, and other important respects. Hopkins and Wilkerson (1965) showed that "parallel" forms within the same standardized achievement-test battery can have dramatically different content validities for a given curriculum, and that a school district's average on the test might differ by one-fifth of a grade equivalent (GE) depending on the particular form that was selected. Publishers of most current standardized achievement tests provide a classification of the skills and content assessed in their tests (see Figure 4–1, p. 103). This breakdown is especially useful in selecting tests for a particular school or school district.

A district's (or a pupil's) pattern of results from standardized tests is partially dependent on the test series being used. Several studies (Findley, 1963b; Stake, 1961; Taylor and Crandall, 1962) revealed that a district's average may vary as much as half a grade equivalent, depending on whether they use, for example, the *California Achievement Test* or the *Metropolitan Achievement Test*.

A portion of the disparity is attributable to differential content validity; that is, one test mirrors the district's objectives and instruction more accurately than another. Some of the disparity may result from differences in the definition of grade equivalents (GE). Some tests use medians, other tests use means to define GE's. When distributions are skewed, the mean and median will yield different "averages." In addition, in some tests "modal" norms have been used—norms based only on students who are of the modal or usual age for their grade. When the underaged and overaged pupils are eliminated from the norm group, the norms become more demanding because more students are nonpromoted than are double promoted, and the former tend to lower the average performance. Another reason for lack of interchangeability of norms on standardized tests is that the reference groups are never completely comparable. Many school districts refuse to permit publishers to use their pupils for norming purposes. For example, in the norming of a recent test, almost one-half of the school districts contacted refused to participate in the test's norming (Hopkins and

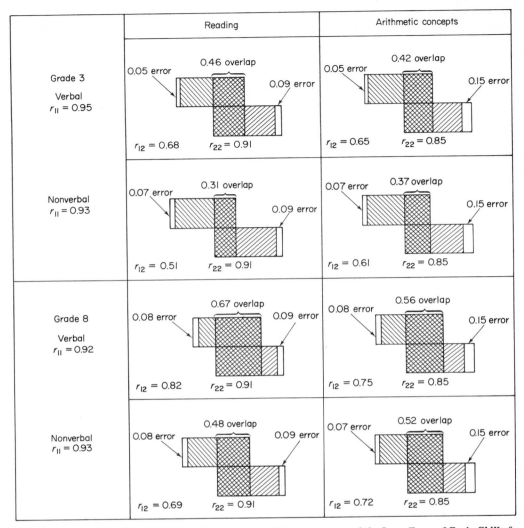

FIGURE 15–2 *Degree of overlapping variance on two achievement areas of the Iowa Tests of Basic Skills for both verbal and nonverbal intelligence (Lorge-Thorndike) tests at two grade levels. Diagrams depict data from the technical manuals for the Lorge-Thorndike Intelligence Tests (Lorge, Thorndike, and Hagen, 1966, pp. 11, 22) and the Iowa Tests of Basic Skills.*

Sander, 1966). The lack of equivalence in norming populations is one of the chief reasons that it is usually best to select a companion set of intelligence and achievement tests (tests normed on the same students) and to employ the same achievement-test series over several grade levels.

    Norming is the weakest link in standardized testing. There are, however, some promising developments on the horizon. Lord (1962a; Lord and Novick, 1968) has developed the theory and procedures by which, through item sampling, only a small portion of testing time is required in the norming process; that is, some students in a class take one short set of items while other students take other sets. Preliminary research on this topic is encouraging (Cook and Stufflebeam, 1967).

Standardized Achievement Tests

Several publishers are now furnishing normative data for individual items. This information has great value for evaluating the success of a class or district's instruction. Figure 15–3 illustrates an analysis of a class's results on a standardized language arts test. Notice that the percent correct for each item is given for the class and for the national norm group. In the class, 82 percent of the pupils used correct capitalization at the beginning of the sentence, whereas 77 percent of the pupils in the national norm group were correct on that question. Information such as that given in Figure 15–3 can help diagnose instructional and curricular weaknesses of a class, school, or school district and can also serve a quality-control function. Often, however, national norms are not the best comparison; norms based on subgroups more like the local system may be preferable.

SRA ACHIEVEMENT SERIES - ITEM ANALYSIS

LANGUAGE ARTS CAPITALIZATION-PUNC. GRAMMATICAL USAGE

SCHOOL | GRADE 3 | SEM 1 | DATE TESTED 10-10-68 | NORMS USED B | ACH BATTERY 3-4 | FORM C | NO. IN GROUP 34 | SRA REF. NO. 26145-008 03349 | PAGE NO. 1

CAPITALIZATION-PUNC. PAGE

ITEM DESCRIPTION	ITEM NUMBER	KEY	NUMBER RESPONDING CORRECTLY	GROUP	NAT'L
CAPITAL LETTER					
BEGINNING OF SENT	4	17 A	28	82	77
NAMES-PROPER NOUNS	3	3 A	26	76	73
	5	3 A	27	79	80
	8	8 B	27	79	67
		9 C	16	47	39
IN FRIENDLY LETTERS	5	2 C	32	94	86
		19 B	25	74	63
IN TITLES	6	4 B	23	68	56
	8	7 B	23	68	57
BEGIN OF DIRECT QUOTE	6	11 B	15	44	48
	8	1 C	9	26	24
IMPROPER NOUNS	6	17 A	24	71	54
		7 B	12	35	42
	8	13 B	9	26	38
PERIOD					
END OF SENTENCE	4	5 C	16	47	42
	5	11 C	13	38	38
	7	14 B	25	74	61
AFTER ABBREVIATION	5	8 B	18	53	40
	8	12 A	17	50	44
QUESTION MARK-QUOTE	6	20 A	15	44	42
COMMA					
FOLLOWING SALUTATION	5	15 B	23	68	59
	8	3 B	24	71	55
COMPLIMENTARY CLOSE	5	10 B	13	38	39
	8	14 C	16	47	38
IN DATES	4	15 C	10	29	47
	5	1 A	24	71	54
		14 B	23	68	34
SEPARATE CITY-STATE	5	9 C	18	53	34
WORDS IN SERIES	6	3 A	18	53	40
	7	5 C	9	26	23
IN DIRECT QUOTATION	4	2 A	23	68	53
	6	6 C	18	22	
IN DIRECT ADDRESS	5	7 B	8	24	33
	7	8 B	17	50	48
	8	10 C	8	24	18

CAPITALIZATION-PUNC. PAGE — COMMA

ITEM DESCRIPTION	ITEM NUMBER	KEY	NUMBER RESPONDING CORRECTLY	GROUP	NAT'L
SUBORDINATE CLAUSE	6	9 A	19	56	46
		18 B	18	53	48
	7	3 C	9	26	25
		7 A	20	59	43
CO-ORDINATE CLAUSE	8	6 C	8	24	21
NONRESTRICTIVE CLAUSE	6	12 B	22	65	46
	7	9 B	20	59	52
INTRODUCTORY ADVERBS	6	15 B	20	59	46
	7	4 A	10	29	23
		11 A	14	41	30
APOSTROPHE					
IN CONTRACTIONS	3	5 C	4	12	19
		13 C	15	44	54
	4	6 B	24	71	66
	5	18 B	32	94	81
SHOWING POSSESSION	3	10 A	24	71	52
		12 B	25	74	68
	4	10 C	24	71	48
		16 B	29	85	65
	7	12 A	17	50	37
	8	4 B	26	76	57
QUOTATION MARKS	7	2 B	12	35	35
		6 C	8	24	22
EXCLAMATION POINT	8	11 B	18	53	51
GRAMMATICAL USAGE					
CORRECT TENSE	3	9 B	30	88	83
	4	7 C	22	65	61
	6	1 C	20	59	46
SUBJECT-VERB AGREEMT	3	2 B	31	91	81
		8 A	30	88	63
	5	12 A	33	97	75
		16 A	31	91	69
	6	6 B	7	21	34

GRAMMATICAL USAGE PAGE

ITEM DESCRIPTION	ITEM NUMBER	KEY	NUMBER RESPONDING CORRECTLY	GROUP	NAT'L
PROBLEM VERBS	3	1 A	27	79	68
		4 C	29	85	61
		6 B	28	82	62
		11 B	26	76	77
		15 A	23	68	51
		17 B	15	47	59
	4	1 B	24	71	54
		4 B	22	65	55
		11 B	27	79	73
		12 C	13	38	27
		13 B	19	56	48
		14 A	20	59	46
	5	5 A	29	85	82
		13 A	32	94	74
		17 B	15	44	52
	6	2 C	25	75	59
		7 B	20	59	56
		10 B	30	88	69
	7	10 C	12	35	29
		13 A	9	26	23
	8	2 C	11	32	39
CHOICE OF PRONOUN	5	4 B	30	88	80
	6	5 A	27	79	69
		8 B	5	15	14
PROBLEM WORDS	3	14 B	29	85	79
		16 A	15	44	59
	4	8 A	30	88	78
		9 B	20	59	51
	5	6 B	17	50	44
	8	5 B	20	59	59
HOMONYMS	3	7 C	17	50	55
	4	3 B	24	71	62
	6	13 A	20	59	48
		14 B	11	32	43
DOUBLE NEGATIVE	6	19 A	4	12	16

SRA Science Research Associates, Inc., 259 East Erie Street, Chicago, Illinois 60611
A Subsidiary of IBM

FIGURE 15–3   A sample report of class performance on each item of a standardized language-arts test, together with national norms for each item. (Reproduced by permission of the publisher, Science Research Associates Copyright © 1967 by Science Research Associates, Inc.)

School vs. Individual Norms

Some tests provide school norms as well as individual student norms. Figure 15–4 shows the difference in the distributions of school averages vs. individual pupil scores. Notice that a score of 15 on the test has a percentile rank of about 76 in the student distribution but a PR of about 99 in terms of school averages; in other words nearly 27 students in 100 earn a score of 15 or more, whereas only one school in 100 has an average of 15 or more. School norms are less valuable than individual norms, but they can complement the individual information when interpreted properly.

Chapter 17 gives guidelines for selecting standardized tests for a school's testing program. In addition to the logical relevance of the items and other technical considerations, one should appraise the kinds of service available, time lag between testing and results, and the types of student and class report.

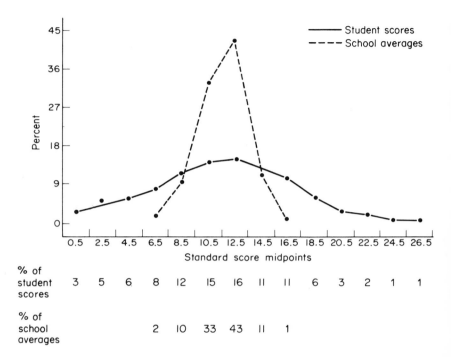

FIGURE 15–4   *Differences between school average percentiles and student percentiles. (Reproduced by permission of the publisher, Science Research Associates. Copyright © 1967 by Science Research Associates, Inc.)*

Interpreting Grade Equivalents

The use of grade-equivalent (GE) norms is perhaps the most common method for reporting results on standardized achievement tests. To interpret GE scores properly one must understand how the grade equivalents are established. How can a third-grade child earn a reading score of 8.0 on a test? Interpolation and extrapolation are two procedures used in the determination of grade equivalents.

Suppose that in the standardization process, a reading test is given during September to students in grades 4, 5, and 6. The means (or medians) for each grade level are determined; suppose the raw-score means were 55, 65, and 70. The respective grade equivalents corresponding to these three scores would be 4.0, 5.0, and 6.0. How does one obtain a GE of 4.5? The difference in the raw-score means of 4.0 and 5.0 is arbitrarily divided into tenths; each tenth corresponds to a GE of .1. A raw score of 60 would yield a GE of 4.5; a score of 68 would yield a GE of 5.6.

This interpolation procedure assumes a constant rate of growth throughout the year. Beggs and Hieronymus (1968) showed that this assumption only roughly approximates the true growth curves in various achievement areas. There are such marked discrepancies in arithmetic over the summer (Bernard, 1966) that the same group may average .5 GE less in September than it did the previous June! The same phenomenon, of course, would result whether GE, percentiles, or stanines were used for describing performance. The safest procedure to prevent interpolation artifacts from contaminating the meaning of scores from standardized achievement tests is to administer the tests during the same period in the school year that was employed in the standardization process.

For some tests the norms were empirically determined at the beginning, middle, and end of the school year so interpolation artifacts are minimal. Norms for other tests were established from a single administration period during the school year; hence, they must rely more heavily on the validity of the interpolation process.

Extrapolation can result in even greater errors in the interpretation of individual scores than does interpolation. Extrapolation is the most common method for establishing GE values at grade levels outside the range of grades to which the test was actually administered. In our interpolation example we gave raw-score means of 55, 65, and 70 for the standardization sample at grades 4.0, 5.0, and 6.0, respectively. Figure 15–5 illustrates the extrapolation and interpolation processes.

Extrapolation is simply a projection of the average performance at some grade levels from the performance of pupils at certain other grade levels. The trend at grades 4, 5, and 6 lead one to assume the mean score at grade 7 would be approximately 73; hence, a score of 73 would receive a GE of 7.0. Similarly a score of 40 might be predicted to correspond to the average performance at grade 3. Extrapolation is obviously a risky process. As the GE values extend beyond the grades actually sampled during the norming, their credibility is lessened. Figure 15–6 is taken from the technical manual of a widely used standardized achievement battery. Notice that all GE values below 4.6 and above 9.6 were extrapolated; thus scores below 4.6 and above 9.6 must be interpreted with great caution. Fortunately there is a salutary trend in test norming to administer a test above and below the actual grade levels for which it was designed; this procedure allows a much stronger basis for attaching meaning to the GE scores. Even with this procedure, extreme GE scores in relation to a pupil's present grade level must be interpreted with caution. A third-grade pupil and a seventh-grade pupil who received GE scores of 5.0 on an arithmetic test would obtain the same raw score, but they would probably obtain them via different routes and have different arithmetic skills. The same caution applies to age scales, such as mental age.

A distinct advantage of GE scores is that they help teachers to realize the true magnitude of individual differences within a single grade level. Figure 15–7 depicts the actual distribution of performance for grades 2.6 through 10.6. Note the very large degree of overlap—about one-sixth of third-grade students are performing better than the average student at grade 4. Note also that the variability in achievement increases with each successive grade level. This is true in all achievement areas and is to be expected because the standard deviation of mental ages increases each year until maturity.

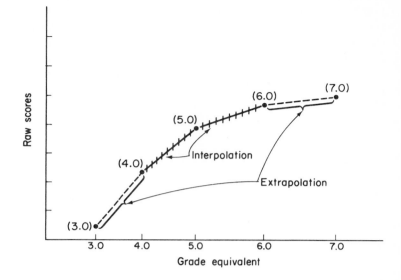

FIGURE 15–5 *Illustration of Interpolation and Extrapolation in establishing grade-equivalent norms.*

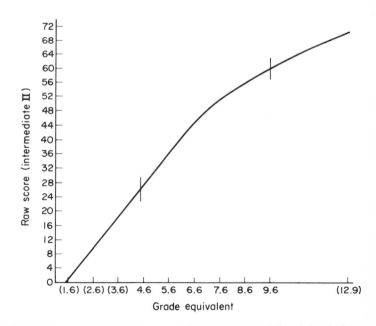

FIGURE 15–6 *Grade norm line—social studies. Values below 4.6 and above 9.6 are extrapolations. (Reproduced from* Stanford Achievement Test, Technical Supplement *[New York: Harcourt Brace Jovanovich, Inc.], Fig. 10, p. 13, by special permission of the publisher. Copyright © 1964–1966 by Harcourt Brace Jovanovich, Inc.)*

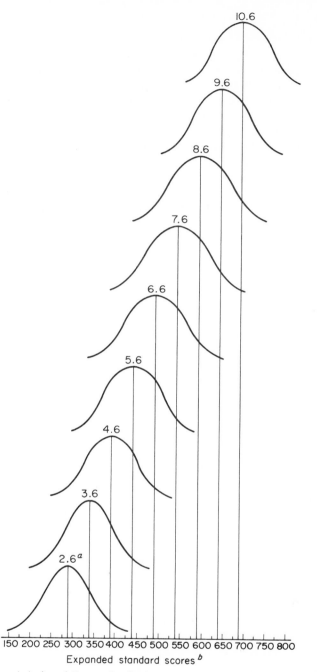

150 200 250 300 350 400 450 500 550 600 650 700 750 800

Expanded standard scores [b]

[a]Test administered during sixth month of school year; grade equivalents of corresponding standard scores are given above the mean of each curve.

[b]Scale employs a mean of 600 and a standard deviation of 100 at grade 10.1

FIGURE 15–7 *An illustration of the great degree of overlap in pupils' achievement performance among grade levels. (Note that approximately one-sixth of grade 2 students [that is, @2.6] received better scores than one-half of grade 3 students [that is, @3.6]. Similarly, approximately one-sixth of grade 3 students received lower scores than one-half of the students in grade 2.) (Reproduced from Technical Memo, January 1969, Expanded Standard Score Scale used in the CTBS, p. 8, by permission of the publisher, CTB/McGraw-Hill, Monterey, California.)*

Grade equivalents can easily be misinterpreted by parents. "If my third-grade child is reading 4.0, why shouldn't he be promoted to grade four?" Parents are unaware of the large degree of individual differences within a given grade as shown in Figure 15–7; thus they do not realize that such a "good" showing on the test will be made by 15 to 20 percent of the pupils in the same third-grade class, or even more in schools where the verbal aptitude is above average. Despite their technical flaws, percentile ranks are probably the preferred method of reporting achievement and aptitude test results to parents.

Another problem with GE scores is that the standard deviations in GE units are not the same for all curricular areas. For example, Table 15–1 shows the standard deviations on the *Iowa Tests of Basic Skills* (ITBS) at grades 3, 5, and 8. Note that these GE scores become more variable with each successive

TABLE 15–1

Standard Deviations in Grade Equivalents for Various Subjects on the Iowa Test of Basic Skills at Grades 3, 5, and 8 (data from the Test Manual)

Type of Test	Grade Level		
	3	5	8
Vocabulary	1.1	1.4	2.0
Reading	1.0	1.4	1.9
Spelling	1.2	1.6	2.2
Language Total	1.1	1.4	2.0
Work-Study Total	.9	1.2	1.8
Arithmetic Total	.8	1.1	1.7
Composite	.9	1.2	1.7

grade. The variability in spelling, reading, vocabulary, and language is consistently larger than that for work-study skills and arithmetic. If a child in grade 3 (3.0) was at the 98th percentile on all tests of the ITBS, his GE scores would vary from about 5.4 for spelling to 4.6 for arithmetic. If the corresponding percentile ranks are reported along with GE's, the chances of misinterpreting them are reduced.

Flanagan (1951, pp. 712–713) summarized the role of GE scores:

> In spite of their many limitations, they [grade equivalents] probably represent the best of available methods for rendering scores "comparable" for elementary school achievement tests. . . . To date the consensus seems to be in favor of the use of grade equivalent scales below grade eight, and some type of [standard score] in high school and college.

The lack of continuity in subject matter after grade 8 is a major reason that the logical meaning of GE scores is greatly reduced beyond that grade. There is little growth in certain basic skills during the high-school grades; consequently, a small increment in performance often results in a large gain in grade-placement units. For example, a GE of 10.7 on the *Comprehensive Tests of Basic Skills*, Language-Mechanics test, corresponds to a raw score of 18, but a GE of 11.9 corresponds to a raw score of 19. This correspondence reflects the smallness of the typical improvement in the eleventh grade of the type of language mechanics measured by this test.

Some standardized tests are accompanied by "expanded standard score scales" that are particularly useful for sequentially evaluating pupil and school growth across several years. These are continuous scales that span several levels of a test. Figure 15–8 illustrates the growth curves of a group and of a student from grade 2 to grade 12. Notice that at grade 8 the student begins to fall behind his class in performance. This type of report is particularly valuable in evaluating an individual's or group's progress.

Diagnostic Use of Test Results

One of the chief uses of standardized achievement and intelligence tests is to identify students who need special attention. Dual standardization is very common today—students in the norming population are given both a battery of achievement tests and a scholastic aptitude test. It is then possible to compare a student's achievement with that of pupils at his grade level and of his same measured scholastic aptitude. His "expectancy" or "anticipated achievement" can be approached empirically. This method of identifying underachieving pupils is far superior to that of comparing a student's percentile ranks on an intelligence test with those on an achievement test—a procedure that will always "find" a large proportion of bright students to be "underachieving" and a corresponding proportion of students with low IQ's achieving "well" in relation to their aptitude. Comparing percentile ranks fails to acknowledge the universal regression effect (Hopkins, 1969).

Figure 15–9 depicts a standard report form for Ann Roberts, who has taken the *Comprehensive Tests of Basic Skills* during the first month of grade 5 (5.1). Raw scores (RS), grade equivalents (GE), anticipated achievement grade equivalents (AAGE), and the national percentile ranks corresponding to the raw scores are given for several achievement areas. The profile chart shows the range within which Ann's true score is likely to lie (her score $\pm$ one standard error of measurement). This chart helps to prevent undue confidence in obtained scores, and encourages the viewing of a score as a band rather than as a precise point.

Ann's raw score of 26 on the reading vocabulary test corresponded to a GE score of 5.1 and a percentile rank of 52. The profile chart shows that her *true* percentile rank is probably (68 percent confidence interval) somewhere between 40 and 63. The AAGE of 5.5 is the average score of students of Ann's grade, age, and CTMM IQ. The "Difference" column for reading vocabulary is blank, which indicates that there is no statistically significant (or reliable) difference between her performance in reading vocabulary and that of other students of the same grade, age, and CTMM IQ.

Ann had an outstanding performance in spelling (8.4); her obtained GE score was three full grade equivalents above her AAGE. Perhaps she needs to devote more attention to arithmetic, in which she is achieving 1.4 GE's below other students of her age, grade, and scholastic aptitude.

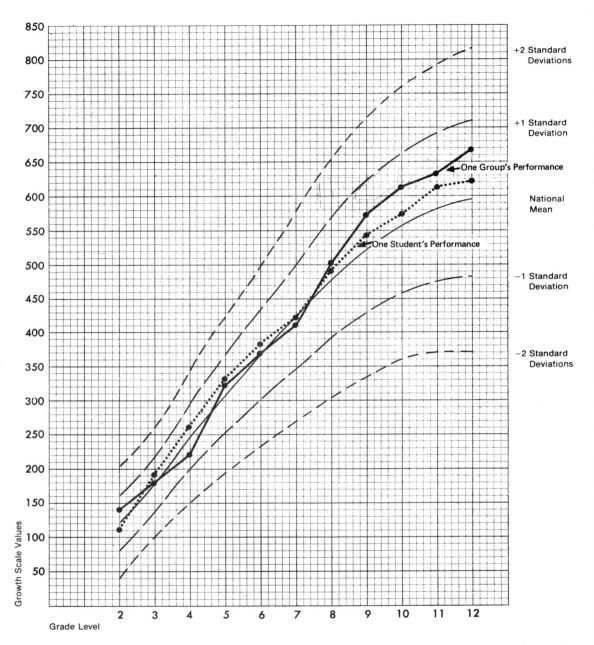

FIGURE 15–8 *Growth curves for one class and one student in the class for grades 2 through 12. Individual growth-scale curves allow a student's performance to be compared both in relation to his group's performance and in relation to national performance. (Reproduced by permission of the publisher, Science Research Associates. Copyright © 1967 by Science Research Associates, Inc.)*

The bottom portion of the CTBS individual test record shows Ann's performance on each item. Her deficiency in arithmetic computation is rather general; she lacks mastery of all basic operations. She appears to be especially

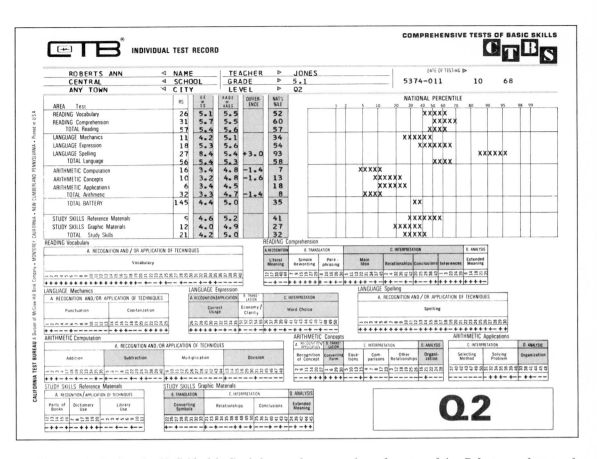

FIGURE 15-9 Sample of individual feedback form used to report the performance of Ann Roberts on a battery of standardized achievement tests. (Reproduced from Individual Test Record for CTBS by permission of the publisher, CTB/McGraw-Hill, Monterey, California.)

lacking in ability to interpret and analyze arithmetic concepts. Ann appears to need a general remedial program in arithmetic. If her CTMM IQ had been lower, for example 80, her arithmetic performance would have been commensurate with her AAGE. If her IQ had been 130, all AAGE values would have increased substantially.

The report of a student's performance in such a complete and explicit form has become feasible only since computers became part of the test scoring and reporting process. This kind of report is more valuable than the typical report of the past, which would have given only the student's IQ, GE scores, and, perhaps, corresponding percentile ranks.

Another illustration of a test report form is given in Figure 15–10, in which an examinee's performance on several tests is shown. Also his achievement levels are compared with those of other students of the same measured aptitude. The results of the student's verbal and numerical aptitude tests appear in the first two columns. His performance on eight subtests of the *Stanford*

APTITUDE—ACHIEVEMENT COMPARISON PROFILE

NAME **DOE, JOHN**   GRADE **7**   SCHOOL **PLEASANT HIGH**   DATE **4-71**

TESTS **JSAT-STANFORD ACH. ADV.**   TEACHER **MRS. BRETNALL**

	APT T1	APT T2	ACH T1	ACH T2	ACH T3	ACH T4	ACH T5	ACH T6	ACH T7	ACH T8	ACH T9	ACH T10	ACH T11
	VERBAL	NUM.	P.MEAN.	SPELL.	LANG.	AR.COM	AR.CON	AR.APP	SOC.ST.	SCIENCE	BAT.MD.		
STANDARD SCORE 1	70	50	80	76	68	33	62	66	67	51	63		

SCALE	VERBAL	NUM.	P.MEAN.	SPELL.	LANG.	AR.COM	AR.CON	AR.APP	SOC.ST.	SCIENCE	BAT.MD.		
97-99													
94-96													
91-93													
88-90													
85-87													
82-84													
79-81			++										
76-78			++	EE									
73-75			++	EE									
70-72	**		++	EE									
67-69	**		++	EE	EE				EE				
64-66	**		++	EE	EE		EE	EE	EE				
61-63	**		++	EE	EE		EE	EE	EE		EE		
58-60	**		++	EE	EE		EE	EE	EE		EE		
55-57	**		++	EE	EE		EE	EE	EE		EE		
52-54	**		++	EE	EE		EE	EE	EE		EE		
49-51	**	**	++	EE	EE		EE	EE	EE	EE	EE		
46-48	**	**	++	EE	EE		EE	EE	EE	EE	EE		
43-45	**	**	++	EE	EE		EE	EE	EE	EE	EE		
40-42	**	**	++	EE	EE		EE	EE	EE	EE	EE		
37-39	**	**	++	EE	EE		EE	EE	EE	EE	EE		
34-36	**	**	++	EE	EE		EE	EE	EE	EE	EE		
31-33	**	**	++	EE	EE	--	EE	EE	EE	EE	EE		
28-30	**	**	++	EE	EE	--	EE	EE	EE	EE	EE		
25-27	**	**	++	EE	EE	--	EE	EE	EE	EE	EE		
22-24	**	**	++	EE	EE	--	EE	EE	EE	EE	EE		
19-21	**	**	++	EE	EE	--	EE	EE	EE	EE	EE		
16-18	**	**	++	EE	EE	--	EE	EE	EE	EE	EE		
13-15	**	**	++	EE	EE	--	EE	EE	EE	EE	EE		
10-12	**	**	++	EE	EE	--	EE	EE	EE	EE	EE		
7-9	**	**	++	EE	EE	--	EE	EE	EE	EE	EE		
4-6	**	**	++	EE	EE	--	EE	EE	EE	EE	EE		
1-3	**	**	++	EE	EE	--	EE	EE	EE	EE	EE		

1 MEAN = 50; STANDARD DEVIATION = 21
*LEVEL OF APTITUDE PERFORMANCE

+ ACHIEVEMENT PERFORMANCE EXCEEDS LEVEL EXPECTED ON BASIS OF APTITUDE PERFORMANCE
− ACHIEVEMENT PERFORMANCE IS BELOW LEVEL EXPECTED ON BASIS OF APTITUDE PERFORMANCE
E ACHIEVEMENT PERFORMANCE IS EQUAL TO LEVEL EXPECTED ON BASIS OF APTITUDE PERFORMANCE

95% LEVEL OF CONFIDENCE

FIGURE 15–10   *Test report form that indicates performance levels and achievement in relation to aptitude.* (Reprinted from H. J. Clawar, An aptitude-achievement comparison profile, Measurement and Evaluation in Guidance, 1969, 2(1): 51, by permission of the author and the American Personnel and Guidance Association. Copyright © 1969 by the American Personnel and Guidance Association.)

Achievement Tests as well as the median on the entire battery are represented by bar graphs composed of EE's, + +'s, or − −'s; these indicate whether his scores are at, above, or below the normal (expected) range of achievement in relation to his aptitude scores. From Figure 15–10 it is obvious that the student performed significantly better than his ability peers in the Paragraph Meaning test, but he was underachieving in arithmetic computation. In all of the other tests his achievement was commensurate with his aptitude. This kind of test

374

reporting should greatly reduce over- and underinterpretation of standardized test results.

Special Problems in Standardized Testing in the Elementary Grades

A test cannot be content-valid unless the items are a representative sample of the curricular objectives and instruction. However, in certain curricular areas such as reading, a common core and sequence of instruction have emerged; in some other curricular areas no such uniform core or sequence exists. This phenomenon is particularly apparent in social studies and science, where great differences in the content and instructional approaches occur among states, districts, and even among schools within a district. These curricular differences have created critical problems in developing content-valid standardized measures for these areas. The approach taken by test publishers has been to emphasize processes and to minimize the emphasis on specific knowledge content—especially for social studies. Standardized tests in science and social studies consequently may not measure some important curricular objectives for a district, school, or class. When interpreting the results from standardized tests, this factor must be considered.

A standardized test designed for a particular grade level sometimes is inappropriate in difficulty for a given school, class, or pupil. If the average IQ score of a fourth-grade class is 85 or 90, more valid scores will result if the class is given the level of the test designed for grade 3 students. When a test is too difficult for a class or a given student, gambling, speed-vs.-accuracy response styles, and chance can result in invalid and misleading scores. A child can receive a near-average score on a standardized test without even reading the items on the test, but by guessing "blindly" on all questions (Hopkins, 1964; Swan and Hopkins, 1965).

The user of standardized tests must realize that the entire educational story is not represented by the results from these tests. For example, only one of the widely used batteries of standardized tests measures the important educational skill of listening. Standardized test data are important, but they remain only major "fragments of the picture."

Special Problems in Standardized Testing in High School

From elementary to high school the nature of the curriculum changes radically. In the elementary grades the curriculum is quite similar for all pupils, but at the high-school level considerable "branching" occurs. There is considerable flexibility even in college-preparatory programs. The common curriculum for all high-school students has virtually disappeared. This is a major reason that there is little meaning in grade-equivalent units for most content areas after grade 8 or 9.

Two approaches have been initiated for the problem of standardized testing in the secondary schools. One approach is represented by the widely used *Iowa Tests of Educational Development* (ITED). The ITED has nine *process-*

oriented tests designed to measure *processes* and *skills* in using information. Thus, testing of specific information is minimized because there is no uniform universe of curricular content. The ITED are general education tests. They predict subsequent performance on the College Board examinations and academic success in college quite well. The nine tests in the ITED battery are:

1. Understanding of basic social concepts
2. Background in the natural sciences
3. Correctness and appropriateness of expression
4. Ability to do quantitative thinking
5. Ability to interpret reading materials in the social studies
6. Ability to interpret reading materials in the natural sciences
7. Ability to interpret literary materials
8. General vocabulary
9. Uses of sources of information

The test titles indicate the global nature and process orientation of the ITED measures. The *general* nature of the tests is a two-edged sword. The ITED do not presuppose a fixed set of courses for the examinees; nevertheless, the general nature of the examinations severely limits their value for the evaluation of the quality of learning and instruction in specific courses such as Algebra I, American History, or Chemistry.

The second approach to standardized testing at the high-school level offers tailor-made tests for specific courses and subjects. These tests are less general and more content-oriented than the ITED tests. Examples of such tests are: the *Nelson Biology Tests, MLA Cooperative Foreign Language Tests, Lankton First-Year Algebra Test, Cooperative English Test, Anderson-Fisk Chemistry Test, Crary American History Test,* and *College Entrance Examination Board achievement test.*[1]

The two approaches can be used so they are mutually complementary. The course-oriented examinations are of greater value in identifying specific weaknesses in a particular curriculum. They offer the teacher useful feedback on his teaching success because norms on an external reference group are available. The general achievement tests are better as a *general* educational quality-control measure; they are not of great value in identifying specific educational deficiencies in a student or a curriculum. Because the ITED are process-oriented and require reasoning and interpretation, they reflect general intelligence to a greater extent than do subject-oriented tests.

Achievement Stability

Although considerable attention has been given to the issue of IQ stability, the related phenomenon of stability and change in scholastic attainment

---

[1] There is a corresponding set of standardized subject examinations for college courses, used primarily to give persons who have acquired their education by unconventional means a chance to receive advanced placement and college credit at many colleges. Tests are available in American Government, General Psychology, Geology, Western Civilization, and several other subjects (see College Entrance Examination Board, 1968b).

has been essentially ignored (Bloom, 1964). Do "slow starters" continue to have ignition trouble, or do they "mature" and eventually achieve normally? Are early differences in achievement only the result of age or maturational differences that eventually disappear? Do children who achieve poorly in the early grades continue to be poor achievers? In other words, "How stable is academic achievement?" Bracht and Hopkins (1970b) studied a large number of children who were given standardized achievement tests during grades 1–7, 9, and 11. They found a high degree of stability and predictability in general academic achievement. The findings indicate that for most pupils the initial success or failure in grade 1 is not likely to represent a temporary pattern or developmental stage. However, a small percentage of individual pupils may make radical changes in their achievement level just as some do with IQ, as discussed in Chapter 14.

General academic achievement at the grade 1 level correlates above .6 with general academic achievement ten years ater. By grade 3 the relationship is increased to about .75, and by the end of the elementary-school period a further increase to above .8 is observed.

Post-organizer

Standardized achievement tests tend to be more general in scope, more process-oriented, and less content-oriented than teacher-made tests. The norms on standardized tests usually offer a comparison with a nationally representative sample of students at the same grade levels and in the same courses.

There is no discrete point at which a test measures intelligence and no longer measures achievement. Intelligence tests are general achievement tests, but they represent an even broader type of achievement than standardized achievement tests do. Although there is considerable overlap between intelligence and achievement tests, each is usually sufficiently unique to justify its use.

Achievement tests with the same label may differ substantially in what they actually measure (see jingle fallacy). Conversely, tests with differing titles may measure little that is unique (see jangle fallacy).

Tests should be selected for a district's testing program only after careful study of the content validity of the available tests and batteries.

It is generally preferable to use a scholastic aptitude test and an achievement battery that have been standardized on the same students so aptitude-achievement comparisons can be made with less error.

The presenting of normative data for each item—a trend among test publishers—promises to be of much greater diagnostic value than the reporting only of total scores.

Grade equivalents are useful units for reporting test results below grade 8 or 9. The reporting of GE scores should be supplemented by standard scores or percentile ranks. The latter are most useful in reporting to parents. Extrapolation of norms attenuates the meaning that can be attached to GE scores that deviate greatly from a pupil's present grade level. Interpolation of norms also creates serious problems in curricular evaluation. For norms to have their clearest meaning, tests should be administered at the same time in the school year that was used in the norming process.

The lack of a uniform, sequential curriculum in certain subject-matter areas restricts the content validity of standardized measures in those areas. Measurements in social studies and science are particularly affected by this problem in the elementary grades.

SUGGESTED READINGS

BEGGS, D. L., and A. N. HIERONYMUS. 1968. Uniformity of growth in the basic skills throughout the school year and during the summer. *Journal of Educational Measurement*, **5**: 91–97.

BLOOM, B. S. 1964. Stability of achievement data. In *Stability and change in human characteristics*. New York: John Wiley & Sons, Inc., Chap. 4, pp. 95–131.

BRACHT, G. H., and K. D. HOPKINS. 1970. Stability of general academic achievement. Paper presented at the annual meeting of the National Council on Measurement in Education, Minneapolis, March, 1970. Reprinted in G. H. Bracht, K. D. Hopkins, and J. C. Stanley. 1972. *Perspectives in educational and psychological measurement*. Englewood Cliffs, N.J.: Prentice-Hall, Inc., Selection 25.

COFFMAN, W. E. 1969. Achievement tests. In R. L. Ebel, ed., *Encyclopedia of educational research*, 4th ed. New York: The Macmillan Company, pp. 7–17.

COX, R. C., and B. G. STERRETT. 1970. A model for increasing the meaning of standardized test scores. *Journal of Educational Measurement*, **7**: 227–228. Reprinted in G. H. Bracht, K. D. Hopkins, and J. C. Stanley. 1972. *Perspectives in educational and psychological measurement*. Englewood Cliffs, N.J.: Prentice-Hall, Inc., Selection 23.

EBEL, R. L. 1961. Standardized achievement tests: Uses and limitations. *National Elementary School Principal*, **40**: 29–32.

———. 1962. Content standard test scores. *Educational and Psychological Measurement*, **22**: 15–25.

———. 1970. Knowledge vs. ability in achievement testing. *Proceedings of the 1969 Invitational Conference on Testing Problems*. Princeton, N.J.: Educational Testing Service, pp. 66–76.

HOPKINS, K. D., and C. J. WILKERSON. 1965. Differential content validity: The California Spelling Test, an illustrative example. *Educational and Psychological Measurement*, **25**: 413–419.

KATZ, M. 1961. Selecting an achievement test: Principles and procedures. *Evaluation and Advisory Service Series*, No. 3, 2nd ed. Princeton, N.J.: Educational Testing Service.

LAVIN, D. E. 1967. *The prediction of academic performance*. New York: John Wiley & Sons, Inc.

Research on relationship of academic success and cognitive, personality, and sociological factors is presented.

LENNON, R. T. 1956. Assumptions underlying the use of content validity. *Educational and Psychological Measurement*, **16**: 294–304.

LESSINGER, L. M. 1970. Accountability in public education. *Proceedings of the 1969 invitational conference on testing problems.* Princeton, N.J.: Educational Testing Service, pp. 109–111. Reprinted in G. H. Bracht, K. D. Hopkins, and J. C. Stanley. 1972. *Perspectives in educational and psychological measurement.* Englewood Cliffs, N.J.: Prentice-Hall, Inc., Selections 26 and 27.

OKADA, T., W. M. COHEN, and G. W. MAYESKE. 1969. *Growth in achievement for different racial, regional and socio-economic groupings of students.* Technical Paper Number 1, May 16th. Office of Program Planning and Evaluation, Division of Elementary and Secondary Programs. Washington, D. C.: Office of Education U. S. Department of Health, Education and Welfare.

SEIBEL, D. W. 1968. Measurement of aptitude and achievement. Chapter 8 in D. K. Whitla, ed., *Handbook of measurement and assessment in behavioral sciences.* Reading, Mass.: Addison-Wesley Publishing Company, Inc., pp. 261–314.

STAKE, R. E., and J. T. HASTINGS. 1964. Review of the Stanford Achievement Battery, 1964. *Personnel and Guidance Journal*, **43**: 178–184. Reprinted in G. H. Bracht, K. D. Hopkins, and J. C. Stanley, 1972. *Perspectives in educational and psychological measurement.* Englewood Cliffs, N. J.: Prentice-Hall, Inc. Selection 24.

16

INTEREST, PERSONALITY, AND SOCIAL MEASUREMENT

In Chapter 12 we discussed informal methods of affective measurement; there also are many published measures of personal and social characteristics. Their principal use in schools is in vocational counseling, where interests and personality as well as aptitudes and abilities are important considerations.

Standardized measures of affective characteristics should not be administered by the classroom teacher unless he has had special training; the dangers and likelihood of misinterpreting them, especially the personality inventories, are much greater than with standardized ability tests. If a teacher has some general understanding of measures of typical performance, however, he can work more effectively with his colleagues who are counselors or school psychologists.

Many high-school and college students who are anxious to know more about themselves so they can better define their academic or vocational futures have become familiar with self-report interest inventories. A student wants to know what kind of vocational activities he finds most appealing. Are his scientific interests stronger than his literary interests? Is the pattern of his interests similar to that of school teachers, chemists, automobile mechanics, or forest rangers? These are the kinds of question interest inventories can help answer.

Vocational Interest Inventories

The first systematic effort to measure interests appears to have been made in 1915 at the Carnegie Institute of Technology, where James Miner developed a questionnaire to assist students in their vocational choices. Giant steps forward   *380* in interest appraisal were taken in 1927 when Strong published the first edition of his *Vocational Interest Blank* (SVIB) and in 1939 when Kuder made available the initial form of the *Kuder Preference Record* (KPR). Buros (1965) cited approximately 50 different published measures of vocational interests, but the SVIB and the KPR have dominated the field for many years.

STRONG VOCATIONAL INTEREST BLANK

The Strong inventory was designed to distinguish successful men in a given occupational group from men in general. Strong thought that the interests typical of any one occupational group would differ from a people-in-general group and at least a little from any other occupational group. He collected 400 items in which an individual could indicate his interests and preferences in a wide range of activities, as well as indicate what *he himself* considered to be his present abilities. Instead of grouping items in similar-interest clusters and devising a number of scales as the KPR does, Strong simply gave the test to the members of many different occupational groups. For each occupational group he determined which items were chosen more (or less) frequently than they were by men in general. From these differences he derived empirically based scoring scales for each group. Consequently an individual taking the test can ascertain whether his interests resemble those of artists, architects, printers, morticians, and so on. Scoring scales have been developed for 55 occupations, from artist to production manager and from minister to real estate salesman. Strong was not prejudicial in choosing which items would make up each given scale; the *actual* interest choices of the different groups decided the weights of the items for each scale. The success and prestige of the SVIB is due to the extensive research involved in its formulation. It has few competitors. It is interesting that Kuder has adopted a rather similar scoring approach in the development of his second interest test, the *Kuder Preference Record—Occupational* (Form D).

Although examinees are asked to choose between competing occupations, most of the 399 items on the 1966 version of the SVIB require the individual to indicate his preference by marking a phrase *D* for "dislike," *I* for "indifferent," or *L* for "like," as in the following three artificial examples (not from the SVIB itself):

Moving a piano	*D I L*	
Multiplying one number by another	*D I L*	
Purchasing a new automobile	*D I L*	

How *should* successful computer programmers, say, respond to "Moving a piano"? We might make a shrewd guess that more programmers than men in general would mark it L, but only actual data will tell whether they in fact do. Each item is scored once for each occupational scale to which it contributes. Scoring weights are determined by the discrepancies between the markings of the occupational group and the group of men in general. In the computer-programmer scale, for example, a $+1$ weight for a response indicates that it occurs more frequently among computer programmers than among men in general, and a −1 weight indicates that it occurs less frequently. Responses that do not differentiate between computer programmers and men in general do not appear in the computer-programmer scale, regardless of how frequently they were chosen by computer programmers. An examinee's total raw score on each occupation scale is the sum of the +1 and −1 weights of his various responses. The raw scores for each scale are converted to T-scores (mean = 50, $\sigma = 10$). The SVIB must be scored separately for each occupation. A list of 55 occupations on which scales have been developed is shown in Figure 16–1. The use of the SVIB is illustrated in Figure 16–1 via the sample profile and case study taken from the manual (Strong and Campbell, 1966).

The shaded area shows the interquartile range (25–75 percentiles) of men in general. The four scales at the bottom of the interest profile in Figure 16–1 reflect Specialization Level (SL) (that is, generalist vs. specialist orientation); Occupation Level (OL) (that is, unskilled vs. professional interest pattern); Masculinity-Feminity (MF) (that is, female vs. male *interest* pattern, not virility); and the recently developed Academic Achievement (AACH) scale, which was developed by contrasting high and low academic achievers. This scale is related to grade-point average in high school and college (*r*'s are above .3), and to the highest academic degree an individual is apt to secure (Strong and Campbell, 1966, pp. 19–20).

The SVIB for men is generally considered to be superior in quality to the form for women, partly because it was prepared more carefully. For occupations in which women compete directly with men, it may be desirable to administer the men's form to women, rather than using the women's form.

When empirical or criterion keying is used, such as that on the SVIB discussed above, one must plan in advance to cross-validate the keying of the scales in order to determine whether he is doing more than merely capitalizing on the peculiar characteristics of the occupational samples he has drawn. This is especially important when the sample is small and/or the number of variables to be used is large. This might be done, for example, by initially securing 1,000 computer programmers and 1,000 men in general (see Figure 16–2). A random 500 of each group would be used to establish one set of weights for the items. These weights would then be tried on the other two 500's to see how well they "work." Similarly, weights might be obtained for the second two 500's and tried out on the first two 500's. For example, the validity of the AACH scale for predicting college grades fell from .52 to .36 on the cross-validation. The schematic illustration of such double cross-validation is shown in Figure 16–2. Further details are too complex to be included in this book (see Mosier, 1951; Katzell, 1951).

KUDER INTEREST INVENTORIES

There are two principal Kuder scales, the *Kuder Preference Record—Vocational* (KPR-V) and the *Kuder Preference Record—Occupational* (KPR-O).

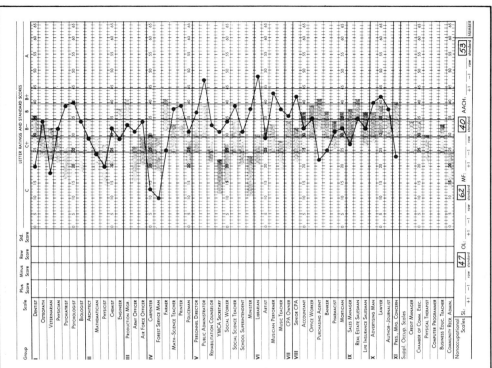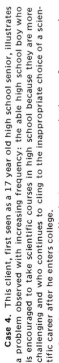

Case 4. This client, first seen as a 17 year old high school senior, illustrates a problem observed with increasing frequency: the able high school boy who is encouraged to take scientific courses in high school because they are more challenging and who continues to cling to the inappropriate choice of a scientific career after he enters college.

Case 4 was a somewhat effeminate young man who has an A— average in a large suburban high school, and who sought help in deciding whether to study aeronautical engineering or geology. He also wanted help in choosing between attending a large private university and a renowned institute of technology. He listed his hobbies as collecting stamps, old weapons, and antiques, and also writing. He was fond of science fiction and politics, and he belonged to several science clubs.

On a test of scholastic aptitude, he ranked in the upper 10 per cent of college freshmen, with slightly more ability, relative to other students, in the linguistic scores than in the quantitative scores. Other aptitude and achievement measures were high. On the SVIB he showed greatest strength in the social-science and verbal—linguistic occupations, and the profile gave no support to selecting a career in the natural sciences.

The counselor suggested that while he probably had the ability to pursue almost any academic field, the interest inventory results indicated that he likely would not be satisfied in any of the "hard" sciences.

The young man was advised to suspend judgment about a vocation, to give more consideration to social sciences and literary fields, He was encouraged by his high aptitude scores but distressed by the counselor's suggestions. He talked of the coming "space age" and seemed unable to relinquish a perception of himself as a rocket expert in an age when such men would have enormous prestige. After three interviews devoted to discussion of the tests and their implications, the client agreed to attend the university rather than the technological institute, but to major in engineering.

The client returned eighteen months later, reporting that he had spent a year studying engineering but that he had not done well in mathematics and was disappointed in the field. He wondered if he might not switch to some mathematical science. The counselor encouraged further exploration, including the social sciences.

Although the client was not seen again, he ultimately changed to a major in political science. His name frequently appeared in the campus newspaper as president of the student union and as a leader of a local student branch of a national political party. Five years after the initial contact he was a graduate student in political science. He thus seems to have ultimately made a vocational choice in line with his high school SVIB profile.

FIGURE 16–1 Profile for Case Study 4 on the Strong Vocational Interest Blank. (Reproduced from Edward K. Strong, Jr., Manual for Strong Vocational Interest Blanks for Men and Women, revised by David P. Campbell [Stanford, Calif.: Stanford University Press], by permission of the publisher, Stanford University Press. Copyright © 1959, 1966 by the Board of Trustees of the Leland Stanford Junior University.)

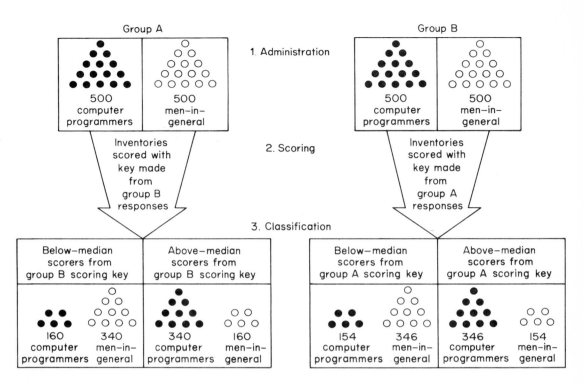

FIGURE 16–2 *Schematic illustration of double cross-validation: scoring weights from each half applied to the other. Computer programmers and men in general randomly chosen.*

Both KPR scales consist of many sets of three phrases each, of the "You like most to . . ." variety, such as this actual item (No. 6):

    R. Play a game that requires mental arithmetic
    S. Play checkers
    T. Work mechanical puzzles

The examinee is to indicate which one of the three activities he likes most, and which one he likes least. This is equivalent to ranking the three activities in order of preference, because obviously the one he does not mark ranks in the middle. Each of the 100 KPR-O items has this forced-choice triad (three-part) form.

There are 120 different combinations of 3 things each taken from 10 things $[(10 \cdot 9 \cdot 8)/(3 \cdot 2 \cdot 1) = 120]$, so with 10 different phrases one can create 120 sets of three phrases each. On the other hand, if each phrase differs from every other phrase, you need $3 \times 100 = 300$ phrases to yield 100 triadic items. Most of the KPR-O phrases are different.

Empirical keying is employed on the KPR-O just as with the SVIB. Let us examine the scoring of the above item for five keys. First, this item does not contribute to the Verification (sincerity vs. faking) scale. Not surprisingly, by empirical scoring you get 1 point on the bank cashier scale if you most like to "Play a game that requires mental arithmetic." You get 1 point on the Librarian scale if you most like to "Play checkers." You get 1 point on the "X-ray Technician" scale if you most like to "Work mechanical puzzles." You get 1 point on the Pharmaceutical Salesman scale if you *least* like to "Work mechanical puzzles." Thus these four occupational scales use four of the six possible like-most and like-least responses to the item. Other scales probably use the like-least responses for mental arithmetic and checkers, too.

There are 100 items to be marked. Your total score on a scale is merely the total number of points you receive. There are 119 holes in the Bank Cashier scoring stencil, but no one can earn a score as high as that because in a number of items two "Most" or two "Least" markings are keyed, and the examinee is instructed to mark just one "Most" and one "Least" in each triad. Scores of 61 or higher are extremely characteristic of bank cashiers, as contrasted with the men-in-general group. The Librarian scoring stencil has 146 holes, with 63 points or more indicating close resemblance to male librarians in the way that they react to KPR-O items.

In the cross-validation group, only 20 percent of the men in general received scores above the cutting point of the Librarian scale, when the cutting point between men in general and male librarians who like their work is half-way between the means of these groups. This shows that high scores on the Librarian scale are more characteristic of such male librarians than of men in general. The chief methodological difference between Strong's approach and Kuder's forced-choice scheme is that the former uses a considerable number of rating-scale type items that one may mark as he pleases—all *L*, for instance, or all *I*—whereas the Kuder uses a ranking triadic item that may be more resistant to response sets caused by the tendency to prefer one category on a rating scale. Kuder requires in effect that the examinee mark exactly 100 "Mosts," one per item, and exactly 100 "Leasts," one per item. Strong does not require the examinee to mark one-third of the 400 items *D*, one-third *I*, and one-third *L*, although he does use some forced-choice items elsewhere in the VIB.

The Strong VIB has the advantage over the KPR-O of long development and much more research and predictive-validity information.

The KPR-V has probably been more widely used than any other interest inventory. The 168 items include a great variety of activities, and the scoring system determines the examinee's relative preference strength on ten distinct scales: outdoor, mechanical, computational, scientific, persuasive, artistic, literary, musical, social-service, and clerical (see Figure 16–3). The KPR-V, which can be handscored, is designed to detect general areas of interest rather than those pertinent to a particular occupation. This capacity to detect general areas is considered to be an advantage for high-school application but a disadvantage for college use, where more explicit vocational interest differentiation is needed.

The examinee's interest in ten broad interest areas is depicted on the standard profile sheet shown in Figure 16–3, which also provides some interpretive assistance for the student. Note that the KPR-V is an *ipsative* rather than a *normative* measure; that is, it shows *relative* intraindividual interests but not overall interest. Whether Bob has more scientific interest than Bill has cannot be ascertained from the KPR-V scores; they show only the relative standing of the interest areas *within* each person. The failure to recognize this ipsative property frequently creates consternation for those attempting to resolve differences in results when an examinee has taken the SVIB and the KPR-V.

Your INTEREST PROFILE

Your profile on the *Kuder Preference Record—Vocational* shows your interest in the ten important areas listed across the top of the chart. The profile will also help you learn how you compare with other people.

The lines you drew on the chart show whether your interest is high, average, or low. If your score is above the top dotted line in any column, it is a high score and shows that you like activities in that area. If your score is between the two dotted lines, your interest is about average. If your score is below the bottom dotted line, it is a low score and shows that you dislike activities of that type.

Like most people, you are probably high in some areas, low in some, and average in others. Look at your highest score first. This score shows the type of activities you probably like best. If you have more than one score above the top dotted line, you have a combination of high interests.

Look at your low scores, too. They should be considered in any plans you make because they indicate the kinds of activities you probably do not enjoy. Remember that high interests are not better or worse than low, nor are some interests better than others. It is your own *pattern* of interests that counts.

Here is what your scores on the *Preference Record* mean:

OUTDOOR interest means that you prefer work that keeps you outside most of the time and usually deals with animals and growing things. Forest rangers, naturalists, and farmers are among those high in outdoor interests.

MECHANICAL interest means you like to work with machines and tools. Jobs in this area include automobile repairmen, watchmakers, drill press operators, and engineers.

COMPUTATIONAL interest means you like to work with numbers. A high score in this area suggests that you might like such jobs as bookkeeper, accountant, or bank teller.

SCIENTIFIC interest means that you like to discover new facts and solve problems. Doctors, chemists, nurses, engineers, radio repairmen, aviators, and dieticians usually have high scientific interests.

PERSUASIVE interest means that you like to meet and deal with people and to promote projects or things to sell. Most actors, politicians, radio announcers, min-

isters, salesmen, and store clerks have high persuasive interests.

ARTISTIC interest means you like to do creative work with your hands. It is usually work that has "eye appeal" involving attractive design, color, and materials. Painters, sculptors, architects, dress designers, hairdressers, and interior decorators all do "artistic" work.

LITERARY interest shows that you like to read and write. Literary jobs include novelist, historian, teacher, actor, news reporter, editor, drama critic, and book reviewer.

MUSICAL interest shows you like going to concerts, playing instruments, singing, or reading about music and musicians.

SOCIAL SERVICE interest indicates a preference for helping people. Nurses, Boy or Girl Scout leaders, vocational counselors, tutors, ministers, personnel workers, social workers, and hospital attendants spend much of their time helping other people.

CLERICAL interest means you like office work that requires precision and accuracy. Jobs such as bookkeeper, accountant, file clerk, salesclerk, secretary, statistician, and traffic manager fall in this area.

The occupations listed for each area on this profile are only examples. Your counselor can help you think of many others that are suggested by your pattern of interests. He can also tell you about many books and pamphlets that will help you learn more about these occupations. You may find that many school courses and leisure-time activities fit into your high interest areas.

Another form of the *Preference Record*, the *Personal*, will help you find out more about the types of things you like to do. It will help you discover, for example, how much you like meeting new people, whether you prefer situations you are familiar with, if you would rather work with ideas or things, how much you prefer pleasant social situations, and if you like to direct others. Your scores in these areas, too, will help you plan your career.

What you can do well depends, of course, on many things in addition to interest. Your abilities are particularly important. Many abilities can be measured by tests. Here, again, your counselor is the person to see.

Try to get as much information as you can about your interests, abilities, and the jobs you want to consider. The more you know about yourself, the more opportunity you have to make wise plans for your future.

FIGURE 16–3   Kuder Preference Record-Vocational Profile Sheet by G. Frederic Kuder, published by Science Research Associates, Chicago. (Reproduced by permission of G. Frederic Kuder.)

Reliability and Validity of Interest Inventories

For some published interest tests little or no adequate information is available concerning their validity and reliability. The critical reviews found in Buros's *Mental Measurement Yearbooks* provide invaluable guidance and an important quality-control function for prospective users. Our comments will exclusively concern the SVIB and KPR inventories and may or may not be characteristic of other instruments.

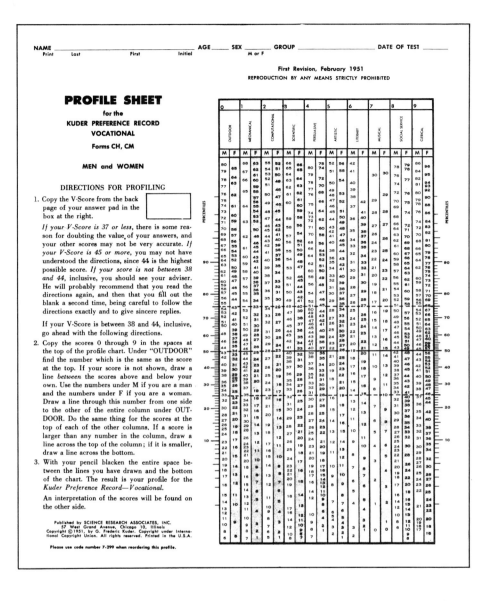

Although internal-consistency reliability estimates are satisfactory evidence of short-term stability in interest profiles, interest measurement over a long period of time cannot be expected to be stable until interests themselves have crystallized. Consequently, there is considerable fluctuation in interest profiles of students below age 17 or 18 on the SVIB and on the KPR (Crites, 1969). Moderate stability is achieved by college age, and fairly high stability is achieved by the end of the college years (D.P. Campbell, 1966a, b). A stability coefficient of .58 was reported for college freshman tested 15 years later (Trinkaus, 1954). A 22-year retest correlation of .67 for college seniors was found by Campbell (1966a, b) for the SVIB.

The results of several studies have shown that the Kuder and Strong inventories can be faked (Garry, 1953) and that the "accuracy" of the faked responses is correlated (about .4) with IQ (Durnall, 1954). Thus efforts to use these measures for selection or employment purposes have not been very successful. Falsification of interest is unlikely in an educational context, however, since there would rarely be a motive to fake.

MEASURED VS. EXPRESSED INTERESTS

Although there is a considerable relationship between expressed and measured interests ($r \approx .5$) (Frandsen and Sessions, 1953), they are far from interchangeable. Haganah (1953) found that the measured interests agreed with expressed interests about two-thirds of the time for those claiming business interests, but there was agreement in the science area in only one case in three. Super and Overstreet (1960) found that more than half of a sample of ninth-grade boys wished to enter occupations that appeared inappropriate for them in terms of the intellectual level required.

In Project TALENT, approximately 14,000 representative grade 12 students were asked about their career plans (Flanagan et al., 1962), which were then classified into the broad categories of college-science (31 percent), college-nonscience (19 percent), noncollege-technical (22 percent), and noncollege-nontechnical (29 percent). Five years later a follow-up study was conducted to determine the careers they were then pursuing. The percentages of people in each original group who continued in the same broad categories of college-science, college-nonscience, noncollege-technical, and noncollege-nontechnical were 31, 56, 51, and 55 percent, respectively (see Flanagan, 1969, p. 1338).

Expressed interests are not necessarily less valid than measured interests; in fact, some studies show expressed interests to be the better predictor of one's ultimate occupation (Flanagan and Cooley, 1966; Wightwick, 1945). Such evidence does not attenuate the validity of measured interest, because many factors other than interest determine one's occupation. For students from the upper social class, where prestige factors limit the "acceptable" occupations one may pursue, McArthur and Stevens (1955) found that expressed interests predicted better than measured interest; for middle-class subjects the reverse was true.

The likelihood of being dissatisfied with one's work has been shown to be three times greater for those who choose a line of work inconsistent with their measured interests as for those whose occupation and measured interests are consistent (Kuder, 1963).

INTERESTS, ABILITIES, AND GRADES

Contrary to popular opinion, little relationship exists between abilities and corresponding interests (Darley and Haganah, 1955; Perrone, 1964). Interests are, however, related to perceived abilities (McCall and Moore, 1965), which suggests the need for systematic feedback to students about their performance on standardized tests. Table 16–1 shows the correlations between the KPR-V interests and the various abilities measured by the *Differential Aptitude Tests* (DAT) for a group of male high-school seniors. Although a moderate relationship exists in the mechanical and computational-numerical areas, the other inter-relationships are low. Note the *r* of only .05 between clerical interest and ability.

Interests generally correlate poorly (below .3) with grades in relevant specific courses or fields (Brokaw, 1956). Even the Academic Achievement (AACH) scale of the SVIB increases the multiple correlation only from .59 to .63

TABLE 16–1

Correlation Coefficients among Various Interests (Kuder Preference Record) and Abilities (Differential Aptitude Tests)

Kuder Scales	Differential Aptitude Tests							
	Verbal	Numerical	Abstract	Space	Mechanical	Clerical	Spelling	Sentences
Mechanical	.13	−.09	.06	.19	.38	−.32	−.28	−.05
Computational	.18	.54	.32	.12	.08	.27	.21	.22
Scientific	.16	.17	.25	.20	.44	−.09	.17	.07
Persuasive	−.05	−.06	−.06	−.15	−.15	.01	.16	.04
Artistic	−.03	−.36	.00	.15	.11	.05	−.18	−.15
Literary	.10	.06	−.28	−.21	−.24	.05	.27	.14
Musical	.02	.28	.12	.12	−.02	.41	−.05	.03
Social Service	−.12	−.14	−.12	−.27	−.37	.00	−.04	−.09
Clerical	−.02	.24	.11	.08	−.12	.05	−.02	.19

SOURCE: Data on 63 twelfth-grade boys, reprinted from G. K. Bennett, H. G. Seashore, and A. G. Wesman, *Differential Aptitude Tests*, Forms L and M, Fourth Edition Manual (New York: The Psychological Corporation), p. A-17, by permission of the publisher. Copyright © 1947, 1952, 1959, 1963, 1966 by The Psychological Corporation, New York. All rights reserved.

for predicting college GPA from high-school rank and a scholastic aptitude test (Strong and Campbell, 1966, p. 19); however, this degree of improvement might be difficult to obtain using solely cognitive measures. Measured interests do predict students' ratings of satisfaction with a field of study, but these factors have little relationship to grades (French, 1961).

The educational value of interest measures was illustrated in Berdie's (1955) study in which the scores on vocational interest tests were shown to be more highly related to the curriculum college students selected than were achievement, aptitude, or personality tests; personality tests were the poorest indication of college major. Researchers in many studies have shown that measured interests have validity (Levine and Wallen, 1954; Strong, 1953) for predicting occupations. Table 16–2 illustrates the predictive validity of the SVIB 18 years after it was administered to 663 college freshmen (Strong and Campbell, 1966). The chances of employment in a given occupation were 88 in 100 for those with a T-score of 55 or above in that occupation; the chances were only 17 in 100 of entering an occupation in which a T-score of 30 or below was attained. Interest tests also forecast satisfaction in a job (Perry, 1955); men who change occupations have lower interest scores before entering that occupation than those who continue (Strong, 1943).

The prediction of occupational *success* is somewhat different from occupational tenure. In the few studies that have been done, the investigators have reported low to moderate correlations, but almost without exception the criteria appeared to be quite unreliable and, hence, unpredictable. Strong did report correlations of about .4 for a group of insurance agents.

A scale has been developed only recently that is especially oriented to the skilled and semiskilled occupations. The *Minnesota Vocational Interest Inventory* (MVII), which follows the SVIB approach, resulted from more that ten years of empirical research. Keys have been developed for 21 specific occupations

TABLE 16-2

Predictive Validity of SVIB Scales over 18 Years
(1938 Scales; N = 663 Students)

Scores on Any Scale	Letter Ratings	Chances in 100 of Employment in That Occupation[a]
55 to 70	A+	88
45 to 54	A−	74
40 to 44	B+	62
35 to 39	B	49
30 to 34	B−	36
Below 30	C	17

SOURCE: Reprinted from Edward K. Strong, Jr., *Manual for Strong Vocational Interest Blanks for Men and Women*, revised by David P. Campbell (Stanford, Calif.: Stanford University Press, 1966), Table 16, p. 44, by permission of Stanford University Press. Copyright © 1959, 1966 by the Board of Trustees of the Leland Stanford Junior University.
[a] Assumes all occupations are equally represented in population.

such as truck driver, electrician, and baker. This inventory may have greater value for non-college-bound students with less scholastic aptitude (Hall, 1966) than the SVIB and the KPR-O.

In interpreting any interest profile, one must remember that: (1) the duties of many jobs change with time, (2) many jobs with the same name differ considerably, and (3) there is a wide diversity of activities within most occupations (see D. P. Campbell, 1968a; J. N. McCall, 1965). The jingle and jangle fallacies are apparent in job titles just as they are in test labels.

In summary, interests tests are of little practical value by themselves, but when considered together with aptitude and achievement patterns they can be a useful aid for helping a student select a career pattern or course of study. A comprehensive report form that gives both ability and interest scores for an examinee, as well as his chances of success in various academic and occupational pursuits, is illustrated in Figure 16-4. Its values for self-guidance are obvious.

The Measurement of Personality Variables

CONCEPTUALIZING THE HUMAN PERSONALITY

Men have always categorized and evaluated the personalities of their contemporaries. The simplest form of personality evaluation is in the construction of various *typologies* under which individuals can be classified. The four temperaments of ancient times—sanguine, melancholy, phlegmatic, and choleric—

Comparative Guidance and Placement Program

1970-71

CGP

STUDENT REPORT

NAME AND ADDRESS	SEX	BIRTH DATE	SOCIAL SECURITY NO.	TEST DATE	ADV SCOR	HIGH SCHOOL
JANE DOE 123 MAIN STREET RADFORD, VIRGINIA 24141	F	7/17/52	123-45-6789	05/70	14	123456

COLLEGE AND CURRICULUM

STATE COMMUNITY COLLEGE
3276 SEC GENERAL

This report is written in a kind of shorthand, which is explained and interpreted in the booklet USING YOUR CGP REPORT. Be sure to ask your counselor for a copy of the booklet if you do not already have one.

COMPARATIVE INTEREST INDEX SCORES PROFILE

	YOUR SCORES
MATHEMATICS	12
PHYSICAL SCIENCES	18
ENGINEERING TECHNOLOGY	18
BIOLOGY	20
HEALTH	21
HOME ECONOMICS	24
SECRETARIAL	28
BUSINESS	20
SOCIAL SCIENCES	15
FINE ARTS	14
MUSIC	31

YOUR TEST SCORES AND PERCENTILE RANKS

	VERBAL	SEN TENCES	TEAR ZON	MIDDLE COMP	LETTER GROUP	ACAD MOTIV
YOUR TEST SCORES	54	50	47	60	58	56	41
NATIONAL PERCENTILE RANK	59	46	81	40	80	72	17
LOCAL PERCENTILE RANK	59	50	82	51			

MATHEMATICS TEST TAKEN		A	ALGEBRA

YOUR HIGH SCHOOL GRADES

	OVERALL	ENGLISH	MATH
	C	B+	D

ENGLISH & MATHEMATICS PLACEMENT FORECAST

COURSES	E110	E101	E099	M110	M101	M099
ABOVE AVERAGE	03	05	08	02	03	04
AVERAGE	04	03	02	03	04	04
BELOW AVERAGE	03	02	1-	05	03	02

PERFORMANCE FORECAST

TYPE OF PROGRAM		TRANSFER				OCCUPATIONAL/TECHNICAL			OCCUPATIONAL/VOCATIONAL	
PROGRAM AREA	SCIENCE AND AGRICULTURE	BUSINESS	LIBERAL ARTS	EDUCATION	FINE ARTS	TRADES & IND. TECH SCIENCE AGRICULTURE	BUSINESS	PUBLIC SERVICE	HEALTH	TRADES & IND. TECH SCIENCE AGRICULTURE	BUSINESS	PUBLIC SERVICE	HEALTH
ABOVE AVERAGE	*	05	03	03		*	07	*			**	
AVERAGE	**	03	03	04		**	02	***			**	
BELOW AVERAGE	***	02	04	03		***	01				*	

FINANCIAL NEED INDICATOR

COLLEGE COSTS	$1400 OR BELOW	$1401-2000	$2001-3000	OVER $3000
YOUR NEED	N	N	S	S

THIS IS A GENERAL INDICATOR OF YOUR NEED FOR ASSISTANCE.
If on S, C or * appears in any of the boxes, see your counselor or financial aid officer.

N-NO NEED
S-SOME NEED
C-CONSIDERABLE NEED
* -NEED MORE INFORMATION

ASSISTANCE GUIDE

YOU ASKED FOR HELP WITH	
READING SPEED AND COMPREHENSION	X
STUDY TECHNIQUES	X
FINDING PARTTIME OR FULLTIME EMPLOYMENT	X
FINDING HOUSING	
FINANCIAL AID	X
EDUCATIONAL AND VOCATIONAL COUNSELING	
PERSONAL COUNSELING	
LOCAL QUESTION	4567 89012

(OVER) 123

Student Identification.

College and Curriculum.

Aptitudes play a most important role in vocational choice. The Student Report provides eight different scores reported on a common scale in **National Percentile Ranks** and **Local Percentile Ranks** for English and mathematics measures at institutions that have participated in the program.

Because secondary school achievement relates closely to performance in post-secondary education, a student and his counselor should consider **High School Grades** as well as test data in making educational and vocational plans. A student's self-reported high school grades are listed on the Student Report to call attention to the importance of this information and to provide the counselor with some data if nothing more is available.

In the **Placement Forecast** on the Student Report, a student and counselor see probable levels of performance in specific English and mathematics classes of their own college. This information should give a student understanding about the proper beginning course that offers him a reasonable opportunity for success.

In the **Comparative Interest Index** section of the report, a student sees a profile of his interest pattern in 11 areas that relate to curricular choice. By using the student interpretive booklet he can compare this interest pattern with those of other students in specific curriculums. He may find that his interest pattern is consistent with those of others who enter his intended curriculum, or he may change or modify his curricular choice if serious inconsistencies exist.

The report's **Financial Need Indicator** alerts a financial aid counselor and student that there may be a need for financial help. It should provide a starting point to determine specific financial need and to see how this need can best be met.

Additional information that identifies special student needs is given on the report in the **Assistance Guide.** This information alerts counselors to special needs expressed by a student as they act to meet such needs or respond to requests for assistance. It also alerts a student that he could seek help in these areas. Several special concerns can be identified.

To be meaningful, aptitude and interest measures have to be looked at in terms of individual institutions. The Student Report's **Performance Forecast** provides specific information that applies to the institution a student will attend. For example, Jane Doe attending State Community College can see her probable chance for success in as many as 14 different curriculums. At colleges that have not yet completed a validity study on which to base specific predictions (stated as chances in 10), the **Performance Forecast** states general predictions (asterisks[*]) based on data from other institutions surveyed by the program. She is able to see in which curriculums she could reasonably expect to succeed, and in which curriculums she may have difficulty. Again, her early thinking may be supported by these data, or she may change her original decision on the basis of the **Performance Forecast.**

FIGURE 16-4 *A sample Student Report showing results from an ability and an interest test, along with performance expectancies on various academic and occupational criteria. (Reproduced from Twenty-one Years Later: ETS Today, p. 80, by permission of the College Entrance Examination Board and the Educational Testing Service.)*

comprised a classification based on a supposed predominance in an individual of one of the four bodily "humours," or fluids—blood, bile, phlegm, or choler. A still popular typology, suggested by the Swiss psychoanalyst C. G. Jung, is introversion-extroversion. Traces of typological psychology remain in personality theory, but more elaborate methods of assessment have been devised in a growing effort to compass the diversity of human personality. Measurement theory has naturally accompanied the development of personality theory. The tests and other evaluative methods used by psychological investigators were constructed for a particular research problem, but there are many "standardized personality tests." Buros (1965) lists 196 published personality tests; they are exceeded in number only by achievement tests.

TRAITS MEASURED BY DIRECT OBSERVATION

In trait assessment by direct observation, a sample of behavior that manifests the trait in question is observed and analyzed. A widely reported study was the Character Education Inquiry of Yale University researchers Hartshorne and May (1928), in which they assessed such traits as truthfulness, honesty, and persistence in children by subjecting them to situational tests of these traits. Hartshorne and May found that most of the traits investigated depended strongly on the situation; that is, a child might cheat on an examination but not steal pennies. Thus they cast doubt on the then-current belief that a child is either wholly honest or wholly dishonest; honesty did not emerge as a single, unitary characteristic of individuals.

The wartime Office of Stategic Services (OSS, 1948) was interested in selecting highly qualified men for risky undercover operations. The assessment staff felt that such traits as energy, initiative, effective intelligence, emotional stability, and leadership would be indispensable in this sort of work, so a number of situational tests were devised to measure the degree of these and other attributes. In one situation, the subject had to build a five-foot cube of giant Tinkertoys with the aid of two workmen. Unknown to the subject, the two helpers were psychologists who did everything possible to obstruct his progress and to belittle him. His reactions under such conditions were later evaluated in terms of the traits being sought. In another trial called the stress interview, the candidate was given a short time to invent a story to cover the fact that he had been caught going through secret governmental papers. In a subsequent third-degree "grilling," his reactions were again weighed.

TRAIT MEASUREMENT THROUGH SELF-REPORT

Today's personality tests are largely of the paper-and-pencil, self-report variety in which the examinee is presented with a series of questions describing typical behavior patterns. His score will then consist of the number of questions answered in a direction supposedly displaying those traits. Sometimes a self-report test measures only one trait dimension, such as security-insecurity or high anxiety-low anxiety. At other times, a test can be devised and scored to measure several traits at once; for example, the *California Psychological Inventory* (CPI) yields 18 different scores, such as sociability, dominance, sense of well-being, self-control, tolerance, and flexibility.

The grandfather of all such devices is the *Woodworth Personal Data Sheet*; it was devised during World War I to facilitate the psychiatric screening of draftees. It consisted of 116 yes-no questions describing typical symptoms of neurotic behavior. "Normals" averaged about 10 psychoneurotic answers, but those with neurotic complications averaged close to 40 such answers (Franz, 1919). High scorers would then be more intensively interviewed and evaluated. The first 36 items from the *Woodworth Personal Data Sheet* are shown in Figure 16–5. By taking the inventory yourself, you can gain insight into some of the difficulties encountered in assessing personality.

A number of presumedly "unidimensional" inventories were developed in the twenties and thirties to determine the strength of a variety of personality traits. It remained for psychologist Robert Bernreuter to demonstrate that *one* test could measure simultaneously a number of personality traits. To do this he gathered a great number of self-report questions and determined which of them discriminated between high and low scorers on each of four tests, which respectively measured "introversion-extroversion," "ascendance-submission," "neurotic tendency," and "self-sufficiency." By this method, he found that a given item might correlate well with more than one of the unidimensional tests; by judicious selection, he was able to produce a 125-item test, the responses to which could be variously combined to produce four separate scores, each of which correlated highly with the unidimensional test it was expected to replace.

Further refinement in the development of self-report personality scales was introduced by John C. Flanagan (1935), who maintained that since the four Bernreuter scales showed significant intercorrelation (for example, people scoring very high on the introversion scale tended to score similarly on the neuroticism scale), the traits could not be called independent and that, therefore, each separate scale did not necessarily have a precise psychological meaning. Flanagan overcame this difficulty by subjecting the Bernreuter test to a trait or factor analysis. After examining the item correlations, he proposed that only two separate factors are needed to account for the score patterns produced by a great number of individuals. He defined these factors as the self-confident, socially aggressive vs. the self-conscious, emotionally unstable dimension and the sociable vs. the nonsociable dimension. This method of defining personality traits is analogous to the factor-analytic method of determining mental abilities and has become a favorite device for producing multidimensional personality tests. Three of the more prominent tests are the *Guilford-Zimmerman Temperament Survey*, which yields ten scores on traits such as general activity, ascendance, sociability, emotional stability, and friendliness; Cattell's *Sixteen Personality Factor Questionnaire*, which yields scores on such trait pairs as aloof vs. warm, confident vs. insecure, tough vs. sensitive, conventional vs. eccentric, conservative vs. experimenting; and *Edwards Personal Preference Schedule*, which yields scores on 15 personality needs—need for achievement, order, autonomy, affiliation, change, aggression, and so on.

A number of things plague those who try to treat self-report items in the same way that they consider ability items. There are, however, technical methods for meeting the problems:

1. A personality inventory can be administered twice to the same indi-

1. Do you usually feel well and strong?	yes	*no*
2. Do you usually sleep well?	yes	*no*
3. Are you frightened in the middle of the night?	*yes*	no
4. Are you troubled with dreams about your work?	*yes*	no
5. Do you have nightmares?	*yes*	no
6. Do you have too many sexual dreams?	*yes*	no
7. Do you ever walk in your sleep?	*yes*	no
8. Do you ever have the sensation of falling when going to sleep?	*yes*	no
9. Does your heart ever thump in your ears so that you cannot sleep?	*yes*	no
10. Do ideas run through your head so that you cannot sleep?	*yes*	no
11. Do you feel well rested in the morning?	yes	*no*
12. Do your eyes often pain you?	*yes*	no
13. Do things ever seem to swim or get misty before your eyes?	*yes*	no
14. Do you often have the feeling of suffocating?	*yes*	no
15. Do you have continual itching in the face?	*yes*	no
16. Are you bothered much by blushing?	*yes*	no
17. Are you bothered by fluttering of the heart?	*yes*	no
18. Do you feel tired most of the time?	*yes*	no
19. Have you ever had fits of dizziness?	*yes*	no
20. Do you have queer, unpleasant feelings in any part of the body?	*yes*	no
21. Do you ever feel an awful pressure in or about the head?	*yes*	no
22. Do you often have bad pains in any part of the body?	*yes*	no
23. Do you have a great many bad headaches?	*yes*	no
24. Is your head apt to ache on one side?	*yes*	no
25. Have you ever fainted away?	*yes*	no
26. Have you *often* fainted away?	*yes*	no
27. Have you ever been blind, half-blind, deaf, or dumb for a time?	*yes*	no
28. Have you ever had an arm or leg paralyzed?	*yes*	no
29. Have you ever lost your memory for a time?	*yes*	no
30. Did you have a happy childhood?	yes	*no*
31. Were you happy when 14 to 18 years old?	yes	*no*
32. Were you considered a bad boy?	*yes*	no
33. As a child did you like to play alone better than to play with other children?	*yes*	no
34. Did the other children let you play with them?	yes	*no*
35. Were you shy with other boys?	*yes*	no
36. Did you ever run away from home?	*yes*	no

FIGURE 16-5 *The first 36 items of the Woodworth Personal Data Sheet. The "neurotic" response to each item is italicized here, but of course not on the inventory itself.* (*Reproduced from* P. M. Symonds, Diagnosing personality and conduct [*New York: Century Company, 1931*], p. 175, *by permission of Appleton-Century-Crofts.*)

viduals after a *short* interval of time, preferably with the order of the items rearranged the second time. The correlation between scores the first and second times tells how stable they are. If scores fluctuate wildly from one time to another, they cannot be useful. (Many self-report devices can be expected to show considerable fluctuation in scores over a short period of time because of actual fluctuations in the individual, even when errors of measurement and situationally distorting aspects are small.)

2. To attempt to reduce the faking problem various "lie" scales have been devised for personality inventories. The usual procedure is to insert items to which a particular response very likely indicates intent to deceive, such as "Have you ever been somewhat unhappy at any time?" Since every mortal has his unhappy moments, however fleeting they may be, a "No" response to this question would be suspect. It   *394*

follows that answers to other items may also be suspect. The Kuder tests have a V-scale designed to detect gross dishonesty.

The MMPI   The most thoroughly studied paper-and-pencil adjustment inventory is the *Minnesota Multiphasic Personality Inventory* (MMPI), which first appeared in 1940. Its items are declarative sentences with which the individual either agrees or disagrees. Scores are secured for a number of psychiatric categories (depression, hypochondriasis, schizophrenia, and so on) and for masculine vs. feminine interests. A tremendous amount of research and re-analysis of the MMPI has been done since its appearance. Because the MMPI is a complex instrument, the consequences of misinterpretation can be very serious. Highly trained administrators and interpreters are required. More than perhaps any other self-report personality test the MMPI should not be used by school personnel. In the MMPI one's responses are compared with various psychiatric groups, who themselves are not defined explicitly enough in meaningful terms. Despite the extensive developmental work on this instrument, it has been shown to have no validity for predicting relevant criteria such as success of student teaching (Gough and Pemberton, 1952; Michaelis, 1954) or performance in clinical psychology training (Snyder, 1955). Hathaway and Monachesi (1963), however, found the MMPI to have some slight validity for predicting delinquent behavior among high school students.

The MTAI   The *Minnesota Teacher Attitude Inventory* (MTAI) has been widely used to study teacher attitudes and has been frequently recommended in selecting prospective teachers (Getzels and Jackson, 1963, p. 517). Each item is empirically weighted on how it discriminated between 100 "superior" and 100 "inferior" teachers (according to principals' ratings) who responded anonymously to many Likert-type items, such as "Without children life would be dull," "Children should be seen and not heard," and so on. Correlations above .4 were reported between MTAI results and the ratings of principals and pupils (Leeds, 1950). A critical flaw that restricts the generalizability of Leeds' findings was that the participating teachers responded anonymously; consequently a "need" or motive to fake was greatly reduced. Rabinowitz (1954) showed that education students have no difficulty in simulating the attitudes of permissive or authoritative teachers when motivated to do so. When anonymity was not involved, subsequent studies (Day, 1959; Oelke, 1956; Popham and Trimble, 1960; Sandgren and Schmidt, 1956) generally failed to find any relationship between MTAI scores and teaching success great enough to be of any practical value.

A statistically significant relationship between the MTAI and certain criteria was reported in a few studies, but statistical significance does not insure practical significance. Popham and Trimble (1960) reported a highly significant difference (.01 level) in MTAI means of 72 "superior" and 72 "inferior" student teachers. This difference represented a correlation (point-biserial)[1]

---

[1] A point-biserial correlation coefficient is the appropriate Pearson product-moment correlation coefficient when one of the variables is a true dichotomy.

of only .24, which, since both groups were equal in number, indicates that the mean of the "superior" group was .24 standard deviations above the composite mean. Similarly the inferior group had a mean z-score in the composite distribution of $-.24$. The magnitude of this difference is depicted in Figure 16–6, which shows two normal distributions with a difference in means of $.5\sigma$; this represents a point-biserial correlation of .25. (The ordinary r between the MTAI scores and the ratings of *all* the teachers, including the average ones, is probably considerably less than .24.)

Day (1959) found a predictive validity coefficient of .28 for the MTAI and principals' ratings, but Callis (1953) found coefficients of only .18 and .19 for the same criterion in two other studies.

The MTAI has little apparent promise in teacher selection. In a research context where the anonymity of the respondent can be preserved, the MTAI may have some utility, especially as a way to help teacher trainees consider some of their school-related attitudes. For this, however, the empirical scoring system (based on too few cases, anyway) can be abandoned, as Yee and Kriewall (1969) recommended more generally.

Evaluation of Personality Inventories   Self-report personality measures are afflicted with the difficulties of affective assessment described in Chapter 12 (see. pp. 298–301) to a greater extent than any other kind of test. They are easily fakable (Braun and Asta, 1968), although some (such as KPR and MMPI) contain scales for detecting the naive, flagrant prevaricator. The job applicant describes himself much more favorably than does the college student (Herzberg, 1954).

Semantic problems and criterion inadequacy are very serious drawbacks to successful self-report personality assessment. Ghiselli and Barthol (1953) surveyed 113 studies in which personality inventories were used for employment selection; they found a median validity coefficient of only .25, which is too low to be of any real practical value.

Current personality inventory scores have generally been of little or no value for predicting future success either in school, on the job, or in one's personal living. We believe no useful purpose is served by giving a personality or adjustment inventory, except perhaps in certain research projects.

PROJECTIVE TECHNIQUES

Psychologists have had difficulty making good theoretical sense of a third personality dimension—the "why" or motivational aspect. A motive is a psychological state of the individual that is inferred from his behavior. Thus if a person begins to eat, his motive is hunger; if he struggles for success, his motive is ambition; if he acts uncharitably, his motive is selfishness. One of the founders of modern social psychology, William McDougal (1923), listed primary human motives (he called them instincts) that included curiosity, pugnacity, self-assertion, reproduction, and repulsion. Further thought, however, led theorists to believe that such lists of motives really were only *descriptions* of a wide range of human behavior. Rather than explaining anything, they simply provided another way to categorize outwardly similar behaviors. The number of such

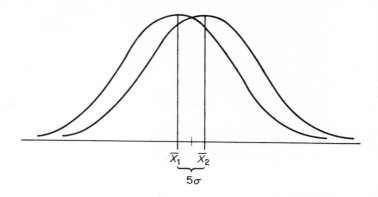

FIGURE 16–6   *The magnitude of difference and overlap accompanying a difference in means of .5σ—that is, a point-biserial correlation of .25.*

motives or categories depended solely on the grouping preferences at work. As one critical wag observed, if a person twiddles his thumbs, need one infer a thumb-twiddling motive?

This sort of thinking led many psychologists to suggest that aside from physiological necessities such as those for food, air, and rest, the motivation concept should be reformulated. The minimum assumption to be made in explaining human action is that the individual will set goals whose attainment provides satisfaction, pleasure, or gratification. The particular goals of any one person, however, will depend partially on his history of rewards and punishments; these in turn probably depend on the value systems of his environment —parents, social groups, and general culture. Thus if a culture reinforces academic success, the behavior leading to such goals will be rewarded and there should be many "educated" individuals.

In this formulation, the motive concept differs from the trait concept only in degree of generality. Motives predict behavior in a wide variety of differing environments; traits refer to more specific responses in highly specified conditions. For our purposes, the most important question concerns the measurement of human motives.

The Rorschach and the TAT   Clinical psychologists frequently use two instruments, the Rorschach Inkblot Test and the *Thematic Apperception Test* (TAT), or variants of them in making many of their personality assessments. They are called "projective tests" because a person is expected to project into the ink blots or the ambiguous pictures his needs, wants, desires, aversions, fears, anxieties, and so on. Procedures for administering, scoring, and interpreting the two tests are quite different, but they have in common their ambiguous stimuli, the "nonsensical" ink blots or the provocative pictures. The well-known Rorschach Inkblot Test (see Figure 16–7) is the classic measure of this kind. The subject is shown one blot at a time and is asked what he sees in it. The examiner notes not only the content of the responses, but also such things

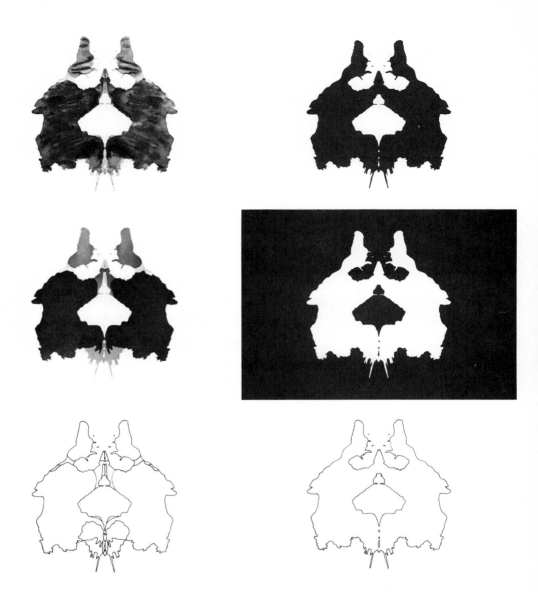

FIGURE 16–7 *Card II and experimental modifications of the Rorschach. (Adapted by permission from material provided by E. Earl Baughman; original blot courtesy Hans Huber Publishers.)*

as the use of the whole blot instead of the use of details, the injection of movement into the blots, and the use of color and white spaces in making a response. Elaborate systems attempt to relate the various perceptual modes to such personality variables as impulsiveness, sensitivity, and emotional stability. Since its appearance in 1921, the Rorschach technique has stimulated much controversial literature; Buros (1965) lists more than 3,000 references pertaining to the Rorschach. Its scientific value as a yardstick of personality, however, is yet to be established.   *398*

Harvard psychologist Henry Murray (1938) proposed that motives are a person's "inner concerns" and that if we learn what these concerns are, we may predict much of his behavior. We can learn of the concerns by listening to a person tell spontaneous, imaginative stories in response to picture cues, such as those used in Murray's *Thematic Apperception Test* (TAT) (see Figure 16–8). By analyzing the content of a series of these spontaneous, imaginative stories according to well-defined rules, the investigator hopes to identify the presence or absence, as well as the strength, of one or more "motives."

We shall not discuss how the TAT or Rorschach is scored. (There are several scoring procedures.) Much background in the psychology of personality and in clinical psychology is required before one is sufficiently well equipped to attempt to use projective techniques. Many measurement specialists have far less regard for projective techniques than do most clinical psychologists. To

FIGURE 16–8   One of the TAT cards. (Reprinted from Henry Alexander Murray, Thematic apperception test [Cambridge, Mass.: Harvard University Press], by permission of the publisher. Copyright 1943 by the President and Fellows of Harvard College.)

some of the former, the Rorschach and TAT rate little higher than the reading of tea leaves. Validity is not well established psychometrically even for the Rorschach and the TAT, much less for newer projective techniques. Perhaps a great part of the reason for their popularity with clinical psychologists rests on what might be called "faith validity" assumed by the users.

Several persons have attempted to devise multiple-choice versions of the Rorschach to replace or at least precede the much more arduous interview procedure by which the Rorschach is usually administered. Examples are the *Holtzman Inkblot Technique* (Holtzman et al., 1961) and the experimental version being tried by the California Test Bureau (Stone, 1958). It is yet uncertain as to whether the objectively scored projective techniques will be useful.

Guilford (1959, p. 313) reviewed the status of Rorschach validity up to 1959 and concluded:

> In spite of the widespread popularity and use of the Rorschach ink blots, the reliabilities of scores tend to be relatively low, and validities, although quite varied, are generally near zero. This statement regarding validity applies to use of the instrument in discriminating pathological from normal individuals, for diagnosis of more particular pathologies such as anxiety, for indicating degree of maladjustment in the general population, and for predicting academic and vocational success.

Six years later, after reviewing the research on the Rorschach, Jensen (1965, p. 509) concluded "the rate of scientific progress in clinical psychology might well be measured by the speed and thoroughness with which it gets over the Rorschach."

Other Projective Techniques   Another very popular projective technique is the *Draw-a-Person Test* presented by Machover (1949). The examinee is provided with paper and pencil and asked to draw a person. After the first drawing is completed, the examinee is asked to draw a person of the sex opposite to that of the first drawing. Every aspect of the drawings is purported to have psychological significance: size, position, order of drawing persons and parts of the body, clothing, shading, omission, background, and so on. Reliability and validity data on such measures are very poor (see Anastasi, 1968, pp. 507–508).

Several "copying" measures have become popular in recent years. Most are a derivative of the *Bender Visual Motor Gestalt Test* shown in Figure 16–9. The subject is asked simply to copy each design. There are several different scoring procedures for this test, but rotation of figures, omission, and distortion are the principal factors in its evaluation (Bender, 1970). "Copying" measurements appear to have some validity for predicting reading failure (DeHirsch et al., 1966) and for identifying persons with perceptual difficulty and certain types of brain damage. Their value for personality appraisal has not been clearly demonstrated.

Evaluation of Projective Techniques   Despite their widespread use by clinical and school psychologists, the validity of projective techniques is highly suspect when studies that are not vulnerable to criterion contamination are excluded. The status of unstructured projective techniques is the same today

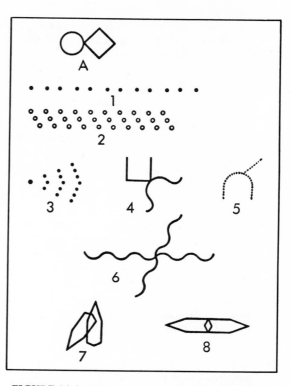

*FIGURE 16–9 The Bender Visual Motor Gestalt Test.
(Reproduced from Dr. Lauretta Bender, A Visual
Motor Gestalt Test and Its Clinical Use, American
Orthopsychiatric Association, Research Monographs
[1938], p. 41, by permission of the author and the
American Orthopsychiatric Association, Inc. Copyright
1938 by the American Orthopsychiatric Association, Inc.)*

as it was when they were harshly evaluated by Eysenck (1959, pp. 276–277),
who concluded:

1. There is no consistent meaningful and testable theory underlying modern
   projective devices.
2. The actual practice of projective experts frequently contradicts the putative
   hypotheses on which their tests are built.
3. On the empirical level, there is no indisputable evidence showing any kind
   of marked relationship between global projective test interpretation by
   experts and psychiatric diagnosis.
4. There is no evidence of any marked relationship between Rorschach scoring
   categories combined in any approved statistical fashion into a scale, and
   diagnostic category, when the association between the two is tested on a
   population other than that from which the scale was derived.
5. There is no evidence for the great majority of the postulated relationships
   between projective test indicators and personality traits.
6. There is no evidence for any marked relationship between projective test
   indicators of any kind and intellectual qualities and abilities as measured,
   estimated, or rated independently.

401

7. There is no evidence for the predictive power of projective techniques with respect to success or failure in a wide variety of fields where personality qualities play an important part.

8. There is no evidence that conscious or unconscious conflicts, attitudes, fears, or fantasies in patients can be diagnosed by means of projective techniques in such a way as to give congruent results with assessments made by psychiatrists independently.

9. There is ample evidence to show that the great majority of studies in the field of projective techniques are inadequately designed, have serious statistical errors in the analysis of the data, and/or are subject to damaging criticisms on the grounds of contamination between test and criterion.

INTERVIEWS

Perhaps the most widely used assessment procedure is the interview. During a lifetime one converses with persons in many situations, and usually he evaluates the remarks he hears. The "formal" interview differs from casual conversation in that it has structure and explicit purpose. It can be considered an oral test. It differs from tests, however, in that the interviewer may adjust his questions to the answers he is getting and thereby probe and explore. In this respect the interview is analogous to an individual intelligence test used by a clinical psychologist to "test the limits"—that is, to ask many questions not in the test manual that the examinee's responses suggest. Since such questions are unique to the examinee, his answers cannot be compared with the answers of other examinees, who are asked different questions. A main strength of the usual test is that it compares all examinees on the same questions. When one departs from this model, whether with a test or a "flexible" interview, he loses direct comparability of responses. This may permit the interviewer's prejudices and biases to operate freely.

The price of flexibility is subjectivity of interpretation. Suppose that you are chairman of the admissions committee of Midstate College. Five hundred high-school graduates have applied for admission to the freshman class at M.C., but only two hundred can be accepted. Which 40 percent will you accept? You know for each applicant his rank in his high-school graduating class, his verbal and quantitative academic aptitude test scores, and his scores on three achievement tests. You decide that there should be an interview with each applicant. Who will do the interviewing, and how? You do not see how you could get a really qualified faculty member to devote the time necessary for interviewing. (Perhaps you would not know which are "qualified.") Professor Jones prefers one kind of student, Professor Smith another, and Professor Doe another. You hesitate to ask five professors to interview 100 students each, for they do not have comparable frames of reference; this would be like giving five different tests, one test to each 100 students, and trying to compare the 500 students to each other.

You do not want to assign a routine administrative assistant to do the interviewing because he might recommend rejection of the students whom the faculty desires. For instance, if the assistant was a mediocre high-school student, he may be subconsciously prejudiced against students who ranked high in their graduating classes. Usually, he would not state his objections this way, but would say that the applicant lacked poise, or sincerity, or "creativity." Amateur interviewers frequently develop pet questions that they consider to have high validity, but that validity is rarely if ever proved. For example, one interviewer of prospective teachers always asks, "Do you take yourself seriously?" Those who respond "Yes" are automatically rejected. "From personal experience" the interviewer is sold on his technique, but it probably has little if any positive validity; in fact, the best-qualified candidates might even be rejected.

When properly planned and conducted, interviews can be of some value for certain purposes, such as assessing the person's congeniality and warmth. At best, interviews probably add little to the prediction of most objective criteria when the best objective predictors are used. Interviews may even hurt predictability by interfering with the efficacy of the objective predictors, as when an academically inferior school superintendent refuses to employ females as principals. Interviews for academic selection are greatly overrated. Academic predictors such as previous grades, verbal and quantitative aptitude, and scores on achievement tests are usually vastly more important than poise and acting ability at an interview, rationalizations of previous inadequacies, and eloquent promises to study hard. The single best predictor of future success is past success.

The contribution of interviews to academic prediction can be studied in a given situation, but the interviewers and their procedures may change from year to year; therefore, it is difficult to generalize across time even within one setting, and much harder to determine the validity of *the* interview in general.

Meehl (1954) found that the simple statistical use of one or two test scores was generally better in predicting or revealing a person's status than judgments made by trained and experienced persons via interviews and other informal observational techniques. Frequently ignored is the effect of the interviewer on the interviewee's behavior. Untrained interviewers tend to "shape" the interviewee's responses by the reinforcement they unconsciously provide verbally and by gestures. This "shaping" has contaminated much research in which the interview method was used.

The prime value of the interview is probably for imparting information and aiding the interviewee to make good choices on the basis of all the information he has. Interviews can be friendly, helpful sessions, if the evaluating of the interviewee by interviewer is minimized in favor of mutual concentration on helping the former make wise choices. This is the guidance function of interviews. It is widely applicable in schools and colleges. Interviews may also be of value in academic, athletic, and occupational recruiting (see Bingham, Moore, and Gustad, 1959).

SOCIOMETRIC TECHNIQUES

Sociometry is the study of interrelationships among members of a group—that is, its social structure: how each individual is perceived by the group. Sociometry was launched in 1934 with the publication of Moreno's *Who Shall Survive*. Bonney (1960, p. 1319) described the rationale as follows:

> The major underlying sociometric method is that within all groups, such as a
> school class or teaching staff, in which considerable interaction is allowed,

there emerges an informal organization among the members based on varying degrees of positive and negative interpersonal feelings, and that these preferences and aversions are significant factors in the morale and efficiency of this group.

Various techniques that we have discussed such as Q-sort, semantic differential, or rating scales can be used to rate others as well as oneself. Special sociometric techniques have been devised for the social appraisal of individuals and groups.

The Sociogram   Teachers may study the social structure of a classroom by asking students to make certain *meaningful* choices such as the following: With which student would you rather study tomorrow's arithmetic lesson? With which three pupils would you rather play at recess? Which two pupils would be the most fun at a party at your home?

A more complex variation is to present the personality sketch of a hypothetical pupil and ask each youngster to name, say, the three persons in the class who seem to him most like the individual described.

We illustrate the sociometric process with actual data from a fourth-grade class that contained 14 girls and 17 boys.[2] The teacher gave each child a dittoed sheet that read as follows:

My three best friends in this class are:
1. My very best friend _____
2. My second best friend _____
3. My third best friend _____

The results are shown in Table 16–3, where the capital letters from A through N designate girls, and the small letters from a through q represent boys.

How does one read Table 16–3? Begin with Girl A. In *row A* we see that she chose Girl D as her very best friend, because there is the number 1 at the intersection of row A and column D. Girl A listed Girl C as her second best friend. Girl A listed Boy c as her third best friend.

Who chose Girl A? Look at *column A*, where you see from top to bottom the following numbers: 1 (first choice of Girls D and N and Boy k), 2 (second choice of Girls C, F, and G and Boy d), and 3 (third choice of Boys c and f). Thus Girl A was named by nine pupils—three times as first choice, four times as second choice, and twice as third choice. You will find the summary 3, 4, and 2 in column A of the first three rows below the choices.

In the lower left quadrant of Table 16–3 you can see that Girl A was chosen by four boys, but no other girl was chosen by more than one boy. You also can determine that no girl chose only boys, but Boy k chose only girls. Did any girl choose Boy k? No, but k was the *first* choice of Boy o.

If we give 3 points for being chosen as "very best friend," 2 points for "second best friend," and 1 point for "third best friend," the highest scorers are Girl A and Boy a, each with 19 points, even though Girl A was chosen by

[2] We thank Elaine M. Williams for lending us a term paper that she had prepared in a graduate course at the University of Wisconsin. We have slightly rearranged a portion of her data.

TABLE 16–3

Choices of Three Best Friends by a class of 14 Girls and 17 Boys

		Girls Chosen													Boys Chosen																
		A	B	C	D	E	F	G	H	I	J	K	L	M	N	a	b	c	d	e	f	g	h	i	j	k	l	m	n	o	p	q
Girls Chose	A			2	1													3														
	B					2				3													1									
	C	2					3											1														
	D	1		3			2																									
	E		1				2												3													
	F	2			1																			3								
	G	2		3																		1										
	H		1							3		2																				
	I		1			3																		2								
	J				2	1																			3							
	K		2	1														3														
	L					2											1	3														
	M				2											1						3										
	N	1			2	3																										
Boys Chose	a																				2	1			3							
	b																1	2						3								
	c	3															1	2														
	d	2															1							3								
	e					2															1											
	f	3	1													2																
	g	1																			2							3				
	h									2								1												3		
	i	2																1			3											
	j															1	2		3													
	k	1		3		2																										
	l						2									1																
	m																2		3					1								
	n																2	1											3			
	o																		3				2		1							
	p																1	3	2													
	q																		1													
1st choice		3	4	1	2			1								5	3	3	1	2	2	1	1		1	1						
2nd choice		4	1	1	1	2	3	2	1	1	1	1				2	3		2	1	2		1	1								
3rd choice		2		3		2		1		2								3	3	2		2		2	1		2	1	1	1		
Times chosen		9	5	4	3	4	3	3	2	3	1	1				7	6	6	6	5	4	3	2	3	2	1	2	1	1	1		
"Score"		19	14	8	8	6	6	5	5	4	2	2	0	0	0	19	15	12	10	10	10	5	5	4	4	3	2	1	1	1	0	0
		A	B	C	D	E	F	G	H	I	J	K	L	M	N	a	b	c	d	e	f	g	h	i	j	k	l	m	n	o	p	q

two more pupils than Boy a. This happens because Boy a was chosen as very best friend by five pupils, resulting in 15 points, whereas Girl A was chosen as very best friend by only three pupils, yielding 9 points. For Girl A the computation is $(3 \times 3) + (4 \times 2) + (2 \times 1) = 19$. For Boy a it is $(5 \times 3) + (2 \times 2) = 19$.

The lowest scorers, whom nobody chose, are Girls *L*, *M*, and *N* and Boys *p* and *q*. They may be the fourth best or fifth best friends of some of the pupils, but they weren't listed as first, second, or third. In Table 16–3 the girls are arranged in order of total number of points from *A* with most to *L*, *M*, and *N* with least. The boys are arranged in the same way.

Every girl listed three names, but Boys *e*, *l*, and *q* did not. Inspect rows *e*, *l*, and *q* to see which choices they omitted. (Do you suppose that fourth-grade boys typically are less careful about such tasks than fourth-grade girls or that some of the boys have fewer close friends than the girls do?)

The 31 very-best-friend choices went to just 15 pupils. How many of these were mutual choices—for example, where Mary listed Susan as her very best friend and Susan listed Mary as hers? By searching in Table 16–3 we see that *A* chose *D* and was chosen by *D*, that *B* chose *f* and was chosen by *f*, that *C* chose *c* but was not chosen by *c*, and so on. The five mutual-first-choice pairs are *AD*, *Bf*, *ag*, *bc*, and *eh*. Fifteen mutual first choices were possible.

It might have been better to ask each pupil to name his (or her) very best friend and second-best friend *of each sex*, rather than just the three best friends. Girl *E*, for instance, listed Girl *B* as her very best friend, but Girl *B* listed Boy *f* as her very best friend and Girl *E* as her second best friend, probably meaning that Girl *E* is her best *girl* friend.

Girl *A*, the most-chosen pupil, has perfect mutuality with all three of her choices. She listed Girl *D* as her very best friend, and Girl *D* listed her likewise. She chose Girl *C* as her second best friend, and Girl *C* reciprocated. She named Boy *c* as her third best friend, and he named her as his third best friend.

Girl *B*'s three choices all named her as very best friend. Girl *C* listed Boy *c* as her very best friend, but he did not choose her at all, instead choosing boys for 1 and 2 and designating her second best friend, *A*, as his third best friend.

One could analyze these 89 "chose" and "was chosen by" listings for a long time, uncovering various interesting relationships. It is rather time-consuming to do this from a two-way table such as Table 16–3, so often a sociogram like the one in Figure 16–10 is constructed to depict mutualities more graphically. Note that all girls except *L* are at the left. *L* chose two boys and was not chosen by anyone, as was also true of *M*. *N*, however, chose only girls (and was chosen by nobody), so she appears at the left. The two "stars," *A* and *a*, are in the center near each other, though neither chose the other. Interestingly, *A* was chosen by four boys, but *a* chose no girls and was chosen by only one. At age 10 he is a "boy's boy."

Arrangement of the sociogram follows definite rules, but because of the enormous number of ways that the "chosen" and "choosers" can be depicted in two dimensions, some variations from teacher to teacher for identical data can be expected. In general, "isolates" (unchosen pupils) are near the periphery, while "stars" (much-chosen pupils) are near the center. Because we used *A* and *a* to represent the most-chosen pupils, *B* and *b* the next-most-chosen ones, and so on, letters at the start of the alphabet tend to be in the middle of Figure 16–10 while letters nearer the end (*M*, *N*, *p*, *q*) are further out.

For clarity, girls are doubly denoted by a capital letter in a circle, and boys are identified by a small letter in a square.

Solid black lines represent first choices, white lines second choices, dashed

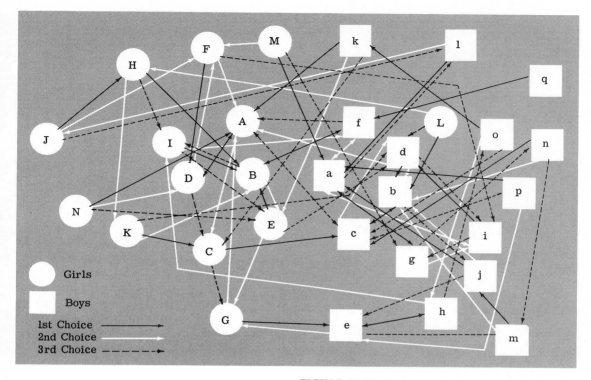

lines third choices. Arrows with points on each end represent mutual choices. For example, *A* and *D* chose each other as "very best friend"; *A* and *C* were mutual "second best friends"; and *A* reciprocated with *c* for "third best friend." Inspection of the table will convince you that strict mutualities, indicated by the double-headed arrows, are rare except for mutual "very best friends" (that is, mutual first choices).

The sociogram drawn in Figure 16–10 has two special limitations (Bonney, 1960). For groups of thirty or more the diagram becomes too complicated to be interpreted easily, unless only first choices are included. In addition, considerable trial-and-error is required before an effective placement of the individuals can be determined.

The *target diagram* shown in Figure 16–11 is a less common but probably a more usable way of depicting sociometric data from groups as large as those found in most classrooms. Figure 16–11 portrays the same data as those shown in Figure 16–10. Four concentric circles distinguish among the students; roughly one-fourth of them are represented in each of the four areas. Typically, boys are placed in one half, girls in the other. The *stars* are found near the center, the *isolates* and *fringers* near the periphery. Arrows can, however, be drawn in the same manner as in the conventional sociogram. In many situations, ease of construction and interpretation of the target diagram allows sociometric analyses that would not be possible with the conventional graphic method illustrated in Figure 16–10.

School Central

Teacher Williams

Level or Grade 5

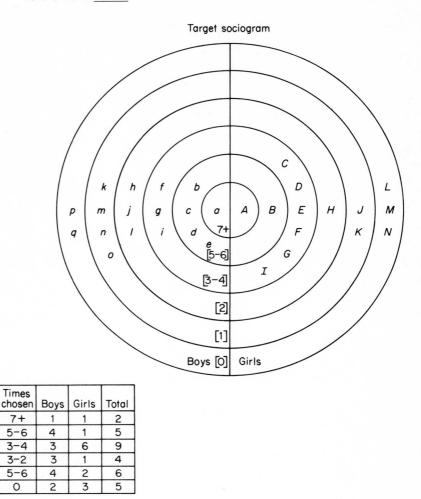

FIGURE 16–11 "Target" sociogram based on data in Table 16–3.

Times chosen	Boys	Girls	Total
7+	1	1	2
5–6	4	1	5
3–4	3	6	9
3–2	3	1	4
5–6	4	2	6
0	2	3	5

"Guess Who" Technique   This technique is one of the simplest methods of obtaining peer judgments. Each student is asked to list the student or students (if any) who match a series of brief descriptions that may include negative as well as positive characteristics. When negative descriptions are included, it is important that the response be optional for the student.

Hartshorne and May (1928) presented the techniques as a guessing game for young children, hence its name, the "guess who" technique. Some excellent   **408**

> Below are some word pictures of members of your class. Read each statement and write down the names of the persons whom you think the descriptions fit.
>   REMEMBER: One description *may* fit several persons. You may write as many names as you think belong under each.
>   The same person may be nominated for more than one description.
>   Write "myself" if you think the description fits you.
>   If you cannot think of anyone to match a particular description, go on to the next one.
>   You will have as much time as you need to finish. Do not hurry.

A series of behavior descriptions follows, such as:

> Someone who always seems rather sad, worried, or unhappy.
> Someone who is very friendly, who is nice to everybody.

Torrance (1962) suggested using the "guess who" approach to evaluate different aspects of creative thinking. Sample items include: "Who has the most original or unusual ideas?" "Who in your class does the most inventing or developing of new ideas, gadgets, and such?"

The results from an actual "guess who" application in a sixth-grade class are shown in Table 16–4. The assessment was a part of a case study of student number 11, who, because of her maladaptive behavior, had been referred to the school psychologist. The teacher's suspicions were dramatically confirmed by peer judgments obtained by the "guess who" technique. Note that pupil 11 was listed as "not liked" by all but one of her peers. No other student was so identified by even one student. Her one nomination for "best friend" was from her own ballot.

From such a self-picture by a class the teacher can identify pupils who most need help. Notice the "quiet" pupils, 15, 18, 22, and 34. Although pupil 15 was perceived as the quietest, he was listed as the best friend by two other students; the other three quiet students were not nominated by any peer. Only one of the four received a single identification with "happy" by a peer, whereas each of the four was deemed "unhappy" by at least one peer.

The principal advantage of the "guess who" technique is its usability. It requires only a few minutes to administer and to tabulate and can assess several dimensions within a group. The sociogram is limited to a single question—a separate figure or table is required for each item.

Reliability and Validity of Sociometric Data   Gronlund (1955) reported a median test-retest reliability coefficient of .76 for sociometric choices over a four-month interval for elementary-school children. From his extensive study of sociometric literature, Bonney (1960, p. 1321) reported: "It seems fair to conclude that there is indeed a strong tendency for the members of a group to maintain quite similar sociometric ranks over several weeks or several months. . . ."

The immediate validity of sociometric data appears to be quite satisfactory (Mouton et al., 1955) when certain precautions are taken. The confidentiality of the information must be perceived by the group, otherwise many negative

Pupil No.	Positive Characteristics (10)										Negative Characteristics (11)											Sum of Positive Traits	Sum of Negative Traits
	Quiet	Most Active in Games	Best Liked	Not Bossy	Polite	Works Well with Others	Happy	Tidy	Takes Care of Things	Best Friend	Restless	Talkative	Silent	Not Liked	Bossy	Not Polite	Does Not Take Care of Things	Unhappy	Untidy	Wastes Time	Does Not Work Well with Others		
1 A.B.		14	2	1			2		1	2						1			1			22	2
2 B.L.								1	1	1					1							3	1
3 B.C.			2			4		1	2	3									1			12	1
4 C.R.								1	1		1					1	1		1		1	2	5
5 E.R.											1	4				6	2	1	2	3	2	0	21
6 B.B.				4	1	1		1											3		1	7	4
7 C.J.									1		1	1				3	1			2	1	1	9
8 E.J.	1	1		2				1	2	2												9	0
9 E.T.			1								1							1	1	2	1	1	6
10 G.P.		2	5	2	2	3	7	2	2	3	2				9						2	28	13
11 H.C.			1					3		1	14	2		34	5	6	22	17	9	15	9	5	133
12 H.S.						1				1	23					5	2	2	2	7	4	2	45
13 H.C.									1	1									1	1	1	2	3
14 J.J.						2																2	0
15 L.J.	13			7	4	1		3	3	2					17				2			33	19
16 M.E.				1	1	1			1						1			1		3	1	4	6
17 M.S.			1		1	3	1		2						2	2			1	1		8	6
18 M.C.	6				3	2	1	1							3				2			13	5
19 M.M.						1	1													1	1	2	2
20 N.R.				1				1	1						1	1				5	3	3	10
21 O.R.					1						1					1						1	2
22 O.S.	6		1	3	6		1	9	2						2	1			1			28	4
23 R.D.					1	8			1		1								1	1	1	10	4
24 R.P.		2	5	1	4	1	2	7								6	1	1				22	8
25 S.M.										1						1	1	2	2		3	1	9
26 S.D.							2		2							3						4	3
27 S.V.			5			1	3	2	1	3	1					1	1		1	2		15	6
28 F.J.				1							1	1			1	1						1	4
29 T.R.		16	15	2	7	4	3		1	4	1											52	1
30 T.K.							1	1	1	2	1								1			5	2
31 T.B.				1	1	2	3		1										1			8	1
32 W.B.				1		2												1	1			3	2
33 M.E.				1	1		2	4	1	2		1				1					1	11	3
34 D.C.	9			3	4	1								10			1	3				17	14
35 A.E.										1					1	1				3	3	1	8
36 B.S.				2	4	1		2	4	1				1		1			1			14	3

SOURCE: Courtesy of Frank Thompson, principal of Hillgrove School, La Puenta, California.

[a] Numbers indicate the frequency with which each student was associated with the "guess who" description by his classmates.

perceptions and interrelationships will not be expressed. A second requirement is that the members of the group know each other quite well. This requirement reduces the value of sociometric data in large schools in which students change classes each period. Sociometric data have had, and will probably continue to have, their greatest utility at the elementary-school level.

Sociometric techniques should be meaningful to the students and should provide useful data for the teacher. Nothing beneficial can be expected to happen merely because each pupil has been asked, for example, to list his three best friends. Responses to this kind of question constitute the starting point from which the ingenious teacher studies the social structure of his classroom and devises ways to help it facilitate his teaching. He may try to alter the structure slightly in carefully thought-out ways, such as by forming study groups of low mutuality in the hope that this will permit the "friendless" to make friends. The teacher needs to understand the social psychology of his group rather well in order to do this extensively or radically. He is well advised to proceed with caution, but to proceed. The "isolates," such as *L, M, N, p,* and *q* in Figure 16-11, may need special help.

When properly obtained, according to Bonney (1960, p. 1323), sociometric data have validity for the following classroom uses:

> (a) to form subgroups which are composed of persons who have indicated preferences for each other, (b) to study changes in interpersonal relations and in the social structure of a group over a particular time interval, (c) to determine the extent to which students of different racial, religious, and social-class grouping accept each other, (d) to locate individuals and small groups of individuals who are outstanding centers of influence in a particular population in order to utilize their social prestige in the management of the group, and (e) to locate individuals who are isolates or fringers in order to plan some kind of assistance for them so that they may achieve some degree of recognition and feeling of belonging.

Sociometric information can also be useful in parent conferences, to enable parents to understand better how their child is perceived by his classmates.

Appraising Socioeconomic Status

The concept of socioeconomic status (SES) is widely used in education, sociology, and psychology. SES is closely related to many educational characteristics of pupils such as achievement motivation, dropping out of school, and academic achievement. Occupation is an important SES ingredient; its relationship to intelligence is graphically illustrated in Figure 14-15 (p. 351). Since the concept of SES is so pervasive, it is useful to understand how it is measured, even though it is it is rarely assessed formally, except in research studies.

The methods of assessing SES have evolved largely from sociology and social psychology. Several different SES measures have been devised; all of them employ some combination of the following: educational level, occupational level, kind of residence, amount of income, source of income, and dwelling area.

The most widely used SES measure is the *Index of Status Characteristics* (ISC) (Warner, Meeker, and Eells, 1949), which uses four factors to arrive at an ISC score, which is then converted to one of five social classes.

Occupation[3]

1. Professionals and proprietors (such as established physicians, lawyers, certified public accountants, major executives, "gentlemen" farmers).
2. Minor professionals and proprietors (such as beginning or less successful physicians, lawyers, and so on, owners of large farms).
3. Semiprofessionals (such as salesmen and cashiers).
4. Skilled workers (such as bookkeepers, factory foremen, sheriffs, railroad engineers).
5. Medium-skill workers (such as telephone operators, carpenters, plumbers, barbers, firemen).
6. Semiskilled workers (such as taxi and truck drivers, gas station attendants, waitresses).
7. Unskilled workers (such as laborers, miners, janitors).

Source of Income

1. Inherited wealth.
2. Earned wealth.
3. Profits and professional fees.
4. Salary and commissions.
5. Wages, determined by an hourly rate.
6. Private relief.
7. Public relief and nonrespectable income.

Housing

1. Excellent houses: very large single-family dwellings surrounded by large landscaped yards.
2. Very good houses, but not as large as those in the first category.
3. Good houses, more conventional and less ostentatious than the first two categories.
4. Average houses, conventional single-family dwellings.
5. Fair houses, smaller houses whose condition is not quite as good as those houses in category 4.
6. Poor, badly run-down houses.
7. Very poor houses, surrounded by debris.

Dwelling Area

1. Very high status area.
2. High status area.
3. Above average area.

---

[3] See Bonjean, Hill, and McLemore (1967, pp. 442–448) for detailed explanation of each category.

4. Average area containing workingmen's homes.
5. Below average area; close to factories or railroads.
6. Low status area; run-down and semi-slums.
7. Very low status area; slum.

Warner had earlier included amount of education and amount of income, but since these factors were found to be largely redundant with the four above, they were eliminated from the scale.

The Index of Status Characteristics (ISC) is arrived at by using the category ratings from the four factors in the following equation:

$$\text{ISC} = (4 \times \text{Occupation}) + (3 \times \text{Source of income}) + (3 \times \text{House type}) + (2 \times \text{dwelling area}).$$

For example, if one is classified into categories 3, 4, 2, 3 for occupation, source of income, house type, and dwelling area, respectively, he receives a total ISC score of

$$\text{ISC} = (4 \times 3) + (3 \times 4) + (3 \times 2) + (2 \times 3) = 36.$$

A social class rating as defined by Warner (Warner, Meeker, and Eells, 1949) is then assigned according to the ISC score:

ISC Score	Social Class Rating
12–22	Upper class
23–37	Upper-middle class
38–51	Lower-middle class
52–66	Upper-lower class
67–84	Lower-lower class

HOLLINGSHEAD'S INDEX

Because of the difficulty and cost of obtaining residential information, other SES scales have been devised that do not require it. One of the most common is Hollingshead's (Hollingshead and Redlich, 1957) *Two-Factor Index of Social Position*.[4] Hollingshead's scale is popular partially because it is easy to use—the index requires only an occupational and educational scale, each of which is divided into seven levels.

Occupational Scale[5]

1. Major executives of large concerns, major professionals, and proprietors.
2. Lesser professionals and proprietors, and business managers.
3. Administrative personnel, owners of small business, and minor professionals.

---

[4] Material from the *Two Factor Index of Social Position* as it appeared in Bonjean, Hill, and McLemore (1967, pp. 381–385) is included by courtesy of Dr. August B. Hollingshead.

[5] See Bonjean, Hill, and Mclemore (1967, pp. 442–448) for detailed explanation of each category.

4. Clerical and sales workers, and technicians.
5. Skilled trades.
6. Machine operators and semiskilled workers.
7. Unskilled employees.

Educational Scale

1. Professionals (Master's degree, doctorate, or professional degree).
2. College graduates.
3. 1–3 years college or business school.
4. High-school graduates.
5. 10–11 years of schooling.
6. 7–9 years of schooling.
7. Under 7 years of schooling.

A total Index of Social Position (ISP) score is arrived at by using the following equation:

$$ISP = (7 \times \text{Occupation rating}) + (4 \times \text{Education rating}).$$

Thus, a carpenter (5) with nine years of school (6) would have a total ISP score of $(7 \times 5) + (4 \times 6) = 59$. Hollingshead classifies the scores in five priorities as indicated below:

Social Class	Scores
I	11–17
II	18–27
III	28–43
IV	44–60
V	61–77

OTHER SES SCALES AND USES

Several similar measures may be found in excellent compendiums by Shaw and Wright (1967); Bonjean, Hill, and McLemore (1967); and Miller (1967).

The scales have important uses in research studies in which SES may be a relevant variable. For example, Harper (1970) investigated the effects of a cognitive stimulating treatment in relation to pupils' SES level and found that the treatment had different effects for high-SES than for low-SES pupils.

Eckland (1964) found that most male college freshmen of modest academic aptitude persisted to eventual graduation if their parents were of fairly high SES, but less so if they were of low SES. Thus, the SES of one's parents has some relationship to one's likelihood of educational and life success; however, the relationship is not extremely close. Many persons move up or down the SES "ladder"—some of them a great distance.

Post-organizer

The value of standardized interest tests is most apparent for vocational guidance purposes. The classic tests are *Strong's Vocational Interest Blank* and the *Kuder Preference Record-Vocational* (KPR-V). The KPR-V measures several areas of interest and is generally preferable for high-school use. During the high-school years there is considerable fluctuation in interests, which must be considered in interpreting students' profiles. Measured interests have little relationship with abilities, although they are related to occupational choice and job satisfaction.

Personality assessment is difficult and imprecise with current tests and techniques. Self-report personality inventories are vulnerable to semantic difficulties, self-deception, faking, and criterion inadequacy. Such measures have rarely been shown to yield information of any practical value. Projective techniques are not easily faked, but their unique assessment difficulties greatly limit their usefulness for personality appraisal.

Sociometric techniques can help one understand the status and dynamics of groups such as a class of students. The "guess who" technique is particularly useful, since it yields information on several dimensions and requires little time to administer and tabulate.

Measures of socioeconomic status are often useful in research studies but have limited value for individual or classroom use. The simpler background ones, however, can provide teachers with information about their pupils.

SUGGESTED READINGS

ALLISON, J., S. J. BLATT, and C. N. ZIMET. 1968. *Interpretation of psychological tests*. New York: Harper & Row, Publishers.

ANASTASI, A. 1968. *Psychological testing*, 3d ed. New York: The Macmillan Company.
    Chapters 17–20, pp. 437–546, give a thorough treatment of the topics of personality and interest measurement.

BANAKA, W. H. 1971. *Training in depth interviewing*. New York: Harper and Row, Publishers.

BONJEAN, C. M., R. J. HILL, and S. D. McLEMORE. 1967. *Sociological measurement: An inventory of scales and indices*. San Francisco: Chandler Publishing Company.

BONNEY, J. M. 1960. Sociometric methods. In C. W. Harris, ed., *Encyclopedia of educational research*, 3d ed. New York: The Macmillan Company, pp. 1319–1324.

CAMPBELL, D. P. 1968a. Changing patterns of interests within the American society. *Measurement and evaluation in guidance*, **1**: 36–49.

———. 1968b. The *Strong Vocational Interest Blank*: 1927–1967. In P. McReynolds, ed., *Advances in psychological assessment*, Vol. I. Palo Alto, Calif.: Science and Behavior Books, pp. 105–130.

CRITES, J. O. 1969. Interests. In R. L. Ebel, ed., *Encyclopedia of educational research*, 4th ed. New York: The Macmillan Company, pp. 678–686.

EYSENCK, J. J. 1959. Rorschach review. In O. K. Buros, ed., *The fifth mental measurements yearbook*. Highland Park, N.J.: The Gryphon Press, pp. 276–278.

FLANAGAN, J. C. 1969. Student characteristics: Elementary and secondary. In R. L. Ebel, ed., *Encyclopedia of educational research*, 4th ed. New York: The Macmillan Company, pp. 1330–1339.

GARDNER, E. F., and G. C. THOMPSON. 1958. Measuring and interpreting social relations. *Test service notebook no. 22.* New York: Harcourt Brace Jovanovich, Inc.

GRONLUND, N. E. 1959. *Sociometry in the classroom.* New York: Harper & Row, Publishers.

JENSEN, A. R. 1965. Review of the Rorschach. In O. K. Buros, ed., *The sixth mental measurements yearbook.* Highland Park, N.J.: The Gryphon Press. Reprinted in G. H. Bracht, K. D. Hopkins, and J. C. Stanley. 1972. *Perspectives in educational and psychological measurement.* Englewood Cliffs, N.J.: Prentice-Hall, Inc., Selection 30.

JOHNSON, O. G., and J. W. BOMMARITO. 1971. *Tests and measurements in child development: A handbook.* San Francisco: Jossey-Bass, Inc.

KUDER, G. F. 1963. A rationale for evaluating interest. *Educational and Psychological Measurement,* **23:** 3–12.

———. 1969. A note on the comparability of occupational scores from different interest inventories. *Measurement and Evaluation in Guidance,* **2:** 94–100.

———. 1970. Some principles of interest measurement. *Educational and Psychological Measurement,* **30:** 205–226. Reprinted in G. H. Bracht, K. D. Hopkins, and J. C. Stanley. 1972. *Perspectives in educational and psychological measurement.* Englewood Cliffs, N.J.: Prentice-Hall, Inc., Selection 28.

MASIA, B. B. 1964. What to look for in a review of a personality inventory. *Personnel and Guidance Journal,* **42:** 1030–1034. Reprinted in G. H. Bracht, K. D. Hopkins, and J. C. Stanley. 1972. *Perspectives in educational and psychological measurement.* Englewood Cliffs, N.J.: Prentice-Hall, Inc., Selection 29.

MEDLEY, D. M., and H. E. MITZEL. 1963. Measuring classroom behavior by systematic observation. In N. L. Gage, ed., *Handbook of research on teaching.* Skokie, Ill.: Rand McNally & Company, Chap. 6, pp. 247–328.

MILLER, D. C. 1967. *Handbook of research design and social measurement.* New York: David McKay Company, Inc.

MORENO, J. L., et al., eds. 1960. *The sociometry reader.* New York: The Free Press.

REMMERS, H. H. 1963. Rating methods in research on teaching. In N. L. Gage, ed., *Handbook of research on teaching.* Skokie, Ill.: Rand McNally & Company, Chap. 7, pp. 329–378.

SHAW, M. E., and J. M. WRIGHT. 1967. *Scales for the measurement of attitudes.* New York: McGraw-Hill Book Company.

SUPER, D. E. 1960. Interests. In C. W. Harris, ed., *Encyclopedia of educational research*, 3rd ed. New York: The Macmillan Company, pp. 728–733.

———, and J. O. CRITES. 1962. *Appraising vocational fitness*, rev. ed. New York: Harper, & Row, Publishers.
      Chapters 16 and 17, pp. 417–513, the nature and measurement of interests.

WARNER, W. L., M. MEEKER, and K. EELLS. 1949. *Social class in America.* Chicago: Science Research Associates.

YEE, A. H., and T. KRIEWALL. 1969. A new logical scoring key for the Minnesota Teacher Attitude Inventory. *Journal of Educational Measurement,* **6:** 11–14.

THE TESTING PROGRAM

One of the chief weaknesses of many attempts to use standardized tests is that there has been no testing *program* worthy of the name. The word *program* has certain important implications of *order, system,* and *planning*. It implies a sequence of events that has been determined after careful thought. Unfortunately, it is the exception rather than the rule when a school district invests the time and effort necessary for a sound program of evaluation and testing. The tests selected and used too often depend more on the quality of the publishers' salesmen than on the quality of the product. There rarely is a systematic program to help teachers properly interpret and use the results of the testing. It is not surprising that many teachers question the value of standardized testing.

One must not assume that the testing *program* should be restricted to the use of standardized tests. Testing programs require the planned use of a variety of tests to supplement the teacher's own testing and other evaluative activities. *Teacher-made tests are a vital part of any complete testing program.* Schools should have a carefully thought-out general policy on such matters as the frequency of testing, the importance of final examinations, the factors to be considered in determining final marks, and, most important, the uses to be made of the results. Results should be viewed cumulatively, so that over the years a number of different student abilities and aptitudes can be assessed.

Regardless of its scope, the complete testing program will ordinarily consist of the following eight stages (in chronological order):

1. Determining the purpose of the program.
2. Selecting the appropriate test or tests.

3. Administering the tests.
4. Scoring the tests.
5. Analyzing and interpreting the scores.
6. Applying the results.
7. Retesting to determine the success of the program.
8. Making suitable records and reports.

Determining the Purpose of the Program

It must be acknowledged that tests are only tools and that measurement is always a means to an end, never an end itself. Thus, the value of any testing program depends on the use made of results. Testing without rhyme, rule, or reason is money, time, and effort wasted. An experienced educator was once heard to say that he had wondered for years what many people did with standard tests after they had been "given." At last he found out. They filed them! A testing program should have a more serious purpose than that. The first step, therefore, in planning a program is to determine its purpose. In so doing, three things should be remembered: the program should be *cooperative*, *practical*, and *definite*. The most common purposes of a testing program were discussed in Chapter 1. They included such uses as identifying underachievers, evaluating curricula, diagnosing learning problems, identifying the academically gifted, grouping and placing students, and several other instructional, administrative, and guidance functions.

A COOPERATIVE PROGRAM

The testing program should not represent the judgment of any one person, but that of a group. It should be a truly cooperative enterprise. The teachers and the administrators should be made to feel that it is "our" program, as indeed it should be. This is not likely to occur if the principal, superintendent, or research department determines the program and then "hands it down" to the classroom teachers. The entire staff should have a voice in determining the purpose of the program and in formulating the plans; they should have the opportunity of participating in it in every way possible from beginning to end. If this is not done, the teachers are not likely to understand the program fully or to appreciate what it is attempting to achieve. Without the enthusiastic cooperation of the entire staff, the program is almost sure to fall short of its highest possibilities. We suggest, therefore, that in a small school or school system the purpose of the program be decided upon after discussion in a general teachers' meeting or series of meetings in which everyone has a chance to participate. In a larger school system, it is better to entrust the responsibility of planning the program to a committee representing all interested groups; the proposed plan should be brought before the entire staff before final action is taken. We cannot emphasize too strongly that the success of the program largely depends on cooperative action. An important part of the program, thus, is educating the staff so they can participate intelligently in it. The teacher's attitude is probably the most important single factor to be considered.

*The Testing
Program*

The general purpose of the testing program is to provide data that will help identify and solve practical educational problems. This usually means that the problems whose solutions are sought will have to do with administration, instruction, research, or some combination of the three. Tests may be used primarily for administrative purposes (such as placement of students), but they can also be used by the classroom teachers for diagnostic purposes. Since 1965, federal legislation in the area of education has increased the need for testing in the schools, to meet legal evaluation and accountability requirements. Schools are required to have a plan for evaluating the success or failure of many new programs that employ federal funds. Such plans frequently involve both standardized and locally constructed tests. For a long time, many educators have been of the opinion that program evaluation and research are legitimate interests of classroom teachers and of administrators.

A DEFINITE PROGRAM

It is not enough that a program be cooperative and practical; it must also be definite. Its scope may be as small as a single subject in one grade or as large as the measurement of an entire school system. A common mistake of a staff inexperienced in the use of tests is to undertake too much. The danger is that the program will drag along until everybody is "fed up" with it. Much of the value of the information sought from the tests will be lost unless the information is made available without delay. It is usually best, particularly with inexperienced teachers, to run the risk of undertaking too small a program rather than one too large.

A mistake often made is in stating the purpose of the program in too general terms. "To improve instruction" is too vague and inclusive. "To motivate study" or "to diagnose weaknesses and provide a basis for remedial instruction" would be better. Best of all would be a still more definite formulation, such as "to motivate study in fifth-grade arithmetic" or "to make a diagnosis of characteristic weaknesses in first-year algebra and to formulate a program of remedial teaching to eliminate them." The purpose should state specifically the nature and the scope of the program to be undertaken. In a long-range program, the purpose for each year will have a definite relationship to the whole. No matter how they are stated, there are two fundamental goals of all measurement: the better understanding of the individual pupil, and assessment of curricular strengths and weaknesses. To accomplish these purposes the information must be as relevant and as complete as possible.

Selecting the Appropriate Test or Tests

After the purpose of the testing program has been determined—and not until then—the selection of tests is in order. In Chapter 4 we emphasized that a test may be superior for one purpose and worthless for another. Great care must be taken to obtain the tests most appropriate for the purpose. Three questions require consideration:

1. Who should select the test or tests?
2. What kinds of test should be used?
3. What is the best procedure for making the selection?

WHO SHOULD SELECT THE TESTS?

In larger school systems, the director of research or of pupil personnel services is often the person most qualified to make the selection. In the selection of achievement tests for specific subjects, the curriculum specialists and teachers of these subjects should be consulted because their knowledge is essential in judging the content validity of the tests. In smaller schools, the major responsibility of selection is usually assumed by the principal or superintendent, or it may be assigned to a guidance counselor. In the selection of achievement tests, a committee of teachers will be helpful for judging the content of the tests. For evaluation that involves a subjective element, it is a sound principle to rely on the combined judgment of a group of competent persons rather than on the judgment of only one individual.

That standardized achievement tests and batteries differ greatly is illustrated in Table 17–1, which provides information on seven batteries of achievement tests designed for the elementary grades (4–6). Note the wide disparity in testing time, length, and especially cost. Table 17–1 should demonstrate the complete lack of interchangeability among standardized achievement-test batteries, even though their descriptive labels are often similar or identical.

TABLE 17–1

*A Comparison of Standardized Achievement-Test
Batteries (Elementary Level) on Several Factors*[a]

Achievement Battery	No. of Subtests	Total Testing Time (Minutes)	Average Minutes per Subtest	Dollar Cost per Battery	Cents Cost per Subtest
1	10	161	16.1	$0.15	1.50¢
2	6	144	24.0	.17	2.83
3	11	279	25.4	.84	7.64
4	10	240	24.0	.25	2.50
5	9	215	23.9	.18	2.00
6	10	480	48.0	.50	5.00
7	7	455	65.0	3.05	43.57

[a] Since the various achievement batteries are continually revised, altered, and repriced, they are not identified by name. The purpose of this table is to show the wide disparity among batteries on several practical factors.

WHAT KINDS OF TEST SHOULD BE USED?

An adequate testing program ordinarily will involve the use of more than one kind of test. It usually will be desirable to use scholastic aptitude (intelligence) and achievement tests at the elementary level. Considerations of continuity and norm comparability make it advisable to limit the testing program to one standard achievement-test battery[1] for determining the present status of the class or school.

For a general survey of the intellectual status of the class or school, one good group test of intelligence will usually be adequately reliable. The interpretation of the achievement tests will be greatly facilitated if they are normed on the same reference group as the intelligence test.

Classroom teachers usually will find a larger place for nonstandardized, teacher-made tests in the solution of instructional problems than will school administrators in the solution of administrative problems. The reverse condition will tend to be true for standardized tests. There is a legitimate place for both kinds of test, but each is superior for some purposes.

WHAT IS THE BEST PROCEDURE?

Regardless of the purpose of the testing program or who makes the selection of tests, it is important that a systematic evaluation procedure be followed. Users of standardized tests will find the information contained in *The Mental Measurements Yearbooks* of great value. The comprehensive character of the tests reviewed in this publication is indicated by Buros' (1970) *Mental Measurements Yearbook Test Index*. The number of tests in each category is also given in Table 17–2.

The *Mental Measurements Yearbooks* (*MMY's*) present critical reviews on every published test. If a test is not new, it has probably been reviewed in earlier *Mental Measurements Yearbooks*, which should be consulted. Buros (1970) has made this easy with his *MMY Test Index* for *MMY* volumes 1–6 that cites such reviews. The *MMY's* and the *MMY Test Index* make it easier for a teacher, guidance counselor, or administrator to decide which tests he would like to inspect. He can then send to the publishers for sample "specimen" sets to compare and contrast.

Many aspects determine the suitability of a given test for given purposes. For many years, test specialists have offered various rating procedures designed to evaluate each of the tests being considered for use so that various characteristics will be considered properly. The following evaluative excerpts are from reviews of the seven *Sequential Tests of Educational Progress* (STEP).[2]

The battery as a whole was discussed independently by four measurement specialists. Each of the seven tests also was reviewed by two or three persons in the fifth and sixth editions of *MMY*. In all, 34 different reviews are provided on some portion or portions of the STEP battery. These reviews offer a great deal of help to the prospective user of the tests, particularly if he reads a number of reviews carefully to average out the preferences of the reviewers.

In the fifth *MMY*, Jackson described the tests, praising various aspects, but he also expressed concern for what

> seems to be an unjustified tendency to offer understanding and application of knowledge as alternatives to the acquisition of factual information. . . . The tests

[1] Nearly every major test publisher has such a battery. The interested educator who helps plan testing programs will want to have test catalogues of the major test publishers and consult the *Mental Measurements Yearbooks*, edited by O. K. Buros.

[2] Essay, listening, mathematics, reading, science, social studies, and writing, published by the Educational Testing Service, Princeton, N.J., 08540.

MMY Test Index	Number of Entries	MMY Test Index	Number of Entries	MMY Test Index	Number of Entries
Achievement Batteries	54	Miscellaneous	3	Sensory-Motor	5
Business Education	11	Agriculture	5	Hearing	19
Bookkeeping	8	Scoring Devices	27	Motor	6
Miscellaneous	8	Courtship and Marriage	14	Vision	30
Shorthand	24	Driving and Safety Education	22		
Typewriting	18	Education	46	Social Studies	33
English	103	Etiquette	7	Contemporary Affairs	13
Composition	11	Handwriting	5	Economics	8
Literature	56	Health and Physical Education	45	Geography	18
Speech	17	Home Economics	34	History	52
Spelling	31	Industrial Arts	14	Political Science	31
Vocabulary	37	Listening Comprehension	2	Sociology	5
Fine Arts	2	Philosophy	2	Vocations	9
Art	12	Psychology	9		
Music	29	Record and Report Forms	26	Clerical	38
Foreign Languages	6	Religious Education	21	Interests	55
English	13	Socioeconomic Status	5		
French	46	Test Programs	9	Manual Dexterity	14
German	23	Multi-Aptitude Batteries	25	Mechanical Ability	50
Greek	2	Personality			
Hebrew	6	Nonprojective	308	Miscellaneous	38
Italian	10	Projective	78		
Latin	22	Reading	86	Selection and Rating Forms	28
Russian	6	Diagnostic	25		
Spanish	30	Miscellaneous	11	Specific Vocations	1
Intelligence		Oral	14	Accounting	2
Group	208	Readiness	19	Dentistry	2
Individual	56	Special Fields	18	Engineering	22
Specific	26	Speed	6	Law	2
Mathematics	58	Study Skills	45	Medicine	3
Algebra	39	Science	44	Miscellaneous	20
Arithmetic	103	Biology	31	Nursing	13
Calculus	3	Chemistry	41	Research	4
Geometry	135	Miscellaneous	16	Selling	31
Miscellaneous	1	Physics	31	Skilled Trades	14
Trigonometry	8			Supervision	11
				Transportation	8

SOURCE: Buros, 1970.

in mathematics, science, and social studies might well be improved by increasing the proportion of items requiring factual knowledge not obtainable by reading a supplied passage; reading with understanding is not, after all, the primary objective in these areas.

He continued with

a more serious question to be raised with respect to the STEP series. . . . In their desire to keep clear of specific subject matter, the authors have apparently tended to arrive at something not too far from a *set* of measures of general intelligence. Further evidence in this connection, particularly in regard to intercorrelations among the tests of the different STEP series, will be awaited with interest. The basic similarity among certain reading, science, and social studies items . . . leads to the expectation that these may be uncomfortably high [p. 64].

Layton prefaced his critique with the following cautions:

> The STEP authors have attempted a tremendous task in designing and developing the STEP materials. Actually, the development project has only just begun. Consequently, in the early stages of the project this review may be too critical. A reviewer several years hence may find many of the present criticisms not applicable [p. 67].

Layton then argued that too high a price has been paid for the "sequential" feature, which attempts to span grades 4 through 14.

Diekhoff wrote of the STEP Essay Test:

> Accepting as he does the assumption that the best test of writing is writing, this reviewer does not see how it could be done much better. The essay topics are appropriate to the several school levels. The sample essays present clear differences in quality—one wishes student themes were always so clearly "high," "low," or "middle" [p. 357].

Julian C. Stanley and Sister M. Jacinta Mann concluded in their review: "Overall, the STEP Science tests meet excellently the need for a well planned, coordinated survey series stressing application of common curricular material to familiar situations." To them, however, "The great amount of reading these tests require is somewhat disturbing . . . , even though the test authors do have an explicit rationale for their long contexts" (p. 804).

In the sixth *MMY*, Seashore observed that "whether the *basic idea* of STEP will dominate the field remains to be seen. STEP and the *Iowa Tests of Educational Development* represent a common trend away from achievement tests which bear a close relation to the curriculum" (p. 105).

Reviewers do not always agree on the characteristics a test should have. For example, in contrast to Jackson's concern about inattention to facts, Stanley and Mann fear that the STEP science test is oriented too heavily toward factual knowledge instead of toward comprehension, application, analysis, synthesis, and evaluation. Such discrepancies motivate Buros to select at least two, and preferably three, independent reviewers for each new test. Only the Listening Test is reviewed by two persons; each other STEP test is reviewed by three independent reviewers or sets of reviewers.

THE APA-AERA-NCME TEST STANDARDS

In Table 17–3 we provide a list of factors that should be considered in evaluating a standardized test. Of course, the validity issue is the most crucial. In addition to the broad categories in Table 17–3, persons involved with test selection should study carefully the 36-page booklet, *Standards for Educational and Psychological Tests and Manuals*, produced by a joint committee of the American Psychological Association (APA), the American Educational Research Association (AERA), and the National Council on Measurement in Education (NCME). The recommendations are made under six major

TABLE 17-3
Relevant Factors in Evaluating
Published Tests

Validity Information
   Content
   Construct
   Criterion-related
   Item Development and selection
Reliability Information
   Type: internal consistency
              test-retest
              parallel form
              long and short term
Norms
   Representativeness of reference group
   Types of converted scores available
   Date of standardization
Usability
   Examinee appropriateness
   Ease of administration
   Cost (booklets, answer sheets, scoring)
   Time required (administration and scoring)
   Machine or hand scoring
   Aids for interpretation and recording
   How does test fit into the total testing
       program and sequence?
Comments of Reviewers[3]

headings: dissemination of information, interpretation, validity, reliability, administration and scoring, and scales and norms. The single most important feature of the recommendations is, perhaps, the treatment of validity. Several excerpts will help reveal the tenor of the recommendations, though of course the serious student will want to read the recommendations himself.

The introduction to the section on validity in the APA-AERA-NCME report (1966, p. 12) is given below. (We considered a number of these concepts in Chapter 4.)

> Validity information indicates to the test user the degree to which the test is capable of achieving certain aims. Tests are used for several types of judgment, and for each type of judgment a different type of investigation is required to establish validity. For purposes of describing the uses for three kinds of validity coefficients, we may distinguish three of the rather numerous aims of testing:
>
> 1. The test user wishes to determine how an individual performs at present in a universe of situations that the test situation is claimed to represent.
> 2. The test user wishes to forecast an individual's future standing or to estimate an individual's present standing on some variable of particular significance that is different from the test.
> 3. The test user wishes to infer the degree to which the individual possesses some hypothetical trait or quality (construct) presumed to be reflected in the test performance.

---

[3] In addition to the *Mental Measurements Yearbooks*, the *Journal of Educational Measurement*, the *Personnel and Guidance Journal*, *Measurement and Evaluation in Guidance*, and several other professional journals publish reviews of new or revised tests.

Thus, a vocabulary test might be used to measure present vocabulary, to predict college success, to discriminate schizophrenics from organics, or to make inferences about "intellectual capacity." To determine how suitable a test is for each of these uses, it is necessary to gather the appropriate validity information.

Following the rather extensive discussion of validity, the report presents numerous recommendations that are classified as "ESSENTIAL," "VERY DESIRABLE," or "DESIRABLE." Examples of each category are:

C1. The manual should report the validity of the test for each type of inference for which it is recommended. If its validity for some suggested interpretation has not been investigated, that fact should be made clear. ESSENTIAL.

Comment: It is incorrect to use the unqualified phrase "the validity of the test." No test is valid for all purposes or in all situations or for all groups of individuals. Any study of test validity is pertinent to only a few of the possible uses of or inferences from the test scores.

If the test is likely to be used incorrectly for certain areas of decision, the manual should include specific warnings. For example, the manual for a writing skills test states that the test apparently is not sufficiently difficult to discriminate among students "at colleges that have selective admissions" [p. 15].

C6.7. To ensure the continued correct interpretation of scores, the validity of the suggested interpretations should be rechecked periodically and the results reported in subsequent editions of the manual. VERY DESIRABLE.

Comment: Job requirements, conditions of work, and the types of person entering an occupation often change materially with the passage of time. Similarly the meanings of clinical categories, the nature of therapeutic treatment, and the objectives in any school course change. So also will the difficulty and psychological meaning of test items. Hence, the reader should be in a position to judge the extent to which scales are obsolete. Criterion data for the psychologist scale of a much used interest test were gathered in 1927. Subsequent research showed that these psychologists were no longer representative of the field. The current manual reports the date (1948) of the validating studies for the revised key. With the growth of mathematical psychology on the one hand, and of private clinical practice on the other, this scale may, in certain aspects, again be obsolescent [p. 22].

C6.71. If the validity of a suggested test interpretation has not been checked within 15 or 20 years, the test should be withdrawn from general sale and distributed, if at all, only to persons who will conduct their own validity studies. DESIRABLE [pp. 22–23].[4]

Before adopting it, you can check off the characteristics of a test against the APA-AERA-NCME recommendations, supplemented by reviews in the *Mental Measurements Yearbooks*. This may seem to be a long, somewhat tedious process, but it is your best guarantee of using wisely the large number of pupil-hours and teacher-hours allotted to testing. We shall not offer any scale for rating tests, other than the brief outline in Table 17–3, because the technical recommendations themselves can serve this evaluative function best.

A very useful source for obtaining a quick general evaluation of standard-

[4] Reprinted from American Psychological Association, American Educational Research Association, and National Council on Measurement in Education, *Standards for educational and psychological tests and manuals* (Washington, D.C.: American Psychological Association, Inc., 1966), pp. 15 and 22–23, by permission of the American Psychological Association.

ized tests at the elementary-school level is the *CSE Elementary School Test Evaluations* (Hoepfner and Klein, 1970). Published tests in the affective, cognitive, and psychomotor domains are given numerical ratings that depict the judged quality of each instrument in 24 categories pertaining to technical considerations (validity, reliability, norms, and so on) and practical ones (such as administration ease, time). These ratings should be viewed only as a quick general assessment and obviously are not substitutes for either the *MMY* reviews or a more intensive test evaluation for a given purpose in a particular situation. Brownell (1937) pointed out "some neglected criteria for evaluating classroom tests" that go beyond the recommendations discussed above. Does the test:

1. Elicit from the pupils the desired types of mental processes?
2. Enable the teacher to observe and analyze the thought processes which lie back of the pupil's answers?
3. Encourage the development of desirable study habits?
4. Lead to improved instructional practice?
5. Foster wholesome relationships between teacher and pupils?

Brownell's criteria are especially important for achievement tests. Such tests can be evaluated by means of Bloom's *Taxonomy of educational objectives* (Bloom et al., 1956) in which the higher thought processes of comprehending, applying, analyzing, synthesizing, and evaluating are emphasized as being important steps beyond the purely factual—but of course basic and essential—*knowledge* level.

In selecting a test for a particular purpose, consider the grade level at which it is to be administered. Test authors and publishers tend to be too optimistic about the range of usefulness of their tests. For example, a reading test that is supposed to be suitable for grades 3 through 8 may be too difficult for half the students in the typical third grade and too easy for the abler students in the eighth grade. A test usually discriminates best among a group of students if the average score obtained is halfway between the chance level and the perfect score (that is, the mean, when corrected for chance, is about one-half of the maximum score), and if very few students make chance or perfect scores. Remember, however, that for diagnostic and mastery tests the discriminating function among students may be relatively unimportant. If one high-school student in a class misses a problem such as $7 \times 8 =$ _____, the information is valuable to the teacher even if all other students answer these basic arithmetic items correctly.

Ingredients of the Testing Program

The frequency with which achievement tests should be used will depend mainly on the purpose they are to serve. Most purposes, however, will require at least a series of tests administered every year in elementary school and every two years thereafter. Many achievement tests have norms for one or two periods during the year (such as the middle and the end of the year) but for no other time. When tests are given at these periods, comparisons with norms are easiest and most defensible. Some studies have shown a considerable decline in knowledge of certain subjects by the end of the summer vacation (Beggs and Hieronymus, 1968). This decline would seem to favor giving the tests at the time of the school year that was used in norming them.

AUTUMN OR SPRING TESTING?

There are advantages in having the tests administered in the fall. Some pupils will enter the school for the first time, and their status in the group can best be determined by administering tests to all the pupils. The results can be reported for the class as a group, and hence are more easily disseminated and available to the teachers. The teachers will then have the entire school year in which to remedy any deficiencies revealed. Testing in the autumn avoids the undesirable practice of cramming or putting pressure on teachers to make a good showing. Since the students in a given classroom have been in several different classes during the previous year, it is less likely that the results will be inappropriately used to evaluate individual teachers. End-of-year testing may encourage some teachers to teach for the test rather than to follow the objectives of the local curriculum guides (Tyler, 1960; Hopkins, 1964a).

On the other hand, administering the tests at the end of the school year makes it possible for the information to serve several purposes. It can aid some of the decisions about promotions, educational guidance, and sectioning the next grade. It seems likely that an analysis of the errors revealed in spring testing could serve as a basis for remedial teaching in the succeeding grade almost as well as autumn testing data, although sometimes changes may occur during summer vacation. Spring testing has greater value for curricular evaluation. A chief drawback of spring testing is that no information is then available on students moving into the district in the summer, which is the period of greatest family mobility. Districts frequently administer some tests at the beginning and some at the end of the school year, as in the illustrative testing program shown in Table 17–4, which outlines the standardized testing program of the Boulder Valley School District (Boulder, Colorado). Achievement is assessed annually in the first seven grades and every two years thereafter. This is a highly desirable pattern not only for curricular evaluation but also for individual students; testing can ascertain whether problem areas for the students have been remedied or not, confirm achievement and aptitude levels, and so on.

TABLE 17–4

An Illustration of a Testing Program for a School District (Boulder Valley Public Schools 1970 Standardized Testing Schedule)

Test	Grade Level													Month of Testing
	K	1	2	3	4	5	6	7	8	9	10	11	12	
Metropolitan Readiness Test	×													March
Metropolitan Achievement Tests		×	×	×										March
Lorge-Thorndike Intelligence Test		×	a	a	×	a	a	×	a	×	a	×	a	October
Iowa Tests of Basic Skills					×	×	×	×	a					September
Iowa Tests of Educational Development										×	a	×	a	November

a New pupils only.

The district administers intelligence tests in grades 1, 4, 7, 9, and 11. There is general agreement that the same pupils need not take intelligence tests every year, but there is also agreement that possible fluctuations on group tests are great enough to warrant giving such tests several times during the K–12 sequence. The fluctuations are likely to be larger in the primary grades (Hopkins and Bracht, 1971b). A plan preferable to that shown in Table 17–4 would be to give intelligence tests every two years beginning with grade 3. The reading readiness tests are more valuable than intelligence tests at grade 1 (Hopkins and Sitkie, 1969) and are less likely to be misinterpreted. The IQ scores from group tests at grade 1 are very unstable (Hopkins and Bracht, 1971b).

In recent years, testing in grades 11 and 12 by outside agencies such as the College Entrance Examination Board (verbal and quantitative scholastic aptitude, plus as many as three or more achievement tests), the American College Testing Program, and the National Merit Scholarship Corporation have provided high schools and colleges with a wealth of comparative information about students. This can be used wisely for guidance and selection, in helping the student make thoughtful and satisfying educational and vocational choices. Such information may make extensive ability testing by the senior high school staff unnecessary.

There is some disagreement on the best time of year to give intelligence tests. If the tests are to have maximum value, they should be administered at approximately the same time as achievement tests so a pupil's performance can be related to his measured scholastic aptitude. The reliability and validity of the test may be increased by postponing testing until after at least two weeks of the school year. There is a growing tendency to administer scholastic aptitude tests for college entrance in the senior year of high school and achievement tests late in the junior year or the senior year. This is obviously necessary if such tests are to be used in counseling seniors on the advisability of continuing their education. Interim testing is necessary, because usually a few pupils will transfer into the school system who have not had intelligence tests, and there will be other pupils for whom teachers doubt the validity of the existing record.

WHO SHOULD ADMINISTER THE TESTS ?

The American Psychological Association established guidelines (*Ethical Standards of Psychologists*, 1953) to restrict the purchase and the use of published tests to qualified persons. Three categories of tests were defined:

Level A. Tests that can be administered, scored and interpreted adequately with the aid of the manual and some orientation. Standardized achievement tests are an example.

Level B. Tests for which some technical knowledge of test development is required along with related statistical concepts necessary to a proper interpretation of test results. General intelligence tests, aptitude tests, and interest inventories fall into this category. Misinterpretation and misuse can do greater harm than for tests in level A. Almost every teacher administers and interprets (in some fashion) tests in this category.

Level C. Tests that require supervised training and experience for proper administration and interpretation and a substantial understanding of testing and supporting psychology. Individual intelligence tests, projective techniques, and other personality tests are examples of level C measures.

Although these guidelines are helpful, it is not always easy to tell who is really competent to administer standardized tests. Level C tests such as individual intelligence tests (for example, the Stanford-Binet or Wechsler intelligence scales) should be administered only by persons who have had special training. Every school or school system should have persons available who are well qualified to give individual tests.

THE TEACHER AND TEST ADMINISTRATION

When group tests are used for research or program evaluation in which the performance of one group is to be compared with that of another group, they should usually be given either by one person or by a small group of specially trained examiners. In an ordinary testing program, the regular classroom teachers can administer the group tests if they are given proper orientation and supervision. Teacher administration of standardized tests can be a significant contaminant (Hopkins, Lefever, and Hopkins, 1967), but this effect can be greatly minimized with proper training. The viewpoint of the pioneer measurement specialist William McCall (1936) seems as sound today as it was when he first stated it:

> Many years ago certain specialists sought to secure a monopoly of the privilege of using standard tests by trying to persuade educators to regard the tests as possessing certain mystic properties. A few of us with Promethean tendencies set about taking these sacred cows away from the gods and giving them to mortals. Can teachers be entrusted with tests? If not, then teachers ought not to be trusted with 90 percent of their present functions. We now entrust them with the far more difficult task of teaching reading, creating concepts, and building ideals. Let us not strain at a gnat when we have swallowed fifty elephants.

It is not sound policy to take the examiners' competence for granted. One of the best plans is to have the group of examiners observe a demonstration of the administration of the tests to be used. An effective demonstration with a regular class can be followed by a discussion with the examiners of the procedure they have seen. Competence is perhaps best achieved by having each teacher administer the test to himself or to some other person before he administers it to the class. If questions arise, they can be settled in a conference with the person in charge of the program before the examiner administers the test to his own students. It has been found that if such measures are taken, the regular classroom teachers can obtain virtually the same results with group tests as can be obtained by special examiners (see Goodwin, 1966).

CONTROLLED TEST ADMINISTRATION

In many schools the directions are given over the "intercom" while the teachers serve as proctors. Closed-circuit television has also been used successfully for test administration (see Burr, 1963; Curtis and Kropp, 1961; Fargo et al., 1967).

Although procedures for administering group intelligence tests and achievement tests are not beyond the mastery of classroom techers and school administrators, some difficulties may arise. Good group testing may be even more difficult than individual testing. The conditions for the test must be favorable and as similar as possible to the conditions prevailing when the test was normed. The tests usually have been given in the familiar environment of the pupils' own classrooms. It is well always to have the tests given at regular class time without permitting them to encroach on lunch hour or play time. It is desirable not to have tests just before or just after an important event, such as a holiday, a school party, or an athletic contest. Precautions should be taken to avoid distractions and interruptions during the test. It is a good plan to attach to the outside of the classroom door a card that reads: *Testing. Please Do Not Disturb.* Pupils should be instructed to remove everything from the tops of their desks except two well-sharpened pencils with good erasers. Some tests required special pencils to permit machine scoring, but this is no longer necessary with current scoring machines. The examiner should also have several extra pencils for children who forget theirs. All these things must be done to insure favorable testing conditions. Pupils unfamiliar with the use of special answer sheets will need some orientation and, perhaps, practice.

A group test usually can be successfully administered by anyone who meets the following three requirements. First, he must be able to read well. Good silent reading is required for the mastery of the directions printed in the manual that accompanies the test. Good oral reading ability is required because the directions to the pupils should be *read*, not recited from memory. To undertake to give the test from memory is to run a serious risk of leaving out an important word or phrase or of paraphrasing the directions in such a way as to change their meaning. But the examiner should be so familiar with the manual that the directions can be read with proper emphasis in a clear voice just loud enough to be heard throughout the room. The administrator's aim should be to make the meaning understood without arousing pupil anxiety or hostility, but the pupils should take the task seriously.

The second requirement for administering a test is accurate timing. If the test has a single time limit of 20 minutes or more, an ordinary wall clock or pocket watch is satisfactory. When a pocket watch is used, set its hands to some convenient time such as the beginning of an hour and give the starting signal just as the second hand reaches 12. It will usually help students and examiner alike to have a clock in the room, preferably at the front, which shows everyone the correct time.

The aim should be to keep time to the second. On most tests the signal to start is, "Ready, go!" or "Ready, begin!" When this signal is given, the examiner should note—that is, write down—the *exact* time—hour, minute, and second. This should be *recorded immediately*, preferably on a small card or specially prepared blank. The record for Test 1 would look like this:

Test 1	Hr.	Min.	Sec.
Time test began............	9	0	0
Time allowed..............		5	
Time to stop	9	5	0

Experienced examiners know that *it is never safe to trust one's memory to keep the time.* A written record must be made.

The third requirement for administering a test is the ability to follow directions accurately. The manual should be followed verbatim; no deviation is permissible. Altering directions can have definite effects on examinee performance (Lamb, 1967; Yamamoto and Dizney, 1965). To modify the directions or time limits in any way violates the standardization procedure. The norms are made on the assumption that a specified procedure is to be used. As a part of the preliminary instructions, pupils are almost always told not to ask any questions after the test starts. Occasionally a pupil forgets this instruction and holds up his hand to ask a question. The examiner should walk over to him and, if it is a reading test or an intelligence test whose purpose is following directions, should say in a quiet voice, "Read it carefully and do just what it says." If it is an achievement test and the pupil is concerned about where to put his answer or some other point of mechanics that does not involve the answer to a question in the test or modify the directions already given, it is permissible to set the pupil at ease without causing disturbance. The teacher should be free to say or do anything that does not disturb or delay pupils at work, that does not help the individual child do the things for which he is being tested, and that does get him to work again after something has distracted him. Examples of permissible statements are: "Yes, you may change your answer if you decide it is wrong," "Just work on the side of the sheet; you do not need scratch paper," "When you have finished the first column go right on to the next one," and "No, you must not go back to a test you have completed." Examples of improper statements would include references to the time remaining for a given test, special statements about guessing, suggestions about pacing, and so on, if they were not specifically allowed in the directions to the test administrator. *In case of doubt, the examiner should err on the side of saying nothing.* While the test is in progress the examiner must be alert constantly to see that the pupils neither help nor hinder each other nor are distracted by external factors. A test is more than a measuring device; it presents a standardized situation in which to observe pupil behavior. Anything observed during the progress of the test that may cast light upon the interpretation of the results should be carefully recorded. The group should be carefully proctored throughout. Almost every class has one or more students who will cheat if given the opportunity. When the time is up, students should be told to put their pencils down and turn their test copies over; otherwise some will continue to work while the tests are being collected.

Scoring the Tests

It is desirable to have the tests scored as quickly as possible and with the highest possible degree of accuracy. The best system is the one that accomplishes these objectives with the minimum expenditure of money, time, and energy. There are two questions involved: Who should score the tests? What technique should be used?

WHO SHOULD SCORE THE TESTS?

There are several extremely fast electronic test-scoring machines. It is desirable for any school system to consider having the tests it uses machine-scored, rather than burdening the administrative staff and teachers with this essentially clerical operation at which people are far less efficient than machines. By negotiating with major test companies, the superintendent or his representative may be able to contract for "package deals" that include, at reasonable rates, rental of test booklets and answer sheets; accurate, fast scoring; and reporting of desired scores and other statistics. He may also want to request supervisory assistance for administering the tests. In these ways he disrupts teaching as little as possible while he secures exactly the information he needs, which may even include counts of the various responses to individual test items if such data are wanted for diagnostic purposes. By renting tests and answer sheets, he eliminates storing and inventory problems. He will always be using the current forms of the tests, whereas if he purchased copies it might be necessary to continue using an obsolescent form because of the expense of buying the later version.

Therefore, *we recommend that electronic-machine scoring be used as much as possible*, freeing teachers and administrators from costly, inefficient clerical labor. Since standardized tests are often scored locally by a variety of persons, we give certain suggestions for improving manual procedures. When objective tests with special answer sheets are used, scoring by cut-out cardboard stencils can be quite efficient. In kindergarten and the primary grades separate answer sheets cannot be handled without disadvantage to some children (Hayward, 1967); therefore, answers should be marked in test booklets and machine scoring cannot be used. Ideally, each answer sheet should be scored independently by two scorers. If they do not agree, the answer sheet should be rescored.

Sometimes, especially in larger systems, the hand-scoring is done by a clerical staff at a central bureau. Scoring sometimes is done by advanced students under supervision, but the most common method seems to be to have the work done by the teachers. Except in the larger systems where there is a bureau of research or testing equipped with special facilities, the scoring is probably best done by the classroom teachers. Not only can the teacher do the work promptly, but he can perhaps learn something of value about the kinds of error made on the achievement tests. It is important to get the scoring done without producing an unfavorable attitude toward it on the part of the teachers. Some schools have found it advisable to dismiss classes at noon when the testing is in progress, so the teachers can devote the afternoon to the work of scoring. This would seem an effective way of emphasizing the important fact that *teaching and testing are intimately related processes*.

WHAT TECHNIQUES SHOULD BE USED?

Every reasonable precaution should be taken to assure a high degree of scoring accuracy. Phillips and Weathers (1958) found that 28 percent of teacher-scored standardized tests contained errors (see. p. 149). It must not be assumed, merely because the directions are clear, the key complete, the separate answer sheets well designed, and the process objective, that perfect protection against errors is afforded. Two distinct kinds of error occur in scoring: *constant errors* and *variable errors*. A common example of the former is misunderstanding the scoring directions—for instance, by counting omissions the same as errors when using a correction-for-chance scoring formula. Such errors are especially serious because there is no possibility of their offsetting each other according to any so-called "law of averages." Variable errors sometimes tend to make the score too high and at other times too low. Although such errors may do serious harm to individual pupils, they tend to cancel each other in group measures such as averages. Examples of variable errors are errors resulting from carelessness, errors in counting the scores, errors in entering the scores on the front of the test booklet or on the record sheet, and errors in adding up the total score. Some of the most serious errors found are not in marking the paper but in counting and in addition.

Accurate scoring cannot be taken for granted. The first step is to prevent the occurrence of errors. The scorers must be *taught* how to score the papers and not merely *told* how to do it. They should be given an opportunity to study the manual and the scoring keys, and whenever possible an actual demonstration of scoring should follow. It is valuable to check carefully the first few papers marked by beginners to detect errors at the outset. This procedure should reveal any constant errors and the principal kinds of variable error. It is usually desirable to have each page, part of the test, or answer sheet scored through all the papers in a set before going on to the second page, part of the test, or answer sheet. If the scorers work in groups, as is usually desirable, each one can specialize in marking one part of the test and pass the test when scored to the next scorer, who is specializing in marking the next part of the test. This procedure will reduce the risk of error and increase the speed of scoring. It is usually an especially poor technique to have one person read the answers while the scorers mark the papers. This is slow, because the slowest scorer sets the pace. It also increases the risk of error, owing to the possibilities of scorers' losing their place or failing to hear correctly.

Colored pencils are desirable. Scorers will save time by marking only the incorrect and omitted items. It is, of course, unnecessary to mark the items after the last one the pupil attempts, but it is well to draw a horizontal line across the test under the last item attempted. Figure 17–1 illustrates the scoring of an alternative-response test of word meaning; the formula Score $= R - W$ was used.

Keeping a simple written record of who marks, checks, transcribes, or totals each part of the test reduces the likelihood of error. If the scoring is organized systematically, such a record on a mimeographed sheet can be easily attached to each package of tests when scored, as shown in Figure 17–2.

Despite these preventive measures, certain errors are likely to occur. The safest plan is to have each set of papers marked a second time by different scorers using pencils of a different color. If a complete rescoring does not seem practical, a sampling method may be followed. Each fifth or tenth paper, for example, may be selected and carefully rescored; if only an occasional minor error is found, the whole set may be safely accepted. But if frequent or serious errors are found in these sample papers, the entire set should be rescored. It is important to have some person other than the original scorer check the totals for each part of the test and for the whole test, all substitutions in the scoring formulas, all transcribing of scores, and all transmuting of point scores into

TEST 3. WORD MEANING

When two words mean the SAME, draw a line under "SAME."
When they mean the OPPOSITE, draw a line under "OPPOSITE."

SAMPLES	fall—drop	**same**—opposite		
	north—south	same—**opposite**		
1	expel—retain	same—**opposite**	1	
2	comfort—console	**same**—opposite	2	
3	waste—conserve	same—**opposite**	3	
4	monotony—variety	same—**opposite**	4	
5	quell—subdue	**same**—opposite	5	
6	major—minor	**same**—opposite	6	—
7	boldness—audacity	**same**—opposite	7	
8	exult—rejoice	same—**opposite**	8	—
9	prohibit—allow	same—opposite	9	O
10	debase—degrade	**same**—opposite	10	
11	recline—stand	same—**opposite**	11	
12	approve—veto	same—**opposite**	12	
13	amateur—expert	**same**—opposite	13	—
14	evade—shun	**same**—opposite	14	
15	tart—acid	same—**opposite**	15	—
16	concede—deny	same—opposite	16	O
17	tonic—stimulant	**same**—opposite	17	
18	incite—quell	**same**—opposite	18	—
19	economy—frugality	**same**—opposite	19	
20	rash—prudent	same—**opposite**	20	
21	obtuse—acute	same—opposite	21	O
22	transient—permanent	same—opposite	22	O
23	expel—eject	**same**—opposite	23	
24	hoax—deception	same—opposite	24	O
25	docile—submissive	**same**—opposite	25	
26	wax—wane	same—opposite	26	O
27	incite—instigate	same—opposite	27	O
28	reverence—veneration	same—opposite	28	O
29	asset—liability	same—opposite	29	O
30	appease—placate	same—opposite	30	O

Right ..15.. *Wrong* ..5.. *Score* ..10..

***FIGURE 17–1** An illustration of the procedure followed in scoring Test 3 of the Terman Group Test of Mental Ability, Form A.* (*Copyright by World Book Company.*)

derived scores.[5] It is possible to locate many serious errors by examining closely the profile of each individual pupil on all tests with this form of record. Any score much higher or much lower than the general level should be suspect. When two or more tests are used that purport to measure the same function, any serious discrepancies should be scrutinized, on the supposition that a high

[5] Derived scores are obtained from tables of norms. The raw scores are expressed in some other unit, such as an age, percentile rank, or standard score. The interpretation of these units was discussed in Chapters 2, 3, and 15.

STANDARD TEST SCORING RECORD

Name of Test *Modern School Achievement Test* Form ____1____

School *Williamsdale* _____ Grade ____4____

No.	Scored by	Errors	Checked by	Comment
1.	Mary Anderson	5	John Long	In Adding
2.	Julia Jones	0	Mabel Adams	not reduced to lowest terms
3.	James Johnson	3	Lee Cross	
4.	Jeanette Long	4	Ed Howard	Decimals
5.	Jessie Lee	20	William Jameson	Misunderstood Directions
6.	Alma Wright	0	Jed Smith	
7.	Walter Justice	2	Ruth Alton	Carelessness
8.	Oscar Wilson	2	Ray Kelley	"
9.	Mildred White	1	June Hunt	
10.	Anna Camp	3	Harry Luther	"

Transcribed by	Errors	Checked by	Comment
Betty Brown	0	Walter Coleman	
Edith Raymond	1	Elizabeth Kent	

Scores added by	Errors	Checked by	Comment
Judson Allon	1	Alice James	Too low by 100

Norms, etc., by	Errors	Checked by	Comment
Edsel Havey	0	Susan Clay	

Class record by	Table made by	Median by	Graph by
Martha Rule	Bill Tate	Norma Gill	Sarah Garr

FIGURE 17–2 A sample standard test-scoring record.

positive correlation is to be expected. The standard of absolute accuracy should be accepted by all scorers. *The possibilities of serious injustice to individual pupils by errors in scoring should be recognized fully.*

Analyzing and Interpreting the Scores

After the tests have been scored and checked, the results must be analyzed and interpreted. Both processes are done together, for analysis is worthless   **435** without interpretation, and interpretation is impossible without analysis. Analysis is of two main kinds, statistical and graphical. Before either can be undertaken, however, there is the important preliminary step of classification and tabulation. An analysis of errors appearing in the test papers is usually of major importance to the classroom teacher. Chapters 2 and 3 are concerned with a discussion of the comprehensive problem of analysis and interpretation; only an outline will be given here to indicate the steps involved:

1. Classification and tabulation of scores.
2. Statistical analysis of scores.
3. Graphical analysis and representation.
4. Use of norms and standards.
5. Analysis of errors.

In a complete testing program all five of these steps will receive attention, although not always to the same degree. If the primary purpose of the testing program is diagnosis, for example, the fourth step would be relatively unimportant and the fifth step quite important. The reverse would be true of a program whose main objective is a study of the comparative efficiency of various grades, classes, and schools.

Applying the Results

The application of the results is the crux of the testing program. Everything that has been done before is preliminary. The value of the tests depends in the last analysis on the use made of the results. Most standardized achievement tests provide helpful suggestions for the use of test results in the improvement of instruction.

The uses of the results depend on the purpose of the program. In several chapters we considered in some detail procedures to be followed for several administrative and instructional problems. It will be sufficient at this point to give some idea of how the procedure varies with the purpose.

Suppose that the purpose of the tests is to determine the present status of a particular school in order to improve it and that the test data are before the principal. The question now is, what is to be done? On the basis of the test scores and other pertinent data, such as the teachers' estimates, health reports, age-grade status, and the like, several pupils are given trial promotions to the next higher grades. A small group of pupils, whose achievement and intelligence scores are well below the central tendency of their respective grades, is organized as an ungraded class which is assigned to a specially trained teacher. With appropriate differentiation in curricula and methods, ability groups are also organized in several grades and classes.

Suppose also that the primary purpose of the testing program is to determine whether the teaching emphasis is correct in the various subjects in the grades, but the test results show that most of the grades are strong in arithmetic and spelling, about average in reading, and weak in language and the social studies. Now what is to be done? The principal has the teachers meet and presents the situation with tables, graphs, and interpretive comment. Then they discuss the findings. One or more committees are appointed to study the situation and to make recommendations at a later meeting. After discussion and deliberation, they decide upon a course of action and anticipate improvement in the weaker subjects.

The procedure will be slightly different in essential respects if the primary purpose is diagnosis and remedial work in reading. The test results should be analyzed in detail in each grade. An analysis of the test papers, item by item, is often very revealing. Special effort should be made to locate the specific nature of the reading difficulties. There may be found some general weaknesses, such as the inability to use the index and table of contents in a book, or possibly to locate the central idea in a paragraph. In addition, there are usually weaknesses that appear in some pupils and not in others. Some of these will not be revealed by the usual paper-and-pencil reading tests but will require special tools and techniques. After considering these facts, the staff will try to plan a remedial program to be followed during the year.

The essential point in all these cases is that *something is done about the situation revealed by the test scores*. To fail to apply the results promptly in some practical way is to fail in the testing program.

Retesting to Determine the Success of the Program

Most testing programs stop with applying the results—if indeed, they go that far. But there is another essential step. After reasonable time has been allowed for a trial of the remedial measures that were agreed upon, a checkup should be made to determine the success of the program. Most tests are not sufficiently accurate to reveal progress during a period shorter than one-half year. A comparable form of the test or tests used in the first testing should be employed in retesting. If this is not done, it will usually be very difficult to express the results in terms sufficiently comparable to make an accurate measure of progress. Of course, not all the change from one form to another can be correctly attributed solely to the remedial program. Some of it is doubtless due to practice effect (familiarity with the test itself), part of it to instruction outside the school, part of it to natural growth, and part to difference between forms.[6] Often, however, the improvement will be so dramatic that it indicates beyond a reasonable doubt the effectiveness of the program attempted. At other times the improvement will be disappointingly small. It is then usually wise to modify the remedial program in view of the results obtained.

It is essential that the success of the remedial program is not taken for granted; a definite effort must be made to assess its effectiveness. To fail to do this is to leave the testing program incomplete. There is no better reason for

[6] If two forms of the test are available, it is probably wise to administer form A to half the students at the beginning of the year and form B to the other half of the students. At the end of the year those students who first took form A can take form B, and vice versa. This procedure permits one to determine whether forms A and B are equally difficult. For a way to ascertain this statistically, see Stanley (1955).

TO THE PARENTS

Scores on the Metropolitan Achievement Tests, like scores on any other test, are just one form of information about the student. They will be useful to the extent to which they are properly understood by all concerned. By knowing and understanding the strengths and weaknesses of your child, it may be possible for you to provide help and encouragement where it is most needed.

Basically, the eleven Metropolitan tests seek to measure the student's progress in the following areas of learning:

Reading. Understanding main ideas and seeing relationships among them, knowing the literal meaning of words and passages, and reading for retention.

Spelling. Correct spelling of commonly used words.

Language. Proper use of grammar, punctuation and structure.

Language Study Skills. Familiarity with standard references and other sources of information.

Social Studies. Three tests covering (1) understanding and interpretation of various types of social studies information (maps, graphs, etc.); (2) knowledge of words and terms used in social studies; (3) knowledge of facts and information relative to history, government, economics, and sociology.

Mathematics. Two tests—*Computation and Concepts,* and *Analysis and Problem Solving*—measure basic computational and problem-solving abilities.

Science. The *Scientific Concepts and Understandings Test* measures understanding of scientific terms and concepts, while the *Science Information Test* covers knowledge and understandings in general science, chemistry, biology, and physics.

How to Understand the Profile Chart. The profile on the other side of this form is a graphic picture of your child's achievement in each of the eleven tests. The scores are recorded as "stanines" based on a STAndard NINE-point scale ranging from very low (1) to very high (9). These scores show the student's standing in comparison with scores earned by a large sample of other students at the same grade level.

Percentile ranks are also given. A percentile rank of 40 means that the student scored as well as or better than 40 % of the group on which the percentiles are based. Percentile ranks do *not* represent the per cent of correct answers on a test.

The numbers circled on the Profile indicate the different levels of achievement earned by your child in the tests. Small differences of one or two stanines from one subject to another should not be given too much attention. However, any noticeable differences, or an over-all pattern of high or low scores may suggest the need for consultation among parents, teachers, counselors, and the student. Consultation should also be arranged if you desire further information about these tests or about your child's progress in school.

FIGURE 17–3 Above, an individual profile chart and report to parents for the Metropolitan Achievement Tests, High School Battery. Below, reverse side of chart. (Reproduced from Metropolitan Achievement Tests by special permission of the publisher. Copyright © 1958–1962 by Harcourt Brace Jovanovich, Inc.)

Metropolitan Achievement Tests

HIGH SCHOOL BATTERY

INDIVIDUAL PROFILE CHART AND REPORT TO PARENTS

Name _____

Grade _____ Age _____
years   months

Date of Birth _____

Date of Testing _____

Teacher _____

Norms: National ☐ _____ Form: Am ☐
Local ☐   type   Bm ☐

This Profile Chart provides information on the student's progress in important areas of the curriculum. Stanine scores in the shaded area on the right represent average achievement; scores 1, 2, and 3, below average achievement; and scores 7, 8, and 9, superior achievement. Information on interpreting the Profile may be found on the reverse side of this sheet.

Tests	1 Reading	2 Spelling	3 Language	4 Language Study Skills	5 Study Skills	6 Vocabulary	7 Information	8 Comp. and Conc.	9 Anal. and Prob. S.	10 Conc. and Und.	11 Information
					Social Studies			Mathematics		Science	
%-ile Ranks											
Stanines											
Above Average	9	9	9	9	9	9	9	9	9	9	9
	8	8	8	8	8	8	8	8	8	8	8
	7	7	7	7	7	7	7	7	7	7	7
Average	6	6	6	6	6	6	6	6	6	6	6
	5	5	5	5	5	5	5	5	5	5	5
	4	4	4	4	4	4	4	4	4	4	4
Below Average	3	3	3	3	3	3	3	3	3	3	3
	2	2	2	2	2	2	2	2	2	2	2
	1	1	1	1	1	1	1	1	1	1	1

To plot the scores: Enter the percentile rank and stanine score for each test in the boxes above the arrows. In each column, below the boxes, circle the number that is the same as the stanine score in the box directly above it. Join the circles with straight lines.

taking the efficiency of the remedial program on faith than there was for taking the earlier results of teaching on faith.

Making Suitable Records and Reports

Certain records and reports are essential to the success of the testing program. They should not all be relegated to the end of the program; some of them are essential to the last three stages discussed.

In general, it may be said that five groups have an interest in knowing what the tests show: pupils, teachers, administrators, parents, and the general public. Naturally, the nature of the report will vary somewhat with the group to whom it is made, and the nature of the record with the specific function it is to serve. In Chapter 4 we considered some ways test results may be used. Most tests provide the user with specific examples of how results can be meaningfully summarized and reported. For many standardized tests special forms are available to facilitate a proper interpretation of the results to the student and his parents. Figure 17–3 shows such a pupil profile chart designed to be given to students and parents. A more elaborate example is depicted in Figure 17–4. The performance of Jane Doe on the STEP mathematics and science tests has been recorded for illustration. The chance of misinterpretation is greatly reduced by such aids.

Post-organizer

We considered eight steps in the testing program, from determining the purpose of the program to making suitable records and reports. Good testing requires thought, time, and money, but probably in no other way can teachers learn as much about pupils in such a short period of time. The better the planning is, the more that can be learned per dollar spent. The designing of a good testing program requires that tests be evaluated in terms of validity, reliability, and norms, as well as cost, time required, and other practical considerations.

Epilogue

We conclude the body of *Educational and Psychological Measurement and Evaluation*, leaving the appendixes and indexes to supplement the knowledge you have acquired in Chapters 1 through 17. We hope that you will continue to learn about measurement. Many colleges and universities provide courses beyond the basic one, such as test construction, test theory, individual intelligence testing, attitude and personality assessment, and factor analysis. Also, a number of test publishers offer excellent free articles on measurement topics. Finally, you can keep up-to-date by reading professional journals such as *Educational and Psychological Measurement*, the *Journal of Educational Measurement*, and *Measurement and Evaluation in Guidance*. But most immediately helpful to you may be the many references in this book and in its companion volume, *Perspectives in Educational and Psychological Measurement*. We wish you continued growth in knowledge of measurement and evaluation.

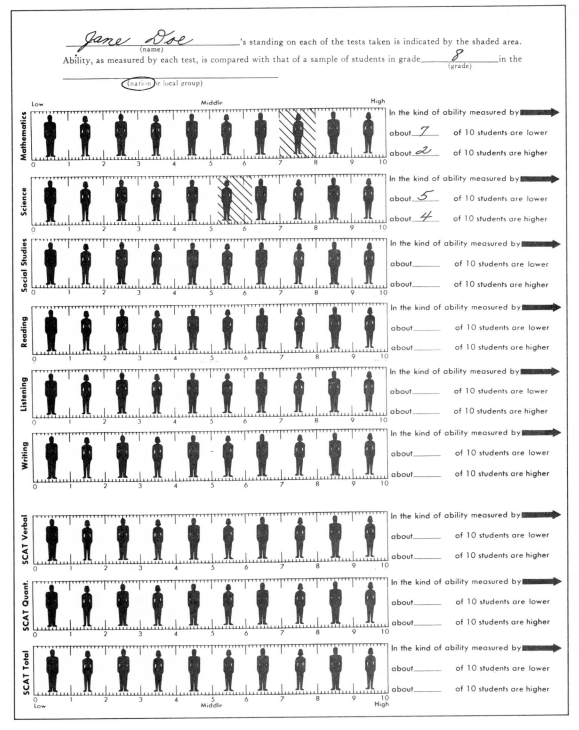

FIGURE 17–4 *Individual Profile Chart from the Sequential Tests of Educational Progress. (Copyright © 1958 by Educational Testing Service. All rights reserved. Reproduced by permission.)*

STEP
Mathematics ... measures your ability to understand numbers and ways of working with them (for example, addition and division), such symbols as $+$, $\sqrt{}$, and $<$, relationships between objects in space, how two changing things can depend on each other (for example, distance and speed), how to draw conclusions from facts, and how to make estimations and predictions when you do not have all the information. Mathematics teachers call these concepts *number and operation, symbolism, measurement and geometry, function and relation, deduction and inference,* and *probability and statistics.*

STEP
Science ... measures your ability to recognize and state problems relating to science, to select ways of getting information about the problems, to understand and judge the information you get, to predict what the solutions to these problems may be, and to work with symbols and numbers used in science problems. Some of the questions are about biology materials; some are about chemistry, physics, meteorology, astronomy, and geology. All of the questions present science in practical situations (for example, in the home, on the farm, and at work).

STEP
Social Studies ... measures your ability to understand the kinds of social studies materials which a citizen in a democracy should be able to deal with. These include maps, graphs, cartoons, editorials, debates, and historical documents. There are questions about history, geography, economics, government, and sociology.

STEP
Reading ... measures your ability to read materials and then answer questions about what you have read. These questions ask you to remember specific things the author said, to understand what he meant and why he might have said what he did, and to criticize his ideas. The reading materials include directions, announcements, newspaper and magazine articles, letters, stories, poetry, and plays.

STEP
Listening ... measures your ability to listen to materials and then answer questions about what you have heard. The Listening test is very much like the Reading test except, of course, you *hear* instead of *see* the things you are asked to remember, understand, or criticize.

STEP
Writing ... measures your ability to criticize materials written by other students in terms of the ways they are organized or written. The questions ask you to pick out errors or weaknesses in the writing and choose revisions which best correct the errors or weaknesses. The materials were written by students in schools and colleges in various parts of the United States; they include letters, answers to test questions, school newspaper articles, announcements, essays, outlines, directions, and stories.

SCAT
Verbal ... measures your ability to understand sentences and give the meanings of words. This ability is most important in such school courses as English, foreign languages, and social studies (history, civics, etc.).

SCAT
Quantitative ... measures your ability to perform operations with numbers and to solve mathematics problems stated in words. This ability is most important in such school courses as mathematics and science.

SCAT
Total ... combines your scores on SCAT Verbal and SCAT Quantitative to provide the *single* best measure of your general capacity to do the work of the next higher level of schooling.

AMERICAN PSYCHOLOGICAL ASSOCIATION; AMERICAN EDUCATIONAL RESEARCH ASSOCIATION; NATIONAL COUNCIL ON MEASUREMENT IN EDUCATION. 1966. *Standards for educational and psychological tests and manuals*. Washington, D.C.: American Psychological Association, Inc.

ANDERSON, S. B., and M. H. MAIER. 1963. 34,000 pupils and how they grew. *Journal of Teacher Education*, **14:** 212–216.

BADAL, A. W., and E. P. LARSEN. 1970. On reporting test results to community groups. *NCME Measurement in Education*, **1:** 1–12.

BAUERNFEIND, R. H. 1963. *Building a school testing program*. Boston: Houghton Mifflin Company.

BUROS, O. K. 1972. *The seventh mental measurements yearbook*. Highland Park, N.J.: Gryphon Press.

CHAUNCEY, H., and J. E. DOBBIN. 1963. *Testing: Its place in education today*. New York: Harper & Row, Publishers.

EDUCATIONAL TESTING SERVICE. 1958. *Large-scale program of testing for guidance*. Princeton, N.J.: ETS.

———. 1961. Selecting an achievement test: Principles and procedures (*Evaluation Advisory Series*). Princeton, N. J.: ETS.

———. 1969. Locating information on educational measurement: Sources and references (*Evaluation and Advisory Series*). Princeton, N.J.: ETS.

FINDLEY, W. G., ed. 1963. The impact and improvement of school testing programs. *Sixty-second yearbook of the National Society for the Study of Education, Part II*. Chicago: University of Chicago Press.

GOLDMAN, L. 1969. Tests should make a difference. *Measurement and Evaluation in Guidance*, **2:** 53–59. Reprinted in G. H. Bracht, K. D. Hopkins, and J. C. Stanley. 1972. *Perspectives in educational and psychological measurement*. Englewood Cliffs, N.J.: Prentice-Hall, Inc., Selection 33.

HOEPFNER, R., and S. KLEIN. 1970. *CSE elementary school test evaluations*. Los Angeles: Center for the Study of Evaluation, University of California at Los Angeles, Graduate School of Education.

HOLLAND, J. L. 1966. *The psychology of vocational choice: A theory of personality types and model environments*. Waltham, Mass.: Blaisdell.

LESSINGER, L. M. 1970. Accountability in public education. *Proceedings of the 1969 invitational conference on testing problems*. Princeton, N. J.: Educational Testing Service, pp. 109–111. Reprinted in G.H. Bracht, K. D. Hopkins, and J. C. Stanley. 1972. *Perspectives in educational and psychological measurement*. Englewood Cliffs, N.J.: Prentice-Hall, Inc., Selection 26. Also see Selection 27.

PRESCOTT, G. A. n.d. Test administration guide. *Test Service Bulletin* No. 102. New York: Harcourt Brace Jovanovich, Inc.

RUSSELL SAGE FOUNDATION. 1969. Proposed principles for management of school records. *Guidelines for the collection, maintenance, and dissemination of pupil records*. New York: Russell Sage Foundation. Reprinted in G. H. Bracht, K. D. Hopkins, and J. C. Stanley. 1972. *Perspectives in educational and psychological measurement*. Englewood Cliffs, N. J.: Prentice-Hall, Inc., Selection 34.

THOMPSON, A. 1958. Tentative guidelines for proper and improper practices with standardized achievement tests. *California Journal of Educational Research*, **9**(4): 159–166.

TRAXLER, A. E. n.d. Fundamentals of testing for parents, school boards, and teachers. *Test Service Notebook* No. 27. Harcourt Brace Jovanovich, Inc. Free.

————. 1959. Ten essential steps in a testing program. *Education*, **79**: 1–6.

Appendixes

appendix A

A GLOSSARY OF
MEASUREMENT TERMS

This list of common measurement and statistical terms is based on *A Glossary of 100 Measurement Terms*, by Roger T. Lennon (assisted by Claude F. Bridges, John C. Marriott, Frances E. Crook, and Blythe C. Mitchell),[1] and *A Glossary of Measurement Terms*, published by the California Test Bureau.[2] We made a moderate number of deletions and additions in order to suit some of the definitions to the discussion in the book.

As Dr. Lennon points out:

> This glossary of technical terms used in educational and psychological measurement is primarily for persons with limited training in measurement, rather than for the specialist. The terms defined are the more common or basic ones such as occur in test manuals and simple research reports. In the definitions, niceties of usage have sometimes been sacrificed for the sake of brevity and, it is hoped, clarity. . . . There is not complete uniformity among writers in the measurement field with respect to the usage of certain technical terms; in cases of varying usage, either these variations are noted or the definition offered is the one that the writer judges to represent the "best" usage.

This glossary is meant to supplement the subject index of *Educational and Psychological Measurement and Evaluation*, not to supplant it. Of course, a textbook provides much more detail and many more concepts than a glossary can.

---

[1] Adapted from *A Glossary of 100 Measurement Terms* (Test Service Notebook No. 13), distributed by Harcourt Brace Jovanovich, Inc. Reproduced by special permission.
[2] Adapted from *A Glossary of Measurement Terms* by permission of the publisher, CTB/McGraw-Hill, Monterey, California.

Academic aptitude   The combination of native and acquired abilities that is needed for school work; likelihood of success in mastering academic work, as estimated from measures of the necessary abilities. (Also called **scholastic aptitude**.)

Accomplishment Quotient (AQ)   The ratio of educational age to mental age: EA ÷ MA. (Also called *Achievement Quotient*.)

Achievement Age   The age for which a given achievement-test score is the real or estimated average score. For example, a representative sample of children 13 years and 4 months old averages 148 points on a certain achievement test battery, so any child who scores 148 points on that battery has an Achievement Age of 13 years and 4 months. (See **Age equivalent, Mental Age**.)

Achievement test   A test that measures the extent to which a person has "achieved" something—acquired certain information or mastered certain skills, usually as a result of specific instruction.

Age equivalent   The age for which a given score is the real or estimated average score. (See **Achievement Age, Mental Age**.)

Age norms   Values representing typical or average performance for persons of various age groups.

Age-grade table   A table showing the number or percent of pupils of various ages in each grade; a distribution of the ages of pupils in successive grades.

Alternate-form reliability   The closeness of correspondence, or correlation, between results on alternate (that is, equivalent or parallel) forms of a test; thus, a measure of the extent to which the two forms are consistent or reliable in measuring whatever they do measure. (Also called *parallel-form reliability*.) (See **Reliability, Reliability coefficient, Standard error of measurement**.)

Aptitude   A combination of abilities and other characteristics, whether native or acquired, known or believed to be indicative of an individual's ability to learn or achieve in some particular area. Thus, "musical aptitude" would refer broadly to that combination of physical and mental characteristics, motivational factors, and conceivably other characteristics that is conducive to acquiring proficiency in the musical field. Some authorities exclude motivational factors, including interests, from the concept of "aptitude," but the more comprehensive use seems preferable. The layman may think of "aptitude" as referring only to some inborn capacity; the term is no longer so restricted in its psychological or measurement usage.

Arithmetic mean   The sum of a set of scores divided by the number of scores. (Commonly called **average**, or **mean**.)

Average   A general term applied to measures of central tendency. The three most widely used averages are the **arithmetic mean**, the **median**, and the **mode**.

Battery   A group of several tests standardized on the same population, so that results on the several tests are comparable. Sometimes loosely applied to any group of tests administered together, even though not standardized on the same subjects.

Ceiling   The upper limit of ability measured by a test.

Chronological Age (CA)   A person's actual age, usually expressed in years and months to the nearest month.

Class analysis chart   A chart, usually prepared in connection with a battery of achievement tests, that shows the relative performance of members of a class on the several parts of the battery.

Coefficient of correlation (*r*)   A measure of the degree of relationship or "going-togetherness" between the two sets of measures for the same group of individuals. The correlation coefficient most frequently used in test development and educational research is the *Pearson (Pearsonian) r*, so named for Karl Pearson, who first derived its formula, or as the *product-moment r*, to denote the mathematical basis of its calculation. Unless otherwise specified, "correlation" usually means the product-moment correlation coefficient, which ranges from .00, denoting complete absence of relationship, to 1.00, denoting perfect correspondence, and may be either positive or negative.

Completion item   A test question calling for the completion (filling in) of a phrase, sentence, or whatever, from which one or more parts have been omitted.

Correction for chance   A reduction in score for wrong answers, sometimes applied in scoring true-false or multiple-choice questions. It is intended to yield more accurate rankings of examinees in terms of their true knowledge. Measurement specialists differ about how well it does this. Scores to which such corrections have been applied—such as rights minus wrongs, or rights minus some fraction of wrongs—are often spoken of as "corrected for guessing" or "corrected for chance." (Also called *correction for guessing*.)

Correlation   Relationship or "going-togetherness" between two scores or measures; tendency of one score to vary concomitantly with the other, as the tendency of students of high IQ to be above average in reading ability. The existence of a strong relationship—that is, a high correlation—between two variables does not necessarily indicate that one has any causal influence on the other. (See **Coefficient of correlation.**)

Criterion   A standard by which a test may be judged or evaluated; a set of scores, ratings, or the like, that a test is designed to predict or to correlate with. (See **Validity.**)

Cross-validation   The process of checking whether a decision derived from one set of data is truly effective when this decision is applied to another independent, but comparable, set of data.

Decile   Any of the nine percentile points (scores) in a distribution that divide the distribution into ten equal parts; every tenth percentile. The first decile is the 10th percentile, the ninth decile the 90th percentile, and so on.

Deviation   The amount by which a score differs from some reference value, such as the mean, the norm, or the score on some other test.

Deviation IQ   See **Intelligence Quotient.**

Diagnostic test   A test used to "diagnose"—that is, to locate specific areas of weakness or strength and to determine the nature of weaknesses or deficiencies; it yields measures of the components or subparts of some larger body of information or skill. Diagnostic achievement tests are most commonly prepared for the skill subjects—reading, arithmetic, spelling.

Difficulty Index   The percent of some specified group, such as students of a given age or grade, who answer an item correctly.

Discriminating power   The ability of a test item to differentiate between persons possessing much of some trait and those possessing little. The *discrimination index* indicates this property of an item.

Distracter   Any of the incorrect choices in a multiple-choice or matching item. (Also sometimes called *foil, decoy,* or *incorrect option.*)

Distribution (Frequency distribution)   A tabulation of scores from high to low, or low to high, showing the number of individuals who obtain each score or fall in each score interval.

Educational Age (EA)   See **Achievement Age.**

Equivalent form   Any of two or more forms of a test that are closely alike with respect to the nature of the content and the difficulty of the items included, and that will yield very similar average scores and measures of variability for a given group. Also sometimes called *parallel,* alternate, or *comparable* form, though usually the three terms are not exact synonyms.

Error of measurement   See **Standard error of measurement.**

Extrapolation   In general, any process of estimating values of a function beyond the range of available data. As applied to test norms, the process of extending a norm line beyond the limits of actually obtained data, in order to permit interpretation of extreme scores. This extension may be done mathematically by fitting a curve to the obtained data or, as is more common, by less rigorous methods, usually graphic. Considerable judgment on the test-maker's part enters into any extrapolation process, which means that extrapolated norm values are likely to be to some extent arbitrary.

Face validity   Refers to the acceptability of the test and test situation by the examinee or user, in terms of apparent uses to which the test is to be put. A test has face validity when it appears to measure the variable to be tested.

Factor   In mental measurement, a hypothetical trait, ability, or component of ability that underlies and influences performance on two or more tests, and hence causes scores on the tests to be correlated. The term "factor" strictly refers to a theoretical variable, derived by a process of **factor analysis**, from a table of intercorrelations among tests; but it is also commonly used to denote the psychological interpretation given to the variable—that is, the mental trait assumed to be represented by the variable, such as verbal ability or numerical ability.

Factor analysis   Any of several methods of analyzing the intercorrelations among a set of variables such as test scores. Factor analysis attempts to account for the interrelationships in terms of some underlying "factors," preferably fewer in number than the original variables; and it reveals how much of the variation in each of the original measures arises from, or is associated with, each of the hypothetical factors. Factor analysis has contributed to our understanding of the organization or components of intelligence, aptitudes, and personality; and it has pointed the way to the development of "purer" tests of the several components.

Forced-choice item   Broadly, any multiple-choice item in which the examinee is *required* to select one or more of the given choices. The term is best used to denote a special type of multiple-choice item in which the options, or choices, are (1) of equal "preference value"—that is, chosen equally often by a typical group, but (2) of differential discriminating ability—that is, such that one of the options discriminates between persons high and low on the factor that this option measures, while the other options do not.

Frequency distribution   See **Distribution.**

Grade equivalent   The grade level for which a given score is the real or estimated average.

Grade norm   The average score obtained by typical pupils of given grade placement. (See **Norms, Modal age.**)

Group test   A test that may be administered to a number of individuals at the same time by one examiner.

Individual test   A test that can be administered to only one person at a time.

Intelligence Quotient (IQ)   Originally, the ratio of a person's mental age to his chronological age (MA/CA) or, more precisely, especially for older persons, the ratio of mental age to the mental age normal for chronological age (in both cases multiplied by 100 to eliminate the decimal). More generally, IQ is a measure of brightness that takes into account both score on an intelligence test and age. A **deviation IQ** is such a measure of brightness, based on the difference or deviation between a person's obtained score and the score that is normal for the person's age.

The following table shows a slight adaptation of the classification of IQ's offered by Terman and Merrill for the Stanford-Binet test, indicating the percent of persons in a normal population who fall in each classification. This table is roughly applicable to tests yielding IQ's having standard deviations of about 16 points (not all do). It is important to bear in mind that any such table is arbitrary, for there are no inflexible lines of demarcation between "retarded" and "borderline," or other adjacent classes.

Classification	*IQ*	*Percent of All persons*
Highly gifted	140 and above	1
Gifted	130–139	2.5
Superior	120–129	8
Above average	110–119	16
Normal or average	90–109	45
Below average	80–89	16
Dull or borderline	70–79	8
Retarded	60–69	2.5
Severely retarded	59 and below	1

Interpolation   In general, any process of estimating intermediate values between two known points. As applied to test norms, it refers to the procedure used in assigning interpreted values (such as grade or age equivalents) to scores between the successive average scores actually obtained in the standardization process. In reading norm tables, it is necessary at times to *interpolate* to obtain a norm value for a score between scores given in the table; for example, in the table given here, an age value of 12-5 would be assigned, by interpolation, to a score of 118.

Score	Age Equivalent
120	12-6
115	12-4
110	12-2

Inventory test   As applied to achievement tests, a test that attempts to cover rather thoroughly some relatively small unit of specific instruction or training. The purpose of an inventory test, as the name suggests, is more in the nature of a "stock-taking" of an individual's knowledge or skill than an effort to measure in the usual sense. The term sometimes denotes a type of test used to measure achievement status prior to instruction.

Many personality and interest questionnaires are designated "inventories," since they appraise an individual's status in several personal characteristics, or his level of interest in a variety of types of activities.

Item   A single question or exercise in a test.

Item analysis   The process of evaluating single test items by any of several methods. It usually involves determining the difficulty value and the discriminating power of the item, and often the correlation with some criterion.

Kuder-Richardson formula(s)   Formulas for estimating the reliability of a test from information about the individual items in the test, or from the mean score, standard deviation, and number of items in the test. Because the Kuder-Richardson formulas permit estimation of reliability from a single administration of a test, without the labor involved in dividing the test into halves, their use has become common in test development. The Kuder-Richardson formulas are not appropriate for estimating the reliability of speeded tests. (See **Speed test.**)

Matching item   A test item calling for the correct association of each entry in one list with an entry in a second list.

Mean   See **Arithmetic mean.**

Median   The middle point (or score) in a distribution; the 50th percentile; the point that divides the group into two equal parts. Half of the group of scores fall below the median and half above it.

Mental Age (MA)   The age for which a given score on an intelligence test is average or normal. If a score of 55 on an intelligence test corresponds to a mental age of 6 years, 10 months, then 55 is presumably the average score that would be made by an unselected group of children 6 years, 10 months of age. (See **Achievement Age, Chronological Age.**)

Modal age   The age or age range that is most typical or characteristic of pupils of specified grade placement.

Modal-age norms   Norms based on the performance of pupils of modal age for their respective grades, which are thus free of the distorting influence of under-age or over-age pupils.

Mode   The score or value that occurs most frequently in a distribution.

Multiple-choice item   A test item in which the examinee's task is to choose the correct or best answer from several given answers, options, or alternatives.

Multiple-response item   A special type of multiple-choice item in which two or more of the given choices may be correct.

N* or *n   The symbol commonly used to represent the number of cases in a distribution, study, or whatever.

Norm line   A smooth curve drawn through the mean or median scores of successive age or grade groups, or through percentile points for a single group.

Normal distribution   A distribution of scores or measures that in graphic form has a distinctive bell-shaped appearance. The graph of a normal distribution is known as a *normal curve* or *normal probability curve*. In a normal distribution, scores or measures are distributed symmetrically about the mean, with as many cases at various distances above the mean as at equal distances below it, and with cases concentrated near the average and decreasing in frequency the further one departs from the average, according to a precise mathematical equation. The assumption that mental and psychological characteristics are distributed normally has been useful in much test-development work.

Normalized standard scores   Standard scores that are forced to be normally distributed by converting the percentile equivalents of raw scores to the corresponding standard scores along a normal curve. They are most frequently expressed with a mean equated to 50 and a standard deviation equated to 10.

Norms   Statistics that describe the test performance of specified groups, such as pupils of various ages or grades in the standardization group for a test. Norms are often assumed to be representative of some larger population, as of pupils in the country as a whole. Norms are descriptive of average, typical, or mediocre performance; they are not to be regarded as standards, or as desirable levels of attainment. Grade, age, and percentile are the most common types of norm.

Objective test   A test in the scoring of which a single answer key is used, so that scorers cannot disagree as to whether responses are to be scored right or wrong. It is contrasted with a "subjective" test, such as the usual essay examination, to which different scorers may assign different scores, ratings, or grades.

Omnibus test   A test (1) in which items measuring a variety of mental operations are all combined into a single sequence rather than being grouped together by type of operation, and (2) from which only a single score is derived, rather than separate scores for each operation or function. Omnibus tests make for simplicity of administration: one set of directions and one overall time limit usually suffice.

Percentile   A point in a distribution below which falls the percent of cases indicated by the given percentile. Thus the 15th percentile denotes the point below which 15 percent of the scores fall. The percent of scores in a distribution equal to or lower than a given score is termed the *percentile rank* of that score.

Performance test   As contrasted with *paper-and-pencil test*, a test requiring motor or manual response on the examinee's part, generally but not always involving manipulation of concrete equipment or materials. "Performance test" is also used in another sense, to denote a test that is actually a work-sample, and in this sense it may include paper-and-pencil tests—as, for example, a test in accountancy, or in taking shorthand, or in proofreading, where no materials other than paper and pencil may be required, but where the test response is identical with the behavior about which information is desired.

Personality test   A test intended to measure one or more of the non-intellective aspects of an individual's mental or psychological makeup. Personality tests include the so-called *personality inventories* or *adjustment inventories* which seek to measure a person's status on such traits as dominance, sociability, and introversion by means of self-descriptive responses to a series of questions; *rating scales* which call for rating, by one's self or another, of the extent to which a subject possesses certain characteristics; *situation tests*, in which the individual's behavior in simulated lifelike situations is observed by one or more judges and evaluated with reference to various personality traits; and *opinion* or *attitude inventories*.

Power test   A test intended to measure level of performance rather than speed of response, hence one in which there is either no time limit or a very generous one, or in which the items are arranged from easiest to most difficult so that most examinees exhaust their knowledge before time is called.

Practice effect   The influence of previous experience with a test on a later administration of the same test or a similar test; usually, an increase in the score on the second testing, attributed to increased familiarity with the directions, kinds of questions, and so on. Practice effect is greatest when the interval between testings is small, when the materials in the two tests are very similar, and when the initial test-taking represents a relatively novel experience for the subjects.

Product-moment coefficient   See **Coefficient of correlation**.

Profile   A graphic representation of the results on several tests, for either an individual or a group, when the results have been expressed in some uniform or comparable terms. This method of presentation permits easy identification of areas of strength or weakness, but differences in the scores that constitute an individual's profile tend to be rather unreliable.

Prognosis (Prognostic) test   A test used to predict future success or failure in a specific subject or field.

Projective technique (Projective method)   A method of personality study in which the subject responds as he chooses to a series of stimuli such as inkblots, pictures, unfinished sentences, and so on. So-called because of the assumption that under this free-response condition the subject "projects" into his responses manifestations of personality characteristics and organization that can, by suitable methods, be scored and interpreted to yield a description of his basic personality structure. The Rorschach (inkblot) technique and the Murray *Thematic Apperception Test* and variations thereof are the most commonly used projective methods.

Quartile   One of three points that divide the cases in a distribution into four equal groups. The first quartile, or 25th percentile, sets off the lowest fourth of the group; the second quartile is the same as the 50th percentile, or median; and the third quartile, or 75th percentile, marks off the highest fourth.

Quartile deviation   One half the distance between the 25th and 75th percentiles—a measure of variability. (Also called the *semi-interquartile range*.)

r   See **Coefficient of correlation**.

Random sample   A sample of the members of a population drawn in such a way that every member of the population has an equal and independent chance of being included—that is, drawn in a way that precludes the operation of bias or selection. The purpose in using a sample thus free of bias is, of course, that the sample be fairly "representative" of the total population, so that sample findings may be generalized to the population. A great advantage of random samples is that formulas are available for estimating the expected variation of the sample statistics from their true values in the total population; in other words, we know how precise an estimate of the population value is given by a random sample of any given size.

Range   The difference between the lowest and highest scores obtained on a test by some group.

Raw score   The first quantitative result obtained in scoring a test—usually the number of right answers, number right minus some fraction of number wrong, time required for performance, number of errors, or similar direct but unconverted measure of performance.

Readiness test   A test that measures the extent to which an individual has achieved a degree of maturity or acquired certain skills or information needed for undertaking successfully some new learning activity. Thus a *reading readiness test* indicates the extent to which a child has reached a developmental stage where he may profitably begin a formal instructional program in reading.

Recall item   An item that requires the examinee to supply the correct answer from his own memory or recollection, as contrasted with a **recognition item**, in which he need only identify the correct answer. For example, "Columbus discovered America in the year ___?___ " is a recall item, whereas "Columbus discovered America in (a) 1425 (b) 1492 (c) 1520 (d) 1546" is a recognition item.

Recognition item   An item requiring the examinee to recognize or select the correct answer from among two or more given answers. (See **Recall item**.)

Regression effect   Tendency for a predicted score to be relatively nearer the mean of its series than the score from which it was predicted is to the mean of its series. For example, if we predict school marks from an intelligence test, we will find that for all pupils who have IQ's two standard deviations above the mean, the mean of their predicted school marks will be less than two standard deviations from the mean of the school marks.

Reliability   The extent to which a test is consistent in measuring whatever it does measure; dependability, stability, relative freedom from errors of measurement. Reliability is usually estimated by some form of **reliability coefficient** or by the **standard error of measurement.**

Reliability coefficient   The coefficient of correlation between two forms of a test, between scores on repeated administrations of the same test, or between halves of a test, properly corrected. These three coefficients measure somewhat different aspects of reliability, but all are properly spoken of as reliability coefficients. (See **Alternate-form reliability**, **Split-half coefficient**, **Test-retest coefficient**, **Kuder-Richardson formula(s).**)

Representative sample   A sample that corresponds to or matches the population of which it is a sample with respect to characteristics important for the purposes under investigation—for example, in an achievement-test norm sample, proportion of pupils from each state, from various regions, from segregated and nonsegregated schools, and so on.

Scholastic aptitude   See **Academic aptitude.**

Skewness   The degree to which a unimodal (one-peak) curve departs from symmetry.

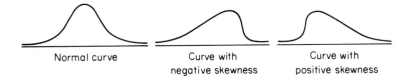

Normal curve   Curve with negative skewness   Curve with positive skewness

Sociometry   Measurement of the interpersonal relationships prevailing among the members of a group. By means of sociometric devices, such as the *sociogram*, an attempt is made to discover the patterns of choice and rejection among the individuals making up the group—which ones are chosen most often as friends or leaders ("stars"), which are rejected by others ("isolates"), how the group subdivides into clusters or cliques, and so on.

Spearman-Brown formula   A formula giving the relationship between the reliability of a test and its length. The formula permits estimation of the reliability of a test lengthened or shortened by any amount, from the known reliability of a test of specified length. Its most common application is in the estimation of reliability of an entire test from the correlation between the two halves of the test (*split-half reliability*).

Speed test   A test in which performance is measured by the number of tasks performed in a given time. Examples are tests of typing speed and reading speed. Some other tests are *speeded* if an appreciable number of examinees do not have time to reveal what they know. The opposite of a speed test is a **power test**.

Split-half coefficient   A coefficient of reliability reflecting the correlation of scores on one half of a test with scores on the other half. Generally, but not necessarily, the two halves consist of the odd-numbered and the even-numbered items.

Standard deviation (σ, s, SD)   A measure of the variability or dispersion of a set of scores. It is the positive square root of the **Variance** of the scores. The more the scores cluster around the mean, the smaller the standard deviation. In a normal distribution, 68 percent of the scores are within one standard deviation of the mean.

Standard error of measurement   An estimate of the magnitude of the "error of measurement" in a score—that is, the **standard deviation** of the difference between obtained scores and corresponding **true scores**. The standard error is an amount such that in about two-thirds (68%) of the cases the obtained score would not differ by more than one standard error from the true score.

Standard score   A general term referring to any of a variety of "transformed" scores, in terms of which raw scores may be expressed for reasons of convenience, comparability, ease of interpretation, and so on.

The simplest type of standard score is that which expresses the deviation of an individual's raw score from the average score of his group in relation to the standard deviation of the scores of the group. Thus:

$$\text{standard score } (z) = \frac{\text{raw score} - \text{mean}}{\text{standard deviation}}.$$

By multiplying this ratio by a suitable constant and by adding or subtracting another constant, we may obtain standard scores having any desired mean and standard deviation. Such standard scores do not affect the relative standing of the individuals in the group or change the shape of the original distribution.

More complicated types of standard score may yield distributions differing in shape from the original distribution; in fact, they are sometimes used for precisely this purpose. **Normalized standard scores** are examples of this latter group.

Standardization sample   Refers to that part of the reference population which is selected for use in norming a test. This sample should be representative of the reference population in essential characteristics, such as geographical location, age, and grade. (Also called *norm sample* and *reference group*.)

Standardized test   A systematic sample of performance obtained under prescribed conditions, scored according to definite rules, and capable of evaluation by reference to normative information.

Stanine   One of the steps in a nine-point scale of standard scores, usually normalized. The stanine (short for *standard-nine*) scale has values from one to nine, with a mean of five and a standard deviation of two.

Stencil key   A scoring key that, when positioned over an examinee's responses either in a test booklet or, more commonly, on an answer sheet, permits rapid identification and counting of all right answers. Stencil keys may be perforated in positions corresponding to positions of right answers, so that only right answers show through when the keys are in place; or they may be transparent, with positions of right answers identified by circles, boxes, and so on printed on the key.

Strip key   A scoring key arranged so that the answers for items on any page or in any column of the test appear in a strip or column that may be placed alongside the examinee's responses for easy scoring.

Survey test   A test that measures general achievement in a given subject or area, usually with the connotation that the test is intended to measure group status, rather than to yield precise measures of individuals.

T-score   A standard score scale (usually normalized) employing a mean of 50 and a standard deviation of 10.

Test-retest coefficient   A type of reliability coefficient obtained by administering the same test a second time after a short interval and correlating the two sets of scores.

True-false item   A test question or exercise in which the examinee's task is to indicate whether a given statement is true or false.

True score   A score entirely free of random errors of measurement. True scores are hypothetical values never obtained by testing, which always involves some measurement error. A true score is sometimes defined as the average score of an infinite series of measurements of a particular examinee with the same or exactly equivalent tests, assuming no practice effect or change in that examinee during the testing.

Validity   The extent to which a test does the job for which it is used. Validity, thus defined, has different connotations for various kinds of test and, accordingly, different kinds of validity evidence are appropriate for them. For example:

1. The validity of an achievement test is the extent to which the content of the test represents a balanced and adequate sampling of the outcomes (knowledge, skills, and so on) of the course or instructional program it is intended to cover (*content, face,* or *curricular validity*). It

is best evidenced by a comparison of the test content with courses of study, instructional materials, and statements of instructional goals, and by critical analysis of the processes required in responding to the items.

2. The validity of an aptitude, prognostic, or readiness test is the extent to which it accurately indicates future learning success in the area for which it is used as a predictor (*predictive validity*). It is evidenced by correlations between test scores and measures of later success.

3. The validity of a personality test is the extent to which the test yields an accurate description of an individual's personality traits or personality organization (*status* or *concurrent validity*). It may be evidenced by agreement between test results and other types of evaluation, such as ratings or clinical classification, but only to the extent that such criteria are themselves valid. Somewhat related to status validity is *construct validity*, but the latter is more theoretically oriented and better grounded in the logic of psychological science.

The traditional definition of validity as "the extent to which a test measures what it is supposed to measure" seems less satisfactory than the above, since it fails to emphasize that the validity of a test is always specific to the purposes for which the test is used, and that different kinds of evidence are appropriate for appraising the validity of various types of test.

Validity of a test *item* usually refers to the discriminating power of the item—its ability to distinguish between persons having much and those having little of some characteristic. This use of the term should probably be avoided, because such discrimination is related more to reliability than validity.

Variance   A measure of the dispersion (that is, the heterogeneity or scatter) of a set of scores. Its square root is the **Standard deviation**.

z-score   A standard score expressed in standard deviation units; hence, its mean is 0 and its standard deviation is 1.

ANSWERS TO QUESTIONS
FOLLOWING CHAPTER 2

1. **C.** $(4 + 5 + 7 + 6 + 4)/5 = 26/5 = 5.2$
2. **C.** Only two of the five options (C and E) contain measures of central tendency; the standard deviation, quartile deviation, and range are measures of variability. Since the arithmetic mean is a function of every score in the distribution, its value would reflect "the undue influence of a few extreme salaries." Whether the highest-paid worker made $5,000 or $50,000 is wholly inconsequential so far as the size of the median is concerned.
3. **D.** When arranged in numerical order, these scores are: 4, 4, **5,** 6, 7. The middle score (midscore) is 5.
4. **D.** The 60th percentile is defined as the point in a distribution below which lie 60 percent of the scores and above which lie 40 percent of the scores.
5. **A.** The difference reflects only the dispersion or variability.
6. **A.** Q_3 is the 75th percentile, and the median is the 50th percentile. Twenty-five percent of the scores lie between these two points, since $75 - 50 = 25$.
7. **C.** $(1 + 1 + 3 + 3)/4 = 2$.
8. **B.** $s = \sqrt{\dfrac{\Sigma (X - \bar{X})^2}{n}} = \sqrt{\dfrac{(1 - 2)^2 + (1 - 2)^2 + (3 - 2)^2 + (3 - 2)^2}{4}}$

    $= \sqrt{\dfrac{4}{4}} = 1$.
9. **B.** $z = \dfrac{\text{score} - \text{mean}}{\text{SD}} = \dfrac{70 - 80}{20} = \dfrac{-10}{20} = -.5$.
10. **D.** $50 + 10(-.5) = 50 - 5 = 45$.
11. **E.** Three tied scores of 95 occur. If there were no ties, these three places would have ranks of 4, 5, 6. Since one score of 95 is as good as another, we assign the average of 4, 5, and 6 (which is 5) to each of the three scores. *460*

Note that $4 + 5 + 6 = 15$, the same as the sum of the new ranks: $5 + 5 + 5 = 15$. Whether or not ties occur, the sum of a certain number (N) of consecutive ranks beginning with 1 will always be $[N(N + 1)]/2$. If there are 9 ranks, as in this question, their sum will be $(9 \times 10)/2 = 45$.

12. **B.** Absolute values greater than 1.0 are mathematically impossible.

13. **A.**

14. **C.** An r of 0 has the least possible predictive value. The closer to 0 r gets, *regardless of sign*, the poorer prediction becomes.

15. **E.** The r discussed in Chapter 2 simply cannot be greater than $+1.00$ or -1.00, except when computational errors are made.

16. **B.** $r_{\text{Ranks}} = 1 - \dfrac{6 \sum D^2}{N(N^2 - 1)}$

$$= 1 - \frac{6[(1 - 2)^2 + (2 - 1)^2 + (3 - 5)^2 + (4 - 4)^2 + (5 - 3)^2]}{5(25 - 1)}$$

$$= 1 - \frac{60}{120} = .50.$$

17. **D.** If the correlation is statistically significant at the .05 level, this means there is no more than a 5 percent chance that the true correlation (that is, the parameter) between the two variables is zero.

18. **B.** When a distribution is skewed negatively, the "tail" points to the left.

19. **B.** The arithmetic mean is a measure of central tendency; the standard deviation is a measure of variability.

20. **C.** Q_3 is the 75th percentile; the median (Q_2) is the 50th percentile.

21. **E.** Both the mean and the standard deviation are based upon all scores in the distribution; the median and Q are both percentile measures. Also, the mean is used with the SD, while the median is used with Q. The analogy is: a certain kind of measure of central tendency is to a similar sort of measure of variability as another kind of measure of central tendency is to its related measure of variability.

22. **D.** Fifty percent of all the measures in a distribution always lie between Q_3 and Q_1. In a normal (so-called "bell-shaped") distribution, 68 percent of all cases lie within one standard deviation of the mean.

23. **A.** The arithmetic mean is the most reliable measure of central tendency, the mode the least reliable; the standard deviation is the most reliable measure of variability, the range the least reliable.

24. **B.** The standard deviation is a linear distance along the base line of a frequency distribution.

25. **E.** When correlation is positive, high scores on one test tend to go with high scores on the other test, while low scores tend to go with low scores. This is a direct relationship. When correlation is negative, high scores on one test go with low scores on the other, and vice versa. This is an inverse relationship.

OBJECTIVES FOR AN INTRODUCTORY UNIT IN BEGINNING ALGEBRA, "USING LETTERS FOR NUMBERS"[1]

Classification in Bloom's Taxonomy	Percentage Weight of Objective		Number of Items Testing this Objective	Percent of Total Items
k[a]	20%	1. To learn the meaning of some of the important words used in algebra: algebraic expression — factor — product base — formula — quotient coefficient — inverse — substitution difference — like terms — symbol equation — literal number — sum exponent — parentheses — term — power — unlike terms	10	22
k	10%	2. To gain knowledge of the order of operation in evaluating expressions and of the rules for operating with zero, with parentheses, with exponents, and with like and unlike terms.	6	14
k	5%	3. To be able to recognize illustrations of the commutative principle.	1	2
k	5%	4. To comprehend the notion of using letters to stand for numbers.	1	2
c[a]	20%	5. To translate mathematical symbolism into verbal statements and vice versa.	6	14
ap[a]	25%	6. To learn how to add, subtract, multiply, divide, and find powers of literal numbers.	14	31

[1] This preliminary formulation of objectives for a 2- to 3-week introductory unit was prepared as a class exercise in a test-construction course by Sister M. Jacinta Mann and Mr. Edward Sasse, experienced teachers of mathematics.

Classification in Bloom's Taxonomy	Percentage Weight of Objective		Number of Items Testing this Objective	Percent of Total Items
ap	10%	7. To develop facility and accuracy in substitution in and evaluation of algebraic expressions and formulas.	5	11
an[a]	5%	8. To gain skill in comprehending the interrelationships among these basic algebraic ideas.	2	4
Affective domain		9. To develop a realization of the importance of algebra in the modern world. (Perhaps best evaluated by observation.)	—	—
Affective domain		10. To create a friendly attitude toward mathematics.	—	—
Totals	100%		45	100

[a] In the cognitive domain, *k*nowledge, *c*omprehension, *ap*plication, and *an*alysis.

Definitions, Instructional Procedures, and Evaluation

1. *To learn the meaning of some of the important words used in algebra.*

How Taught: A vocabulary list is compiled day by day (left on front board) as the new words arise. The student is, therefore, conscious of what new words he is expected to know and what their correct spelling and syllabication are. Continual review is interspersed with class work where the words arise.

Evaluation: 1. unit test
2. quizzes
3. oral questioning in continual review discussions mentioned above
4. observing the student's actual use of these words—for example, when the student asks about "the sign of the second term" instead of pointing to it and asking "What's the sign supposed to be?"

2. *To gain knowledge of the order of operation in evaluating expressions and of the rules for operating with zero, with parentheses, and with like and unlike terms.*

How Taught: As these rules arise and are explained and illustrated, the students add the names of the rules next to their vocabulary list. They are required then to study them so that in oral drill they can repeat the various rules *in their own words*. This all takes place, of course, simultaneously with learning to apply the rules in problems.

Evaluation: 1. unit test
2. quizzes
3. oral drill in class

3. *To be able to recognize illustrations of the commutative principle.*

How Taught: As are the vocabulary words. The principle could be added to that list.

Evaluation: 1. unit test
              2. quizzes
              3. class discussion with oral questioning

464

*Objectives for
An Introductory
Unit in
Beginning
Algebra,
"Using Letters
for Numbers"*

4. *To comprehend the notion of using letters for numbers.*

How Taught: A class discussion of symbolization in general should precede the particular use of it in algebra. Then the idea must permeate all future discussions until it is felt that every child is familiar and friendly with the *xyz*'s. There are available some excellent audio-visual aids in this area.

Evaluation: 1. unit test (difficult to form questions)
              2. oral discussion

5. *To translate mathematical symbolism into verbal statements and vice versa.*

How Taught: There is no substitute for oral and written drill in this matter. The drill material can be composed of quite interesting and meaningful examples.

Evaluation: 1. unit test
              2. quizzes
              3. oral and board drill

6. *To learn how to add, subtract, multiply, divide, and find powers of literal numbers.*

How Taught: These skills are taught simultaneously with the rules mentioned in Objective 2. There needs to be much drill on the various skills and the combinations of them. This drill is achieved by way of blackboard work, oral work, and written homework assignments. The "spelling bee" type of game may be useful to employ here. Ninth graders usually still have sufficient simplicity to enjoy them.

Evaluation: 1. unit test
              2. quizzes
              3. oral drill and homework assignments

7. *To develop facility and accuracy in substitution in and evaluation of algebraic expressions and formulas.*

How Taught: Same as Objective 6; in this case the type of problem lends itself to composition of interesting drill material.

8. *To gain skill in comprehending the interrelationships among these basic algebraic ideas.*

How Taught: As each new term is taught, it should be related to the others in the list, always encouraging the pupil to *discover* the relationship himself.

Evaluation: Same as Objective 2

9. *To develop a realization of the importance of algebra in the modern world.*

10. *To create a friendly attitude toward mathematics.*

How Taught: Objectives 9 and 10 cannot (effectively) be taught for *directly* but must be kept in mind through every activity. The teacher must have achieved these objectives in his own "self," so that they will "rub off" on the students. Many little surprise opportunities will arise for the alert teacher to utilize.

Bulletin boards planned by students and teacher together, films on the subject, and field trips to local industries can aid in the achievement of these objectives.

Evaluation: 1. observation of individuals in class and out of class
2. discussion with the study hall teacher and parents

At the end of the unit, attainment of Objectives 1–8 was tested by items at appropriate levels of Bloom's *Taxonomy.*

PUBLISHERS OF STANDARDIZED TESTS

The following list includes every significant test publisher indexed on pages 1597–1606 of Oscar K. Buros, ed., *The sixth mental measurements yearbook* (Highland Park, N.J.: Gryphon Press, 1965). Asterisks indicate major publishers.

AMERICAN GUIDANCE SERVICES, Inc., 720 Washington Ave., S. E., Minneapolis, Minn. 55414

AUSTRALIAN COUNCIL FOR EDUCATIONAL RESEARCH, Frederick St., Hawthorn E.2, Victoria, Australia

BOBBS-MERRILL COMPANY, Inc. 4300 East 62nd St., Indianapolis, Ind. 46206

BUREAU OF EDUCATIONAL MEASUREMENTS, Kansas State Teachers College, Emporia, Kansas 66801

*CALIFORNIA TEST BUREAU, Del Monte Research Park, Monterey, Calif. 93940

CONSULTING PSYCHOLOGISTS PRESS, INC., 577 College Ave., Palo Alto, Calif. 94306

EDUCATIONAL RECORDS BUREAU, 21 Audubon Avenue, New York, N.Y. 10032

*EDUCATIONAL TESTING SERVICE, Princeton, N.J. 08540

GRUNE & STRATTON, INC., 381 Park Ave., South, New York, N.Y. 10016

*HARPER & ROW, PUBLISHERS, 49 East 33d St., New York, N.Y. 10016

*HARCOURT BRACE JOVANOVICH, INC., 757 Third Ave., New York, N.Y. 10017

*HOUGHTON MIFFLIN COMPANY, 2 Park St., Boston, Mass. 02107

INSTITUTE FOR PERSONALITY AND ABILITY TESTING, 1602 Coronado Dr., Champaign, Ill. 61820

NATIONAL FOUNDATION FOR EDUCATIONAL RESEARCH IN ENGLAND AND WALES, The Mere, Upton Park, Slough Bucks, England

Newnes Educational Publishing Company Ltd., Tower House, 8–11 Southampton St., Strand, London W.C. 2, England

Ohio Scholarship Tests, Stat C, Department of Education, 751 Northwest Blvd., State of Ohio, Columbus, Ohio 43212

*Psychological Corporation, 304 East 45th St., New York, N.Y. 10017

Psychometric Affiliates, 1743 Montery, Chicago, Ill. 60643

Public Personnel Association, 1313 East 60th St. Chicago, Ill. 60637

Richardson, Bellows, Henry & Co., Inc. 324 Balter Bldg., New Orleans, La. 70112

Scholastic Testing Service, Inc., 3374 West Devon Ave., Chicago, Ill. 60106

*Science Research Associates, Inc., 259 East Erie St., Chicago, Ill. 60611

Sheridan Supply Co., P. O. Box 837, Beverly Hills, Calif. 90213

C. H. Stoelting Co., 424 North Homan Ave., Chicago, Ill. 60624

University of London Press Ltd., Little Paul's House, Warwick Square, London E.C. 4, England

Western Psychological Services, Box 775, Beverly Hills, Calif. 90213

Publishers of Standardized Tests

Bibliography

ABRAMSON, T. 1969. The influence of examiner race on first-grade and kindergarten subjects' Peabody Picture Vocabulary Test scores. *Journal of Educational Measurement,* **6**(4): 241–246.

ADAMS, G. S. 1964. *Measurement and evaluation in education, psychology, and guidance.* New York: Holt, Rinehart and Winston, Inc.

AHMANN, J. S., and M. D. GLOCK. 1969. *Evaluating pupil growth: Principles of tests and measurement,* 3d ed. Boston: Allyn and Bacon, Inc.

AIKEN, L. R., JR. 1963. The grading behavior of a college faculty. *Educational and Psychological Measurement,* **23**(2): 319–322.

ALLISON, D. E. 1970. Test anxiety, stress, and intelligence-test performance. *Canadian Journal of Behavioral Science,* **2**: 26–37.

ALLISON, J., S. J. BLATT, and C. N. ZIMET. 1968. *Interpretation of psychological tests.* New York: Harper & Row, Publishers.

AMERICAN PSYCHOLOGICAL ASSOCIATION. 1953. *Ethical standards of psychologists.* Washington, D.C.: American Psychological Association.

AMERICAN EDUCATIONAL RESEARCH ASSOCIATION, and NATIONAL COUNCIL ON MEASUREMENT IN EDUCATION. 1966. *Standards for educational and psychological tests and manuals.* Washington, D.C.: American Psychological Association, Inc.

AMMONS, MARGARET. 1969. Objectives and outcomes. In R. L. Ebel, ed., *Encyclopedia of educational research,* 4th ed. New York: The Macmillan Company, pp. 908–914.

ANASTASI, A. 1958. Heredity, environment, and the question "How?" *Psychological Review,* **65**(4): 197–208.

————. 1964a. Culture-fair testing. *Educational Horizons,* **43**(1): 26–30. Reprinted in

G. H. Bracht, K. D. Hopkins, and J. C. Stanley, eds. 1972. *Perspectives in educational and psychological measurement.* Englewood Cliffs, N.J.: Prentice-Hall, Inc., Selection 20.

———. 1964b. Some current developments in the measurement and interpretation of test validity. *Proceedings of the 1963 Invitational Conference on Testing Problems.* Princeton, N.J.: Educational Testing Service.

———. 1968. *Psychological testing,* 3d ed. New York: The Macmillan Company.

ANDERSON, H. R., and E. F. LINDQUIST. 1960. Revised by David K. Heenan. *Selected test items in world history,* 3d ed.: *Bulletin No. 9.* Washington, D.C.: National Council for the Social Studies.

———. 1964. Revised by Harriet Stull. *Selected test items in American history: Bulletin No. 6.* Washington, D.C.: National Council for the Social Studies.

ANDERSON, R. 1970. Comments on Professor Gagne's paper entitled "Instructional variables and learning outcomes." In M. C. Wittrock and D. E. Wiley, eds. *The evaluation of instruction.* New York: Holt, Rinehart and Winston.

ANDERSON, R. D. 1967. Has the objective been attained? *Science and Children,* **5**(2): 33–36.

———, A. DeVITO, O. E. DYRLI, M. KELLOGG, L. KOCHENDORFER, and J. WEIGAND. 1970. Performance objectives: A blueprint for action. Chapter 2 in *Developing children's thinking through science.* Englewood Cliffs, N.J.: Prentice-Hall, Inc.

ANDERSON, R. H. 1966. The importance and purposes of reporting. *National Elementary School Principal,* **45**: 6–11.

ANDERSON, S. B. 1952. Sequence in multiple choice item opinions. *Journal of Educational Psychology,* **43**: 364–368.

———, and M. H. MAIER. 1963. 34,000 pupils and how they grew. *Journal of Teacher Education,* **14**: 212–216.

ANGOFF, W. H. 1971a. Scales, norms, and equivalent scores. In R. L. Thorndike, ed., *Educational measurement,* 2d ed. Washington, D. C.: American Council on Education, Chap. 15.

———, ed. 1971b. *The College Board admissions testing program.* New York: College Entrance Examination Board.

ARMITAGE, J. H. 1967. *Analysis of citizenship goals in social studies instruction.* Doctoral dissertation, University of Colorado. University Microfilms, No. 68-10,601. *Dissertation Abstracts,* **29**:(2): 396-A, 397-A (August 1968).

ARMSTRONG, R. J., and R. F. MOONEY. 1969. Confidence testing: Is it reliable? Paper read at the annual meeting of the National Council on Measurement in Education, Los Angeles, February.

ASHBAUGH, E. J. 1924. Reducing the variability in teachers' marks. *Journal of Educational Research,* **9**: 185–198.

ASHBURN, R. R. 1938. An experiment in the essay-type question. *Journal of Experimental Education,* **7**: 1–3.

ASTIN, A. W. 1970. *Predicting academic performance in college.* New York: The Free Press.

AUSUBEL, D. P. 1961. The use of advance organizers in the learning and retention of meaningful verbal learning. *Journal of Educational Psychology,* **52**: 266–274.

AYRES, L. P. 1918. History and present status of educational measurements. *Seventeenth yearbook of the National Society for the Study of Education, Part II.* Bloomington, Ill.: Public School Publishing Co.

BADAL, A. W., and E. P. LARSEN. 1970. On reporting test results to community groups. *NCME Measurement in Education,* **1**: 1–12.

BAGLEY, W. C. 1900. On the correlation of mental and motor ability in school children. *American Journal of Psychology*, **12**: 193–205.

BAIRD, L. L., L. A. MUNDAY, and W. J. FEISTER. 1969. A study of grading standards. Paper prepared for the annual meeting of the National Council on Measurement in Education, Los Angeles, February.

BAKER, F. B. 1965. Origins of the item parameters X_{50} and beta as a modern item analysis technique. *Journal of Educational Measurement*, **2**: 167–180.

———. 1971. Automational test scoring, reporting, and analysis. In R. L. Thorndike, ed., *Educational measurement*, 2d ed. Washington, D.C.: American Council on Education, Chap. 8.

BANAKA, W. H. 1971. *Training in depth interviewing*. New York: Harper and Row, Publishers.

BARCH, A. M. 1957. The relation of departure time and retention to academic achievement. *Journal of Educational Psychology*, **48**: 352–358.

BARCLAY, J. R. 1968. *Controversial issues in testing*. Boston: Houghton Mifflin Company.

BARRON, F. 1968. The measurement of creativity. In D. K. Whitla, ed., *Handbook of measurement and assessment in behavioral sciences*. Reading, Mass.: Addison-Wesley, pp. 348–366.

BARTON, W. A., JR. 1931. Improving the true-false examination. *School and Society*, **34**: 544–546.

BAUERNFEIND, R. H. 1963. *Building a school testing program*. Boston: Houghton Mifflin Company.

BAUMAN, D. J. 1970. The development and comparison of measures of science interest of secondary school science students. Doctoral dissertation, University of Colorado, Laboratory of Educational Research.

———, G. V GLASS, and S. A. HARRINGTON. 1969. The effects of the position of an "Organizer" on learning meaningful verbal material. Boulder: University of Colorado, Laboratory of Educational Research.

BAYLEY, N. 1955. On the growth of intelligence. *American Psychologist*, **10**: 805–817.

———, and M. H. ODEN. 1955. The maintenance of intellectual ability in gifted adults. *Journal of Gerontology*, **10**: 91–107.

BEGGS, D. L., and A. N. HIERONYMUS. 1968. Uniformity of growth in the basic skills throughout the school year and during the summer. *Journal of Educational Measurement*, **5**(2): 91–97. Reprinted in G. H. Bracht, K. D. Hopkins, and J. C. Stanley (eds). 1972. *Perspectives in educational and psychological measurement*. Englewood Cliffs, N. J.: Prentice-Hall, Inc., Selection 5.

BENDER, L. 1970. Use of the Visual Motor Gestalt Test in the diagnosis of learning disabilities. *Journal of Special Education*, **4**(1): 29–39.

BENNETT, G. K., and J. E. DOPPELT. 1956. Item difficulty and speed of response. *Educational and Psychological Measurement*, **16**: 494–496.

———, H. G. SEASHORE, and A. G. WESMAN. 1966. *Differential Aptitude Tests*, 4th ed. Manual, Forms M and L. New York: The Psychological Corporation.

BERDIE, R. F. 1955. Aptitude, achievement, interest, and personality tests: A longitudinal comparison. *Journal of Applied Psychology*, **39**(2): 103–114.

BERG, H. D. 1958. Suggestions for increasing the thought content of objective test items. Mimeographed, 9 pp.

———. 1961. Evaluation in social science. Chapter 4 in P. L. Dressel, ed., *Evaluation in higher education*. Boston: Houghton Mifflin Company.

————, ed. 1967. Evaluation in social studies. *Thirty-fifth yearbook of the National Council for the Social Studies.* Washington, D.C.: The Council.

BERNARD, J. 1966. Achievement test norms and time of year of testing. *Psychology in in Schools,* **3**: 273–275.

BINET, A. 1911. *Les idées modernes sur les enfants.* Paris: Flammarion.

————, and T. SIMON. 1908. Le développement de l'intelligence chez les enfants. *L'Année psychologique,* **14**: 1–94.

————. 1916. *The development of intelligence in children.* Translated by Elizabeth S. Kite. Baltimore: The Williams & Wilkins Company.

BINGHAM, W. V., B. V. MOORE, and J. GUSTAD. 1959. *How to interview,* 4th ed. New York: Harper & Row, Publishers.

BIRD, D. E. 1953. Teaching listening comprehension. *Journal of Communication,* **3**: 127–130.

BIRREN, J. E. 1960. Psychological aspects of aging. In P. R. Farnsworth, ed., *Annual Review of Psychology,* Vol. 11. Palo Alto: Annual Reviews, Inc. pp. 161–198.

BLACK, H. 1963. *They shall not pass.* New York: William Morrow & Company, Inc.

BLACK, J. 1961. *The Q-sort method in personality assessment and psychiatric research.* Springfield, Ill.: Charles C Thomas, Publisher.

BLESSUM, W. T. 1969. *Annual Report 1968–1969, Medical Computer Facility.* Irvine, Calif.: University of California, Irvine, California College of Medicine.

BLOOM, B. S. 1956. The 1955 normative study of the tests of general educational development. *School Review,* **64**: 110–124.

————. 1961. Quality control in education. *Tomorrow's teaching.* Oklahoma City: Frontiers of Science Foundation, pp. 54–61.

————. 1964. *Stability and change in human characteristics.* New York: John Wiley & Sons, Inc.

————, M. D. ENGELHART, G. J. FURST, W. H. HILL, and D. R. KRATHWOHL. 1956. *Taxonomy of educational objectives* (subtitle: The classification of educational goals): *Handbook I, The cognitive domain.* New York: David McKay Company, Inc. Portions reprinted in G. H. Bracht, K. D. Hopkins, and J. C. Stanley (eds). 1972. *Perspectives* in *educational and psychological measurement.* Englewood Cliffs, N. J.: Prentice-Hall, Inc., Selection 12.

BOAG, A. K., and M. NEILD. 1962. The influence of the time factor on the scores of the Triggs Diagnostic Reading Test as reflected in the performance of secondary school pupils grouped according to ability. *Journal of Educational Research,* **55**(4): 181–183.

BOERSMA, W. C. 1967. The effectiveness of the evaluative criteria as a stimulus for school improvement in eleven Michigan high schools. Doctoral dissertation, University of Michigan, 184 pp.

BONJEAN, C. M., R. J. HILL, and S. D. McLEMORE. 1967. *Sociological measurement: An inventory of scales and indices.* San Francisco: Chandler Publishing Company.

BONNEY, M. E. 1955. Social behavior differences between second grade children of high and low sociometric status. *Journal of Educational Research,* **48**: 481–495.

————. 1960. Sociometric methods. In C. W. Harris, ed., *Encyclopedia of educational research,* 3d ed. New York: The Macmillan Company, pp. 1319–1324.

BORGARDUS, E. 1925. Measuring social distance. *Journal of Applied Sociology,* **9**: 299–308.

————. 1933. A social distance scale. *Sociology and Sociological Research,* **17**: 265–271.

BORING, E. G. 1961. The beginning and growth of measurement in psychology. *Isis*, **52**(168): 238–257.

BRACHT, G. H. 1967. The comparative values of objective and essay testing in undergraduate education: Implications for valid assessment of instruction. Unpublished master's thesis, University of Colorado.

———, and G. V Glass. 1968. The external validity of experiments. *American Educational Research Journal*, **5**: 437–474.

BRACHT, G. H., and K. D. HOPKINS. 1968. Comparative validities of essay and objective tests. Research Paper No. 20. Boulder: University of Colorado, Laboratory of Educational Research.

———. 1970a. The communality of essay and objective tests of academic achievement. *Educational and Psychological Measurement*, **30**: 359–364.

———. 1970b. *Stability of general academic achievement.* Paper presented at the annual meeting of the National Council on Measurement in Education, Minneapolis, March. Reprinted in G. H. Bracht, K. D. Hopkins, and J. C. Stanley, eds., 1972. *Perspectives in educational and psychological measurement.* Englewood Cliffs, N.J.: Prentice-Hall, Inc., Selection 25.

———, and J. C. STANLEY, eds. 1972. *Perspectives in educational and psychological measurement.* Englewood Cliffs, N.J.: Prentice-Hall, Inc.

BRADWAY, K. P., C. W. THOMPSON, and R. B. CRAVENS. 1958. Preschool IQ's after twenty-five years. *Journal of Educational Psychology*, **49**(5): 278–281.

BRAUN, J. R., and P. ASTA. 1968. Effects of faking instructions on sales motivation inventory scores. *Journal of Educational Measurement*, **5**(4): 339–340.

BRENNER, M. H. 1964. Test difficulty reliability and discrimination as functions of item difficulty order. *Journal of Applied Psychology*, **48**(2): 98–100.

BRIDGMAN, C. S. 1964. The relation of the upper-lower item discrimination index, *D*, to the bivariate normal correlation coefficient. *Educational and Psychological Measurement*, **24**(1): 85–90.

BROKAW, L. D. 1956. Technical school validity of the Airman Activity Inventory. *AFPTRC Development Report*, 56–109.

BROWNELL, W. A. 1937. Some neglected criteria for evaluating classroom tests. *National Elementary School Principal*, **16**: 485–492.

BRYNER, E. 1918. A selected bibliography of certain phases of educational measurement. *Seventeenth yearbook of the National Society for the Study of Education, Part II*. Bloomington, Ill.: Public School Publishing Co., pp. 161–190.

BURACK, B. 1961. Have you checked machine scoring error lately? *Vocational Guidance Quarterly*, **9**: 191–193.

BURBA, D. V., and W. S. CORLISS. 1963. *A study of the results of a questionnaire concerning attitudes of children toward report cards.* Birmingham, M. Ch., unpublished.

BUROS, O. K., ed. 1938, 1941, 1949, 1953, 1959, 1965, 1972. *The Mental Measurements Yearbook* (first through seventh). Highland Park, N.J.: Gryphon Press.

———. 1961. *Tests in print.* Highland Park, N.J.: Gryphon Press.

———, ed. 1970. *Personality tests and reviews: Including an index to the Mental Measurements Yearbooks.* Highland Park, N.J.: Gryphon Press.

BURR, W. L. 1963. Empirical relationships among modes of testing, modes of instruction and reading levels: In sixth-grade social studies. *Journal of Experimental Education*, **31**(4): 433–435.

BURT, C. 1955a. The evidence for the concept of intelligence. *British Journal of Educational Psychology*, **25**: 158–177.

———. 1955b. The meaning and assessment of intelligence. *Eugenics Review*, **47**(2): 81–91.

———. 1958. The inheritance of mental ability. *American Psychologist*, **13**: 1–15.

———. 1966. The genetic determination of differences in intelligence: A study of monozygotic twins reared together and apart. *British Journal of Psychology*, **57**: 137–153.

BURTON, N. W. 1968. *Course evaluation inventory.* Boulder: University of Colorado, Laboratory of Educational Research.

CALDWELL, E., and R. HARTNETT. 1967. Sex bias in college grading. *Journal of Educational Measurement*, **4**: 129–132.

CALLIS, R. 1953. The efficiency of the Minnesota Teacher Attitude Inventory for predicting interpersonal relations in the classroom. *Journal of Applied Psychology*, **37**: 82–85.

CAMPBELL, D. P. 1966a. Stability of interests within an occupation over 30 years. *Journal of Applied Psychology*, **50**: 51–56.

———. 1966b. Stability of vocational interests within occupations over long time spans. *Personnel and Guidance Journal*, **44**: 1012–1019.

———. 1968a. Changing patterns of interests within the American society. *Measurement and Evaluation in Guidance*, **1**: 36–49.

———. 1968b. The Strong Vocational Interest Blank: 1927–1967. In P. McReynolds, ed., *Advances in psychological assessment.* Vol. I. Palo Alto, Calif.: Science and Behavior Books, pp. 105–130.

CAMPBELL, D. T. 1969. Reforms as experiments. *American Psychologist*, **24**: 409–429.

———, and D. W. FISKE. 1959. Convergent and discriminant validation by the multitrait-multimethod matrix. *Psychological Bulletin*, **56**: 81–105.

CAMPBELL, D. T., and J. C. STANLEY. 1966. *Experimental and quasi-experimental designs for research.* Skokie, Ill.: Rand McNally & Company.

CAMPBELL, J. T., T. L. HILTON, and B. PITCHER. 1967. *Effects of repeating on test scores of the Graduate Record Examinations.* Graduate Record Examinations Special Report 67-1, Educational Testing Service.

CARROLL, J. B. 1968. Review of Guillford's *The nature of human intelligence. American Educational Research Journal*, **5**(2): 249–256.

CATTELL, R. B. 1963. Theory of fluid and crystallized intelligence: A critical experiment. *Journal of Educational Psychology*, **54**: 1–22.

CAVANAUGH, M. C., I. COHEN, D. DUNPHY, E. A. RINGWALL, and I. D. GOLDBERG. 1957. Prediction from the Cattell Infant Intelligence Scale. *Journal of Consulting Psychology*, **21**(1): 33–37.

CHADWICK, E. 1864. Statistics of educational results. *The Museum*, **3**: 480–484.

CHAMBERS, A. C., K. D. HOPKINS, and B. R. HOPKINS. 1972. Anxiety, physiologically and psychologically measured: Its effects on mental test performance. *Psychology in the Schools*, in press.

CHASE, C. I. 1964. Relative length of options and response set in multiple choice items. *Journal of Educational Measurement*, **1**(1): 38, also *Educational and Psychological Measurement*, **24**(4): 861–866.

————. 1968. The impact of some obvious variables on essay test scores. *Journal of Educational Measurement*, **5**(4): 315–318.

CHAUNCEY, H., and J. E. DOBBIN. 1963. *Testing: Its place in education today.* New York: Harper & Row, Publishers.

CHAUNCEY, H., and T. L. Hilton. 1965. Are aptitude tests valid for the highly able? *Science*, **148**(3675): 1297–1304.

CHURCHILL, W. D., and S. E. SMITH. 1966. The relationship of the 1960 Revised Stanford-Binet Intelligence Scale to intelligence and achievement test scores over a three-year period. *Educational and Psychological Measurement*, **26**: 1015–1020.

CLARK, C. A. 1968. The use of separate answer sheets in testing slow-learning pupils. *Journal of Educational Measurement*, **5**(1): 61–64.

CLAWAR, H. J. 1969. An aptitude-achievement comparison profile. *Measurement and Evaluation in Guidance*, **2**(1): 50–52.

CLEARY, T. A. 1968. Test bias: Prediction of grades of Negro and white students in integrated colleges. *Journal of Educational Measurement*, **5**(2): 115–124.

————, and T. L. HILTON. 1968. An investigation of item bias. *Educational and Psychological Measurement*, **28**(1), 61–75.

CLEMANS, W. W. 1971. Test administration. In R. L. Thorndike, ed., *Educational measurement*, 2d ed. Washington, D. C.: American Council on Education, Chap. 7.

COCHRAN, R. E., and C. C. WEIDEMANN. 1934. "Explain" essay vs. word answer fact test. *Phi Delta Kappan*, **17**: 59–61, 75.

————. 1937. A study of special types of tests. *Phi Delta Kappan*, **19**: 113–115, 131.

COFFMAN, W. E. 1966. On the validity of essay tests of achievement. *Journal of Educational Measurement*, **3**(2): 151–156. Reprinted in G. H. Bracht, K. D. Hopkins, and J. C. Stanley, eds. 1972. *Perspectives in educational and psychological measurement.* Englewood Cliffs, N.J.: Prentice-Hall, Inc., Selection 16.

————. 1969a. Achievement tests. In R. L. Ebel, ed., *Encyclopedia of educational research*, 4th ed. New York: The Macmillan Company.

————. 1969b. Concepts of achievement and proficiency. In *Proceedings of the 1969 Invitational Conference on Testing Problems.* Princeton, N.J.: Educational Testing Service, pp. 3–11.

————. 1971. Essay examinations. In R. L. Thorndike, ed., *Educational measurement*, 2d ed. Washington, D.C.: American Council on Education, Chap. 10.

————, and D. KURFMAN. 1968. A comparison of two methods of reading essay examinations. *American Educational Research Journal*, **5**(1): 99–107.

————, COLEMAN, W., and E. E. CURETON. 1954. Intelligence and achievement: The "jangle fallacy" again. *Educational and Psychological Measurement*, **14**: 347–351.

COLLEGE ENTRANCE EXAMINATION BOARD. 1962. *College Board score reports: A guide for counselors.* Princeton, N.J.: CEEB.

————. 1968a. *Effects of coaching on Scholastic Aptitude Test.* Princeton, N.J.: CEEB.

————. 1968b. *A description of the subject examinations.* Princeton, N.J.: CEEB.

CONANT, J. B. 1963. *The education of American teachers.* New York: McGraw-Hill Book Company.

COOK, D. L. 1955. An investigation of three aspects of free response and choice type tests at the college level. Doctoral dissertation, State University of Iowa. 377 pp.

————, and D. L. STUFFLEBEAM. 1967. Estimating test norms from variable size item and examinee samples. *Journal of Educational Measurement*, **4**(1): 27–33.

COOK, W. W. 1950. Achievement tests. In W. S. Monroe, ed., *Encyclopedia of educational research*. New York: The Macmillan Company, pp. 1461–1478.

————. 1951. The functions of measurement in the facilitating of learning. Chapter 1 in E. F. Lindquist, ed., *Educational measurement*. Washington, D.C.: American Council on Education.

COX, R. C., and B. G. STERRETT. 1970. A model for increasing the meaning of standardized test scores. *Journal of Educational Measurement*, **7**: 227–228. Reprinted in G. H. Bracht, K. D. Hopkins, and J. C. Stanley, eds, 1972. *Perspectives in educational and psychological measurement*. Englewood Cliffs, N.J.: Prentice-Hall, Inc., Selection 23.

CREMIN, L. A. 1961. *The transformation of the school*. New York: Alfred A. Knopf.

CRITES, J. O. 1969. Interests. In R. L. Ebel, ed., *Encyclopedia of educational research*, 4th ed. New York: The Macmillan Company, pp. 678–686.

CRONBACH, L. J. 1942. Studies of acquiescence as a factor in true-false tests. *Journal of Educational Psychology*, **33**: 401–415.

————. 1946. Response sets and test validity. *Educational and Psychological Measurement*, **6**: 475–494.

————. 1950. Further evidence on response sets and test design. *Educational and Psychological Measurement*, **10**: 3–31.

————. 1951. Coefficient alpha and the internal structure of tests. *Psychometrika*, **16**: 297–334.

————. 1969a. Heredity, environment, and educational policy. *Harvard Educational Review*, **39**: 338–347.

————. 1969b. Validation of educational measures. *Proceedings of the 1969 Invitational Conference on Testing Problems*. Princeton, N.J.: Educational Testing Service, pp. 35–52. Reprinted in G. H. Bracht, K. D. Hopkins, and J. C. Stanley. eds., 1972. *Perspectives in educational and psychological measurement*. Englewood Cliffs, N.J.: Prentice-Hall, Inc., Selection 9.

————. 1970. *Essentials of psychological testing*, 3d ed. New York: Harper & Row, Publishers.

————. 1971. Test validation. In R. L. Thorndike, ed., *Educational measurement*, 2nd ed. Washington, D.C.: American Council on Education. Chap. 14.

————, and H. AZUMA. 1962. Internal-consistency reliability formulas applied to randomly sampled single-factor tests: An empirical comparison. *Educational and Psychological Measurement*, **22**(4): 645–665.

CRONBACH, L. J., and L. FURBY. 1970. How we should measure change—or should we? *Psychological Bulletin*, **74** (1): 68–80.

CRONBACH, L. J., G. C. GLESER, H. NANDA, and N. RAJARATNAM. 1971. *The dependability of behavioral measurements: Multifacet studies of generalizability*. New York: John Wiley & Sons.

CRONBACH, L. J., and P. E. MEEHL, 1955. Construct validity in psychological tests. *Psychological Bulletin*, **52**: 281–302.

CRONBACH, L. J., N. RAJARATNAM, and G. C. GLESER. 1963. Theory of generalizability: A liberalization of reliability theory. *British Journal of Statistical Psychology*, **16**(2): 137–163.

CUNNINGHAM, R., et al. 1951. *Group behavior of boys and girls*. New York: Columbia University Press.

CURETON, E. E. 1969. Measurement theory. In R. L. Ebel, ed., *Encyclopedia of educational research*, 4th ed. New York: The Macmillan Company, pp. 785–804.

CURETON, L. E. 1971. The history of grading practices. *NCME Measurement in Education*, **2**, No. 4 (May), pp. 1–8.

CURTIS, F. D., W. C. DARLING, and N. H. SHERMAN. 1943. A study of the relative values of two modifications of the true-false test. *Journal of Educational Research*, **36**: 517–527.

CURTIS, H. A., and R. P. KROPP. 1961. A comparison of scores obtained by administering a test normally and visually. *Journal of Experimental Education*, **29**: 249–260.

DADOURIAN, H. M. 1925. Are examinations worth the price? *School and Society*, **21**: 442–443.

DARLEY, J. G., and T. HAGANAH. 1955. *Vocational interest measurement: Theory and practice*. Minneapolis: University of Minnesota Press.

DARRELL, D. S. 1970. *The accuracy of short-cut estimates for standard deviation of raw score distributions on teacher-made tests*. Paper read at annual meeting of the National Council on Measurement in Education, Minneapolis, March.

DAVIDSON, W. M., and J. B. CARROLL. 1945. Speed and level components in time-limit scores: A factor analysis. *Educational and Psychological Measurement*, 1945, **5**: 411–427.

DAVIS, F. B. 1951. Item selection techniques. In E. F. Lindquist, ed., *Educational measurement*. Washington, D.C.: American Council on Education.

DAY, H. P. 1959. A study of predictive validity of the MTAI. *Journal of Educational Research*, **53**: 37–38.

DEHIRSCH, K., J. J. JANSKY, and W. S. LANGFORD. 1966. *Predicting reading failure*. New York: Harper & Row, Publishers.

DIEDERICH, P. B. 1964. *Short-cut statistics for teacher-made tests*. Princeton: Educational Testing Service, Evaluation and Advisory Service Series, No. 5, p. 19.

DI VESTA, F. J., and W. DICK. 1966. The test-retest reliability of children's ratings on the semantic differential. *Educational and Psychological Measurement*, **26**: 605–616.

DIZNEY, H. F., P. R. MERRIFIELD, and O. L. DAVIS, JR. 1966. Effects of answer-sheet format on arithmetic test scores. *Educational and Psychological Measurement*, **26** (2): 491–493.

DOWNIE, N. M. 1967. *Fundamentals of measurement: Techniques and practices*, 2d ed. New York: Oxford University Press, Inc.

DRESSEL, P. L., ed. 1961. *Evaluation in higher education*. Boston: Houghton Mifflin Company.

———, and J. SCHMIDT. 1951. *An evaluation of the tests for general educational development*. Washington, D.C.: American Council on Education.

DROEGE, R. C., A. C. CRAMBERT, and J. B. HENKIN. 1963. Relationship between G.A.T.B. aptitude scores and age for adults. *Personnel and Guidance Journal*, **41**: 502–508.

DUBOIS, P. H. 1966. A test-dominated society: China, 1115 B.C.–1905 A.D. In A.

Anastasi, ed., *Testing problems in perspective*. Washington, D.C.: American Council on Education, pp. 29–38.

————. 1970. *A history of psychological testing*. Boston: Allyn and Bacon, Inc.

DUNCAN, A. J. 1947. Some comments on the Army General Classification Test. *Journal of Applied Psychology*, **31**: 143–149.

DUNN, T. F., and L. G. GOLDSTEIN. 1959. Test difficulty, validity, and reliability as functions of selected multiple-choice item construction principles. *Educational and Psychological Measurement*, **19**(2): 171–179.

DURNALL, E. J., JR. 1954. Falsification of interest patterns on the Kuder preference record. *Journal of Educational Psychology*, **45**: 240–243.

DUROST, W. N. 1954. Present progress and needed improvements in school evaluation programs. *Educational and Psychological Measurement*, **14**: 247–254.

————. 1962. *Manual for interpreting Metropolitan Achievement Tests*. New York: Harcourt Brace Jovanovich, Inc.

DYER, H. S. 1967a. The discovery and development of educational goals. *Proceedings of the 1966 Invitational Conference on Testing Problems*. Princeton, N.J.: Educational Testing Service, pp. 12–24. Reprinted in G. H. Bracht, K. D. Hopkins, and J. C. Stanley , eds. 1972. *Perspectives in educational and psychological measurement*. Englewood Cliffs, N.J.: Prentice-Hall, Inc., Selection 2.

————. 1967b. Needed changes to sweeten the impact of testing. *Personnel and Guidance Journal*. **45**: 776–780. Reprinted in G. H. Bracht, K. D. Hopkins, and J. C. Stanley , eds. 1972. *Perspectives in educational and psychological measurement*. Englewood Cliffs, N.J.: Prentice-Hall, Inc., Selection 32.

EBEL, R. L. 1954. Procedures for the analysis of classroom tests. *Educational and Psychological Measurement*, **14**: 352–364.

————. 1956. Obtaining and reporting evidence on content validity. *Educational and Psychological Measurement*, **16**: 269–282.

————. 1960. Some tests of competence in educational measurement. *The seventeenth yearbook of the National Council on Measurements Used in Education*. Ames, Iowa: National Council on Measurements Used in Education, pp. 93–104.

————. 1961a. Improving the competence of teachers in educational measurement. *Clearing House*, **36**(2): 67–71.

————. 1961b. Must all tests be valid? *American Psychologist*, **16**: 640–647. Reprinted in G. H. Bracht, K. D. Hopkins, and J. C. Stanley, eds. 1972. *Perspectives in educational and psychological measurement*. Englewood Cliffs, N.J.: Prentice-Hall, Inc., Selection 8.

————. 1961c. Standardized achievement tests: uses and limitations. *National Elementary School Principal*, **40**: 29–32.

————. 1962a. Content standard test scores. *Educational and Psychological Measurement*, **22**: 15–25.

————. 1962b. Measurement and the teacher. *Educational Leadership*, **20**: 20–24.

————. 1963. The relation of testing programs to educational goals. In W. G. Findley, ed., *The sixty-second yearbook of the National Society for the Study of Education, Part II*. Chicago: University of Chicago Press, pp. 28–44.

————. 1964. The social consequences of educational testing. *Proceedings of the 1963 Invitational Conference on Testing Problems*. Princeton, N.J.: Educational Testing Service. Reprinted in G. H. Bracht, K. D. Hopkins, and J. C. Stanley, eds. 1972. *Perspectives in educational and psychological measurement.* Englewood Cliffs, N.J.: Prentice-Hall, Inc., Selection 1.

————. 1965a. Confidence weighting and test reliability. *Journal of Educational Measurement,* **2**(1): 49–57.

————. 1965b. *Measuring educational achievement.* Englewood Cliffs, N.J.: Prentice-Hall, Inc.

————. 1967. The relation of item discrimination to test reliability. *Journal of Educational Measurement,* **4**(3): 125–128.

————. 1968. The value of internal consistency in classroom examinations. *Journal of Educational Measurement,* **5**(1): 71–73.

————. 1970a. The case for true-false test items. *School Review,* **78**: 373–389.

————. 1970b. Some limitations of criterion-referenced measurement. Paper presented at the American Educational Research Association, Minneapolis, 1970. Reprinted in G. H. Bracht, K. D. Hopkins, and J. C. Stanley, eds. 1972. *Perspectives in educational and psychological measurement.* Englewood Cliffs, N.J.: Prentice-Hall, Inc., Selection 14.

————. 1970c. Knowledge vs. ability in achievement testing. *Proceedings of the 1969 Invitational Conference on Testing Problems.* Princeton, N.J.: Educational Testing Service, pp. 66–76.

————, and D. E. DAMRIN. 1960. Tests and examinations. In C. W. Harris, ed., *Encyclopedia of educational research,* 3d ed. New York: The Macmillan Company, pp. 1502–1517.

ECKLAND, B. K. 1964. College dropouts who came back. *Harvard Educational Review,* **34**: 404–420.

EDUCATIONAL POLICIES COMMISSION. 1961. *The central purpose of American education.* WASHINGTON, D.C.: National Education Association.

EDUCATIONAL TESTING SERVICE. n.d. *Making your own tests.* Princeton, N.J.: ETS.

————. 1958. *Large-scale program of testing for guidance.* Princeton, N.J.: ETS.

————. 1960. *A description of the College Board Scholastic Aptitude Test.* Princeton, N.J.: ETS.

————. 1961. Judges disagree on qualities that characterize good writing. *ETS Developments,* **9**: 2.

————. 1963. *Multiple choice questions: A close look.* Princeton, N.J.: ETS. Reprinted in G. H. Bracht, K. D. Hopkins, and J. C. Stanley, eds. 1972. *Perspectives in educational and psychological measurement.* Englewood Cliffs, N.J.: Prentice-Hall, Inc., Selection 15.

————. 1966. Are aptitude tests unfair to Negroes? ETS investigates two kinds of "Bias." *Educational Testing Service Developments,* **14**(1): 1–4.

————. 1969a. Bias in selection tests and criteria studies by ETS and U.S. Civil Service. *ETS Developments,* **17**: 2. This is a brief summary of ongoing research by J. T. Campbell, F. R. Evans, R. L. Flaugher, M. H. Mahoney, L. Norris, L. W. Pike, and D. A. Rock of ETS.

————. 1969b. *Locating information on educational measurement: Sources and references* (Evaluation and Advisory series). Princeton, N.J.: ETS.

EDWARDS, A. L. 1957. *The social desirability variable in personality assessment and research.* New York: The Dryden Press, Inc.

EELLS, K., et al. 1951. *Intelligence and cultural differences.* Chicago: University of Chicago Press.

EELLS, W. C. 1961. Population center. *Science* (September), **134**: 797.

EISS, A. F. and M. B. HARBECK. 1969. *Behavioral objectives in the affective domain.* Washington, D.C.: National Education Association.

ENGELHART, M. D. 1964. *Improving classroom testing: What research says to the teacher.* Booklet No. 31. Washington D. C.: National Education Association.

————. 1965. A comparison of several item discrimination indices. *Journal of Educational Measurement*, **2**(1): 69–76.

ESCALONA, S. K., and A. MORIARTY. 1961. Prediction of schoolage intelligence from infant tests. *Child Development*, **32**: 597–605.

EYSENCK, H. J. 1959. Rorschach review. In O. K. Buros, ed., *The fifth mental measurements yearbook.* Highland Park, N.J.: Gryphon Press, pp. 276–278.

————. 1971. *Race, intelligence and education.* London: Maurice Temple Smith Ltd.

FALLS, J. D. 1928. Research in secondary education. *Kentucky School Journal*, **6**: 42–46.

FARGO, G. A., D. C. CROWELL, M. H. NOYES, R. Y. FUCHIGAMI, J. M. GORDON, and P. DUNN-RANKIN. 1967. Comparability of group television and individual administration of the Peabody Picture Vocabulary Test: Implications for screening. *Journal of Educational Psychology*, **58**(3): 137–140.

FELDHUSEN, J. F. 1964. Student perceptions of frequent quizzes and post-mortem discussions of tests. *Journal of Educational Measurement*, **1**(1): 51–54.

FELDT, L. S., and A. E. HALL. 1964. Stability of four item discrimination indices over groups of different average ability. *American Educational Research Journal*, **1**: 35–46.

FERGUSON, L. W. 1952. *Personality measurement.* New York: McGraw-Hill Book Company, 1952.

FERRELL, G. V. 1951. *High school holding power—an analysis of certain internal factors.* Doctoral dissertation, George Peabody College for Teachers.

FESTINGER, L., and D. KATZ. 1953. *Research methods in the behavioral sciences.* New York: Dryden Press.

FINDLEY, W. G. 1956. Rationale for evaluation of item discrimination statistics. *Educational and Psychological Measurement*, **16**: 175–180.

————, ed. 1963a. The impact and improvement of school testing programs. *Sixty-second yearbook of the National Society for the Study of Education, Part II.* Chicago: University of Chicago Press.

————. 1963b. Purpose of school testing programs and their efficient development. In W. G. Findley, ed., 1963a, pp. 1–27.

FINLEY, C. J. 1963. A comparison of the California Achievement Test, Metropolitan Achievement Test and Iowa Test of Basic Skills. *California Journal of Educational Research* (March) **14**(2): 79–88.

FISHMAN, J. A., et al. 1964. Guidelines for testing minority group children. *Journal of Social Issues*, **20**: 127–145.

FLANAGAN, J. C. 1935. *Factor analysis in the study of personality.* Stanford, Calif.: Stanford University Press.

————. 1937. A proposed procedure for increasing the efficiency of objective tests. *Journal of Educational Psychology*, **28**: 17–21.

————. 1951a. Units, scores, and norms. In E. F. Lindquist, ed., *Educational measurement.* Washington, D. C.: American Council on Education.

————. 1951b. The use of comprehensive rationales in test development. *Educational and Psychological Measurement*, **11**: 151–155.

————. 1952. The effectiveness of short methods for calculating correlation coefficients. *Psychological Bulletin*, **49**: 342–348.

————. 1969. Student characteristics: Elementary and secondary. In R. L. Ebel, ed., *Encyclopedia of educational research*, 4th ed. New York: The Macmillan Company, pp. 1330–1339.

————, and W. W. COOLEY. 1966. *Project Talent: One-year follow-up studies*. Pittsburgh: University of Pittsburgh Press.

FLANAGAN, J. C., et al., 1962. *Design for a study of American youth*, vol. 1: *The talents of American youth*. Boston: Houghton Mifflin Company.

FLAUGHER, R. L., M. H. MAHONEY, and R. B. MESSING. 1967. *Credit by examination for college-level studies: An annotated bibliography*. New York: College Entrance Examination Board.

FLEMING, E. S., and R. G. ANTTONEN. 1970. Teacher expectancy or my fair lady. In John Pilder, ed., *Abstracts/One: 1970 Annual Meeting Paper Session*, Washington, D.C.: American Educational Research Association, p. 66.

FRANDSEN, A. N., and A. D. SESSIONS. 1953. Interests and school achievement. *Educational and Psychological Measurement*, **13**: 94–101.

FRANKEL, E. 1960. Effects of growth, practice, and coaching on Scholastic Aptitude Test Scores. *Personnel and Guidance Journal*, **38**: 713–719.

FRANZ, S. I. 1919. *Handbook of mental examination methods*. New York: The Macmillan Company.

FRASE, L. T. 1967. Learning from prose material: Length of passage, knowledge of results, and position of question. *Journal of Educational Psychology*, **58**: 266–272.

FREDERIKSEN, N., and D. S. MELVILLE. 1954. Differential predictability in the use of test scores. *Educational and Psychological Measurement*, **14**: 647–656.

FRENCH, J. W. 1957. What English teachers think of essay testing. *The English Journal*, **46**: 196–201.

————. 1961. Aptitude and interest score patterns related to satisfaction with college major field. *Educational and Psychological Measurement*, **21**: 287–294.

————. 1962. Effect of anxiety on verbal and mathematical examination scores. *Educational and Psychological Measurement*, **22**(3): 553–564.

————, and R. E. DEAR. 1959. Effect of coaching on an aptitude test. *Educational and Psychological Measurement*, **19**(3): 319–330.

FRICKLE, B. G., and J. MILLMAN. 1957. Who benefits from high school testing? *High School Journal*, **41**: 71–74.

FURST, E. J. 1958. *Constructing evaluation instruments*. New York: David McKay Company, Inc.

GAGE, N. L., P. J. RUNKEL, and B. B. CHATTERJEE. 1960. *Equilibrium theory and behavior change: An experiment in feedback from pupils to teachers*. Urbana: Bureau of Educational Research, University of Illinois. (Mimeographed.)

GARBER, H. 1967. The digital computer simulates human rating behavior. In J. T. Flynn and H. Garber, *Assessing behavior: Readings in educational and psychological measurement*. Reading, Mass.: Addison-Wesley Publishing Company, Inc.

GARDNER, E. F. 1962. Normative standard scores. *Educational and Psychological Measurement*, **22**: 7–14.

———. 1970. Interpreting achievement profiles—uses and warnings. *NCME Measurement in Education: A Series of Special Reports of the National Council on Measurement in Education*, **1**(2).

———, and G. G. THOMPSON. 1958. Measuring and interpreting social relations. *Test service notebook No.* **22**. New York: Harcourt Brace Jovanovich, Inc.

GARLOCK, J., R. S. DOLLARHIDE, and K. D. HOPKINS. 1965. Comparability of scores on the Wide Range and the Gilmore Oral Reading Tests. *California Journal of Educational Research*, **16**: 54–57.

GARRY, R. 1953. Individual differences in ability to fake vocational interests. *Journal of Applied Psychology*, **37**: 33–37.

GERBERICH, J. R. 1956. *Specimen objective test items, a guide to achievement test construction.* New York: David McKay Company, Inc.

———, H. A. GREENE, and A. N. JORGENSEN. 1962. *Measurement and evaluation in in the modern school.* New York: David McKay Company, Inc.

GETZELS, J. W., and P. W. JACKSON. 1963. The teacher's personality and characteristics. In N. L. Gage, ed., *Handbook of research on teaching.* Skokie, Ill.: Rand McNally & Company, pp. 506–582.

GHISELLI, E. E., and R. P. BARTHOL. 1953. The validity of personality inventories in the selection of employees. *Journal of Applied Psychology*, **37**: 18–20.

GLASER, R. 1963. Instructional technology and the measurement of learning outcomes: Some questions. *American Psychologist*, **18**: 519–521.

———, and A. J. NITKO. 1971. Measurement in learning and instruction. In R. L. Thorndike, ed., *Educational measurement*, 2d ed. Washington, D.C.: American Council on Education, Chap. 17.

GLASS, G. V 1971. The growth of evaluation methodology. *No. 7 of the AERA Curriculum Evaluation Monograph Series.* Skokie, Ill.: Rand McNally & Company.

———, and J. C. STANLEY. 1970. *Statistical methods in education and psychology.* Englewood Cliffs, N.J.: Prentice-Hall, Inc.

GLASS, G. V, and D. E. WILEY. 1964. Formula scoring and test reliability. *Journal of Educational Measurement*, **1**(1): 43–47.

GLASSER, W. 1969. *Schools without failure.* New York: Harper & Row, Publishers.

GODDARD, H. H. 1910a. Four hundred feebleminded children classified by the Binet method. *Pedagogical Seminary*, **17**: 387–397.

———. 1910b. A measuring scale for intelligence. *The Training School*, **6**: 146–155.

———. 1911. Two thousand normal children measured by the Binet measuring scale of intelligence. *Pedagogical Seminary*, **18**: 232–259.

GODSHALK, F. I., F. SWINEFORD, W. E. COFFMAN, and EDUCATIONAL TESTING SERVICE. 1966. *The measurement of writing ability.* New York: College Entrance Examination Board.

GOLDMAN, L. 1969. Tests should make a difference. *Measurement and Evaluation in Guidance*, **2**: 53–59. Reprinted in G. H. Bracht, K. D. Hopkins, and J. C. Stanley, eds. 1972. *Perspectives in educational and psychological measurement.* Englewood Cliffs, N.J.: Prentice-Hall, Inc., Selection 33.

GOODENOUGH, F. L. 1949. *Mental testing*. New York: Holt, Rinehart and Winston, Inc.

GOODWIN, W. L. 1966. Effect of selected methodological conditions on dependent measures taken after classroom experimentation. *Journal of Educational Psychology*, **57**: 350–358.

GORDON, M. A. 1953. A study of the applicability of the same minimum qualifying scores for technical schools to white males, WAF, and Negro males. Technical Report 53–54. San Antonio, Texas: Human Resources Research Center, Lackland Air Force Base.

GOSLIN, D. A. 1963. *The search for ability: Standardized testing in social perspective.* New York: Russell Sage Foundation.

———. 1967a. The social impact of testing. *Personnel and Guidance Journal*, **45**: 676–682. Reprinted in G. H. Bracht, K. D. Hopkins, and J. C. Stanley, eds. 1972. *Perspectives in educational and psychological measurement.* Englewood Cliffs, N.J.: Prentice-Hall, Inc., Selection 31.

———. 1967b. *Teachers and testing.* New York: Russell Sage Foundation.

GOUGH, H. G., and W. H. PEMBERTON. 1952. Personality characteristics related to success in practice teaching. *Journal of Applied Psychology*, **36**: 307–309.

GOZALI, J. and E. L. MEYER. 1970. The influence of the teacher expectancy phenomenon on the academic performance of educable mentally retarded pupils in special classes. *Journal of Special Education*, **4**: 417–424.

GRAFF, K. 1965. The high school equivalency program. *Vocational Guidance Quarterly*, **13**: 297–299.

GRANICH, L. A. 1931. A technique for experimenting on guessing in objective tests. *Journal of Educational Psychology*, **22**: 145–156.

GREENE, K. B. 1928. The influence of specialized training on tests of general intelligence. *The 27th yearbook, National Society for the Study of Education, Part I*, pp. 421–428.

GROBMAN, H. 1968. Evaluation activities of curriculum projects. *AERA Monograph Series in Curriculum Evaluation*, No. 2. Chicago: Rand McNally & Co. p. 93.

GRONLUND, N. E. 1955. The relative stability of classroom social status with unweighted and weighted sociometric choices. *Journal of Educational Psychology*, **46**: 345–354.

———. 1959. *Sociometry in the classroom.* New York: Harper & Row, Publishers.

———. 1968. *Constructing achievement tests.* Englewood Cliffs, N. J.: Prentice-Hall, Inc.

GROSS, M. L. 1962. *The brain watchers.* New York: Random House, Inc.

GROTELUESCHEN, A., and D. D. SJOGREN. 1968. Effects of differentially structured introductory materials and learning tasks. *American Educational Research Journal*, **5**(2): 191–202.

GUILFORD, J. P. 1936. *Psychometric methods.* New York: McGraw-Hill Book Company.

———. 1950. Creativity. *American Psychologist*, **14**: 469–479.

———. 1954. *Psychometric methods*, 2d ed. New York: McGraw-Hill Book Company.

———. 1959. *Personality.* New York: McGraw-Hill Book Company.

———. 1965. *Fundamental statistics in psychology and education*, 4th ed. New York: McGraw-Hill Book Company.

———. 1967. *The nature of human intelligence*. New York: McGraw-Hill Book Company.

———. 1968. The structure of intelligence. In D. K. Whitla, ed., *Handbook of measurement and assessment in behavioral sciences*. Reading, Mass.: Addison-Wesley Publishing Company, Inc., Chap. 7.

———, B. FRUCHTER, and H. P. KELLEY. 1959. Development and application of tests of intellectual and special aptitudes. *Review of Educational Research*, **29**: 26–41.

GUILFORD, J. P., and J. I. LACEY, eds. 1947. *Printed classification tests. Army Air Forces aviation psychology research program reports, Report 5*. Washington, D.C.: U.S. Government Printing Office.

GUSTAV, A. 1963. Response set in objective achievement tests. *Journal of Psychology*, **56**: 421–427.

GUTTMAN, L. 1947. The Cornell technique for scale and intensity analysis. *Educational and Psychological Measurement*, 7: 247–279.

HABERMAN, M. 1970. The relationship of bogus expectations to success in student teaching (Or, Pygmalion's illegitimate son). In *Abstracts/One:* 1970 *Annual Meeting Paper Sessions*. Washington, D.C.: American Educational Research Association, p. 66. Critique session: "The Pygmalion effect: A teacher's expectations," John L. Hayman, chairman.

HADLEY, S. T. 1954. A school mark—fact or fancy? *Educational Administration and Supervision*, **40**: 305–312.

HAGANAH, T. 1953. *A normative study of the revised Strong Vocational Interest Blank for Men*. Doctoral dissertation, University of Minnesota.

HAKSTIAN, A. R. 1971. The effect on study methods and test performance of objective and essay examinations. *Journal of Educational Research*, **64** (7): 319–324.

HALL, D. W. 1966. The Minnesota Vocational Interest Inventory. *Journal of Educational Measurement*, 3(4): 337–341.

HAMBLETON, R. K. 1968. The effects of item order and anxiety on test performance and stress. Paper presented at the annual meeting of the American Educational Research Association, Chicago, February 8–10.

HAMILTON, C. H. 1950. Bias and error in multiple-choice tests. *Psychometrika*. **15**: 151–168.

HARPER, H. E. 1970. *The identification of socio-economic differences and their effect on the teaching of readiness for "new math concepts" in the kindergarten*. Final report: Project No. 9-H-004, U.S. Department of Health, Education and Welfare, Office of Education, Bureau of Research.

HARRIS, C. W., ed. 1963. *Problems in measuring change*. Madison: University of Wisconsin Press.

HARTSHORNE, H., and M. A. MAY. 1928. *Studies in deceit*. New York: The Macmillan Company.

HASHIMOTO, Juji. 1959. Test no yokoku koka ni tsuite (The effect of announcement of the coming test). *Japanese Journal of Educational Psychology*, **6**: 217–222, 265.

HASTINGS, J. T. 1966. Curriculum evaluation: The why of the outcomes. *Journal of Educational Measurement*, 3: 27–32.

HATHAWAY, S. R., and E. D. MONACHESI. 1963. *Adolescent personality and behavior*. Minneapolis: University of Minnesota Press.

HAWES, G. R. 1964. *Educational testing for the millions: What tests really mean for your child*. New York: McGraw-Hill Book Company.

HAWKES, H. E., E. F. LINDQUIST, and C. R. MANN. 1936. *The construction and use of achievement examinations*. Boston: The Houghton Mifflin Company.

HAYWARD, P. 1967. A comparison of test performance on three answer sheet formats. *Educational and Psychological Measurement*, 27(4, pt. 2): 997–1004.

HEDGES, W. D. 1966. *Testing and evaluation for the sciences in the secondary school*. Belmont, Calif.: Wadsworth Publishing Company, Inc.

HELMSTADTER, G. C. 1970. *Research concepts in human behavior*. New York: Appleton-Century-Crofts.

HENRY, N. B., ed. 1946. The measurement of understanding. *Forty-fifth yearbook of the National Society for the Study of Education*, Part I. Chicago: University of Chicago Press.

HENRYSSON, S. 1963. Correction of item-total correlations in item analysis. *Psychometrika*, 28: 211–218.

———. 1971. Gathering, analyzing, and using data on test items. In R. L. Thorndike, ed., *Educational measurement*, 2d ed. Washington, D. C.: American Council on Education, Chap. 5.

HENSLEY, H., and R. A. DAVIS. 1952. What high-school teachers think and do about their examinations. *Educational Administration and Supervision*, 38: 219–228.

HERZBERG, F. 1954. Temperament measures in industrial selection. *Journal of Applied Psychology*, 38: 81–84.

HICKLIN, N. J. 1962. A study of long-range techniques for predicting patterns of scholastic behavior. Unpublished Ph.D. thesis, University of Chicago.

HIERONYMOUS, A. N., and J. B. STROUD. Comparability of IQ scores on five widely used intelligence tests. *Measurement and Evaluation in Guidance*, 2(3): 135–140.

HILL, W. H., and P. L. DRESSEL. 1961. The objectives of instruction. Chapter 2 in P. L. Dressel, ed., *Evaluation in higher education*. Boston: Houghton Mifflin Company.

HILLS, J. R. 1971. Use of measurement in selection and placement. In R. L. Thorndike, ed., *Educational measurement*, 2d ed. Washington, D.C.: American Council on Education, Chap. 19.

———, and J. C. STANLEY. 1968. Prediction of freshman grades from SAT and from Level 4 of SCAT in three predominantly Negro state colleges. *Proceedings, 76th annual convention, American Psychological Association*, pp. 241–242.

———, and STANLEY. 1970. Easier test improves prediction of Black students' college grades. *Journal of Negro Education*, 39, 320–324.

HOEPFNER, R. 1967. Review of the Torrance Tests of Creative Thinking. *Journal of Educational Measurement*, 4(3): 191–192.

———, and S. KLEIN. 1970. *CSE elementary school test evaluation*. Los Angeles: Center for the Study of Evaluation, UCLA Graduate School of Education.

HOEPFNER, R., and M. O'Sullivan. 1968. Social intelligence and IQ. *Educational and Psychological Measurement*, 28: 339–344.

HOFFMANN, B. 1962. *The tyranny of testing*. New York: Crowell-Collier and Macmillan, Inc.

HOLLAND, J. L. 1966. *The psychology of vocational choice: A theory of personality types and model environments*. Waltham, Mass.: Blaisdell Publishing.

HOLLINGSHEAD, A. B., and F. C. REDLICH. 1957. *Two factor index of social position.* New Haven, Conn.: Published by the authors.

HOLT, J. 1968. *How children fail.* New York: Pitman Publishing Corporation.

HOLTZMAN, W. H., et al. 1961. *Inkblot perception and personality—Holtzman technique.* Austin: University of Texas Press.

HONZIK, M. P., J. W. MACFARLANE, and L. ALLEN. 1948. The stability of mental test performance between two and eighteen years. *Journal of Experimental Education,* **17**: 309–324.

HOPKINS, K. D. 1964a. Evaluating pupil achievement: A critical look at provincial and standardized testing. *The British Columbia Fourth School Principals' Conference,* 107–113.

———. 1964b. Extrinsic reliability: Estimating and attenuating variance from response styles, chance, and other irrelevant sources. *Educational and Psychological Measurement,* **24**(2): 271–281. Reprinted in G. H. Bracht, K. D. Hopkins, and J. C. Stanley, eds. 1972. *Perspectives in educational and psychological measurement.* Englewood Cliffs, N. J.: Prentice-Hall, Inc., Selection 10.

———. 1969. Regression and the matching fallacy in quasi-experimental research. *Journal of Special Education,* **3**(4): 329–336.

———, and M. BIBELHEIMER. 1971. Five-year stability IQ's from language and non-language group tests. *Child Development,* **42**: 645–649.

HOPKINS, K. D., and G. H. BRACHT. 1971a. A longitudinal study of constancy of reading performance. In *Diagnostic Viewpoints in Reading,* 103–112.

———. 1971b. The stability and change of language and non-language IQ Scores. Final Report, Project No. O-H-O24. Office of Education, Bureau of Research, U. S. Department of Health, Education and Welfare.

HOPKINS, K. D., J. C. DOBSON, and O. A. OLDRIDGE. 1962. The concurrent and congruent validities of the Wide Range Achievement Test. *Educational and Psychological Measurement,* **22**: 791–793.

HOPKINS, K. D., A. R. HAKSTIAN, and B. R. HOPKINS. 1973. Validity and reliability consequences of confidence weighting. *Educational and Psychological Measurement,* in press.

HOPKINS, K. D., and B. R. HOPKINS. 1964. Intraindividual and interindividual positional preference response styles in ability tests. *Educational and Psychological Measurement,* **24**(4): 801–805.

HOPKINS, K. D., D. W. LEFEVER, and B. R. HOPKINS. 1967. TV vs. teacher administration of standardized tests: Comparability of scores. *Journal of Educational Measurement,* 4(1): 35–40.

HOPKINS, K. D., and L. McGUIRE. 1966. Mental measurement of the blind: The validity of the Wechsler Intelligence Scale for Children. *International Journal for Education of the Blind,* **15**: 65–73.

HOPKINS, K. D., and D. L. SANDER. 1966. Review of the Academic Ability Test. *Journal of Educational Measurement,* 3(1): 81–83.

HOPKINS, K. D., and E. G. SITKIE. 1969. Predicting grade one reading performance: Intelligence vs. reading readiness tests. *Journal of Experimental Education,* 37(3): 31–33.

HOPKINS, K. D., and C. J. WILKERSON. 1965. Differential content validity: The California Spelling Test, an illustrative example. *Educational and Psychological Measurement,* **25**(2): 413–419.

HORN, J. L. 1966. Some characteristics of classroom examinations. *Journal of Educational Measurement,* 3(4): 293–295.

————. 1967. Intelligence—why it grows, why it declines. *Trans-action*, **5**: 23–31.

————, and R. B. CATTELL. 1966. Refinement and test of the theory of fluid and crystallized general intelligence. *Journal of Educational Psychology*, **57**: 253–270.

HOYT, D. P., and L. A. MUNDAY. 1966. *Your college freshmen.* Iowa City, Iowa: The American College Testing Program.

HULTEN, C. E. 1925. The personal element in teachers' marks. *Journal of Educational Research*, **12**: 49–55.

HUNKINS, F. P. 1969. Effects of analysis and evaluation questions on various levels of achievement. *Journal of Experimental Education*, **38**: 45–58.

HUSÉN, T. 1951. Undersökningar rörande sambanden mellan somatiska föhållanden och intellektuell prestationsformága. *Särtryck ur Tidskrift i militär Hälsovárd*, 76: 41–74.

INGLE, R. B., and G. DE AMICO. 1969. The effect of physical conditions of the test room on standardized achievement test scores. *Journal of Educational Measurement*, **6**(4): 237–240.

JACKSON, P. W., and H. M. LAHADERNE. 1967. Scholastic success and attitude toward school in a population of sixth graders. *Journal of Educational Psychology*, **58**(1): 15–18.

JACKSON, R. A. 1955. Guessing and test performance. *Educational and Psychological Measurement*, **15**: 74–79.

JACOBS, J. N., and J. L. FELIX. 1968. Testing the educational and psychological development of preadolescent children—ages 6–12. *Review of Educational Research*, **38**: 19–29.

JACOBS, S. S. 1968. Bias in the keying of standardized tests: A reexamination. *Journal of Educational Measurement*, **5**(4): 335–336.

JENKINS, W. L. 1946. A short-cut method for σ and r. *Educational and Psychological Measurement*, **6**: 533–536.

JENSEN, A. R. 1965. Review of the Rorschach. In O. K. Buros, ed., *The sixth mental measurements yearbook*. Highland Park, N. J.: Gryphon Press. Reprinted in G. H. Bracht, K. D. Hopkins, and J. C. Stanley, eds. 1972. *Perspectives in educational and psychological measurement*. Englewood Cliffs, N.J.: Prentice-Hall, Inc., Selection 30.

————. 1968a. Another look at culture-fair testing. In Thomas A. Shellhammer, chrmn., Measures for educational planning, *Seventeenth annual western regional conference on testing problems*. Princeton, N.J.: Educational Testing Service, pp. 50–104.

————. 1968b. Social class, race, and genetics: Implications for education. *American Educational Research Journal*, **5**(1): 1–42.

————. 1969. How much can we boost IQ and scholastic achievement? *Harvard Educational Review*, **39**: 1–123. Reprinted in G. H. Bracht, K. D. Hopkins, and J. C. Stanley, eds. 1972. *Perspectives in educational and psychological measurement*. Englewood Cliffs, N.J.: Prentice-Hall, Inc., Selection 19.

JOHNSON, A. P. 1951. Notes on a suggested index of item validity. *Journal of Educational Psychology*, **42**: 499–504.

JOHNSON, F. W. 1911. A study of high school grades. *School Review,* **19**: 13–24.

JOHNSON, O. G., and J. W. BOMMARITO. 1971. *Tests and measurements in child development:* A handbook. San Francisco: Jossey-Bass, Inc.

JOSÉ, J., and J. J. CODY. 1971. Teacher-pupil interaction as it related to attempted changes in teacher expectancy of academic ability and achievement. *American Educational Research Journal,* **8**: 39–50.

JOURNAL OF EDUCATIONAL PSYCHOLOGY. 1921. Intelligence and its measurement: a symposium. *Journal of Educational Psychology,* **12**: 123–147, 195–216, 271–275.

JURGENSEN, C. E. 1966. Advisory panel appraises suitability of USES testing. *Industrial Psychologist,* 1966, **4**: 41–44.

JURS, S., and K. D. HOPKINS. 1971. Jenkins' short-cut deviations: Its accuracy with non-normal distributions. Paper presented to the National Council on Measurement in Education, New York.

KAHN, S. B. 1968. The relative magnitude of speed and power in SCAT. *Journal of Educational Measurement,* **5**(4): 327–330.

KAISER, H. F. 1958. A modified stanine scale. *Journal of Experimental Education,* **26**: 261.

KARLINS, J. K., M. KAPLAN, and W. STUART. 1969. Academic attitudes and performance as a function of a differential grading system: An evaluation of Princeton's pass-fail system. *Journal of Experimental Education,* **37**(3): 38–50.

KATZ, M. R., ed. 1959. *ETS builds a test.* Princeton, N.J.: Educational Testing Service.

———. 1961. Selecting an achievement test: Principles and procedures. *Evaluation and Advisory Service Series,* No. 3, 2d ed. Princeton, N.J.: Educational Testing Service.

———, D. W. SEIBEL, and J. A. CONNOLLY. 1961. Testing . . . testing. . . . *Junior Libraries,* **7**: 14–20. Reprinted, with additions, by Educational Testing Service as "Take a reading in measurement."

KATZELL, R. A. 1951. Cross-validation of item analysis. *Educational and Psychological Measurement,* **11**: 5–28.

KATZMAN, M. T., and R. S. ROSEN. 1970. The science and politics of national assessment. *The Record,* **70**(4): 571–586.

KEARNEY, N. C. 1953. *Elementary school objectives.* New York: The Mid-Century Committee on Outcomes in Elementary Education, Russell Sage Foundation.

KELLEY, T. L. 1927. *Interpretation of educational measurements.* New York: World Book Company.

———. 1939. The selection of upper and lower groups for the validation of test items. *Journal of Educational Psychology,* **30**: 17–24.

KENDRICK, S. A., and C. L. THOMAS. 1970. Education for socially disadvantaged children: Transition from school to college. *Review of Educational Research,* **40**: 151–179.

KLEIN, S. P., and F. M. HART. 1968. The nature of essay grades in law school. *Research Bulletin* 68-6. Princeton, N. J.: Educational Testing Service.

KLINGER, E., and H. H. GEE. 1960. The study of applicants, 1958–58. *Journal of Medical Education,* **35**: 120–133.

KLUGMAN, S. F. 1944. The effect of money incentive versus praise upon the reliability and obtained scores of the revised Stanford-Binet test. *Journal of General Psychology,* **30**: 255–269.

KNAPP, R. R. 1960. The effects of time limits on the intelligence test performance of Mexican and American subjects. *Journal of Educational Psychology*, **51**(1): 14–20.

KOSTICK, M. M., and B. M. NIXON. 1953. How to improve oral questioning. *Peabody Journal of Education*, **30**: 209–217.

KRATHWOHL, D. R. 1965. Stating objectives appropriately for program, for curriculum, and for instructional materials development. *Journal of Teacher Education*, **16**: 83–92.

———, and D. PAYNE. 1971. Defining and assessing educational objectives. In R. L. Thorndike, ed., *Educational measurement*, 2d ed. Washington, D.C.: American Council on Education, Chap. 2.

KRATHWOHL, D. R., et al. 1964. *Taxonomy of educational objectives: Handbook II, Affective domain.* New York: David McKay Company, Inc.

KREIT, L. H. 1968. The effects of test-taking practice on pupil test performance. *American Educational Research Journal*, **5**(4): 616–625.

KROPP, R. P., H. W. STOKER, and W. L. BASHAW. 1966. *The construction and validation of tests of the cognitive processes as described in the taxonomy of educational objectives.* Cooperative Research Project No. 2117. Washington, D.C.: Office of Education, U.S. Department of Health, Education, and Welfare.

KRUEGER, W. C. F. 1929. The effect of overlearning on retention. *Journal of Experimental Psychology*, **12**: 71–78.

KUDER, G. F. 1963. A rationale for evaluating interests. *Educational and Psychological Measurement*, **23**(1): 3–12.

———. 1969. A note on the comparability of occupational scores from different interest inventories. *Measurement and Evaluation in Guidance*, **2**: 94–100.

———. 1970. Some principles of interest measurement. *Educational and Psychological Measurement*, **30**: 205–226. Reprinted in G. H. Bracht, K. D. Hopkins, and J. C. Stanley, eds. 1972. *Perspectives in educational and psychological measurement.* Englewood Cliffs, N.J.: Prentice-Hall, Inc, Selection 28.

———, and M. W. RICHARDSON. 1937. The theory of the estimation of test reliability. *Psychometrika*, **2**: 151–160.

KURFMAN, D. 1968. *Teacher-made test items in American history.* Bulletin No. 40. Washington, D.C.: National Council for the Social Studies.

KURTZ, A. K., and M. A. BERTIN. 1958. Reappraisal of marking practices. *Educational Research Bulletin*, **37**: 67–74.

LA FAVE, L. 1964. Essay tests can be standardized. *Science*, **146**: 171.

———. 1966. Essay vs. multiple-choice: Which test is preferable? *Psychology in the Schools*, **3**: 65–69.

LAMB, G. S. 1967. Teacher verbal cues and pupil performance on a group reading test. *Journal of Educational Psychology*, **58**: 332–336.

LANGE, A., I. J. LEHMANN, and W. A. MEHRENS. 1967. Using item analysis to improve tests. *Journal of Educational Measurement*, **4**(2): 65–68.

LATHROP, R. L., 1961. A quick-but-accurate-approximation to the standard deviation of a distribution. *Journal of Experimental Education*, **29**: 319–321.

LAVIN, D. E. 1967. *The prediction of academic performance.* New York: John Wiley & Sons, Inc.

LEEDS, C. H. 1950. A scale for measuring teacher-pupil attitudes and teacher-pupil rapport. *Psychological Monograph*, **64**(6, Whole No. 312).

LENNON, R. T. 1956. Assumptions underlying the use of content validity. *Educational and Psychological Measurement*, **16**: 294–304.

———. 1964. Norms: 1963. In *Proceedings, Invitational Conference on Testing Problems*, 1963. Princeton, N. J.: Educational Testing Service, pp. 13–22. Reprinted in G. H. Bracht, K. D. Hopkins, and J. C. Stanley, eds. 1972. *Perspectives in educational and psychological measurement*. Englewood Cliffs, N.J.: Prentice-Hall, Inc., Selection 4.

———. 1969. Scores and norms. In R. E. Ebel, ed., *Encyclopedia of educational research*, 4th ed. New York: The Macmillan Company.

LERNER, D., ed. 1965. *Cause and effect*. New York: The Free Press.

LESSINGER, L. M. 1970. Accountability in public education. *Proceedings of the 1969 Invitational Conference on Testing Problems*. Princeton, N. J.: Educational Testing Service, pp. 109–111. Reprinted in G. H. Bracht, K. D. Hopkins, and J. C. Stanley, eds. 1972. *Perspectives in educational and psychological measurement*. Englewood Cliffs, N.J.: Prentice-Hall, Inc., Selection 26.

LEVINE, P. R., and R. WALLEN. 1954. Adolescent vocational interests and later occupation. *Journal of Applied Psychology*, **38**(6): 428–431.

LEVINE, R. S., and W. H. ANGOFF. 1958. *The effects of practice and growth on scores on the Scholastic Aptitude Test*. Statistical Report 58-6. Princeton, N.J.: Educational Testing Service.

LINDEN, K. W., and J. D. LINDEN. 1968. *Modern mental measurement: A historical perspective*. Boston: Houghton Mifflin Company.

LINDQUIST, E. F. 1935. Cooperative achievement testing. *Journal of Educational Research*, **28**: 519.

———. 1944. The use of tests of accreditation of military experience and in the educational placement of war veterans. *Educational Record*, **25**: 357–376.

———, ed. 1951. *Educational measurement*. Washington, D. C.: American Council on Education.

———. 1968. *The impact of machines on educational measurement*. Bloomington, Ind.: Phi Delta Kappa, Inc.

———, and A. N. HIERONYMUS. 1964. Use and interpretation of test results. In *Manual for administrators, supervisors, and counselors: Iowa Tests of Basic Skills*. Boston: Houghton Mifflin Company. Reprinted in G. H. Bracht, K. D. Hopkins, and J. C. Stanley, eds. 1972. *Perspectives in educational and psychological measurement*. Englewood Cliffs, N.J.: Prentice-Hall, Inc., Selection 22.

LINDVALL, C. M., and A. J. NITKO. 1969. Criterion-referenced testing and the individualization of instruction. Paper presented at the annual meeting of National Council on Measurement in Education.

LINS, L. J. 1950. Probability approach to forecasting university success with measured grades as the criterion. *Educational and Psychological Measurement*, **10**: 386–391.

LITTLE, E., and J. CREASER. 1966. Uncertain responses on multiple-choice examinations. *Psychological Reports*, **18**: 801–802.

LIVINGSTON, S. A. 1972. Criterion-referenced applications of classical test theory. *Journal of Educational Measurement*, **9** (in press).

LORD, F. M. 1952. The relation of the reliability of multiple-choice tests to the distribution of item difficulties. *Psychometrika*, **17**: 181–194.

———. 1955. A survey of observed test-score distribution with respect to skewness and kurtosis. *Educational and Psychological Measurement*, **15**: 383–389.

———. 1956. A study of speed factors in tests and academic grades. *Psychometrika*, **21**(1): 31–50.

————. 1959. Test norms and sampling theory. *Journal of Experimental Education,* **27**: 247–263.

————. 1962a. Estimating norms by item-sampling. *Educational and Psychological Measurement,* **22**(2): 259–267.

————. 1962b. Test reliability—a correction. *Educational and Psychological Measurement,* **22**(3): 511–512.

————. 1963. Formula scoring and validity. *Educational and Psychological Measurement,* **23**(4): 663–672.

————, and M. R. NOVICK. 1968. *Statistical theories of mental test scores.* Reading, Mass: Addison-Wesley Publishing Company, Inc.

LORGE, I. 1952. Speed of response as a factor in mental "decline" with age. In R. G. Kuhlen and G. G. Thompson, eds. *Psychological studies of human development.* New York: Appleton-Century-Crofts, Inc., pp. 173–179.

————, and L. KRUGLOV. 1952. A suggested technique for the improvement of difficulty prediction of test items. *Educational and Psychological Measurement,* **12**: 554–561.

LORGE, I., R. L. THORNDIKE, and E. HAGEN. 1966. The Lorge-Thorndike intelligence tests: Multi-level edition. Boston: Houghton Mifflin Company.

LUDLOW, H. G. 1956. Some recent research on the Davis-Eells games. *School and Society,* **84**: 146–148.

LYMAN, H. B. 1971. *Test scores and what they mean.* 2d ed. Englewood Cliffs, N.J.: Prentice-Hall, Inc.

————. 1968. *How to take a test.* New York: McGraw-Hill Book Company, tape recording (#75488, 21 minutes.)

MCARTHUR, C., and L. B. STEVENS. 1955. The validation of expressed interests as compared with inventoried interests: A fourteen-year follow-up. *Journal of Applied Psychology,* **39**: 184–189.

MCASHAN, H. H. 1970. *Writing behavioral objectives.* New York: Harper & Row, Publishers.

MCCALL, J. N. 1965. Trends in the measurement of vocational interest. *Review of Educational Research,* **35**: 53–62.

————, and G. D. MOORE. 1965. Do interest inventories measure estimated abilities? *Personnel and Guidance Journal,* **43**: 1034–1037.

MCCALL, W. A. 1920. A new kind of school examination. *Journal of Educational Research,* **1**: 33–46.

————, ed. 1936. *The Test Newsletter.* Teachers College, Columbia University, December.

MCDOUGAL, W. 1923. *An introduction to social psychology,* 15th ed. Boston: John W. Luce.

MCGUIRE, C. 1963. Research in the process approach to the construction and analysis of medical examinations. *The twentieth yearbook of the National Council on Measurement in Education,* pp. 7–16.

MCKEACHIE, W. J., YI-GUANG LIN, and W. Mann. Student ratings of teacher effectiveness: Validation Studies. *American Educational Research Journal,* **8**: 435–445.

MCLAUGHLIN, K. F. 1964. *Interpretation of test results.* Washington, D.C.: U.S. Government Printing Office.

MCMORRIS, R. F. 1971. Evidence on the quality of several approximation for commonly used measurement statistics. Paper presented to the National Council on Measurement in Education, New York.

McNemar, Q. 1964. Lost: Our intelligence. Why? *American Psychologist*, **19**: 871–882.

Machover, K. 1949. *Personality projection in the drawing of the human figure: A method of personality investigation.* Springfield, Ill.: Charles C Thomas, Publisher.

Mager, R. F. 1962. *Preparing instructional objectives.* San Francisco: Fearon Publishers. (Programmed.)

Mann, H. 1845. Report of the annual examining committee of the Boston grammar and writing schools. *Common School Journal*, **7**: 326–336.

Marcus, A. 1963. The effect of correct response location on the difficulty level of multiple-choice questions. *Journal of Applied Psychology*, **47**(1): 48–51.

Marshall, J. C. 1967. Composition errors and essay examination grades re-examined. *American Educational Research Journal*, **4**(4): 375–385.

———, and J. M. Powers. 1969. Writing readability, composition errors, and essay grades. University of Missouri-St. Louis. Paper presented at the annual meeting of the National Council on Measurement in Education, Los Angeles, February 6–8.

Marso, R. N. 1970a. Classroom testing procedure, test anxiety, and achievement. *Journal of Experimental Education*, **38**(3): 54–58.

———. 1970b. Test item arrangement, testing time and performance. *Journal of Educational Measurement*, **7**(2): 113–118.

Masia, B. B. 1964. What to look for in a review of a personality inventory. *Personnel and Guidance Journal*, **42**: 1030–1034. Reprinted in G. H. Bracht, K. D. Hopkins, and J. C. Stanley, eds. 1972. *Perspectives in educational and psychological measurement.* Englewood Cliffs, N.J.: Prentice-Hall, Inc., Selection 29.

Masling, J. 1959. The effects of warm and cold interaction on the administration and scoring of an intelligence test. *Journal of Consulting Psychology*, **23**: 336–341.

Mason, G. P., and R. E. Odeh. 1968. A short-cut formula for standard deviation. *Journal of Educational Measurement*, **5**: 319–320.

Mayo, S. T. 1967. *Pre-service preparation of teachers in educational measurement.* Final report. Chicago: Loyola University.

———. 1968. The methodology and technology of educational and psychological testing. *Review of Educational Research*, **38**: 92–101.

———. 1970. Mastery learning and mastery testing. *Measurement in Education: A series of special reports of the National Council on Measurement in Education*, **1**(3).

———, R. C. Hunt, and F. Tremmel. 1969. A mastery approach to the evaluation of learning statistics. Paper presented to the National Council on Measurement in Education, Los Angeles.

Meade, J. E., and A. S. Parkes. 1966. *Genetic and environmental factors in human ability.* London: Oliver & Boyd, Ltd.

Medley, D. M., and H. E. Mitzel. 1963. Measuring classroom behavior by systematic observation. In N. L. Gage, ed., *Handbook of research on teaching.* Skokie, Ill.: Rand McNally & Company, Chap. 6, pp. 247–328.

Meehl, P. E. 1954. *Clinical versus statistical prediction: A theoretical analysis and a review of the evidence.* Minneapolis: University of Minnesota Press.

Merwin, J. C., and E. F. Gardner. 1962. Development and application of tests of educational achievement. *Review of Educational Research*, **32**: 40–50.

Metfessel, N. S., and G. Sax. 1957. Response set patterns in published instructors' manuals in education and psychology. *California Journal of Educational Research*, **8**(5): 195–197.

————. 1958. Systematic biases in the keying of correct responses on certain standardized tests. *Educational and Psychological Measurement*, **18**: 58–62.

MEYER, M. 1908. The grading of students. *Science*, **27**: 243–250.

MEYER, W. J., and A. W. BENDIG. 1961. A longitudinal study of the Primary Mental Abilities Test. *Journal of Educational Psychology*, **52**(1): 50–60.

MICHAEL, J. J. 1968a. The reliability of a multiple-choice examination under various test-taking instructions. *Journal of Educational Measurement*, **5**(4): 307–314.

————. 1968b. Structure of intellect theory and the validity of achievement examinations. *Educational and Psychological Measurement*, **28**: 1141–1149.

————, and W. B. MICHAEL. 1969. The relationship of performance on objective achievement examinations to the order in which students complete them. *Educational and Psychological Measurement*, **29**(2): 511–513.

MICHAEL, W. B. 1969. Prediction. In R. L. Ebel, ed., *Encyclopedia of educational research*, 4th ed. New York: The Macmillan Company, pp. 982–993.

————, A. F. HAERTZKA, and N. C. PERRY. 1953. Errors in estimates of item difficulty obtained from use of extreme groups on a criterion variable. *Educational and Psychological Measurement*, **13**: 601–606.

MICHAELIS, J. U. 1954. The prediction of success in student teaching from personality and attitude inventories. *University of California Public Education*, **11**: 415–481.

MILLER, D. C. 1967. *Handbook of research design and social measurement*. New York: David McKay Company, Inc.

MILLMAN, J. 1961. Multiple-choice test item construction rules. Ithaca, N.Y.: Cornell University Press. (Mimeographed, 7 pp.)

————, C. H. BISHOP, and R. EBEL. 1965. An analysis of test-wiseness. *Educational and Psychological Measurement*, **25**(3): 707–726.

MILLMAN, J. and J. LINDLOF. 1964. The comparability of fifth-grade norms of the California, Iowa and Metropolitan achievement tests. *Journal of Educational Measurement*, **1**: 135–137.

MILLMAN, J., and W. PAUK. 1969. *How to take tests*. New York: McGraw-Hill Book Company.

MOLLENKOPF, W. G. 1960. Time limits and the behavior of test takers. *Educational and Psychological Measurement*, **20**(2): 223–230.

MONROE, W. S. 1945. Educational measurement in 1920 and 1945. *Journal of Educational Research*, **38**: 334–340.

————, and R. E. CARTER. 1923. *The use of different types of thought questions in secondary schools and their relative difficulty for students*. Bulletin No. 14. Urbana: Bureau of Educational Research, University of Illinois.

MOORE, J. C., R. E. SCHUTZ, and R. L. BAKER. 1966. The application of a self-instructional technique to develop a test-taking strategy. *American Educational Research Journal*, **3**: 13–17.

MORENO, J. L. 1934. *Who shall survive?* Washington, D.C.: Nervous and Mental Disease Publishing Co.

————, et al., eds. 1960. *The sociometry reader*. New York: The Free Press.

MOSIER, C. I. 1951. Problems and designs of cross-validation. *Educational and Psychological Measurement*, **11**: 5–28.

————, C. MYERS, and H. G. PRICE. 1945. Suggestions for the construction of multiple-choice test items. *Educational and Psychological Measurement*, **5**: 261–271.

MOULY, G. J. 1970. The science of educational research. New York: Van Nostrand Reinhold Co.

————, and SR. MARY EDGAR, R.S.M. 1958. Equivalence of IQ's for four group intelligence tests. *Personnel and Guidance Journal* (May), **36**: 623–626.

MOUTON, J. S., et al., 1955. The validity of sociometric responses. *Sociometry*, **18**: 7–48.

MOYNIHAN, P. 1971. Seek parity of educational achievement, Moynihan urges. *Report on Educational Research* (March 3), 3(5): 4.

MURPHY, G. 1949. *Historical introduction to modern psychology*, rev. ed. New York: Harcourt Brace Jovanovich, Inc.

MURRAY, H. A., et al. 1938. *Explorations in personality*. New York: Oxford University Press.

MYERS, C. T. 1962. The relationship between item difficulty and test validity and reliability. *Educational and Psychological Measurement*, **22**(3): 565–571.

MYERS, S. S. 1961. The kinds of thinking required in current mathematics tests. *New Jersey Mathematics Teacher*, **18**: 11–15.

NATIONAL ASSESSMENT OF EDUCATIONAL PROGRESS. 1970. First assessment of results reported to public. *National Assessment of Educational Progress*, 3(3): 1–2.

NATIONAL EDUCATION ASSOCIATION. 1963. School entrance age—policies and exceptions. *NEA Research Bulletin*, **41**: 77–78.

————. 1967. National Education Association report to parents. *NEA Research Bulletin*, **45**: 51–53.

NELL, W. 1963. *A comparative investigation of teacher assigned grades and academic achievement in the Aztec Junior High, New Mexico*. Society for the Study of Education: *Educational Research Bulletin*, pp. 15–16.

NELSON, M. J. 1969. Intelligence and special aptitude tests. In R. L. Ebel, ed., *Encyclopedia of educational research*. New York: The Macmillan Company, pp. 667–677.

NOBLE, C. E., J. L. NOBLE, and W. T. ALCOCK. 1958. Prediction of individual differences in human trial-and-error learning. *Perceptual and Motor Skills*, **8**: 151–172.

NORMAN, R. D. 1954. The effects of a forward-retention set on an objective achievement test presented forwards or backwards. *Educational and Psychological Measurement*, **14**: 487–498.

NOVICK, M. R., and C. LEWIS. 1967. Coefficient alpha and the reliability of composite measurements. *Psychometrika*, **32**: 1–13.

NUNNALLY, J. C. 1967. *Psychometric theory*. New York: McGraw-Hill Book Company.

OELKE, M. C. 1956. A study of student teachers' attitudes toward children. *Journal of Educational Psychology*, **47**: 193–196.

OHLSEN, M. M. 1963. Interpretation of test scores. In W. G. Findley, ed. The impact and improvement of school testing programs. *The sixty-second yearbook of the National Society for the Study of Education, Part II*. Chicago: University of Chicago Press, pp. 254–294.

OKADA, T., and W. M. COHEN. 1969. Growth in achievement curves by student socio-economic status and racial-ethnic group membership. Paper presented at the annual meeting of the American Educational Research Association, Los Angeles, February 5–8.

————, and G. W. Mayeske. 1969. *Growth in achievement for different racial, regional and socio-economic groupings of students.* Technical Paper Number 1, May 16. Office of Program Planning and Evaluation, Division of Elementary and Secondary Programs. Washington, D.C.: Office of Education/U.S. Department of Health, Education and Welfare.

Oldridge, O. A. 1963. *An experimental study of two guidance emphases in the elementary school.* Doctoral dissertation, University of Southern California University Microfilms, 1963, No. 63–5061. *Dissertation Abstracts,* **24**(2): 632–633 (August 1963).

————, and A. A. Allison. 1968. Wechsler Preschool and Primary Scale of Intelligence (WPPSI). *Journal of Educational Measurement,* **5**(4): 347–348.

Osgood, C. E., G. J. Suci, and P. H. Tannenbaum. 1957. *The measurement of meaning.* Urbana: University of Illinois.

OSS Assessment Staff. 1948. *Assessment of men: Selection of personnel for the Office of Strategic Services.* New York: Rinehart.

Owens, T. R., and D. L. Stufflebeam. 1969. An experimental comparison of item sampling and examinee sampling for estimating test norms. Paper presented at the annual meeting of the National Council on Measurement in Education Los Angeles, February 6–8.

Owens, W. A. 1953. Age and mental abilities: A longitudinal study. *Genetic Psychology Monographs,* **48**: 3–54.

————. 1966. Age and mental abilities: A second adult follow-up. *Journal of Educational Psychology,* **57**: 311–325.

Page, A. 1960. To grade or retrograde. *College English,* **21**: 213–216.

Page, E. B. 1958. Teacher comments and student performance: A seventy-four classroom experiment in school motivation. *Journal of Educational Psychology,* **49**(4): 173–181.

————. 1966. The imminence of grading essays by computer. *Phi Delta Kappan,* **47**: 238–243.

Palmer, O. 1961. Sense or nonsense? The objective testing of English composition. *English Journal,* **50**: 314–320.

————. 1962. Seven classic ways of grading dishonestly. *English Journal,* **51**: 464–467.

Payne, D. A. 1963. A note on skewness and internal consistency reliability estimates. *Journal of Experimental Education,* **32**(1): 43–46.

————. 1968. *The specification and measurement of learning outcomes.* Waltham, Mass.: Blaisdell Publishing Company.

Peak, H., and E. G. Boring. 1926. The factor of speed in intelligence. *Journal of Experimental Psychology,* **9**: 71.

Perrone, P. A. 1964. Factors influencing high school senior's occupational preference. *Personnel and Guidance Journal,* **42**: 976–980.

Perry, D. K. 1955. Validities of three interest keys for U.S. Navy yeomen. *Journal of Applied Psychology,* **39**: 134–138.

Peters, F. R. 1956. Measurement of informal educational achievement by the GED tests. *School Review,* **64**: 227–232.

PHILLIPS, B. N., and G. WEATHERS. 1958. Analysis of errors in scoring standardized tests. *Educational and Psychological Measurement*, **18**: 563–567.

PIDGEON, D. A., and A. YATES. 1957. Experimental inquiries into the use of essay-type English papers. *British Journal of Educational Psychology*, **27**: 37–47.

PLUMLEE, L. B. 1964. Estimating means and standard deviations from partial data—an empirical check on Lord's item sampling technique. *Educational and Psychological Measurement*, **24**(3): 623–630.

POLLACZEK, P. P. 1952. A study of malingering on the CVS abbreviated individual intelligence scale. *Journal of Clinical Psychology*, **8**: 75–81.

POOLE, R. L. 1969. An examination of cognitive processes elicited by test items as a function of the taxonomy of educational objectives and selected cognitive factor abilities. Paper presented at the Annual Meeting of the National Council on Measurement in Education, Los Angeles, February.

POPHAM, W. J., and T. R. HUSEK. 1969. Implications of criterion-referenced measurement. *Journal of Educational Measurement*, **6**: 1–10. Reprinted in G. H. Bracht, K. D. Hopkins, and J. C. Stanley, eds. 1972. *Perspectives in educational and psychological measurement*. Englewood Cliffs, N.J.: Prentice-Hall, Inc., Selection 13.

POPHAM, W. J., and R. R. TRIMBLE. 1960. The Minnesota Teacher Attitude Inventory as an index of general teaching competence. *Educational and Psychological Measurement*, **20**: 509–572.

PRESCOTT, G. A. n.d. Test administration guide. *Test Service Bulletin* No. 102. New York: Harcourt Brace Jovanovich, Inc.

RABINOWITZ, W. 1954. The fakability of the Minnesota Teacher Attitude Inventory. *Educational and Psychological Measurement*, **14**: 657–664.

REMMERS, H. H. 1963. Rating methods in research on teaching. In N. L. Gage, ed., *Handbook of research on teaching*. Skokie, Ill.: Rand McNally & Company, Chap.7.

RICE, J. M. 1897. The futility of the spelling grind: I. *Forum*, **23**: 163–172; II. *Ibid.*, 409–419.

RICHARDS, J. M., JR., and S. W. LUTZ 1968. Predicting student accomplishment in college from the ACT assessment. *Journal of Educational Measurement*, **5**(1): 17–29.

RINSLAND, H. D. 1938. *Constructing tests and grading in elementary and high school subjects*. Englewood Cliffs, N.J.: Prentice-Hall, Inc.

ROBERTSON, G. J. n.d. Innovation in the assessment of individual differences: development of the first group mental ability test. *Normline*, **1**(2): New York: Harcourt Brace Jovanovich Inc. Reprinted in G. H. Bracht, K. D. Hopkins, and J. C. Stanley, eds. 1972. *Perspectives in educational and psychological measurement*. Englewood Cliffs, N.J.: Prentice-Hall, Inc., Selection 18.

ROBINSON, D. 1970. National assessment assessed: General optimism, but doubts linger on. *Phi Delta Kappan*, **52**(1): 67–68.

RODGER, A. G. 1936. The application of six group intelligence tests to the same children, and the effects of practice. *British Journal of Educational Psychology*, **6**: 291–305.

ROELFS, R. M. 1955. Trends in junior high school progress reporting. *Journal of Educational Research*, **49**: 241–249.

ROEMER, R. E. 1965. Nine-year validity study of predictors of medical school success. *Journal of Educational Research*, **59**(4): 183–185.

ROSENTHAL, R., and L. JACOBSON. 1968. *Pygmalion in the classroom: Teacher expectation and pupils' intellectual development.* New York: Holt, Rinehart and Winston, Inc. Reviewed in *Contemporary Psychology* by Richard E. Snow, **14**(4): 197–199 (1969).

ROSS, C. C., and J. C. STANLEY. 1954. *Measurement in today's schools,* 3d ed. Englewood Cliffs, N.J.: Prentice-Hall, Inc.

ROTHKOPF, E. Z. 1966. Learning from written instructive materials: An exploration of the control of inspection behavior by test-like events. *American Educational Research Journal,* **3**: 241–249.

RUCH, G. M. 1929. *The objective or new-type examination.* Glenview, Ill.: Scott, Foresman and Company.

RUEBUSH, B. K. 1963. Anxiety. In the Yearbook Committee and Associated Contributors, H. W. Stevenson, J. Kagan, and C. Spiker, eds., Child psychology: *The sixty-second yearbook of the National Society for the Study of Education.* Chicago: University of Chicago Press.

RULON, P. J. 1939. A simplified procedure for determining the reliability of a test by split halves. *Harvard Educational Review,* **9**: 99–103.

———. 1941. Problems of regression. *Harvard Educational Review,* **11**: 213–223.

RUNDQUIST, E. A., and B. F. SLETTO. 1936. *Personality in the depression.* Minneapolis: University of Minnesota Press.

RUSSELL, I. L., and A. T. WELLINGTON. 1955. Personality: Does it influence teachers' marks? *Journal of Educational Research,* **48**: 561–564.

RUSSELL SAGE FOUNDATION. 1969. *Guidelines for the collection, maintenance and dissemination of pupil records. Report of a conference on the ethical and legal aspects of school record keeping.* Sterling Forest, N.Y.: Russell Sage Foundation. Reprinted in G. H. Bracht, K. D. Hopkins, and J. C. Stanley, eds. 1972. *Perspectives in educational and psychological measurement.* Englewood Cliffs, N.J.: Prentice-Hall, Inc., Selection 34.

RYANS, D. G. 1960. *Characteristics of teachers.* Washington, D.C.: American Council on Education.

SABERS, D. L., and R. D. KLAUSMEIER. 1971. Accuracy of short-cut estimates for standard deviation. *Journal of Educational Measurement,* **8**, 335–339.

SANDERS, N. M. 1966. *Classroom questions: What kinds?* New York: Harper & Row, Publishers.

SANDGREN, D. L., and L. G. SCHMIDT. 1956. Does practice teaching change attitudes toward teaching? *Journal of Educational Research,* **49**: 673–680.

SARASON, S. S., G., MANDLER, and P. G. CRAIGHILL. 1952. The effect of differential instructions on anxiety and learning. *Journal of Abnormal and Social Psychology,* **47**: 561–565.

SARASON, S. B., et al. 1960. *Anxiety in elementary school children.* New York: John Wiley & Sons, Inc.

SAX, G., and A. CARR. 1962. An investigation of response sets on altered parallel forms. *Educational and Psychological Measurement,* **22**(2): 371–376.

SAX, G., and L. S. COLLET. 1968. The effects of differing instructions and guessing formulas on reliability and validity. *Educational and Psychological Measurement,* **28**: 1127–1136.

SAX, G., and T. R. CROMACK. 1966. The effects of various forms of item arrangements on test performance. *Journal of Educational Measurement*, 3(4): 309–311.

SAX, G., and M. READE. 1964. Achievement as a function of test difficulty level. *American Educational Research Journal*, 1: 22–25.

SAYLOR, G. 1970. National Assessment: Pro and con. *The Record*, 70(4): 588–597.

SCANNELL, D. P., and J. C. MARSHALL. 1966. The effect of selected composition errors on grades assigned to essay examinations. *American Educational Research Journal*, 3: 125–130.

SCATES, D. E. 1947. Fifty of objective measurement and research in education. *Journal of Educational Research*, 41: 241–264.

SCHAIE, K. W., and C. R. STROTHER. 1968. A cross-sequential study of age changes in cognitive behavior. *Psychological Bulletin*, 70: 671–680.

SCHOER, L. A. 1970. *Test construction: A programmed guide.* Boston: Allyn and Bacon, Inc.

SCHULTZ, M. K., and W. H. ANGOFF, 1956. The development of new scales for the aptitude and advanced tests of the Graduate Record Examinations. *Journal of Educational Psychology.* 47(5): 285–294.

SCHUMACHER and GEE. 1961. The relationship between initial and retest scores on the Medical College Admission Test. *Journal of Medical Education*, 36: 129–133.

SCHWARZ, J. C. 1967. A new procedure for administering objective tests to large classes. *Journal of Educational Measurement*, 4(3): 167–168.

SCIENCE RESEARCH ASSOCIATES, INC. 1963. *ITED (The Iowa Test of Educational Development). How to use the test results: A manual for teachers and counselors.* Chicago: Science Research Associates, Inc.

SCRIVEN, M. 1967. The methodology of evaluation. In R. W. Tyler, R. M. Gagné, and M. Scriven, *Perspectives of curriculum evaluation.* Skokie, Ill.: Rand McNally & Company, pp. 39–83.

———. 1970. Discussion. *Proceedings of the 1969 Invitational Conference on Testing Problems.* Princeton, N. J.: Educational Testing Service, pp. 112–117.

SEASHORE, C. E. 1899. Some psychological statistics. *University of Iowa Studies in Psychology*, 2: 1–84.

SEASHORE, H. G., and J. H. RICKS, JR. 1950. Norms must be relevant. *Test Services Bulletin* No. 39. New York: The Psychological Corporation.

SECHREST, L. 1963. Incremental validity: a recommendation. *Educational and Psychological Measurement*, 23: 153–158.

SEIBEL, D. W. 1968. Measurement of aptitude and achievement. In D. K. Whitla, ed., *Handbook of measurement and assessment in behavioral sciences.* Reading, Mass.: Addison-Wesley Publishing Company, Inc., Chap. 8.

SHAW, M. E., and J. M. WRIGHT. 1967. *Scales for the measurement of attitudes.* New York: McGraw-Hill Book Company.

SHELDON, M. S., and A. G. SORENSON. 1960. On the use of Q-techniques in educational evaluation and research. *Journal of Experimental Education*, 29: 143–151.

SHEPHERD, E. M. 1929. The effect of the quality of penmanship on grades. *Journal of Educational Research*, 19(2): 102–105.

SHERRIFFS, A. C., and D. S. BOOMER. 1954. Who is penalized by the penalty for guessing? *Journal of Educational Psychology*, 45: 81–90.

SILVERSTEIN, A. B., P. J. MOHAN, R. E. FRANKEN, and D. E. RHONE. 1964. Test anxiety and intellectual performance in mentally retarded school children. *Child Development*, **35**: 1137–1146.

SIMPSON, R. H. 1944. The specific meanings of certain terms indicating different degrees of frequency. *Quarterly Journal of Speech*, **30**: 328–330.

SIMS, V. M. 1931. The objectivity, reliability, and validity of an essay examination graded by rating. *Journal of Educational Research*, **24**: 216–223.

SINICK, D. 1956. Encouragement, anxiety, and test performance. *Journal of Applied Psychology*, **40**(5): 315–318.

SLAKTER, M. J. 1967. Risk taking on objective examinations. *American Educational Research Journal*, **4**(1): 31–43.

———. 1969. Generality of risk taking on objective examinations. *Educational and Psychological Measurement*, **29**: 115–128.

———, R. A. KOEHLER, and S. H. HAMPTON. 1970. Grade level, sex, and selected aspects of test-wiseness. *Journal of Educational Measurement*, **7**(2): 119–122.

SLATER, R. D. 1964. The equivalency of IBM mark-sense answer cards and IBM answer sheets when used as answer formats for a precisely-timed test of mental ability. *Journal of Educational Research*, **57**: 545–547.

SMITH, A. Z., and J. E. DOBBIN. 1960. Marks and marking systems. In C. W. Harris, ed., *Encyclopedia of educational research*, 3d ed. New York: The Macmillan Company.

SMITH, E. R., and R. W. TYLER. 1942. *Appraising and recording student progress.* New York: Harper & Row, Publishers,

SMITH, H. 1955. *The purposes of higher education.* New York: Harper & Row, Publishers.

SNOW, R. E. 1969. Unfinished pygmalion, review of Rosenthal and Jacobson's *Pygmalion in the classroom. Contemporary Psychology*, **14**: 197–199.

SNYDER, W. U. 1955. The personality of clinical students. *Journal of Counseling Psychology*, **2**: 47–52.

SODERQUIST, H. 1936. A new method of weighting scores in a true-false test. *Journal of Educational Research*, **30**: 290–292.

SOLOMON, R. J. 1965. Improving the essay test in the social studies. In H. D. Berg, ed., *Evaluation in social studies*. Washington, D. C.: National Council for Social Studies, pp. 137–153.

SPAIGHTS, E. 1965. Accuracy of self-estimation of junior high school students. *Journal of Educational Research*, **58**(9): 416–419.

SPEARMAN, C. 1904. "General intelligence," objectively determined and measured. *American Journal of Psychology*, **15**: 206–219.

———. 1923. *The nature of intelligence and the principles of cognition.* London: The Macmillan Company.

———. 1927. *The abilities of man.* New York: The Macmillan Company.

SPRINTHALL, N. A. 1964. A comparison of values among teachers, academic underachievers, and achievers. *Journal of Experimental Education*, **33**(2): 193–196.

STAKE, R. E. 1961. "Overestimation" of achievement with the California Achievement Test. *Educational and Psychological Measurement*, **21**(1): 59–62.

———. 1967. The countenance of educational evaluation. *Teachers College Record*, **68**: 523–540.

————, and J. T. HASTINGS. 1964. Review of the Stanford Achievement Battery, 1964. *Personnel and Guidance Journal*, **43**: 178–184. Reprinted in G. H. Bracht, K. D. Hopkins, and J. C. Stanley, eds. 1972. *Perspectives in educational and psychological measurement*. Englewood Cliffs, N.J.: Prentice-Hall, Inc., Selection 24.

STAKE, R. E., and D. D. SJOGREN. 1964. Activity level and learning effectiveness. NDEA Title VII, Project No. 753. Lincoln: University of Nebraska.

STALNAKER, J. M. 1936. The problem of the English examination. *Educational Record*, **17**(Suppl. No. 10): 41.

————. 1951. The essay type of examination. Chapter 13 in E. F. Lindquist, ed., *Educational measurement*. Washington, D.C.: American Council on Education.

————. 1961. Research in the National Merit Scholarship program. *Journal of Counseling Psychology*, **8**: 268–271.

STANLEY, J. C. 1954. Psychological correction for chance. *Journal of Experimental Education*, **22**: 297–298.

————. 1955. Statistical analysis of scores from counterbalanced tests. *Journal of Experimental Education*, **23**: 187–207.

————. 1957. K-R 20 as the stepped-up mean item intercorrelation. *Yearbook of the National Council on Measurements Used in Education*, **14**:78–92.

————. 1958. The ABCs of test construction. *NEA Journal*, **47**: 224–226.

————. 1960a. College studies and college life in Belgium. *College Board Review*, **40**: 10–14.

————. 1960b. Teacher-made tests as approaches to convergence of measurement and instruction. *Proceedings of the Ninth Annual Western Regional Conference on Testing Problems* of Educational Testing Service.

————. 1964. *Measurement in today's schools*, 4th ed. Englewood Cliffs, N.J.: Prentice-Hall, Inc.

————. 1966. Rice as a pioneer educational researcher. *Journal of Educational Measurement*, **3**(2): 135–139.

————. 1967. A design for comparing the impact of different colleges. *American Educational Research Journal* (May), **4**(3): 217–228.

————. 1968. Maximum possible Kuder-Richardson formula 20 coefficients for test scores from constant, rectangular, and rectangular-normal distributions of difficulties of dichotomously scored zero-chance-success items. *Proceedings, 76th Annual Convention, American Psychological Association*.

————. 1971a. Predicting college success of the educationally disadvantaged. *Science*, **171**: 640–647.

————. 1971b. Reliability. In R. L. Thorndike, ed., *Educational measurement*, 2d ed. Washington D.C.: American Council on Education, Chap. 13.

————. 1971c. Reliability of test scores and other measurements. In L. C. Deighton, *The encyclopedia of education*. New York: The Macmillan Company. Reprinted in G. H. Bracht, K. D. Hopkins, and J. C. Stanley, eds. 1972. *Perspectives in educational and psychological measurement*. Englewood Cliffs, N.J.: Prentice-Hall, Inc., Selection 6.

————, and E. Y. BEEMAN. 1956. Interaction of major field of study with kind of test. *Psychological Reports*, **2**: 333–336.

STANLEY, J. C., and D. L. BOLTON. 1957. A review of Bloom's *Taxonomy of educational objectives*. *Educational and Psychological Measurement*, **17**: 631–634.

STANLEY, J. C., and A. C. PORTER. 1967. Correlation of Scholastic Aptitude Test score with college grades for Negroes versus whites. *Journal of Educational Measurement*, **4**: 199–218.

STANLEY, J. C., and M. D. WANG. 1970. Weighting test items and test-item options, an overview of the analytical and empirical literature. *Educational and Psychological Measurement*, **30**: 21–35.

STARCH, D. 1913. Reliability and distribution of grades. *Science*, **38**: 630–636.

———, and E. C. ELLIOT. 1912. Reliability of grading high school work in English. *Scholastic Review*, **20**: 442–457.

———. 1913. Reliability of grading high school work in mathematics. *Scholastic Review*, **21**: 254–259.

STECKLEIN, J. E. 1955, 1956. *Bulletins on classroom testing* of the Bureau of Institutional Research, University of Minnesota, Minneapolis, Nos. 4, 5, and 6 (1955) and 7 (1956): "How to write multiple-choice test items," "How to write true-false test items," "How to write matching test items," and "How to measure more than facts with multiple-choice items."

STEIN, Z., and M. SUSSER. 1970. Mutability of intelligence and epidemiology of mild mental retardation. *Review of Educational Research*, **40**: 29–67.

STEPHENSON, W. 1953. *The study of behavior: Q-technique and its methodology*. Chicago: University of Chicago Press.

STERN, G. G. 1963. Measuring noncognitive variables in research on teaching. In N. L. Gage, ed., *Handbook of research on teaching*. Skokie, Ill.: Rand McNally Company, Inc., Chap. 9.

STEVENSON, H. W. 1961. Social reinforcement with children as a function of CA, sex of examiner, and sex of subject. *Journal of Abnormal and Social Psychology*, **63**: 147–154.

STEWART, N. 1947. AGCT scores of Army personnel grouped by occupation. *Occupations*, **26**: 5–41.

STODOLA, Q. C., D. E. PETERSON, and M. O. HOLOIEN. 1965. Some practical uses of data processing methods in classroom testing and student personnel services. *Journal of Educational Measurement*, **2**: 117–118.

STONE, C. W. 1908. *Arithmetical abilities and some factors determining them*. New York: Columbia University Press.

STONE, J. B. 1958. *Structured-objective Rorschach test, preliminary edition*. Monterey, Calif.: California Test Bureau.

STONE, J. C. 1922. *The teaching of arithmetic*. Chicago: Benj. H. Sanborn & Co.

STOREY, A. G. 1968. The versatile multiple-choice item. *Journal of Educational Research*, **62**(4): 169–172.

STRONG, E. K., JR. 1943. *Vocational interests of men and women*. Stanford, Calif.: Stanford University Press.

———. 1953. Validity of occupational choice. *Educational and Psychological Measurement*, **13**: 110–121.

———, revised by D. P. CAMPBELL. 1966. *Strong Vocational Interest Blank: Manual*. Stanford, Calif.: Stanford University Press.

STUFFLEBEAM, D. L. 1966. A depth study of the evaluation requirement. *Theory Into Practice*, **5**: 121–133.

SUPER, D. E., ed. 1958. *The use of multifactor tests in guidance:* Washington, D.C.: American Personnel and Guidance Association.

———. 1960. Interests. In C. W. Harris, ed., *Encyclopedia of educational research*, 3d ed. New York: The Macmillan Company, pp. 728–733.

———, W. F. BRAASCH, and J. B. SHAY. 1947. The effect of distractions on test results. *Journal of Educational Psychology*, **38**: 373–377.

Super, D. E., and J. O. Crites. 1962. *Appraising vocational fitness*, rev. ed. New York: Harper & Row, Publishers.

Super, D. E., and P. L. Overstreet. 1960. *The vocational maturity of ninth grade boys.* New York: Teachers College, Columbia University.

Swan, R. J., and K. D. Hopkins. 1965. An investigation of theoretical and empirical chance scores on selected standardized group tests. *California Journal of Educational Research*, **16**: 34–41.

Swineford, F. 1938. The measurement of a personality trait. *Journal of Educational Psychology*, **29**: 295–300.

———. 1941. Analysis of a personality trait. *Journal of Educational Psychology*, **32**: 438–444.

———, and P. M. Miller. 1953. Effects of directions regarding guessing on item statistics of a multiple-choice vocabulary test. *Journal of Educational Psychology*, **44**(3): 129–139.

Symonds, P. M. 1931. *Diagnosing personality and conduct.* New York: Century.

Tate, M. W. 1948. Individual differences in speed of response in mental test materials of varying degrees of difficulty. *Educational and Psychological Measurement*, **8**: 353–374.

Taylor, E. A., and J. H. Crandall. 1962. A study of the "norm-equivalence" of certain tests approved for the California state testing program. *California Journal of Educational Research*, **13**(4): 186–192.

Terman, L. M. 1954. The discovery and encouragement of exceptional talent. *American Psychologist*, **9**: 221–230.

———, and M. A. Merrill. 1937. *Measuring intelligence.* Boston: Houghton Mifflin Company.

———. 1960. *Stanford-Binet Intelligence Scale.* Boston: Houghton Mifflin Company.

Thomas, C. L., and J. C. Stanley. 1969. Effectiveness of high school grades for predicting college grades of black students: A review and discussion. *Journal of Educational Measurement*, **6**: 203–215.

Thompson, A. 1958. Tentative guidelines for proper and improper practices with standardized achievement tests. *California Journal of Educational Research* (September), **9**(4): 159–166.

Thorndike, E. L. 1904. *Introduction to the theory of mental and social measurements.* New York: Teachers College, Columbia University.

———. 1910. *Handwriting.* New York: Bureau of Publications, Teachers College, Columbia University.

———. 1918. The nature, purposes, and general methods of measurements of educational products. *The seventeenth yearbook of the National Society for the Study of Education, Part II*, p. 16.

———. 1922. Measurement in education. *The twenty-first yearbook of the National Society for the Study of Education, Part I.*

———. 1926. *The measurement of intelligence.* New York: Teachers College, Columbia University.

Thorndike, R. L. 1949. *Personnel selection.* New York: John Wiley & Sons, Inc.

———. 1951. Reliability. In E. F. Lindquist, ed., *Educational measurement.* Washington, D.C.: American Council on Education.

THORNDIKE, R. L. 1963a. The concepts of over- and underachievement. New York: Columbia University, Teachers College, Bureau of Publications.

———. 1963b. Some methodological issues in the study of creativity. *Proceedings of the* 1962 *Invitational Conference on Testing Problems.* Princeton, N.J.: Educational Testing Service. Reprinted in G. H. Bracht, K. D. Hopkins, and J. C. Stanley, eds. 1972. *Perspectives in educational and psychological measurement.* Englewood Cliffs, N.J.: Prentice-Hall, Inc., Selection 21.

———. 1964a. Educational decisions and human assessment. *Teachers College Record,* **66**: 103–112.

———. 1964b. Reliability. *Proceedings of* 1963 *Invitational Conference on Testing Problems.* Princeton, N.J.: Educational Testing Service. Reprinted in G. H. Bracht, K. D. Hopkins, and J. C. Stanley, eds. 1972. *Perspectives in educational and psychological measurement.* Englewood Cliffs, N.J.: Prentice-Hall, Inc., Selection 7.

———. 1968. Review of Rosenthal and Jacobson's *Pygmalion in the classroom. American Educational Research Journal,* **5**(4): 708–711.

———. 1969a. Helping teachers use tests. *Measurement in Education: A Series of Special Reports of the National Council on Measurement in Education,* **1**(1).

———. 1969b. Marks and marking systems. In R. L. Ebel, ed., *Encyclopedia of educational research,* 4th ed. New York: The Macmillan Company, pp. 759–766. Reprinted in G. H. Bracht, K. D. Hopkins, and J. C. Stanley, eds. 1972. *Perspectives in educational and psychological measurement.* Englewood Cliffs, N.J.: Prentice-Hall, Inc., Selection 17.

———, ed. 1971. *Educational measurement,* 2d ed. Washington, D.C.: American Council on Education.

———, and G. A. GALLUP. 1944. Verbal intelligence of the American adult. *Journal of General Psychology,* **30**: 75–85.

THORNDIKE, R. L., and E. P. HAGEN. 1969. *Measurement and evaluation in psychology and education,* 3d ed. New York: John Wiley & Sons, Inc.

THURSTONE, L. L. 1927. A law of comparative judgment. *Psychological Review,* **24**: 273–286.

———. 1938. Primary mental abilities. *Psychometric Monographs,* **1**.

———. 1955. The differential growth of mental abilities. Paper No. 14. Psychometric Laboratory, University of North Carolina.

———. 1959. *The measurement of values.* Chicago: University of Chicago Press.

TIEDEMAN, D. V. 1952. Has he grown? *Test Service Notebook* No. 12. New York: Harcourt Brace Jovanovich, Inc., 4 pp.

———, and E. J. CHAVE. 1929. *The measurement of attitude.* Chicago: University of Chicago Press.

Time Magazine. 1967. Testing: Toward national assessment. January 27, p. 61.

TINKELMAN, S. N. 1971. Planning the objective test. In R. L. Thorndike, ed., *Educational measurement,* 2d ed. Washington, D. C.: American Council on Education.

TORRANCE, E. P. 1962. *Guiding creative talent.* Englewood Cliffs, N.J.: Prentice-Hall, Inc.

TRAUB, R. E., R. K. HAMBLETON, and B. SINGH. 1968. Effects of promised reward and threatened penalty on performance of a multiple-choice vocabulary test. Unpublished manuscript, The Ontario Institute for Studies in Education.

TRAXLER, A. E. n.d. Fundamentals of testing for parents, school boards, and teachers. *Test Service Notebook* No. 17. Harcourt Brace Jovanovich, Inc.

————. 1959. Ten essential steps in a testing program. *Education*, **79**: 1–6.

————, and H. A. ANDERSON. 1935. The reliability of an essay examination in English. *School Review*, **43**: 534–539.

TRINKAUS, W. K. 1954. The permanence of vocational interests of college freshmen. *Educational and Psychological Measurement*, **14**: 641–646.

TRYK, H. E. 1968. Assessment in the study of creativity. In P. McReynolds, ed., *Advances in psychological assessment*, vol. 1. Palo Alto, Calif.: Science and Behavior Books, Inc., Chap. 3.

TUCKMAN, J., and I. LORGE. 1954. The influence of changed directions on stereotypes about aging: Before and after instruction. *Educational and Psychological Measurement*, **14**: 128–132.

TUDDENHAM, R. D. 1969. Intelligence. In R. L. Ebel, ed., *Encyclopedia of educational research*. New York: The Macmillan Company, pp. 654–664.

————, and M. M. SNYDER. 1954. Physical growth of California boys and girls from birth to 18 years. *Child Development*, **1**: 183–364.

TYLER, L. E. 1956. The GED tests—Friends or foes? *California Journal of Educational Research*, **3**(2): 66–71.

————. 1958. The stability of patterns of primary mental abilities among grade school children. *Educational and Psychological Measurement*, **18**(4): 769–774.

TYLER, R. W. 1960. What testing does to teachers and students. *The* 1959 *Invitational Conference on Testing. Problems*. Princeton, N. J.: Educational Testing Service, p. 11.

————, ed. 1969. Educational evaluation: New roles, new means. *The sixty-eighth yearbook of the National Society for the Study of Education, Part II*. Chicago: The University of Chicago Press.

UNDERWOOD, B. J. 1964. Laboratory studies of verbal learning. In E. R. Hilgard, ed., Theories of learning and instruction, *The sixty-third yearbook of the National Society for the Study of Education*. Chicago: University of Chicago Press.

VALLANCE, T. R. 1947. A comparison of essay and objective examination as learning experience. *Journal of Educational Research*, **41**: 279–288.

VERNON, P. E. 1950. *The structure of human abilities*. London: Methuen & Co., Ltd.

————. 1954. Symposium on the effect of coaching and practice in intelligence tests. *British Journal of Educational Psychology*, **24**: 57–63.

————. 1962. The determinants of reading comprehension. *Educational and Psychological Measurement*, **22**(2): 269–286.

————, and G. D. MILLICAN. 1954. A further study of the reliability of English essays. *British Journal of Statistical Psychology*, **7**(Part II): 65–74.

VOTAW, D. F. 1936. The effect of "do not guess" directions on the validity of true-false and multiple-choice tests. *Journal of Educational Psychology*. **27**: 699–704.

WAHLSTROM, M., and F. J. BOERSMA. 1968. The influence of test-wiseness upon achievement. *Educational and Psychological Measurement*, **28**: 413–420.

WALBERG, H. J. 1967. Scholastic aptitude, the National Teacher Examinations, and teaching success. *Journal of Educational Research*, **61**(3): 129–131.

WALKER, H. M. 1929. *Studies in the history of statistical method.* Baltimore: Williams & Wilkins Company.

———. 1950. Statistical understandings every teacher needs. *High School Journal,* 33: 30–36.

WALLEN, N. E. 1962. Development and application of tests of general mental ability. *Review of Educational Research,* 32: 15–24.

WANG, M. D., and J. C. STANLEY. 1970. Differential weighting: A review of methods and empirical studies. *Review of Educational Research,* 40(5): 663–705.

WARNER, W. L., M. MEEKER, and K. EELLS. 1949. *Social class in America.* Chicago: Science Research Associates.

WATERS, L. K. 1967. Effect of perceived scoring formula on some aspects of test performance. *Educational and Psychological Measurement,* 27(4, pt. 2): 1005–1010.

WECHSLER, D. 1958. *The measurement and appraisal of adult intelligence,* 4th ed. Baltimore: Williams & Wilkins Company.

———. 1967. *Manual for the Wechsler Preschool and Primary Scale of Intelligence.* New York: The Psychological Corporation.

WEIDEMANN, C. C. 1933. Written examination procedures. *Phi Delta Kappan,* 16: 78–83.

———. 1941. Review of essay test studies. *Journal of Higher Education,* 12: 41–44.

WEISS, R. A. 1961. The effects of practicing a test: A review of the literature. *Research Memorandum* 61–12. Princeton, N.J.: Educational Testing Service.

WEITMAN, M. 1965. Item characteristics and long-term retention. *Journal of Educational Measurement,* 2(1): 37–47.

WEITZMAN, E., and W. J. MCNAMARA. 1946. Apt use of the inept choice in multiple-choice testing. *Journal of Educational Research,* 39: 517–522.

WESMAN, A. G. 1952. Reliability and confidence. *Test Service Bulletin* No. 44. New York: The Psychological Corporation.

———. 1971. Writing the test item. In R. L. Thorndike, ed., *Educational measurement,* 2d ed. Washington, D.C.: American Council on Education, Chap. 4.

WEVRICK, L. 1962. Response set in a multiple-choice test. *Educational and Psychological Measurement,* 22(3): 533–538.

WHITCOMB, M. A. 1958. The IBM answer sheet as a major source of variance on highly speeded tests. *Educational and Psychological Measurement,* 18(4): 757–759.

WHITE, E. E. 1886. *The elements of pedagogy.* New York: American Book Company.

WHITE, H. B. 1932. Testing as an aid to learning. *Educational Administration and Supervision,* 18: 41–46.

WIGHTWICK, M. I. 1945. *Vocational interest patterns.* Contributions to Education, No. 900. New York: Teachers College, Columbia University.

WILBUR, P. H. 1969. Positional responses set in multiple choice examinations. Paper presented at the meeting of the National Council on Measurement in Education, Los Angeles, February 1969.

WILEY, D. E., J. R. COLLINS, and G. V GLASS. 1970. *Sources of variation in multiple-choice test performance.* Research Paper 37, Laboratory of Educational Research, University of Colorado, Boulder.

WILLIAMS, J. E., and J. K. ROBERSON. 1967. A method for assessing racial attitudes in preschool children. *Educational and Psychological Measurement,* 27: 671–689.

WILLIAMSON, M. L., and K. D. HOPKINS. 1967. The use of "none-of-these" versus homogeneous alternatives on multiple-choice tests: Experimental reliability and validity comparisons. *Journal of Educational Measurement*, **4**(2): 53–58.

WISSLER, C. 1901. The correlation of mental and physical tests. *Psychological Review, Monograph Supplements*, **8**(16), 62 pp.

WODTKE, K. H. 1964. Some data on the reliability and validity of creativity tests at the elementary school level. *Educational and Psychological Measurement*, **24**(2): 399–408.

WOLFLE, D. 1965. Psychological testing and the invasion of privacy. *Science*, **150**: 1773.

WOMER, F. B. 1965. Test norms: Their use and interpretation. Washington, D.C.: National Association of Secondary School Principals.

———. 1970. *What is National Assessment?* Ann Arbor, Mich.: National Assessment of Educational Progress. Reprinted in G. H. Bracht, K. D. Hopkins, and J. C. Stanley, eds. 1972. *Perspectives in educational and psychological measurement*. Englewood Cliffs, N.J.: Prentice-Hall, Inc., Selection 3.

———, and N. K. WAHI. 1969. Test use. In R. L. Ebel, ed., *Encyclopedia of educational research*, 4th ed. New York: The Macmillan Company, pp. 1461–1469.

WOOD, D. A. 1960. *Test construction: Development and interpretation of achievement tests*. Columbus, Ohio: Charles E. Merrill Books, Inc.

WOODRING, P. 1966. Are intelligence tests unfair? *Saturday Review* (April 16), 79–80.

WOODRUFF, A. D., and M. W. PRITCHARD. 1949. Some trends in the development of psychological tests. *Educational and Psychological Measurement*, **9**: 105–108.

WORTHEN, B. R., and J. R. SANDERS. 1972. *Educational evaluation: Theory and practice*. Worthington, Ohio: Charles A. Jones Publishing Company.

WRIGHT, W. H. E. 1944. The modified true-false item applied to testing in chemistry. *School Science and Mathematics*, **44**: 637–639.

WRIGHTSMAN, L. S., JR. 1962. The effects of anxiety, achievement motivation, and task importance upon performance on an intelligence test. *Journal of Educational Psychology*, **53**(3): 150–156.

WRIGHTSTONE, J. W. 1957. Do students benefit from testing? *High School Review*, **41**: 75–78.

WRINKLE, W. L. 1956. *Improving marking and reporting practices in elementary and secondary schools*. New York: Holt, Rinehart and Winston, Inc.

YAMAMOTO, K. 1962. A study of the relationships between creative thinking abilities of fifth-grade teachers and academic achievement. Doctoral dissertation, University of Minnesota, Minneapolis.

———, and H. F. DIZNEY. 1965. Effects of three sets of test instructions on scores on an intelligence scale. *Educational and Psychological Measurement*, **25**: 87–94.

YATES, A. J., et al. 1953, 1954. Symposium on the effects of coaching and practice in intelligence tests. *British Journal of Educational Psychology*, **23**: 147–154; **24**: 1–8, 57–63.

YEE, A. H., and T. KRIEWALL. 1969. A new logical scoring key for the Minnesota Teacher Attitude Inventory. *Journal of Educational Measurement*, **6**: 11–14.

ZILLER, R. C. 1957. A measure of the gambling response set in objective tests. *Psychometrika*, **22**: 289–292.

ZIRKEL, P. A., and E. G. MOSES. 1971. Self-concept and ethnic group membership among public school students. *American Educational Research Journal*, **8**: 253–266.

NAME INDEX

Abramson, T., 148
Adams, G. S., 99, 195
Ahmann, J. S., 319
Aiken, L. R., Jr., 288, 310
Alcock, W. T., 347
Allen, L., 336
Allison, A. A., 84, 333
Allison, D. E., 140
Allison, J. S., 415
Allport, G. W., 228, 261
Ammons, Margaret, 172-73
Anastasi, A., 52, 59, 79, 113, 140, 151-53, 168, 301, 358, 361, 400, 415
Anderson, H. A., 203
Anderson, H. R., 264
Anderson, R., 187
Anderson, R. D., 183, 195
Anderson, R. H., 303
Anderson, S. B., 192, 442
Angoff, W. H., 85, 87, 91, 99, 138
Anttonen, R. G., 151
Armitage, J. H., 296
Armstrong, R. J., 147
Ashbaugh, E. J., 160
Ashburn, R. R., 199
Asta, P., 396
Astin, A. W., 113
Ausubel, D. P., 11
Ayres, L. P., 158, 168
Azuma, H., 126-127, 132

Badal, A. W., 442
Bagley, W. C., 325
Baird, L. L., 306, 310
Baker, A. O., 220
Baker, F. B., 164, 268
Baker, R. L., 138
Baldwin, T. S., 264
Banaka, W. J., 415
Barch, A. M., 141
Barclay, J. R., 12
Barron, F., 358
Barrett, E. R., 240
Barthol, R. P., 396
Barton, W. A., 226
Bashaw, W. L., 179
Bauernfeind, R. H., 442
Bauman, D. J., 11, 282, 296
Bayley, N., 336
Beauchamp, W. L., 220, 222, 229
Beck, R. L., 222
Beeman, E. Y., 207
Beggs, D. L., 367, 378, 427
Bender, L., 400-401
Bendig, A. W., 345
Bennet, R. W., 271
Bennett, G. K., 128, 141, 352, 355-56, 389
Berdie, R. F., 389
Berg, H. D., 216-17, 246-47, 264
Bernard, J., 367
Bertin, M. A., 319

[1] Does not include bibliographic citations, pp. 469-507.

509

Ebel, R. L., 6, 13, 36, 79, 100, 102, 113, 132, 138, 141-42, 144, 147, 154, 168, 170, 180, 187, 195, 215, 230, 234, 236, 264, 267, 269, 272-73, 280, 307-8, 312, 319-20, 359, 378, 415
Eckland, B. K., 414
Edgar, Mary, Sr., 345
Edwards, A. L., 299
Eells, K., 150, 412, 416
Eiss, A. F., 301
Elliot, E. C., 159, 303
Engelhart, M. D., 52, 173, 265, 268, 270-71, 281, 308
Escalona, S. K., 336
Eysenck, H. J., 359, 401, 415

Falls, J. D., 159-60
Fargo, G. A., 148, 429
Feister, W. J., 306, 310
Feldhusen, J. F., 8
Feldt, L. S., 381
Felix, J. L., 9
Ferguson, L. W., 284
Ferrell, G. V., 62
Finch, F. H., 239
Findley, W. G., 7, 13, 99, 268, 281, 363, 442
Fishman, J. A., 151
Fiske, D. W., 112-13
Flanagan, J. C., 125, 166, 185, 213, 370, 388, 393, 415
Flaugher, R. L., 10
Fleming, E. S., 151
Flynn, J. T., 265
Foley, J. J., 264
Frase, L. T., 11
Frandsen, A. N., 388
Frankel, E., 139
Franz, S. I., 393
French, J. W., 140, 153, 183, 389
Frickle, B. C., 11
Fruchter, B., 182
Furby, L., 310
Furst, E. J., 173

Gage, N. L., 290, 302, 416
Gallup, G. A., 336
Garber, H., 202, 205, 265
Gardner, E. F., 93, 99, 100, 265, 416
Garlock, J., 109
Garry, R., 388
Gates, A. I., 240
Gee, H. H., 89, 138
Gerberich, J. R., 255, 265
Getzels, J. W., 395
Ghiselli, E. E., 396
Glaser, R., 186, 188, 195
Glass, G. V., 9, 11, 29, 48, 60, 68, 70, 72, 79, 144-45, 340
Glasser, W., 303, 307
Gleser, G. C., 117
Glock, M. D., 319
Goddard, H. H., 327

Godshalk, F. I., 198, 201, 203
Godshalk, R., 215
Goldman, L., 429
Goodenough, F. L., 323, 327
Goodwin, W. L., 148-49, 429
Gordon, M. A., 151
Gordon, W. E., 203
Goslin, D. A., 3, 5, 13, 197
Gough, H. G., 395
Gozali, J., 151
Graff, K., 82
Granich, L. A., 142
Greene, H. A., 227-28, 265
Greene, K. B., 139
Gregory, C. A., 222
Grobman, H., 279
Gronlund, N. E., 265, 409, 416
Gross, M. L., 11
Grotelueschen, A., 11
Guilford, J. P., 141-42, 164, 182, 201, 269, 324, 334-35, 356-57, 359, 400
Gustad, J., 403
Gustav, A., 141
Guttman, L., 296

Haberman, M., 151
Hadley, S. T., 306
Haertzka, A. F., 269
Haganah, T., 388
Hagen, E. P., 125, 307, 364
Hakstian, A. R., 147, 206-7, 215
Hall, A. E., 281
Hall, D. W., 390
Hambleton, R. K., 144, 192
Hamilton, C. H., 143
Hampton, S. H., 137
Harbeck, M. B., 301
Hardy, D. P., Jr., 219
Harper, H. E., 414
Harrington, S. A., 11
Harris, C. W., 170, 310, 320, 415-16
Hart, F. M., 205
Hartnett, R., 306
Hartshorne, H., 392, 408
Hashimoto, Juji, 148
Hastings, J. T., 9, 195, 264, 301, 379
Hawes, G. R., 13
Hawkes, H. E., 198, 236, 249, 255
Hayward, P., 149
Hedges, W. D., 179, 195, 265
Helmstadter, G. C., 298
Henkin, J. B., 336
Henry, N. B., 265
Henrysson, S., 268, 272, 281
Hensley, H., 207
Herzberg, F., 396
Hicklin, N. J., 310
Hieronymous, A. N., 359, 367, 378, 427
Hill, W. H., 173, 196
Hill, R. J., 412-15
Hills, J. R., 151, 153, 310
Hilton, T. L., 138, 150, 153, 198
Hoepfner, R., 346, 356-57, 426, 442
Hoffman, B., 11, 198

Acquiescence response set, 141-42
Administrative factors in test performance, 148-50
Affective domain, 174, 282-301
  assessment of, 282-301
  problems in assessment, 298-301
  taxonomy of, 282-83
Age norms, 90
Ambiguity of test items, 234
American College Testing Program (ACT), 428
Anchor test, 91
Anonymity in self-reporting, 296, 301
Anticipated achievement, 93
Anxiety, test, 140-41
Army Alpha, 329
Army Beta, 329
Army General Qualification Test (AGQT), 350, 352
Assessment (*see* Measurement)
Attenuation, correction for, 340
Attitude measurement (*see* Affective assessment)
Average, 18, 73

Behavioral objectives, 173
Bell-shaped curve (*see* Normal distribution)
Bender Visual Motor Gestalt Test, 400-401

Binet-Simon scales, 326
Biserial correlation coefficient, 72, 278-79
Bloom's taxonomy of objectives, 173-80

Calibrated norms, 91
California Test of Mental Maturity, 341, 354
Carryover-effects in essay scoring, 200
CAVD Tests, 333
Central tendency, 16-28
  mastery test items for, 74-78
  measures of, 24-28
  programmed materials pertaining to, 16-21
  comparisons among, 25-28
  mean, 18, 24-28
  median, 17, 24-28
  mode, 16, 25-28
Chance scores, 144
  correction formulas, 143-47
Classification, use of tests for, 10
Classroom tests, construction of, 188-94
Coaching effects, 139-40
Coefficient of stability, 122-24
Coefficient of validity (*see* Validity coefficients)
Cognitive domain, 173-74
College Entrance Examination Board, 428
Completion-type items, 221-26
Concurrent validity, 109-11

---

[1] Glossary terms are not included in the subject index, but should be consulted separately for an abbreviated treatment of many concepts.